Semantic Web Engineering in the Knowledge Society

Jorge Cardoso
SAP Research, Germany

Miltiadis Lytras
Athens University of Economics and Business, Greece

INFORMATION SCIENCE REFERENCE

Hershey · New York

Director of Editorial Content:	Kristin Klinger
Director of Production:	Jennifer Neidig
Managing Editor:	Jamie Snavely
Assistant Managing Editor:	Carole Coulson
Typesetter:	Larissa Vinci
Cover Design:	Lisa Tosheff
Printed at:	Yurchak Printing Inc.

Published in the United States of America by
Information Science Reference (an imprint of IGI Global)
701 E. Chocolate Avenue, Suite 200
Hershey PA 17033
Tel: 717-533-8845
Fax: 717-533-8661
E-mail: cust@igi-global.com
Web site: http://www.igi-global.com

and in the United Kingdom by
Information Science Reference (an imprint of IGI Global)
3 Henrietta Street
Covent Garden
London WC2E 8LU
Tel: 44 20 7240 0856
Fax: 44 20 7379 0609
Web site: http://www.eurospanbookstore.com

Library of Congress Cataloging-in-Publication Data

Semantic Web engineering in the knowledge society / Jorge Cardoso and Miltiadis Lytras, editors.

    p. cm.

  Includes bibliographical references and index.

  Summary: "This book lays the foundations for understanding the concepts and technologies behind the Semantic Web"--Provided by publisher.

  ISBN 978-1-60566-112-4 (hardcover) -- ISBN 978-1-60566-113-1 (ebook)

  1. Semantic Web. 2. Intelligent agents (Computer software) 3. Web site development. 4. Information society. I. Cardoso, Jorge, 1970- II. Lytras, Miltiadis D., 1973-

  TK5105.88815.S4338 2009

  025.04--dc22

                        2008014461

British Cataloguing in Publication Data
A Cataloguing in Publication record for this book is available from the British Library.

All work contributed to this book is original material. The views expressed in this book are those of the authors, but not necessarily of the publisher.

Editorial Advisory Board

Table of Contents

Detailed Table of Contents

Deborah L. McGuinness, Tetherless World Constellation, Rensselaer Polytechnic
Institute (RPI), and Stanford University, KSL, USA

Vasco Furtado, University of Fortaleza, UNIFOR, Brazil

Paulo Pinheiro da Silva, University of Texas at El Paso (UTEP), USA

Li Ding, Tetherless World Constellation, Rensselaer Polytechnic Institute (RPI), and
Stanford University, KSL, USA

Alyssa Glass, Stanford University, KSL, USA

Cynthia Chang, Tetherless World Constellation, Rensselaer Polytechnic Institute (RPI),
and Stanford University, KSL, USA

This chapter introduces the concept of explanation for Semantic Web applications by providing motivation, description, and examples. The Inference Web explanation toolkit that provides support for a broad range of explanation tasks ranging from explaining deductive reasoning, to information extraction, to hybrid integrated learning systems is described. The authors argue that an explanation solution, such as the one they endorse, is required if we are to realize the full potential of hybrid, distributed, intelligent Web agents that users can trust and use.

Victor Rodriguez-Herola, Dirección de Sistemas de Defensa y Seguridad, ISDEFE,
S.A., Spain

The North Atlantic Treaty Organisation (NATO) is shifting towards Net-centric operations paradigms driven by the nature of the new missions that the Alliance will likely be facing in the coming years. This new situation has forced the Alliance to pursue the achievement of the so-called NATO Network-Enabled Capability (NNEC). In this framework, the concept of a system of systems should give way to the new paradigm of federation of services, where any capability needs to be seen as a loosely-coupled service. From any perspective of these services, one of the biggest issues will be to discover available services and, more importantly, the information provided for such services that can be consumed. For this purpose, the authors present the use of Semantic Web as a technology that will facilitate the explicit description of the services available on the Net and eventually help in selecting the right services as well as mediate between service consumers and service providers, so information is given a well-defined meaning and is comprehensible. Based on the foundations of the Semantic Web, the authors propose a concept demonstrator called SISearch, where well defined vocabularies from apparently different domains are defined using ontology languages. Then, these different vocabularies are interpreted with respect to the vocabulary defined by a potential service consumer. Assisted by this interpretation and by inference services, the SISearch will translate both consumer-based queries to service provider specific-queries (using different vocabularies), and aggregate and interpret the results with respect to the service consumer vocabulary. This approach will allow an extension to new potential service consumer or service providers without having to develop specific modules or components.

Chapter III

Vassileios Tsetsos, University of Athens, Greece
Vassilis Papataxiarhis, University of Athens, Greece
Stathes Hadjiefthymiades, University of Athens, Greece

Personalization techniques provide optimized access to content and services based on the preferences and characteristics of each individual user. Currently, many applications, either Web-based or not, call for personalized behavior. Obviously, such behavior leads to an increased demand for knowledge management, since personalization is based on user profiles, user preferences, usage policies, and other knowledge components. The main topic of this chapter is the investigation of how well Semantic Web technologies apply to personalized applications. Semantic Web is a relatively new platform for developing (distributed) knowledge-based applications that have gained great popularity over the last few years. Hence, this chapter surveys the most prominent techniques for personalization in the context of the Semantic Web. It discusses and compares different approaches to architectural and engineering techniques and other issues relevant to this hot topic. The chapter provides foundational knowledge on this topic, as well as a discussion of some key implementation issues.

Chapter IV

Marco Brambilla, Politecnico di Milano, Italy
Federico M. Facca, Leopold-Franzens-Universität Innsbruck, Austria

This chapter presents an extension to Web application conceptual models toward Semantic Web. Conceptual models and model-driven methodologies are widely applied to the development of Web applications because of the advantages they grant in terms of productivity and quality of the outcome. Although some of these approaches are meant to address Semantic Web applications too, they do not fully exploit the whole potential deriving from interaction with ontological data sources and from semantic annotations. The authors claim that Semantic Web applications represent an emerging category of software artifacts, with peculiar characteristics and software structures, and hence need some specific methods and primitives for achieving good design results. In particular, the contribution presented in this chapter is an extension of the WebML modeling framework that fulfils most of the design requirements emerging in the new area of Semantic Web. The authors generalize the development process to cover Semantic Web needs and devise a set of new primitives for ontology importing and querying. The chapter also presents a comparison of the proposed approach with the most relevant existing proposals and positioned with respect to the background and adopted technologies.

> *Florian Fuchs, Siemens AG, Corporate Technology, Intelligent Autonomous Systems, Germany*
>
> *Michael Berger, Siemens AG, Corporate Technology, Intelligent Autonomous Systems, Germany*
>
> *Michael Pirker, Siemens AG, Corporate Technology, Intelligent Autonomous Systems, Germany*

This chapter discusses the potential of semantically processing monitoring data in industrial applications such as condition-based maintenance and monitoring of complex systems and infrastructure networks. It points out the particular requirements involved and gives a comprehensive and structured overview of current approaches and engineering solutions in these fields. As a case study for engineering industrial end-to-end solutions, it presents the design and prototype implementation of a decision support system in the railway domain

> *Florence Amardeilh, Mondeca, France and Université Paris 10, France*

This chapter deals with issues related to semantic annotation and ontology population within the framework defined by the Semantic Web (SW). The vision of the Semantic Web—initiated in 1998 by Sir Tim Berners-Lee—aims to structure the information available on the Web. To achieve that goal, the resources, textual or multimedia, must be semantically tagged by metadata so that software agents can exploit them. The idea developed in this chapter is to combine the information extraction (IE) tools with knowledge representation tools from the SW for the achievement of the two parallel tasks of semantic annotation and ontology population. The goal is to extract relevant information from the resources based on an ontology, then to populate that ontology with new instances according to the extracted information, and finally to use those instances to semantically annotate the resource. Despite all integration efforts, there is currently a gap between the representation formats of the linguistic tools used to extract information and those of the knowledge representation tools used to model the ontology and store the instances or the semantic annotations. The stake consists in proposing a methodological reflexion on the interoperability of these technologies as well as designing operational solutions for companies and, on a broader scale, for the Web.

> *Abdul-Rahman Mawlood-Yunis, Carleton University, Canada*
> *Michael Weiss, Carleton University, Canada*
> *Nicola Santoro, Carleton University, Canada*

Local mappings between peers with different knowledge representations, and their correctness, are prerequisite for the creation of emergent semantics. Yet, often approaches to emergent semantics fail to distinguish between permanent and transient mapping faults. This may result in erroneously labelling peers as having incompatible knowledge representations. In turn, this can further prevent such peers from interacting with other semantically related peers. This chapter will explore the issue of semantic mapping faults. This issue has not received enough attention in the literature. Specifically, it will focus on the effect of non-permanent semantic mapping faults on both inclusiveness of semantic emergence and robustness of applications and systems that use semantic mappings. A fault-tolerant emergent semantics algorithm with the ability to resist transient semantic mapping faults is also provided.

Chapter VIII

This chapter highlights the benefits of semantics for analysis of the collaboration network in a bibliography dataset. Metadata of publications was used for extracting keywords and terms, which can be the starting point towards building taxonomy of topics. The aggregated effect of the topics over all publications of an author can be used to determine his or her areas of expertise. We also highlight the value of using taxonomy of topics in searching for experts on a given topic.

Chapter IX

In this chapter we discuss the approaches to find, extract, and structure information from natural language texts on the Web. Such structured information can be expressed and shared using the standard Semantic Web languages and hence be machine interpreted. In this chapter we focus on two tasks in Web information extraction. The first part focuses on mining facts from the Web, while in the second part presents an approach to collect community-based metadata. A search engine is used to retrieve potentially relevant texts. From these texts, instances and relations are extracted. The proposed approaches are illustrated using various case-studies. We show that we can reliably extract information from the Web using simple techniques.

Chapter X

This chapter introduces the UML profile for OWL as an essential instrument for bridging the gap between the legacy relational databases and OWL ontologies. Authors address one of the long-standing relational database design problems where initial conceptual model (a semantically clear domain conceptualization ontology) gets "lost" during conversion into the normalized database schema. The problem is that such "loss" makes database inaccessible for direct query by domain experts familiar with the conceptual model only. This problem can be avoided by exporting the database into RDF according to the original conceptual model (OWL ontology) and formulating semantically clear queries in SPARQL over the RDF database. Through a detailed example, authors show how UML/OWL profile is facilitating this new and promising approach.

Chapter XI

Sören Auer, University of Pennsylvania, USA & Institut für Informatik, Universität Leipzig, Germany

In this chapter, authors provide a brief overview on the recently emerging concepts Social Software and Web 2.0. Both stress the adaptive, agile methodological character of communication and collaboration. In order to lift the adaptive collaboration and communication patterns of Social Software and the Web 2.0 towards a truly semantic collaboration, we outline an adaptive knowledge engineering methodology—RapidOWL. It is inspired by adaptive software development methodologies from software engineering and emphasises support for small end-user contributions to knowledge bases.

Chapter XII

Ansgar Bernardi, German Research Center for Artificial Intelligence (DFKI) GmbH, Kaiserslautern, Germany
Stefan Decker, National University of Ireland, Ireland
Ludger van Elst, German Research Center for Artificial Intelligence (DFKI) GmbH, Kaiserslautern, Germany
Gunnar Aastrand Grimnes, German Research Center for Artificial Intelligence (DFKI) GmbH, Kaiserslautern, Germany
Tudor Groza, National University of Ireland, Ireland
Siegfried Handschuh, National University of Ireland, Ireland
Mehdi Jazayeri, University of Lugano, Switzerland
Cédric Mesnage, University of Lugano, Switzerland
Knud Möller, National University of Ireland, Ireland
Gerald Reif, University of Lugano, Switzerland
Michael Sintek, German Research Center for Artificial Intelligence (DFKI) GmbH, Kaiserslautern, Germany
Leo Sauermann, German Research Center for Artificial Intelligence (DFKI) GmbH, Germany

This chapter introduces the general vision of the Social Semantic Desktop (SSD) and details it in the context of the NEPOMUK project. It outlines the typical SSD requirements and functionalities that were identified from real world scenarios. In addition, it provides the design of the standard SSD architecture together with the ontology pyramid developed to support it. Finally, the chapter gives an overview of some of the technical challenges that arise from the actual development process of the SSD.

This chapter is about uncertainty representation and reasoning for the Semantic Web (SW). We address the importance, key issues, state-of-the-art approaches, and current efforts of both the academic and business communities in their search for a practical, standard way of representing and reasoning with incomplete information in the Semantic Web. The focus is on why uncertainty representation and reasoning are necessary, its importance to the SW vision, and the major issues and obstacles to addressing uncertainty in a principled and standardized way. Although some would argue that uncertainty belongs in the "rule layer" of the SW, we concentrate especially on uncertain extensions of ontology languages for the Semantic Web.

The Semantic Web technology needs to be thoroughly evaluated for providing objective results and obtaining massive improvement in its quality; thus, the transfer of this technology from research to industry will speed up. This chapter presents software benchmarking, a process that aims to improve the Semantic Web technology and to find the best practices. The chapter also describes a specific software benchmarking methodology and shows how this methodology has been used to benchmark the interoperability of ontology development tools, employing RDF(S) as the interchange language.

Preface

The Knowledge Society is not a utopia or a phrase typically found in political speeches. Computer Science, Semantic Web, and Information Science communities have years of valuable experience that can contribute to the design, implementation, and launch of applications for the awareness and realization of the Knowledge Society.

After working and researching for many years in Web Engineering domains, we have decided to compile an edition which will help students, researchers, and practitioners utilize promising Semantic Web technologies. From the beginning we had in mind to promote a balanced discussion of key theoretical topics combined with a practical orientation. With the support and contribution of more than 40 academics and practitioners around the world, the manuscript "Semantic Web Engineering in the Knowledge Society" is finally in your hands.

Many papers have been written and many statements have been articulated to describe the Semantic Web. From a technical perspective, the current World Wide Web is syntactic and the content itself is only readable by humans. The Semantic Web proposes the mark-up or annotation of the content on the Web using formal ontologies that structure underlying data for the purpose of comprehensive and transportable machine understanding. Academia has been working on several solutions, applications, and examples to illustrate how the use of semantics can greatly enhance the integration and interoperability of information systems. Nevertheless, many professionals in the industry believe that there is a lack of guiding principles that would enable them to deploy end-to-end solutions in a straightforward and effortless way. Having this requirement in mind, this edition describes aspects and issues that have considerable importance in the development of end-to-end solutions. Such contributions include research on knowledge modeling, ontology design methodologies, ontology tools, approaches for semantic annotation, and inferencing and reasoning.

The main objective of the book is to lay the foundations for understanding the concepts and technologies behind the Semantic Web. Organizations and professionals are striving for literature that guides them in the development of end-to-end applications and systems that use semantics. While the industry is willing to use semantics, academia has not yet been shown how to systematically employ Semantic Web technologies to deploy a new breed of systems. This book aims to provide relevant theories, tools, and methodologies to develop semantic applications. It is written for students and professionals who want to improve their understanding of how semantics and ontologies can be used inside organizations. It also studies how semantics are applied to each of the steps of the lifecycle of semantic applications and how semantics can help address critical issues of reuse, integration, and interoperability.

A variety of relevant topics and solutions are discussed in 14 chapters and include the following areas:

- Modeling knowledge
- The Semantic Web Engineering agenda
- Expressing knowledge
- Syntax, semantics, and pragmatics
- Ontology design methodologies
- Ontology languages
- Ontology tools
- Semantic annotation
- Inferencing and reasoning
- Industrial use of semantics: Case studies
- Knowledge society and semantics: Case studies
- Research on semantics: Open fields
- The future of the Semantic Web

This book provides valuable answers to frequent problems that academia and industry commonly face when implementing Semantic Web-based solutions. In each chapter, a key concern of Semantic Web Engineering is discussed.

This edition represents another valuable contribution to the available literature on Semantic Web and knowledge representation on the Web. Therefore, we invite you to be part of the exciting Semantic Web Engineering Community and we look forward to your comments, ideas, and suggestions for upcoming editions.

March 2008
Jorge Cardoso, SAP Research, Germany
Miltiadis D. Lytras, Open Research Society, Greece

Chapter I
Explaining Semantic Web Applications

Deborah L. McGuinness
Tetherless World Constellation, Rensselaer Polytechnic Institute (RPI),
and Stanford University, KSL, USA

Vasco Furtado
University of Fortaleza, UNIFOR, Brazil

Paulo Pinheiro da Silva
University of Texas at El Paso (UTEP), USA

Li Ding
Tetherless World Constellation, Rensselaer Polytechnic Institute (RPI),
and Stanford University, KSL, USA

Alyssa Glass
Stanford University, KSL, USA

Cynthia Chang
Tetherless World Constellation, Rensselaer Polytechnic Institute (RPI),
and Stanford University, KSL, USA

ABSTRACT

In this chapter, we introduce the concept of explanation for Semantic Web applications by providing motivation, description, and examples. We describe the Inference Web explanation toolkit that provides support for a broad range of explanation tasks ranging from explaining deductive reasoning, to information extraction, to hybrid integrated learning systems. We argue that an explanation solution such as the one we endorse is required if we are to realize the full potential of hybrid, distributed, intelligent Web agents that users can trust and use.

INTRODUCTION

Question answering on the Semantic Web (SW) typically includes more processing steps than database retrieval. Question answering can be viewed as an interactive process between a user and one or more intelligent software agents. Using queries, user preferences, and context, intelligent agents may locate, select and invoke services and, if necessary, compose these services to produce requested results. In other words, the web paradigm shifts from one where users mainly retrieve explicitly stated stored information to a paradigm where application results are answers to potentially complex questions that may require inferential capabilities in addition to information retrieval. Web applications with question answering capabilities may still use information retrieval techniques to locate answers, but they may also need to use additional semantics such as encoded term meanings to support additional methods of information access (such as targeted database queries or knowledge base queries) along with information manipulations (such as reasoning using theorem provers, or inductive or deductive methods). Examples of this new, more complex reality include the automatic composition of web services encoded in OWL-S or semi-automatic composition of services as provided by workflows. Ontology-enhanced search is another example of how Semantic Web technology can provide and is providing new directions for a category of "smart" search applications. Many other SW applications are emerging with a common theme of increasing knowledge and autonomy. This new context generates an additional requirement for effective use of SW applications by typical users: *applications must provide explanation capabilities showing how results were obtained*. Explanations are quickly becoming an essential component in establishing agent credibility (e.g., Glass et al, 2008) and result credibility (e.g., Del Rio and Pinheiro da Silva, 2007) by providing process transparency, thereby increasing user understanding of how results are derived. Explanations can also identify information sources used during the conclusion derivation process. In the context of the SW, explanations should be encoded in a way that they can be directly or indirectly consumed by multiple agents, including both human users and software systems.

In this chapter we describe explanation as a special kind of pervasive SW functionality, in the sense that a SW application may need to provide transparency concerning its results. We first analyze some distinct application paradigms in the SW context, and for each paradigm we identify explanation requirements. We then describe a general framework, called Inference Web (IW) (McGuinness and Pinheiro da Silva, 2004) that includes the Proof Markup Language (PML) (McGuinness, et al., 2007, Pinheiro da Silva, McGuinness, Fikes, 2006), a modularized ontology describing terms used to represent provenance, justifications and trust relations. IW includes a set of tools and methods for manipulating PML-encoded result justifications. Using Inference Web, and its PML interlingua, applications may provide interoperable and portable explanations that support intelligent, interactive application interfaces. After the description of the IW framework and the PML interlingua, we will exemplify how PML and IW have been used to explain the results and behaviors of a wide range of applications including intelligent personal agents, information extraction agents, and integrated learning agents.

A CONCEPTUAL FRAMEWORK FOR EXPLAINING RESULTS FROM SEMANTIC WEB APPLICATIONS

We investigate the correspondence between SW application paradigms and their explanation requirements.

Semantic Web Application Characterization

SW applications are geared to take advantage of vast amounts of heterogeneous data with potentially varying amounts of semantic markup. They concentrate on identifying and meaningfully combining available semantic markup in order to derive complex results. Below we briefly characterize the SW applications features considered important from an explanation perspective: collaboration, autonomy, and use of ontologies.

Collaboration

Collaboration requires agents to interact and share knowledge with the common goal of solving a particular problem. Collaboration raises issues concerning how to create, use, and share a combination of provenance, trust and reputation throughout distributed reasoning processes. Wikis, for example, are gaining popularity as collaborative tools for human agents, although they do not provide a precise infrastructure for recording and reusing provenance information. A *Semantic Wiki* is a wiki application enhanced with Semantic Web technologies that support wiki content annotation that goes beyond simple structured text and untyped hyperlinks. Semantic Wikis provide the ability to represent metadata about content, term meanings, and inter-relationships. Provenance support is typically somewhat limited, in both ordinary wikis and in semantic wikis, to keeping track of which author (if a login authentication process is included) made which updates and when.

Content Management Systems (CMS) are one of the most common uses of wikis for knowledge management. Semantic Wikis aim to enhance ordinary wikis by allowing users to make their internal knowledge more explicit and formal, enabling search methods that go beyond simple keyword search. In this case, provenance information may be included in these searching capabilities. Other collaborative systems are aimed at Personal Information Management (PIM) or community knowledge management. The ability to store project history, and to utilize tools that access and perform intelligent queries over this history, is one of the benefits brought by Semantic Wikis used for content management.

The collaborative characteristic is also prominent in applications developed via the integration of multi-agent systems and Semantic Web services. In this situation, collaborating agents are software programs such as digital assistants that manage electronic information. These collaborating agents can proactively engage in tasks on behalf of their users to find, filter, assess and present information to the user in a more appropriate manner (Maes, 1994). Several types of multi-agent applications have been developed such as office organization (Pyandath & Tambe, 2002); technical support (Sullivan et al. 2000); and information retrieval (Rhodes et al., 1996). Again, most of these collaborating agents provide little support for storing and retrieving provenance information about how they work internally, and in particular, they provide only limited access to information about how they collaborate. However, end user activities may require the integration of multi-agent systems and Semantic Web services. Personal agents may also need user models, to allow them to better perform tasks in compliance with user needs and preferences.

Distributed solutions for multi-agent problems can alternatively be represented using a reactive multi-agent architecture. In these domains, the individual agents have little autonomy. The "intelligence" used to solve problems comes from intensive inter-agent communication. This paradigm is typically used on the web, where heterogeneity and loosely-coupled distributed systems are common. Thus, interactions between agents or system components must not be rigidly specified at design time, but opportunistically built though the use of new services as they become available. Prior knowledge of such services is thus not necessary (and often not practical nor desirable). Instead, agents must discover services by accessing a *service description* that can be semantically described by means of ontologies in which descriptive expressions or concepts are attached to services.

Autonomy

An individual agent's autonomy controls its ability to act independently. Barber and Martin (1999) consider an agent's degree of autonomy with respect to a particular goal that the agent is actively pursuing. Within this context, they define the degree of autonomy to be (1) the degree to which the decision making process was used to determine how that goal should be pursued; and (2) how free the agent is from intervention by other agents. Traditional web-based applications have very little autonomy, since they primarily take direct input from the user and retrieve information consistent with the query. For example, a typical web search engine's primary interaction mechanism is based on communication between the user and the search engine. The degree of autonomy of the search engine is said to be low because the user is required to reformulate and resubmit the query when the original query is not satisfactorily answered by the engine. In contrast with typical search engines, SW applications have more autonomy while pursuing goals. For example, online shopping agents have autonomy over how to find answers to shopping queries concerned with product location, price comparison, or rating information. ShopBot can make several autonomous decisions, such as which content sources to use, which services to call and compose, and how to enhance the query with background representation information, all in an attempt to answer the user's question as efficiently and usefully as possible. In general,

the development of autonomous problem-solving software agents in the Semantic Web is increasingly gaining popularity.

Use of Ontologies

Semantic Web applications are increasingly using large amounts of heterogeneous semantic data from multiple sources. Thus, the new generation of Semantic Web applications must be prepared to address issues associated with data of varying quality. Intelligence in these large-scale semantic systems comes largely from the system's ability to operate effectively with large amounts of disparate data.. In this context, ontologies are used to support information integration as well as to identify inconsistencies between data coming from multiple sources. Ontologies are being used to provide declarative specifications of term meanings. Agents can then decide to use a term meaning as specified in a particular ontology, and when multiple agents decide to use the same definition of a term (for example by referencing the same term in the same ontology), they can communicate more effectively. Usage of the same term, now with the same meaning, helps improve consistency across applications.

Content search and context search are other typical uses of ontologies. In content search, search engines use background knowledge bases to enhance queries and thus improve results. When the background knowledge bases contain term definitions, semantic query engines may be able to retrieve answers that are inferred by the query, no longer restricting the search to exact user-provided terms. Search engines can go beyond statistical clustering methods, which while effective, have limitations largely associated with training data sets. In context search, search engines may consider the user's context when processing a search. For example, a search engine may utilize a user's geographic location as well as known preferences when retrieving answers. Information about geographic location and preferences may be encoded in background ontologies.

Ontologies describing domain knowledge, user preferences, and problem areas are often used in creating agents with reasoning capabilities. These ontologies are often used to establish a common vocabulary among multiple agents. Personal agents' learning capabilities are also important, as such capabilities can increase the agents' level of autonomy (e.g., the Cognitive Assistant that Learns and Organizes (CALO, 2008). Personal agents can act alone or communicate with others in order to accomplish their task; in these cases, ontologies describing communications protocols are also necessary.

Explanation Issues

Given these Semantic Web application features which impact the need for explanation, we identify a set of criteria for analyzing the required explanations. These criteria include such issues as whether explanations are expected to be consumed by humans or machine agents; varying characteristics of these agents; and the resulting types of explanations that should be provided.

Explanation Types

System transparency allows users to see how answers are generated and how processes within and among agents have evolved to support answer generation. Transparency allows users to access lineage information that often appears hidden in the complex Semantic Web network. Note that explanations should be viewed as a web of interconnected objects recording source information, source assertions and assumptions, intermediate results, and final results instead of as a single "flat" annotation. Results from Semantic Web applications may be derived from a series of information manipulation steps, each of which applies a primitive information manipulation operation, e.g., an inference or extraction rule, on some antecedents and produces a conclusion. Note that an information manipulation step may be any kind of inference and is not limited to those that are used in sound and complete reasoners. Thus this representation can handle statistical methods, standard logical inference, or even non-logical information transformation methods. A justification may be viewed as a transaction log of information manipulation steps. When a user requests a detailed explanation of what has been done or what services have been called, it is important to be able to present an explanation based on this justification. These transaction logs may be quite detailed, so it is also important to be able to provide explanations that are abstractions of these logs.

Another kind of explanation can be obtained from provenance metadata that contains annotations concerning information sources, (e.g., when, from where, and by whom the data was obtained). Provenance metadata connects statements in a knowledge base to the statement sources such as web pages and publications, including annotations about data collection or extraction methods. Criticality of provenance is evident. Users demand detailed provenance metadata before they will accept and believe answers (e.g., Cowell, et al, 2006; Del Rio and Pinheiro da Silva, 2007). In some settings such where an initial evaluation of usefulness is made, provenance metadata (e.g., source, recency, and authoritativeness) is the only information that users need.

Trust in the Semantic Web is another subject of growing importance in the explanation context. Trust representation, computation, combination, presentation, and visualization present issues of increasing importance for Semantic Web applications, particularly in settings that include large decentralized communities such as online social networks (e.g., McGuinness, et. al, 2006).

Human or Machine Consumption

Semantic Web applications typically require explanation for both human and machine consumption. Software agents require representation of justifications, provenance and trust in a standard format in order to enable interoperability. An interoperable justification specification can be used to generate explanations of an agent's reasoning process as well as of the sources used by the agent during the problem solving process. Explanations aimed at either humans or software agents can be generated from the internal justification, provenance, and trust representations. When the explanations are aimed at humans, the explanations must also include human computer interface (HCI) considerations. For instance, the display of an explanation may take into consideration the level of expertise of the user, e.g., expert or non-expert, as well as the context of the problem (e.g., Del Rio and Pinheiro da Silva, 2007a). HCI researchers have approached the explanation problem by proposing intelligent question-answering systems (e.g., Maybury, 2003), intelligent help systems (e.g., Lieberman and Kumar, 2005), and adaptive interfaces (e.g., Wagner and Lieberman, 2003).

Visualization Capabilities

Explanations can be viewed as Semantic Web metadata representing how results were obtained. In distributed settings such as the Web, representation interoperability is paramount. A variety of "user friendly" rendering and delivery modes are required to present information to different types of users in varying contexts. As explanations may need to be delivered to users with a variety of skill levels, visual representation must be flexible, manageable, extensible, and interoperable. Additionally, corresponding presentation modes need to be customizable and context-dependent, and need to provide options for abstract summaries, detailed views, and interactive follow-up support.

We consider several possible presentation modes. Implemented interfaces for each of these views can be seen in McGuinness, et al, 2006.

Global View. The entire process of explanation may be presented via a graphical display of a justification graph. The idea is to provide a view of the global structure of the reasoning process used by a question answering system. Common issues include how portions of information composing the explanation will be presented (for example, whether they are displayed in an English translation of the justification encoding, or in the reasoner's native language); or whether to restrict the depth and width of the explanation graph (e.g., with using notions such as lens magnitude and width options in the Inference Web browser). A useful feature in these kinds of views is to provide clickable hot links to enable access to additional information.

Focused View. Merely providing tools for browsing an execution trace is not adequate for most users. It is necessary to provide tools for visualizing the explanations at different levels of granularity and focus, for instance, to focus on one step of the justification, and to display that step using a natural language template style for presentation. Further focus on explanations can be provided by suggested context-appropriate follow up questions.

Filtered View. Alternative options may also be chosen, such as seeing only the assertions (ground facts) upon which a given result depended; only the sources used for ground assertions; or only the assumptions upon which the result depended. Another possible view is the collection of sources contributing information used to derive the result. Some users are willing to assume that the reasoning is correct, and as long as only reliable and recent knowledge sources are used, they are willing to believe the result. Initially, these users may not want to view all the details of the information manipulations (but they do want the option of asking follow-up questions when necessary).

Abstraction View. Machine-generated justifications are typically characterized by their complexity and richness of details that may not be relevant or interesting to most users. Filtering explanation information and providing only one type of information (for example, only showing the information sources) are some of the strategies used to deal with the large volume of data in justifications. These strategies translate the detailed explanation into a more abstract and understandable one.

In fact, this diversity of presentation styles is critical for broad acceptance of SW results. As we have interviewed users both in user studies (e.g., Cowell, et al, 2006; Del Rio and Pinheiro da Silva, 2007; Glass, et al., 2008) and in ad hoc requirements gathering, it was consistently true that broad user communities require focus on different types of explanation information and on different explanation formats. For any user segment that prefers a detailed trace-based view, there is another complementary and balancing user segment that requires an extensively filtered view. This finding results in the design and development of the trace-based browser, the explainer with inference step focus, multiple filtered follow-up views, and a discourse-style presentation component.

Explanation Issues vs. Semantic Web Application Characteristics

Having independently considered facets of both complex Semantic Web contexts and requirements for successful explanations, we now address how these issues relate to each other, providing requirements for explaining a broader range of SW applications.

Explanation and Collaboration

Trust and reputation are important issues in the context of collaborative applications and have been studied in the context of traditional wikis like Wikipedia (e.g., McGuinness, Zeng et al., 2006).

The advent of semantic wikis introduces new concerns and requirements in terms of explanation. Autonomy among SW agents is continuously increasing, and if users are expected to believe answers from these applications, SW applications must support explanations. This requirement becomes even more important when SW applications collaborate to generate complex results.

As personal agents mature and assume more autonomous control of their users' activities, it becomes more critical that these agents can explain the way they solve problems on behalf of humans. The agents must be able to tell the user why they are performing actions, what they are doing, and they must be able to do so in a trustable manner. Justifications and task processing explanations are essential to allow personal agents to achieve their acceptance goals. In addition, the learning skill presented by some personal agents amplifies the need for explanation since it introduces a degree of variability resulting from learning results. Justifications concerning agent's internal reasoning for learning new knowledge as well as explanations concerning usage of knowledge sources are examples of what must be explained. Distributed reasoning requires explanation capabilities to help users understanding the flow of information between the different agents involved in a problem solving process. These capabilities also allow users to understand the process taken by the distributed problem solvers. Additionally, provenance explanations are of interest since users might want to know information about each one of the learners and problem solvers used, as well as wanting to know information about each source of information that was used. Issues of trust and reputation are particularly likely to modify user's trust in agents' answers.

Explanation and Autonomy

In applications for which the degree of autonomy is low (for instance, a Google-based search query), no explicit explanation is provided. One could assume that aspects of explanatory material are implicitly embedded in the answers. In such settings, the user needs to have enough information to understand the context of the answers (e.g., the links selected by the query engine represent an information retrieval response to the query, and the answers include links to the sites containing the information). It is assumed that explaining why a search engine has selected a set of links is implicitly understood by the user (for instance, the search engine considers the provided answers to be the best responses, with some suitable definition of best which may rely on reverse citations, recency, etc.). The existence of a ranking mechanism is fundamental for the success of the interaction process because query reformulation depends on that ability. Understanding the process that led the search engine to provide an answer to a query facilitates the process of query refinement.

Even applications with low degrees of autonomy may experience demand from users for some forms of explanation. Users may want to know how a search engine got its answers, for example, if the answers were selected using certain purchased keywords or other advertising promotions, or if the answers depended on out-of-date source material. The information needs to be presented in an understandable manner, for instance, by displaying answers using purchased keywords in a different style.

Justifications become even more important in applications with higher degrees of autonomy. Autonomous agents can follow complex inference process, and justifications are an important tool for them to provide understandable information to end users.

Explanations and Ontologies

Ontologies can be used effectively to support explanations for a wide array of applications, ranging from relatively simple search applications to complex autonomous problem solving. For example, consider a contextual database search agent which considers user preferences when answering queries. Explanations of why a given solution was provided in a given context are particularly important when the solution does not match the user's specified preferences. Similarly, explanations are important when a particular contextual query results in different answers in different contexts (for example, when answers are dependent on the user's geographic location).

INFERENCE WEB: AN ONTOLOGY-ENHANCED INFRASTRUCTURE SUPPORTING EXPLANATIONS

We now explore Inference Web in the context of addressing the problem of providing explanations to justify the results and behaviors of Semantic Web services and applications. IW provides tools and infrastructure for building, maintaining, presenting, exchanging, combining, annotating, filtering, comparing, and rendering information manipulation traces, i.e., justifications. IW services are used by agents to publish justifications and explanations for their results that can be accessible digitally – on the web, on a local file system, or distributed across digital stores. Justification data and explanations derived from justifications are encoded using terms defined by the Proof Markup Language (PML) justification, provenance, and trust ontologies. The PML ontologies are specified in OWL and are easily integrated with Semantic Web applications. The ontologies include terms such as sources, inference rules, inference steps, and conclusions as explained later.

PML is an on-going, long-term effort with several goals and contributions to explaining Semantic Web application results and behaviors. Our earlier version of PML focused on explaining results generated by hybrid web-based reasoning systems, such as the question answering systems of DARPA's High Performance Knowledge Base program and its subsequent Rapid Knowledge Formation program. The requirements obtained for this initial explanation phase were similar to explanation requirements gathered for expert systems where knowledge bases were generated from reliable source information and using trained experts. Information in these systems was assumed to be reliable and recent. Thus, agent users only needed explanations about information manipulation steps, i.e. how the results were derived in a step by step manner from the original knowledge base via inference. In this setting, explanations concerning information sources used to derive results were not required.

As automated systems become more hybrid and include more diverse components, more information sources are used and thus users are seldom in a position to assume that all information is reliable and current. In addition to information manipulation, users may need explanations about information provenance. Under certain circumstances, such as intelligence settings that motivated DTO's Novel Intelligence for Massive Data program, provenance concerns often dwarfed all others when explanations were required (Cowell, et. al., 2006).

As automated systems begin to exploit more collaborative settings and input may come from many unknown authoring sources, notions of trust and reputation may become more critical. Meta information may be associated with authoring sources such as "I trust Joe's recommendations" or "I trust population data in the CIA World Factbook"). In these situations the meta-information may be user authored. In other settings, trust or reputation information may be calculated using techniques such as link analysis or revision analysis (Zeng, et.al. 2006).

Our goal is to go beyond explanation for traditional knowledge-based systems, and instead address explanation needs in a wide range of situations. We have settings where three different aspects of explanation sometimes dominate to the point that the other aspects are of secondary consideration. We thus took on a rationalization and redesign of our original representation Interlingua so that it could be modular. We can now support applications that only desire to focus on provenance (initially or permanently ignoring issues related to information manipulation and trust.). While these applications may later expand to include those concerns, they need not import ontologies with terms defined for those situations.

Using PML

To illustrate how PML supports explanation generation, we use a simple wine agent scenario. While this example is intentionally oversimplified, it does contain the question answering and explanation requirements in much more complicated examples. We have implemented a wine agent (Hsu, McGuinness, 2003) that suggests descriptions of wines to go with foods. The agent uses PML as its explanation interlingua, and a theorem prover capable of understanding and reasoning with OWL and outputting PML (Fikes, et. al., 2003)). The agent is capable of making wine recommendations to coordinate with meal courses (such as "Tony's specialty"). Before customers choose to follow the agent's recommendation, they may be interested in knowing a description of Tony's specialty, so that they can evaluate if the suggested wine pairing meets their desires. In this scenario, they would find that Tony's specialty is a shellfish dish and the wine agent suggests some white wines as potential matches. The user may want to know how the description of the matching wine was produced, and if the wine agent used other sources of information, such as commercial online wine web sites or hand built backend databases.

In some intelligence settings, e.g., (Cowell, et. al., 2006, Murdock, et. al., 2006), users often want to ask questions about what sources were relied on to obtain an answer. In some military settings, e.g., (Myers, et. al., 2007), users often want to ask what the system is doing, why it has not completed something, and what learned information was leveraged to obtain an answer. In other settings, such as collaborative social networks, users may be interested in either reputation as calculated by populations or trust as stated and stored by users, e.g., (McGuinness, et. al., 2006b). These setting are further elaborated in the following section.

Our PML explanation ontologies include primitive concepts and relations for representing knowledge provenance. Our original version of PML (Pinheiro da Silva et al., 2003) provided a single integrated ontology for use in representing information manipulation activities, the extended version of PML (called PML 2) improves the original version by modularizing the ontologies and refining and expanding the ontology vocabulary. This also broadens the reach covering a wider spectrum of applications for the intelligence, defense, and scientific communities. The modularization serves to separate descriptive metadata from the association metadata to reduce the cost of maintaining and using each module. The vocabulary expansion refines the definition and description structure of existing PML concepts; and it also adds several new primitive concepts to enrich expressiveness. For example, instead of simply serializing a piece of information into a text string, PML uses the concept of information as the universal reference to any piece of data, and enables explicit annotation (for instance, of format, language, and character encoding) about the string that serializes the piece of information.

PML provides vocabulary for three types of explanation metadata:

- The provenance ontology (also known as PML-P) focuses on annotating identified-things (and in particular, sources such as organization, person, agent, services) useful for providing lineage.
- The justification ontology (also known as PML-J) focuses on explaining dependencies

among identified-things including how one identified-thing (e.g., information) is derived from other identified-things (e.g. information, services, agents).

- The trust relation ontology (also known as PML-T) focuses on representing and explaining belief assertions.

Provenance Ontology

The goal of the provenance ontology (also called PML-P[a]) is to annotate the provenance of information, e.g., which sources were used, who encoded the information, etc. The foundational concept in PML-P is *IdentifiedThing*. An instance of IdentifiedThing refers to an entity in the real world, and its properties annotate its metadata such as name, description, creation date-time, authors, and owner. PML-P includes two key subclasses of IdentifiedThing motivated by knowledge provenance representational concerns: *Information* and *Source*.

The concept Information supports references to information at various levels of granularity and structure. It can be used to encode, for example, a formula in logical languages or a natural language text string. PML-P users can simply use the value of information's *hasRawString* property to store and access the content of the referred information as a string. They may optionally annotate additional processing and presentation instructions using PML-P properties such as *hasLanguage*, *hasFormat*, *hasReferenceUsage* and *hasPrettyNameMappingList*. Besides providing representational primitives for use in encoding information content as a string, PML-P also includes primitives supporting access to externally referenced content via *hasUrl*, which links to an online document, or *hasInfoSourceUsage*, which records when, where and by whom the information was obtained. This concept allows users to assign an URI reference to information. The example below shows that the content of a piece of information (identified by

#info1) is encoded in the Knowledge Interchange Format (KIF) language and is formatted as a text string. The second example below shows that the content of information (identified by #info_doc1) can be indirectly obtained from the specified URL, which also is written in KIF language.

```
<pmlp:Information rdf:about="#info1">
  <pmlp:hasRawString>(type TonysSpe-
cialty SHELLFISH)
  h</pmlp:hasRawString>
  <pmlp:hasLanguage rdf:re-
source= "http://inferenceweb.stan-
ford.edu/registry/LG/KIF.owl#KIF" />
  <pmlp:hasFormat>text</pmlp:hasFormat>
</pmlp:Information>
```

```
<pmlp:Information rdf:about="#info_
doc1">
  <pmlp:hasURL>http://iw.stanford.
edu/ksl/registry/storage/docu-
ments/tonys_fact.kif</pmlp:hasURL>
  <pmlp:hasLanguage rdf:re-
source= "http://inferenceweb.stan-
ford.edu/registry/LG/KIF.owl#KIF" />
```

```
</pmlp:Information>
```

The concept source refers to an information container, and it is often used to refer to all the information from the container. A source could be a document, an agent, or a web page, and PML-P provides a simple but extensible taxonomy of sources. The Inference Web Registry (McGuinness and Pinheiro da Silva, 2003) provides a public repository for registered users to pre-register metadata about sources so as to better reuse such metadata. Our current approach, however, does not demand a centralized or virtual distributed registry; rather, it depends on a search component that finds online PML data and provides search service for users' inquiry.

```
<pmlp:Document rdf:about="#STE">
  <pmlp:hasContent rdf:resource="#info_
doc1"/>
  </pmlp:Document>
```

In particular, PML-P provides options for encoding finer grained references to a span of a text through its *DocumentFragmentByOffset* concept.

Figure 1. Raw text fragment with highlighted segment used by text analytics components and represented in PML 2

This is a sub-class of Source and *DocumentFragment*. The example below shows how the offset information about #ST can be used to highlight the corresponding span of text (see Figure 1). This type of encoding was used extensively in our applications that used text analytic components to generate structured text from unstructured input as explained below.

```
<pmlp:DocumentFragmentByOffset rdf:
about="#ST">
    <pmlp:hasDocument rdf:
resource="#STE"/>
    <pmlp:hasFromOffset>62</pmlp:has-
FromOffset>
    <pmlp:hasToOff-
set>92</pmlp:hasToOffset>
</pmlp:DocumentFragmentByOffset>
```

As our work evolved, a number of our applications demanded more focus on provenance. We became increasingly aware of the importance of capturing information about the dependency between information and sources, i.e. when and how a piece of information was obtained from a source. PML 2 has a more sophisticated notion of *SourceUsage*. The encoding below simply shows how PML represents date information identifying when a source identified by #ST was used.

```
<pmlp:SourceUsage rdf:
about="#usage1">
    <pmlp:hasUsageDateTime>2005-10-
17T10:30:00Z</pmlp:hasUsageDateTime>
    <pmlp:hasSource rdf:resource="#ST"/>
</pmlp:SourceUsage>
```

Besides the above concepts, PML-P also defines concepts such as *Language*, *InferenceRule*, and *PrettyNameMapping*, which are used to represent metadata for application processing or presentation instructions.

Justification Ontology

The goal of the justification ontology is to provide concepts and relations used to encode traces of process executions used to derive a conclusion. A justification requires concepts for representing conclusions, and information manipulation steps used to transform/derive conclusions from other conclusions, e.g., step antecedents.

A *NodeSet* includes structure for representing a conclusion and a set of alternative information manipulation steps also called *InferenceSteps*. Each InferenceStep associated with a NodeSet provides an alternative justification for the NodeSet's conclusion. The term NodeSet is chosen because it captures the notion that the NodeSet concept can be used to encode a set of nodes from one or many proof trees deriving the same conclusion. The URI of a NodeSet is its unique identifier, and every NodeSet has exactly one URI.

The term inference in InferenceStep refers to a generalized information manipulation step, so it could be a standard logical step of inference, an information extraction step, a simple computation process step, or an assertion of a fact or assumption. It could also be a complex process such as a web service or application functionality that may not necessarily be describable in terms of more atomic processes. InferenceStep properties include *hasInferenceEngine* (the agent who ran this step), *hasInferenceRule* (the operation taken in this step), *hasSourceUsage*, *hasAntecedentList* (the input of this step), and others.

PML2 supports encodings for several typical types of justifications for a conclusion. Three justification examples are as follows:

An unproved conclusion or goal. A NodeSet without any InferenceStep can be explained as an inference goal that still needs to be proved. Unproved conclusions happen when input information encoded in PML2 is provided to an agent.

```
<pmlj:NodeSet  rdf:about="#answer1">
<pmlp:hasConclusionrdf:resource="#info1"/>
 </pmlp:hasConclusion>
   </pmlj:NodeSet>
```

Assumption. The conclusion was directly asserted by an agent as an assumption. In this case, the conclusion is asserted by a source instead of being derived from antecedent information.

Direct assertion. The conclusion can be directly asserted by the inference engine. In this case, the conclusion is not derived from any antecedent information. Moreover, direct assertion allows agents to specify source usage. The following example shows that "'(type TonysSpe-

cialty SHELLFISH)' has been directly asserted in Stanford's Tony's Specialty Example as a span of text between byte offset 62 and byte offset 92 as of 10:30 on 2005-10-17"

```
<pmlj:NodeSet  rdf:about="#answer2">
 <pmlp:hasConclusion rdf:resource="#info1"
/>
    <pmlp:isConsequentOf>
    <pmlp:InferenceStep rdf:about="step2">
    <pmlp:hasInferenceEngine rdf:resource=
"http://inferenceweb.stanford.edu/registry/IE/
JTP.owl#JTP" />
    <pmlp:hasInferenceRule  rdf:resource=
"http://inferenceweb.stanford.edu/registry/
```

Figure 2. Trace-oriented explanation with several follow-up question panes

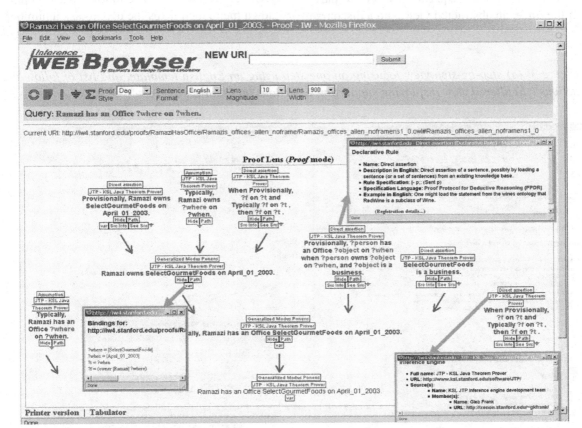

DPR/Told.owl#Told" />
        <pmlp:hasSourceUsage rdf:
resource="#usage1" />
    </pmlp:InferenceStep>
    </pmlp:isConsequentOf>
    </pmlj:NodeSet>

TOOLS FOR MANIPULATING EXPLANATION IN PML

To address the need to support multiple visualization modes for explanation, Inference Web provides rich presentation options for browsing justification traces, including a directed acyclic graph (DAG) view that shows the global justification structure, a collection of hyperlinked web pages that allows step-by-step navigation, a filtered view that displays only certain parts of the trace, an abstracted view, and a discourse view (in either list form or dialogue form) that answers follow-up questions.

Global View. Figure 2 depicts a screen shot from the IW browser in which the *Dag* proof style has been selected to show the global structure of the reasoning process. The sentence format can be displayed in (limited) English or in the reasoner's native language, and the depth and width of the tree can be restricted using the lens magnitude and lens width options, respectively. The user may ask for additional information by clicking hot links. The three small panes show the results of asking for follow-up information about an inference rule, an inference engine, and the variable bindings for a rule application.

Focused View. In Figure 3a, our explainer interface includes an option to focus on one step of the trace and display it using an English template style for presentation. The follow-up action pull down menu then helps the user to ask a number

Figure 3. (a) step-by-step view focusing on one step using an English template, and list of follow-up actions; (b) filtered view displaying supporting assertions and sources

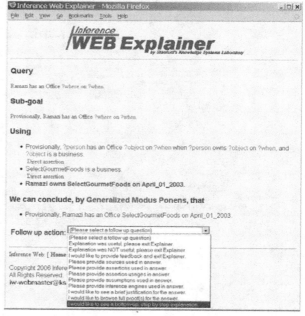

of context-dependent follow-up questions.

Filtered View. Figure 3b is the result of the user asking to see the sources.

Abstraction View. Inference Web approaches this issue with two strategies:

- Filter explanation information and only provide one type of information (such as what sources were used). This strategy just hides portions of the explanation and keeps the trace intact.
- Transform the explanation into another form. The IW abstractor component helps users to generate matching patterns to be used to rewrite proof segments producing an abstraction. Using these patterns, IW may provide an initial abstracted view of an explanation and then provide context appropriate follow-up question support.

The IW abstractor consists of an editor that allows users to define patterns that are to be matched against PML proofs. A matching pattern is associated with a rewriting strategy so that when a pattern is matched, the abstractor may use the rewriting strategy to transform the proof (hopefully into something more understandable). An example of how a proof can be abstracted with the use of a generic abstraction pattern is shown in Figure 4. In this case, the reasoner used a number of steps to derive that crab was a subclass of seafood. This portion of the proof is displayed in the *Dag* style in the middle of Figure 4 (inside the blue round-angled box). The user may specify an abstraction rule to reduce the multi-step proof fragment into a one-step proof fragment (class-transitivity inference) on the left side of Figure 4.

We are building up abstraction patterns for domain independent use, e.g. class transitivity as

Figure 4. Example of an abstraction of a piece of a proof

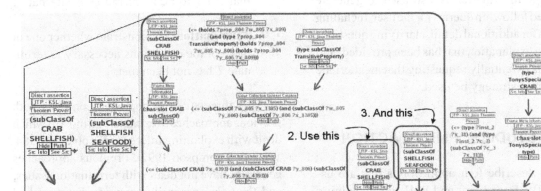

well as for domain-dependent use. It is an ongoing line of research to consider how best to build up a library of abstraction patterns and how to apply them in an efficient manner.

Discourse View. For some types of information manipulation traces, particular aspects or portions of the trace are predictably more relevant to users than others. Additionally, the context and user model can often be used to select and combine these portions of the trace, along with suggestions of which aspects may be important for follow-up queries. Particularly for these types of traces, IW provides a *discourse view*, which selects trace portions and presents them in simple natural language sentences. In this interaction mode, the full details of the inference rules and node structure are kept hidden from the user. Individual nodes, provenance information, and metadata associated with those nodes, are used as input for various explanation strategies, which select just the information relevant to the user's request and provide context-sensitive templates for displaying that information in dialogue form. This same information is also used to generate suggested follow-up queries for the user, including requests for additional detail, clarifying questions about the explanation that has been provided, and questions essentially requesting that an alternate explanation strategy be used.

CASE STUDIES: PML IN ACTION

We will describe four applications that are using the IW framework and PML for explaining semantic information and behavior. We selected four applications that can be categorized differently following the conceptual framework.

Cognitive Personal Assistants: CALO Example

IW and PML have been used by a DARPA-sponsored cognitive agent system called CALO that can be told what to do, reason with available knowledge, learn from experience, explain its recommendations, and respond robustly to surprise. The cognitive agent's actions are supported by justifications that are used to derive and present understandable explanations to end-users. These justifications reflect both how the actions support various user goals, and how the particular actions chosen by the agent were guided by the state of the world. More specifically, our approach to PML task justification breaks down the justification of a question about a particular task T into three complementary strategies, described here using terminology from SPARK (Morley & Myers 2004), the task engine used by CALO:

- **Relevance:** Demonstrate that fulfilling T will further one of the agent's high-level goals, which the user already knows about and accepts
- **Applicability:** Demonstrate that the conditions necessary to start T were met at the time T started (possibly including the conditions that led T to be preferred over alternative tasks)
- **Termination:** Demonstrate whether one or more of the conditions necessary to terminate T has not been met.

This three-strategy approach contrasts with previous approaches to explanation, most of which dealt with explaining inference (Scott et al. 1984, Wick & Thompson 1992). Previous approaches generally have not dealt with termination issues, and they also generally have not distinguished between relevance and applicability conditions. These are critical aspects of task processing and thus are important new issues for explanation.

Behavior Justification in PML

In CALO context, PML documents contain encodings of *behavior justifications* using PML node sets. A task execution justification is always a justification of why an agent is executing a given task *T*. The final conclusion of the justification is a sentence in first order logic saying that *T* is currently being executed. There are three antecedents for this final conclusion, corresponding to the three strategies discussed above. Each antecedent is supported by a justification fragment based on additional introspective predicates.

It is important to note that all the task processing justifications share a common structure that is rich enough to encode provenance information needed to answer the explanation requests we have identified so far. By inspecting the execution state via introspective predicates, explanation components can gather enough provenance information to support a wide range of explanations.

Text Analytic Information Manipulations: KANI Example

KANI (Knowledge Associates for Novel Intelligence) (Welty, et. al., 2005, Murdock, et. al., 2006) is a DTO-sponsored intelligence analyst hybrid system that combines large scale information extraction with knowledge representation. In this section we focus on the relevance of provenance to support explanations of hybrid systems utilizing statistical and deductive inference.

In this setting, we can view all information manipulation steps in a PML justification as a kind of inference. We then generated a taxonomy of text analytic processes and tasks that can be viewed as inferences. The taxonomy was motivated by the need to describe and explain the dominant extraction tasks in UIMA[b], without overloading the system with more information than would be useful. One key was to generate a taxonomy that is adequate to accurately describe extraction task functionalities and simultaneously abstract enough to be able to hide details of the tasks from end users. Another key was to support explanations to end users of the integrated system, not authors of software components debugging their products.

We divided text extraction into three primitive areas: annotation, co-reference, and integration. We describe each briefly. Annotation tasks make assertions about spans of text that recognize a type or argument. Annotation inferences include:

1. **Entity recognition:** Determines that some span of text refers to an entity of a specified type. For example, a component could take the sentence "Tony Gradgrind is the owner of Tony's Foods" (the restaurant serving Tony's Specialty) and conclude that characters 0 to 14 of that sentence refer to some entity of type Person.

2. **Relation recognition:** Assigns a relation type to a span (e.g., a sentence describes a relation of type Owner).

3. **Relation annotation argument identification:** Determines and assigns values to the roles of a relation (e.g., a particular person is a participant in a given ownership relation instance).

Co-reference inferences utilize annotation inferences and further identify that multiple text spans actually refer to the same entity or relation.

1. **Entity identification:** Determines that a set of entity annotations refer to a particular instance.

2. **Relation identification:** Determines that a set of relation annotations refer to a particular relation instance.

3. **Extracted entity classification:** Determines that a particular co-referenced entity has a particular type. (e.g., the type of the entity referred to by "Gradgrind" is Person).

4. **Knowledge integration** inferences include mapping inferences providing access to provenance.

5. **Entity mapping:** Determines that an entity instance in the KB is derived from a set of entities and relation instances.

6. **Relation mapping:** Determines that a relationship in the target KB is derived from a set of entity and relation instances.
7. **Target entity classification:** Determines that an entity instance is an instance of an entity type in the target ontology.

We have registered these inferences in the IW registry and we use these information manipulation steps to explain all of the UIMA components used in our prototype system, which provides intelligence analyst support for analyzing documents and evaluating results of text statements.

Text Analytic Manipulation Descriptions

We use our taxonomy of text analytic manipulations in declarative descriptions encoding what was done to generate the extracted knowledge bases. UIMA generates a large extracted knowledge database containing its conclusions. We needed to take that as input (potentially augmented) and generate interoperable proof descriptions (a PML document) as an output.

The software component that produces PML documents for UIMA-based analysis processes begins with a specified result from a specified Extended Knowledge Database (EKDB) (e.g., TonyGradgrind is the Owner of TonysFoods). It follows the links in the EKDB from that conclusion back to the intermediate results and raw input that led to it. From these intermediate results, it is able to produce inference steps encoded in PML that refer to the corresponding tasks in the taxonomy. For example, if the EKDB records that characters 0 to 14 of some sentence were labeled as a Person and that this labeling was identified as specifying an occurrence of TonyGradgrind then the component would create an Entity Recognition inference step in PML for that labeling as well as coreference step for the result that the labeling is an occurrence of TonyGradgrind.

Transparent Accountable Data Mining: TAMI Example

TAMI (Weitzner, et. al., 2006) is an NSF-sponsored privacy-preserving system funded in the Cybertrust program. The idea is to provide transparency into the usage of data that has been collected, so that people may be able to see how data that has been collected about them has been used. In any accountable system, explanations are essential for providing transparency into the usage of information along with claims of compliance with privacy policies.

Usage policies are encoded concerning which organizations can use information for particular purposes. (The project specifically aims at usage instead of collection policies, so it is only use and reuse that is a topic for explanations). A transaction log is collected, which encodes data transfer information concerning transfers, policies, purposes, and organizations. Reasoning engines are used that evaluate the validity of transfer actions based on the encoded policies. These engines are instrumented to encode justifications for their determinations in PML, so that explanations can be provided about justified or unjustified transfers.

This system can be leveraged in a number of examples. One use case is in the explanation of justified or unjustified arrests. It is possible that data collected in compliance with rules for a particular purpose by an authorized agency may be reused to support a number of other conclusions. One prototype demonstration system in TAMI looks at arrests and then checks to see if they are justified according to their appropriate or inappropriate reuse of data that has been collected. Inference Web can then be used to explain why the system has determined that an arrest is legally justified or unjustified.

Integrated Learning Systems: GILA Example

GILA (Generalized Integrated Learning Architecture) is a DARPA-sponsored intelligent agent that integrates the results of multiple learners to provide intelligent assistant services. The initial domain is airspace control order deconfliction. GILA uses multiple independent learning components, a meta reasoning executive, and other components to make recommendations about ways to resolve conflicts in an existing airspace control order. In order to be operational, it must be able to explain its recommendations to end users and auditors. In addition, the explanations may be uses by learners and the meta executive to choose appropriate recommendations and assign credit and blame.

DISCUSSION

Explanation has been an active line of research since at least the days of expert systems, where explanation research largely focused on explaining rule-based systems. Today, explanation in rule systems is once again a research. Rule systems are now being integrated into hybrid settings, and now explanation must be done on both the rule components and the setting in which conclusions from those rule components are integrated and used. Also, theorem proving systems, such as Description Logic Reasoners, historically integrated explanation capabilities after usage increased and broadened. Early description logics that were broadly used, such as CLASSIC and LOOM provided some notion of explanation (e.g., McGuinness, 1996) in either insight into a trace or a proof theoretic-based approach to explanation. More recent explanation demands have inspired current generation tableaux-based DL reasoners to include some notion of explanation focusing on provenance, axiom usage, and clash detection (e.g., Parsia, et al, 2005, Plessers

and Troyer, 2006). While all of these efforts are useful and important, today's explanation systems need to handle a much broader range of question answering styles and thus demand much more versatility and interoperability for their explanation infrastructure. Simultaneously, the infrastructure needs to be modular so that users with limited scope can support their applications without the burden of extra (unwanted) overhead. In our research on explaining provenance, we have recently modularized our explanation interlingua and the supporting background ontologies so that clients *only* interested in explaining provenance may use our infrastructure with the freedom of importing only the required modules.

Explanation requirements often arise in many settings that do not simply use standard deductive reasoning components. Our work, for example, has taken us into the realm of explaining text analytic components and a wide range of machine learning components. As a result, we have explored and are continuing to explore representation, manipulation, and presentation support for explaining systems that may use statistical, incomplete, and/or uncertain reasoning paradigms. Explanation research has also branched out into settings such as collaborative social networks, and we have engaged in research aimed particularly at explaining systems embedded in or leveraging large distributed communities. In many of the more recent research areas, we have found many requirements concerning trust, ranging from trust calculation to trust propagation, as well as presentation issues related to filtering by trust.

One relatively active area of provenance explanation is in the field of scientific applications. Increasingly, virtual collections of scientific data are being enabled by semantic technology (e.g., Virtual Observatories such as the Virtual Solar Terrestrial Observatory (McGuinness, et al, 2007). Such repositories are much more likely to be usable and to be used when provenance is maintained and available concerning where the data came from. More recently, there has been emphasis on additionally explaining the workflow from which it was produced. Thus, there is an emerging emphasis on explaining scientific provenance and workflow.

FUTURE RESEARCH DIRECTIONS

We have active research plans in a number of areas related to explanation.

1. **Learning.** Increasingly hybrid systems are depending on individual or multiple learning components to provide either ground facts or sometimes procedures. We are currently working multiple learning component authors to provide explanation components for learned information and learned procedures.
2. **Provenance.** The importance of provenance seems to be growing in many fields and we are focusing on providing relatively lightweight explanation solutions for provenance. We are also exploring special purpose needs of interdisciplinary scientific applications with respect to provenance.
3. **Trust.** Our current trust model is relatively simplistic and we are investigating ways of providing more representational primitives, methods for automatically suggesting trust ratings, and methods for intelligently combining and explaining combined trust values.
4. **Evaluation.** We have developed a PML validator that checks to see if an encoding is valid PML. We are extending that to provide an ontology evaluation module that not only checks for syntactic and semantic correctness, but also reviews (and explains findings concerning) ontology modeling styles.

CONCLUSION

In this chapter, we have explored the growing field of explanation. We noted that as applications become more autonomous, complex, collaborative, and interconnected, the need for explanation expands. We presented a modular interlingua capable of representing explanations that focus on provenance, justifications, and trust. We also presented the Inference Web infrastructure for manipulating explanations in a wide range of application settings. We provided examples in a diverse set of domains showing different settings where explanations are required, and then described how Inference Web and PML are being used to meet these needs. We also presented a number of different presentation paradigms for explanations.

ACKNOWLEDGMENT

We have benefited greatly by working with a number of excellent collaborators including Bill Murdock, Chris Welty, and Dave Ferrucci from IBM and Andrew Cowell, Dave Thurman, and colleagues from Battelle on NIMD, Michael Wolverton, Karen Myers, David Morley from SRI on CALO, Danny Weitzner, Tim Berners-Lee, Lalana Kagal, Chris Hanson, Gerry Sussman, Hal Abelson, Dan Connolly, Sandro Hawke, Kay Waterman, and colleagues from MIT on TAMI, and a large contingent of collaborators on GILA including Ken Whitebread, Martin Hofmann, Phil DiBona, Steve Wilder from Lockheed Martin and collaborators in multiple universities on the project related to learners and meta reasoning. This work has been partially supported by contract numbers: 55-00680, PO TT0687676, 5710001895-2, 2003*H278000*000, HR0011-05-0019, and F30602-00-1-0579.

REFERENCES

Barber, K., & Martin, C. (1999, May 1). Agent autonomy: Specification, measurement, and ydnamic adjustment. In *Proceedings of the Autonomy Control Software Workshop at Autonomous Agents 1999* (Agents '99), 8-15. Seattle,WA.

CALO (2008). http://www.ai.sri.com/project/CALO

Cowell, A.J., McGuinness, D.L., Varley, C.F., & Thurman, D.A. (2006). Knowledge-worker requirements for next generation query answering and explanation systems. In the *Proceedings of the Workshop on Intelligent User Interfaces for Intelligence Analysis, International Conference on Intelligent User Interfaces* (IUI 2006), Sydney, Australia.

Del Rio, N., & Pinheiro da Silva, P. (2007, June). Identifying and explaining map imperfections through knowledge provenance visualization. *Technical report UTEP-CS-07-43a*, University of Texas at El Paso, El Paso, TX.

Del Rio, N., & Pinheiro da Silva, P. (2007a, November 26-28). Probe-It! Visualization support for provenance. In *Proceedings of the Third International Symposium on Visual Computing (ISVC 2007)*, Lake Tahoe, NV/CA.

Dent, L., Boticario, J., McDermott, J. et al. (1992). A personal learning apprentice. In *Proceedings of the 10 National Conference on Artificial Intelligence*, San Jose, California: AAAI Press, pp. 96-103.

Dzbor, M., Motta, E., & Domingue, J.B. (2004). Opening up magpie via semantic services. In McIlraith et al. (eds), The Semantic Web - ISWC 2004, *Third International Semantic WebConference*. Hiroshima, Japan. *Lecture Notes in Computer Science*, 3298,Springer-Verlag.

Glass, A., McGuinness, D., & Wolverton, M. (2008). Toward establishing trrust in adaptive agents. In *Proceedings of the International Conference on Intelligent User Interfaces (IUI'08)*, Gran Canaria, Spain. Also, KSL Technical Report KSL-07-04.

Guha, R., & McCool, R. (2003). Tap: A Semantic Web platform. *Computer Networks, 42*(5), 557-577.

Hyvönen, E., Mäkelä, E., Salminen, M., Valo, A., Viljanen, K., Saarela, S., Junnila, M., & Kettula, S. (2005). MuseumFinland - Finnish museums on the Semantic Web. *Journal of Web Semantics, 3*(2), 25.

Huynh, D., Mazzocchi, S., Karger, D. (2005, November 6-10). Piggy bank: Experience the Semantic Web inside your Web browser. In Gil et al. (eds), *The Semantic Web - ISWC 2005, 4th International Next Generation Semantic Web Applications ISWC 2005*. Galway, Ireland. *Lecture Notes in Computer Science*, 3729 Springer-Verlag.

Lashkari, Y., Metral, M., & Maes, P. (1994). Collaborative interface agents. In *Proceedings of the 12 National Conference on Artificial Intelligence*. Seattle, WA: AAAI Press, pp. 444-450.

Lieberman, H., & Kumar, A. (2005, September). Providing expert advice by analogy for on-line help, *IEEE/ACM Conference on Web Intelligence & Intelligent Agent Technology*, Compiègne, France.

Lopez, V., Motta, E., & Uren, V. (2006, June 11-14). PowerAqua: Fishing the Semantic Web. In York Sure and John Domingue (eds.), *The Semantic Web: Research and Applications, 3rd European Semantic Web Conference, ESWC 2006*, Budva, Montenegro. *Lecture Notes in Computer Science 4011*, Springer, ISBN 3-540-34544-2.

Maes, P. (1994). *Agents that reduce work and information overload communications of the ACM, 37*(7), 31-40.

Maybury, M. (2003). New directions on question and answering, *AAAI Spring Sysmposium,* TR-SS-03-07, Stanford, CA.

McGuinness, D. L. (1996). Explaining reasoning in description logics. Ph.D. Thesis, Rutgers University. Technical Report LCSR-TR-277. Rutgers Department of Computer Science Technical Report Series.

McGuinness, D.L., & Pinheiro da Silva, P. (2004, October). Explaining answers from the Semantic Web: The inference Web approach. *Journal of Web Semantics, 1*(4), 397-413.

McGuinness, D.L., Ding, L., Glass, G., Chang, C., Zeng, H., & Furtado, V. (2006a) Explanation interfaces for the Semantic Web: Issues and models. Presented in the *3rd International Semantic Web User Interaction Workshop (SWUI'06),* Co-located with the *International Semantic Web Conference*, Athens, Georgia, USA.

McGuinness, D.L., Zeng, H., Pinheiro da Silva, P., Ding, L., Narayanan, D., & Bhaowal. M. (2006b, May 22). Investigations into trust for collaborative information repositories: A Wikipedia case study. *WWW2006 Workshop on the Models of Trust for the Web (MTW'06)*, Edinburgh, Scotland.

McGuinness, D.L., Ding, L., Glass, G., Chang, C., Zeng, H., & Furtado, V. (2006a) Explanation interfaces for the Semantic Web: Issues and models. Presented in the *3rd International Semantic Web User Interaction Workshop (SWUI'06),* Co-located with the *International Semantic Web Conference*, Athens, Georgia, USA.

McGuinness, D.L., Ding, L., Pinheiro da Silva, P., & Chang, C. (2007). A modular explanation interlingua. In the *Proceedings of the Explanation-aware Computing Workshop (ExaCt-2007)* co-located with the *Association for the Advancement of Artificial Intelligence*, Vancouver, BC.

McGuinness, D., Fox, P., Cinquini, L., West, P., Garcia, J., Benedict, J.L., & Middleton, D. (2007a,

July 22-26). The virtual solar-terrestrial observatory: A deployed Semantic Web application case study for scientific research. In *proceedings of the Nineteenth Conference on Innovative Applications of Artificial Intelligence (IAAI-07)*. Vancouver, BC, Canada.

Morley, D., & Myers, K. (2004). The SPARK agent framework. In *Proceedings of the Third International Joint Conference on Autonomous Agents and Multi Agent Systems (AAMAS-04),* New York, NY.

Mota, E., & Sabou, M. (2006). *Next generation Semantic Web applications*, ASWC.

Murdock, J.W., McGuinness, D.L., Pinheiro da Silva, P., Welty, C., & Ferrucci, D. (2006, November 5-9). Explaining conclusions from diverse knowledge sources. In the *Proceedings of the Fifth International Semantic Web Conference,* Athens, Ga.

Parsia, B., Sirin, E., & Kalyanpur, A. (2005) Debugging owl ontologies. In the *Proceedings of the World Wide Web Conference*, pp. 633-640.

Plessers, P, & Troyer, O. D. Resolving inconsistencies in evolving ontologies. In the *Proceedings of the European Semantic Web Conference*, pp. 200-214.

Popov, B., Kiryakov, A., Kirilov, A., Manov, D., Ognyanoff, D., & Goranov, M. (2003). KIM – A Semantic Annotation Platform. In D. Fensel, K. Sycara, and J. Mylopoulos (eds.), *The Semantic Web - ISWC 2003, Second International Semantic Web Conference. Lecture Notes in Computer Science*, 2870, Springer-Verlag.

Pynadath, D.V., & Tambe, M. (2002). Electric elves: Adjustable autonomy in real-world multiagent environments. In socially intelligent agents – *Creating relationships with computers and robots.* Kluwer Academic Publishers.

Rhodes, B.J., & Starner, T. (1996). Remembrance agent: A continuously automated information retrieval system. *Proceedings, First international Conference on the Practical Application of Intelligent Agents and Multi-Agent Technology.* London, UK.

Schraefel, M.C., Shadbolt, N.R., Gibbins, N., Glaser, H., & Harris, S. (2004). CS AKTive space: Representing computer science in the Semantic Web. In *Proceedings of the 13th International World Wide Web Conference.*

Sullivan, D., Grosz, B., & Kraus, S. (2000). Intention reconciliation by collaborative agents. In *Proceedings of the Fourth International Conference on Multi-Agent Systems, IEEE Computer Society Press*, Boston, MA.

Wagner, E., & Lieberman, H. (2003, January). End-user debugging for electronic commerce. *ACM Conference on Intelligent User Interfaces*, Miami Beach.

Weitzner, D.J., Abelson, H., Berners-Lee, T., Hanson, C.P., Hendler, J., Kagal, L., McGuinness, D.L., Sussman, G.J., Krasnow-Waterman, K. (2006). Transparent accountable inferencing for privacy risk management. *Proceedings of AAAI Spring Symposium on The Semantic Web meets eGovernment.* Stanford University, USA: AAAI Press Also available as MIT CSAIL Technical Report-2006-007 and Stanford KSL Technical Report KSL-06-03.

Welty, C., Murdock, J.W., Pinheiro da Silva, P., McGuinness, D.L., Ferrucci, D., & Fikes, R. (2005). Tracking information extraction from intelligence documents. In *Proceedings of the 2005 International Conference on Intelligence Analysis (IA 2005),* McLean, VA, USA.

ADDITIONAL READINGS

Explanation Infrastructure:

Foundational paper: Deborah L. McGuinness and Paulo Pinheiro da Silva. Explaining Answers from the Semantic Web: The Inference Web Approach. *Journal of Web Semantics. 1*(4). 397-413, October 2004.

Diverse Explanation Presentation Paradigms: Deborah L. McGuinness, Li Ding, Alyssa Glass, Cynthia Chang, Honglei Zeng and Vasco Furtado. Explanation Interfaces for the Semantic Web: Issues and Models. Presented in *the 3rd International Semantic Web User Interaction Workshop(SWUI'06),* Co-located with the International Semantic Web Conference, Athens, Georgia, USA, November 6, 2006.

Explanation Interlingua:

Newest version: McGuinness, D.L.; Ding, L., Pinheiro da Silva, P., and Chang, C. A Modular Explanation Interlingu . Proceedings of the 2007 Workshop on Explanation-aware Computing (ExaCt-2007), Vancouver, Canada, July 22-23, 2007.

Original version: Paulo Pinheiro da Silva, Deborah L. McGuinness and Richard Fikes. A Proof Markup Language for Semantic Web Services. *Information Systems.* Volume 31, Issues 4-5, June-July 2006, Pages 381-395. Previous version, technical report, Knowledge Systems Laboratory, Stanford University.

Explanation and Trust Requirements Studies:

In Intelligence Settings: Cowell, A.; McGuinness, D.L.; Varley, C.; Thurman, D. Knowledge-Worker Requirements for Next Generation Query Answering and Explanation Systems. In the Proceedings of the Workshop on Intelligent User Interfaces for Intelligence Analysis, International Conference on Intelligent User Interfaces (IUI 2006), Sydney, Australia. 2006.

In Cognitive Assistant Settings: Glass, A.; McGuinness, D.L.; Wolverton, M. Toward Establishing Trust in Adaptive Agents. International Conference on Intelligent User Interfaces (IUI'08), Gran Canaria, Spain, 2008.

Selected Applications

Explaining Task Processing in Learning Settings: McGuinness, D.L.; Glass, A.; Wolverton, M.; Pinheiro da Silva, P. Explaining Task Processing in Cognitive Assistants that Learn. Proceedings of the 20th International FLAIRS Conference (FLAIRS-20), Key West, Florida, May 7-9, 2007.

Explaining Data Mining and Data Usage: Weitzner, D.J.; Abelson, H.; Berners-Lee, T.; Hanson, C.P.; Hendler, J.; Kagal, L.; McGuinness, D.L.; Sussman, G.J.; Waterman, K.K. Transparent Accountable Data Mining: New Strategies for Privacy Protection. Proceedings of AAAI Spring Symposium on The Semantic Web meets eGovernment. AAAI Press, Stanford University, Stanford, CA, USA, 2006.

Explaining Text Analytics: J. William Murdock, Deborah L. McGuinness, Paulo Pinheiro da Silva, Christopher Welty and David Ferrucci. Explaining Conclusions from Diverse Knowledge Sources. The 5th International Semantic Web Conference (ISWC2006), Athens, Georgia, USA, November 5th - 9th, 2006.

Explaining Intelligence Applications: Christopher Welty, J. William Murdock, Paulo Pinheiro da Silva, Deborah L. McGuinness, David Ferrucci, Richard Fikes. Tracking Information Extraction from Intelligence Documents. In Proceedings of the 2005 International Conference on Intelligence Analysis (IA 2005), McLean, VA, USA, 2-6 May, 2005.

Explanation, Trust, and Collaborative Systems:

Deborah L. McGuinness, Honglei Zeng, Paulo Pinheiro da Silva, Li Ding, Dhyanesh Narayanan, and Mayukh Bhaowal. Investigations into Trust for Collaborative Information Repositories: A Wikipedia Case Study. WWW2006 Workshop on the Models of Trust for the Web (MTW'06), Edinburgh, Scotland, May 22, 2006.

Ilya Zaihrayeu, Paulo Pinheiro da Silva and Deborah L. McGuinness. IWTrust: Improving User Trust in Answers from the Web. Proceedings of 3rd International Conference on Trust Management (iTrust2005), Springer, Rocquencourt, France, 2005.

Zeng, H.; Alhossaini, M.; Ding, L.; Fikes, R.; McGuinness, D.L. Computing Trust from Revision History. The 2006 International Conference on Privacy, Security and Trust (PST 2006) Markham, Ontario, Canada October 30 -- November 1, 2006.

Patricia Victor, Chris Cornelis, Martine De Cock, Paulo Pinheiro da Silva. Towards a Provenance-Preserving Trust Model in Agent Networks. Proceeding of the WWW'06 Workshop on Models of Trust for the Web (MTW'06), Edinburgh, Scotland, May 22, 2006.

Patricia Victor, Chris Cornelis, Martine De Cock, Paulo Pinheiro da Silva. Gradual Trust and Distrust in Recommender Systems. Fuzzy Sets and Systems (to appear).

ENDNOTES

[a]   The OWL encoding of PML-P is available at: http://iw.stanford.edu/2006/06/pml-provenance.owl

[b]   http://www.research.ibm.com/UIMA/

Chapter II
Industrial Use of Semantics:
NNEC Semantic Interoperability

Victor Rodriguez-Herola

Dirección de Sistemas de Defensa y Seguridad, ISDEFE, S.A., Spain

ABSTRACT

The North Atlantic Treaty Organisation (NATO) is shifting towards Net-centric operations paradigms driven by the nature of the new missions that the Alliance will likely be facing in the coming years. This new situation has forced the Alliance to pursue the achievement of the so-called NATO Network-Enabled Capability (NNEC). In this framework, the concept of a system of systems should give way to the new paradigm of federation of services, where any capability needs to be seen as a loosely-couple service. From the perspective of any of these services, one of the biggest issues will be to discover available services and, more importantly, the information provided for such services can be consumed. For this purpose, we present in this chapter the use of Semantic Web as a technology that will facilitate the explicit description of the services available on the Net that will eventually help in selecting the right services. The technology will also mediate between service consumers and service providers, so information is given a well-defined meaning and is comprehensible. Based on the foundations of the Semantic Web, we propose a concept demonstrator called SISearch, where well defined vocabularies from apparently different domains are defined by using ontology languages. Then, these different vocabularies are interpreted with respect to the vocabulary defined by a potential service consumer. Assisted by this interpretation and by inference services, the SISearch will translate both consumer-based queries to service provider specific-queries (using different vocabularies), and aggregating and interpreting the results with respect to the service consumer vocabulary. This approach will allow extending to new potential service consumer or service providers without having to develop specific modules or components.

INTRODUCTION

NATO member states are facing new challenges and new threats. NATO structure has changed considerably in the last fifteen years. The traditional strategic models, where enemy power could equalize those of the Alliance countries, are no longer of use.

A relevant example is the threat of terrorist attacks – asymmetric warfare – which cannot be focused on an organised state with traditional military forces. Another relevant example is related to the operations in which NATO is directly involved, from the Balkan crises to Afghanistan stabilisation operations. In any of these cases, these are peacekeeping operations which were not initially contemplated by the Alliance and, which became more striking, the new situation required information exchange with non-NATO Nations that are present on theatre. Furthermore, the response time needed in these situations, from force deployment to *CIS* (Communications and Information Systems) deployment, is not in tune with the past rigid structure.

These are some of the reasons that have forced to clearly define a new structure of the Alliance that would give response to the above mentioned challenges, *NATO Response Force* (NRF) (NATO, 2007b) being a representative of a more dynamic and ready to deploy forces. Along with this new restructuring comes a new set of necessary CIS capabilities adapted to more dynamic forces and to unforeseen operations, unlike those fixed stovepiped self-contained systems developed for very well known situations. This new paradigm (as opposed to the stovepipe paradigm) is the so-called *NATO Network Enabled Capability* (NNEC) (Buckman, 2005).

NNEC can be defined as net-centric environment, resembling the Grid concept (Foster et al., 1999), where systems are no more considered monolithic elements eventually connected at some point in time, but they are considered as specific net-centric functionalities or services.

Moreover, these services will be connected and disconnected over time and, thus, must advertise their presence automatically. Besides, whenever any consumer service needs information, it will need a mechanism by which it discovers available and adequate services. The possibility of finding relevant information will enable any services, applying the necessary filtering, to have a better situational awareness and an enhanced coordination and force reaction.

The above descriptions make the case for specifying an Interoperability Framework by which NATO and National services will interoperate in this new environment. Several Research & Development initiatives within NATO are exploring different existing and promising technologies in order to enable and implement the interoperability requirements defined by NNEC. As a common ground, it is assumed that any net-centric solution should consider the Internet as a model: the ability of accessing any type of information, the possibilities of making available any type of information and the ability of dynamically discovering services.

Based on the foundations of the Semantic Web (W3C, 2007), we propose a concept demonstrator called *Semantic Interoperability Search* (*SISearch*), where well defined vocabularies from different domains are defined by using ontology languages. Then, these different vocabularies are interpreted with respect to the vocabulary defined by a potential service consumer. Assisted by this interpretation, the SISearch will translate both consumer-based queries to service provider specific-queries (using different vocabularies), and aggregating and interpreting the results with respect to the service consumer vocabulary.

This approach will allow extending to new potential service consumers or service providers without having to develop specific modules or components. It will be needed a way to declaratively exposing the new vocabulary and defining interpretations with respect to the consuming service. This will be achieved by being able to reason or infer information out of the vocabulary descriptions or ontologies. We provide an architecture that shields these generic capabilities and eventually have been used for service and information discovery in the SISearch demonstrator.

Section 2 presents the Interoperability problem seen from the perspective of NATO. In Section 3, an introduction to Semantic Interoperability concepts are given and, then, an approach by using linking ontologies is presented in Section 4. Section 5 outlines the overall architecture of the SISearch prototype developed by NC3A. Finally the major conclusions drawn from the present work are covered in Section 6.

THE INTEROPERABILITY PROBLEM

Interoperability is one of the fundamental elements that characterize NATO. This means that, in any operation in which NATO is leading, the countries members must contribute not only with troops in a cohesive way, but also must deploy all the necessary CIS and Functional Systems in order to support operations: and they have to work seamlessly. NATO can, in some cases, be in charge of the basic CIS infrastructure, but it cannot replace in any case the national systems.

NATO does not specify explicitly which CIS each member country should use, meaning each nation has their own specific system with potentially unique definitions. However these systems must communicate with each other or be capable of transferring information between each other in a safe, trustworthy and complete way. Therefore, NATO, through the collaboration of all the signatory countries, must develop a set of specifications (standard agreement – STANAG) (NATO, 2007) that assure interoperability at all the levels of the OSI model; from communications interoperability, to network interoperability to application interoperability.

At the communications level, which during many years was practically the only means of interoperability between the member states, the existing standards are quite stable, having undergone slight adaptations over time. At the network level, interoperability has evolved much quicker; protocols like TCP/IP have prevailed as one of the most stable.

When we reach the application layer, new protocols and variations of existing ones have appeared at a greater rate. This has meant an additional effort to make specific standards with respect to the information and how to structure and formalize this information. The traditional method of information interoperability has been based mainly on messages following a format and specific syntax (i.e. NATO, 2008). Interoperability between systems has become more and more sophisticated by the replication of data structures based on a common data model. The number of message formats and the number of *common data models* have been increasing based on the different requirements in line with the diverse levels of information interoperability required, or on the different technological capacities of the member nations.

This explosion of diverse standards at the level of information interoperability is key but was seen, at the time, as controllable because it was only required on a point-to-point basis (i.e. System A ⇔ System B interoperating synchronously or asynchronously). At this point we can exclude the *tactical data link* community (TDL) (Nierle, 1996) which makes use of radio transmission to broadcast (multicast) their information. So to date two types of interoperability architecture have basically existed: An architecture based on a *common data model* and an architecture based on the specification of a *bilateral model*.

The Common Data Model

The architecture based on a *common data model* (see Figure 1) is based on the principle of the translation or adaptation of the information instances in a specific internal system model to a

Figure 1. Common data model

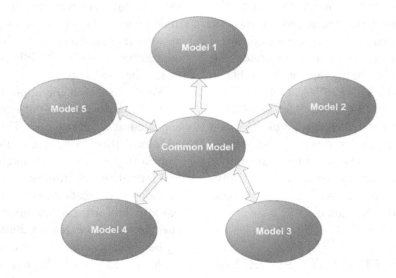

common or intermediate data model or scheme shared with one or more other systems. Therefore, before transmitting the information from one system to another (point to point) the information must be adapted and be translated to this common schema. Once the consuming system receives the instances of data it will have to perform another translation into their internal data model.

In some cases, some national systems have been developed from the beginning considering this common model and, therefore, the reception and later information processing are facilitated since the translation to the internal model is reduced to the minimum (that comes to be practically the common model itself). In other occasions, the national systems have been developed following their own data model and closer to their own requirements and specifications. This forces to maintain two data models, the internal one and the one that is used for a possible transference to another system.

This architecture is known as *N problem*, since being *N* systems with different internal data model with respect to the common one, they are to make at least *2N* translations from the own data models to the common data model and vice versa.

An advantage of this architecture is that the number of translations that a system must make to transmit the information is reduced to one, or to two, if we considered that some systems must translate the information received from the common model to the internal model.

But some *logistics* disadvantages exist, since any modification of the common model must simultaneously have the approval of the people in charge of all the involved systems and, at the same time, these modifications implies changes, sometimes substantial changes, of the own system. This implies that the change cycle is considerably spaced. For example, in the case of *Multinational Interoperability Programme* (MIP, 2005) the life cycle of a version of the common model (well-known as *Command and Control Information Exchange Data Model* - C2IEDM) is two years, that is to say, the adaptation of the systems to a new change takes, as a minimum two years. We will see later that this approach may not be the most appropriate for current and future requirements.

Figure 2. Bilateral model

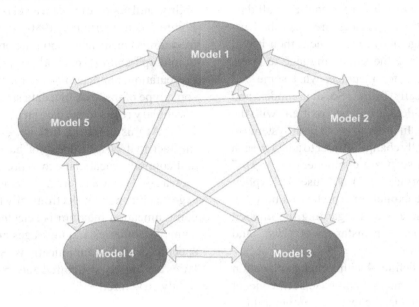

The Bilateral Model

In the architecture based on a *bilateral model* (see Figure 2), a specific model is defined for every two systems that wish to interchange information. This model varies based on the requirements and of the type of information. In this case, each system will have to adapt to as many models as different types of information and formats are wanted to interchange with other so many systems.

This architecture has come to be known as N^2 *problem*, since being N systems each one with a different model of information, there will be N^2-N adaptations or translations.

There is an evident disadvantage in this approach, since the number of adaptations that each system must do is excessive if the number of systems (strictly speaking, the number of different information models) that must interoperate with is high. But it has the advantage, however, of the flexibility, that is to say, the necessary time so that a system is adapted in such a way that it can interchange information with a new system, it is considerably smaller than if the model needs a consensus between all the people in charge of the systems. In anyone of the cases, this approach is also unsuitable for the present and future situations.

PRINCIPLES OF SEMANTIC INTEROPERABILITY

Semantic Interoperability (SI) postulates for specifying an XML-based formal language that will enable the mutual understanding of the interchanged data between two or more entities (Sølvberg et al., 2002). This language will enhance the syntactical nature of XML with ancillaries for interpreting a domain or system specific vocabulary. Furthermore, this language is devised to be interpreted by "intelligent" services. By "intelligent" we refer to the ability of an application to provide implicit answers from explicit knowledge and applying specific rules (Baader et al., 2003).

Intuitively, we are to imagine that any system that provides information in a Net-centric environment it will also make explicit the data model associated to that information. If all data model from all the services are described using the language above mentioned, then it will be possible to use the same language to "say" or interpret that, for instance, what some call "*Unit*" others call "*Track*". So, data models and transformation details will be "written" with the same language. In order to avoid both systems to programmatically change in order to adapt to each other model, a software component or "*agent*" (Russell & Norvig, 2003) will use the explicit models and the explicit interpretations between them to provide answers regarding the implicit "similarities" between instances of "*Unit*" and instances of "*Track*".

So to better define SI, a thorough explanation of each of the terms that compose such concept will be given, that is, the term "interoperability" and the term "semantic".

Interoperability

Interoperability is basically the ability that two or more entities (i.e., systems) have to work or operate together. In order to achieve that, a medium, a message and a formal vocabulary are needed to construct the message.

Each of these three components can be applied at different levels of interoperability. It can be applied to a human interoperability: In NATO it has been concluded that the medium is the air or a piece of paper, the message is referring to the oral or written message and the vocabulary has been constrained to English and/or (in some cases) French syntax. It can also be applied at the technical level, that is, at the communications level. In this case, there are several medium, like air (i.e., satellite communication for a broad reach, wireless in a local area), electrical medium (i.e. cable); the message it uses to be some packets of 0's and 1's and the vocabulary range from TDL to TCP/IP, etc.

It can be given further examples of interoperability until application data level is reached – see Figure 3 (Zimmermann, 1980). In this case, the medium is constructed upon the previous layers of interoperability – network, transport, session, presentation, application - the message refers to some type of instance of a data structure and the vocabulary refers to the data structure or schema itself. At this point the first issues arise due to the fact that NATO does not have a universal and common vocabulary to express any type of messages – we are referring of course to a message that is to be sent electronically for whichever communication medium is selected. Moreover, some vocabularies and messages are bound to a specific kind of communications. Some vocabularies are loosely structured and some others are tightly structured.

Figure 3. The OSI model

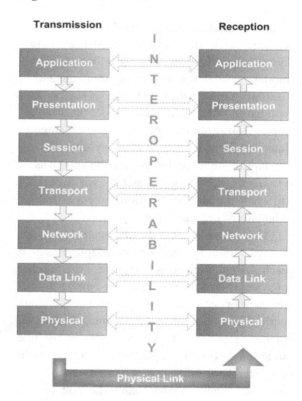

Besides the medium, the message and the vocabulary, it is needed a syntax, that is, some rules that constrains how the different parts of the vocabulary can be put together. And even in this case, different types of syntax at the data interoperability level can be applied, because there are different types of syntax when "writing" a message; from MTF (Message Text Format), with a very loosely structured syntax, to C2IEDM based information exchange, with a very tightly structured syntax.

As mentioned before, NATO have been successful in achieving some agreements (STANAGs) on how this interoperability at the different levels should be and some of them co-exist at the same level, depending on the objectives and the context they are to be used; as an example, it would be excessive to send a sophisticated database instance for replication through a 64 Kb bandwidth line, so a message based replication is more appropriate.

Some common ground has been found in order to identify a common syntax – not a common vocabulary – that would be used to construct our messages. And that common syntax is XML (Bray et al., 2006). XML is independent from the medium, independent of the message to be constructed and independent of the vocabulary to be used. Moreover, it allows the definition of vocabulary and the definition of how the terms of a vocabulary are put together. In a single word: Metalanguage, a language that is able to create languages. With XML is possible to re-adapt the messages, vocabulary and syntax and be able to exchange those XML-based messages between systems that generate and consume different ones. This is achieved because XML is built by using a universal vocabulary, based on the standards ISO-8879 (Goldfarb, 1991).

XML is the foundation for many of the most relevant and emerging standards in the international arena: from XSD (XML Schema Definition) and XSL (XML Style sheet) (Thompson et al., 2004) to define vocabularies, define structures and assist in the transformation, to SOAP (Simple Object Access Protocol) (Gudgin et al., 2007) and WSDL (Chinnici et al. 2007) for the basic Web Services Standards and from standardized (BEPL (Alves et al., 2006), WS-Security (Nadalin et al., 2004), WS-Notification (Graham et al., 2006)...) to non-standardized but standards de-facto (XMPP (Saint-Andre, 2004), JXTA (Oaks et al., 2002)...) for other kind of functionalities.

XML has been embraced as the *lingua franca* not only for Internet but also within NATO, as it has been understood that is a well-suited language to create message vocabularies or even to create data instance replications. Some examples can be seen in the ongoing effort to formalize in XML the different (T)DL specifications; or the NVG (NATO Vector Graphics) a specific extension to SVG (Scalable Vector Graphics) (Ferraiolo, Jun & Jackson, 2003); several kind of message-based standards, like AdatP-3 and OTH-Gold (Muller, 2000) are providing XML Schemas representation of their traditional vocabularies.

Semantic

Besides the four interoperability pillars mentioned before (medium, message, vocabulary, syntax), it is obviously needed a mechanism by which it is understood what the message coming from a specific medium, using a specific vocabulary and "written" with a specific syntax means.

It was said before that having this message in XML would be sufficient. It may happen that the message is in a structure and with a vocabulary that the receiving systems are unable to process. It is formalised in XML and a universal XML parser can be used in order to get all the bits and pieces of it but, what can it be done with it? At least there are XML parsers available commercially or open source. Back in time a new parser had to be developed for each and every specific message and when the number of different message syntax was increasing, the number of message-specific parser developed grew accordingly.

To date, the way to overcome the issue of "understanding" an XML-based vocabulary and structure is to get software engineers and developers from the different systems at stake to discuss and figure out how to understand the message, the vocabulary and the syntax associated with the types of messages to exchange. The structure of the message contained in the so called XML Schema Definition (XSD) can be shared and a new component in the system that will be able to get messages based on such schema and map it to our internal vocabulary and our internal syntax can be built. In summary, it is the human intervention that makes the semantic of the messages be understood and extracted. Then, of course, such understanding can be programmatically registered with a new component for the system. A non-programmatic approach would be to generate an XML style sheet that would translate from one message structure to internal message structure of the system; but again, this is only a syntactic translation.

In a dynamic and flexible environment where services will come and go, where new types of information will be registered, where unanticipated services and information will be available, this approach is not the most appropriate. And this is exactly the scenario depicted by the NNEC, so an enhancement to the syntactic interface must be provided.

It is necessary an interoperability framework that will accelerate the readiness of the services providing and consuming the information, taking into account that the time for programmatic adaptation of any of the systems must be reduced to the minimum. This can only be achieved if every service is able to explicitly describe the model associated to the information provided - and how to retrieve the information from the service itself - so the vocabulary can be interpreted with respect to others. This interpretation or semantic (also called ontologies), will be used for adapting (interpreting) any message based on a specific external model to the own model without hav-

ing to programmatically change any services nor translating our information to an external model. Therefore, the flexibility and readiness will be guaranteed.

The NNEC FS Executive Summary (Buckman, 2005) pointed out ontologies as one of the key Information and Integration element:

"Military specific vocabularies require the participation of military experts, not only to define the core vocabularies for various COIs [Communities of Interest] but to also define the semantic relationships that exist between the words themselves (i.e. ontologies). This standardization activity is key to information interoperability at all levels of maturity, key to future concepts of information security and key to the use of machine based reasoning / agent based technology that will provide the foundation for meeting the longer term objectives for IIS and the NII in general." (Buckman, 2005)

Semantic Interoperability

Figure 4 depicts a situation where a symbol which can be seen on a map, it is a geo-location entity, which is a army battalion unit - at least that is what a Land Command and Control System may express— and its speed and cursor have been given by a TDL-to-TCP/IP converter, thanks to its message delivery mechanism, giving information about tracks on the ground; and the Intelligence system says that it is an enemy army battalion unit, since they have reports from intelligence analyst regarding that same area.

The above picture describes, by the use of graphs, the semantic linkages between different parts of disparate vocabularies. That is precisely the aim of Semantic Interoperability. Semantic Interoperability is simply a formal layer on top of the already existing interoperability layers (see Figure 5) (Berners-Lee, 2007). We had a medium, a message, a vocabulary and syntax. We have realised that XML is the perfect meta-language

Figure 4. Description example using different vocabularies

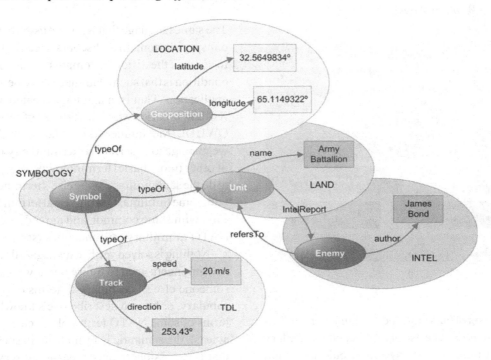

for defining vocabulary, syntax and building up the message. For Semantic Interoperability, XML is perfect because, as a meta-language, it will be able to create a proper language to **describe** the semantic of a domain. A domain, in simple words, is the vocabulary, the syntax and the associated messages used for a specific purpose.

Note that the word "*describe*" has been stressed. This is simple: the way to define the semantic of some message or the parts that form this message is by describing its components with respect to other components. For example, we may say that "*a unit is a military organisation whose structure is prescribed by a competent authority*", which means that we describe *unit* saying that is also a *military organisation* and has some specific attributes, like *structure* and, by the way, needs to be *prescribed* by a *competent authority*.

This is what we do every single day of our life: We know what we know because we connect our knowledge to previous knowledge or to just new acquired knowledge. We describe new things in terms of what we already know and what we are learning.

It is not intended (yet) to apply Semantic Interoperability to natural language. We are trying to apply Semantic Interoperability mainly to structured information that use to be in databases. Database systems structure its data precisely describing entities in terms of other entities and its relationships with them – Entity-Relationship Diagram is a perfect example (Chen, 1976). Some other information is not in databases, like real-time messages that are passed through in some well-known syntax. But still, there is a vocabulary and there is a way of describing major knowledge in terms of the common terminology.

So it is for sure that in each domain, in each domain application, there is a way of describing the major vocabulary constructs in terms of a

Figure 5. Semantic extension to OSI Layers – The Semantic Web layer cake

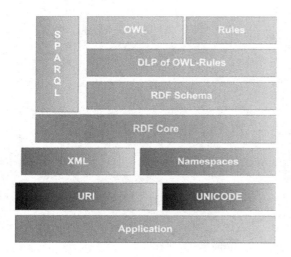

LINKING ONTOLOGIES

The same language that has to be used to describe our specific domain of discourse needs to be used to connect the different domains. Again, the only condition is that such a language must be an XML application. That is, a language created by using XML ancillaries which in the case of SISearch is OWL DL (McGuinness & van Harmelen, 2004). If we manage to describe our terminology in terms of other (more basic) terminologies, it is possible to do the same with someone else's terminology or with some (minimal but) universal terminology or even with some common and agreed category of NATO or military terminologies (see Figure 6).

Nothing is solved yet, because again developers and engineers need to figure out how to describe someone else's vocabulary in terms of one's vocabulary, or how to describe one's knowledge in terms of some NATO terminology category. But at least, the semantic is formalised in such a way that it is possible to apply reasoning services to identify equivalent concepts or concept subsumption (Baader et al., 2003).

Whenever someone tells you *something*, whenever someone makes an assertion or whenever someone asks a question, you need to put that *something* in the perspective of what you know. If some system asserts that an *entity with id "urn:uuid:334aacd23332d998f" is a military organisation with a particular structure prescribed by a superior*, it can be said that *"urn: uuid:334aacd23332d998f" is a Unit*. Such conclusions can be drawn because some descriptions of Unit were provided earlier and because some reasoning functionalities were applied, that is, some knowledge based on what is known and on what it has just been learnt can be inferred.

We need some artefact, some piece of software that will be able to tell if something is right or wrong, if something is true or false, if something exists or does not exist and even if the validity or existence of something cannot be told as there

common set of building blocks *within that application or domain*. The use of a universal vocabulary or structure that every system should use is not encouraged. Whatever is known and you can be said, must be within the domain knowledge. This, on the one hand, gives more flexibility as any domain applications are in control of what they want to say and how they want to describe it; and on the other hand, facilitates the process of making domain data available as it is so close to the domain vocabulary description, almost a one-to-one relation.

So there is the semantic of an application. The reason of all this approach comes when an application or service needs to engage with other systems, either by receiving other system's message or by sending its messages to other systems. In any case, the service will be sending its data on "*its way*" that is, using its vocabulary, using its description, using its syntax; the only condition is that it should be in XML. The other system will do the same. How they are going to understand each other is part of the major role Semantic Interoperability can play and will be presented in the following section.

Figure 6. Different levels of interpretation

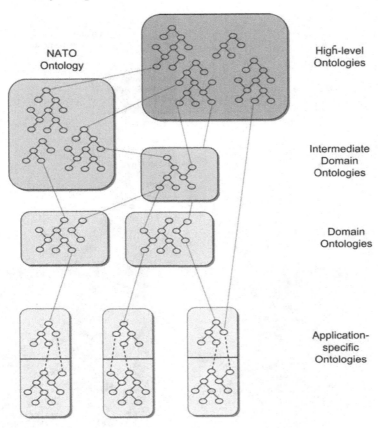

is not enough information. That is only achievable if there is a proper way of describing our domain or domains (the set of what we know), there is a proper way of telling new facts or asking about the validity of some facts (the set of what we are learning, the set of questions) and, more importantly, there is a set of well defined rules to reason on these two previous sets, in the same way we have got internalized in our mind our reasoning rules. That piece of software is an Inference Engine or Service.

If this Inference Service is generic enough, it will be able to work with any type of terminology, for any type of domain and for any purpose that implies reasoning on description of terminologies

and instantiation of such terminology. And if such is the case, then there is no need to programmatically do any changes on any system, but just declaratively adapt the interpretation that exists - that is, the linkages between our vocabulary and other's vocabulary and/or a NATO terminology category. Thus, it will be possible to put yet another system's terminology in the perspective of our own set of terms.

Ontology Linking Approach

As it is mentioned in (Pulvermacher et al., 2004), there exists several approaches with respect to linking ontologies or ontology connections.

Figure 7. Ontology linking concept

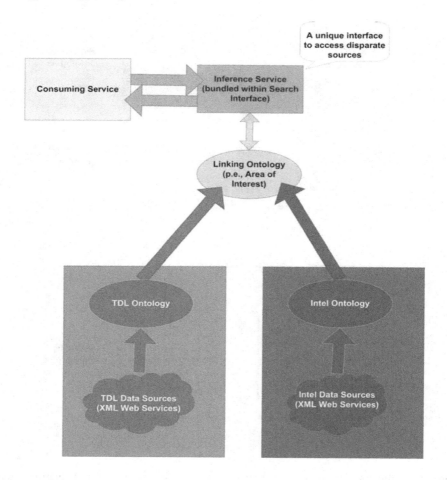

However, none of them completely offers an automated form to make these connections or interpretations.

What it is obvious is the necessity of considerable knowledge in the specific domains that are considered in the linking. This means that the aid of the subject matter experts at design and development time is mandatory, not only with respect to the domain ontologies and the corresponding applications involved in the linking process, but also with respect to the terms or concepts of the ontologies to be interpreted.

Figure 7 shows the approach taken by *SISearch*. In this case, based on the query made by a consumer service and a linking ontology, the inference service could infer the terms that should be considered at the time of generating the queries for each of the information sources to be invoked. The consumer service does not need to know what sources are available and how to access these sources, but simply to generate the query based on a series of generic arguments like area (Area of interest) and/or a time interval.

These generic terms could be declared and described in the linking ontology and behave

Figure 8. Example of ontology linking

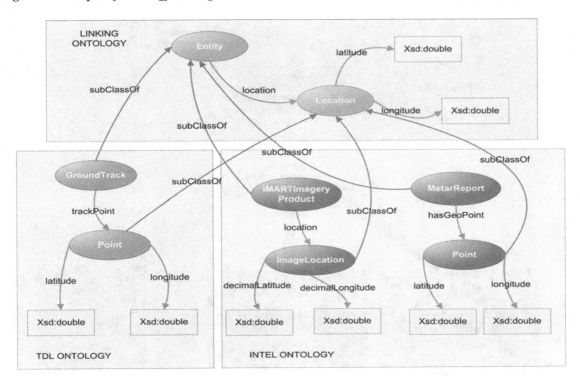

like generic element that would be connected or interpreted with respect to more specific terms defined in each of the domain ontologies. A simple example to show the concept of ontology linking is depicted in Figure 8.

Taking into account the ontology linking in Figure 8, the inference service will verify what data sources or services are available, what data type they can offer and what terms or concepts should be included as part of the queries to be made which the services can understand.

Once the replies from the different services are received (with the terminology of the corresponding domain), the inference service would perform an instance checking and would establish the linking ontology concept that would subsume the term associated to each of the instances.

Thanks to the ability that any description logic language has for extending new concept expres-

sion, as OWL DL does, we will be able to add new knowledge as long as we do not break the consistency of our knowledge base. This means that we could add new domain ontologies and simply extend the linking ontology to connect the new concepts of interest with those defined either in the linking ontology, or in any other ontology. This approach is depicted in Figure 9, where ontology for Land Command and Control systems is added.

By making this extension and by being able to locate new information sources, the same architecture could generate the specific queries for these new services and interpret the information (instances) coming from new services. And this can be done without any consumer systems to be re-programmed in order to consider the existence of services with new types of information.

Figure 9. Ontology linking extension

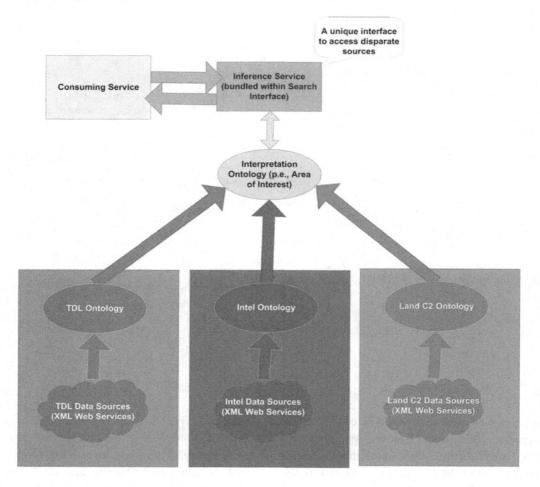

SISEARCH ARCHITECTURE

The objective of the SISearch prototype is twofold: it not only serves as confirmation that semantic interoperability is optimal for the integration of information coming from diverse systems based on different data models, but it also confirms that this is the architecture that better adapts to the NNEC concept and the optimization of the information flow in this environment.

This architecture has two basic principles: dynamic discovery of available services pro-

viding relevant information, and information discovery by the invocation of selected services and integration of the multiple responses. It is in the latter where we will apply the semantic interoperability, but it will also have a relevant role in the former.

We will describe the architecture of SISearch, starting with a generic or operational view, that is, what main objectives are to be covered by SISearch.

Figure 10. SISearch operational view

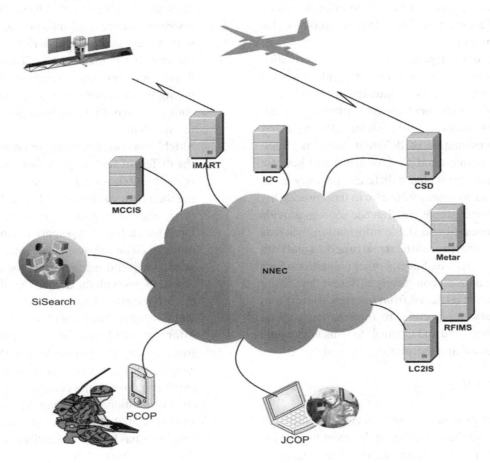

Operational View

In a Net-centric environment, systems do not have to be seen like monolithic and vertical elements where either interoperability does not exist, or message interchange is made via the traditional and hierarchical methods. One of the paradigms of the NNEC is that information has to be accessible even though it has not been processed. Therefore, information must be available in such a way that can be consumed and be interpreted.

Figure 10 shows a generic view of how NNEC should facilitate any system or component to be seen like a service offering data and information. In this environment, SISearch is a prototype that shows the capacity of semantic interoperability to facilitate the availability of information and its interpretation. This way, information can be represented in an integrated and coherent form, in spite of its great heterogeneity and different state (from information pre-processed by the human intervention or low level data barely processed).

In order to discover the information that is provided by each of the services, it is necessary SiSearch to be able to find those ones that are available. Thus, every service has to advertise its presence and, in addition, to offer details on how to access it and the domain ontology that makes use of.

Figure 10 depicts some of the information sources that have been used for validating the SISearch concept and architecture. It is beyond the scope of this chapter to provide thorough details of these systems. They were selected because they are representative of different domains (Intelligence domain and TDL domain) and because information provided is different, not only in the detail and complexity but also in their processing states. For example, intelligence sources provide well processed and stable information, whereas TDL systems provide near real time data and with a transient nature. Several other validations have been made with completely different data, from information retrieved from Internet, useful from a military perspective, to information coming from Command and Control systems where data is processed and thoroughly checked.

System View

SISearch provides a single service interface that will enable the discovery of different type of information from different data sources, aggregate such information and provide it to the service consumer as a coherent response. The SISearch relies on the Inference Services for both translating the initial query to the data asset-specific query (and their underlined vocabulary) and aggregating and associating the instances of the different types of information discovered in order to provide the response.

The intention of the SI Search is to:

1. **Serve as a mediation service for retrieving information from different sources:** SISearch makes use of ontologies in order to describe a domain or service-specific vocabulary. By linking these different ontologies together in a semantic manner, the SI Search is able to get information from disparate sources and interpret or adapt it with respect to the consumer's vocabulary, the one that it understands. Thus, the SI Search will mediate among services applying the necessary transformation in the data by interpreting the linkages between the vocabularies.

2. **Shield consumer services from details of the different service provider interfaces:** By enabling consumer services querying using their own vocabulary, SI Search release them from having to create specific interfaces for each of the potential information providers. The only work consumer services need to do is linking their own vocabularies or ontologies with the domain ontologies of the service providers.

3. **Help in correlation and association of information:** Once information is retrieved from sources, it is put together in the Inference Service in order to provide an aggregated response to the consumer. By doing so, information items may be correlated and associated, if the ontology used by the consumer has been made with provision for this capabilities. This way, the reasoning capabilities of the Inference Service will be able to find implicit relations out of the explicit information.

4. **Support extensibility of its interfaces:** SISearch has been designed with extensibility in mind. Both, the interface to the consumer and the interface to the different providers can be extended to take into consideration other exchange mechanism. SI Search source code provide an abstract interface at both ends that can be easily implemented and extended.

So far, SI Search provides a SPARQL interface (Clark, 2006) at both, the consumer and the provider side. That is, any service can pose a query to the SI Search using the SPARQL specifications (Prud'Hommeaux & Seaborne, 2007).

The Inference Service

The inference service is an attempt to wrap up some of the core functionality required from a range of services which deal in RDF (Carroll & Klyne, 2004) and OWL, taking on the responsibility of "understanding" OWL-DL and parsing RDF, reducing the complexity and amount of hard-wiring in those external services.

The intentions of the inference service are to:

1. **Shield the user from the complexities of parsing and interpreting RDF and OWL:** While the Semantic Web offers a great deal in return for a little investment, that investment is still rather high for the average service developer. This is mostly as a result of tool and library support being as yet neglected by the major IDEs and programming languages, which have only in the last few years begun to support XML as a core data format.

2. **Allow different inference engines to be used:** By abstracting the common functionalities of different inference engines, the Inference Service provides a common interface to different back-end implementations. Since different inference engines offer different levels of functionality, for instance balancing out speed versus expressiveness, or speed versus memory requirements, we can use an inference engine that is suited to the particular use that the inference service will be put to. Currently implemented back end inference engines (reasoners) are Pellet 1.4 (Sirin & Parsia, 2004), Sesame 2.0 (Broekstra et al., 2002) and RACER (Haarslev & Möller, 2001).

3. **Implement a Query Translation process:** Based on the available query types and registered services. Section *5.3.2 Query Translation Discussion* provides a thorough discussion on this functionality.

The service is available either directly using Java, or as a SOAP based Web service. The following sections broadly categorize the architecture and show some standard interactions.

Query Translation Discussion

The query translation service (Li & Horrocks, 2003) that is performed by the Inference Service is based on the Data Integration concept defined in (Levy, 2000) as the mechanism to provide a uniform interface to various data sources so as to enable users to focus on specifying what they want. In the SISearch particular case, the data sources are assumed to provide a Web service interface where the query language is SPARQL and the result is given in RDF.

Designing a Data integration system and, thus the Inference Service, is a complex task. Two of the most important ones are described in (Borgida, Lenzerini & Rosati, 2003):

- The specification of the content of the various data sources
- The process of computing the answer to queries posed to the data integration system, based on the specification of the sources.

In the case of the former, this has been explained in section 4 of this chapter. That is, by using a linking ontology, it is possible to describe specific domain ontologies (those of the data sources) with respect to more generic ones defined by the linking ontology.

In (Borgida, Lenzerini & Rosati, 2003), the specification of the data sources content is provided at two level, the conceptual level, which

Table 1.

$$rfims: RFIAttachment \subseteq concept: Entity$$
$$rfims: RequestTemporalScope \subseteq concept: Entity$$
$$rfims: suspendDateTime \subseteq_{property} concept: dateTime$$
$$rfims: lastTimeInformationOfValue \subseteq_{property} concept: dateTime$$

contains a conceptual representation of the sources and of the reconciled integrated data; and the logical level, which contains a representation of the sources in terms of a logical data model.

Again, the conceptual level is formed by the Enterprise Conceptual Schema, representing the global concepts, the Source Conceptual Schema, representing concepts related to the data residing in the data source; and the Domain Conceptual Schema which is the union of both the previous elements and the inter-schema relationships (Catarci and Lenzerini, 1993).

From the SISearch and the Inference Service point of view, the conceptual level comprises,

- A set of descriptions of data sources with respect to the vocabulary they "understand", that is, each data source is related to its ontologies,
- The representation of global concepts which will be used in the generic query that users (or consumer services) will send to the SISearch.
- The representation of source specific concepts that describe the data contained in the data source (source ontologies).

- The linking ontology, which can be seen as the Domain Conceptual Schema, with the caveat that the relationships are defined between source concepts and global concepts.

Some examples of inter-schema relationships defined in the linking ontology are shown in Table 1:

The first assertion states that the concept denoted by rfims:RFIAttachment in source RFIMS is a subconcept of the one denoted by concept: Entity in the Enterprise or Global Conceptual Schema.

The logical level provides a description of the logical content of each source. This logical ontology or schema is normally defined by using the relational logical model underpinning the data source (Borgida, Lenzerini & Rosati, 2003).

In the case of the SISearch, it is up to every source provider to make the relationship between the internal logical data model and the source ontology. The internal logical schema can be seen as the "private" source ontology and the source

Table 2.

```
PREFIX rdf: <http://www.w3.org/1999/02/22-rdf-syntax-ns#>
PREFIX concept: <http://si.nc3a.nato.int/ontologies/2005/07/genericConcepts#>
SELECT ?ent
 WHERE { ?ent rdf:type concept:Entity .
 ?ent concept:dateTime ?date .
 FILTER ( (xsd:dateTime(?date) < xsd:dateTime("2003-10-20T09:30:00GMT")) &&
 (xsd:dateTime(?date) > xsd:dateTime("2003-10-20T08:30:00GMT")) )
}
```

Table 3.

```
PREFIX rdf: <http://www.w3.org/1999/02/22-rdf-syntax-ns#>
PREFIX rfims: <http://si.nc3a.nato.int/ontologies/2005/05/rfims#>
SELECT ?i ?j ...
 WHERE { ?i rdf:type rfims:RFIAttachment .
 ?i rfims:creationDateTime ?d1 .
 ?j rdf:type rfims:RequestTemporalScope .
 ?j rfims:suspendDateTime ?d2 .
 ?j rfims:lastTimeInformationOfValue ?d3 .
 FILTER ( (xsd:dateTime(?d1) < xsd:dateTime("2003-10-20T09:30:00GMT")) &&
 (xsd:dateTime(?d1) > xsd:dateTime("2003-10-20T08:30:00GMT")) &&
 (xsd:dateTime(?d2) < xsd:dateTime("2003-10-20T09:30:00GMT")) &&
 (xsd:dateTime(?d2) > xsd:dateTime("2003-10-20T08:30:00GMT")) &&
 ... )
}
```

ontology, which is at the conceptual level, can be seen as the "public" source ontology.

The most relevant role of the Inference Service is to translate queries posed to the SISearch over the global view, that is, by using the global concepts, into specific queries over each of the "public" source ontologies, and to answer the queries by accessing the sources Web services in a transparent way. If a query is considered as a view over, say, the global ontology instances, then the queries rewritten by the Inference Service for each of the sources by using the inter-schema relationships between the global ontology and the "public" source ontologies (for example the subsumption assertions depicted above) are to be seen as local views over the "public" source ontologies instances and, more importantly, as sub-views of the global view.

For example, having the following query over the global view is shown in Table 2 and using the previous subsumption assertions, the following query is generated for the RFIMS source is shown in Table 3.

The answer given by the RFIMS Web service will be a sub-view of the initial query and, if any other source is posed with its respective query, the corresponding answer will also be a sub-view of the global one. The Inference Service will retrieve and integrate all the answers and will reply as a single answer to the initial query.

RELATED WORK

Ontology mapping and data integration are very well documented subjects. We have provided some initial works on data integration that the current approach is based on. Regarding ontology mapping, there are several frameworks like MAFRA (Maedche et al., 2002) or OIS (Calvanese, Giacomo & Lenzerini, 2001) which aim at creating a meta-ontology language for defining mapping between different domain ontologies (MAFRA) or mappings are defined by queries (OIS). A very comprehensive ontology mapping survey can be found in (Kalfoglou & Schorlemmer, 2005), where different frameworks, techniques and tools are covered.

These two approaches mentioned above may very well fit the SISearch requirements and, in fact, they all share the idea that one unique global ontology is not suitable in a federated environment. However, one of the basic ideas from the inception of SISearch was that of using standards (or W3C recommendations) like RDF, OWL and SPARQL and not creating a new layer over them. In fact, SISearch is an attempt of applied research for achieving semantic interoperability in a loosely coupled confederated universe of services that will form the future NATO Network Enabled Capabilities (NNEC). Therefore, it tries to take the best out of the current academic work and following the standards and recommendation regarding Semantic Web as much as possible. The more internationally accepted the standards are the easier they will be accepted by the member Nations.

In the case of MAFRA, the concept of semantic bridges is used and a specific vocabulary for defining the mapping rules is created. Our approach was to start by using the semantic implicit to OWL for defining the mapping rules and taking advantage of the associated reasoning. The drawback that was found is the limited expressiveness for defining complex rules. If the meta-ontology language defined by MAFRA or any other meta-ontology language for mapping is standardised or broadly used, it is obvious that this extra vocabulary should be used instead.

In (Li & Horrocks, 2003), OWL is used as the query language and, in fact, any description logics based language is suitable as a query language (Li & Horrocks, 2003). This can be named as "query by example". In SISearch, we initially made use of this approach but decided to move to SPARQL once it was accepted as a W3C Candidate recommendation. Furthermore, it was easy to generate a SPARQL Web service by using D2R Server (Bizer & Cyganiak, 2008), a tool that provides an easy RDF-based mapping language between the database logical schema and the source ontology (in our terminology, between the "private" source ontology and the "public" source ontology).

CONCLUSION

Semantic Web can be one of the main pillars to obtain interoperability at the information level. The use of a language and a common syntax to represent the data model implicit to any application, as well as to represent information instances, enable semantic interoperability; the capacity to be able to share not only the information but the model that underpins this information.

Another additional advantage is the possibility of being able to interpret a model with respect to another one and, indeed, using the same language. Again, interoperability is the beneficiary, since this interpretation can also be shared with other organizations as models are.

The concept of Semantic Web allows breaking the barrier of the existing interoperability architectures. The interpretation or linking does not have to be made with respect to a common model or between models but it is possible to be based on already existing previous interpretations. Therefore, one makes sure that the complexity using Semantic Web will be less than $O(N^2)$.

It is indeed the linking ontology that connects the models or ontologies of the different domains. And this linking ontology can change in time, either because it adds new domain ontologies to the discourse or because new associations between terms of diverse ontologies are defined. In the specific case of the SISearch prototype, a static linking ontology has been defined, that is to say, the application knows it beforehand and "knows" where to obtain it from. In a real situation, this interpretation might start as an empty set and, as ontologies are discovered, a user with sufficient knowledge of what these ontologies represent, could make the necessary interpretations between the terms of, for example, two different ontologies or define a concept as superclass of two different domain ontology concepts. This process of human interpretation would be registered in the linking ontology and would serve as starting point for searching over the domains at hand. Obviously, these interpretations could be refined in an evolutionary form.

There are current initiatives in NATO for specifying an ontology development framework. This would allow on the one hand to make the domain vocabularies visible and, on the other hand to accelerate the process of interpretation between the different domains. The use of a generic or conceptual terminology would benefit this process, although the use of it might not be mandatory. For example, it would be of great interest to be able to define generic ontologies that widely represent concepts used by all the domains, like those related to spatial locations or vocabularies that represent generic concepts like tracks (sequence of points in time and space).

This process would create a synergy which all actors would benefit from. No longer each application should support its own linking, but it would exist a whole Web of interpretations that any application, by using the inference service, could "navigate". That is to say, when we received information about a specific instance, we could navigate through the graph and go from one vocabulary to another thanks to the fact that we have access to the interpretations between models.

FUTURE RESEARCH DIRECTIONS

SISearch prototype is driving the current Semantic Interoperability initiatives within NATO, not only in the standardization process but also supporting new operational paradigms that will improve the information exchange mechanism among different systems. In any of the cases, new challenges are ahead and can be found in the Semantic Web stack layers depicted by Sir Tim Berners-Lee.

One of those challenges has got to do with the fact that different domain ontologies present diverse complexity when referring to the same concepts. This makes difficult a smooth linking process as there is no direct interpretation. Thus, a closer look to OWL 1.1 (Patel-Schneider & Horrocks, 2007) and its new constructs should be pursued for facilitating ontology linking.

It is assumed that any resource can be referred by a URI and that such a resource might be defined by different systems with different URIs. One of the main issues that need further investigation is how to define global unique URIs for resources so any systems can express facts about the very same resource by using the same URI.

Semantic Web has been partially used for discovering service by describing such services using RDF and a well defined vocabulary. This has to be extended in order to provide a more sophisticated discovery terminology and support selection of services and their composition. Several specifications have arisen lately but none of them has found widespread acceptance. In the other hand, some new initiatives that rely on inference services for discovery, selection and composition have been proposed and it will be worth it to follow them up.

The critical path in SISearch performance is in the ABox reasoning process once results are retrieved from provider services and uploaded to the ABox inference service, as the computational complexity depends on the level of expressiveness used in the ontologies at hand. It is necessary to investigate what is the minimum expressiveness that will fulfil all the requirements in terms of domain ontologies, conceptual ontologies and linking ontologies development and, at the same time, will provide the maximum performance.

If the graph obtained by aggregating the results of the different provider services is considerably large, no matter how simple the ontology is, the time consumed by the inference service to make any instance checking or realisation will be also considerably long. This time could be reduced if reasoning can be done in a distributed way, in parallel or incrementally, without having to aggregate first all the responses (and thus, waiting until the slower service has provided its result) and then reason over the resulting graph.

SPARQL is becoming more and more important as a promising query and protocol specification for information discovery. Right now it is in its infancy which means that there is a long way ahead, not only from a theoretical point of view regarding the complexity of certain parts of the syntax, but also from a practical point of view about how to optimise the query translation process in the scope of the Semantic Interoperability paradigm depicted in this chapter.

Finally, there are two important orthogonal functionality that must be taken into account with respect to information assurance: One of them is related to security labelling, by which different part of the graph will be identified as having different level of security and will have to be filtered whenever information cross from one security domain to the other. The other functionality has got to do with trust and, by extension, with provenance: it is necessary to identify which parts of the graph have been asserted by the different information providers when aggregating information. At any point in time, any consuming service might apply different trust criteria and sift the graph based on who provides the information.

ACKNOWLEDGMENT

My first thoughts go to Alex Tucker and Ilker M. Karakas for their incredible programming and development skills and his sharp contributions; without them, most of the ideas reflected in the SISearch prototype would have never been a reality. Our discussions with Jan Vlug, Donato Griesi, Leo Breebaart and Arno Bijl have always improved this work. I thank Dr. Sven Kuehne for his insight and clarifications regarding the connections between the application ontologies up to the high-level ontologies; he is the person that came with the diagram depicted in Figure 6. One of the persons that has made the most in order to let the project be known, be understood and be respected is Dave Clarke; something that we have learned during the last two years is that an R&D project needs someone to keep it running through the ups and downs. I also want to thank Dario Cadamuro for always giving a "healthy" reality check whenever we went too "technical". Finally I am grateful to Troy Turner, our mentor in Allied Command for Transformation (ACT) for defending the funding of this project against all odds, and the NATO C3 Agency for letting me publish this work.

REFERENCES

Alves, A., Arkin, A., Askary, S., Bloch, B., Curbera, F., & Goland, Y. (2006). *Web services business process execution language (WS-BPEL) Version 2.0* (Committee Draft): Organization for the Advancement of Structured Information Standards (OASIS).

Baader, F., Calvanese, D., MacGuinness, D.L., Nardi, D., & Patel-Schneider, P. (Eds.) (2003). *The description logic handbook: Theory, implementation, and applications.* United Kingdom: Cambridge University Press.

Berners-Lee, T. (2007). Web Services - Semantic Web. Retrieved May, 2007 from http://www.w3.org/2003/Talks/05-gartner-tbl.

Bizer, C., Cyganiak, R. (2008). *Publishing Databases on the Semantic Web.* Retrieved February, 2008 from http://www4.wiwiss.fu-berlin.de/bizer/d2r-server/publishing.

Borgida, A., Lenzerini, M., & Rosati, R. (2003). Description logics for data bases. In Baader, F., Calvanese, D., MacGuinness, D.L., Nardi, D., Patel-Schneider, P. (Eds.) (2003). *The Description Logic Handbook: Theory, Implementation, and aApplications* (pp. 472-494). United Kingdom: Cambridge University Press.

Bray, T., Paoli, J., Sperberg-McQueen, C. M., Maler, E., & Yergeau, F. (2006). *Extensible Markup Language (XML) 1.0 (Fourth Edition)* (W3C Recommendation). Retrieved May, 2007 from http://www.w3.org/TR/xml/.

Broekstra, J., Kampman, A., & van Harmelen, F. (2002). Sesame: A generic architecture for storing and querying RDF and RDF schema. *First International Semantic Web Conference*, No. *2342*, 54-68: Springer Verlag.

Buckman, T. (2005). *NATO network enabled capability feasibility study: Executive summary.* (Executive Summary). Brussels, Belgium: NATO

Consultation, Command and Control Agency (NC3A).

Calvanese, D., De Giacomo, G., Lenzerini, M. (2001, August). Ontology of integration and integration of ontologies. In *Proceedings of the 9th International Conference on Conceptual Structures* (ICCS'01), Stanford, CA, USA, August 2001.

Carroll, J.J., Klyne, G. (2004). *Resource description framework (RDF): Concepts and abstract Syntax* (W3C Recommendation). Retrieved May, 2007 from http://www.w3.org/TR/rdf-concepts/.

Catarci, T., & Lenzerini, M. (1993). Representing and using interschema knowledge in cooperative information systems. *Journal of Intelligent and Cooperative Information Systems*, 2(4), 375-398.

Chen, P. (1976). The entity-relationship model - Toward a unified view of data. *ACM Transactions on Database Systems, 1*(1), 9-36 .

Chinnici, R., Moreau, J-J., Ryman, A., & Weerawarana, S. (2007). *Web services description language (WSDL) Version 2.0 Part 1: Core language* (W3C Proposed Recommendation). Retrieved May, 2007 from http://www.w3.org/TR/wsdl20/.

Clark, K. (2006). *SPARQL Protocol for RDF* (W3C Candidate Recommendation). Retrieved May, 2007 from http://www.w3.org/TR/rdf-sparql-protocol/.

Ferraiolo, J., Jun, F., & Jackson, D. (2003). Scalable vector graphics (SVG) 1.1 Specification (W3C Recommendation). Retrieved May, 2007 from http://www.w3.org/TR/SVG11/.

Fielding, R.T. (2000). *Architectural styles and the design of network-based software architectures*. Doctoral dissertation, University of California, Irvine, CA, USA.

Foster, I., Kesselman, C., Nick, J., & Tuecke, S. (Eds.) (1999). *The grid: Blueprint for a new computing infrastructure*. San Francisco, CA, USA: Morgan-Kaufmann Publishers Inc.

Goldfarb, C.F. (1991). *The SGML handbook*. New York, USA: Oxford University Press.

Graham, S., Hull, D., & Murray, B. (2006). *Web services base notification 1.3 (WS-BaseNotification)* (Public Review Draft): Organization for the Advancement of Structured Information Standards (OASIS).

Gudgin, M., Hadley, M., Mendelsohn, N., Moreau, J-J., & Nielsen, H. F. (2007). *SOAP Version 1.2 Part 1: Messaging framework (Second Edition)* (W3C Recommendation). Retrieved May, 2007 from http://www.w3.org/TR/soap12-part1/.

Haarslev, V., & & Möller, R. (2001). *RACER system description. Hamburg*, Germany: University of Hamburg, Computer Science Department.

Levy, A. Y. (2000). Logic-based techniques in data integration. In Jack Minker, editor, *Logic Based Artificial Intelligence*. Kluwer Academic Publishers, 2000.

Li, L., & Horrocks, I. (2003, May). A software framework for matchmaking based on Semantic Web technology. *Paper presented at WWW2003*, Budapest, Hungary.

Maedche, A., Motik, B., Silva, N., & Volz, R. (2002). MAFRA – A mapping framework for distributed ontologies in *Knowledge Engineering and Knowledge Management: Ontologies and the Semantic Web*, Volume 2473(/2002), :pp. 69-75. Springer Berlin / Heidelberg.

McGuinness, D.L., & van Harmelen, F. (2004). *OWL Web ontology language* (W3C Recommendation). Retrieved May 2007 from http://www.w3.org/TR/owl-features/.

Muller, K. (2000, June). *NATO and XML*. Paper presented at XML Europe 2000, Paris, France.

Multilateral Interoperability Programme – MIP (2005). *Command and control information exchange data model (C2IEDM) sSpecifications.* Retrieved May, 2007 from http://www.mip-site.org/publicsite/03-Baseline_2.0/C2IEDM-C2_Information_Exchange_Data_Model/C2IEDM-Main-UK-DMWG-Edition6.15e-2005-12-02.pdf.

Nadalin, A., Kaler, C., Monzillo, R., & Hallan-Baker, P. (2004). *Web services security: SOAP message security 1.0 (WS-Security 2004)* (OASIS Standard): Organization for the Advancement of Structured Information Standards (OASIS).

NATO (2007). *NATO Standardization Agreements.* Retrieved May, 2007 from http://www.nato.int/docu/standard.htm#STANAG.

NATO (2007b). *NATO Response Force (NRF).* Retrieved May, 2007 from http://www.nato.int/issues/nrf.

NATO (2008). *NATO Ground Moving Target Indicator Format (GMTIF).* Retrieved January, 2008 from http://www.nato.int/docu/stanag/4607/4607_home.htm.

Nierle, J. E. (1996). *Internetworking: Technical sStrategy for iImplementing the nNext gGeneration Internet pProtocol (IPV6) in the Marine Corps tTactical dData nNetwork.* Msc. Thesis, Naval Postgraduate School, Monterey, CA, USA.

Oaks, S., Gong, L., & Traversat, B. (2002), *JXTA in a nNutshell.* Sebastopol, CA, USA: O'Reilly & Associates, Inc.

Patel-Schneider, P.F., & Horrocks, I. (2007*). OWL 1.1 Web oOntology lLanguage – Overview.* Retrieved May, 2007 from http://webont.org/owl/1.1/overview.html

Prud'Hommeaux, E., & Seaborne, A. (2007). *SPARQL Query Language for RDF* (W3C Working Draft). Retrieved May, 2007 from http://www.w3.org/TR/rdf-sparql-query/.

Pulvermacher, M.K., Stoutenburg, S., & Semy, S. (2004). *Net-centric sSemantic lLinking: An approach for eEnterprise sSemantic iInteroperability.* (Tech. Paper). Bedford, Massachusetts, USA: The MITRE Corporation.

Russell, S.J., & Norvig, P. (2003). *Artificial iIntelligence: Aa modern approach.* Upper Saddle River, N.J.: Prentice Hall.

Saint-Andre, P. (Ed.) (2004). *Extensible mMessaging and pPresence pProtocol (XMPP): Core* (RFC 3920): Jabber Software Foundation.

Sirin, E., & Parsia, B. (2004, May). Pellet: An OWL DL rReasoner. *Paper presented at Workshop on Application Design, Development and Implementation Issues in the Semantic Web,* New York, NY, USA.

Sølvberg, A., Hakkarainen, S., Brasethvik, T., T., Su, X., & Matskin, M. (2002, October). *Concepts on eEnriching uUnderstanding and rRetrieving the sSemantics on the Web.* ERCIM News No. 51, October 2002.

Thompson, H., Beech, D., Maloney, M., & Mendelsohn, N. (2004). *XML sSchema Part 1: Structures sSecond eEdition* (W3C Recommendation). Retrieved May, 2007 from http://www.w3.org/TR/xmlschema-1/.

W3C (2007). *Semantic Web.* Retrieved May, 2007 from http://www.w3.org/2001/sw.

Zimmermann, H. (1980, April). OSI rReference mModel - The ISO mModel of aArchitecture for oOpen sSystems iInterconnection. *IEEE Transactions on Communications, vol. 28*(, no. 4), April 1980, pp. 425 - 432.

ADDITIONAL READING

Baader, F., Calvanese, D., MacGuinness, D.L., Nardi, D., Patel-Schneider, P. (Eds.) (2003). *The Description Logic Handbook: Theory, Imple-*

mentation, and Applications. United Kingdom: Cambridge University Press.

Berman, F., Fox, G., & Hey, A.J.G. (Ed.) (2003) . *Grid computing: Making the global infrastructure a reality*. West Sussex, England: John Wiley & Sons Ltd.

Visser, U. (2004). *Intelligent Information Integration for the Semantic Web*. Berlin Heidelberg, Germany: Springer-Verlag.

Staab, S., & Stuckenschmidt, H. (Eds.) (2006). *Semantic Web and Peer-to-peer*. Berlin Heidelberg, Germany: Springer-Verlag.

Li, L., & Horrocks, I. (2003, May). *A Software Framework For Matchmaking Based on Semantic Web Technology*. Paper presented at WWW2003, Budapest Hungary.

Pulvermacher, M.K., Stoutenburg, S., & Semy, S. (2004). *Net-centric Semantic Linking: An approach for Enterprise Semantic Interoperability*. (Tech. Paper). Bedford, Massachusetts, USA: The MITRE Corporation.

APPENDIX: QUESTIONS FOR DISCUSSION

1. Which areas of defence can gain from Semantic Web technologies?

As seen throughout this chapter, one of the areas that might take advantage of the use of Semantic Web technologies is Data integration. From an interoperability stand point, the way data can be shared is by establishing a formal framework for expressing such data and, by extension, being able to aggregate and associate them. This capability is key for achieving what is known as Common Operational Picture (COP), by which data from different systems can be grouped, linked and associated in a common and shared situational picture.

Mediation is a very broad term for referring to some capabilities that can work on behalf of certain requester. The concept introduced by SISearch is clearly in this direction and it is precisely because it leans on Semantic Web principle that such mediation services are possible. Mediation will be key when exchanging information between different security network domains, as it will help to a clear separation of concerns and a better security administration: each network will specify a single interface to access to data without having to broaden the number of internal accessible services, which can pose serious security threats.

Semantic Web can not only provide a formal framework for expressing data but it can also be used for formalising the way to describe services and, similarly, there are some new technologies that are facilitating the information discovery process. Thus, these technologies will definitely be a key actor in the NATO standardisation agreements to come.

Finally Semantic Web technologies can definitely play a major role in information and security management at all level. This include the framework for describing information depicted above (let us not forget that RDF stands for *Resource Description Framework*, that is, meta-data) and the ability to describe service security policies and reason over them in order to ensure that security policies from different security domains does not collide.

2. At this stage, what is the level of penetration of Semantic Web technologies in defence?

Nowadays, Semantic Web is considered an experimental technology for defence. There are no main operational systems relying on these technologies. Nevertheless, there is a growing awareness of the different existing specifications and it is becoming clear that for any information and knowledge management effort to be successful, a way of describing the different concepts implicit in the data is needed. This is precisely one of the areas where Semantic Web is being used in order to formalise taxonomies and ontologies.

With respect to the other areas highlighted in the previous question, the NNEC feasibility study presented a technology roadmap that would inject their capabilities to the overall NNEC concept. It is foreseen that Semantic Web will be a major contributions from 2010 onwards, not only for standardisation but also for data integration, mediation and service and information discovery. This will be possible once this technology become mainstream of major open source and commercial products, which will facilitate its adoption by defence procurement agencies.

3. From a defence perspective, what are the major challenges Semantic Web technologies should cope with to be successful?

Some of the major challenges have been introduced in the *Future Research Directions* section. Distributed reasoning is one of the most challenging for data integration and mediation support. So far, reasoning is done over the aggregated data but some new mechanisms and algorithms must be devised in order to enhance the reasoning performance and the ability to work in a distributed environment where information is not centralised, which is the assumption taken by NNEC.

If anything characterise a defence environment is the concern for security. In NNEC this translates to information assurance. It implies mechanisms to assure that information is trusted, reliable, exchanged in an integral form and only accessible to those with appropriate authorisation. So far Semantic Web technologies have been devised in order to let as much data as possible be accessed and visible. New specifications that will extend the current ones are needed in order to assure that information is available following the information assurance tenets described above.

4. Apart from the Semantic Web technologies referred in this chapter, what other technologies will make relevant contributions for Semantic Web to be successful for defence?

For service description and composition support, which are key elements for service discovery and service mediation, there are some specifications like OWL-S, WSDL-S, WSMO or SWSF that are worth taking into account in the future. Each of them tries to tackle one specific part of the Semantic Web Service concepts and none of them have been openly embraced by any major standardisation organisation. It is needed a more harmonised approach that pushes for a consolidated specification in this important area.

Related to the concept of information assurance introduced in the previous question, it is necessary to formalise and standardise the several academic contributions on the subject of *named graphs* in support of information provenance and trust.

Rules are integral part of ontologies and, in fact, the different constructs devised in OWL (Lite, DL or Full) are to be considered as rules. Nevertheless, there are other types of rules (i.e., production rules) within the conceptualisation of a domain – that is, the domain ontology – which, albeit not preserving the decidability of reasoning over certain ontologies, are considered key artefacts for describing service constraints or supporting information mediation. In this respect SWRL is a good candidate to keep track of, but so far there has not been a decisive initiative to make it a W3C recommendation.

Chapter III
Personalization Based on Semantic Web Technologies

Vassileios Tsetsos
University of Athens, Greece

Vassilis Papataxiarhis
University of Athens, Greece

Stathes Hadjiefthymiades
University of Athens, Greece

ABSTRACT

Personalization techniques provide optimized access to content and services, based on the preferences and the characteristics of each individual user. Nowadays many applications, either Web-based or not, call for personalized behavior. Obviously, such behavior leads to an increased demand for knowledge management, since personalization is based on user profiles, user preferences, usage policies, and other knowledge components. The main topic of this chapter is the investigation of how well Semantic Web technologies apply to personalized applications. Semantic Web is a relatively new platform for developing (distributed) knowledge-based applications that has gained great popularity in previous years. Hence, this chapter surveys the most prominent techniques for personalization in the context of the Semantic Web. It discusses and compares different approaches to architectural and engineering techniques and other issues relevant to this hot topic. The chapter provides foundational knowledge on this topic, as well as discussion on some key implementation issues.

INTRODUCTION

Nowadays we witness a shift in many computing paradigms. Firstly, the Web is evolving from a Web of documents, and content in general, to a Web of applications and services. The so-called Web 2.0 has paved the way for social networking through many innovative applications. Moreover, the vision of Semantic Web (SW) has been realized to a certain degree and has produced many modern and useful tools[1] for knowledge engineering and management.

On the other hand, all application domains, either Web-based or not, call for advanced user experience. The human has come to the center of the computing environments (i.e., human-centered computing) and this implies that systems should become more personalized. Such personalization aims at increasing efficiency and effectiveness, hiding complexity or adding intelligence to the man-machine interaction.

In the present chapter, we investigate how the merging of the aforementioned paradigms (i.e., Web-oriented knowledge technologies and personalized applications) can be performed. We do not deal with a specific type of applications, but rather try to describe a framework for designing and developing such applications. Some assumptions made are that applications exploit domain semantics and adhere to a model-driven design. We call them Semantic Web Enabled Applications (SWEA). Before delving into the technical part of the chapter, we should give some definitions that will clarify some terms and concepts discussed in the following sections.

Definition 1. *Semantic Web Enabled Application (SWEA).* An application or service component that is relying on Semantic Web technologies. This may be a Semantic Web application or any other application that exploits the respective technologies (e.g., semantic TV). In practice, they are applications that are built with software engineering methods based on SW ontologies and/or rules (Happel, 2006).

Definition 2. *Adaptable and Adaptive System.* A system is called "adaptable" when it allows a user to adapt the behavior of the system to her current needs and preferences. On the other hand, an "adaptive" system supports this capability in an autonomous way. In particular, it knows and/or captures the user needs (preferences, interests, experience etc.) and it automatically adapts itself to these inferred needs. These definitions are in line with those given in (Baldoni, 2005).

Definition 3. *Personalization.* The process of delivering content and/or services to a user based on her preferences, interests, needs, and context in general. The purpose of this process is to *adapt* the content/services to the specific user characteristics in order to achieve optimum performance (the definition of "performance" is domain-dependent).

Consequently, we call an application as "personalized" or "user adaptive" if it is aware of the user profile, can detect the user context and needs and is able to adapt itself in order to meet these needs. As already mentioned, in this chapter we deal with personalized SWEAs.

The chapter is organized as follows. *Semantic Web for Personalization* provides a discussion on the current status regarding Semantic Web and personalized applications. *Architecture of a Personalized Semantic Web Enabled Application* presents a reference architecture for personalized SWEAs. Some issues about user modeling are elaborated in *User Modeling*. In *Rule-based Adaptation* we present some background knowledge and discussion on rule-based personalization. The chapter concludes with several directions for future research.

SEMANTIC WEB FOR PERSONALIZATION

As expected from the increasing demand for user-centered applications, there have been proposed many approaches for personalizing applications. In general, each approach is tailored to the specific requirements of the target application (see also the following subsection). Among these approaches one can find several technical solutions and this is an evidence that there is no globally accepted and generic methodology for enabling personalization.

In this chapter we discuss how the emerging Semantic Web technologies can satisfy the requirements of personalized applications and aid developers in developing them. Recently, many advances have been observed in the SW area, such as maturity of ontology description and query languages, development of rule languages, stable and production versions of reasoning engines and development tools, etc. These advances enable the use of SW technologies and methods in more and more real-world knowledge-based applications. An indication that supports this claim is the adoption of SW technologies by many researchers working on personalized and adaptive systems. Such systems are surveyed in the following paragraphs. On the other hand, there are still some issues that can pose limitations to personalized SWEAs. Some advantages and disadvantages regarding the suitability of SW technologies for personalization purposes are summarized in Table I (derived from common experience; some of them are elaborated in subsequent sections).

Table I. Pros and cons of SW- and knowledge-based personalization

Advantages	Disadvantages
<ul><li>Explicit description of the application semantics through ontologies</li><li>Model-driven design of personalized applications</li><li>Efficient reasoning with subsets of First Order Logic</li><li>Serialization of SW data based on XML, which is both machine-interpretable and human-readable</li><li>Ontology reuse and alignment to existing models</li><li>Modularity of knowledge base through well established ontological engineering</li><li>Transparency of the adaptive behavior of the personalized system through the use of natural form of knowledge (such as rules)</li><li>Existence of quite mature development tools (e.g., editors, Application Programming Interfaces)</li></ul>	<ul><li>Limited expressiveness of current modeling elements due to the well-known "expressiveness vs. tractability tradeoff"[2] (Baader, 2003)</li><li>Limitations to SW reasoning (i.e., no efficient algorithms for various types of inferences)[3] (Borgida, 2003)</li><li>Low industry adoption due to the difficulty in structuring and populating knowledge bases, in conjunction with the fact that there are not many "practical" ontologies and there are no well-established automatic population methods (e.g., for profile extraction).</li></ul>

Examples of Personalized Applications in WWW and Semantic Web

In this section we present some personalized applications from diverse domains. The common denominator of all these applications is that they are oriented towards a knowledge-based approach. Most of them exploit some means of formal knowledge representation techniques (e.g., ontologies and rules). However the reader should note that we do not aim to fully describe the internals of these applications.

A common category of applications that require personalization is context-aware services, and mainly location-based services (e.g., navigation, tracking or emergency services). Conventional context-aware services rely only on contextual conditions external to the user. In more advanced scenarios, service executions are also affected by user abilities, interests and preferences. For example, consider the case of a user that uses a wheel chair to move around. In this scenario, a navigation service should capture that knowledge and present to the user paths that do not include stairways or escalators. Semantic Web technologies provide an efficient way to store and exploit that kind of information using ontologies, rule languages and reasoning modules. Some personalized location-aware applications that have been developed so far can be found in (Gartner, 2004; Tsetsos, 2006; Kikiras, 2006).

An ever growing family of personalized applications is related with e-learning. Many organizations have already adopted online learning platforms to provide on-demand training in a wide range of different domains. A related research system, called WLog (Baldoni, 2004), aims at supporting students in structuring their personalized "study plans". Furthermore, another demonstration application of the domain is the Personal Reader for e-learning (Dolog, 2004), which provides a framework for studying learning resources. In particular, Personal Reader makes use of ontologies, rules and query languages, stemming from Semantic Web. Additionally, the application suggests personalized information like useful examples, summary or next-step documents, according to the current knowledge status of the user.

Another domain with relevant applications is that of e-tourism services. For example, consider the case that a visitor in a town wants to schedule a single-day tour. She may like shopping, museums, sightseeing and many other activities. In this case, a Web service or a Web-based system attempts to support the user and recommend a complete activity schedule to her. Various approaches have been proposed and implemented to meet the user interests and offer personalized tour guidance (Srivihok, 2005; Puhretmair, 2002; Ricci, 2002).

In (Kumar, 2002), a personal assistant that provides various functions to the user is proposed. A software agent acts on behalf of a user and manages her diary, filters the emails, adjusts the desktop environment, retrieves useful content from the Web, etc.

In addition, a Personal Publication Reader is presented in (Baumgartner, 2005). This reader takes advantage of Personal Reader Framework (Henze, 2004a; Henze, 2004b) and provides a personalized view of publication information. Specifically, it makes use of reasoning over ontologies, metadata about publication info and data extraction techniques.

Moreover, an ontology-based framework that provides personalization in a multimedia content management environment is proposed in (Vallet, 2005). The main goal is to support user-awareness in a knowledge-driven multimedia system. This framework captures and manages relevant information about the user and the context, making use of knowledge structures, such as user and device models. The overall approach targets at improving the operational quality of the services provided by a media system through SW technologies.

Finally, a TV-recommender system, based on semantic inference, is proposed in (Fernandez, 2006). This system, called AVATAR, captures resources and relationships relevant to the area of Digital-TV and reasons about them through the use of ontologies and appropriate reasoning modules. The main goal of AVATAR is to discover associations between the user preferences and the characteristics of TV-programs for recommending "interesting" TV-programs to the users. A main advantage of the approach is that it avoids suggesting programs similar to those the user has seen in the past.

As one can observe, most of the aforementioned applications focus on personalized content retrieval and recommender systems. These are typical applications that are used for filtering, in an intelligent manner, vast amounts of content.

ARCHITECTURE OF A PERSONALIZED SEMANTIC WEB ENABLED APPLICATION

In this section, a reference architecture for personalized SWEAs is presented. The main components

of this architecture are depicted in Figure 1 and are described in the following paragraphs.

Application Business Logic

The application business logic defines how the SWEA delivers services or content to each end-user in an optimal way, given the current context. Optimality may refer to ease of use, high performance, proactive behavior, efficient content retrieval, filtering and presentation, etc. Business logic should be highly parameterized, based on the adaptation actions decided by the reasoning component, which is described in subsequent paragraphs.

Models and Context

As it has already been stated, the emphasis of this chapter is on model-based personalization. That means that all knowledge relevant to the target application is described through formal models. In the case of SWEAs, the most common way to represent such models is the SW ontology languages, namely the Web Ontology Language (OWL) and/or the Resource Descrip-

Figure 1. General architecture of a personalized Semantic Web enabled application

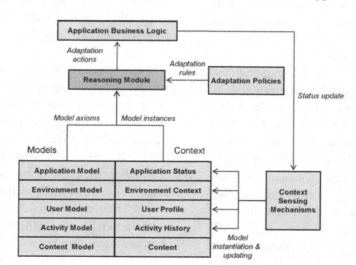

tion Framework Schema (RDFS). The models (i.e., ontologies) may describe various aspects of the overall system architecture. In Figure 1, we identify five main models that are expected to be found on every personalized SWEA (although they might not be always implemented as discrete ontologies):

- **Application model:** Describes application-specific details, such as application states and processes and their semantics.
- **User model:** A mandatory model for every human-centered application. It may describe several aspects of the user profile, such as demographic information, current situation, interests, and preferences. Moreover, it usually specifies a classification of users.
- **Environment model:** Specifies peripheral modeling elements, e.g., the state of the surrounding user environment or from external applications that may affect the behavior of the target application.
- **Activity model:** Describes all possible user interactions with the systems and other activities that can be performed and provide some feedback for future application behavior. In a sense, this model is a formal description of activity logs. For example, the various classes the user is classified over time may be useful information for triggering adaptation actions. The instances of this model capture knowledge that might include information accessed earlier by the user, temporal patterns of the application usage, etc. This type of information is, generally, obtained by the system in a seamless way. Moreover, such information is a common input for profile learning mechanisms.
- **Content model:** Describes the semantics of the content used by the application. It can be safely assumed that in most cases content does not change dynamically.

The abovementioned models are just the schemata for representing application-relevant data. The actual data (i.e., instances or individuals) form the context of each model. For those readers familiar with the Description Logics (DL) (Baader, 2003) terminology, the models comprise the TBox while the contexts constitute the ABox. Usually, we expect to have models that remain rather constant with time, while context data are quite dynamic.

Context Sensing Mechanisms

Updates in user context are captured and inserted into the system by specialized context sensing mechanisms. In general, such mechanisms are comprised by two main processes: *context sensing* and *context translation* (Anagnostopoulos, 2007). The former monitors the various components of the discussed architecture and "senses" value changes in context-relevant parameters, e.g., location of user, environmental temperature, run-time application errors, characteristics of content retrieved by the application etc. The latter represents sensed values in a machine-understandable way, according to the adopted ontologies. Such translation process may require from very simple to very complex data transformation routines. For instance, translation from geometric Global Positioning System (GPS) coordinates to symbolic positions, fuzzy representation of natural world parameters such as speed, etc.

Reasoning Module

This is the module where all actual inference and reasoning regarding the adaptation of the application is implemented. Its inputs are the specific models and facts (i.e., instances) that describe the overall context of the personalized application as well as the possible adaptation decisions that should be made upon assertion of certain facts (i.e., policies). Its outputs are the final adaptation decisions and actions that should be taken by the application in order to better adapt to the user context. Depending on the knowledge representation technique and the expressiveness used for the models and the adaptation policies, this module may undertake various types of inference. For example, if user history is taken into account, statistical processing or temporal reasoning may be required. In typical SWEAs, this module consists of a (DL) reasoner engine and a rule engine. In general, this module can be regarded as a *hybrid reasoning engine*, since additional reasoning tasks are required for the majority of the applications, e.g., fuzzy reasoning.

Adaptation Policies

This is the rule base that describes the possible decisions made in order to personalize the application. They are the glue between the various context elements. The specific grammar and semantics of the rules may vary depending on the desired expressiveness of the adaptation policy. In *Rule Based Adaption*, we survey several formalisms that have been proposed for building such rule bases. In general, the adaptation policies are rather static, mainly for retaining simplicity in their management. However, in some cases, changes in context may trigger changes in the policies, too. In this chapter, we do not deal with (automatic) policy revision and we assume that all rules are either predefined by the application developers or are manually added/updated throughout the application lifecycle (e.g., by the users).

USER MODELING

Definitions

The user model plays a key role in every personalized system. Obviously, given the existing Semantic Web technologies, ontology is the best-suited "tool" for expressing this model. Current SW ontology languages provide many ways of representing user characteristics. However, before delving into more technical topics of ontology-based user modeling, we will discuss various aspects of a (knowledge-based) user model. The first is the *functional aspect*, which divides model elements into categories based on their actual use in the application. Typical categories are:

- **User demographics:** This type of information captures general information of the user. Such information might include user's name, age, e-mail address etc. Typically, it is initially provided by the user.

- **User preferences:** A user might have several preferences concerning her interaction with a system. This information helps the system to provide optimized access, presentation and retrieval of the information to the user. Such preferences may include the interests of the user or her information needs.

- **User capabilities:** A user might also have individual capabilities or disabilities which should affect the way the system performs. For example, in a pedestrian navigation scenario consider a user into a public building that uses a wheelchair. Moreover, assume that the building provides a navigational service to users with smart phones. Obviously, the navigation service should exclude all paths that contain stairs, due to the disability of the user to access them. In another similar situation, a user could have forgotten her glasses so that the personalized application would have to increase the font size during content presentation. Since Universal Access and Design for All (Stephanidis, 2001) are popular trends in modern system design, such capabilities become more and more important during personalization.

The second aspect is the *structural aspect*. Similarly to the definitions in (Cali, 2004), a user model, consists of:

Equation 1.

$$\text{YoungWheelChairedUser} \equiv \exists\text{hasAbility.WheelchairedMobility} \sqcap \exists\text{hasAge}<25$$

- *A set of high-level user classes, UC,* used for classifying users with regard to the specific application domain. For example, in a medical application some candidate user classes might be "Doctor", "FeveredPerson", "DiabeticPerson", etc. The more specific these classes are, the more detailed descriptions they should have (see also discussion on "defined" versus "primitive" classes in the following paragraphs). A user is represented as an instance of one or more UCs.
- *A set of classes representing features of the profile, FC.* These classes constitute the superset of the interests, capabilities and preferences a user may have. The actual features that apply to a user are represented as instances of the respective FCs.
- *A set of relationships (or feature properties), FP,* that assign features (FC instances) to users (UC instances). According to the OWL language, these are binary relationships and are specified as object-properties,
- *A set of attributes, A,* that assign literal values to user characteristics. Typical characteristics might be the name, the age, the sex etc. According to the OWL language, these are modeled as binary relationships and are specified as datatype-properties.

Furthermore, we can treat a user model as a combination of two parts. The *core user model* (CUM) and the *application user model* (AUM). This discrimination is adopted for two reasons: (a) ease of modeling and (b) efficient implementation. Each model has different expressiveness and can support different inferences. The CUM mainly aids the system design and development by providing a controlled vocabulary for the key user-related concepts and their inter-relationships.

Moreover, it is the reusable part of the model, since its concepts and relationships are generic and can be used in diverse applications (we remind the reader that reusability is a foundational principle in the SW). In general, this part contains primitive ontology classes (i.e., expressed through necessary conditions) and is instantiated/populated explicitly and in a top-down manner. For example, the user should explicitly assert in which user class she belongs to and the specific properties she has. Moreover, the system cannot automatically detect if the user state (i.e., user class) has changed due to some change in her context.

The AUM is a more fine-grained model that captures more details of a user profile, thus, enabling more advanced reasoning. The concepts and relationships that comprise it are purely application-dependent, and are usually specified through formal definitions that include necessary and sufficient conditions (i.e., defined ontology classes). A sample concept of AUM is shown in equation 1.

In this model, the user just asserts her properties (ability and age) and is automatically classified by the reasoning engine. Moreover, if some changes occur in her properties, these will also affect her class (i.e., profile update propagation is supported - more details on this follow in a subsequent paragraph). The only difficulty in creating the AUM is that it requires expertise in knowledge engineering.

Of course, depending on the application and how knowledge-intensive it is, only one of the user models may exist. For example, if the user model is used just for providing a shared vocabulary, then no AUM may be needed. In Figure 2, the overlap between the various aspects is shown. Each one of the four quadrants can include any combination of structural elements (e.g., UC, FP).

Figure 2. User model aspects

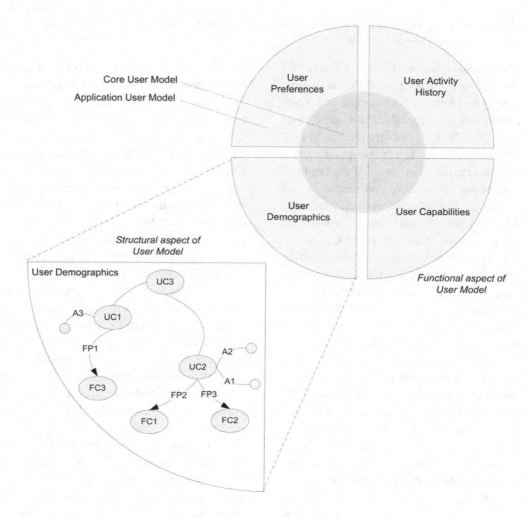

User Ontology Instances

Another issue in multi-user systems is the way the actual user profiles (i.e., ontology instances) are stored. There are two approaches:

Approach A: all user profiles in one file. This approach enables centralized management of all user instances (see also Figure 3a). In particular, all the user instances along with the corresponding user model are stored in a unique file. However, as the number of users increases, the size of this file

also increases. Hence, some limitations regarding the reasoning process arise. Specifically, most DL reasoners cannot deal with arbitrarily large numbers of instances or are proved inefficient, especially for (near) real-time applications. As a result, querying or classifying such sets of instances is a troublesome task. Several approaches have been proposed in order to cope with this issue, e.g., (Horrocks, 2004), but in general it is not advisable to reason over large instance sets. Ontology modularization (d'Aquin, 2006) is not

Figure 3. (a) All the profiles are stored in one file. (b) The user profile of each user is stored in a different file.

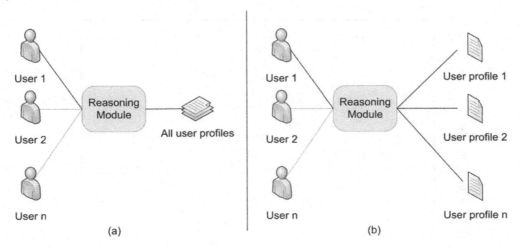

(a)

(b)

a solution either, since it focuses on segmenting the ontology schema and not on partitioning instances.

Approach B: one file for each user profile. This approach (see Figure 3b) may impose some overhead during user model serialization, but enables high scalability for multi-user systems. Moreover, it enables distributed user management, since each user ontology can be published independently of the others. The user could even have a local copy of her profile in order to control its use and ensure that the desired level of privacy is preserved. As a consequence, queries that concern an individual user could be executed for small document files, thus facilitating the reasoning process. On the other hand, a main drawback of this approach is the weakness to process efficiently aggregate queries that require information stored in different user ontologies (e.g., "find all users that have a specific attribute").

Static User Models

In this and the following section, we attempt to evaluate the approaches of Figure 3 in terms of reasoning efficiency. The user ontology used in these tests is relatively small and it contains 46 concepts, 9 object properties and 5 datatype properties. Each user profile contains 33 concept instances as well as 34 property instances. Finally, Bossam (Jang, 2004) was used as the DL reasoning and rule engine.

Figure 4 shows that the time needed to load and classify an ontology increases proportionally to the number of user profiles contained in it. As a result, when the number of user profiles exceeds some hundreds, the reasoning delay becomes a limiting factor for real-time or Web applications that call for small response times. Moreover, the application of a few rules to the same model resulted in a very high execution time even for a limited number of users (e.g., an ontology with 100 user instances gave an execution time of approximately 10 seconds). The purpose of this test is not to demonstrate this quite expected behavior, but to provide some indicative values for the actual execution times that are required by state-of-the-art tools.

Figure 4. Loading and classification performance for the Approach A

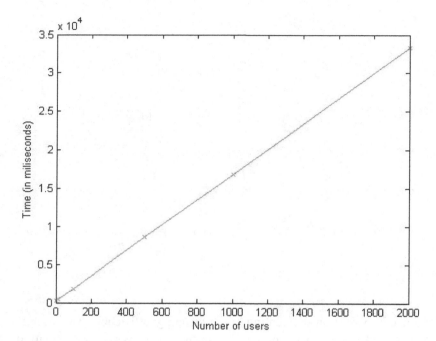

Dynamic User Models

Another issue with user models is that they may be dynamic, i.e., change over time according to the user context. Dynamic user models, add an extra intelligence to the applications, but also introduce some implementation problems. Probably the most important is the performance overheads that result from the re-classification of the user model, on every contextual change.

One good example of this case is when the user model is used to classify the user according to her situation. Consider, for instance, a location-based application that requires capturing knowledge about the mobility situation of the users. Let us assume that we have a property (*hasSpeed*) in the user model that describes the current user speed. Hence, we are able to define the following user classes:

RunningUser ≡ User ⊓ ∃hasSpeed.HighSpeed
WalkingUser ≡ User ⊓ ∃hasSpeed.MediumSpeed
StationaryUser ≡ User ⊓ ∃hasSpeed.LowSpeed

Provided that the speed of a typical user changes while moving, the application should update her profile, by setting the right value to the *hasSpeed* property at regular intervals. This update process implies the re-classification of the user model if, for example, we want to pose queries of the form "identify all the walking users".

However, this re-classification procedure is computationally expensive. In order to assess the reasoning performance on dynamic user models, we use again the testing scenarios of the previous section (approaches A and B). The experiment assumes the modification of these profiles with the following probability values: 0.3, 0.5 and 0.8. This change affects a single property (*hasSpeed*). In particular, the users are initially considered stationary, while, consequently, they are classified as moving, through the change in the value of the aforementioned property.

In Figure 5, the time required to re-classify the aforementioned modified ontologies is presented. Obviously, for Approach A as the number of users increases, the re-classification time also increases, similarly to Figure 4. Any time differences are caused by the optimized re-classification algorithm implemented by the Bossam engine. However, the aforementioned optimization is proved insufficient due to the fact that re-classification is, usually, executed in real-time and, as a consequence, the imposed delay is fully perceivable by the user.

On the other hand, storing user profiles in different files (i.e., Approach B) seems to lead to a more efficient execution of the re-classification process. In order to demonstrate this improvement, we conducted a series of experiments. The user re-classification requests followed a Poisson distribution with a mean inter-arrival time of 1 second. The experimental results show that this approach requires much less time, due to the handling of smaller documents. For example, the mean classification time is about 100 milliseconds, irrespectively of the total number of users. As a result, the efficiency provided by the latter approach can satisfy the requirements imposed by the real-time requirements of applications and minimize the time delay caused by the re-classification process.

A possible solution to avoid re-classification of "large" ontologies is to appropriately modify the queries that involve defined concepts. For instance, it would be inefficient to ask "find all walking users", since this query needs to re-classify all the user instances based on their current speed. Alternatively, one could also ask the query "identify all users with a *MediumSpeed* value

Figure 5. Re-classification performance for the approaches A and B

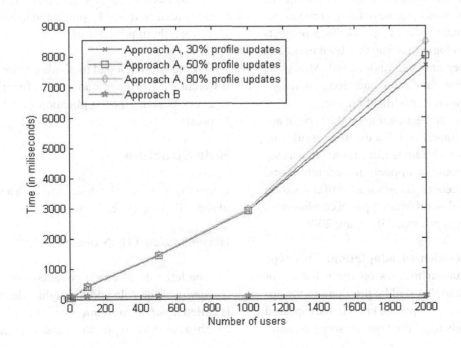

for the *hasSpeed* property". Although these two queries are semantically identical, the latter is not recommended for knowledge-based systems as it is more close to a database querying paradigm. After all, expressive ontologies (which can fully define concepts) are used in order to allow for simple and intuitive queries.

Both queries do not require much time to execute (some tenths of milliseconds, depending on the file size), but the former requires that the ontology is re-classified, and in the case of 2000 user profiles this leads to a time overhead of 8 sec (Figure 5).

RULE-BASED ADAPTATION

In order to achieve personalization, rules play a key role in the automated adaptation of system behavior. In general, modeling the application elements through ontologies provides interoperability, reusability and extensibility to the system, while rules constitute a natural and declarative form for representing the application business logic and/or its desired adaptation. As a result, the integration of rules with the ontology models enables the formation of a framework that represents the adaptation logic in a way that both users and computing elements can understand. Moreover, such integration facilitates knowledge management, maintenance, modification, etc.

Rules may vary depending on the type of adaptation they implement. For example, a rule that detects content relevant to information that a user is accessing could be applied in a content-based adaptation. A generic categorization of adaptation methods, based on different types of conditions in the rule body, is proposed in (Tran, 2006):

- **Content-oriented adaptation:** This type of adaptation focuses on the selection of the content that will be provided to the application user. Specific knowledge captured by models (e.g., the topic of some content)

is used to provide recommendations, based on the activity history, the capabilities and the interests of the user. For example, a personalized application may recommend resources related to content that user has accessed in the past.

- **Navigation-oriented adaptation:** The system exhibits proactive behavior by recommending to the user subsequent processes (tasks) that logically follow her current task or activity. It is also known as task-based adaptation. For instance, the system could decompose large content objects (e.g., restructure the hypertext organization of a Web site) by distributing the content into a number of linked pages and progressively present these pages to her.
- **Presentation-oriented adaptation:** The application presents information or content in an appropriate way, depending on the special features of the individual user. This type of adaptation requires the execution of a number of formatting instructions by the presentation device. For example, the system may have to increase the default font size of all texts that will be presented to a partially visually impaired user.

The abovementioned methods can be seen as different levels of generic adaptation functionality in every personalized application (De Virgilio, In press).

Rule Structure

Generally, a rule can be described with a formula of the following type:

IF *condition(s)* **THEN** *action(s)*

The left side of a rule is called *body* or *antecedents* of the rule and the right side of a rule is called *head* or *consequents* of the rule. In the case of a system that provides personalization, we can think that the antecedents of a rule describe a possible situation of the system, the user, the activity history and the context environment, while the consequents describe a possible adaptation decision. Specifically, the actions of a rule are triggered-executed when all of its *conditions* hold true.

In a sense, rules consolidate the contexts with the adaptive functionality of the personalized application. Practically, the conditions in the rule body are composed of atoms stemming from knowledge representation models. Hence, the antecedents of the rules have to be satisfied by the instances of the respective models. Such instances may refer to the user profile, the environment context, the application status or the activity history of the user. At the same time, the head specifies values for personalization parameters or business logic that should be executed and depends on the desired application behavior.

Semantic Web Rule Language

Semantic Web Rule Language (SWRL) (Horrocks, 2004) is the most common formalism for integrating rules with ontologies in the SW and it is based on a combination of Web Ontology Language (OWL) (Antoniou, 2004) and Rule Markup Language (RuleML, 2007). Since 2004, SWRL is a W3C candidate standard for formalizing the expression of rules in the context of SW. The basic idea behind SWRL is to extend OWL axioms to include Horn-like rules, while maintaining maximum backwards compatibility with OWL syntax and semantics, i.e., the head and body of a rule are generally OWL statements. The latter means that rules and ontologies are combined in the same logical language. Specifically, in the SWRL approach, rules are introduced by adapting existing semantics for rule languages directly in the ontology layer. As a result, the interaction between ontologies and rules is achieved with tight semantic integration.

We can think of SWRL rules as formulae of the following type:

$$a_1 \wedge a_2 \wedge \dots \wedge a_n \rightarrow b_1 \wedge b_2 \wedge \dots \wedge b_m$$

$$(1)$$

where a_i and b_i are atoms. Multiple antecedent atoms are treated as a conjunction, while multiple atoms in the consequent set are treated as separate consequences (i.e., multiple rules with unique consequent in the head). Both antecedent and consequent may consist of a possibly empty set of atoms. An empty antecedent is treated as trivially holding, while an empty consequent implies that not all antecedents can hold at the same time.

Atoms can be of the following forms:

- Concepts, e.g., $C(x)$, where C is an OWL description or data range and x is either a variable, an OWL individual or a data value.
- Object or Datatype properties, e.g., $P(x,y)$, where P is an OWL property and x, y are either variables, individuals or data values.
- $sameAs(x,y)$, $differentFrom(x,y)$ or $builtIn(r,x,\dots)$, where r is a built-in relation and x, y are either variables, individuals or data values.

The set of SWRL built-ins adheres to a modular approach that allows further extensions in the future. Existing built-ins for SWRL provide, between others, arithmetic and time comparison operators.

The main drawback of extending OWL-DL with SWRL rules is that the extended knowledge base (OWL-DL + SWRL) becomes undecidable. Additionally, SWRL does not support negation in atoms, neither in the head nor in the body of a rule. Furthermore, as we can notice in the above formula (1), SWRL rules cannot include disjunctions. As a result, SWRL inserts a number of limitations in rule expressiveness, thus constraining the adaptation functionality of an application.

In the case of an indoor navigation application, some SWRL example rules could be the following:

WheelchairedUser(u) $\wedge$ Stairway(s) $\rightarrow$ isExcludedFor(s,u),

ElderlyUser(u) $\wedge$ Elevator(m) $\rightarrow$ hasPreferentialBonusFor(m,u).

The first rule captures the common knowledge that a suitable path for a wheel-chaired user should not contain stairways, while the second rule provides an advantage to the elevator, since an elderly user wants to eliminate, to the extend possible, walking segments from her route to destination.

Other Approaches

Apart from SWRL, several proposals have been made for integrating rules with SW ontologies, since there is no universal and totally accepted solution in this issue. In this section, we discuss the most prominent approaches in the area. The reader may refer to (Eiter, 2006) for an extensive survey. These approaches can be distinguished into the following categories, depending on the degree of integration between the rule and ontology layers:

1. **Tight semantic integration between ontologies and rules.** In this approach, the existing semantics of rule languages are adapted directly in the Ontology Layer. Specifically, both ontologies and rules are embedded in a common logical language, permitting predicate sharing in a coherent way. In such a framework, rules may be used for defining classes of the ontology. SWRL and Description Logic Programs (DLP) adhere to this approach.

DLP constitutes an intersection of logic programming and Description Logics, proposed

in (Grosof, 2003). Particularly, this approach attempts to define a mapping from Description Logics to logic programming (specifically, to *def-*Horn fragment of First Order Logic that does not contain function symbols), establishing a certain degree of interoperability between them. For example, the following subclass axiom:

C1 $\sqcup$ C2 $\sqsubseteq$ D $\equiv$ D(x) $\leftarrow$ C1(x) $\vee$ C2(x)

becomes disjunction in the body of the corresponding rule:

D(x) $\leftarrow$ C1(x)
D(x) $\leftarrow$ C2(x)

Although, DLP approach covers basic class constructors (like conjunction, disjunction and quantification restrictions), it allows a very restricted expressiveness for the sake of decidability. For instance, DLP excludes negation in class descriptions as well as does not fully support cardinality restrictions.

2. **Strict semantic separation between ontologies and rules.** A strict separation is made between the rule predicates and the ontology elements. In particular, the vocabulary (concepts and predicates) offered by the ontologies is used as a conceptualization of the domain and rules cannot define ontology classes or properties. One of the most interesting approaches is Answer Set Programming (ASP) (Baral, 2003). ASP comprises a knowledge representation formalism, including non-monotonic logic features as well as efficient reasoning support. Moreover, ASP supports disjunction in the head of the rules as well as negation (strong and negation-as-failure) in rule atoms and, in general, retains decidability. The main idea in ASP lies in the semantics and the computation of multiple *answer sets* (or *stable models*) of a program. Specifically,

these answer sets represent different solutions of the program, due to the disjunctions it contains, adding a non-deterministic aspect in ASP. A typical ASP rule can be of the form:

$$a_1 \vee a_2 \vee ... \vee a_N \leftarrow b_1, b_2, ..., b_M$$

where b_i may refer to positive or negated atoms (either strong negated or with negation-as-failure). A simple rule for the navigation scenario follows:

belongsToSelectedPath(X,U) $\vee$ – belongsToSelectedPath(X,U) $\leftarrow$ accessiblePathElementFrom(X, U)

This rule denotes that every path element accessible by a user (e.g., a ramp or a corridor is accessible by a wheel chaired user) either belongs or does not belong to the selected path that the navigation application will present to the user. The negation of this rule is strong and is denoted by the symbol "–". Recently, several solvers, like the one presented in (Leone, 2005), support these features, facilitating the practical adoption of ASP.

Such a combination of logic programs and description-logic knowledge bases under the answer-set semantics is proposed in (Eiter 2004), introducing *description logic programs* (or *dl-programs*). A dl-program (L,P) consists of a knowledge base L in description logics and a set of dl-rules P, applied to L. Such dl-rules are similar to logic programming rules, but may also contain queries to L, allowing rules to derive knowledge from the knowledge base and back. As a consequence, dl-programs permit building rules on top of ontologies and exchanging knowledge they capture or derive. A simple example of dl-program could be:

DL["WheelchairedUser"](X) $\rightarrow$ wheelchairedUser(X).

DL["Stairway"](X) $\rightarrow$ stairwayElement(X).
DL["Escalator"](X) $\rightarrow$ escalatorElement(X).

In the above dl-rules, the operator DL[] denotes a query to the DL ontology, while the right part represents the corresponding predicate (outside of the knowledge base).

Then, the predicate "isExcludedFor" can be defined as:

wheelchairedUser(X), stairwayElement(Y) $\rightarrow$ isExcludedFor(Y,X).
wheelchairedUser(X), escalatorElement(Y) $\rightarrow$ isExcludedFor(Y,X).

Finally, personalization based on Semantic Web techniques may also involve reasoning with incomplete or contradictory information, which usually appears when integrating different ontologies. Defeasible reasoning constitutes a rule-based knowledge representation formalism that permits defining priorities on rules, allowing one to resolve possible conflicts between rules. As a result, this approach provides reasoning about preferences, while preserving consistency of the knowledge base. Such systems are presented in (Bassiliades, 2004; Antoniou, 2005).

Rule Engines

A rule engine constitutes the module that executes the rules of the application and infers new knowledge or triggers actions. Currently, several efficient and usable rule engines have been implemented. Some main representatives are:

Bossam (Jang, 2004) is an inference engine that provides OWL reasoning capabilities. In particular, it is a RETE-based rule engine for reasoning over OWL ontologies, SWRL and RuleML. Bossam has a number of features, including support for both classical negation and negation-as-failure (NAF), disjunctions in the body and conjunctions in the head of rules, Java method calls in SWRL rules (a.k.a. procedural attachments), etc. Finally, it provides an API for managing the engine, loading ontologies and rules, query over documents and other capabilities. Currently, Bossam does not support execution of SPARQL queries, but does provide another query language named Buchingae rule language. Another missing feature is the serialization of the knowledge base to a persistent store (e.g., file system).

RacerPro (RacerPro, 2007) is the commercial name of the RACER software, which constitutes probably the most well-known inference engine for ontologies (written in OWL) in the research community. RacerPro aims to become a universal framework for managing semantic Web ontologies and recently (RacerPro 1.9 release) offered an SWRL rule engine. Racer has been proved as a very efficient DL-reasoner and it has yet to be proved efficient in rule execution, too.

Jena (Jena, 2007) is an open-source Java framework for enabling Semantic Web applications. Among other features, Jena provides a rule-based inference engine (forward and backward chaining), but it does not support SWRL rules. As a result, someone that desires to use Jena as a rule engine has to adopt its own RDF rule language (JenaRules) or to make use of SweetRules tool (SweetRules, 2007) to get a partial mapping from SWRL to JenaRules.

Finally, *Jess* (Jess, 2007) is a rule engine written entirely in Java. Although Jess cannot directly process SWRL rules, the SWRL Tab Protégé plug-in (O'Connor, 2005) offers the capability to translate the OWL ontology plus the SWRL rules in Jess facts and rules. As a result, Jess can be used as reasoning module for executing rules in conjunction with ontologies.

Since this chapter provides also an implementation-oriented view to the Semantic Web technologies used for personalization, we summarize some common problems of existing rule engines:

- **The inference support of the rule engines is not integrated with an ontology classifier.** As a result, new assertions provided by rule execution may violate existing restrictions in the ontology. Similarly, inferred knowledge from ontology reclassification may, in turn, produce knowledge that should automatically trigger rules. Currently, these conflicts are handled manually, by the developer. An ideal solution supposes the existence of a single reasoning module for both rule inference and ontology classification. Figure 6 presents the determined tasks that an integrated inference framework should provide for combining rules with ontologies uniformly.
- **Reasoning over concrete domains.** Concrete data like integers, strings etc. is almost crucial for most applications. OWL-DL

Figure 6. The lifecycle of knowledge in a system combining ontologies with rules

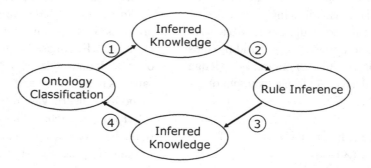

supports concrete domains that can be used as the range type of OWL datatype properties. Some usual examples may be the properties "has Age" with float range or "hasName" with string range. Additionally, SWRL allows using datatype properties as SWRL atoms and also determines a variety of built-ins over concrete domains. Though some existing rule engines support reasoning over concrete domains, many of them do not provide facilities for dealing with such type of knowledge.

- **Non-monotonic reasoning features.** Most of the current rule engines do not fully support non-monotonic reasoning features like negation-as-failure (NAF), due to the open world assumption of Description Logics. However, in practice, it has been proved over the years that closed world reasoning would be useful in Web applications, too (Damasio, 2006). Hence, future inference engine developers should consider incorporating non-monotonic reasoning into their systems.

FUTURE RESEARCH DIRECTIONS

Throughout the chapter, many open or underdeveloped research areas in the domain of personalized SWEAs have been identified. Firstly, more ontology design patterns and more expressive ontology languages should be developed. Since humans live in a physical environment, many of their characteristics are expressed by non-symbolic information, which may also carry uncertainty. This fact has implications for the expressiveness of the modeling languages. This has been recognized by the research community and some extensions have been proposed for SW languages. For example in order to deal with uncertainty some fuzzy extensions to OWL have been proposed in (Sanchez, 2006). However, more research is necessary towards this direction in order to develop reasoning algorithms capable of reasoning with the operators and constructs of these extensions (e.g., fuzzy operators).

However, more expressive modeling languages call for more efficient reasoning and inference engines. In general, tractability is a key issue in the ontological engineering community. Designing efficient algorithms and tools for reasoning with ontologies and rules remains and will, probably, remain a very hot topic in the coming years. Every time a new ontology construct is added to a language, both the semantics and its tractability are affected and new optimizations are needed. As we have shown in previous sections, reasoning efficiency is not of top level even for low-expressiveness ontologies (i.e., not exploiting many axioms).

Another research issue that is raised is that of (semi-)automatic profile extraction and revision. While this is addressed by existing traditional personalized systems, in knowledge-based systems there are still open problems. For example, knowledge revision implies non-monotonic reasoning which is not fully supported by current reasoners, due to the open world assumption of Description Logics. Moreover, typical methods for automatic (profile) learning that employ, for example, probabilistic inferences and learning have not been explored extensively in the context of Semantic Web. In fact, there is some progress in the field of ontology learning, but most works focus on learning from text documents (Cimiano, 2006). Moreover, some works on Web mining exist that are oriented to the personalization problem (Zhou, 2005), but they cannot directly apply to SWEAs. Finally, another interesting approach would be to infer/predict missing profile elements through model clustering. For example, if we have a user A that has many similarities (whatever the similarity measure is) with another user B, then maybe we could infer or predict some missing attributes of A. Obviously, this method applies only to non-unique characteristics, which should be also marked in the user ontology (thus constituting another potential categorization of user model elements).

Another interesting aspect that should be investigated is whether some parts of a personalization framework for SWEAs can be "standardized" to a certain degree. Since we described a model-driven architecture for personalization, some modeling elements and/or design patterns may be shared across different applications (i.e., application-agnostic). It would be interesting if such sub-models/patterns could be identified and specified in order to allow for model reuse and sharing. For example, the demographics section of a user profile could be specified through a community process and constitute an ontology module shared by diverse user models. In other words, and in line with the categorization of *User Modeling*, the elements of the core user model should be identified. Other approaches to the same issue propose cross-application user model exchange (Niedere, 2004). The applicability of these ideas remains an open question that requires more investigation.

Finally, group and collaborating applications is another area that is currently attracting much research interest. This is also reflected by the wide adoption of social networking theories and methods in the Web (actually they are a core element of Web 2.0). Hence, group modeling is expected to be more and more included in future personalized applications. We are not aware of much existing work on knowledge-based group modeling and reasoning and we believe that it is an area that deserves more in-depth research.

SUMMARY

In this chapter several issues on a knowledge-based approach to personalization have been discussed. We have described the components of a reference framework architecture. Our main focus was on user modeling issues and rule-based adaptation. Specifically, we investigated the applicability of Semantic Web technologies and tools to personalized applications. Through an extensive discussion and several experiments we showed that although these technologies are in a relatively mature phase, more improvements should be made in two main directions: reasoning performance and modeling expressiveness. This conclusion does not imply that Semantic Web is incapable of supporting personalized application functionality. However, developers should be aware that many practical issues have not been addressed adequately up to now.

ACKNOWLEDGMENT

This work has been partially funded by the Greek General Secretariat for Research and Technology (GSRT) under grant PENED2003 (No. 03ED173)

REFERENCES

Anagnostopoulos, C. B., Tsounis, A., & Hadjiefthymiades, S. (2007). Context awareness in mobile computing environments. *Wireless Personal Communications 42*(3), 445-464.

Antoniou G., & Bikakis A. (2005). DR-Prolog: A system for reasoning with rules and ontologies on the Semantic Web. *Proceedings From 25th American National Conference on Artificial Intelligence (AAAI)* (pp. 1594-1595), Pittsburgh, Pennsylvania: AAAI Press.

Antoniou, G., & Harmelen, F.V. (2004a). *A Semantic Web primer.* Massachusetts: The MIT Press.

Antoniou, G., Baldoni, M., Baroglio, C., Baumgartner, R., Bry, F., Eiter, T., Henze, N., Herzog, M., May, W., Patti, V., Schaffert, S., Schindlauer, R., & Tompits., H. (2004b). Reasoning methods for personalization on the Semantic

Web. *Annals of mathematics, computing and teleinformatics, 2*(1), *1-24*.

Baader, F., Calvanese, D., McGiuness, D., Nardi, D., & Patel-Schneider, P. (2003). *The description logic handbook: Theory, implementation, and applications.* Cambridge: Cambridge University Press.

Baldoni, M., Baroglio, C., & Henze, N. (2005). Personalization for the Semantic Web, *Reasoning Web, first international summer school 2005, LNCS Tutorial, 3564,* 173-212, Msida, Malta: Springer.

Baldoni, M., Baroglio, C., & Patti, V. (2004). Web-based adaptive tutoring: An approach based on logic agents and reasoning about actions. *Artificial Intelligence Review, 1*(22), *3-39*.

Baral. C. (2003). *Knowledge representation, reasoning and declarative problem solving.* Cambridge, UK: Cambridge University Press.

Bassiliades, N., Antoniou, G., & Vlahavas, I. (2004). *A defeasible logic system for the Semantic Web.* In Principles and Practice of Semantic Web Reasoning (2004), LNCS 3208 (pp. 134-148). St Malo, France: Springer.

Baumgartner, R., Henze, N., & Herzog, M. (2005). The personal publication reader: Illustrating Web data extraction, personalization and reasoning for the Semantic Web. *Lecture Notes in Computer Science, 3532. In 2005 European Semantic Web Conference (ESWC 2005)* (pp. 515-530). Heraklion, Greece: Springer.

Borgida, A., & Brachman, R.J. (2003). *Conceptual modelling with description logics.* In (Baader, 2003), chapter *10,* 349-372.

Cali, A., Calvanese, D., Colucci, S., Di Noia, T., & Donini, F.M. (2004). *A description logic-based approach for matching user profiles,* In Volker Haarslev, Ralf Möller (Eds.), *Proceedings of the 2004 International Workshop on Description Logics (DL2004). 104,* 110-119. Whistler, British Columbia, Canada: CEUR.

Cimiano, P. (2006). *Ontology learning and population from text: Algorithms, evaluation, and applications.* New York, NY, USA: Springer-Verlag.

Damasio, C. V., Analyti, A., Antoniou, G., & Wagner, G. (2006). Supporting open and closed world reasoning on the Web. In José Júlio Alferes, J. Bailey and U. Schwertel (Eds.), *Lecture Notes in Computer Science Vol. 4187,* 149–163. Budva, Montenegro: Springer.

d'Aquin, M., Sabou, M., & Motta, E., (2006). Modularization: A key for the dynamic selection of relevant knowledge components. *Paper presented at First International Workshop on Modular Ontologies, 232,* 15-28. Athens, Georgia, USA: CEUR.

De Virgilio, R., Torlone, R., & Houben, G.J. (In Press). Rule-based adaptation of Web information systems, *World Wide Web Journal,* Springer.

Dolog, P., Henze, N., Nejdl, W., & Sintek, M. (2004). The personal reader: Personalizing and enriching learning resources using Semantic Web technologies. In *Proceedings of the 3nd International Conference on Adaptive Hypermedia and Adaptive Web-Based Systems (AH 2004),* LNCS 3137 (pp. 85–94). Eindhoven, The Netherlands: Springer.

Eiter, T., Ianni, G., Polleres, A., Schindlauer, R., & Tompits, H. (2006). Reasoning with rules and ontologies. In *Proceedings of Summer School Reasoning Web 2006* (pp. 93-127). Lisbon, Portugal: Springer.

Eiter, T., Lukasiewicz, T., Schindlauer, R., & Tompits, H. (2004). Combining answer set programming with description logics for the semantic Web. In *Proceedings KR-2004,* (pp. 141–151), TU Wien: Publisher.

Fernandez, Y. B., Arias, J. J. P., Nores, M. L., Solla, A. G., & Cabrer, M. R. (2006). AVATAR: An improved solution for personalized TV based on semantic inference, *IEEE Transactions on Consumer Electronics* (pp. 223-231). IEEE Consumer Electronics Society.

Gartner, G., Frank, A., & Retscher, G. (2004). Pedestrian navigation system for mixed indoor/outdoor environments - The NAVIO project. In: Schrenk, M. (Ed.): *Proceedings of the CORP 2004 and Geomultimedia04 Symposium* (pp. 165-171). Vienna, Austria.

Grosof, B. N., Horrocks, I., Volz, R., & Decker, S. (2003). *Description logic programs: Combining logic programs with description logic.* In *Twelfth International World Wide Web Conference (WWW 2003)* (pp. 48-57). Budapest, Hungary: ACM.

Happel, H.-J., & Seedorf, S. (2006). *Applications of ontologies in software engineering.* Paper presented at Workshop on Semantic Web Enabled Software Engineering (SWESE) on the 5th International Semantic Web Conference (ISWC 2006), Athens, Georgia, USA.

Henze, N., & Herrlich, M. (2004a). The personal reader: A framework for enabling personalization services on the Semantic Web. In *Proceedings of the Twelfth GI-Workshop on Adaptation and User Modeling in Interactive Systems (ABIS 04)*, Berlin, Germany.

Henze, N., & Kriesell, M. (2004b). Personalization functionality for the Semantic Web: Architectural outline and first sample implementations. In *Proccedings of the 1st International Workshop on Engineering the Adaptive Web (EAW 2004)*, co-located with AH 2004, Eindhoven, The Netherlands.

Horrocks, I., Li, L., Turi, D., & Bechhofer, S. (2004a). *The instance store: DL reasoning with large numbers of individuals.* In *Proc. Of the 2004 Description Logic Workshop (DL-2004),* (pp. 31-40). Whistler, British Columbia, Canada

Horrocks, I., Patel-Schneider, P.F., Boley, H., Tabet, S., Grosof, B., & Dean, M. (2004b). *SWRL: A Semantic Web rule language combining OWL and RuleML*, W3C Member Submission, 21 May 2004. Retrieved June 13, 2007, from http://www.w3.org/Submission/SWRL/.

Jang, M., & Sohn, J-C. (2004). Bossam: An extended rule engine for OWL inferencing. Hiroshima, Japan: In *Workshop on Rules and Rule Markup Languages for the Semantic Web at the 3rd International Semantic Web Conference* (LNCS 3323), (pp. 128-138). Hirosima, Japan: Springer-Verlag.

Jena, A. *Semantic Web framework for java*, Retrieved June 13, 2007, from http://jena.sourceforge.net/

Jess, The rule engine for the Java Platform, Retrieved June 13, 2007, from http://www.jessrules.com/jess/index.shtml

Kay, J., & Lum, A., (2003). Ontology-based User Modelling for the Semantic Web. *10th International Conference on User Modeling, Workshop: Personalisation for the Semantic Web* (pp. 11-19). Edinburgh, Scotland.

Kikiras P., Tsetsos V., & Hadjiefthymiades S. (2006). Ontology-based user modeling for pedestrian navigation systems, *Paper presented at ECAI 2006 Workshop on Ubiquitous User Modeling (UbiqUM)*, Riva del Garda, Italy.

Kumar, S., Kunjithapatham, A., Sheshagiri, M., Finin, T., Joshi, A., Peng, Y., & Cost, R.S. (2002). A personal agent application for the Semantic Web. In *AAAI Fall Symposium on Personalized Agents* (pp. 43-58), North Falmouth, MA: AAAI Press.

Leone, N., Pfeifer, G., Faber, W., Eiter, T., Gottlob, G., Perri, S., & Scarcello F. (2005). The DLV System for Knowledge Representation and Reasoning. ACM Transactions on Computational Logic, ACM

Niedere, C., Stewart, A., Mehta, B., & Hemmje, M. (2004). *A multi-dimensional, unified user model for cross-system personalization. Paper presented at Advanced Visual Interfaces (AVI2004) Workshop on Environments for Personalized Information Access,* Gallipoli, Italy.

O'Connor, M. J., Knublauch, H., Tu, S. W., Grossof, B., Dean, M., Grosso, W.E., & Musen, M.A. (2005). Supporting rule system interoperability on the Semantic Web with SWRL. *Fourth International Semantic Web Conference* (pp. 974-986). Galway, Ireland: Springer.

Puhretmair, F., Rumetshofer, H., & Schaumlechner, E. (2002). Extended decision making in tourism information dystems. *Lecture Notes in Computer Science, 2455*, 57-66. Aix-en-Provence, France: Springer-Verlag.

RacerPro, Retrieved June 13, 2007, from http://www.racer-systems.com/products/racerpro/index.phtml http://www.racer-systems.com/products/racerpro/index.phtml

Ricci, F., Arslan, B., Mirzadeh, N., & Venturini, A (2002). ITR: A case-based travel advisory system, *Lecture Notes in Artificial Intelligence, 6th European Conference on Case Based Reasoning 2416,* 613-627. Aberdeen, Scotland: Springer-Verlag.

RuleML, Rule Markup Initiative, Retrieved June 13, 2007, from http://www.ruleml.org/

Sanchez, E. (2006). *Fuzzy logic and the Semantic Web.* Elsevier Science & Technology.

Sirin, E., Parsia, B., Grau, B. C., Kalyanpur, A., & Katz, Y. (2007). Pellet: A practical OWL-DL reasonerr, *Journal of Web Semantics, 5*(2), 51-53

Srivihok, A., & Sukonmanee, P. (2005). *Intelligent agent for e-Tourism: Personalization travel support agent using reinforcement learning. Proceeding of The 14th International World Wide Web Conference (WWW2005) Workshop.* Chiba, Japan: Keio University.

Stephanidis, C., & Savidis, A. (2001). Universal access in the information society: Methods, tools, and interaction technologies, *Universal Access in the Information Society, 1*(1), 40-55.

SweetRules, *Tools for Semantic Web rules and ontologies, including translation, inferencing, analysis, and uathoring,* Retrieved June 13, 2007, from http://sweetrules.projects.semWebcentral.org/

Tran, T., Cimiano, P., & Ankolekar, A. (2006). Rules for an ontology-based approach to adaptation. In *Proceedings of the 1st International Workshop on Semantic Media Adaptation and Personalization* (pp. 49-54). Athens, Greece: IEEE Computer Society.

Tsetsos, V., Anagnostopoulos, C., Kikiras, P., & Hadjiefthymiades, S. (2006). Semantically-enriched navigation for indoor environments. *International Journal of Web and Grid Services, 2*(4), 473-47., Inderscience Publishers.

Vallet, D., Mylonas, P., Corella, M. A., Fuentes, J. M., Castells, P., & Avrithis, Y. (2005). A semantically-enhanced personalization framework for knowledge-driven media services. *IADIS WWW/Internet Conference (ICWI 2005).* Lisbon, Portugal: IADIS Press.

Weissenberg, N., Gartmann, R., & Voisard, A. (2006). An ontology-based approach to personalized situation-aware mobile service supply. *Geoinformatica 10*(1), 55-90.

Zhou, B., Siu, C., & Fong, A. (2005). Web usage mining for Semantic Web personalization. *Presented at Personalization on the Semantic Web,* Edinburgh, UK.

ADDITIONAL READING

Antoniou, G., Bikakis, A., & Wagner, G. (2004a). A system for non-monotonic rules on the Web. In *Proc. of RuleML-2004* (pp. 23-36), Berlin, Germany: Springer LNCS.

Antoniou, G., & Harmelen, F.V. (2004b). *A Semantic Web primer*. Massachusetts: The MIT Press.

Brusilovsky, P. (2006). Methods and techniques of adaptive hypermedia. *User Modeling and User Adapted Interaction, 6*(2-3), 87–129.

Dolog, P., Henze, N., Nejdl W., & Sintek, M. (2004a). *Personalization in distributed E-Learning environments. International World Wide Web Conference*, New York, USA.

Dolog, P., Henze, N., Nejdl, W., & Sintek, M. (2003). Towards the adaptive Semantic Web. *Principles and Practice of Semantic Web Reasoning* (PPSWR'03) (pp. 51-68), Mumbay, India.

Dolog, P., Henze, N., Nejdl, W., & Sintek, M. (2004b). *The personal reader: Personalizing and enriching learning resources using Semantic Web technologies*. In *Proceedings of the 3nd International Conference on Adaptive Hypermedia and Adaptive Web-Based Systems (AH 2004)*, LNCS 3137 (pp. 85–94). Eindhoven, The Netherlands.

Eiter, T., Ianni, G., Polleres, A., Schindlauer, R., & Tompits, H. (2006). Reasoning with rules and ontologies. In *Proceedings of Summer School Reasoning Web 2006* (pp. 93-127). Lisbon, Portugal: Springer.

Eiter, T., Lukasiewicz, T., Schindlauer, R., & Tompits, H. (2004). Combining answer set programming with description logics for the Semantic Web. In *Proceedings KR-2004*, (pp. 141–151), TU Wien.

Eiter, T., Lukasiewicz, T., Schindlauer, R., & Tompits, H. (2004). Well-founded semantics for description logic programs in the Semantic Web. In *Proceedings RuleML 2004 Workshop, ISWC Conference*, (pp. 81–97), Hiroshima, Japan: Springer.

Henze, N., & Kriesell, M. (2004). Personalization functionality for the Semantic Web: Architectural outline and first sample implementations. In *Proceedings of the 1st International Workshop on Engineering the Adaptive Web (EAW 2004)*, co-located with AH 2004, Eindhoven, The Netherlands.

Heymans, S., & Vermeir, D. (2003). Integrating Semantic Web reasoning and answer set programming. In *Answer Set Programming, Advances in Theory and Implementation, Proc. 2nd Intl. ASP'03 Workshop* (pp. 194–208). Messina, Italy.

Horrocks, I., Patel-Schneider, P.F., Boley, H., Tabet, S., Grosof, B., & Dean, M. (2004b). *SWRL: A Semantic Web rule language combining OWL and RuleML*, W3C Member Submission, 21 May 2004. Retrieved June 13, 2007, from http://www.w3.org/Submission/SWRL/

Kobsa, A. (1993). *User modeling: Recent work, prospects and hazards*. In M. Schneider-Hufschmidt, T. Kuhme, and U. Malinowski, editors, Adaptive User Interfaces: Principles and Practice (pp. 111-128). North Holland.

Kobsa, A. (2001). Generic user modeling systems. *User Modeling and User-Adapted Interaction, 11*, 49–63.

McCarthy, J., & Hayes, P. J. (1969). Some philosophical problems from the standpoint of artificial intelligence. In B. Meltzer & D. Michie (Eds.), *Machine Intelligence 4*, 463-502. Edinburgh: Edinburgh University Press.

OWL, Web Ontology Language, W3C Recommendation, Retrieved June 13, 2007, from http://www.w3.org/TR/owl-ref/

Rich, E. (1978). User modeling via stereotypes. *Cognitive Science, 3*, 329-354.

Tran, T., Cimiano, P., & Ankolekar, A. (2006). Rules for an ontology-based approach to adaptation. In *Proceedings of the 1st International Workshop on Semantic Media Adaptation and Personalization* (pp. 49-54). Athens, Greece.

Webb, G. I., Pazzani, M. J., & Billsus, D. (2001). Machine learning for user modeling. *User Modeling and User-Adapted Interaction, 11*, 19-29.

ENDNOTES

[1]   The Web site *http://www.mkbergman. com/?page_id=325* by Michael K. Bergman provides a rather good collection of SW tools

[2]   The more expressive is an ontology language, the more inefficient are the corresponding reasoning algorithms.

[3]   Datatype reasoning constitutes an example of such difficult reasoning tasks. However, a first approach to support concrete domains, in sense of various numeric and string datatypes, can be found in (Sirin, 2007) where the functionality of the Pellet reasoner is described.

Chapter IV
Building Semantic Web Portals with a Model-Driven Design Approach

Marco Brambilla
Politecnico di Milano, Italy

Federico M. Facca
Leopold-Franzens-Universität Innsbruck, Austria

ABSTRACT

This chapter presents an extension to Web application conceptual models toward Semantic Web. Conceptual models and model-driven methodologies are widely applied to the development of Web applications because of the advantages they grant in terms of productivity and quality of the outcome. Although some of these approaches are meant to address Semantic Web applications too, they do not fully exploit the whole potential deriving from interaction with ontological data sources and from semantic annotations. The authors claim that Semantic Web applications represent an emerging category of software artifacts, with peculiar characteristics and software structures, and hence need some specific methods and primitives for achieving good design results. In particular the contribution presented in this chapter is an extension of the WebML modeling framework that fulfils most of the design requirements emerging in the new area of Semantic Web. The authors generalize the development process to cover Semantic Web needs and devise a set of new primitives for ontology importing and querying. The chapter also presents a comparison of the proposed approach with the most relevant existing proposals and positioned with respect to the background and adopted technologies.

INTRODUCTION AND MOTIVATION

Modern Web applications comprise distributed data integration, remote service interaction, and management of workflow activities, possibly spawned on different peers. In this scenario, a wider attention to the semantics of data and applications is mandatory to allow effective design and evolution of complex systems. Indeed, if semantics of data and applications is known, their integration becomes more feasible. Moreover, explicit semantic annotation of Web applications can facilitate content search and access, and foster a future generation of Web clients that exploit the semantic information to provide better browsing capabilities to customers.

The Semantic Web aims at bringing formal "semantics" to the human-readable information so as to make it machine-readable and allow better and easier automatic integration between different Web applications. To address this challenge, many semantic description languages arose, like RDF, OWL and WSML; some of them are currently W3C Recommendations. All these languages allow to formally model knowledge by means of ontologies: the resulting formal models are the starting point to enable easy information exchange and integration between machines.

These languages are suitable for reasoning and inference, i.e., to deduct more information from the model by applying logical expressions. This makes the modeling task easier since not all the knowledge has to be modeled. These languages are supported by a wide range of tools and APIs, that cover design of knowledge (e.g., Protégé (Noy et al., 2001) and OntoEdit (Sure et al., 2002)), provide storing facilities (e.g., Sesame (Aduna, 2007) and Jena (HP, 2007)), and offer reasoning on the data (e.g., Racer (Racer Systems, 2007) and Pellet (Sirin et al.,2007)). Based on these modeling languages, a set of querying languages have been devised too; among them, we can mention TRIPLE (Sintek & Decker, 2002) and SPARQL (W3C, 2007), a W3C candidate recommendation.

Unfortunately, although the theoretical bases and some technological solutions are already in place for Semantic Web support, the techniques and methodologies for Semantic Web application design are still rather rough. This leads to high costs of implementation for Semantic Web features, even if embedded within traditional Web applications. These extra costs are related not only to the design of the architecture and deployment of the Semantic platforms, but also to the repetitive and continuous task of semantic annotation of contents and application pages.

We claim that conceptual modeling and model-driven development can increase dramatically the efficiency and efficacy of the design and implementation of such applications, by offering tools and methodologies to the designer for specifying semantically-rich Web applications.

The model-driven approach to software development has been proven valid in several application fields and is currently one of the best practices of the software engineering discipline. Developing a Semantic Web application, as with any other kind of software system, is a complex achievement that requires the ability to master a broad spectrum of tasks, jointly performed by a number of persons with different skills for a long timeline. Software engineering and Web engineering (Ceri et al., 2002) demonstrated that following a well organized development process, centered on the appropriate modeling concepts, is essential to overcome the complexity inherent to such kind of developments.

This chapter aims at demonstrating how model-driven design can impact on specification, design, and implementation of Semantic Web portals as well. In the proposed approach, we leverage a conceptual modeling approach for visually designing the Web application domain model and hypertext model. Conceptual modeling works at higher abstraction levels with respect to direct implementation design, thus allowing to specify the application design with a top-down philosophy. The first design steps aim at describing the platform-independent domain and hypertext models, disregarding the low-level details. Further refinements can take more and more into account such details, finally leading to the expected outcome of the work. These approaches take great advantage from the adoption of C.A.S.E. (Computer Aided Software Engineering) tools, which provide facilities for designing and implementing applications according to specific methods and notations. C.A.S.E. tools sometimes include partially or completely automatic code generation too.

As a concrete example of modeling language, we pick WebML (Web Modeling Language) (Ceri et al., 2002), a well known methodology and set of metamodels in the Web engineering environment, and its companion C.A.S.E. tool WebRatio (WebModels s.r.l., 2007).

To discuss our approach and related background technologies, a running example will be used throughout the chapter. We discuss a realistic scenario based on the reuse of existing ontologies available on the Internet that can be easily exploited to create new Semantic Web Portals. In particular, we will consider two ontologies for the musical domain to build a Web application offering access to music contents, considering also users profile information. We combine the MusicBrainz ontology (http://www.musicbrainz. org) for the music domain information; the MusicMoz (http://www.musicmoz.org/) hierarchy to classify music genres; the RDF Site Summary (RSS-DEV Working Group, 2000) for music news; and the Friend Of A Friend (Foaf) ontology (Miller & Brickley, 2000) to describe for user's profiles and relationships among them. The case study application is similar to other existing Semantic Web applications (e.g., http://Foafing-the-music. iua.upf.edu/, http://squiggle.cefriel.it/music/), that provide personalized access to the contents exploiting distributed semantic information. The presented application, although rather simple because of space reasons, can be considered a full-fledged Semantic Web Portal since it aggregates

different sources of information spanned across the Internet and presents them in a structured and user-friendly manner.

Structure of the Chapter

This chapter is organized as follows. The Section *Background* contains a description of the background technologies, metamodels and methodologies for Web engineering and Semantic Web applications (i.e., WebML, OWL, RDF, and so on). The Section *Requirements for Semantic Web engineering* presents a set of requirements that Web Engineering approaches for modeling Semantic Web applications must comply with, according to our analysis; The Section *Modeling Semantic Web application with WebML* proposes our extension of a metamodel for the design of Semantic Web portals (i.e., new primitives and metamodels within the WebML framework); in Section *Case Study: A Music Semantic Portal* we present a realistic Semantic Web portal scenario designed and implemented with the proposed methodology. The Section *Implementation Experience* discusses the architectural and implementation aspects of the proposed approach. Finally Section *Conclusion* and *Future Research Directions* propose a summary of the lesson learned from the research presented and possible research direction starting from the work reported in the chapter.

BACKGROUND

This section presents an overview of the background technologies and relevant work in the field of engineering Semantic Web applications. In particular we first introduce an overview of the most relevant languages adopted for defining and querying ontologies; then we present a review of relevant Web engineering methodologies that cover Semantic Web technologies; a subsequent paragraph is dedicated to introduce WebML, the Web application modelling language that we extend for supporting Semantic Web features (extensions are discussed in Section *Modeling Semantic Web application with WebML*).

Languages for the Semantic Web

Several ontology languages have been developed during the last few years, and they will surely be exploited in the context of the Semantic Web. Some of them are based on XML syntax, such as Ontology Exchange Language (XOL), SHOE (which was previously based on HTML), and Ontology Markup Language (OML), whereas Resource Description Framework (RDF) (W3C, 2004b) and RDF Schema (W3C, 2004c) are languages created by World Wide Web Consortium (W3C) working groups. Later, two additional languages have been built on top of RDF(S) - the union of RDF and RDF Schema - to improve its features: Ontology Inference Layer (OIL) and DAML+OIL. DAML+OIL was submitted to W3C as starting proposal for a new ontology language: OWL (W3C, 2004a). Recently, a new emerging initiative, the Web Service Modeling Ontology (WSMO), introduced a new ontology language called WSML (Fensel et al., 2006). A more detailed discussion can be found in Chapter *Ontology Languages for the Semantic Web: An Overview*. The ontologies adopted in our case study are a mix of RDF(S) and OWL, that are shortly presented in the next paragraphs.

Resource Description Framework and RDF Schema

RDF (W3C, 2004b), developed by the W3C for describing Web resources, allows the specification of the semantics of data based on XML in a standardized, interoperable manner. It also provides mechanisms to explicitly represent services, processes, and business models, while allowing recognition of non explicit information. The RDF data-model is based on *subject, predicate, object* triples, so called RDF statements, to formalize meta-data. RDF is domain independent in that no assumptions about a particular domain of discourse are made. It is up to the users to define their own ontologies for the user's domain in an ontology definition language such as RDF Schema (RDFS) (W3C, 2004c).

RDF statements are based on the concept of *resources*, which can be used in the different roles of the statement. A resource can be everything; a book, a person, a Web page, a CD, a track on a CD, and so on. Every resource is identified by a Uniform Resource Identifier (URI). In the case of a Web page, the URI can be the Unified Resource Locator (URL) of the page. The URI does not necessarily enable the access via the Web to the resource; it simply unambiguously identifies the resource.

The *subject* of a statement is the resource we want to make a statement about. For example if we want to make a statement about a music artist, we need to identify it with a URI (e.g. http://musicbrainz.org/mm/mm-2.1#artist_id1234). The predicate defines the kind of information we want to express about the subject. For example if we want to make a statement about the name of the Artist we can use the URI http://musicbrainz.org/mm/mm-2.1#name that references the property defined in the ontology. The *object* defines the value of the predicate, for example in our case we want to state that the name of artist is "Bono". The object can be a literal, like in this example, or another resource represented by the object's URI.

The statement presented can be written in triple notation as[a]:

<http://musicbrainz.org/mm/mm-2.1#artist_id1234>
<http://musicbrainz.org/mm/mm-2.1#name> "Bono".

RDF supports also an XML syntax for writing and exchanging RDF graphs, called RDF/XML. The RDF/XML representation of the previous statement is:

Figure 1. The graphical representation of a RDF statement.

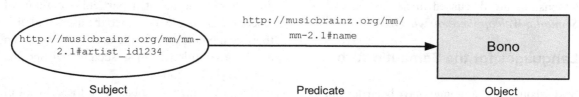

A statement can be represented as a graph too, as depicted in Figure 1.

The RDF data model does not provide mechanisms for defining the relationships between properties (attributes) and resources - this is the role of RDFS (W3C, 2004c). RDFS offers primitives for defining knowledge models that are closer to frame-based approaches[b].

In particular RDFS introduces "meta"-classes that are used to define resource types: rdfs:Class to define RDF classes (concepts); rdfs:Literal to define literal values such as strings and integers; rdfs:Property to define properties. The full RDFS vocabulary and its description can be found in (W3C, 2004c). The following fragment defines the concept artist as previously introduced:

```
<rdfs:Class rdf:about="http://musicbrainz.org/mm/
mm-2.1#Artist"
   rdfs:label="Artist">
  <rdfs:subClassOf
    rdf:resource="http://www.w3.org/2000/01/rdf-
schema#Resource"/>
  </rdfs:Class>
  <rdf:Property
    rdf:about="http://musicbrainz.org/mm/mm-
```

```
2.1#name" rdfs:label="name">
  <rdfs:domain rdf:resource="http://musicbrainz.
org/mm/mm-2.1#Artist"/>
  <rdfs:range rdf:resource="http://www.
w3.org/2000/01/rdf-schema#Literal"/>
  </rdf:Property>
```

RDF and RDFS are not rich enough to completely describe an ontology as they still miss some important concepts within their Description Logic.

Ontology Web Language

OWL (W3C, 2004a) is designed for applications that need to process the content of information instead of just presenting information to humans. Furthermore OWL facilitates greater machine interpretability of Web content than that supported by XML, RDF, and RDF Schema (RDFS) by providing additional vocabulary along with a formal semantics.

OWL provides a number of additional modelling primitives that increase the expressiveness compared to RDFS and solve some shortcomings of RDFS:

- *Cardinality restrictions.* RDFS does not provide any means to restrict the number of distinct values a property may or must take.
- *Disjoint classes.* RDFS does not provide primitives to declare two classes to be disjoint.

- *Set combination of classes*. RDFS does not allow to define new classes by building the union, intersection, or complement of other classes.
- *Special characteristics of properties*. In RDFS is not possible to define that a property is transitive (e.g. greater than), unique (e.g. is mother of), or the inverse of another property.

The following OWL fragment represents a OWL properties and its inverse. The inverseOf element specifies that playedBy is the inverse of plays.

```
<!-- Artist plays a Track-->
<owl:ObjectProperty rdf:ID="http://musicbrainz.
org/mm/mm-2.1#plays">
    <rdfs:domain rdf:resource="http://musicbrainz.
org/mm/mm-2.1#Artist"/>
    <rdfs:range rdf:resource="http://musicbrainz.org/
mm/mm-2.1#Track"/>
</owl:ObjectProperty>


<!-- Track played by an Artist -->
<owl:ObjectProperty rdf:ID="http://musicbrainz.
org/mm/mm-2.1#playedBy">
    <rdfs:domain rdf:resource="http://musicbrainz.
org/mm/mm-2.1#Track"/>
    <rdfs:range rdf:resource="http://musicbrainz.org/
mm/mm-2.1#Artist"/>
    <owl:inverseOf rdf:resource="http://musicbrainz.
org/mm/mm-2.1#plays" />
</owl:ObjectProperty>
```

OWL has three increasingly-expressive sublanguages: OWL Lite, OWL DL, and OWL Full.

- *OWL Lite* supports those users primarily needing a classification hierarchy and simple constraint features.
- *OWL DL* includes all OWL language constructs with restrictions such as type sepa-

ration (a class can not also be an individual or property; a property can not also be an individual or class). OWL DL is so named due to its correspondence with *description logics*, a field of research that has studied a particular decidable fragment of first order logic.

- *OWL Full* gives the maximum expressiveness and the syntactic freedom of RDF with no computational guarantees. For example, in OWL Full a class can be treated simultaneously as a collection of individuals and as an individual in its own right. It is unlikely that any reasoning software will be able to support every feature of OWL Full. For instance, general inference in OWL Full is clearly undecidable as OWL Full does not include restrictions on the use of transitive properties which are required in order to maintain decidability.

Query Languages for the Semantic Web

With the diffusion of RDF data sources, the problem of querying them in a easy way caused the flourishing of many different query languages for RDF based on different principles: some are inspired by SQL, like SPARQL (W3C, 2007) and RQL (Karvounarakis, 2004), others are based on different principles like graph patterns - e.g. TRIPLE (Sintek & Decker, 2002) - and reactive rules - e.g. Algae (Prud'hommeaux, 2004). In depth comparison of the most relevant RDF query languages can be found in (Haase et al., 2004; Furche et al., 2006); while a broader discussion of Web and Semantic Web query languages is presented in (Bailey et al., 2005). In the next paragraph we give some more details on SPARQL since it is probably the most adopted query language for RDF and it is the language adopted by our solution.

SPARQL

SPARQL (W3C, 2007) is a query language that has already reached candidate recommendation status at the W3C, and is on a good way to become the W3C recommendation for RDF querying. Querying RDF data with languages in the SPARQL family amounts to matching graph patterns that are given as sets of triples of subjects, predicates and objects. The triple syntax adopted by SPARQL is based on Turtle (Beckett, 2004). Solutions to SPARQL queries are given in the form of result sets: each result set contains a set of mappings from the variables occurring within the query to nodes of the queried data. For instance, the query that extracts the name and the nationality of all the Artists from the ontology previously presented can be written as:

```
BASE    <http://musicbrainz.org/mm/mm-2.1#>
PREFIX  mm: <http://musicbrainz.org/mm/mm-2.1#>
PREFIX  rdf: <http://www.w3.org/1999/02/22-rdf-
syntax-ns#>
SELECT  ?name ?nationality
WHERE
 { ?id rdf:type mm:Artist .
   ?id  mm:name ?name .
   OPTIONAL
     { ?id  mm:nationality ?nationality .}
 }
```

The WHERE clause specifies the graph pattern to selected data to be mapped to the variables; variables are identified by either ? or $ prefix. The OPTIONAL clause specifies that a certain triple is optional: it is not compulsory that all the returned results contains the triples stated has optional. If the OPTIONAL clause is removed, the results will include only the triples that contain the whole graphical pattern requested. The FROM clause can be used to specifies the URL (or some other identifier) of the data to be queried.

SPARQL includes also other three types of query: the CONSTRUCT query clauses, that create new RDF graphs with data from the RDF graph queried; the DESCRIBE query that return RDF "descriptions" of the resources matching the query part (e.g., the query DESCRIBE mm: u2 returns a RDF graph representing the mm: u2 resource); and the ASK query that return true or false according to the fact that the specified pattern has a solution or not (e.g., the query ASK mm:u2 rdf:type mm:Artist returns true if the resource mm:u2 is an instance of the class mm:Artist).

Methodologies to Design Semantic Web Applications

While design methodologies for traditional Web applications offer rather mature and established solutions methodologies for developing Semantic Web applications are still in an early development phase. Realizing the benefits of the Semantic Web platform (e.g., interoperability, inference capabilities, increased reuse of the design artifacts, etc.) traditional design methodologies are now focusing on designing Semantic Web applications: e.g., OOHDM (Schwabe & Rossi 1998) evolved in SHDM (Lima & Schwabe, 2003). New methodologies like XWMF (Klapsing et al., 2001), OntoWebber (Jin et al., 2001) and Hera (Vdovjak et al., 2003) were specifically designed by considering the Semantic Web peculiarities. Among them, the most complete are Hera and SHDM that are shortly described in the next paragraph.

The Semantic Hypermedia Design Method

SHDM (Lima & Schwabe, 2003) is an ontology-based design methodology. It extends the expressive power of OOHDM (Schwabe & Rossi, 1998) by defining ontologies for each of the OOHDM models. These ontologies are specified in OWL, a more expressive language than RDFS. In the same way as OOHDM, SHDM identifies four different phases: conceptual design, navigation design, abstract interface design, and implementation.

The conceptual design builds the conceptual class schema for the application domain. This schema is described in UML extended with a few new characteristics like the ability to specialize relations. The UML diagram is mapped to an OWL model according to some heuristics rules.

The navigation design defines the navigational class schema and the navigational context schema. The main navigational primitives are navigational classes (nodes), navigational contexts, and access structures. In the same way as for the conceptual class schema, one can specialize navigational

relations. The mappings between the conceptual schema and navigational class schema are defined using RQL. The navigation context allows the description of sets of navigational objects.

The abstract interface design defines the visual aspect of the deployed application by means of the abstract widget ontology and concrete widget ontology. The implementation phase produces a Semantic Web application based on the previous SHDM specifications.

Figure 2 presents the Navigational Class Schema (top part) and the Navigational Context

Figure 2. SHDM navigational design for a Web application based on the case study ontologies: Navigational Class Schema (top part) and Navigational Context Schema (bottom part).

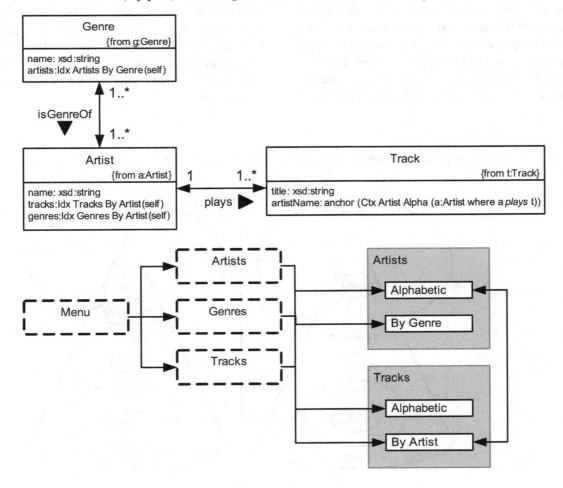

Schema (bottom part) of a simple Web application based on the musicbrainz and musicmoz ontology.

HERA

The Hera Methodology (Vdovjak et al., 2003) is a model driven methodology for designing and developing Web applications using Semantic Web technologies. It is developed from a database perspective; the conceptual modelling (similar to the ER modelling) and the querying of the different Hera models are important issues in the proposed methodology.

The Hera methodology has three main layers: *the conceptual model layer (CM), the application model layer (AM),* and the *presentation model layer (PM).* The first layer describes data content used for generation of hypermedia presentations and makes available data coming from different, possibly heterogeneous data sources; the integration of different data sources is possible thanks to a data integration model (a sub-layer that allows decoupling between the conceptual model and the data sources). The second layer describes the navigation structure and functionality; finally the PM layer describes spatial layout and rendering of hypermedia presentations. An orthogonal layer, called adaptation layer, captures adaptation issues in all the above layers.

By distinguishing these different layers, Hera differentiates at design level between the semantic aspects, the navigational aspects, and the interface aspects of a Semantic Web application.

The core components of the application model layer are called slices. They are associated with a concept from the CM model and may contain properties of the concept or other slices. Different not nested slices may be interconnected by slice relationships, that can be classified in aggregation relationships (e.g., index, tour, indexed guided tour, etc.) or reference relationships (i.e., links with an anchor specified). Slices represent views over the conceptual model and are translated to RQL queries.

Figure 3. An Hera application model based on the case study ontologies

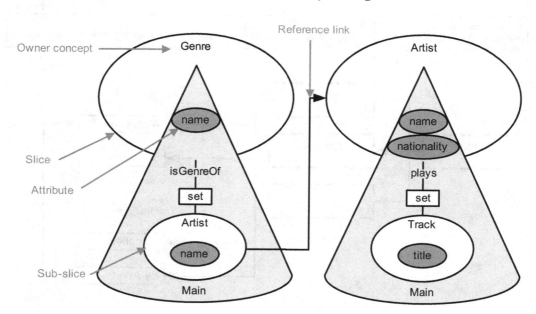

All the HERA models are, as matter of fact, ontologies, and hence a Web application model is a collection of instances of the different model ontologies. Therefore, it is possible to define a fragment of an application model as subclass of another fragment (this applies also the other two models).

Figure 3 presents a fragment of an application model based on the musicbrainz and musicmoz ontology: the first slice on the left represents a page that contains a genre and the set of artists linked to that genre; each artist is linked with a reference link to the artist slice that collects information about the artist an the set of tracks played by the artist.

WEBML

Our approach to Semantic Portals specification is based on WebML (Ceri et al., 2002). In this paragraph we introduce the basic features of WebML; the extension we introduced to model Semantic Web applications is presented later in this chapter. WebML uses conceptual modeling techniques for describing web applications. The WebML design methodology comprises three main phases: data design, hypertext design, and implementation. It provides a visual notation and a XML serialization for the proposed models.

For specifying the data underlying the application, WebML exploits an extended version of the *Entity-Relationship* model, which consists of entities (classes of data elements), and relationships (semantic connections between entities).

The hypertext design defines the navigational structure of the application. WebML also allows designers to describe hypertexts, called *site views*, for publishing and managing content. A site view is a piece of hypertext, which can be browsed by a particular class of users. Multiple site views can be defined for the same application. Site views are then composed of *areas* and *pages*. Areas and pages can be nested in areas. Finally pages are

the containers of elementary pieces of content, called *content units*, typically publishing data retrieved from the database, whose schema is expressed through the data model. In particular, WebML primitives for content publishing denote alternative ways for displaying one or more entity instances: e.g., the *data unit* publishes a single instance of data, the *index unit* a list of data. Unit specification requires the definition of a source and a selector: the source is the name of the entity from which the unit's content is extracted; the selector is a condition, used for retrieving the actual objects of the source entity that contribute to the unit's content.

Between units/pages one can define hyper-textual links as oriented connections. WebML distinguishes several types of links: *navigational*, *automatic*, and *transport* links. These links can carry information from the source to the destination. The information is stored in the link parameters. The navigational links require user intervention, while both automatic and transport links are traversed without user intervention: for automatic links once the source is presented also the associated destination is shown; the transport links do not define navigation and are solely used to transport information.

WebML also supports the specification of content management operations. They allow creating, deleting or modifying an instance of an entity (respectively through the *create*, *delete*, and *modify* units), or adding or dropping a relationship between two entity instances (respectively through the *connect* and *disconnect* units).

Figure 4 presents an example of WebML hypertext model and its underlying E-R model. It shows a single page, which allows the user to see his reviews about music albums. In the *My Home Page* a *Get* unit retrieves the identifier of the current user from the session parameter *CurrentUser* and provides it in input to the following *Data* unit, which publishes the user's personal profile data. The data to be published are restricted by means of a selector condition, specified below the unit.

Figure 4. An example Web page modeled in WebML (left) and its underlying data model (right)

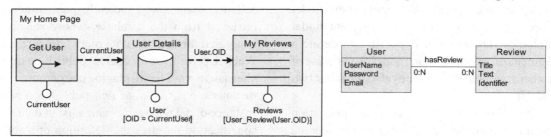

The user identifier is further propagated to the *Index* unit *My Reviews* by means of a transport link. The index unit shows the list of reviews related to the received user identifier.

WebML-based development is supported by the WebRatio CASE tool (WebModels s.r.l., 2007), which offers a visual environment for designing the WebML conceptual schemas, storing them in XML format, and automatically generates the running code (through XSLT model transformations), which is deployed as pure J2EE code.

REQUIREMENTS FOR SEMANTIC WEB ENGINEERING

While Web Engineering managed to bring software engineering practices to the Web development area, no discipline has addressed the peculiar needs of Semantic Web application design. A good methodology for the design of Semantic Web applications must provide additional facilities to the developer, specifically addressing the new needs. To understand them, we define the features of these applications, and then infer the characteristics of the methodologies and models that must be provided to the designer. To collect the requirements that a Semantic Web application should comply with, we analyzed some existing Semantic Web Portals (e.g., http://www.mind-swap.org, http://Foafing-the-music.iua.upf.edu, and http://ontoworld.org) and we extracted the following set of needs:

- **Support of semantic languages:** Semantic Web applications should be aware of and support (i.e., be able to query and manage) different Semantic Languages and metamodels (RDFS, OWL, WSML, …).
- **Semantic application models:** Semantic Web applications should be designed and specified by means conceptual models that include and support semantic descriptions.
- **Flexible integration:** Semantic Web applications should embrace the philosophy of flexibility and heterogeneity integration of Semantic Web.
- **Classes and instances access and queries:** Both domain ontology classes and instances should be easily and seamlessly accessible by Semantic Web applications, through appropriate querying primitives, including data instance and structure queries.
- **Inference and verification:** Ontology-based web applications should exploit available inferring systems on ontological data, both for semantic queries and verification of data.
- **Semantic data sources:** A Semantic Web application relies on semantic data (e.g., ontologies) that offer a machine understandable data description that may be used to populate and generate Web pages and also to provide semantic annotations.
- **Importing and reuse of ontologies:** Semantic Web applications shall allow to: (1) import new (possibly distributed) data

conforming to the Web application ontology; (2) to seamlessly integrate new ontologies, not fitting the default ontology; and (3) to reuse existing and shared ontologies.

From the previous set of characteristics, we derived the following requirements for the conceptual models pursuing the design of Semantic Web applications:

- Semantic Web application models should be aware of and support semantic languages.
- The models themselves should be "semantic", i.e., grant self-annotation and explicit semantic extraction.
- The models should allow flexible integration of heterogeneous sources and applications.
- The models should allow transformations towards a query language able to capture all the aspects of ontologies, including inference, verification, query on instances, and query on classes.
- The models should easily allow: to specify semantic data sources as underlying level of the application; to exploit these sources for populating Web pages, and for (automatically) annotating such Web pages.
- The models shall be able to import and reference distributed data and ontologies, aiming at the reuse and sharing of the knowledge.

MODELING SEMANTIC WEB APPLICATIONS WITH WebML

In this section we give an overview of extensions to the WebML methodology and models that we developed for complying with the requirements of Semantic Web applications (see previous section). WebML showed its flexibility and ease of extension in many other contexts (e.g., Web Services, Processes, Adaptive Web applications, Rich Internet applications): this allowed to con-

solidate and standardize the extension process. Basically, extending WebML for a new design domain (like Semantic Web portals) requires to introduce changes to the overall development process and to the related metamodels (and if required to introduce new metamodels in the development process). In particular, to deal with Semantic Web applications, we analyzed the current aspects of the WebML methodology and provided the proper extensions for each of them: the development process is enriched with steps that allow to describe the tasks related to the design of ontologies and semantics of the web applications/services; the data model is extended to support semantic data sources (i.e., ontologies); the hypertext model is enriched with new primitives that support ontology querying, with particular attention to advanced and inferring queries. Finally the presentation model is extended to allow for semantic annotations of the applications.

Extending the WebML Development Process

The injection of semantics within Web applications requires the extension of the methodology adopted in the development of "traditional" Web applications with additional tasks that formalize the new design steps. Figure 5 depicts the extended version of the development process for Web applications (yellow blocks represent the new tasks we introduced to fulfill Semantic Web application requirements). The original version was proposed in (Ceri et al., 2002) and is adopted with slight variations by most of the existing Web Engineering approaches. We want to stress that this development process is of general purpose and can be used for developing Semantic Web applications regardless of the use of any model-driven technique (actually it is valid also in case of traditional development techniques).

During *Requirements Specification*, a software analyst derives information about the application domain and functional requirements for the

Figure 5. The extended development process for Semantic Web applications, new and modified steps have yellow background

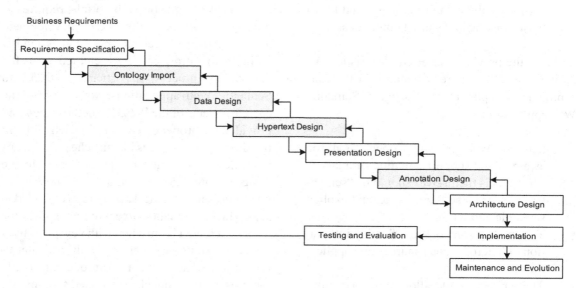

application from the business requirements and produces a detailed and formal specification for application designers. Already at this step some requirements related to semantic aspects can be highlighted and properly formalized. Based on the resulting specification, the designer can select existing domain ontologies to be imported (*Ontology Import*) and integrated in the Web application. Both ontology schemas and ontology instances maybe imported at this point. Never the less, for the Web application design, only ontology schemas are relevant. The imported ontologies can be possibly modified or merged to better suite the Web application purposes with specialized tools like Protégé (Noy et al., 2001). During the *Data Design* phase, the database structure and new ontologies can be created. Then, during the *Hypertext Design* the actual Web application structure is designed; in this phase, new primitives allows to specify how to query ontologies. Notice that the design of interactions with relational data remains unchanged with respect to the standard WebML design techniques. At this point the designer takes decisions about

the *Presentation Design* of the Web application (e.g. design of graphical mock-ups and resources) and about the semantic annotations he wants to include in the rendered pages. The *Annotation Design* enriches the Hypertext Design and relies on the Presentation Design for deciding the actual position, formatting, and display style of annotations. *Architecture Design* mainly concerns the definition of hardware and software components as well as the design of the required network infrastructure. Once an overall application design has been specified, the *Implementation* phase can be carried out. It produces in output the software components (databases, ontologies, HTML templates, business logics, etc.) that build up the actual Web application, running on the selected architecture. During the following *Testing and Evaluation* phase, several tests (regarding e.g. functionality, usability, and performance) validate the application's conformance with respect to the initial business requirements, and could lead to novel derived requirements or modifications of the implementation. After testing, the application is released and undergoes ordinary maintenance and evolution activities. Notice that the waterfall representation may be adjusted for some design experiences, considering that in some cases some steps are not needed at all (e.g., if only imported ontologies are necessary, the data design step can be skipped). We did not depict all the variants for sake of clarity.

In the following paragraphs we discuss in more detail the changes introduced to the development process (yellow blocks in Figure 5).

Extending the WebML Data Model

Current existing model-driven methodologies for Semantic Web applications either evolved from existing ones by extending their data source coverage to ontologies, or have born with native support of semantic data sources.

Although ontology support is obviously necessary for Semantic Web applications design, we think that relational data sources can still provide great added value to Web applications. Relational databases are still a valuable option for modeling portion of domain data where features offered by ontologies are not needed (e.g., hierarchies, polymorphism, reasoning support, …) and where performances are a key issue (e.g., transactional data).

Therefore, allowing seamless interaction between ontologies and databases is a desideratum of current Semantic Web applications. Notice that we do not aim at extending the data model of WebML so as to model ontologies (see Noy et al. 2001), but at allowing Web applications to query imported semantic knowledge together with relational sources. By adopting a conceptual model, like WebML, interaction between ontology instances and database instances can be quite straightforward.

The designer is in charge of carefully deciding what is going to be part of an ontological data source and what is going to part of a relational data source. As data design (both in case of ontologies and databases) in general is an already

consolidated discipline, we do not provide further details in this chapter. The only critical aspect is that the designer needs also to foresee if there is any need of references between the two data sources (e.g., the URI identifier of a Foaf user profile may be referenced in the relational schema to connect some relational attributes).

Extending the WebML Hypertext Model

WebML comes with a basic set of primitives for data access (e.g., *Index* unit, *Multidata* unit, the *Data* unit) that have a general purpose meaning (see Section "Background") and are perfectly fitting in the role of query and navigation primitives for both relational and ontology sources. Indeed, this is a general feature of conceptual models: if the used abstractions are generic enough, they do not need to be changed when their data source grounding is changed. They can be easily extended for supporting the additional expressive power and the different data model of the ontological sources.

For example, in WebML the *Index* unit is extended so that, besides extracting lists of relational instances, allows to produce lists of instances of a particular class within an ontology model. In previous sections we highlighted some requirements related to this kind of query: (1) the possibility to show only direct instances or also inferred instances; (2) the need for querying both instances and classes, thus mixing instances and (sub)classes in the results too. The same principles can be applied to *Multidata* unit and *Data* unit.

The *Hierarchical Index* unit, already defined in WebML, fits perfectly with the ontological data sources since it can be extended to browse and publish a portion of ontology in a hierarchical tree representation: for instance, given a class, it allows to publish the hierarchical tree underlying it, comprising subclasses and instances.

As stressed above, these basic WebML primitives remain valid, nevertheless they require some small extensions to support challenges posed by ontological data sources. Ontologies allow for queries with a wider expressive power and require some different modeling rules for the information within respect to relational data. This reflects into changes in the notations that the primitives must use for defining the conditions and the selection of the data.

Some of the challenges posed by ontologies are:

- There is no distinction between relationships and attributes within the set of properties of a class. E-R style relationships might be considered as ontological properties having an URI as value, and attributes to ontological properties having a literal as value;
- Several Semantic Web framework (e.g., OWL, RDF) assume that any instance of a class may have an arbitrary number (zero or more) of values for a particular property;
- Properties specification may include cardinality constraints and classes as range (and of course domain). In this case, it is possible to publish as values also structured objects and not only atomic attributes.

The revised units allow to model in a visual and simple way queries over ontologies. The data integration between relational data sources and different ontologies can be tackled directly in the Hypertext Model, by exploiting the data flow mechanism provided by WebML. One of the main advantages of WebML is the ability to specify business logic of applications by interconnecting smaller business logic components (units) in chains and passing parameters between them. This allows to define complex business logics composed by units that may query different ontologies or relational data sources and then can exchange information along the chain of transport links in a very easy way. Thus, parameters on the links become the actual contact point between traditional and semantic data and provide the

mechanism for orthogonalizing data issues and hypertext issues.

Advanced Data Access Primitives

Many possible queries, using semantic data sources and semantic query languages, cannot be expressed using the basic data access primitives presented in the previous section. By carefully analyzing the semantic query languages presented at the beginning of the chapter, we introduce a new set of operational primitives that cover advanced queries over ontological data available in these languages. In particular these new units are largely influenced by two languages presented in the background section, namely, SPARQL (W3C, 2007) and RDF Schema syntax (W3C, 2004c). SPARQL was also selected among the various semantic query languages as the one adopted in the implementation of the runtime components (see Section *Implementation Experience*) because of its large software support and because it is probably going to become a W3C Recommendation.

The core set of new units aims to fill the gap between the basic WebML querying primitives and the increased expressive power of semantic languages. The basic primitives can not be combined to design any query that heavily exploits reasoning and mixing between schemas and instances. Thus, the basic WebML primitives miss two of the main assets of semantic languages. For example, they do not allow to infer all the classes an instance belongs to; they do not allow to infer the classes a particular property belongs to (in ontological models, a property can be associated to more than one class, since it is modeled independently from the class itself). The new units (i.e., *SubClassOf, InstanceOf, HasProperty, HasPropertyValue, SubPropertyOf*), described in Table 1, aim at providing explicit support to advanced ontological queries and allow to extract classes, instances, properties, values; to check existence of specific concepts; and to verify whether a relationship holds between two objects. These

Table 1. *The new WebML units for advanced queries on ontologies*

Unit name and Symbol	Input	Output	Description
SubclassOf [ClassName1=?] [ClassName2=?]	c_1, c_2 $c_1, ?$?, c_2	true if c_1 is subclass of c_2 the list of superclasses of c_1 the list of subclasses of c_2	Given two classes, it returns true if the first is subclass of the second. Given a class, it returns the list of its subclasses or superclasses.
InstanceOf [ClassName=?] [Instance=?]	i, c i, ? ?, c	true if i is instance of c the list of classes for i the list of instances of the class c	Given a class and an instance, it returns true if the object is instance of the class. Given a class, it returns the list of its instances. Given an instance, it returns the list of the classes it belongs to.
HasProperty [ClassName=?] [Property=?]	c, p c, ? ?, p	true if the class c has the property p the list of properties of the class c the list of classes having p	Given a class and a property, it returns true if the class includes the property. Given a class, it returns the list of its properties. Given a property, it returns the list of the classes it belongs to.
Has PropertyValue [Property=?] [Value=?]	p, v p, ? ?, v	the list of URIs where the property p has value v the list of possible values for the property p the list of properties with value v	Given a property and a value, it returns the list of resource that has that property with that value. Given a property, it returns the list of all the possible values of the property. Given a value, it returns the list of properties with that value.
Subproperty [Property1=?] [Property2=?]	p_1, p_2 $p_1, ?$?, p_2	true if p_1 is subproperty of p_2 the list of superproperties of p_1 the list of subproperties of p_2	Given two properties, it returns true if the first is subproperty of the second. Given a property, it returns the list of its subproperties or superproperties.

units have a polymorphic behaviour: their business logic and the results returned change according to the configuration of their input parameters. The complete summary of the behaviour of these units is presented in Table 1.

Some other capabilities are needed within Semantic Web applications. For instance, we may need to import at runtime ontologies instances compliant with ontological schemas defined (or imported) at design time; to extract semantic descriptions of ontology portions; or to merge and compose ontologies. To this purpose, we introduce three new units, visually represented in Figure 6. The *Set Composition* operation unit is able to

Figure 6. Symbols of the new WebML semantics management units

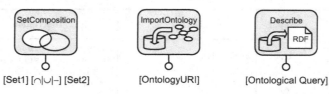

perform classic set operations (i.e., union, intersection, difference) over two input sets of URIs, considering the hierarchy of the URIs involved. E.g. suppose we have two set of classes:

A = {ProgressiveRock, Jazz, Metal}
B = {Rock, JazzFusion}.

In this case, the set operation will give the following results:

A ∩ B = {ProgressiveRock, Metal, JazzFusion}
A ∪ B = {Rock, Jazz}

since Rock is superclass of ProgressiveRock and Metal, and Jazz is superclass of JazzFusion.

The *Import Ontology* unit allows to import at run time ontological data sources consistent with one or more of the ontology models imported at design time. This unit validates imported data against existing schemas and according to the designer choice, allows to store only the url of the newly imported ontology (i.e., it will be remotely queried every time, so modification on the remote source will be propagated to the application) or to import the ontology in the local OWL/RDF repository (i.e., it will be accessed locally, but modifications to the original data will not be propagated to the application). Notice however that in our methodology the navigational model of the Web application cannot be changed dynamically at runtime, thus if the imported ontology contains a new class unrelated with already existing classes queried in the hypertext, these new class will not

be reachable in the navigation of the hypertext.

The *Describe* unit returns the RDF description of an URI, thus enabling data exporting and semantic annotation of pages.

The different advanced querying units are designed such that they can be combined in chains to compose complex business logic pattern that enables reasoning over ontological data. For instance, Figure 7 reports a fragment of the portal that allows to retrieve artists or albums that are correlated to artist searched by the user. The value submitted in the form is passed to an index unit that, by means of a filter, extracts all the Artists whose name contains in the string submitted by the user. The URI of the Artist picked from the index is passed to the *HasPropertyValue* unit. This unit extracts a set of URIs (instances of the class Album or Artist) that have the passed URI as value of the relatedWith property. The set of URIs is then passed to the *InstanceOf* unit that checks if they are instances of the class Artist. In this case, the URIs are passed over through the OK link to an index unit showing a list of Artist, otherwise the URIs are passed on the KO link to publish a list of Album (not shown in the figure).

Extending the Presentation Model to Support Semantic Annotations

Each WebML semantic unit has been designed as able to automatically extract a RDF description of its contents. The designer has to specify in the HTML templates how he wants to use the RDF annotations. This RDF fragments can be used to

Figure 7. A portion of a Semantic Web application described by the new WebML units

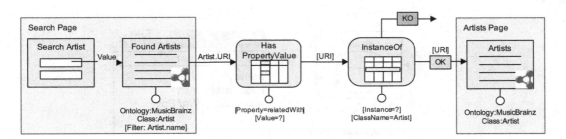

annotate a single portion of the page (the one where the unit is rendered) or they can be aggregated and published together in a single predefined location, as a global semantic annotation of the whole page itself. Annotations can be made visible in the page for user reference or kept hidden in the HTML code if they are meant to be used only by machine readers. The WebML presentation model (that allows to place objects in a page grid, according to appropriate styles) can be exploited for defining how and where semantic annotations are rendered within the generated pages. If advanced annotation is needed, the solution is the *Describe* unit, which allows to query the ontologies to extract complex RDF fragments to be used as annotations. In this way, it is possible to extract semantic fragments also of instances or classes not published in any content unit of the displayed page. Different templates may be applied to different portions of the application according to the requirements of the developed Web application.

For example, the designer may decide to adopt a template that generates RDFa (Adida & Birbeck, 2007) annotations. RDFa is a syntax that expresses the structure underlying the published data using a set of elements and attributes that embed RDF in HTML. An important goal of RDFa is to achieve this RDF embedding without repeating existing HTML content when that content is the structured data. Within our framework RDFa is particularly easy to adopt since published data reflects an ontology schema; each displayed property value can be simply published with the proper reference to its property URI (setting the `property` attribute in the surrounding HTML tag), and reference resource (setting the `about` attribute in the surrounding HTML tag). Once the designer has defined the generic template, correct annotations are extracted in an automated way at runtime according to the underlying ontological model. Figure 8 presents an example of data unit with the relative generated RDFa annotation.

CASE STUDY: A MUSIC SEMANTIC PORTAL

In this section we show a simplified example of a Semantic Web portal modelled with WebML leveraging on the extensions we introduced in the previous section. For the design of the application we adopt the ontologies cited in the Introduction, namely the MusicBrainz ontology, the ontologization of the MusicMoz hierarchy; the RDF Site Summary for music news; and the Friend Of A Friend (Foaf) ontology. The main ontology adopted in the case study application is the MusicBrainz ontology; Figure 9 visually represents a fragment of it. The application includes also a small relational schema that contains registration information for the users, described by the User entity with its login data and the URI of its cor-

Figure 8. An example of data unit with the relative generated RDFa annotation (highlighted in black).

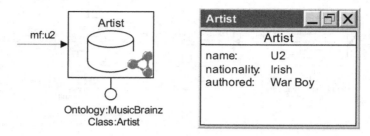

```
<TABLE xmlns:mf="http://example.org/mf#">
  <TR>
    <TD>
      <SPAN property="mf:name" about="mf:u2">U2</SPAN>
    </TD>
  </TR>
  <TR>
    <TD>
      <SPAN property="mf:nationality" about="mf:u2">Irish</SPAN>
    </TD>
  </TR>
  <TR>
    <TD>
      <SPAN property="mf:authored" content="mf:War"
        about="mf:u2">War</SPAN>
      <SPAN property="mf:authored" content="mf:Boy"
        about="mf:u2">Boy</SPAN>
    </TD>
  </TR>
</TABLE>
```

responding Foaf profile, if he has imported one in the Web application.

Figure 10 reports a fragment of the WebML model for the proposed application: content units with the RDF symbol ⌣ use ontological data sources (e.g., *Artists* index unit), while the other units publish data from the a relational database (e.g., *User Data* data unit). The user starts his navigation from the *User Home Page*, where the *Foaf Profile* data unit is published; the user also import a profile if it is not available yet. This part of the application actually shows how integration between ontological data sources and relational data can be achieved using parameters transported

over links: when the user imports the ontology that represents his Foaf profile, he actually stores the URI of the profile in the *User* relational entity; this URI is later used to publish his Foaf profile from the ontology repository according to the database schema.

The user can navigate from *Foaf Profile* data unit to the *Suggestion* page that presents an index of Artist corresponding to his preferences. From here (and from any other page presenting a visual query over the Artist class) the user can browse the *Artist details* page, where detailed information about the selected Artist and his Album are presented. The user can ask for the

Figure 9. A fragment of the MusicBrainz ontology representing Artist, Album, and Track, with the respective relationships

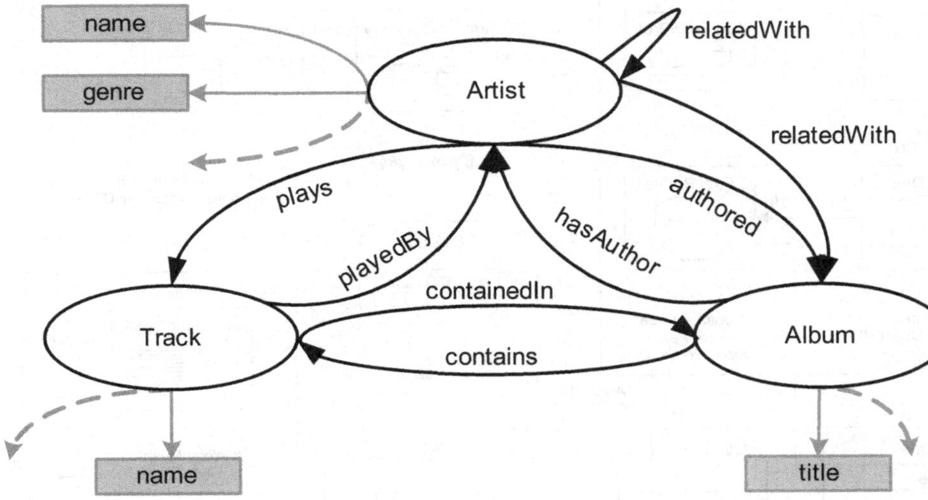

exporting of the RDF description of the `Artist` he is currently browsing. From the *Albums* index unit is possible to reach the *Album Details* page that reports information on the navigated instance of `Album` and its `Track` instances. Then accessing the landmark page *Search by genre* (a landmark page is a page accessible from any point in the hypertext also without an explicit link), the user can navigate a hierarchical representation of the class `Genre`, and then accesses all the `Artist` instances that are related to the selected genre. The *SubClassOf* unit extracts indirect sub-genres of the chosen one, thus allowing to display associated artists. Finally the *News* page reports an index of RSS `Item` and, by selecting an item from the list, the user can display the `Artist` associated with it (thanks to the filter that allows to retrieve `Artist` instances whose name or alias is included in the title or in the description property of the item). New sources of RSS `Item` may be imported adopting the *Import Ontology* unit, such as in the case of the Foaf profile.

IMPLEMENTATION EXPERIENCE

In this section we discuss the architecture design we adopted to implement the presented extensions to the WebML metamodel. These design choices are discussed according to the reference implementation of WebML, the Webratio toolsuite (WebModels s.r.l., 2007). As API to integrate ontologies both in the design environment and in the runtime framework we adopted the Jena framework (HP, 2007), while the reasoning support is obtained by means of the Jena integrated reasoner, or by means of the integration of Pellet (Sirin et al., 2007) with the Jena framework (the choice is made by the designer from the CASE tool). The runtime environment offered by Webratio has been extended exploiting the plug-in mechanism of the toolsuite:

- We devised a general purpose ontology data access layer to be exploited by every unit;
- Then, we developed a runtime Java component and an XML descriptor for each unit.

Figure 10. A portion of a WebML diagram for a Semantic Music Portal

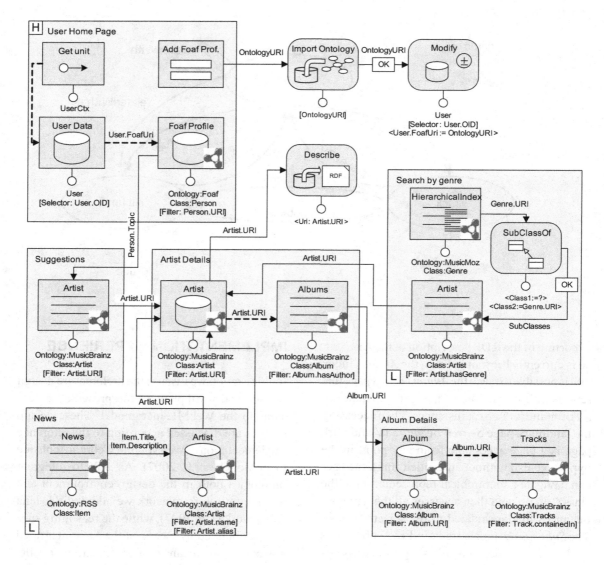

Some extensions were needed on the design time interface too, in order to provide the proper management of ontological sources and units. Figure 11 reports a screenshot of the extended design environment showing the use case Semantic Web application presented in the previous section.

Implementing the Ontological Units

In the WebRatio framework, each unit is implemented by means of a generic class representing the runtime component that is executed for every instance of that kind of unit. Then, for each new unit (including the revisited traditional units that access ontologies) we developed an XML descrip-

Figure 11. The Semantic Web Portal for the Music domain modelled with the WebRatio CASE tool

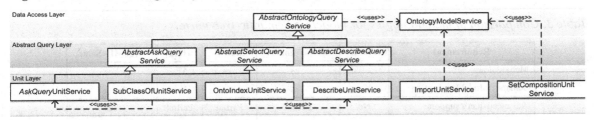

Figure 12. UML class diagram of the class hierarchy of the new implemented units

tor specifying its parameters, its properties, the binding to the implementation classes, and so on. To better clarify the structure of the descriptor, we show two examples of an ontological unit descriptors (see left column of Table 2). By means of an associated XSLT transformation, design time descriptors are translated to runtime descriptors that include automatically generated template of SPARQL queries (right column of Table 2). Units are implemented by Java components that behave according to the logics specified in the runtime descriptors, defined for each instance of the unit.

Table 2. Design time and runtime descriptors for two semantic units

	Design Time Descriptor	Runtime descriptor

Semantic Index unit	```
	<SWINDEXUNIT class="mf:Track" id="swinu1"
	  name="Tracks" ontology="onto1">
	  <DisplayedProperties
	  property="mf:title"/>
	  <DisplayedProperties
	  property="mf:descriptor"/>
	  <SortProperties order="ascending"
	  property="mf:title"/>
	  <Filter boolean="or">
	    <FilterCondition id="fselector1"
	    property="mf:playedBy"
	    predicate="eq" name="Artist"/>
	  </Filter>
	</SWINDEXUNIT>
	``
		``
		<descriptor service="org.webml.onto.
		SWIndexUnitService">
		  <onto>onto1</onto>
		  ...
		  <input-params>
		    <input-param type="mm:Artist"
		    name="swdau2.rdf:ID" />
		  </input-params>
		  ...
		  <query type="SELECT">
		  SELECT DISTINCT ?instance ?p1 ?p2
		  WHERE {?instance rdf:type mm:Track .
		  ?instance mm:title ?p1 .
		  ?instance mm:descriptor ?p2 .
		  ?instance mm:playedBy ?fs1 .
		  FILTER (?fs1 = $swdau2.rdf:ID$)}
		  ORDER BY DESC(?p1)
		  </query>
		</descriptor>
		``

SubclassOf unit	```
	<SUBCLASSOFUNIT id="iof1"
	  name="SubClassOf" ontology="onto1">
	</SUBCLASSOFUNIT>
	``
		``
		<descriptor service="org.webml.onto.
		SubClassOfUnitService">
		  <onto>onto2</onto> ...
		  <input-params>
		    <input-param type="mz:Genre"
		    name="swinu3.rdf:ID" />
		  </input-params>
		  <query type="SELECT">
		  SELECT ?id WHERE
		    {?id rdfs:subClassOf $swinu3.rdf:ID$}
		  </query>
		</descriptor>
		``

Table 3. Comparison of methodologies for modeling Semantic Web portals

Requirement	XWMF	OntoWebber	SHDM	Hera	WebML+Sem.
Methodology	Partial	Yes	Yes	Yes	Yes
Semantic Model Description	Yes	Yes	Yes	Yes	Partial
Advanced query support	No	Partial	Partial	Partial	Yes
Flexible integration	No	Partial	Yes	Yes	Partial
Heterogeneous data sources	No	No	Partial	Partial	Yes
Distributed data sources	No	No	No	Yes	Yes
Reuse of ontologies	Yes	Yes	Partial	Yes	Yes
(Automatic) Annotation	No	No	No	No	Yes
Reasoning Support	No	No	Yes	Yes	Yes

Ontological Data Source Layer

We defined a new data access layer to allow the interaction with ontologies, comprising a set of general purpose Java classes to be reused by all the new units for querying the ontology repositories. These classes provide facilities to import ontologies and to select OWL/RDF classes, properties, and instances (possibly filtered by one or more conditions). The main aspects of the class structure are represented in Figure 12. The *OntologyModelService* enables connections to local and remote ontologies specified at design time or imported at runtime by means of the Import Ontological Source unit. Three abstract classes offer the query services corresponding to the query methods offered by SPARQL on the ontology contents: the *AbstractSelectQueryService* class perform selection over data (SPARQL SELECT query); the *AbstractDescribeQueryService* retrieves the RDF describing a given URI (DESCRIBE query), the *AbstractAskQueryService* verifies simple predicates (ASK query). The AbstractAskQueryService is extended by the *AskQueryService* that is used by some of the advanced querying units to verify predicates (e.g., to check whether a class is subclass of another). In general, ontological unit services use or implement these general purpose services.

CONCLUSION

In this chapter we presented our research on the design of Semantic Web applications; we introduced briefly all the used background technologies and languages that are at the core of our proposal or that are adopted by other well-known frameworks. To ease the comparison of our work with other solutions, we described in detail Hera and SHDM, the most complete existing solutions.

The core of this chapter is the presentation of our extension to the WebML methodology and models for supporting the design and the specification of Semantic Web applications. The described solution provides a full coverage of the development process: it allows the designer to specify basic and advanced queries on ontological data sources, to import existing sources, and to annotate Web pages with semantic descriptions of the contents and of the models. Our approach provides substantial added value with respect to the existing frameworks for Semantic Web application design, although some of them are more advanced on some aspects (e.g., seamless integration of different ontologies).

Table 3 reports a summary that compares the features of the previously cited models for Semantic Web Portals and the WebML extensions presented in this chapter. All the methodologies, except for XWMF, have a complete development methodology that covers all the needed aspects to create a Semantic Web application. They also offer a wide support for ontology languages: basically all the models support both RDF and OWL (except for XWMF). However, our extension is the only one that leverages on Semantic Web query languages to offer advanced query primitives that allow both query on schema and instances, together with simple reasoning patterns over data. Other models (e.g., Hera) offer query on data schema and instances. Hera and OntoWebber offer direct support to data integration by means of an integration model that can be used to query different data schemas using the same query. WebML offers the chance to integrate relational, XML and ontology data sources, while other methodologies seem to support explicitly only ontologies (of course, this issue can be solved by adopting extraction techniques to import other data sources within ontologies).

SHDM does not allow to import ontologies but only to create them from UML diagrams. Then, it offers a tricky way to link these ontologies to the external ones. Only a specific WSDM extension (Casteleyn et al., 2006) provides an approach to annotate pages so as to make them machine readable. Most of the new methodologies offer runtime frameworks that include or allow integration of reasoners, while some of them do not clarify if the reasoning is supported also at design time.

An important factor to assure the success of a design methodology is the existence of CASE tool support, since a powerful methodology that is not accompanied by adequate tools will make the designer tasks very difficult to fulfil. While most of the traditional design methodologies have powerful CASE tools, no established tool support is provided for Semantic Web design, although all the cited methodologies offer some basic tools. We support our proposal with a prototype implementation within the CASE tool WebRatio.

FUTURE RESEARCH DIRECTIONS

Future research will span on several directions: one of the main aspect we want to address is to generalize the way for extending the querying expressive power of the WebML units. Indeed, the provided extensions address some specific additional query power, but if further query expressive power is needed, researchers will need to devise new appropriate units. With a general representation framework, we plan to avoid this burden and to provide a quicker and more compact way for obtaining the results.

Another interesting aspect that was highlighted by this extension experience is related to the traditional way in which WebML provides querying facilities: standard WebML units (index unit, multi-data unit, data unit, and so on) provide both query service and publishing features in one single component (the *unit* specified within the page). Our extensions instead provide components that offer only the query services, without dealing with publishing, which is left to traditional WebML units. This separation of concerns could probably be applied to traditional querying too, so that the two aspects are always kept separate. This would mean a deep rethinking of the WebML

hypertext models. We plan to consider this hint and to study possible solutions to the problem in the immediate future.

Besides pure research topics, we plan to extend and refine our implementation. Future implementation work includes:

- Providing a content integration layer to allow for seamless integration of different ontologies;
- Extensive testing of the new framework, including the application of the approach to real industrial scenarios;
- Integration of existing Eclipse based solutions for ontology editing with in the CASE tool.

REFERENCES

Adida, B., & Birbeck, M. (2007). *Rdfa primer 1.0: Embedding RDF in XHTML*, W3C Working Draft 12 March 2007. Retrieved June 16, 2007, from http://www.w3.org/TR/xhtml-rdfa-primer/

Aduna (2007). *Sesame*. Retrieved June 26, 2007, http://www.openrdf.org/.

Bailey, J., Bry, F., Furche, T., & Schaffert, S. (2005). Web and Semantic Web query anguages: A survey. In J. Maluszinsky and N. Eisinger (Eds.), *Reasoning Web Summer School 2005*, (pp. 35–133). Springer-Verlag.

Beckett, D. (2004). *Turtle - Terse RDF triple language*. Retrieved June 16, 2007, from http://www.dajobe.org/2004/01/turtle/.

Brambilla, M., Celino, I., Ceri, S., Cerizza, D., Della Valle, E., & Facca, F.M. (2006, November 5-9). A software engineering approach to design and development of Semantic Web service applications. In *The Semantic Web - ISWC 2006, 5th International Semantic Web Conference, ISWC 2006, Athens, GA, USA, Proceedings* (pp. 172-186). Springer.

Casteleyn, S., Plessers, & P., Troyer, O.D. (2006, *July 11-14*). Generating semantic annotations during the Web design process. In *Proceedings of the 6th international Conference on Web Engineering (Palo Alto, California, USA). ICWE '06* (pp. 91-92). ACM Press.

Ceri, S., Fraternali, P., Bongio, A., Brambilla, M., Comai, S., & Matera, M. (2002). *Designing data-intensive Web applications*. Morgan Kauffmann

Fensel, D., Lausen, H., Polleres, A., de Bruijn, J., Stollberg, M., Roman, D., & Domingue, J. (2006). *Enabling Semantic Web services: The Web service modeling ontology*. New York: Springer-Verlag.

HP (2007). *Jena a Semantic Web framework for Java*. Retrieved June 26, 2007, http://jena.sourceforge.net.

Furche, T., Linse, B., Bry, F., Plexousakis, D., & Gottlob, G. (2006). RDF querying: Language constructs and evaluation methods compared. In *Proceedings of Summer School Reasoning Web 2006*, Lisbon (pp. 1–52). Springer.

Haase, P., Broekstra, J., Eberhart, A., & Volz, R. (2004, November 7-11). A comparison of RDF query languages. In *Proceedings of the third International Semantic Web Conference, Hiroshima, Japan,* (pp. 502–517). Springer.

Jin, Y., Decker, S., & Wiederhold, G. (2001, July 30-August 1). OntoWebber: Model-Driven ontology-based Web site management. In I.F. Cruz, S. Decker, J. Euzenat, & D.L. McGuinness (Eds.), *Proceedings of SWWS'01, The First Semantic Web Working Symposium,* Stanford University, California, USA. (pp. 529–547)

Karvounarakis, G., Magkanaraki, A., Alexaki, S., Christophides, V., Plexousakis, D., Scholl, M., & K. Tolle (2004). RQL: A functional query language for RDF. In Gray, P., King, P., & Poulovassilis, A. (Eds.), *The Functional Approach to Data Management* (pp. 435–465). Springer-Verlag.

Klapsing, R., Neumann, G., & Conen, W. (2001, November). Semantics in Web engineering: Applying the resource description framework. *IEEE MultiMedia, 8(2),* 62-68. IEEE Computer Society.

Lima, F., & Schwabe, D. (2003). Application modeling for the Semantic Web. In *1st Latin American Web Congress (LA-WEB 2003), Empowering Our Web,, Sanitago, Chile, Proceedings* (pp. 93–102). IEEE Computer Society.

Miller, L., & Brickley, D. (2000). *Foaf project*. Retrieved June 16, 2007, from http://www.Foaf-project.org.

Noy, N.F., Sintek, M., Decker, S., Crubezy, M., Fergerson, R.W., & Musen, M.A. (2001). Creating Semantic Web contents with Protègè 2000. *IEEE Intelligent Systems 16(2),* 60-71. IEEE Computer Society.

Prud'hommeaux, E. (2004). *Algae RDF query language*. Retrieved June 16, 2007, from http://www.w3.org/2004/05/06-Algae/.

Racer Systems (2007). *RacerPro*. Retrieved June 16, 2007, from http://www.racer-systems.com/.

RSS-DEV Working Group (2000). RDF Site Summary (RSS) 1.0. Retrieved June 16, 2007, from http://web.resource.org/rss/1.0/spec.

Schwabe, D., & Rossi, G. (1998, October). An object-oriented approach to Web-based application design. In *Theory and Practice of Object Systems (TAPOS),* 207–225. John Wiley & Sons

Sintek, M., & Decker S. (2002). TRIPLE - A Query, inference, and transformation language for the Semantic Web. In *1st International Semantic Web Conference, ISWC 2002, Chia, Sardinai, Italy, Proceedings* (pp. 364 - 378). Springer.

Sirin, E., Parsia, B., Grau, .B. C., Kalyanpur, A., & Katz, Y. (2007). Pellet: A Practical OWL-DL Reasoner. *Journal of Web Semantic,s 5(2),* 51-53. Elsevier.

Sure, Y., Erdmann, M., Angele, J., Staab, S., Studer, R., & Wenke D. (2002). OntoEdit: collaborative ontology development for the Semantic Web. In *1st International Semantic Web Conference, ISWC 2002, Chia, Sardinai, Italy, Proceedings* (pp. 221 - 235). Springer.

Vdovjak, R., Frasincar, F., Houben, G.J., & Barna, P. (2003). Engineering Semantic Web information systems in Hera. *Journal of Web Engineering, 2(1-2)*, 3-26. Rinton Press

W3C (2004a, February). *OWL Web ontology language overview: W3C recommendation*. Retrieved June 16, 2007, from http://www.w3.org/TR/owl-features/.

W3C (2004b, February). *RDF Primer: W3C recommendation*. Retrieved June 16, 2007, from http://www.w3.org/TR/owl-features/

W3C (2004c, February). *RDF Vocabulary Description Language 1.0: RDF Schema W3C Recommendation*. Retrieved June 16, 2007, from http://www.w3.org/TR/rdf-primer/

W3C (2007, June). SPARQL Query Language for RDF: W3C Candidate Recommendation. Retrieved June 26, 2007, from http://www.w3.org/TR/rdf-sparql-query.

WebModels s.r.l. (2007). *Webratio tool*. Retrieved June 16, 2007, from http://www.webratio.com

ADDITIONAL READING

Berners-Lee, T. (2003). *Web services - Semantic Web talk*. Retrieved June 16, 2007, from http://www.w3.org/2003/Talks/08-mitre-tbl/

Berners-Lee, T., Hendler, J., & Lassila, O. (2001). The Semantic Web. *Scientific American 5(*284*) 34-43.*

Brambilla, M., Ceri, S., Fraternali, P., & Manolescu, I. (2006c). Process modeling in Web applications. *ACM Trans. Softw. Eng. Methodol. 15(4), 360-409.* ACM Press.

Broekstra, J., Kampman, A., & van Harmelen, F. (2002, June 9-12). Sesame: An architecture for storing and querying RDF and RDF schema. In *Proceedings of the First International Semantic Web Conference (ISWC 2002),* Sardinia, Italy, (pp. 54-68). Springer.

De Troyer, O., Casteleyn, S. & Plessers, P. (2007). WSDM: Web semantics design method. In Rossi, G., Pastor, O., Schwabe, D., & Olsina, L. (Eds.), *Web Engineering: Modelling and Implementing Web Applications, Human-Computer Interaction Series, 12,* 303-351. Springer.

Fernandez, M.F., Florescu, D., Levy, A.Y., & Suciu, D. (2000). Declarative specification of Web sites with Strudel. *VLDB Journal 9*(1), 38-55.

Fons, J., Pelechano, V., Albert, M., & Pastor, O. (2003, October 13-16). Development of Web applications from Web-enhanced conceptual schemas. In *Conceptual Modeling - ER 2003, 22nd International Conference on Conceptual Modeling,* Chicago, IL, USA, *Proceedings* (pp. 232–245). Springer.

Karvounarakis, G., Christophides, V., Plexousakis, D., & Alexaki, S. (2001, *October 29-November 2*). Querying RDF descriptions for community Web portals. In *17iemes Journees Bases de Donnees Avancees (BDA'01) Agadir, Maroc Proceedings* (pp. 133–144).

Kifer, M., Lausen, G., & Wu, J. (1995). Logical foundations of object-oriented and frame-based languages. In *Journal of the ACM, 42,* 741-843. ACM Press.

Maedche, A., Staab, S., Stojanovic, N., Studer, R., & Sure, Y. (2003). Semantic portal - The seal approach. In Fensel, D., Hendler, J., & Lieberman, H., (Eds.), *Spinning the Semantic Web* (pp. 317-359). MIT Press, Cambridge, MA.

Murugesan, S., Deshpande, Y., Hansen, S., & Ginige, A. (2001). Web engineering: A new discipline for development of Web-based systems. *Web Engineering, 2016,* 3-13 *Lecture Notes in Computer Science.* Springer.

OMG. (2003). *Model driven architecture guide v1.0.1. Tech. rep., Object Management Group.* Retrieved June 16, 2007, from http://www.omg. org/docs/omg/03-06-01.pdf.

OMG (2006). *Ontology definition metamodel. tech. rep., object management group.* Retrieved June 16, 2007, from http://www.omg.org/cgi-bin/ doc?ad/06-05-01.pdf

Rossi, G., Schwabe, D., & Lyardet, F. (1999, November). Web application models are more than conceptual models. In *18th International Conference on Conceptual Modeling (ER 99), Paris, France, Proceedings* (pp. 239–252). Springer.

Staab, S., Angele, J., Decker, S., Erdmann, M., Hotho, A., Maedche, A., Schnurr, H.-P., Studer, R., & Sure, Y. (2000). Semantic Community Web Portals. *Computer Networks,* 33(1-6) (pp. 473–491). Elsevier.

Staab, S., & Maedche, A. (2001). Knowledge Portals - Ontologies at Work. In *AI Magazine,* 21(2), 63–75. AAAI.

Tzitzikas, Y., Spyratos, N., Constantopoulos, P. & Analyti, A. (2002). Extended Faceted Taxonomies for Web Catalogs. In *Third International Conference on Web Information Systems Engineering, WISE 2002, Singapore, December, 2002* (pp. 192–204). IEEE Computer Society

van der Sluijs, K., Houben, G.J., Broekstra, J. & Casteleyn, S. (2006). Hera-S - Web Design Using Sesame. In *Proceedings of the 6th international Conference on Web Engineering (Palo Alto, California, USA, July 11 - 14, 2006). ICWE '06* (pp. 337–344). ACM Press.

van Harmelen, F., Horrocks, I. & Patel-Schneider, P. (2001). *Reference Description of the DAML+OIL (March 2001) Ontology Markup Language.* Retrieved June 16, 2007, from http:// www.daml.org/2001/03/reference.html

Vdovjak, R., Barna, P. & Houben, G.J. (2003). EROS: Explorer for RDFS-based Ontologies. In *ACM International Conference on Intelligent User Interfaces, IUI 2003, Proceedings* (pp. 330). ACM.

APPENDIX: QUESTIONS FOR DISCUSSION

Beginner

Q1: Are model-driven techniques influenced by technology changes?

A: Model-driven techniques aim at abstracting the modeling layer of applications from the actual implementation layer. I.e., model-driven approaches should capture abstract characteristics of the application field so that their model is resilient to technology changes and to the different implementation platforms that can be chosen. For example, the WebML methodology proposed in this chapter showed how abstraction introduced to handle relational data are still valid for semantic data sources, proving that the abstraction level of the adopted primitives doesn't depend on the underlying implementation and the underlying technologies (SQL or SPARQL). The same discussion applies to SHDM that evolved from OOHDM.

Q2: Why the import and reuse of ontologies is a key requirement for Semantic Web applications?

A: Reuse is one of the key goals of Software Engineering and is usually widely applied to software components and libraries. This aspect is even more emphasized at the level of semantic content specification and usage. Thanks to the introduction of Semantic Web languages, like OWL, also data model can be widely reused and shared. Indeed, one of the key factors for the success of the Semantic Web initiative is the spread of a set of domain ontologies with a wide consensus on their definition. This will enable different applications to be transparently integrated thanks to the fact that they are sharing the same data model.

Intermediate

Q3: Why the adoption of a standard query language is important in the definition of metamodels for Semantic Web applications?

A: The use of a standard query language contributes to abstract furthermore the modeling layer from the actual implementation. Indeed, if the implementation of the conceptual primitives relies on a specific API, this implies the change of the whole querying mechanism (comprising the generation of queries) if a slightly different implementation is chosen. On the other hand, the use of a query language (like SPARQL) enables to change the adopted implementation at the lower level of the adopted query engine. This is particularly evident with relational database technologies, where the SQL language (and possibly some standardized APIs like JDBC/ODBC) allows for (theoretical) total independence from the actual database engine adopted. Semantic Web technologies are still evolving very quickly, therefore a similar decoupling is still missing, but probably the wide adoption of the SPARQL language will provide a similar benefit.

Advance

Q4: The WebML extension for Semantic Web achieves different source integration thanks to parameter passing on the links between WebML components. Is there any other valuable option that still maintains valid the primitives proposed and offer the opportunities to integrated different data sources?

A: This issue can be easily solved by adopting one of the currently available semantic bridges that allows to use a single domain ontology to which heterogeneous data sources can be mapped (e.g., relational databases, ontologies, web services, xml documents). The mapped data sources can then be accessed through queries (e.g. SPARQL queries) to the domain ontology. The adoption of such a technology will affect only the implementation layer, maintaining valid the design primitives proposed and the generated SPARQL queries from the ontology model. The main difference stands on the level where integration occurs: instead of integrating the sources at the application modelling level, sources are integrated at the data design level.

Practical Exercises

Exercise 1. Define a navigation model for allowing users to navigate the popular Wine ontology using the WebML notation (http://www.w3.org/TR/owl-guide/wine.rdf)

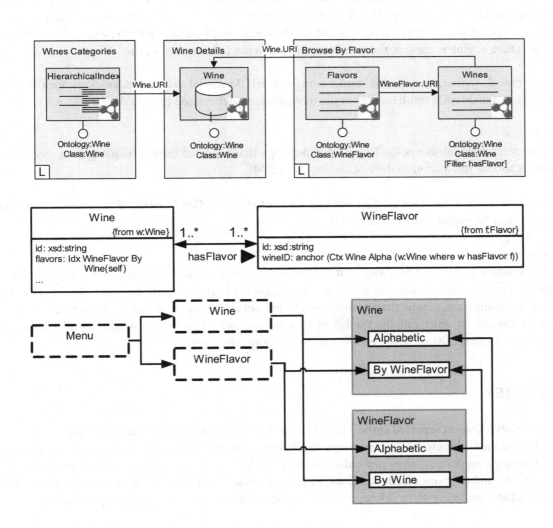

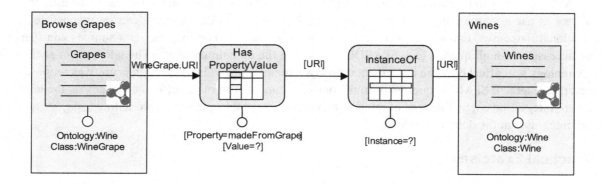

Solution:

The simplest solution is to provide access to the wines directly through the wine categorization provided in the ontology or through flavors. A hierarchical index can be used for browsing the wine categories and selecting a wine. The Wine Details page shows the information of the selected wine.

Two simple index units can be used to display the flavors and hence to show the wines of the selected flavour. Once a wine is chosen, the user is sent to the Wine Details page again.

Exercise 2. Define a navigation model using the SHDM model-driven methodology for the Wine ontology that displays a result similar to the navigation model created in WebML.

Solution:

The content model shows the fragment of ontology that has been used. The navigation model represents a similar navigation to the one shown for WebML

Exercise 3. Model a WebML diagram that allows to select a Grape instance and then retrieves all the classes of Wine that use the selected Grape.

Solution:

The solution consists of an index unit that allows to select instances of class WineGrape, and of a chain of semantic query units that select all the objects made from the chosen grape (the HasPropertyValue unit) and then, among the returned objects, extract all the classes of the elements of the returned objects (InstanceOf unit). Finally, the list of classes is shown in an index. Notice that the parameter *[URI]* represents the set of URIs resulting from the respective queries.

ENDNOTES

[a]   The serialization reported is the TURTLE (Beckett 2004) RDF serialization format.

[b]   Frame based languages are metalanguages that apply the frame concept to the structuring of language properties. They are rather focused on the recognition and description of objects and classes, and relations and interactions are considered as "secondary". They are widely adopted for ontology modeling since inference based on them it's easier than using other paradigms.

Chapter V
Semantic Processing of Monitoring Data in Industrial Applications

Florian Fuchs
Siemens AG, Corporate Technology, Intelligent Autonomous Systems, Germany

Michael Berger
Siemens AG, Corporate Technology, Intelligent Autonomous Systems, Germany

Michael Pirker
Siemens AG, Corporate Technology, Intelligent Autonomous Systems, Germany

ABSTRACT

This chapter discusses the potential of semantically processing monitoring data in industrial applications such as condition-based maintenance and monitoring of complex systems and infrastructure networks. It points out the particular requirements involved and gives a comprehensive and structured overview of current approaches and engineering solutions in these fields. As a case study for engineering industrial end-to-end solutions, it presents the design and prototype implementation of a decision support system in the railway domain.

INTRODUCTION

Maintenance costs represent a significant portion of operating budgets in most industrial sectors. In an effort to reduce these cost, maintenance has evolved over the years from simply reacting to machinery breakdowns (*corrective maintenance,* CM), to performing time-based maintenance (*preventive maintenance,* PM), to today's emphasis on the ability to detect early forms of degradation in *predictive maintenance* (PdM) practices. *Condition-based maintenance* (CBM) is a prerequisite for predictive maintenance. It has been defined as maintenance actions based on actual condition obtained from in-situ, non-invasive tests, operating and condition measurement.

CBM has been adopted by many industries. Among many others, it is used in manufacturing plants, transportation infrastructures such as railways systems, and power networks. Common to all these applications is that sensors and monitoring systems are in place in order to observe and measure particular phenomena. This information is the conceptual basis for assessing the current condition of complex systems and its components.

In reality, however, integration and interpretation of the acquired monitoring data is still inadequate. Today's systems suffer from heterogeneous data sources, where each monitoring system is provided by a different manufacturer and interoperability is usually not supported. This is particularly the case in large-scale infrastructures such as railway and power networks. As a consequence, monitoring data is rarely integrated and related to each other although this would frequently yield more accurate interpretations and therefore more effective maintenance. An example from the railway domain is the alignment of measurements from track-side monitoring systems with measurement from on-train monitoring systems. The suboptimal exploitation of the potentially available monitoring data results in ill-informed decision making on operations and generates unnecessary costs.

The Semantic Web provides promising tools for tackling these problems: Representing monitoring data with respect to ontologies facilitates interoperability among heterogeneous data sources. Engineering a model of states and faults of the monitored system allows using automated reasoning for interpreting collected data. It also results in a declarative model, which can be checked for consistency and facilitates maintenance and extensibility.

Adoption of semantic technologies for these types of industrial applications is still in its infancy. There are several prototypes demonstrating the benefits (e.g. Feng, 2005; Terziyan, 2007; Fuchs, 2006), but no known production systems yet. One reason is the non-availability of standards and implementations: Key W3C standards have only recently been published; others are still work-in-progress (e.g. SPARQL). The same is true for processing tools such as repositories and reasoners, which have only recently achieved a certain level of stability and are still constantly developed further. Another major reason, however, are challenges specific to semantic processing of monitoring data, such as handling the varying quality of real-world data, coping with large data volumes, and providing timely interpretation of the data.

The objectives of this chapter are to argue how monitoring systems can benefit from semantic processing of monitoring data. It presents several industrial use cases and discusses the associated challenges and benefits. Then it focuses on two key areas and provides guidance on (1) how to engineer appropriate ontologies and (2) how to design scalable system architectures for semantic processing of monitoring data. Finally, it illustrates the proposed approach using a case study on infrastructure maintenance in the railway domain.

BACKGROUND AND ADVANTAGES OF THE SEMANTIC APPROACH

This section discusses several industrial use cases that rely on effective monitoring. It identifies the key issues and challenges for its realization. Finally, it points out how the semantic approach can help.

Industrial Applications and Use Cases

We present examples from distributed power network maintenance, railway system maintenance, and supply chain monitoring and reconfiguration.

Power Network Maintenance

The first example is taken from (Terziyan, 2007) as a real world scenario in the domain of distributed power network maintenance at ABB (Distribution Automation).

Localization and removal of faults in distributed power line networks is performed by operation centers with participation of human operators. When a fault is detected, a protection relay sends an alarm and a record of monitoring data to the operation center using a high sampling frequency. Each sub-network in the integral power network is controlled by an operation center. It provides an integrated graphical view of the sub-network, acquires data from the sub-stations, and is capable of remotely controlling relays, switches, and other network components. Operation centers also implement various algorithms such as fault localization and calculation of optimal network reconfiguration. The medium-voltage sub-networks are owned, controlled, and maintained by local companies. Usually, there is no connection between the operation centers of different companies, so information exchange among them is nearly impossible. When a fault affects two different sub-networks, *information exchange* is usually essential in order to provide proper fault localization, network reconfiguration, and network restoration. An inter-organizational monitoring information system could help to resolve this issue.

In addition to the currently utilized data in the power network management (network structure and configuration, feeder relay readings), *contextual information* from external sources (like weather conditions, ongoing forest works, forest fires) can be monitored and integrated. This additional information is used for *risk analysis* by evaluating existing threats to the power network, which could be used to trigger alert states for the maintenance team or reconfiguration of the network. It is also the basis for improved *fault localization* by enhancing the fault localization

algorithms and improved *operator user interfaces* by augmenting the operator's view of the power network with satellite images, for example.

Railway System Monitoring

The second industrial application example is taken from (Fuchs, 2006) as a real-world scenario in the domain of distributed railway system monitoring and decision support at Siemens Transportation Systems. At the highest level of a railway system, the measure of success of the operations and therefore of decision making is compared against predefined targets called Key Performance Indicators (KPIs). Different operational disciplines such as rolling stock (RS) management, traffic management, and infrastructure management use different KPIs. In order to calculate these KPIs, low-level characteristics are monitored and managed. The following section briefly illustrates the complexity and challenges of the monitoring system for railway systems.

One major challenge in many railway systems is the *heterogeneity of the information sources* and produced monitoring data. These include track-side systems that measure features of passing vehicles such as wheel impact forces as well as on-train systems that monitor the condition of tracks when travelling over them. Some systems measure the subtle incremental changes in signals and use these characteristics to make judgements on the condition of the assets. Interoperability is hampered by the incompatibility of format and representation of data. Integration is considered an important requirement for the intelligent management of the system. This is important because firstly, it is possible that information from one part of the system could be useful for decision making in another part of the system. Secondly, the integration and combination of independent information creates more reliable and valuable information.

Other challenges are that railway systems are complex, large-scale, distributed systems with many subsystems and interfaces. For example, there are many interfaces between the operational part (the vehicle) and the supporting part (the track). The train operator must ensure that the facets of the vehicles are in a condition that enables the continued functional operation. The track operator must ensure that track characteristics enable the passage of the trains. Maintaining the compatibility between these low-level interfaces is required.

The complexity of managing these interfaces is increased by the large number of stakeholders involved in the organization of railway systems: Rolling stock operation and fleet management are managed independently from infrastructure and traffic management. Train Operating Companies (TOCs) are responsible for the operation of passenger services over the infrastructure. They usually lease their train fleet from Rolling Stock Companies (ROSCOs) who procure rolling stock and manage upgrades. Train maintenance, however, is performed either in-house by the TOCs or by the train supplier. Infrastructure and traffic management are owned and controlled by the infrastructure operator, who is responsible for management, maintenance, upgrade, and renewal of the infrastructure.

Supply Chain Monitoring

A third application example is taken from (Keller, 2005) as a real world scenario in the domain of distributed supply chain monitoring and reconfiguration at Siemens VDO Automotive.

Supply chains are currently developing towards dynamic Build-To-Order (BTO) supply chains, where production is triggered just-in-time after the customer put the order (e.g. after 5 days) and the product will be personalized to the customer's wishes. The ultimate goal is to realize lot-size-one production, where products are not manufactured in large lot sizes for the mass market anymore, but each order is individually processed for each customer. As a major advantage, this al-

lows to reduce cost as supply chains will require almost no stock for material, part products, and end products. As a prerequisite, the single tiers (component producers, assemblies / OEMs) have to work very efficiently and cooperatively in order to achieve the goal of fast delivery. These supply chains therefore require cooperative planning processes for production, logistics, purchase, and sales. This implies the need for detailed and up-to-date information exchange about capabilities and capacities of each tier and logistics company. Furthermore, new methods like production and transport assignment negotiations are used in order to increase the quality of plans. During runtime (execution phase) tiers must adapt their production based on demand. In case of exceptions the same mechanisms as during the planning phase must guarantee that the problem can be solved dynamically and quickly.

BTO supply chains strongly depend on *fast and reliable information exchange* about the current status of capacities of, for example, transport, production, and stock. These values have to be monitored permanently and delivered to the planning and execution centers at each tier or at a central place.

Summary of Challenges

This subsection identifies core and common challenges for processing monitoring data in industrial applications with respect to the previously presented use cases.

1. **Integrating data from many distributed heterogeneous sources:** All of the industrial use cases above show that data is acquired by different kinds of spatially distributed data sources and that an integration and interoperability is required. This results in additional issues such as potential inconsistency and incompleteness of integrated data.

2. **Handling varying quality of monitoring data:** The correct interpretation of the monitoring data requires meta-data such as where and when the data was measured, using which measuring method and so on. In all use cases these additional information are needed in order to process the measurements properly.

3. **Coping with large data volumes:** The scale of industrial systems implies that huge amounts of monitoring data are permanently generated and have to be handled appropriately.

4. **Providing timely interpretation of data:** The monitoring aspect of many of the presented industrial applications requires exchange and processing of the collected data in time.

5. **Enabling flexible interpretation of collected data:** Depending on the processing objective, the same data must be interpreted in different ways.

6. **Providing declarative descriptions:** In order to maintain such complex monitoring and maintenance systems (e.g. removing or adding new components), also the basic interoperability and data processing mechanisms must be reusable and easily adaptable to new requirements.

In addition, aspects like a secure exchange of the data and the reliability of the connection have to be addressed.

Advantages of the Semantic Approach

Ontology-based representation of monitoring data facilitates integration of data from heterogeneous sources. The semantic approach enables interoperability between different sub-components, sub-networks, and organizations, even if different software systems with usually proprietary data formats are used. Handling varying quality of data is less straightforward to achieve as fuzzy statements are difficult to handle with the semantic approach. However, it is well suited for capturing meta-data, which can then be evaluated through other mechanisms. Coping with large data volumes has previously been of less concern, but is increasingly investigated because most real-world applications face this problem. This is also true for timely interpretation of data, which is a trade-off with expressivity of the knowledge representation formalism as well as knowledge base size. Flexible interpretation of the collected data is well supported as queries can freely be formulated with respect to the ontology. On a higher abstraction level, the ontological representation allows to declaratively specify relevant system states. This system state model can then be exploited for automated reasoning. As a side-effect, this yields a formal model which documents the system behaviour and can be checked for logical consistency. Even more important for industrial use is that such as declarative model dramatically facilitates maintainability and extensibility.

The advantages of utilizing Semantic Web technologies will be shown in detail in the next section and are listed only shortly below:

1. **Seamless integration and interoperability of monitoring data:** We motivate the importance of the integration of real-world data from existing and future sources as well as legacy data.

2. **Consistent and documented model of system states:** We describe the advantages of a formal model of system states and faults.

3. **Higher maintainability and extensibility:** We argue why a declarative model of system states, specified with respect to integrated real-world data, improves maintainability and extensibility of a system.

ENGINEERING INDUSTRIAL APPLICATIONS FOR SEMANTIC PROCESSING OF MONITORING DATA

This section addresses the previously identified issues when realizing semantic processing of monitoring data. We distinguish two problem areas in this context, namely ontology engineering and system design. For each of them, we present existing approaches and discuss their implications. As a case study, the following section will then describe the implementation of the presented aspects in a railway monitoring system.

Ontology Engineering

Semantic technologies require a formal model of the represented data. For semantic processing of monitoring data in industrial applications this means that both sensor measurements and high-level states and faults have to be formally modeled. Model engineering must be carried out involving several different organizations.

Modelling Monitoring Data

With monitoring data we refer to observations about the current state of entities, such as system components, in the relevant part of the world. Modeling this information therefore requires capturing features such as observation type, value, unit of measurement, procedure, time, quality, and other metadata. As one of the major requirements for the envisioned application domain is interoperability, standards are particularly relevant. In the following, we discuss major initiatives in this area.

OGC Sensor Web Enablement: Observations & Measurements

Sensor Web Enablement (SWE) is an initiative by the Open Geospatial Consortium (OGC, 2007), an industry consortium comprising more than 300 companies, government agencies, and universities. It specifies interoperability interfaces and metadata encodings that enable real-time integration of heterogeneous sensors into the information infrastructure. An important part of SWE is the Observation & Measurements (O&M) standard (Cox, 2006).

O&M provides best practices for modelling observations and measurements and additionally specifies XML schemes for representing such data. To this end, it defines important domain terms and the relationships between them. An *Observation* is defined as an event with a result, which has a value describing some phenomenon. In addition,

Figure 1. Event and observation feature types in O&M

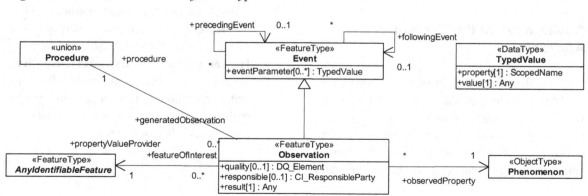

O&M defines and relates the terms *Measurement, Result, Procedure, Feature of Interest, Observed Property, Phenomenon* and *Coverage.*

Conceptual models in O&M are represented using the Unified Modeling Language (UML). See Figure 1 for an example for the model of the *Observation* concept. For each conceptual model, also an XML encoding based on XML Schema is provided.

Advantageous about O&M are its detailed conceptual models about basic terms and their relations. They provide a consistent conceptualization of the observation and measurements domain. Unfortunately, O&M provides only XML schema-based representations of these models and therefore lacks the machine-readable formal semantics required for automated reasoning. Nevertheless, it represents a mature conceptualization of the domain, backed by an established standards organization, and should therefore serve as a basis for an ontology-based model of monitoring data.

Semantic Web for Earth and Environmental Terminology (SWEET)

The Semantic Web for Earth and Environmental Terminology (SWEET) project (http://sweet.jpl.nasa.gov/ontology/) was initiated by the Jet Propulsion Laboratory of NASA as a common semantic framework for the Earth science domain (Raskin, 2003). It provides ontologies for phenomena in the earth, biosphere and sun realm. As such, it also includes specifications about physical phenomena, processes, and substances as well as sensors, space, time, and units. After using DAML+OWL for the first version of SWEET, OWL has been adopted in the meantime as the underlying ontology language.

Although being aimed at earth science in general, the SWEET ontologies cover several aspects that are relevant to monitoring data such as physical phenomena, space, time, units, and sensors. Due to their formal semantics, they can readily be used for reasoning. Modularization into several independent ontologies facilitates reuse. SWEET therefore represents a valuable source for ontologies reuse when formally specifying monitoring data.

Open Systems Architecture for Condition-Based Maintenance (OSA-CBM)

The OSA-CBM specification is a standard architecture for moving information in a condition-based maintenance system. It is published by MIMOSA (Machinery Information Management Open Standards Alliance), a standards body with members from about 50 international companies and some branches of the US Department of Defense.

In accordance with ISO-13374, OSA-CBM primarily defines six functional blocks of CBM systems, as well as the interfaces between those blocks. These blocks are *data acquisition, data manipulation, state detection, health assessment, prognostics assessment,* and *advisory generation.* Furthermore, OSA-CBM provides three types of information: *data, configuration,* and *explanation.* In the context of monitoring data, the information type *data* is the most relevant one as it represents the information or events that each blocks generates. On the data acquisition layer, this would be identical with the monitoring data.

Like OGC's O&M, OSA-CBM is specified using UML and provides XML schemes for representing standard-compliant data. Similar to O&M, it only describes a generic model of metadata and does not provide a taxonomy of monitored features or phenomena. So it is primarily relevant as a representation standard that is used by many existing systems and should therefore be considered with respect to backward-compatibility.

In summary, the O&M provides a very detailed, but generic model of observations and their relevant features. Unfortunately, its semantics are not formally represented. On the other hand, the SWEET ontologies provide several onto-logical models of useful phenomena, but lack generality. OSA-CBM is primarily relevant as a widely-adopted standard that should be taken into account when designing new ontologies. A generic ontological model for monitoring data should combine the respective advantages. An important aspect when modeling sensor-acquired information is also the representation of imperfection and uncertainty (see chapter "Uncertainty Representation and Reasoning for the Semantic Web" for more details).

Modeling System States

Description Logics (DL) are one of the underlying formalism of formal ontologies. They form an important and powerful class of logic-based knowledge representation languages (Baader, 2003). Assessing the current state of a complex system depends on background knowledge about the design of the system and previous experiences with it. Representing this knowledge in a formal way enables machine-processing.

Description Logics are specifically designed for specifying classes of objects. These classes can be defined with respect to other classes (conjunction, disjunction, and complement) as well as with respect to relations (existentially and universally quantified, number restricted, etc.). Furthermore, DLs can express both "necessary" and "necessary and sufficient" relations between two concepts. This approach has been successfully applied, among many others, to configuration problems (McGuinness, 1998), where complex machinery such as telecommunications equipment at AT&T is compiled out of basic components. Given a compilation of components, the consistency of this combination with desired class of system can then automatically be checked.

Analogously, complex system states can be modelled as classes. The "necessary" and "necessary and sufficient" conditions for this state to hold will be encoded in the class definition.

Given a set of observed conditions of components of the complex system, the overall state of the system can then also automatically be derived. This approach to condition-based monitoring has recently been applied in intrusion detection systems for computer networks (Undercoffer, 2004), real-time condition monitoring for substations in power system networks (Feng 2004; Feng, 2005; Schröder, 2007), and condition-based maintenance systems in the railway domain (Fuchs, 2006; Lewis, 2006).

A simple example from the power system domain (Feng, 2004) is the following expression, which provides a set of sufficient conditions in order to determine the cooler status based on the effect that the cooler has on the cooling oil temperature of the transformer:

cooler.on $\doteq$ power.on $\sqcap$ ¬cooler:off $\sqcap$ cooling_oil_temperature.drop $\sqcap$ ambient_temperature.unchanged

Another example from the intrusion detection systems domain is the modelling of the so-called Mitnick attack (Undercoffer, 2004). This is an interesting attack because it is multi-phased and consists of a Denial of Service (DoS) attack, TCP sequence number prediction and IP spoofing. It is modelled with the following expressions:

SystemUnderMitnickAttack $\doteq$ (SystemUnderProbeAttack $\sqcap$
$\exists$connectedTo.SystemUnderProbeAttack) $\sqcup$ (SystemUnderDoSAttack $\sqcap$
$\exists$connectedTo.SystemUnderDoSAttack)
SystemUnderProbeAttack $\doteq$ System $\sqcap$ $\exists$experiencing.Probe
SystemUnderDoSAttack $\doteq$ System $\sqcap$ $\exists$experiencing.DoS.
SynFlood $\doteq$ DoS $\sqcap$ $\exists$tcpEstb.Amount_WA_Normal $\sqcap$
$\exists$tcpSynRec.Rate_WA_Normal
RstProbe $\doteq$ Probe $\sqcap$ $\exists$icmpOutMsg.Rate_WA_Normal $\sqcap$

∃tcpEstabRst.Rate_WA_Normal ⊓
∃tcpOutRst.Rate_WA_Normal

Adopting these basic ideas for specifying system states, a more structured and extensible model can be achieved by referring to fundamental concepts from the condition-based monitoring domain such as *Measurement, Symptom, Fault, Failure* and *State.*

These concepts are usually defined as follows:

- **Measurement:** Value of reading taken of a phenomenon.
- **Symptom:** A qualitative or quantitative measure that shows a particular equipment anomaly, directly or indirectly.
- **Fault:** A defect or imperfection. A fault develops when physical degradation has occurred, but the degradation is not severe enough to be termed as failure. A fault is absolute. This means there is a sufficiently high degree of confidence that a detailed physical examination of the component in question will show a fault that is absolutely supported by the symptom(s).
- **Failure:** The termination of the ability of a component or system to perform a required function.

- **State:** The current status of the monitored system.

The conceptual model of these maintenance concepts and their relationships is illustrated in Figure 2: *Measurements* are defined as described in the previous section. *Symptoms* are defined with respect to one or more measurements that deviate from the expected behaviour of the monitored entity (e.g. an excessive temperature). *Faults* are specified with respect to one or more symptoms. For example, a fault may be the result of one or more symptoms observed about the same system component. Or it may be caused by several symptoms about different components of the same system. A *Failure* is again specified with respect to one or more faults that in combination cause this failure. The *State* of a monitored entity, finally, is defined with respect to the symptoms, faults, and failures that have been detected.

Adopting this approach enables easy extension of the system state ontology, for example if new measurements are to be taken into account. Adding a new reference to a new measurement in the definition of a particular symptom, for example, automatically results in a more detailed definition of all faults and failures taking into account this symptom. See Section 0 for examples from the railway domain.

Figure 2. Conceptual model of basic maintenance concepts

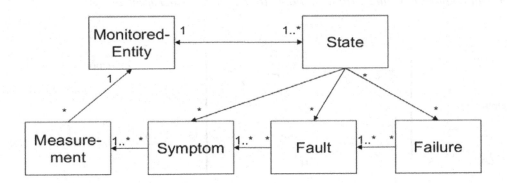

Engineering Inter-Organizational Ontologies

The scale of industrial applications usually spans several organizations and application domains. An appropriate methodology for ontology engineering in these scenarios therefore has to involve multiple stakeholders and domain experts. Several surveys on ontology engineering methodologies are available (Jones, 1998; Fernandez, 1999; Corcho, 2003; Cristani, 2005).

One of the most mature approaches is Methontology (Fernandez, 1997). In contrast to other methodologies, it is very comprehensive as it based on the activities identified in the IEEE standard for software development. Methontology encompasses an ontology development process, a life cycle and particular techniques to carry out each activity. The ontology development process identifies the following tasks for building ontologies: *project management* consisting of planning, control and quality assurance; *development* consisting of specification, conceptualization and formalization; as well as *support activities* such as knowledge acquisition, evaluation, integration and documentation. For each activity in the development process, Methontology defines techniques that have to be carried out, the required output products and how they have to be evaluated. The life cycle models the life cycle of an ontology and the interdependencies with the life cycle of other ontologies.

Recent ontology engineering methodologies also specifically address the requirements of inter-organizational ontology engineering. See the DOLCE-MESS methodology (De Moor, 2006) as an example.

Choosing an appropriate ontology architecture also facilitates inter-organizational ontology engineering. Three generic ontology architectures can be distinguished (see Figure 3):

- A *monolithic* ontology architecture allows the ontology engineer to control the entire ontology. This can result in high coherence (ontology concepts are related to each other in various ways), but also in high coupling (change to one concept will have high impact on other concepts). Using a monolithic architecture with multiple engineers, it is therefore difficult to maintain the consistency of the ontology. Also extensibility of such an ontology is limited.

- A *meshed* ontology architecture, on the other hand, usually exhibits high coherence for the individual sub-ontologies, i.e. within one sub-ontology concepts are highly related. Ontology engineers can be assigned responsibility for particular sub-ontologies. Still, as every ontology may be connected to

Figure 3. Ontology architectures: (a) monolithic, (b) meshed, (c) hierarchical

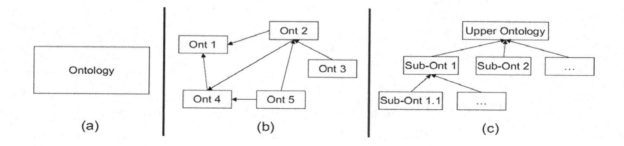

every other ontology, there is frequently high coupling between sub-ontologies. Again, this limits maintainability and extensibility.

- A *hierarchical* ontology architecture still results in high coherence for individual sub-ontologies. It also allows to assign responsibilities for sub-ontologies to particular engineers. At the same time, it enforces low coupling between sub-ontologies, as every sub-ontology is only allowed to refer to its parent ontology. This results in a maintainable and extensible ontology architecture that is suitable for multi-user ontology engineering.

A hierarchical approach therefore offers a good trade-off between modularity and coherence. Popular upper ontologies that can be adopted for this approach include IEEE SUMO and DOLCE (Oberle, 2006). Hierarchical ontology architectures also facilitate reuse of existing ontologies through mapping. See also chapter "Ontology Matching, Mapping, Merging".

System Design: Processing Stages

Processing monitoring data in a semantic way requires an appropriate functional system design. In this section, we identify generic functional building blocks and discuss for each of them, what has to be considered for its implementation in order to meet the previously identified non-functional requirements.

First, monitoring data has to be acquired from sensors and other measurement systems. At this stage, the data is not yet represented with machine-readable semantics. After a preprocessing step, the monitoring data is transformed into an ontology-based representation. This data needs to be managed appropriately. Its formal semantics can then be exploited in a separate reasoning step. This provides a semantically-rich view of

the current state of the system, which can be used by an application.

Preprocessing

In the targeted application domain, monitoring data is produced by a large number of sensors and other measurement systems. For example, a typical power network contains sensors for transformer temperature, transformer noise, transformer frequency and so on. In railway systems there are sensors for the operational status of point machines, for the impact of wheels on tracks as well as hot axle boxes, to name only a few.

These data sources usually produce continuous streams of measurements, which results in huge amounts of data. Depending on the technical specifications of the sensor and the observed phenomena, these measurements may be of varying quality and contain noise. At the same time, data sources are highly distributed. As a consequence, large amounts of data would have to be transmitted. Transmission bandwidth, however, is usually scarce and expensive. Particularly in the case of battery-powered sensors, data transmission is also a major source of energy consumption. Finally, monitoring data consumers usually cannot cope with the details of raw measurements, but required refined data.

This is why measurement systems usually perform preprocessing on the raw signals and provide refined measurement data only. Examples for preprocessing are: *aggregation* (e.g. the computation of so-called key performance indicators such as mean value), *feature extraction* (i.e. the identification of relevant high-level features out of a large amount of low-level features), and *pattern recognition* (i.e. the categorization of raw data to states). A large body of work on highly-specialized methods for these tasks is available taking into account varying quality and historical data. Logic-based knowledge representation technologies such as formal ontologies, however, are usually not suitable at this stage of processing yet.

Transformation to Ontology-Based Representation

After the preprocessing step, monitoring data is available in a refined version and associated with a particular entity (e.g. the status of a point machine, the wear of a rail head, the temperature of a transformer). However, it is still represented in a sensor-specific representation (e.g. a particular XML schema) that does not carry formal semantics and is not associated with other components of the monitored system yet.

This is where the logic-based knowledge representation based on formal ontologies offers distinguishing benefits: It enables semantic interoperability by providing a common formalism for representing monitoring data. At the same time, it allows to capture semantic relationships between measurements that imply particular symptoms, faults, and states (e.g. the overall condition of a locomotive depends on different combinations of the individual states of its components).

At this stage, it is therefore necessary to transform the sensor-specific data representation delivered by sensors to an ontology-based representation with respect to the system ontology. For a particular sensor, this is an invariant transformation from one representation to another, which has to be implemented only once. The transformation is specific to the output format of a particular sensor. Still, if several sensor use the same, e.g. standardized format (see section 0), then transformation modules can be reused.

Data Management

Transforming monitoring data in an ontology-based representation results in large volumes of data that have to be managed appropriately. This includes acquisition, storage, and retrieval of data.

Relational database systems (RDBMS) cannot directly be adopted for this purpose as their underlying data model is based on relations. The data model of formal ontologies, however, is based on triples. This is why there are repositories particularly optimized for storing and retrieving triple-based data, so-called *triple stores*. As the Semantic Web usually adopts RDF as the syntax for representing formal ontologies, these repositories are also frequently called RDF repositories.

Several triple stores such as Sesame (http://www.openrdf.org), Jena/Joseki (http://jena.sourceforge.net, http://www.joseki.org), Redland (http://librdf.org), Kowari (http://www.kowari.org), and OWLIM (http://www.ontotext.com/owlim/) are currently available. They frequently use traditional relational databases for persistency and apply appropriate index structures and mappings between the triple-based and the relational data models. Current challenges for triple stores are to reach a performance level that is comparable with relational databases. Performance evaluations of triple stores (e.g. Lee, 2004) with respect to data volume and retrieval performance provide characterizations of particular triple stores. The choice of a triple store depends on system-specific requirements.

Reasoning

Up to this stage of processing, the monitoring data is uniformly represented with respect to the system ontology. It includes only data that was directly observed by measurement systems. Another major advantage of the ontology-based approach – apart from facilitating interoperability – is that it enables the exploitation of semantic relations represented in the system ontology. This process of making implicitly captured information explicit is performed by so-called *reasoners*.

Reasoners are associated with a *knowledge base* that comprises of a formal ontology (the so-called TBox) and data represented with respect to this ontology (the so-called ABox). Reasoners accept queries formulated with respect to this ontology and return all answers that are *logically entailed* by the current knowledge base (Baader, 2003).

Different inference procedures are used for implementing reasoners: Widely adopted is the tableaux calculus, for example by RacerPro (Wessel, 2005), FaCT++ (Tsarkov, 2006), Pellet (Parsia, 2004), and SHER (Dolby, 2007), while KAON2 (Hustadt, 2004) uses disjunctive datalog. Other systems explore concepts such as answer set programming and hypertableaux calculus (Motik, 2007).

These systems differ in the expressiveness of the Description Logic, the query languages and interfaces they support, the implementation language as well as their performance and scalability. Several recent performance evaluations are available (Motik, 2006; Liebig, 2006; Gardiner, 2006).

All these systems require the complete knowledge base to be available locally. Systems that support distributed knowledge bases (distributed ontologies and/or distributed data) include Distributed Description Logics (Borgida, 2003), e-connections (Kutz, 2003), and Distrea (Fuchs, 2006). Depending on the scale of the monitored system, these may represent the only option for reasoning on the produced monitoring data.

Further approaches to scalable reasoning on distributed monitoring data include hybrid approaches that combined Description Logics-based reasoning with other formalisms.

Application

Various applications will benefit from the increased quality of semantically-processed monitoring data: Condition-based maintenance operations can be optimized, control of manufacturing processes can be improved, and incident handling can be expedited and its quality increased. Implementations on this layer are highly application-specific and will typically include optimization and planning algorithms. In addition to centralized systems, these applications can also be realized as distributed systems.

CASE-STUDY: DECISION SUPPORT FOR INFRASTRUCTURE MANAGEMENT IN RAILWAY NETWORKS

As a concrete application, this section presents our current work on decision support in European rail networks (Fuchs, 2006; Lewis, 2006). Following the structure introduced in the previous section, we describe our approach to system information model engineering and system architecture for an industrial end-to-end solution based on semantic processing of real-world data.

Application Scenario

Track-related infrastructure parts are one of the most important and most expensive building blocks in the railway domain. Both infrastructure owners and train operators aim at an efficient and sustainable use of this important resource. The current trend in this domain focuses on two major aspects: Intelligent avoidance of damage and predictive maintenance.

Today, costly damage to the railway infrastructure happens due to late integration or lack of integration of already available information. For example, already today the European track infrastructure is equipped at many places with Wheel Impact Load Measurement (WILM) sensor systems, which measure the forces that are applied to the track by damaged wheels of trains and wagons. Although this information is collected from many WILM systems along the route of a train, it is currently not used efficiently enough to prevent damage. Because today the process of WILM data collection and processing is a semi-automatic process (sometimes even involving humans sending around a fax), this information is mainly used to determine the trace of a train that caused damage to the infrastructure (e.g. for determining extra fees for the train operator). Intelligent avoidance of damage in this context means that an appropriate speed restriction is dynamically applied to the train during its operation, based on a series of WILM and other measurements. Also, train rerouting or a total stop at the next depot can be considered.

Tracks, on the other side, are surveyed and measured in many different ways: Field staff manually inspects the condition of tracks in regular time intervals, dedicated trains equipped with sensor systems like laser scanners collect information about rail and track wear, and critical infrastructure components such as point machines are equipped with special sensors for monitoring their overall technical condition. Today, all this information is primarily used to understand single aspects about a track segment. For instance, manual inspection can reveal that the ballast of a part of the track is washed out and the sleepers are displaced. On the other hand, a laser scan obtained by a measurement train indicates that the rail profile of one of the rails of the track shows considerable damage. Currently, these two aspects are measured by completely separate systems (human/sensor) and maintenance processes are independent from each other. Integrating this information can help to support predictive maintenance strategies: Observed washout of ballast indicates that the rail profile will eventually be damaged and suggest to schedule unplanned rail maintenance. Detection of rail profile damage leads to extra inspection of sleepers and could suggest unscheduled ballast maintenance.

Infrastructure managers have to decide about the priority of track-related maintenance activities, e. g. the list of track segments that must be maintained within the next maintenance period. They also need to manage wear of the track infrastructure through trains, e. g. by rerouting, speed restricting or stopping damaging trains. Different information sources are the basis for these decisions. A lot more information is already collected today. But this information is either not available or not processed properly at the time the decision has to be made by the infrastructure manager.

For making an informed decision, it is essential to integrate and interpret these real-world data in the overall context in due time.

Ontology Engineering

Providing integrated and useful information to the infrastructure manager in due time requires concise and machine-processable models of the information produced by track-related monitoring systems. As illustrated above with ballast washout and rail profile wear, there are complex interdependencies between different types of monitoring data, which have to be captured in the system information model. Some phenomena may also not be possible to observe directly, but need to be derived from combination of available types of monitoring data. The diversity of monitoring systems such as point machine monitors, WILM sensors, manual track inspections, and trains equipped with sensors, produces monitoring data, which is highly heterogeneous in terms of data volume (e.g. high volume WILM data streams along busy track sections), data quality (e.g. different types of WILM systems providing different data quality), and data frequency (e.g. time intervals between point machine measurements). Availability of monitoring data may also be subject to availability of the measurement system (e.g. measurement systems can be temporally unreachable or data bases can be off-line).

To harmonize these different information sources into a unified system information model, the following core aspects, central for the track-related infrastructure management, have been modelled as an OWL DL ontology: A formalization of the track network, a formalization of measurement data, and a formalization of physical railroad characteristics. In addition to this core model, extension ontologies for specific sensor systems have been modelled to describe monitoring information from heterogeneous systems in a uniform representation.

Figure 4. Overview of the track network model

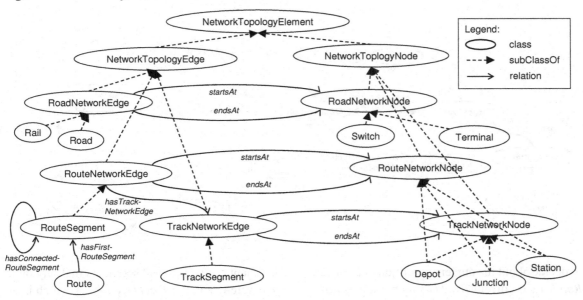

Figure 4 shows the key concepts and relationships of the track network part of the core model. The root concept of the track network formalization is *NetworkTopologyElement*, which is the super concept of the concepts *NetworkTopologyEdge* and *NetworkTopologyNode*. As can be seen, edges can be physical rails and roads (with each road consisting of exactly two rails), tracks (a collection of several parallel roads), and routes (a logical path over a sequence of tracks). The two concepts *TrackNetworkEdge* and *RouteNetworkEdge* model the distinction between the physical track, which is relevant to infrastructure management, and the logical route, which is relevant to traffic management. Each edge is delimited by a start and end node modelled by the properties *startsAt* and *endsAt*. A road is delimited by switches and terminals such as buffer stops. Tracks and routes are both delimited by depots, junctions, and stations. A route, the abstraction used for traffic management, is modelled according to the W3C list ontology pattern (Blomqvist, 2005) to enable the instantia-

tion of a sequence of *RouteSegments* along the *hasConnectedRouteSegment* property.

Figure 5 shows the key concepts and relationships of the measurement part of the core model, which are used to describe the monitoring data collected about different railway systems. An *Observation* represents a plain measurement and can have a number of properties that represent the temporal, spatial, and quality aspects of this measurement. A *Symptom* denotes the detection of a deviation from expected target system behaviour according to the *TargetSystemModel*. A *Fault* represents a further abstraction defined with respect to a set of Symptoms. The *SystemStatus* takes into account available *Observations*, *Symptoms*, and *Faults* and represents the overall condition of the *TargetSystem*.

Figure 6 shows a sample instantiation of the key concepts and relationships for physical track characteristics as part of the core model. As explained above, the *Road* is a physical system, which has many complicated interrelationships between its subcomponents. The two main characteristics

Figure 5. Overview of the measurement model

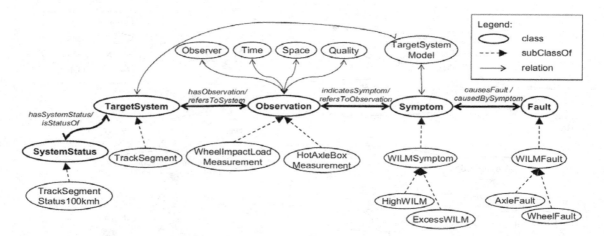

to decide about the current condition of a certain *Road* are its current *TrackGeometry* and its *Rail-Profile*. Basically, the *TrackGeometry*, which is the relative position of the two rails to each other, depends on the *Sleepers* that are themselves embedded in the *Ballast*. *RailProfile*, which is important to find out about critical wear, depends on many other factors like wheel impacts or wheel slips. Furthermore, *TrackGeometry* and *RailProfile* affect each other: A wrong *TrackGeometry* causes an unwanted wear of the *RailProfile* and wrong *RailProfiles* can cause a deviation from the default *TrackGeometry*. Relating these factors in practice in order to classify a *Road* is difficult today for infrastructure managers due to the heterogeneity of information sources. In the system information model, however, these links are all captured and can therefore be exploited by automated reasoning.

As an interesting property of DL-based modelling, these semantics are still useful, even if not complete information is available. This is due to the Open World Assumption (OWA) of DLs as we will explain in the following (see also Figure 6). Consider an important query related to predictive maintenance: In order to schedule maintenance activities, the infrastructure manager wants to identify all road segments with

incipient faults, i.e. road segments that rely on a subsystem (e.g. the *TrackGeometry*), which is in non-critical condition, but which in turn depends on a subsystem, which is already in critical condition (e.g. *Sleepers*). This query could be useful for detecting incipient faults of the road segment. If complete information is available (*TrackGeometry, RailProfile, Sleeper*) it can easily answered by performing an instance check on *road01* for concept *IncipientFaultRoad*. But if the current *TrackGeometry* status was unknown, a DL reasoner would still be able to derive an answer by checking all possible cases: Assuming that *TrackGeometry* status is defined as only either *critical* or *non-critical*, the reasoner investigates both cases. If in both cases *road01* is classified as *IncipientFaultRoad*, it can actually be inferred that this statement holds, even if the exact state of *TrackGeometry* is currently unavailable and therefore unknown.

To further illustrate the application of the parts of the core model, we discuss an example where the track network and measurement model parts are necessary. One can consider the situation where the infrastructure manager must decide about speed restrictions of observed trains travelling along their route. In our simplified example, we

Figure 6. Physical railroad characteristics and incipient fault detection

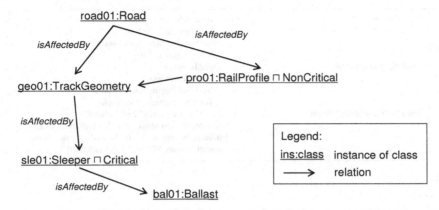

$$TrackGeometry \equiv (TrackGeometry \sqcap Critical) \sqcup (TrackGeometry \sqcap NonCritical)$$
$$IncipientFaultRoad \equiv \exists isAffectedBy.(NonCritical \sqcap \exists isAffectedBy.Critical)$$

consider the case where a route is restricted to 50mph. As explained above, a route is modelled as a sequence of route segments. Therefore, a route with some speed restriction of 50mph is defined as either starting with a route segment, which is restricted to 50mph (*RouteSegment50mph*) or containing some *RouteSegment50mph* (where *hasNextRouteSegment* is transitive, see Figure 7 and Figure 8).

Using the concepts *RouteSegment* and *TrackSegment* as a foundation, *RouteSegment50mph* can be defined with respect to the underlying physical track segment: This segment is restricted to 50mph if the status of the corresponding track segment indicates a restriction to 50mph (*TrackSegmentStatus50mph*). *TrackSegmentStatus50mph* is defined with respect to the monitoring data collected for this track segment.

Figure 7. Example of a route with speed restriction of 50mph

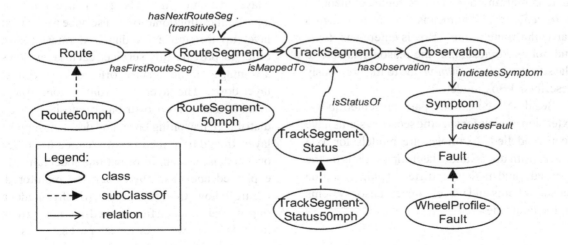

Figure 8. Modeling a route with speed restriction of 50mph (DL syntax)

```
Route50mph              ≡    hasFirstRouteSegment some
                                  (RouteSegment50mph or
                                     (hasNextRouteSegment some
                                     RouteSegment50mph))
RouteSegment50mph       ≡    isMappedTo some
                                  (TrackSegment and
                                     (hasTrackSegmentStatus some
                                     TrackSegmentStatus50mph))
TrackSegmentStatus50mph ≡    isStatusOf some (TrackSegment and
                                  (hasObservation some (WILMMeasurement and
                                  (indicatesSymptom some (WILMSymptom and
                                  (causesFault some WheelProfileFault))))))
```

This combination of the core model and the application-specific extensions enables the automatic inference of the status of a track segment, given a set of monitoring data through the specification of *Observation*, *Symptom*, and *Fault*. A *TrackSegmentStatus50mph* is basically defined as the status belonging to a track segment, which has been measured with some symptom that indicates a *WheelProfileFault*. Now, implicit information can be automatically inferred with a query such as "Find routes, which contain a speed restriction of 50mph". Taking into account the TBox, a DL reasoner can derive that track segments with associated *WheelProfileFaults* have a status of *TrackSegmentStatus50mph*. This implies that a route segment mapped to one of these track segments is a *RouteSegment50mph*. Finally, any route containing one of these route segments is a *Route50mph*. This means that even though a particular route in the ABox is entered as *Route* and not as *Route50mph*, the reasoner is able to classify it as a *Route50mph* due to the previously described TBox model.

Besides the core model parts presented above, extension models for specific sensor systems have been modelled. Examples are models for axle boxes, train doors, and wheel slip systems on the train side, and models for different point machine sensor systems and wheel impact sensor systems on the land side.

System Architecture

Semantics-based railway infrastructure decision support systems must semantically represent and integrate the distributed monitoring information acquired about the rail system. The goal is to provide the infrastructure manager with an intelligent and intuitive interface for posing arbitrary queries (formulated with respect to the system information model) about the monitored state of the system. In a more autonomous version, this system can also proactively inform the user about changing system conditions or important system states.

The dynamics of the sensor data and the distributed generation of sensor data represent major challenges. To cope with this, we designed a layered architecture, where each layer provides a particular functionality as a service to the next layer up through a standardized interface. In order to provide this service, each layer takes advantage of the service offered by the next layer down. The layers are from bottom to top: Transformation layer, distributed repository layer, distributed reasoning layer, and decision support layer. In addition, the overall architecture relies on a concise system information model (already explained above) of the system be monitored. Figure 9 shows this architecture, which provides a step-wise abstraction from sensed monitoring data towards high-level decision support services.

Figure 9. Layered architecture of the semantic decision support system

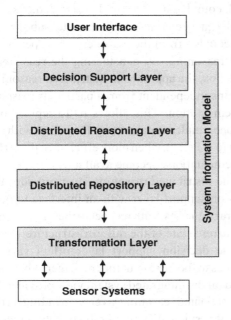

Sensor systems include both real-world sensors as well as legacy information systems like databases that provide the raw monitoring for further processing. Data sources are for example:

- Sensors for wheel impact load, some of which deliver their data in XML schema definition (XSD) based XML format.
- Point machine monitoring devices, which provide their monitoring data in a simple comma separated value (CSV) format.
- Infrastructure legacy databases

Monitoring data is delivered in the proprietary format of the data source. This can happen either in push mode or in pull mode. In push mode new data is automatically sent to the upper layer as soon as it is available. In pull mode the data has to be explicitly requested. The mode of data provisioning depends on the constraints of the data source.

The transformation layer comprises of adapter components which transform the data delivered by the sensor systems into an OWL DL ontology-based representation with respect to the system information model. In detail this means that the raw monitoring information is translated into instances of the ontology of the system information model. These adaptors are specific for each type of sensor or database system. As described above, data formats may include CSV, XML, and others. Representing the monitoring information with respect to the system information model makes this information available to automatic interpretation by DL reasoners. The adapter layer therefore provides the distributed repository layer with monitoring information represented as ABox data.

The distributed repository layer comprises of geographically distributed RDF triple stores like Jena/Joseki (http://jena.sourceforge.net, http://www.joseki.org), Sesame (http://www.openrdf.org), and Redland (http://librdf.org), which are physically located near the monitoring data sources for persisting the ABox data. This way requests for both current and historical monitoring data can be answered. As this information stems from highly distributed systems, it is necessary to store the transformed monitoring information in a distributed manner. This avoids unnecessary data traffic and increases scalability for high data volumes. The distributed repository layer provides the distributed reasoning layer with the relevant ABox data.

The distributed reasoning layer comprises of DL reasoning nodes, which collaboratively reason over ABox data stored across the distributed repositories. Each reasoning node provides access to both the explicitly stated data as well as to implicitly available system data, which can be derived from the explicit data. Therefore the reasoning layer infers information, which is only implicitly expressed based on the system information model, and enables integrated access to information available in the distributed repositories. As monitoring information is stored distributedly in the repositories, it makes sense to also distribute the reasoning: This allows reducing network traffic (not all data must be aggregated at one single place), increases scalability (reasoning load is distributed across many reasoner instances), and increases robustness (no single point of failure). Figure 10 shows the core idea of the realization approach of the distributed reasoning system (Fuchs, 2006). The query to be processed by the reasoning layer is divided into suitable subqueries and handed over to the corresponding reasoners. Each such reasoner might be able to process its subquery. If not, the reasoner forwards (parts of) the query to another reasoner being able to answer the query. The resulting information (the answer to a query) is propagated back to the requesting reasoner and used for further answer generation in turn. The implementation of the distributed reasoning layer was realized based on the RacerPro reasoner (http://www.racer-systems.com; Wessel, 2005) as well as based on the Pellet reasoner (http://pellet.owldl.com; Parsia, 2004). This is to demonstrate that the query engine, which generates subqueries, is decoupled from the reasoner, which performs local reasoning: By considering the reasoner a black box, the approach to distributed reasoning remains independent from a particular reasoner implementation. This allows us to replace one reasoner implementation (e.g. RacerPro) with another (e.g. Pellet), when more efficient or powerful implementations become available.

The distributed reasoning layer provides the decision support layer with an interface to pose arbitrary queries, with respect to the TBox, about the current state of the rail infrastructure.

The decision support layer offers various services to the infrastructure manager, which are based on the integrated system view provided by the distributed reasoning layer. Depending on the kind of service, different problem solving algo-

Figure 10. Illustration of distributed reasoning approach

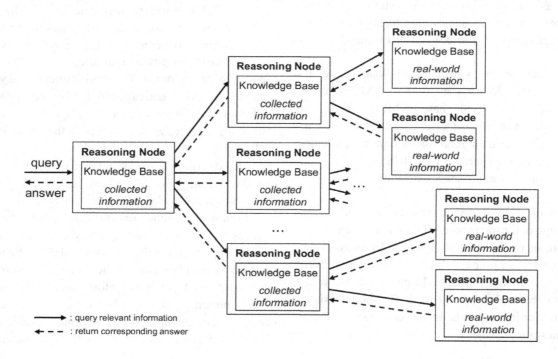

126

rithms are applied, for instance constraint satisfaction, planning, or rule-based mechanisms.

The interfaces between the decision support and distributed reasoning layer, the distributed reasoning and distributed repository layer, and the distributed repository and transformation layer are both realized as push as well as pull mechanisms. This means that a layer may either directly request the necessary information from the layer below, or register with the layer below to get informed about newly available information. These mechanisms are implemented with the SPARQL protocol (Kendall, 2006) and SOAP messages, which are formulated in SPARQL (Prud'hommeaux, 2006; Beckett, 2006) and RDF (Manola, 2004), exchanged as part of this protocol.

Since the SPARQL protocol does not provide any support for asynchronous interaction, a new format following the message exchange patterns "In-Only" and "Out-Only" of the WSDL Specification (Chinnici, 2007) was used.

Lessons Learned

Engineering a software system capable of monitoring large-scale, highly distributed and heterogeneous infrastructures like railway networks requires extra care and consideration of many different factors. In the following we present some of them, which we became aware of during our work on the system described above. Taking into account these issues right from the start can decrease the overall system engineering time and improve the outcome.

Know the monitoring systems well: Very often monitoring systems measure system characteristics by means of one or more methods such as inductive loops, optical systems, sonar systems, and so on. Raw measurements are therefore frequently represented in terms of current or voltage levels. Usually, preprocessing is already applied by the monitoring system and higher-level monitoring data is provided, for example forces (in Newton) derived from voltage measurements. Clarifying

right at the beginning the exact semantics and units of measurement of the provided monitoring data avoids confusion and waste of time when modeling the important characteristics of the respective measurement systems. This is also important in order to keep the resulting model as concise as possible.

Abstract away from particular monitoring systems: In addition to detailed understanding of each monitoring system, data source-independent semantic types of monitoring data have to be identified. For instance, monitoring systems from different manufacturers but providing the same type of monitoring data may be part of the overall system. An important engineering decision is whether to introduce models for each monitoring system variant or to generalize all variants to one type of monitoring data. The lesson learned is to avoid modelling manufacturer-specific variants as far as possible. It should be considered only if there are good reasons for introducing such a level of detail for a particular monitoring system. Not being careful about this step of abstraction will result in oversized system information models that are difficult to maintain and inefficient at runtime.

Identify the necessary level of abstraction of the monitoring system: Based on the knowledge about the monitoring system (the conceptual model of the monitoring system), it is helpful to think in the next stage about the level of abstraction that is necessary to introduce when modelling this system. For instance, many monitoring systems provide a possible output range for their measurements. In a model of this system it is not always necessary to reflect each possible single value of such ranges. Often, after talking to domain experts, one can identify upper and lower limits of specific systems states. This enables the application of the value partition ontology design pattern (Rector, 2005): It suggests to introduce a small set of expressive intervals of monitoring measurements (like "low", "medium" and "high"), each one belonging to one such system state and covering parts of the overall monitoring system output range. By introducing value partitions for numerical monitoring data, dealing with so-called concrete domains can be avoided. The purpose of concrete domains is to enable the definition of concepts with reference to concrete qualities of their instances such as the weight, age, duration, and spatial extension. This would be a natural approach for dealing with numerical data. However, the use of concrete domains carries several difficulties (Lutz, 2003) and most existing tools still lack efficient support for concrete domain reasoning. This is why we currently represent monitoring data using the value partition design pattern.

In fact, system information models not providing such an abstraction from real-world systems already at this low level tend to suffer from data congestion at runtime, due to an overwhelming number of instances of monitoring data to be processed.

Consider the history of monitoring data: Measuring the system state at one discrete point in time and abstracting this measurement into the high-level system view imposed by the system information model can already help to master many monitoring related situations and answer queries posed to the monitoring system. But there are at least as many other situations and queries that depend on the current measurement and several measurements before that one. Therefore a very important point to consider right from the start of the system design is to enable the management of historical monitoring data. Even worse, one clearly has to differentiate between and deal with the history of raw monitoring data and the history of monitoring data already represented in the form of the system information model. Some system characteristics, reflected in the system information model, might only be derived based on the history of the raw monitoring data (i.e. the plain outputs of a monitoring system). Other system characteristics can also be derived, based solely on model level monitoring information.

Having a clear idea, which type of monitoring information history will be necessary and to what extend, will prevent you from engineering an inappropriate system.

Anticipate key queries the system will have to answer: System monitoring is always dedicated to answer queries that are relevant for system operation. For example, queries about incipient faults and required maintenance (predictive maintenance) or queries about the optimal use of a system must be answered. Like software has to be designed and implemented towards the requirements that were identified in the first phases of a software engineering process, the questions that a system information model must be able to answer must be well understood in advance and guide the design of the system information model through all phases of the engineering process. A failure to do so at an early stage of the engineering process of the system information model will result in many iterations of model changes, which will not necessarily result in system information model improvements.

Take into account automatic inference: Based on the knowledge about the questions a system must be able to handle and the understanding of the different monitoring systems that must be modelled, the usage of the model and the monitoring data (in the form of model instances) must be considered and tested throughout the development of the system information model. Realizing system information models in the form of, for example, OWL DL ontologies and populating them with monitoring data will only provide real benefit if they are processed automatically at runtime. Reasoning engines such as DL reasoners can be used for this. Still, response times depend on the particular reasoner implementation, the complexity of the query, and the design of the ontology. An ontology engineer should therefore aim at realizing system information models that are as lean and as concise as possible, while reflecting all necessary system characteristics. Using unnecessary complicated or expressive constructs, results in suboptimal system performance at runtime. The only way to guarantee good performance of automatic processing of system information models at runtime is the continuous testing of the system information model with real-world monitoring data and real world queries to the system. A failure to do so will result in systems not applicable under real world conditions.

Think about runtime aspects at design time: Monitoring systems have very different characteristics, depending on their special application. For example, at runtime some of them might only produce very few data within larger time frames (their internal preprocessing can be a reason for such a behavior), others will provide high data volumes in the form of continuous data streams. Taking into account such characteristics of the monitoring systems to be integrated in one system information model will help to decide how to engineer the model properly. Again, keeping the model and the reasoning based on this model as lean and as simple as possible will help to make the resulting application robust and fast enough to cope with real world situations.

CONCLUSION

Semantic processing of monitoring data holds out many benefits: A rich semantic model of monitoring data and system states provides a solution to today's interoperability problems between different monitoring systems. It facilitates the integration of data from different sensors in order to achieve more accurate interpretations. It also enables automatic reasoning and flexible querying of the available data based on the formal semantics. On the other hand, system architectures have to be able to cope with the large amounts of semantically-annotated data. We identified the basic functional steps and for each steps provided an overview of existing tools and approaches. Finally, we demonstrated the idea of semantic processing of monitoring with a case study from the railway domain.

FUTURE RESEARCH DIRECTIONS

Semantic processing of monitoring data is still in its infancy. The first major reason for this is the lack of appropriate ontologies. Currently available standards are based on semi-formal UML models and only syntactically standardized as XML schemes. So a major future challenge is the development of ontologies for monitoring data. These should be generic enough to allow for standardization. At the same time, they have to capture a sufficient amount of semantics in order to support rich reasoning. In addition, more elaborate methodologies for inter-organizational ontology engineering are required.

An important aspect for the representation of monitoring data is capturing of uncertainty. This may not only require appropriate models, but also the extension of the underlying formalisms. There are already several approaches for extending different Description Logics with probabilities. It has to be investigated whether these are sufficient for the representation and reasoning on monitoring data.

Another aspect is handling temporal information. Temporal relations are very important for interpreting monitoring data. Still, standard Description Logics do not provide special constructs for this. It has to be investigated whether ideas from temporal logics and other formalisms can be adopted.

Another major challenge for semantic processing of monitoring data is scalability. Some progress has been made for triple stores recently by leveraging mature relational databases or by re-using database techniques. Reasoning procedures, however, have theoretical limitations with respect to scalability. These are addressed by optimizing existing algorithms such as tableaux algorithms. After having focus on terminological reasoning at first, recent implementations specifically aim to accelerate reasoning over large ABoxes, i.e. instance data. Due to inherent computational complexity of highly expressive Description Logics such as the one adopted for OWL DL, however, investigation of less expressive, but better tractable Description Logics is worthwhile. An example for this is the Description Logic EL (Baader, 2003). Also novel approaches to reasoning algorithms, for example a recently proposed hypertableaux algorithm may yield better average-case runtimes. Finally, it is important for reasoning procedures to support incremental reasoning where updates to the instances data (i.e. ABox) can efficiently be handled.

A third major challenge is distributed system architectures and distributed data management of ontology-based data. Although being highly distributed in nature, there are few applications of the Semantic Web that reach this scale today. This is why more research is needed on the effects of distribution and optimal levels of distribution for ontology-based systems.

REFERENCES

Beckett, D., & Broekstra, J. (2006). *SPARQL query results XML format.* W3C. http://www.w3.org/TR/rdf-sparql-XMLres/

Blomqvist, E., & Sandkuhl, K. (2005). Patterns in ontology engineering: Classification of ontology patterns. In *International Conference on Enterprise Information Systems (ICEIS2005), 3,* 413-416. Setubal: INSTICC.

Borgida, A., & Serafini, L. (2003). Distributed description logics: Assimilating information from peer sources. *Journal of Data Semantics, 2800/2003,* 153-184.

Chinnici, R., Haas, H., Lewis, A., A., Moreau, J., Orchard, D., & Weerawarana, S. (2007). *Web services description language (WSDL).* Version 2.0 Part 2: Adjuncts. W3C, http://www.w3.org/TR/wsdl20-adjuncts/

Corcho, O., Fernández-López, M., & Gómez-Pérez, A. (2003). Methodologies, tools and languages for building ontologies: Where is their meeting point? *Data Knowledge Engineering, 46*(81), 41-64.

Cox, S.J.D. (2006). *Observations and measurements.* OpenGIS Discussion Paper, OGC document 05-087r4.

Cristani, M., & Cuel, R. (2005). A survey on ontology creation methodologies. *International Journal on Semantic Web & Information Systems, 1*(2), 49-69.

De Moor, A., De Leenheer, P., & Meersman, R. (2006). DOGMA-MESS: A meaning evolution support system for interorganizational ontology engineering. In *14th International Conference on Conceptual Structures (ICCS 2006),* pp. 189-202. Aalborg, Denmark: Springer.

Dolby, J., Fokoue, A., Kalyanpur, A., Kershenbaum, A., Schonberg, E., & Srinivas, K. (2007). Scalable semantic retrieval through summarization and refinement. In *22nd AAAI Conference on Artificial Intelligence (AAAI-07),* pp. 209-304. Vancouver, British Columbia: AAAI Press.

Feng, J. Q., Wu, Q. H., & Fitch, J. (2004). An ontology for knowledge representation in power systems. In *Control 2004 Conference, 35,* 1-5. University of Bath, UK.

Feng, J. Q., Smith, J. S., Wu, Q. H., & Fitch, J. (2005). Condition assessment of power system apparatuses using ontology systems. In *Transmission and Distribution Conference,* pp. 1-6. Dalian, China: IEEE/PES.

Fernández-López, M., Gómez-Pérez, A., & Juristo, N. (1997). Methontology: From ontological art towards ontological engineering. In *AAAI Spring Symposium on Ontological Engineering,* pp 33-40. Stanford: AAAI Press.

Fernández-López, M. (1999). Overview of methodologies for building ontologies. In *IJCAI Workshop on Ontologies and Problem-Solving*

Methods, pp. 1-12. Stockholm, Sweden: CEUR Publications.

Fuchs, F., Lewis, R., Pirker, M., Roberts, C., Berger, M., & Langer, G. (2006). Applying semantic technologies to railway decision support. In *Semantics 2006 International Conference*, pp. 217-227.Vienna: Oesterreichische Computer Gesellschaft.

Fuchs, F., Henrici, S., Pirker, M., Berger, M., Langer, G., & Seitz C. (2006). Towards semantics-based monitoring of large-scale industrial systems. In *Conference on Computational Intelligence for Modelling, Control and Automation*, pp. 261-266. Sydney: IEEE Computer Society.

Fuchs, F., & Berger, M. (2006). Towards scalable retrieval of distributed and dynamic ontology instances. In *5th International Semantic Web Conference (ISWC), Workshop Scalable Semantic Web Knowledge Base Systems*, pp. 89-100. Athens, GA, USA: Springer LNCS 4273.

Gardiner, T., Tsarkov, D., & Horrocks, I. (2006). Framework for an automated comparison of description logic reasoners. In *5th International Semantic Web Conference (ISWC)*, pp. 654-667. Athens, GA, USA: Springer LNCS 4273.

Hustadt, U., Motik, B., & Sattler, U. (2004). Reducing SHIQ⁻ description logic to disjunctive datalog programs. In *9th International Conference on Knowledge Representation and Reasoning (KR2004)*, pp. 152-162. Whistler, BC, Canada: AAAI Press.

Jones, D.M., Bench-Capon, T.J.M., & Visser, P.R.S. (1998). Methodologies for ontology development. In *15th World Computer Congress, Conference on Information Technology and Knowledge Systems*. Budapest: IFIP.

Keller et al. (2005). *State of the art of supporting ICT systems for collaborative planning and execution within supply networks*. Deliverable D4.2/5.2. of the ILIPT project. Available through http://www.ilipt.org.

Kendall, G. C. (2006). *SPARQL Protocol for RDF*. W3C. http://www.w3.org/TR/rdf-sparql-protocol/

Kutz, O., Lutz, C., Wolter, F., & Zakharyaschev, M. (2003). E-Connections of description logics. In *International Workshop on Description Logics*. Rome, Italy: CEUR-WS.

Lee, R. (2004). *Scalability report on triple store applications* (SIMILE project report). Cambridge: Massachusetts Institute of Technology.

Lewis, R., Fuchs, F., Pirker, M., Roberts, C., & Langer, G. (2006). Using ontology to integrate railway condition monitoring data. In *Conference on Railway Condition Monitoring (RCM)*, pp. 149-155. Birmingham, UK: IET.

Liebig, T. (2006). *Reasoning with OWL – System support and insights* (Technical Report 2006-04). Ulm: Ulm University.

Lutz, C. (2003). Description logics with concrete domains—A survey. *Advances in Modal Logics*, (4), 265-296.

Manola, F., & Miller, E. (2004). *RDF primer*. W3C. http://www.w3.org/TR/rdf-primer/

McGuinness, D. L., & Wright, J. R. (1998). An industrial strength description logic-based configurator platform. *IEEE Intelligent Systems*, *13*(4), 69-77.

Motik, B., & Sattler, U. (2006). A comparison of reasoning techniques for querying large description logic ABoxes. In *13th International Conference on Logic for Programming Artificial Intelligence and Reasoning*, pp. 227-241. Phnom Penh, Cambodia: Springer LNCS 4246.

Motik, B., Shearer, R., & Horrocks, I. (2007). A hypertableau calculus for *SHIQ*. In *International Workshop on Description Logics, pp. 419-426. Brixen, Italy: CEUR.*

Oberle, D., Ankolekar, A., Hitzler, P., & al. (2006). *DOLCE ergo SUMO: On foundational and domain models in SWIntO (SmartWeb Integrated Ontology)* (Technical Report). Karlsruhe: University of Karlsruhe, AIFB.

OGC (Open Geospatial Consortium), Inc. (2007). *Sensor Web enablement WG*. Retrieved June 4, 2007, from http://www.opengeospatial.org/projects/groups/sensorweb

Parsia, B., & Sirin, E. (2004). Pellet: An OWL DL reasoner. In *International Semantic Web Conference (ISWC)*. Hiroshima, Japan: Springer LNCS.

Prud'hommeaux, E., & Seaborne, A. (2006). *SPARQL Query Language for RDF*. W3C. http://www.w3.org/TR/rdf-sparql-query/

Raskin, R. (2003). Semantic Web for earth and environmental terminology (SWEET). In *3rd Annual Earth Science Technology Conference*. Earth Science Technology Office, NASA.

Rector, A. (2005). Representing specified values in OWL: "value partitions" and "value sets". *W3C Best Practice Working Group Note*, http://www.w3.org/TR/swbp-specified-values.

Schröder, A., Laresgoiti, I., Werlen, K., Schowe-von der Brelie, B., & Schnettler, A. (2007). Intelligent self-describing power grids. In *International Conference on Electricity Distribution*. Vienna, Austria: CIRED.

Terziyan, V., & Katasonov A. (2007). *Global understanding environment: Applying Semantic Web to industrial automation*. Retrieved December 12th, 2007, from University of Jyvaskyla, Department for Artificial Intelligence: http://www.cs.jyu.fi/ai/papers/Chapter_Emergent_Technologies_IS-2007.pdf

Tsarkov, D., & Horrocks, I. (2006). Fact++ Description logic reasoner: System description. In *International Joint Conference on Automated Reasoning (IJCAR 2006)*, pp.292-297. Springer LNCS 4130.

Undercoffer, J. (2004). *Intrusion etection: Modeling system state to detect and classify aberrant behaviors*. Doctoral dissertation, University of Maryland, Baltimore.

Undercoffer, J., Joshi, A., Finin, T., & Pinkston, J. (2004). A target centric ontology for intrusion detection: Using DAML+OIL to classify intrusive behaviors. *Knowledge Engineering Review*, 18, 221-241.

Wessel, M., & Möller, R. (2005). *A high performance Semantic Web query answering engine*. In *International Workshop on Description Logics (DL2005)*. Edinburgh, UK: CEUR.

ADDITIONAL READING

Baader, F., Calvanese, D., McGuinness, D., Nardi, D., & Patel-Schneider, P. (2003). *The description logic handbook*. Cambridge University Press.

Brachman, R., & Levesque, H. (2004). *Knowledge representation and reasoning*. Morgan Kaufmann Publishers, Inc.

Debenham, J. (2001). *Knowledge engineering: Unifying knowledge base and database design*. Springer.

Fensel, D. (2004). *Ontologies: A silver bullet for knowledge management and electronic commerce*. Springer.

Huth, M., & Ryan, M. (1999). *Logic in computer science: Modelling and eeasoning about systems*. Cambridge University Press.

McGuinness, D. L., & Wright, J. R. (1998). An industrial strength description logic-based configurator platform. *IEEE Intelligent Systems, 13*(4), 69-77.

Russel, S., & Norvig, P. (2003). *Artificial intelligence: A modern approach*. Prentice Hall International.

APPENDIX: QUESTIONS FOR DISCUSSION

Beginner

1. What are the characteristics of monitoring systems that can benefit from using formal semantics?
    Answer: large-scale, heterogeneous data sources, complex dependencies
2. What aspects must be considered in the beginning of the model specification phase?
    Answer: see the *Lessons Learned* section.
3. What are the challenges and pitfalls when engineering ontologies with multiple engineers?
    Answer: see the *Engineering Inter-Organizational Ontologies* section.
4. What options do you have for managing ontology-based data?
    Answer: see the *System Design* section.

Intermediate

5. How would you structure an ontology to guarantee extensibility in later stages?
    Answer: hierarchical structure, established upper ontology
6. What are differences between OWL lite, OWL DL and OWL Full?
    Answer: OWL is very limited in expressivity, but there are tractable inference procedures. OWL DL is an expressive DL for which still a decidable inference procedure exists. OWL Full is undecidable.

Advanced

7. How can you capture the semantics of high-level system states in an extensible and maintainable way?
    Answer: see the *Ontology Engineering Section*.
8. Which constructs in OWL DL are computationally expensive and should therefore be avoided if possible in order to maximize reasoning performance?
    Answer: use datatypes instead of nominals, avoid inverse properties, beware of cyclic axioms.

Practical Exercises

*   Imagine a system to be monitored and some real-world monitoring systems. Now use OWL DL for engineering a system information model that covers the relevant aspects of these systems.
*   Create several ontology modules belonging to some real-world systems and structure them in a hierarchical order. Then try to use the same ontologies, but introduce a meshed architecture. Compare the advantages and disadvantages of each approach.
*   Write a small program producing random measurements from a real-world monitoring system. Engineer a small ontology for this monitoring system. Connect the ontology with the random data generator. Find out about the problems related to the history of data and the problems that arise when increasing the speed of data generation. Try to query the system at runtime and observe the performance depending on the different level of complexity of the queries you send to reasoning systems working on the ontology.

• Imagine a simplified technical system consisting of real-world monitoring systems. Think about different system states that have to be detected. Model the system states and formulate appropriate queries. Find out how difficult it is to develop correct and consistent models. Check if you formulated the queries correctly by implementing an OWL DL ontology and using a DL reasoner to answer your queries.

Chapter VI
Semantic Annotation and Ontology Population

Florence Amardeilh
Mondeca, France and Université Paris 10, France

ABSTRACT

This chapter deals with issues related to semantic annotation and ontology population within the framework defined by the Semantic Web (SW). The vision of the Semantic Web, initiated in 1998 by Sir Tim Berners-Lee, aims to structure the information available on the Web. To achieve that goal, the resources, textual or multimedia, must be semantically tagged by metadata so that software agents can utilize them. The idea developed in this chapter is to combine the information extraction (IE) tools with knowledge representation tools from the SW for the achievement of the 2 parallel tasks of semantic annotation and ontology population. The goal is to extract relevant information from the resources based on an ontology, then to populate that ontology with new instances according to the extracted information, and finally to use those instances to semantically annotate the resource. Despite all integration efforts, there is currently a gap between the representation formats of the linguistic tools used to extract information and those of the knowledge representation tools used to model the ontology and store the instances or the semantic annotations. The stake consists in proposing a methodological reflexion on the interoperability of these technologies as well as designing operational solutions for companies and, on a broader scale, for the Web.

INTRODUCTION

This chapter deals with semantic annotation and ontology population in the context of the Semantic Web (SW). The aim of the Semantic Web is to structure information available on the Web. To achieve that goal, resources, both textual and multimedia, must be semantically enriched with metadata to allow software agents to use them. Explicit representation of the contents of

Web-based resources is enabled by ontologies. Ontologies play a major part in semantic annotation, since they define the concepts, attributes and relations used to annotate the document content. The ontology constrains the vocabularies and knowledge instances allowed as metadata for any given application. For example, an article may be annotated by a metadata "author" which the value should be an instance of the concept "Person". But if it is essential for a Semantic Web application to rely on an ontology for the realization of this semantic annotation task, it is also important that the knowledge base, associated with this ontology, contains the instances to be used for semantic annotation. For example, the value of the metadata "author" might be "Florence Amardeilh", an instance of the concept "Person" in a particular knowledge base. This is why the purpose of the ontology population task is to enrich (semi-)automatically the knowledge base with new instances of the concepts, attributes and relations defined by the ontology model.

First the chapter proposes definitions of semantic annotation and ontology population (section 2). It then describes each dimension of semantic annotation, a dimension in turn being composed of a set of characteristics. Those dimensions must be carefully taken into account when implementing a new solution for semantic annotation and ontology population. The differences between these two tasks are highlighted as well as their mutual interaction to generate new content for applications.

Second, the chapter presents the current state-of-the-art of semantic annotation and ontology population solutions, from both research and business perspectives (section 3). The capabilities of these solutions and their limitations are explained in order to indicate the future challenges to be solved in these fields during the next few years.

Third, the chapter presents a framework composed of modular software components, allowing maximum flexibility with respect to the needs and objectives for a new application

(section 4). The chapter highlights the problems resolved by these components, in particular those from the annotation and instances consolidation task and from the maintenance of the different terminologies.

Finally, the chapter illustrates how the proposed framework can be used in a complete project involving information extraction, terminological and ontological resource enrichment, semantic annotation and terminology update (section 5). It describes a methodology in five stages, based on the software engineering recommendations. It aims to provide simple and effective instructions for the realization of a concrete semantic annotation or ontology population application within a company. It eases the burden of creating such an application by defining the roles of the different actors, the objectives of each step, the actions, the means and the set of deliverables needed to assess the success of the target system. It has already been successfully put into practice in various semantic annotation and ontology population projects.

The main objectives of the chapter are:

- To provide a clear description of Semantic Annotation and its close relationship to Ontology Population;
- To illustrate the components required to create a complete semantic annotation application;
- To provide a simple but efficient methodology to assist users in implementing such an application in an industrial context.

SEMANTIC ANNOTATION VERSUS ONTOLOGY POPULATION

The word **annotation** is a derivative of the Latin term '*annotare*', meaning "to note; to annotate", i.e. "to accompany a text with annotations, remarks, comments". Therefore, an annotation corresponds to "the action of annotating, with the result of this action as being a critical or explanatory note which accompanies a text". It is important to understand that an annotation alone often does not make sense. It is always associated to the object which is annotated. This is why annotations are regarded as **metadata**. As Handschuh (2005) explains, if a metadata is a data on data, an annotation constitutes a particular case of metadata since it represents new data attached to a resource. At this point it is important to clarify the concept of **resource** as used throughout this chapter: it may correspond to a whole document or only to a fragment thereof; it can contain text, image, sound, video or a combination. In the context of the World Wide Web, it is identified and accessible via a URL address (Laublet, 2007).

The annotation of resources is an old tradition in the world of documentation and libraries. The DIGITAL Library Federation (DLF), an association comprising the fifteen most important American libraries in the United States, defined three kinds of annotation which can be added to resources of a numerical library (Handschuh, 2005):

- The **administrative annotation** (Laublet, 2007) indicates information associated with the creation and maintenance of the resource such as "which, what, where and how". Since the advent of the Web, the Dublin Core language has become a standard for defining an administrative annotation. Its descriptors include author, title, source, editor, date of publication, language, etc.
- The **structural annotation** connects parts of resources in order to constitute a logical representation of a document and may help the navigation inside the annotated resource (Rinaldi, 2003).
- The **descriptive annotation** describes a resource with respect to its content, i.e. it will identify the concepts mentioned in the resource, their relations as well as their instances (Laublet, 2007; Rinaldi, 2003).

For example the "Politician" concept could have the instances "George Bush", "Tony Blair" and "Jacques Chirac".

In this chapter we are mainly interested in the descriptive annotation. The content of a document can be analyzed from various angles. Euzenat (2005) distinguishes in particular three structures that constitute different orthogonal views of the descriptive annotation: the *grammatical structure* to analyze the relations between phrases, the *rhetorical structure* to underline the argumentation of a text and the *logical structure* to question the sense of a document.

Within the Semantic Web, a descriptive annotation is generally called **semantic annotation** (Prié, 2004). As stressed by Laublet (2007), the term "semantic" is ambiguous but it indicates the intent to highlight the meaning of a document's content in a more or less formal way according to the logic theory. Therefore, the semantic annotations aim to express the "semantics" of a resource's content in order to improve its comprehension, its searchability and thus its reuse by end-users. Consequently, we define semantic annotation as a **formal representation of content, expressed using concepts, relations and instances as described in an ontology, and connected to the original resource**.

Let's recall here that these instances are usually stored in a knowledge base, like KIM (Kiryakov, 2005) or ITM (Amardeilh, 2004), independently from the annotated resource. As such, they can be re-used for annotating other resources. The action of adding new instances to a knowledge base that is constrained by an ontology is called **ontology population** or **knowledge base enrichment**. Some semantic annotation tools are able to populate an existing ontology using the semantic annotations created for a given resource, unless the ontology is already pre-populated with all the possible instances of the domain. It is interesting to note that some tools, such as Melita (Ciravegna,

2002), do not directly aim at annotation, but rather consider annotation as a means for capturing a domain's knowledge to populate the corresponding ontology.

Note: The notion of **ontology population** has to be clearly distinguished from that of **ontology enrichment**. In this second case, it is not a question of adding new instances to existing concepts, but rather of adding new concepts or properties to the formal model of the ontology.

According to the above definition of semantic annotation, we can define a **semantic annotation tool** as a software application which inserts and manages semantic annotations related to a given resource. Within the Semantic Web, the semantic annotation tools use an ontology, or at least a formal model, which formalizes and structures the annotations produced according to the concepts and constraints defined by the model. These semantic annotation tools aim to reduce the burden of manually annotating Web pages. Most of the tools have evolved to include increasingly automated features thanks to the techniques resulting from the Information Extraction (IE) and Machine Learning (ML) fields. In addition to the traditional manual annotation user interface, tools employing these methods are able to suggest a set of semantic annotations related to the analyzed resource to the user. A semantic annotation tool can also be used to *populate an ontology*, i.e. to instantiate the knowledge base containing the instances of the reference ontology. If the Semantic Web approach is mainly devoted to the automated production of semantically annotated resources, the knowledge acquisition field considers semantic annotation as a means of enriching a knowledge base thanks to the annotated documents. These two approaches have given rise to a collection of similar tools.

DIMENSIONS OF SEMANTIC ANNOTATION

It is impossible to perform an exhaustive study of the available semantic annotation tools since this area is attracting much investment and attention and is in constant evolution. New tools or new versions of existing tools are continually being released. There are also several conferences and workshops covering semantic annotation and its derivatives knowledge acquisition, ontology population and maintenance, etc. Nevertheless, we can identify a certain number of *dimensions* when speaking of semantic annotation and tools. These dimensions describe the nature of the resources, the formal models used for annotation, the degree of automation of annotation creation, their storage with respect to the annotated resource and their use by software agents. We present here each of those dimensions and how they are handled by the different versions of existing annotation tools. In the remainder of the chapter, we only consider annotation tools applicable to textual resources, but it should be noted that there are also tools or projects to perform semantic annotation of multimedia resources.

Nature of the Resources

As we mentioned, a resource can be the entire document or only a fragment thereof. It can contain different types of information: text, image, sound, video, etc. Textual resources can differ in their degree of structure. Therefore the nature of the content plays a major role in the creation of the semantic annotations. For example, if the resource contains textual fragments, methods and tools from the Natural Language Processing (NLP) field can be used to create some annotations. With respect to the content of the documents, one notes that semantic annotation tools, and in particular those offering a (semi-)automated process, are mainly focussed on identifying named entities.

They are less interested in extracting attributes or even relations. Any relations that are extracted tend to be very high level, e.g. the fact that a Person is member of an Organization, or that an Organization is located in a given Place. However within some Semantic Web applications, in particular the ones intended for industrial companies, it is an absolute necessity to be able to collect all the semantics of a domain in a more precise way than these basic relations. This is only possible by using fine-grained linguistic analysis and domain-oriented extraction rules.

Structuring the Formal Models

The formal models that define the semantic annotations can be structured to different degrees. Administrative annotations are generally based on the the DublinCore standard, even if the properties' values are usually not normalised strings, e.g. as in Figure 1.

As these annotation values are in natural language, they have the disadvantage of being targeted at human users as opposed to software agents. Analysis a natural language expression is a very complex task for a machine. Traditionally, linguistic analysis of a text is organized in different levels dealing with the internal structure of the words (morphology), their organization in phrases and sentences (syntax), and the analysis of the words and sentences' sense (semantics) (Sowa, 2000). Each level generates its proper set of predetermined annotations, also called

tags in this context, as they directly mark the corresponding textual unit with the result of the specific linguistic analysis. These tags can then be used by the next level of analysis.

Let's focus more closely on the semantic analysis which is at the core of all the mechanisms of language comprehension, making it possible to analyze, translate and interpret the sentences and thus the texts. Two great families of formalisms are used to build semantic representations: on the one hand structures such as frames, semantic networks or conceptual graphs (Sowa, 2000) and, on the other hand logical formalisms such as predicate logic, also known as first order logic (Bouillon, 1998). Compared to morphology and syntax, work in semantics has not reached the same level of development. It is much more complex to describe and formalize than the former. It is also more difficult to implement in operational systems, which are limited to applications where the semantic analysis is applied to the analysis of a perfectly delimited domain. In addition, as Habert (2005) underlines it, most of the annotations until now are provided in proprietary formats. The annotations were developed as an output of specific software tools with no thought of interoperability between software agents. Yet it is absolutely crucial for industrial applications to deal with a consensual standard format and a formal representation so that annotations can be created, exploited and maintained by various users, whether they are human or software.

An ontology, such as defined within the Knowledge Engineering field, represents both

Figure 1. Example of an annotation using the DublinCore "dc:subject" property to annotate the content of a document about "Francis Ford Coppola's birth

this consensus object for humans and a formal object allowing use by software agents (Laublet, 2007). Its representation took inspiration from semantic networks and description logics theory. It is composed of concepts (or classes), properties (relations or attributes) and constraints that define and specify the use cases of these concepts and properties. An ontology can be described in a formal language such as RDF(S) or OWL, both recommendations of the W3C. The standardization of the annotation formats is essential to build compatible and interoperable applications. Among the tools studied, all were developed between 2000 and 2006 and we can very clearly notice an evolution of the annotation languages used according to the recommendations made by the W3C. Indeed, the first tools like SHOE Knowledge Annotator (Heflin, 2001), OntoAnnotate (Staab, 2001a; Staab, 2001b) or MnM (Vargas-Vera, 2001) used non-standard languages, respectively SHOE, HTML-A and OCML. Then with the emergence of RDF and DAML+OIL, these preceding formats became inoperative: the existing tools migrated

towards RDF and/or DAML+OIL whereas the new ones of course directly used these languages for representing their annotations. More recently, annotations generated in OWL appeared. RDF however remains a standard for annotations, OWL being rather used for the ontology population task. An annotation in this context connects the content of the text to the instances of the concepts or even properties as described in the domain ontology, cf. Figure 2. The fact of using the semantics of these concepts and properties to create the annotations makes it possible to assign these semantics to the content of the resource and thus make it usable by software agents.

A limited number or tools, such as KIM (Kiryakov, 2005) or AeroDAML (Kogut, 2001), impose the use of a generic reference ontology upon the end-user. More generally, the choice of the ontology is left to the end-user so that she can implement the annotation task according to her needs. These ontologies are modelled on the domain concerned by the application. They can be accessed locally or loaded from a Web

Figure 2. Example of a semantic annotation corresponding to the domain ontology used

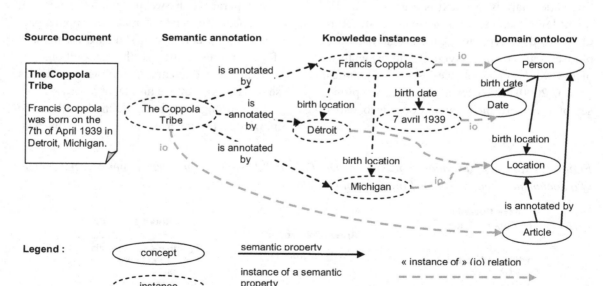

site depending on their availability. Most of the tools now support the OWL format as they have evolved in accordance with the evolution of the languages and standards defined for the Semantic Web. However few tools provide functionality beyond research and navigation in one or more ontologies. Leaving aside tools which integrate an ontology editor such as SMORE (Kalyanpur, 2005) or OntoMat (Staab, 2001b), ontology maintenance is almost never supported by the present generation of annotation tools even if this task directly impacts annotation maintenance. This is an important challenge and ontology maintenance could be supported by additional functionalities in the current user interfaces. A final type of maintenance is the population of an ontology with new instances resulting from the annotations. And it is also interesting to exploit these new instances in order to enrich the lexicons of the IE tools. For example, an extraction rule based on a regular expression can extract a company name. This company's instance is added to the knowledge base either automatically or after end-user validation. In return, the company's name is sent to the lexicon used by the IE tool. Thus, when a new document is parsed, the fact that this company's name now belongs to the lexicon will automate its recognition and its extraction. This return on investment can progressively improve the results of an IE tool on a particular domain but this task is rarely taken into account by the existing annotation tools.

Automating the Annotations' Creation

An automated process can be defined as operated by "machines" whereas a manual process is operated by a human being. Machines here correspond to the computers, and more precisely to the software agents. We distinguish fully automated processes, i.e. without any intervention of a human being in its execution, from partially automated processes, i.e. that the intervention of a

human is necessary upstream for the preparation of the process or downstream for the validation of the produced results.

In a manual semantic annotation process, the human annotator selects the resource to be annotated in a user interface, chooses the formal model to represent the semantic annotations and creates new annotations respecting the constraints imposed by the formal model (Kahan, 2001; Handschuh, 2001). But the automation of the annotation process is a vital step towards the simplification of the knowledge acquisition task. The tools thus evolved to provide the end-user with automatic or semi-automatic support based on the techniques resulting from the Information Extraction (IE) domain. A fully automated process uses algorithms based on statistical models or on the exploitation of the redundancy of some relevant terms over a corpus (Cimiano, 2004; Dill, 2003b). Nevertheless, their pertinence is limited and their annotations often not exploitable in a real enterprise application. The annotation tools which rely on this method are only viable for R&D projects in laboratories, on an experimental basis. During the past few years semi-automatic processes showed that they could provide considerable help to human annotators. They generally integrate an Information Extraction engine. The construction of such an engine is carried out according to two methods: either the manual creation of the extraction patterns (Vargas-Vera, 2002b; Popov, 2003), or their supervised training (Handschuh, 2002; Dingli 2003b).

- Manual creation of the extraction patterns:

The Information Extraction engine uses a set of rules manually defined by an experienced user, generally a linguist. These rules are based on regular expressions (for example a regular expression to extract a date can be of the form "dd/mm/yyyy") or on the results of more thorough linguistic analyses (for example if the parsing finds a subject representing a named entity of type Person, a verb meaning the birth and an adverbial phrase representing a named entity of type Location, then one can annotate this sentence as being the birthplace of the person). The set of rules is then compiled in a finite-state transducer. The transducer parses the whole corpus and annotates it according to the previously defined rules. The linguistic analysis can be more or less fine-grained. This kind of extraction pattern is relevant for annotating semi-structured and more important unstructured texts. Nevertheless, since the manual definition of the rules is based on domain-oriented linguistic expressions, this method strongly depends on that domain and rule modification is often difficult. Writing these patterns can become extremely tedious, especially if the objective is to extract semantically rich information. Annotation tools like KIM (Kiryakov, 2005) ArtEquAkt (Kim, 2002) or Onto-H (Benjamins, 2005) implement this type of IE engine.

- Supervised learning of the extraction patterns:

The supervised training method results in systems that are able to learn how to annotate a given corpus. The human annotator initiates this training by manually annotating a subset of the corpus. Then these annotations are used as examples in the extraction engine which deduces new rules from them: simple regular expressions based either on the language or on the document's structure. For example, it may use the HTML or XML elements contained in the document. The human annotator can also bootstrap the training by providing a set of basic rules. The extraction engine is then able to learn how to annotate resources by repeatedly redefining these regular expressions, either by generalization or by specialization. It also exploits the corrections provided progressively by the human annotator until it reaches an acceptable quality threshold. Once the training phase is completed, the ex-

traction engine can automatically annotate the remainder of the corpus.

Supervised annotation tools, like MnM (Vargas-Vera, 2002b), Melita (Dingli, 2003a) or OntoMat (Handschuh, 2002), use the Amilcare (Ciravegna, 2003) engine: it learns how to recognize the entities which will be annotated by training itself on a corpus made up of previously annotated documents. This method is well adapted to very structured documents (e.g. those produced from databases) or semi-structured ones (e.g. Web pages) in which constructions are sufficiently simple and fixed to allow linguistic or structural regular expressions to be easily learned without generating too many irrelevant annotations. This technique requires the tagging of a significant number of documents so that the training can reach a satisfactory level of relevance. In addition, not only must the training corpus be consequential, but its annotations must be "good" examples in order to optimize the training phase and to obtain pertinent results for the annotation task. We note that it is not always easy to create or to find this type of sufficiently annotated corpus.

Consequently annotation tools such as Armadillo (Ciravegna, 2004) or SemTag (Dill, 2003a) were created to address the issues raised by the annotated corpora required for supervised extraction systems. They implemented various statistical techniques based on the analyzed corpus used for training extraction systems. For example, PANKOW shows how the distribution of Hearst patterns on the Web can be used to deduce the annotation from entities. Nevertheless, the users of these annotation systems, which can be entirely automated, must be aware of their limits: these systems appear to provide relevant results only on strongly structured content. It should be noted however that applications for processing large corpora e.g. when annotating the Web, prefer an imperfect annotation to no annotation at all. Another problem with IE tools is the extraction of relations. This extraction is crucial for the tagging of ontological information and the creation of intelligent documents. Most of the IE systems can identify the concepts and their instances but rarer are those detecting explicit semantic relations between these instances. For this reason, the ontology population task cannot be complete without the manual intervention of the end-user. For certain applications, this can constitute a major disincentive to the choice of such tools due to their lack of richness, coverage and precision.

Storing the Annotations and their Resources

The annotations can be either "embedded in" or "separated from" the document source. An annotation is considered "embedded" when it is added directly to the document's content. This document can then be updated on the initial Web site, in the company's Content Management System (CMS), or simply saved locally on a computer for later re-use. On the contrary, a "separated" or "standoff" annotation is stored outside the source document. Not only must the annotation itself be stored, but the link to the annotated resource must also be preserved so as to be able to find all the annotations corresponding to a specific resource. The advantage of a standoff annotation is that it becomes possible to annotate any resource, including those not owned by the application. This is particularly true when annotating Web pages. The disadvantage lies in the fact that if the document source is modified or removed, the annotations become obsolete or orphaned. Within the Semantic Web, the resources and the annotations are generally stored apart, as in Annotea (Kahan, 2001) or AktiveDoc (Lanfranchi, 2005). On the other hand, in an organization like a company, the annotations can be directly stored within the document when the company is of course the owner of the document. This is the case for SemanticWord (Tallis, 2003) or even MnM (Vargas-Vera, 2002b).

Another subtle nuance exists between the notions of **annotation server**, e.g. Annotea (Kahan, 2001) or SemTag's Label Office (Dill, 2003a), and **knowledge base**. An annotation server can store knowledge and a knowledge base is able to store annotations. However, let us specify that, in the case of an annotation server, the annotation is explicitly linked to a resource and its value may point to an ontology's instance, even if this instance is stored outside the annotation server. On the contrary, a knowledge base is created to store the ontology's instances. Metadata attached to one instance can indicate the document's name or URL that originated the instance's creation in the knowledge base. But the instances exist as such, independently from the annotations or the documents that produced them. These instances are inter-connected, providing a network of knowledge for the particular domain.

The approach selected will impact the annotation maintenance process with respect to the annotated document. When the annotations are not stored with the document source, it is necessary to have a process making it possible to preserve the conformity of the annotations with the annotated document. This task is extremely tedious and complex. However, separate storage also has its advantages. Dissociating the semantic from the content facilitates the re-use of the document but also of its annotations. That allows launching queries on heterogeneous resources as if they belonged to the same knowledge base. It also eases the production of various perspectives of the same document, e.g. for users with different roles and different access rights. This is why most of the annotation tools ultimately propose both methods of annotation storage in order to allow the end-user to choose the best solution for her application, e.g. SHOE KA (Heflin, 2001), COHSE (Bechhofer, 2003) or the different versions of Ont-O-Mat (Staab, 2001a; Staab, 2001b; Handschuh, 2002).

Using and Interfacing the Annotations

Semantic annotation enables several applications including semantic-based information search, categorization, and composition of documents. The more formal the annotation model is, the more "intelligent" the services suggested by this annotation can be. Indeed, the software agents will be able to infer new knowledge, to reason on this knowledge and consequently to improve the results of the information search or to surface an implicit meaning contained in the source document.

One of the most common environments for annotating is a Web browser, a natural result since most of the annotation tools are designed to be used within the Semantic Web. Even when used within a more industrial context such as in companies, it has the advantage of being a very familiar technology. Another frequent environment consists of independent Java applications containing an ontology navigator and/or a document editor. Both of these environments mainly focus on Web formats such as HTML and XML, leaving aside other formats used in an enterprise or industrial context such as MS Word or PDF.

Few of the tools implementing an ontology navigator or providing the ontology population function have advanced functionalities to support the user in validating or adding annotations with respect to the constraints and restrictions modelled in the reference ontology. Only the various versions of Ont-O-Mat (Staab, 2001a; Staab, 2001b; Handschuh, 2002) assist the end-user with those tasks. But more recent tools, e.g. SMORE (Kalyanpur, 2005), understood that the semantic annotation and ontology population processes must be controlled in order to guarantee the integrity and the coherence of the corresponding knowledge bases. Some tools can be interfaced with external tools, e.g. the annotation server Annotea (Kahan, 2001). Most of the annotation tools resulting from university research are open-source in order to support community testing and improvement.

Discussion

To sum up, within the Semantic Web, the objective is to describe the content of the resources by annotating them with unambiguous information in order to support their exploitation by software agents. However, the current Web data are still too often written in natural language as it is oriented towards its human users and not the machine ones. The natural language being essentially too ambiguous, one needs to develop formal and semantically explicit alternatives. As a matter of fact, the annotation task for the Semantic Web consists in analysing a resource in order to provide the same content enriched with a set of semantic annotations based on a formal knowledge representation, usually an ontology.

Indeed, this ontology represents the concepts, attributes and relations of a particular domain and can be implemented in a knowledge representation language such as OWL. The semantic annotations are structured according to this ontology and their values point towards the ontology's instances or concepts. Other terminological resources, such as a thesaurus, can also be used as semantic value of the annotation in order to provide a different point of view on the resource. Each semantic annotation tool has particular characteristics, more and more directed towards assisting humans with the creation of the annotations. The level of automation depends on the IE engine integrated within the tool. The annotations can be stored in an annotation server, embedded or separated from the source document, or within a knowledge base. As a result, they can be used to improve the information retrieval systems, to populate an existing ontology, to even help with creating new ontologies.

Nevertheless, the existing tools are more or less resulting from university research. In spite of a fast evolution of the languages and standards, mainly due to the rise of the Semantic Web, the tools are still not adapted to the concrete uses of the real world. And for the companies to integrate them in their applications, some major limitations still exist that we absolutely need to overcome:

1. The annotation tools are intrinsically linked to their IE engine used to extract information from the texts and thus to annotate them. We are convinced that they should be dissociated so that the annotation tool can use such or such IE engine to better fit the targeted application's needs.

2. The IE engines are mainly based on a supervised training process. These systems are perhaps powerful on a (semi-)structured content. But on the Web and in the companies' corpora, unstructured contents are the ones containing potentially new strategic information, among them the semantic relations between entities. That information is the most difficult to apprehend (Aussenac, 2000). Therefore, it is necessary to give priority to IE systems based on various fine-grained linguistic analysis so as to better identify this strategic information and its semantics.

3. It is imperative to provide support to the end-user, particularly when the objective also consists in populating an ontology. The processes and the interfaces must not only present him with suggestions, but they must also be able to guide him by taking into account the constraints and restrictions modelled in the domain ontology. The question of the annotations' integrity and the knowledge base's consistency is of primary importance to obtain a true operating profit with regards to the results provided by such a solution.

In the remainder of this chapter, we present a framework for developing a new kind of semantic annotation tool which can also be used to populate an ontology. This framework is oriented towards solving concrete use cases in the industrial world. Nevertheless, rather than «to reinvent the wheel», we rely on existing Knowledge Representation and Natural Language Processing tools. The goal of the framework is to define a gateway between these two categories of tools. The gateway must also take into account the inherent problems due to interfacing two types of tools, having different inputs/outputs. But thanks to our experience in building several annotation applications for various companies (Amardeilh, 2005a; Amardeilh, 2005b, Amardeilh, 2006b), we know how to handle these issues in our proposed framework.

ONTOPOP, A SEMANTIC ANNOTATION & ONTOLOGY POPULATION FRAMEWORK

The OntoPop framework proposes a set of software components recommended for processing a corpus in order to perform the semantic annotation and ontology population tasks. These components are the following (cf. Figure 3): the Information Extraction Module, the Information Consolidation Module & the Information Storage Module.

The framework was developed with the following requirements in mind:

- **Mapping the structure of the ontology and the structure of the linguistic extractions**, modelled in separate ways. Annotating a document and/or populating an ontology must not impose new constraints on the way the terminological and ontological resources are modelled nor on the format produced by the IE tools.

- **Completeness**. The framework must be able to map all information given by the IE tools while remaining independent from the IE tool used in the process.

- **Standardisation**. The framework must produce Semantic Web compliant formats such as RDF and OWL.

Figure 3. The architecture of the OntoPop framework

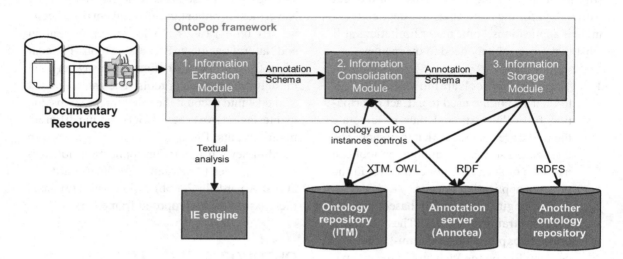

- **Consistency**. The instances created in the knowledge base and the semantic annotations produced must be consistent with the ontology model.
- **Ease of implementation**. Mapping IE tools with KR tools requires different kind of expertise (from the domain, linguistic, and knowledge representation). Thus, the chosen solution must be based on an iterative process the human users can easily understand.
- **Capacity to evolve**. The framework must be able to take into account evolutions of both the ontological resources and the IE tools.

The Information Extraction Module

The first step of the annotation workflow consists in extracting all relevant information relating to the concerned domain from a set of documents. The Information Extraction Module connects to the chosen IE engine that analyzes every document according to its lexicons and its set of extractions patterns. It locates the information to be extracted in each document and tags it in order to generate a **conceptual tree** as the output. This term

"conceptual tree" describes the results of the IE engines, being the ones produced by Amilcare, GATE or IDE™ for example, although they do not truly correspond to a "tree of concepts" (to the ontological sense).

As shown in Figure 4, its root generally represents the document analyzed by the IE engine. Each node of the tree consists of a semantic tag (prefixed by the symbol "/") and the value of the textual unit to which this tag was attributed (indicated in brackets). Other information, such as the lemma of this textual unit or its position in the text, can also be associated to the semantic tags if needed. In Figure 4, the document's root has the semantic tag "/article" and its title "The Coppola Tribe" corresponds to the value.

Consequently, one needs to map the semantic tags from the conceptual tree resulting of the linguistic analysis with the concepts, attributes and relations modelled in the domain ontology of the target application. Not only is it necessary to correctly interpret the semantics provided by the conceptual trees but also to take into account the gap that may exist between the two modes of knowledge representation.

Figure 4. Extract of the conceptual tree produced by linguistic analysis performed by the IE tool IDE™ on the article "The Coppola Tribe" published in Elle magazine (the tree is translated from French)

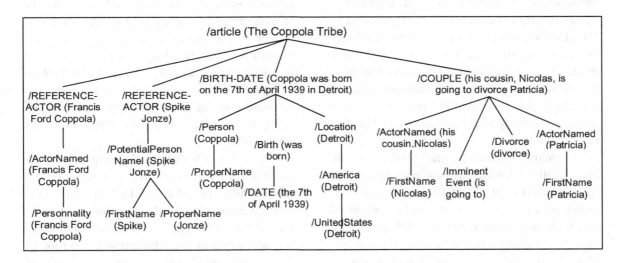

In the existing solutions, annotation tools are closely linked and dependent on the mapping carried out between the two modes of knowledge representation. As an example, OntoMat, in its S-CREAM version (Handschuh, 2005), recognizes that its integration with the Amilcare IE tool is made of "ad hoc" and specific mapping rules. This mapping could not be used to integrate another IE tool. However, we want to emphasize the fact that a semantic annotation and/or ontology population tool should be able to easily plug in a new IE engine according to the target application's needs. For example, in a use case requiring the resolution of the co-reference, the annotation tool

Figure 5. Mastering the gap from IE to semantic representation

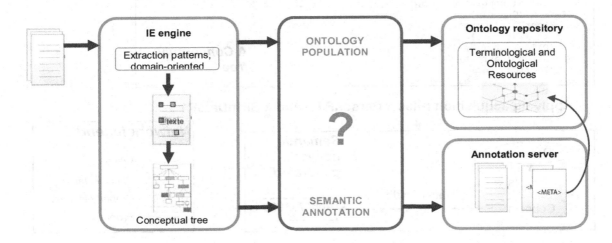

could map to GATE's conceptual trees whereas if the use case involves identification of complex scenarios, the annotation tool could rather exploit the more detailed conceptual trees provided by IDE. Dissociating the IE system from the annotation tool allow us to provide more flexibility and modularity for the target applications. But to do so, we need to find a generic solution to fill the existing gap as presented in Figure 5. It is thus necessary to design a gateway between these two representations.

The solution that we recommend takes the form of declarative rules, called Knowledge Acquisition Rules (KAR) (Amardeilh, 2006a). These rules map one or more semantic tags of a conceptual tree with an element (concept, attribute or relation) of the domain ontology. Concretely a rule identifies the semantic tag which will trigger the annotation or population process. It is also able to take into account the context of the semantic tag in the conceptual tree in order to solve a certain number of ambiguities.

Since a conceptual tree can be represented as a XML document, the Information Extraction Module makes use of the XML family of languages to compile and execute the KARs. As an example, if the linguistic analysis of the sentence «Coppola was born on April 7, 1939 in Detroit» produces the conceptual tree located at the top of Figure 6, then the application of the created KARs defined for this application will create the semantic network located at the bottom of Figure 6. This semantic network associates the attribute «Date of birth» having the value «April 7, 1939» with the instance «Coppola» of class «Personality».

From a methodological perspective, the Knowledge Acquisition Rules constitute the gateway foundations between the linguistic results and the semantic knowledge representation. From a software solution perspective, they are the essential ingredient to enable correct operation of the ontology population and semantic annotation processes.

The Information Consolidation Module

The second phase is operated by the Information Consolidation Module. This module is subdivided

Figure 6. Applying knowledge acquisition rules on a conceptual tree to produce the associated semantic network

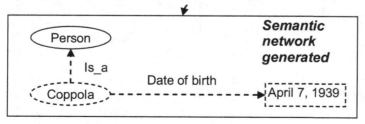
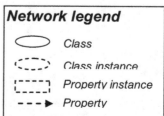

in two components: one dedicated to ontology population and one to semantic annotation. The application of the KARs to the conceptual trees produces an Annotation Schema composed of a semantic network in case of ontology population and/or a set of semantic annotations, according to the target application's objectives. This Annotation Schema must be controlled and consolidated, in particular by checking its validity against the ontological model as well as verifying the absence of any redundancy. The semantic network must be the first to be controlled. Thus, the controlled instances can be created and used to consolidate the potential semantic annotations.

As indicated in (Alani, 2003), rare are the tools for ontology population or semantic annotation which describe, or even mention, the consolidation phase in their workflows. However, this phase is extremely important to maintain the integrity and the quality of the application's referential. In fact, most of them rely only on manual validation to check the generated annotations or instances. Some annotation tools, like OntoMat (Handschuh, 2001; Handschuh, 2002) or SMORE (Kalyanpur, 2003b), have an ontology editor which allows the end-users to control the domain and range constraints on the created annotations. From the ontology population's point of view, only one project, ArtEquAkt (Alani, 2003), was concerned by the consolidation phase and clearly specified it.

In this project, Alani et al. define four problems related to the integration of new instances in a knowledge base: duplicated information, geographical consolidation, temporal consolidation and inconsistent information. For each problem, they explain what are the consolidation operations needed to solve them:

- **Duplicated information:** Merging the instances with the same label, merging the instances if possessing a common set of attributes, merging the attributes when identical (name, value);

- **Geographical consolidation:** Using relations of synonymy and specialization in a geographical thesaurus, such as the Thesaurus of Geographic Names (TGN), clarifying location names using contextual analysis in the document's content or associated semantic network;

- **Temporal consolidation:** Reasoning on the dates to identify them in a precise manner, clarifying the dates using contextual analysis in the document's content or associated semantic network;

- **Inconsistent Information:** Using frequency of extraction as a proof for precision.

Their approach to solving these problems consists of instantiating the knowledge base with the information extracted from the documents and then applying a consolidation algorithm based on a set of heuristics and methods of terminological expansion. This algorithm uses the lexical base WordNet in order to automate the process performed on the instances of the knowledge base.

- Consolidation operations proposed by OntoPop

A contrario, in order to preserve the integrity of the knowledge base, this consolidation phase must be carried out before the creation of the instances in the referential. As we said, the semantic network and the semantic annotations resulting from the linguistic analysis are analyzed in depth to raise any ambiguity, any inconsistency or any conflict with already existing information. Thus, only new and consistent information is created, yet preserving the integrity of the referential and thus improving the quality of the target application. We studied the various possible cases of instances and annotations' creation. We deduced two axes of consolidation:

- The first axis defines the ontological element concerned, i.e. an instance of a class, of an attribute, of a relation, a thesaurus descriptor or a semantic annotation;

- The second axis defines the constraints to be checked, i.e. non redundancy, the domain and range restrictions and the element's cardinality.

The second axis must be adapted according to the ontological element consolidated. Indeed for an instance of class as for a thesaurus descriptor, it is not necessary to control the domain and range restrictions. But, rather the domain restriction on a class instance could be thought as verifying if the correct class was attributed to the instance. The same way, the range restriction for an attribute can be understood as checking the data type awaited by the knowledge base: is it a character string, a numeric, an address URL or a date? According to these axes, we define all

the operations of consolidation recommended by OntoPop in the Annotation and Acquisition Module, cf. Table 1.

If the instances, the descriptors or the annotations are rejected by the consolidation phase, they must be saved in a "buffer" in order to be subsequently proposed to the end-user for correction and validation. We consider that any knowledge is exploitable even if it requires human intervention. Nevertheless, the knowledge that is not conform to the ontology model should not make the referential inconsistent. This is why it is kept separate from the valid instances and annotations.

- Human validation

In the case of a semi-automated application, the end-user has to validate the results generated by the application (cf. Figure 4 & Figure 6) in order

Table 1. Operations of consolidation performed accordingly to the two axes defined

Elements vs. Constraints	Class instance	Attribute instance	Relation instance	Thesaurus descriptor	Semantic annotation
Duplicate information	Control the existence of the instance in the KB by: → querying its label or its aliases → querying its mandatory attributes	Control the existence of an attribute for a given instance by: → querying the attribute type on the given instance and verifying its value	Control the existence of a relation between instances by: → querying the relation type on each instance and verifying their values	Control the existence of a descriptor in a thesaurus by: → querying its label, synonyms, orthographic variants or translations	Control the existence of an annotation linked to a given document by: → querying the annotation type in the document and verifying its value
Domain or class restriction	Control the instance's membership of the relevant class or one of its subclasses	Control the class of the instance to which that attribute is linked compared to its modelled domain	Control the class of the instance to which that relation is linked compared to its domain	No control, new descriptor added as default in the « Candidate Descriptor »'s class	Control the class of the instance to which that annotation is linked compared to its domain
Range or data type restriction	No control	Control the value of the attribute compared to its modelled data type (string, date, number, etc.)	Control the values (instance references) of the relation compared to its range	No control	Control the value (instance or descriptor reference) of the annotation versus its range
Cardinality	No control	Control the number of existing attributes of that type related to the given instance	Control the arity of the relation: unary relations are not valid	No control	No control

to verify its performance and quality. A single user interface, such as OntoPop's (cf. Figure 7), enables the validation of both the semantic annotations and created instances simultaneously. The user can edit them, modify them, add new ones or remove them. Each of these actions is constrained by the ontology model so that the user cannot add inconsistencies to the knowledge base or to the semantic annotations. The annotations and instances that were rejected at the automated consolidation process are also presented to the user. She can easily accept new information considered as relevant that the consolidation process did not succeed in solving automatically. This information can also be merged with existing instances or annotations.

To sum up, the consolidation phase implemented in this Module consists of:

- Controlling the instances and semantic annotations according to the ontology model

(domain and range restrictions, cardinalities), to the knowledge base, and to controlled vocabularies such as a thesaurus or reference tables;
- Providing a user interface for validating the results obtained automatically.

The Information Storage Module

Once the Annotation Schema has been fully consolidated by the previous module, it can then be stored in an ontology repository such as ITM or OWLIM, in an annotation server such as Annotea, or even on a file system. As for the IE engine used by the target application, the Information Storage Module should be able to use any ontology repository or annotation server for saving the valid semantic network or the valid semantic annotations created by the application. Indeed, thanks to the application's parameters, the Information Storage Module knows in which format the An-

Figure 7. The « Annotations » tab in the validation user interface

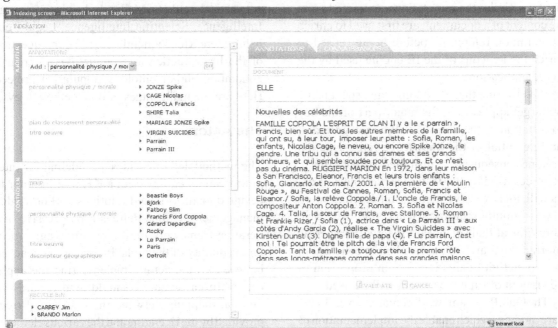

notation schema must be serialised (OWL, RDF, XTM, others…) and to which support it must connect to in order to save the results.

The Lexicons Maintenance Module

A fourth possible module of OntoPop's framework relates to the enrichment of the IE engine's lexicons from the instances created in the knowledge representation tool. A Lexicons Maintenance Module "listens to" all creations, modifications or deletions which are performed either automatically by the Information Storage Module, or manually by the end-users of the knowledge representation tool.

Each time a terminological or ontological resource is created, modified or deleted in the referential, the Lexicons Update Module generates a copy of that resource and transfers it to the IE engine in order to update its lexicons. The IE engine can then create a new entry in the appropriate lexicon, update the entry corresponding to this resource in the case of a modification, or even remove this entry from the lexicon. These three principal stages of OntoPop's lifecycle define a virtuous circle: the annotations, extracted from the content of a document, are first used to enrich the common referential before being reused to enrich the lexicons of the IE engine used by the target application.

We presume that after some time spent using the target application, the major part of the key information of the domain will be integrated in the referential of the knowledge representation tool, and consequently transmitted to the linguistic resources used by the IE tool. Thus, the end-users will not have to validate as much information as was initially required. Hence, they will have more time at their disposal for activities such as information search or publication. In conclusion, the productivity gains increase in proportion to the amount of time the system will be used.

The OntoPop framework contains several software modules which enable the implementation of domain-oriented applications for ontology population and/or semantic annotation. The knowledge base's enrichment phase, based on the information extracted by the IE engine and subsequently annotated, is supplemented by capitalizing on the end-user's feedback. This feedback takes place not only during validation of the suggestions formulated by the application but also during manual enrichment of the knowledge base via its standard edition interface. It thus allows the augmentation of the linguistic resources used by the extraction engine. The process of ontology population and semantic annotation can thus be regarded as a virtuous circle. Moreover, constant attention is applied to maintain the knowledge base's integrity at each phase of the process, and more particularly at the consolidation phase thanks to a set of algorithms and heuristics.

THE ONTOPOP'S PROJECT METHODOLOGY

The OntoPop framework was implemented and tested in various industrial applications in different vertical markets: Media, Industry, Economic Intelligence, Scientific Intelligence, Legal Publishing, etc. Consequently, it raises the question of the best practice for conducting a semantic annotation and/or ontology population project. Here are the main stages of this methodology.

The Actors

The methodology provides a guideline for integrating an IE engine with a KR tool in order to design domain-oriented solutions for knowledge management. It thus defines a progressive and iterative framework until a common agreement on the quality of the tools' integration is reached between all the actors implementing the application. In particular, it should tend towards an optimal mapping between the conceptual trees provided by the IE engine and the various elements modelled in the KR tool of the application. By optimal, we mean that the mapping is the richest, the most complete and as relevant as possible for a given application.

The OntoPop methodology helps the various human actors to work in a progressive and iterative way during the concrete implementation of the proposed framework. These actors can be classified according to their role and their expertise in the methodology:

- **The domain expert**, most often the client himself, who specifies the application's needs and scope, who provides the existing terminological and ontological resources if any and who validates the entire solution provided by the other actors;
- **The linguist**, who is in charge of the linguistic development needed to adapt the IE tool chosen for the domain according to a representative corpus of textual resources;
- **The ontologist**, who models the domain ontology and loads all the data from a legacy application if any (databases, thesaurus, terminologies, knowledge bases, etc.) in the knowledge representation tool;
- **And the integrator**, who is in charge of mapping the results of the IE engine and the KR tool and of all that relates to the implementation of the solution from a technical point of view.

The Five Stages

We previously stated that the KA rules constitute the core of the OntoPop framework. They are an important requirement to the correct implementation and use of the target application. It is the role of the integrator to model these rules, on the basis of the information provided by the linguist, the domain expert and the ontologist. In order to define these rules it is necessary, for any project or domain, to evaluate the development workload

required for each tool used by the target application. To do so, it is thus necessary:

a. To estimate the information extraction capability for a new domain and the attainable level of coverage based on a representative corpus of documents from that domain, and

b. To model the domain ontology by taking into account the coverage targeted by the new application and the potential reuse of any available data from any legacy applications in the company.

The expert provides all the necessary support to understand the key points of the studied domain, the application's objectives and its limits. As such, he must provide concrete and precise answers to:

- A set of general questions, such as:
  - Is the application dedicated to ontology population, semantic annotation or both?
  - Should the application be entirely automated or semi-automated with a manual validation process by the end-users?
  - Are there existing functional and technical requirements for the target application?
  - What are the key failings, if any, in the existing application that must be addressed by the target application?
  ...
- A set of document-oriented questions, such as:
  - What are the existing and future documentary flows to consider in the target application?
  - Which textual documents or resources are representative of the domain concerned by the target application?
  - What textual documents or resources must be manipulated by the target application?

○ What are the formats of the textual documents of the target application (Word, PDF, XML, HTML...)? ...

• A set of knowledge management-oriented questions, such as:

○ Are there some databases, or preferably knowledge bases, used by the current application? Do they have to be recovered by the target application?

○ Are there some terminological resources (taxonomies, lexicons, thesaurus...) defined in the actual application or external to it but still related to the domain concerned by the target application that can be re-used?

○ Should the current data be re-used in the target application?

○ Should the data structure (schema or formal model) be maintained as is or is it possible to entirely rethink that structure?

○ Should the documents previously annotated by the current application be re-annotated according to the new ontology model? ...

It is also important to be able, as soon as possible, to share the specific needs and issues of the target application. The common coverage between the results produced by the IE engine and domain modelled through the ontology should be rapidly identified. To do so, documents such as the structure of both the conceptual trees and the ontology, must be shared between the various actors in order to produce a first integration within the shortest time possible. That integration will then be iteratively developed, tested and refined before being finally validated by the domain expert. Figure 8 shows some of the exchanges required by the methodology between the various actors during the implementation of the target solution.

Based on these considerations, the OntoPop methodology is composed of the following stages:

Figure 8. Roles and exchanges between the actors in the OntoPop methodology

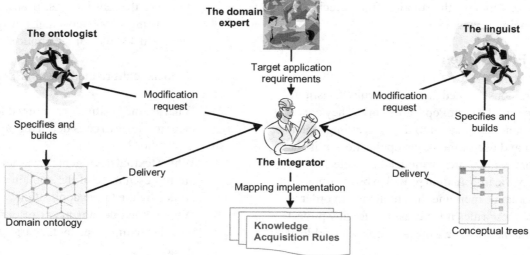

Figure 9. The methodology overview

	Study Phase	Structuring Phase	Mapping Phase	Validation Phase	Delivery Phase
Objectives	Assessment of the data to process by the target application as well as their sources - Definition of the domain's coverage	Definition of the conceptual tree's structure Definition of the domain-ontology model	Mapping the conceptual trees with the ontological elements Implementation of the KARs	Validation of the application's results Reiteration of the Mapping or Structuring stages if adjustments needed	Delivery of the application User Training Maintenance of the application
Actions	- Studying the application's domain, its requirements and the existing - Studying the documentary corpus - Defining the application's perimeter - Defining the tools' coverage	Fine-grained study of the application's needs and of the content of its actual data sources Exchanges on the future structure of the conceptual trees Exchanges on the future ontology model Regularly analysing their overlap	Implementing the ontology in the KR tool Drawing the parallel between the linguistic tags and the ontological elements Context analysis for each linguistic tag Implementing the knowledge acquisition rules	Constituting the testing corpus of the domain Measuring the linguistic resources quality Measuring the mapping quality Correcting the rules Improving the linguistic resources and/or the ontology Validating the results	Delivering and installing the components Installing the application for end-users
Means	- The expert provides the different existing data sources used to model or to be recovered - Interviews with the expert to define the application's needs - Kick-off meeting between the various actors	Regular exchanges between the expert, the ontograph and the linguist Meeting to validate the models with the participation of the integrator	Fine-grained analysis of the conceptual trees resulting from the linguistic process Bilateral meetings between the linguist and the integrator	Bilateral meetings between the integrator and the linguist to test the results obtained and to decide on necessary changes either in the linguistic resources or in the ontology model	Validation meeting between all the actors Training of the end-users and of the system administrator
Deliverable	- General specifications of the target application - Schemas or models of the actual data sources: databases, knowledge bases, thesaurus, etc. - Corpus of textual documents representative of the application's domain	First version of the domain ontology with its documentation First version of the linguistic resources with the detailed specifications of the resulting conceptual trees' structure First version of the « Linguistic vs. ontology Mapping Table »	New version of the domain ontology and its documentation New version of the linguistic resources and their documentation The « Linguistic vs. ontology Mapping Table » completed with the created Knowledge acquisition rules	New version of the domain ontology New version of the linguistic resources The validated mapping Testing reports about the mapping for each rule and the coverage rate between the tools Updated « Linguistic vs. ontology Mapping Table » with validated elements	The IE and KR tools (if not already installed) Final domain ontology + documentation Final linguistic resources + documentation Final mapping (KARs) Updated « Linguistic vs. ontology Mapping Table » Quality reports

1. **The Study Stage.** Discussion about the data to manage (the corpus to analyse, the knowledge to model and the metadata to produce) between the linguist, the ontologist, the integrator and the client: they evaluate the work load required to adapt each tool to the domain, they estimate the capacity of extraction of the IE tool for a new domain and the coverage that can be obtained on the representative corpus, they define the targeted coverage for the new application and thus the concepts to be modelled, while considering transitioning the existing data to the new model.

2. **The Structuring Stage.** Structuring the semantic tags resulting from IE into a conceptual tree and modelling the domain ontology: the integrator identifies as soon as possible the overlapping and the missing information in the conceptual trees or in the

ontology model to adjust them according to the client's needs; the integrator, the ontologist and the linguist produce a synchronised development plan; they exchange specification documents such as the structure of the conceptual trees produced by the IE tool and the ontology model for the application domain to facilitate the integrator's task.

3. **The Mapping Stage.** Mapping each element defined in the domain ontology with the semantic tags contained in the conceptual trees in order to create a set of Knowledge Acquisition Rules, as discussed above.

4. **The Validation/Quality Stage.** Validation of the produced semantic annotations and knowledge base instances: the integrator tests the implemented mapping and the client validates the complete new application solution. If improvements are needed, users reiterate the methodology phases from the Structuring stage.

5. **The Delivery Stage.** Delivery of the application to the client and its subsequent maintenance.

For each phase, we identified the objectives, the actions, the means and the deliverables that should be completed and exchanged by the various actors. We summarized these important points in Figure 9 to provide a global view of the methodology for easier application.

CONCLUSION

At Mondeca, we implemented several applications for different clients in various domains such as Legal Publishing (Amardeilh, 2005a), Media Publishing (Amardeilh, 2005b; Amardeilh, 2006b), Economic or Scientific Intelligence (Amardeilh, 2004), etc. That experience helped us to find the best way to optimize the deployment of domain-oriented semantic annotation and ontology population applications. We analysed the problems

with the existing applications in order to provide each relevant actor concrete the means to avoid repeating them. The OntoPop framework and the proposed project methodology are both results of this expertise we gained. We designed the OntoPop framework with a maximum of flexibility and modularity to adapt any Semantic Annotation or Ontology Population application's needs. The organisation in the three main components, Information Extraction, Information Consolidation and Information Storage, allows each of them to connect to an independent external tool for either processing a textual analysis or storing the annotations. A set of configuration files provides all the parameters needed to organise the target application workflow.

FUTURE RESEARCH DIRECTION

We are presently transitioning the OntoPop framework within the context of the European IST project "Transitioning Applications to Ontologies" (TAO)[a], based on a Service Oriented Architecture (SOA). The goal aims at using a set of semantic web services for connecting to the final application but also at defining an internal workflow based on a set of services between the various components of the framework. The main point to be developed is about the consolidation algorithm. It would be very interesting if we could compose this algorithm with web services: one for verifying the consistency with the ontology model, one for avoiding the redundancy with existing instances in the knowledge base, one for reasoning and inferring new annotations or new instances, one for comparing reusing existing annotations if the contents are similar, etc. A lot needs to be done about that consolidation algorithm. As we previously stated, rare are the annotation tools that perform such activities on their extraction results, only presenting them to the end-user for a manual validation.

Some other research directions concern the semantic annotation of multimedia contents, the improvement of the information extraction engine for unstructured texts (and more particularly the extraction of semantic relations and the recognition of entities anaphora and co-references), the ergonomics of the user interfaces for validation and knowledge instances enrichment…

REFERENCES

Amardeilh, F., & Francart, T. (2004). A Semantic Web portal with HLT capabilities. *Actes du Colloque Veille Stratégique Scientifique et Technologique (VSST'04)*, *2*, 481-492, Toulouse, France.

Amardeilh, F., Laublet, P., & Minel, J.-L. (2005a). Annotation documentaire et peuplement d'ontologie à partir d'extractions linguistiques. Actes de la Conférence Ingénierie des Connaissances (IC'05), Nice, France, pp. 160-172.

Amardeilh, F., Laublet, P., & Minel, J.-L. (2005b). Document annotation and ontology population from linguistic extractions. *Proceedings of the International Conference on Knowledge Capture (KCAP'05)*, Banff, Canada, pp. 161-168.

Amardeilh, F. (2006a). OntoPop or how to annotate documents and populate ontologies from texts. *Proceedings of the Workshop on Mastering the Gap: From Information Extraction to Semantic Representation (ESWC'06), CEUR Workshop Proceedings*, *187*, Budva, Montenegro. Retrieved February 21, 2008, from http://ftp.informatik. rwth-aachen.de/Publications/CEUR-WS/Vol-187/11.pdf

Amardeilh, F., Carloni, O., & Noel, L. (2006b). PressIndex: A Semantic Web press clipping application. *Proceedings of the ISWC 2006 Semantic Web Challenge*, Athens, Georgia, USA.

Aussenac, N., & Seguela, P. (2000). Les relations sémantiques : Du linguistique au formel. *Cahiers de grammaire*, Numéro spécial « Sémantique et Corpus », *25*, 175-198 Presses de l'UTM, Toulouse.

Bechhofer, S., Goble, C., Carr, L., Kampa, S., & Hall, W. (2003). COHSE: Conceptual open hypermedia service. *Annotation for the Semantic Web*, Handschuh S., & Staab, S. (Eds.), Frontiers in artificial intelligence and applications, Volume 96, 193-211. IOS Press, Springer-Verlag.

Benjamins, V.R., Contreras, J., Blázquez, M., Niño, M., García, A., Navas, E., Rodríguez, J., Wert, C., Millán, R., & Dodero, J.M. (2005). ONTO-H: A collaborative semiautomatic annotation tool. *Proceedings of the 8th International Protégé Conference*. Madrid, Spain.

Cimiano, P., Handschuh, S., & Staab, S. (2004). Towards the self-annotating Web. *Proceedings of the 13th International World Wide Web Conference (WWW'04)*, pp. 462-471. New York, USA: ACM Press

Ciravegna, F., Dingli, A., Petrelli, D., & Wilks, Y. (2002). User-system cooperation in document annotation based on information extraction. *Proceedings of the 13th International Conference on Knowledge Engineering and Management (EKAW'02)*, LNCS 2473, Springer-Verlag, Madrid, Spain, pp. 122-138.

Ciravegna, F., & Wilks, Y. (2003). Designing adaptive information extraction for the semantic web in Amilcare. *Annotation for the Semantic Web*, Handschuh, S., & Staab, S. (Eds.), Frontiers in Artificial Intelligence and Applications, Volume 96, IOS Press, Springer-Verlag, pp. 112-127.

Ciravegna, F., Chapman, S., Dingli, A., & Wilks, Y. (2004). Learning to harvest information for the Semantic Web. *Proceedings of the 1st European Semantic Web Symposium (ESWS'04)*, Springer-Verlag, Heraklion, Crete, Greece, pp. 312-326.

Dill, S., Eiron, N., Gibson, D., Gruhl, D., Guha, R., Jhingran, A., Kanungo, T., Rajagopalan, S., Tomkins, A., Tomlin, J.A., & Zien, J.Y. (2003a). SemTag and Seeker: Bootstrapping the Semantic Web via automated semantic annotation. *Proceedings of the 12th International World Wide Web Conference (WWW'03)*, ACM Press, Budapest, Hungry, pp. 178-186.

Dill, S., Eiron, N., Gibson, D., Gruhl, D., Guha, R., Jhingran, A., Kanungo, T., Mccurley, K.S., Rajagopalan, S., & Tomkins, A. (2003b). A case for automated large-scale semantic annotation. *Journal of Web Semantics, Science, Services and Agents on the World Wide Web, 1*(1), 115-132. Elsevier.

Dingli, A. (2003a). Next generation annotation interfaces for adaptive information extraction. *Proceedings of the 6th Annual Computer Linguists UK Colloquium (CLUK'03)*, Edinburgh, UK.

Dingli, A., Ciravegna, F., & Wilks, Y. (2003b). Automatic semantic annotation using unsupervised information extraction and integration. *Proceedings of the Workshop on Knowledge Markup and Semantic Annotation (KCAP'03)*, Sanibel, Florida.

Euzenat, J. (2005). L'annotation formelle de documents en 8 questions. *Ingénierie des connaissances*, Teulier R., Charlet J & Tchounikine P. (Eds.), L'Harmattan, Paris, pp. 251-271.

Habert, B. (2005). *Instruments et ressources électroniques pour le français*, Collection «L'essentiel Français», Ophrys, Paris, p. 169

Heflin, J., & Hendler, J. A. (2001). A portrait of the Semantic Web in action. *IEEE Intelligent Systems, 16*(2), 54-59. IEEE.

Handschuh, S., Staab, S., & Maedche, A. (2001). CREAM - Creating relational metadata with a component-based, ontology-driven annotation. *Proceedings of the Knowledge Capture Conference (KCAP'01)*, Banff, Canada, pp. 76-83.

Handschuh, S., Staab, S., & Ciravegna, F. (2002). S-CREAM - Semi-automatic creation of metadata. *Proceedings of the 13th International Conference on Knowledge Engineering and Management (EKAW'02)*, LNCS 2473, Springer-Verlag, Madrid, Spain.

Handschuh, S. (2005). *Creating ontology-based metadata by annotation for the Semantic Web.* PhD Thesis, Karlsruhe University, p. 225.

Kahan, J., Koivunen, M.R., Prud'Hommeaux, E., & Swick, R. (2001). Annotea: An open RDF infrastructure for shared Web annotations. *Proceedings of the 10th International World Wide Web Conference (WWW'01)*, ACM Press, Hong-Kong, pp. 623-632.

Kalyanpur, A., Parsia, B., Sirin, E., Cuenca-Grau, B., & Hendler, J. (2005). Swoop: A 'web' ontology editing browser. *Journal of Web Semantics, 4*(2).

Kim, S., Alani, H., Hall, W., Lewis, P., Millard, D., Shadbolt, N., & Weal, M. (2002). Artequakt: Generating tailored biographies with automatically annotated fragments from the Web. *Proceedings of the Workshop on Semantic Authoring, Annotation & Knowledge Markup (SAAKM'02)*, Lyon, France, pp. 1-6.

Kiryakov, A., Popov, B., Terziev, I., Manov, D., Kirilov, A., & Goranov, M. (2005). Semantic annotation, indexing, and retrieval. *Journal on Web Semantics, Science, Services and Agents on the World Wide Web, 2*(1), 49-79. Elsevier.

Kogut, P., & Holmes, W. (2001). AeroDAML: Applying information extraction to generate DAML annotations from Web pages. *Proceedings of the Workshop on Knowledge Markup and Semantic Annotation (KCAP'01)*, Victoria, Canada. Retrieved February 21, 2008, from http://semannot2001.aifb.uni-karlsruhe.de/positionpapers/AeroDAML3.pdf

Lanfranchi, V., Ciravegna, F., & Petrelli, D. (2005). Semantic Web-based document: Editing and browsing in AktiveDoc. *Proceedings of the 2ⁿᵈ European Semantic Web Conference (ESWC'05)*, LNCS 3532, Springer-Verlag, Heraklion, Crete, Greece, pp. 623-632.

Laublet, P. (2007). Web Sémantique et ontologies. *Nouvelles Technologies Cognitives et Concepts des Sciences Humaines et sSociales, 1.* Humanités Numériques, Hermès, Paris.

Popov, B., Kiryakov, A., Manov, D., Kirilov, A., Ognyanoff, D., & Goranov, M. (2003). Towards Semantic Web information extraction. *Proceedings of the Human Language Technologies Workshop (ISWC'03)*, Sanibel, Florida, pp. 1-22.

Prié, Y., & Garlatti, S. (2004). Méta-données et annotations dans le Web Sémantique. *Le Web sémantique*, Charlet, J., Laublet, P., & Reynaud, C. (Ed.), Hors série de la *Revue Information - Interaction - Intelligence* (I3), *4*(1), 45-68. Cépaduès, Toulouse.

Rinaldi, F., Dowdall, J., Hess, M., Ellman, J., Zarri, G.-P., Persidis, A., Bernard, L., & Karanikas, H. (2003). Multilayer annotations in Parmenides. *Proceedings of the Knowledge Markup and Semantic Annotation Workshop*, Sanibel, Florida, USA, pp.33-40.

Sowa, J. (2000). *Knowledge representation: Logical, philosophical and computational foundations*, Brooks Cole Publishing Co., Pacific Grove, p. 594.

Staab, S., Maedche, A., & Handschuh, S. (2001a). An annotation framework for the Semantic Web. *Proceedings of the 1ˢᵗ International Workshop on MultiMedia Annotation*, Tokyo, Japan.

Staab, S., Maedche, A., & Handschuh, S. (2001b). *Creating metadata for the Semantic Web: An annotation framework and the human factor.* Technical Report, AIFB Institut, Karlsruhe University, Germany, p. 25.

Tallis, M. (2003). Semantic word processing for content authors. *Proceedings of the Knowledge Markup and Semantic Annotation Workshop (SEMANNOT'03)*, CEUR Workshop Proceedings, 101, Sanibel, Florida. Retrieved February 21, 2008, from ftp.informatik.rwth-aachen.de/Publications/CEUR-WS/Vol-101/Marcelo_Tallis.pdf

Vargas-Vera, M., Domingue, J., Motta, E., Buckingham Shum, S., & Lanzoni, M. (2001). Knowledge extraction by using an ontology-based annotation tool. *Proceedings of the Workshop Knowledge Markup & Semantic Annotation (KCAP'01)*, Victoria, Canada, pp. 5-12.

Vargas-Vera, M., Motta, E., Domingue, J., Lanzoni, M., Stutt, A., & Ciravegna, F. (2002a). MnM: Ontology driven tool for semantic markup. *Proceedings of the Workshop on Semantic Authoring, Annotation & Knowledge Markup (SAAKM'02)*, Lyon, France, pp. 43-47.

Vargas-Vera, M., Motta, E., Domingue, J., Lanzoni, M., Stutt, A., & Ciravegna, F. (2002b). MnM: ontology driven semi-automatic and automatic support for semantic markup. *Proceedings of the 13ᵗʰ International Conference on Knowledge Engineering and Management (EKAW'02)*, LNCS 2473, Springer-Verlag, Madrid, Spain, pp. 379-391.

ADDITIONAL READING

Benjamins, V.R., Contreras, J., Corcho, O., & Gómez-Pérez, A. (2002). Six challenges for the Semantic Web. *Proceedings of the Workshop on the Semantic Web (KR'02)*, Toulouse, France.

Bontcheva, K., & Cunningham, H. (23003). The Semantic Web: A new opportunity and challenge for human language technology. *Proceedings of the Workshop on Human Language Technology for the Semantic Web and Web Services at the Second International Semantic Web Conference (ISWC'03)*, Sanibel Island, Florida.

Buitelaar, P., Declerck, T., Calzolari, N., & Lenci, A. (2003). Towards a language infrastructure for the Semantic Web. *Proceedings of the Workshop on Human Language Technology for the Semantic Web and Web Services in the International Semantic Web Conference (ISWC'03)*, Sanibel Island, Florida.

Contreras, J., & Benjamins, R. (2003). *Annotation tools and services*, Delivrable D3.1, Esperonto Services Project, 67 p.

Corcho, O. (2006). Ontology-based document annotation: Trends and open research problems. *International Journal of Metadata, Semantics and Ontologies*, *1*(1), 47-57. Inderscience.

Handschuh, S., & Staab, S. (2003, Eds.). *Annotation for the Semantic Web*. Frontiers in Artificial Intelligence and Applications, *96*. IOS Press, Springer-Verlag.

Maynard, D. (2005). Benchmarking ontology-based annotation tools for the Semantic Web. *Proceedings of the Workshop "Text Mining, E-Research and Grid-enabled Language Technology" in the UK E-Science Programme All Hands Meeting (AHM2005)*, Nottingham, UK.

Reeve, L. & Han, H. (2005). Survey of semantic annotation platforms. *Proceedings of the Symposium on Applied Computing (SAC'2005)*, Santa Fe, New Mexico, USA, pp. 1634 - 1638.

Sazedj, P., & Pinto, S. (2005). Time to evaluate: Targeting annotation tools. *Proceedings of the 5th International Workshop on Knowledge Markup and Semantic Annotation (semAnnot'05)*, CEUR

Workshop Proceedings, Vol. 185. Retrieved February 21, 2008, from ftp.informatik.rwth-aachen.de/Publications/CEUR-WS/Vol-185/semAnnot05-04.pdf

Stevenson, M., & Ciravegna, F. (2003). Information extraction as a Semantic Web technology: Requirements and promises. *Proceedings of the Adaptive Text Extraction and Mining Workshop at the 14th European Conference on Machine Learning (ECML'03)*, Cavtat-Dubrovnik, Croatia.

Stojanovic, L., Stojanovic, N., & Handschuh, S. (2002). Evolution of metadata in ontology-based knowledge management systems. *Proceedings of Experience Management 2002*, Berlin, Germany, pp. 65--77.

Uren, V., Cimiano, P., Handschuh, S., Vargas-Vera, M., Motta, E., & Ciravegna, F. (2006). Semantic annotation for knowledge management: requirements and a survey of the state-of-the-art. *Journal of Web Semantics*, Science, Services and Agents on the World Wide Web, *4(*1), 14-26. Elsevier.

Valarakos, A., Paliouras, G., Karkaletsis, V., & Vouros, G. (2004). Enhancing ontological knowledge through ontology population and enrichment. *Proceedings of the 14th International Conference on Knowledge Engineering and Knowledge Management (EKAW'04)*, LNAI 3257, Springer-Verlag, Whittlebury Hall, UK, pp. 144-156.

ENDNOTE

[a]   TAO project website: http://www.tao-project.eu

Chapter VII
Fault–Tolerant Emergent Semantics in P2P Networks

Abdul-Rahman Mawlood-Yunis
Carleton University, Canada

Michael Weiss
Carleton University, Canada

Nicola Santoro
Carleton University, Canada

ABSTRACT

To survive in the 21st century, enterprises need to collaborate. Collaboration at the enterprise-level presupposes the interoperability of the underlying information systems. Access to heterogeneous information sources must be provided transparently while maintaining their autonomy. Further, the availability of nearly unlimited information calls for efficient and precise information retrieval, which can be achieved by making the semantics embedded in information sources explicit. Solving the semantic interoperability problem becomes imperative to the success of information search and retrieval applications and enterprises that rely on them. Inspired by self-organizing systems found in biology, physics, and computing, the approach of emergent semantics has been proposed as a solution to the semantic interoperability problem. Emergent semantics refers to the bottom-up construction of interoperable systems, in which semantically related peers are discovered and linked together during the normal operation of the system. Individual information source providers will provide mappings (so-called semantic bridges) between their own local and semantically related foreign information sources. Emergent Semantics in a peer-to-peer (P2P) network is the lowest common knowledge, semantically relevant concepts, among all the peers of the network. Local mappings between peers with different knowledge representations, and their correctness, are prerequisites for the creation of emergent semantics. Yet, approaches to emergent semantics often fail to distinguish between permanent and transient mapping faults. This may result in erroneously labeling peers as having incompatible knowledge representations. In turn, this can further prevent such peers from interacting with other semantically related peers . This is because, in emergent semantics, peers use past interactions to determine which peers they will interact with in future collaborations. This chapter will explore the issue of semantic mapping faults. This issue has not received enough attention in the literature. Specifically, it will focus on the effect of non-permanent semantic mapping faults on both inclusiveness of semantic emergence and robustness of applications and systems that use semantic mappings. A fault-tolerant emergent semantics algorithm with the ability to resist transient semantic mapping faults is also provided. The contributions of this chapter are: (a) an analysis of the impact of the semantic mapping faults on the inclusiveness of semantic knowledge sharing in P2P systems, (b) a preliminary solution to the problems created by semantic mapping faults in P2P semantic knowledge sharing systems, and (c) a qualitative analysis of the causal links between fault causes and fault types. The rest of this chapter is organized as follows. Section II provides broad discussion and literature review about semantic interoperability problem among heterogeneous information source. Section III defines what we mean by a semantic mapping fault and the types of faults. Section IV lists sources of semantic mapping faults. Section V classifies temporal semantic mapping faults. Section VI describes the emergent semantics approach. Section VII presents an algorithm to eliminate the harmful effects of transient mapping faults on emergent semantics (fault-tolerant emergent semantics). Section VIII concludes the chapter and Section IX identifies directions for future work.

BACKGROUND

In today's globally connected and digitalized world, the ability to exchange information, provide services and carry out business worldwide has become an essential requirement for many government agencies and departments, interest groups, businesses, etc. The need for transparent exchange of information and doing business on the global scale is faced with the *semantic heterogeneous information representation* problem among autonomous and distributed information source providers.

Existing information sources are *scattered* around the world. They are stored in repositories located in different government departments, research labs, universities, interest groups, enterprises, etc. The stored information is represented heterogeneously along different aspects. For example, data or information can be in XML files[b], relational tables, HTML files, RDF[c] documents

etc. Further, when the same type of representation format is used for storing information, the information modeling, the structure and semantics of concepts used in the modeling may vary among different information source providers.

An example of *semantic differences* would be using *different* vocabularies to refer to the same physical or conceptual object by different information representations: one's "zip code" is somebody else's "area code"; or using the *same* vocabulary to refer to *different* conceptual or physical real life objects in different representations: a "terminal" for one is a computer monitor, but a "station" for somebody else.

In the distributed environment, information source providers are autonomous. In other words, information source providers have control on their local information sources. They could make changes, update, remove or restrict the access to their information sources. Consequently, in order for various businesses and service applications and systems to be able to cooperate and exchange information in the environment described above, they need to overcome the barrier of heterogeneity between semantic information representations.

In the sections below, we will delineate how a common ontology and emergent semantics help resolve the issue of semantic heterogeneity, and review existing literature on the different approaches for solving the problem.

Ontology-Enabled Semantic Reconciliation

Common ontologies and shared semantics (Gruber, 1993) have been used for semantic reconciliation, recognizing similarities and enabling information exchange to overcome the representational differences. Knowledge engineers and domain experts use concepts from common ontologies to model the area of interest (e.g. medicine, education, tourism) where concept meanings are shared and agreed upon by members of the domain, i.e. individuals commit to the meanings assigned to vocabularies used to describe the domain.

To enable information exchange among multiple independent ontologies for the same domain or among ontologies from overlapping domains, an upper ontology is utilized as mediator. Concepts from independent ontologies are mapped to the common ontologies and from common ontologies to the other independent ontologies. This procedure continues back and forth and for as much as needed.

Several global ontologies have been constructed including OpenCyc, SUO/SUMO, UNPSC etc (Gomez-Perez, 2004). Despite some usefulness of this approach and the existing number of common upper ontologies, the prominent problems with this type of work are the maintenance and scale up difficulties as ontology domain concepts change or evolve over time. It is hard to have an ontology which is comprehensive and highly agreed upon. Thus, to date, there is no privileged or standard common ontology in use for any domain.

More recently, contextualization, or use of local ontologies, has been suggested by some authors (Bonifacio, 2002 ; Bouquet, 2003; Ghidini) as a strategy for modeling information sources. Following this paradigm, individual information source providers (be they Web site owners, operators of peers in a semantic P2P network, or database designers) will annotate their information sources with semantics in their own ontologies. These semantics will be provider-specific, and reflect the information provider's knowledge of the application domain, experience, or culture. This implies a shift from large and centralized to smaller and possibly simpler distributed ontologies.

However, contextualization also imposes new restrictions. Allowing users to create their own local data representations and semantics raises heterogeneous representation problem, e.g. problem of semantic incompatibility among the interacting information sources. To resolve the heterogeneity problem (i.e. enable independent and autonomous information sources to communicate with one another) we need to provide semantic mappings, i.e. translations between semantically related peers.

Local Translation and Emergent Semantics

Emergent behavior is a well-known phenomenon in biology, physics and (distributed) computing. For example, several optimization and network routing techniques have been inspired by the way the behavior of an ant colony as a whole emerges from local interactions between individual ants. [d] Similarly, local cooperation between robots in multi-robot systems for search and rescue operations has been modeled after the formation of flocks of birds (Bahceci, 2003).

Inspired by emergent behavior, the approach of *emergent semantics* has been proposed as a solution to the semantic interoperability problem among autonomous, heterogeneous information sources with local ontologies. Emergent semantics refers to the bottom-up construction of interoperable systems, in which semantically related peers are discovered and linked together during normal operation of the system—as part of regular search and query forwarding operations. Under this approach, individual information source providers provide semantic mappings (so-called *semantic bridges*) between their own local and semantically related foreign information sources (Aberer, 2003, 2004; Larry, 2006; Staab, 2002). This implies a shift from large and centralized approach to a decentralized approach with smaller ontologies. Bottom-up construction of emergent semantic enables consensus reaching on the semantics of concepts used in distributed local ontologies. This in turn paves the way for the knowledge sharing among independent and autonomous peers. Emergent Semantics in a P2P network is the *lowest common knowledge* among all peers' contextual ontologies in the network.

The decentralized approach, not only puts the scalability problem behind, but also if used with simpler ontologies—ontologies with less expressive power and less restricted language—mainly taxonomy, causes dramatic change in the scale of semantic Web applications and semantic information exchange in P2P applications. This is because simplicity encourages users to annotate their information sources with semantics (Rousset, 2004), to understand and make use of others' ontologies.

The decentralized semantic reconciliation approach is especially attractive for semantic search and query forwarding in peer-to-peer (P2P) network (Staab, 2006). This is not only because the information peers bring to the network is heterogeneous and their meanings need to be reconciled in order to improve the search and query results, but also because P2P network is dynamic and the decentralized approach performs dynamic semantic mapping.

Using dynamic semantic mapping, concepts that constitute the query are the only ones which need to be translated and it is done on the fly, i.e. during system operation. This approach suits the P2P dynamic network well and is much preferred over the pre-defined mappings of all concepts among semantically connected peers.

Local mappings between peers with different knowledge representations, and their correctness are a prerequisite for the creation of emergent semantics. Yet, often approaches to emergent semantics fail to distinguish between permanent and *transient* mapping faults. This may result in the erroneous labeling of peers as having incompatible knowledge representations. In turn, this can further prevent such peers from teaming up with other semantically related peers in the future. This is because, in emergent semantics, peers use past interactions to determine which peers they will interact with in future collaborations.

The importance of tolerating non-permanent faults (also known as noise) has long been recognized in hardware and software reliability studies. Non-permanent faults include transient, but also intermittent faults (which are recurring transient faults; for definitions of these terms see Section 3). Methods for controlling the effects of non-permanent faults form an important part of disciplines such as fault-tolerance (Bondavalli, 1997, 2000; Pizza, 1998) and evolutionary game theory (see e.g. Axelrod, 97; Wu, 1995 for a discussion of noise in the iterated prisoner's dilemma).

We argue that Web information systems must also tolerate non-permanent faults. This is particularly true for mission-critical applications such as security and business-to-business applications. Discarding a viable source of information, or preventing a valuable business partner from participating in business transactions just because of transient faults will negatively impact the level of accuracy of the collected information in the security case, and could jeopardize potential financial gains in business-to-business applications.

Existing Approaches

We observed from the literature review that approaches to solve semantic interoperability problem are somewhat different from each other. The existing works could be roughly classified into to four different inter-related classes: Local Mapping and Query Translation, Collaboratively Building Ontologies and Consensus Reaching, Pattern Extraction or Structure Similarity and Tagging and Social Networks. The names are related to the way each approach tries to reconcile the semantic differences among different information source representations. Below is a short a description of each approach.

Local Mapping and Query Translation

The underlying working environment for this approach is mostly a P2P network and a common theme among systems belongs to this approach is the use of local mapping to achieve some form of knowledge sharing and cooperation. In other words, peers have their own local representations and local mappings, i.e. translations between local information presentations are provided to enable information exchange among communicating peers. Examples of systems that use this approach include Chatty Web (Aberer, 2003), OBSERVER (Mena, 2000), Piazza (Halevy, 2003), H-Match (Castano, 2003), KEx (Bonifacio, 2002), Bibsiter (Haase, 2004) and SomeWhere (Rousset, 2006). For a short survey about these systems, the reader is encouraged to see (Mawlood, 2007).

Collaborative Building of Ontologies and Consensus Reaching

An engineering methodology for building ontology collaboratively and reaching consensus on concept definition and domain conceptualization has been suggested by Tempich (2004, 2005). The procedure starts by building general core ontology then, individual users extend the core ontology and adapt it to their local needs. After using the core ontology, users are asked to send feedback to a centralized authority regarding what should and should not be part of the core ontology. The centralized authority will look after user's suggestions and updates the core ontology accordingly. Authors of the methodology assert that after several iterations, a stable and shared common ontology will emerge.

Pattern Extraction or Structure Similarity

Distributed Emergence System (DistES) (Fergus, 2003) and Constructing consensus ontologies for semantic web (Stephens, 2001) are examples of the systems which use structure similarity among distributed ontologies to solve the interoperability problem. DistES protocol is based on the evolutionary algorithm for discovering and merging knowledge in P2P environment. Each peer owns local ontology represented in hierarchical structure. Peers extend their knowledge by querying other peers, selecting best result among the query answers and merging the selected result with local ontology. The process of selecting foreign concepts and forging concept relations for integration with local data is based on their frequency of occurrence in the query answers. Concepts and concept relation with high occurrence, i.e., appeared in multiple query answers; will be selected for merging with local data, those with fewer occurrences are ignored. Thus, the end result information source structure, i.e. emerging ontology, manifests the general consensus among peers who participated in the interaction. Similarly, Stephens (2001) uses the occurrence rate of concepts and concept relations among multiple, small and related ontologies used for web annotation to construct a merged ontology on the fly. The newly constructed ontology is then presented to the user for further refining.

Tagging and Social Networks

The launch of the social book marking Web site "del.icio.us" [e], the photo sharing service "Flickr"[f] and others opened-up a new way of categorizing Web information sources, i.e. building ontologies collaboratively by large numbers of Web users.

A network of English words made of *numerous tags* used by independent users for labeling the *same online document* forms the basis for ontology creation by this strategy. Similarly, using *same tag* by numerous independent users to refer to some *resource* is the basis for creation of online communities around using common resources, i.e. share common interest (Mika, 2005). Currently, serious discussion and interest have been devoted to social networking and collaborative building ontologies in academia. Several works following this strategy have been surveyed in Staab (2005).

We will extend or build upon these existing techniques by eliminating/ reducing the effect of the temporal mapping faults which confronts the semantic information flow. In our system we will try to overcome two fundamental problems of the existing systems: the lack of fault tolerance and the inability to distinguish permanent from non-permanent semantic mapping faults. The ability to resist semantic mapping fault helps in building a robust system. It also prevents peer's unwarranted removal from future participation on further collaboration events. This implies an intelligent use of peer's past collaboration to determine future decision on further collaboration in a best possible way.

SEMANTIC MAPPING FAULTS

In this section we define what we mean by a *semantic mapping fault*, and identify different types of faults based on notions from fault tolerance literature.

Faults

A *fault* is an incorrect semantic mapping, or the failure to map between concepts from different ontologies. We say that a fault occurs when (1) a concept in one ontology is mapped to a semantically unrelated concept in a different ontology, or (2) a concept in one ontology cannot be mapped to an existing semantically related concept in a different ontology.

Formally we can express this definition as follows. Assume we have two ontologies $O1 = \{C, P, R\}$ and $O2 = \{C^\backslash, P^\backslash, R^\backslash\}$ where C and $C^\backslash$ are sets of concepts, P and $P^\backslash$ are sets of concept properties and R and $R^\backslash$ are sets of relations between concepts. Given two semantically equivalent concepts or their instances[g] $c \in C$ and $c^\backslash \in C^\backslash$ such that $c \equiv c^\backslash$ we say that a fault occurs if either one of the following is true:

- c is mapped to a semantically unrelated concept $x \in C^\backslash$ such that $x \neq c$.
- c cannot be mapped to a semantically related concept $c^\backslash \in C$, i.e. the mapping process incorrectly leads to nil.

The fault-tolerance literature classifies faults based on their duration. Accordingly, we distinguish between permanent, transient and intermittent faults.

Permanent Faults

A *permanent fault* is a fault that continues to exist, unless some outside action takes place to remove its underlying cause.

For example, any attempt to map between two concepts from two unrelated ontologies, i.e., two ontologies from different domains, will result in a permanent fault. This situation will continue indefinitely, unless, e.g., a change is made in the mapping semantics linking the ontologies.

Transient Faults

A *transient fault* is a type of fault that appears once, and remains in place for a short period of the time.

A transient fault may corrupt the data of a system, but the system will remain operational. It is a statistical fault, and it is hard to predict when exactly it will happen. For example, the change of a company's stock symbol can result in a transient semantic mapping fault, if either the propagation of the change notification to related peers or applications is delayed, or the related peers or applications are unable to incorporate the change immediately.

Intermittent Faults

An *intermittent fault* is a fault that occurs periodically. It appears for a short period of time, disappears, and then reappears repeatedly.

For example, in a situation where ontology modification is not a full substitution of one ontology by another, it is possible for semantically related peers to continue operating. In the described scenario, there can be intermittent faults. Faults will occur, because there are situations, when related peers are unable to interpret the meaning of concepts in the modified ontologies.

Although transient and intermittent faults manifest very similarly, they are quite different. While the first one is generated from temporal condition, the second one is the result of unstable system. Also, the intermittent fault could be fixed by removing the unstable component from the system, but transient faults cannot be eliminated.

The diagram in Figure 1 is one way that the three types of errors can be visualized. A semantic mapping can either be correct (no fault) or incorrect (faulty). In the case of a permanent fault, once the status of the mapping changes from no fault to faulty, it remains faulty. For a transient fault, the mapping will be faulty for some time

Figure 1. Fault types

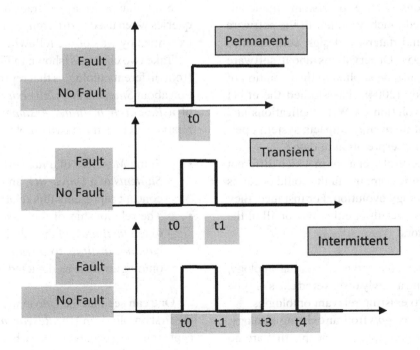

interval. In the case of an intermittent fault, the status of the mapping repeatedly changes between no fault and faulty.

CAUSES OF NON-PERMANENT SEMANTIC MAPPING FAULTS

In this section, we discuss situations that can cause non-permanent (transient or intermittent) semantic mapping faults. Our intention is not to be comprehensive, but to illustrate the need for handling (either by tolerating or guarding against) temporary mapping faults. The causes of faults discussed below include ontology evolution, query context and static mapping, temporal nature of data, unavailability of data sources, and misbehavior of peers.

Ontology Evolution

Ontologies evolve as existing components/elements are replaced with new components, or components are modified. The evolution of software and its consequences on system functionality has received much attention in the software engineering and database design communities (Roddick, 1995). Observations about software evolution can also be applied to the evolution of ontologies. Noy (2004a) has studied the effect of ontology evolution on Web applications and concludes that it strongly impacts system operability and the interpretation of data [h].

There are several scenarios in which different types of semantic mapping faults could occur as a result of ontology evolution. For instance, they could occur as a result of either one or all of the following factors:

*   *Adding new concepts* to an existing ontology, e.g. adding a newly discovered class or type of drug to existing relevant ontologies.
*   *Deleting concepts* from an existing ontology. Outdated concepts or concepts that are no

longer used or useful may be deleted from the ontology.
*   *Changes in concept meaning.* A changed meaning can result in the removal or addition of a concept relation or property.

An example of a change in ontology by adding new properties is attaching a concept for hydrogen as a new type of fuel to the concept car. Removing a relation that links the concept floppy drive to the concept PC is another example of a change in ontology, e.g. for a PC maker who no longer supports floppy drives in its product configurations

Query Contexts and Static Mapping

Static mapping is a mapping without consideration of the *context* in which a concept is used, i.e. the relations and properties of a concept. It is a *term-by-term* association. For example, if a concept x is mapped statically to another concept y; mapping will always produce the same results no matter the context of x.

Static mapping may generate faulty answers to queries when used in different contexts. This can explained by way of the following example.

Take two concepts (shown in Figures 2 and 3) from different ontologies that represent information about *Students* at a *University* and *Members* of a *Research Institute*. *Assume* the following relations between the two ontologies:

*   Some *Members* of a *Research Institute* are *Students* of a *University*, and the *Employer* concept represents this relation.
*   The relationship of the *Research Institute* to the *Institute* and the relationship of *Educational Institute* to *Institute* from the two ontologies were as depicted in Figure 4.

One can see that the *University* concept from the first ontology and the *Research Institute* concept from the second ontology become semantically equivalent, i.e.

University ≡ Research Institute.

This is possible, because the *Institute* concept from both ontologies can be declared in the mapping table as equivalent concepts.

Consider the effect of the static mapping from *Institute* to *Institute* on the following two queries:

Q_1: List the *Names* of all *Members* of *Institutes*

When this query is posed on both ontologies, it asserts that University ≡ Institute. However, consider the second query:

Q_2 List the *Names* of all Members of *Educational Institutes*

The relation University ≡ Institute no longer holds, and its assumption will result in a fault.

That is, while the semantic correspondance between the concepts resulted in a correct answer to the first query, it resulted in fault for the second query. This scenario is a good example of an *intermittent* fault. Every time the static mapping between *University* and Research *Institute* is used, a fault will occur, but not if it is not used. The work of (Ouksel, 1999) further elaborates on the effect of context and static mapping on faults.

Figure 2. Representation of the concept student at a university

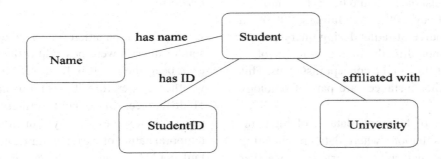

Figure 3. Representation of the concept member of a research institute

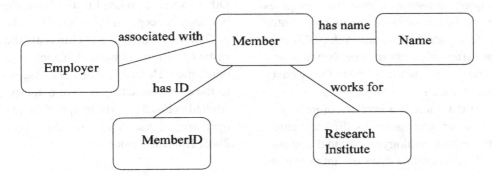

Figure 4. Two different institute concept representations

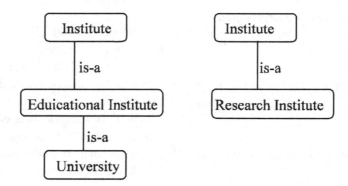

Temporal Nature of Data

While in pervious examples we talked about *concept mapping faults*, concept instances could also lead to transient or intermittent faults. Even though different researchers have different views on whether instances should be part of ontology or not (e.g. Lacy, 2005; McGuiness, 2003)[i], an important source of faults during query answer evaluation, not directly in mapping, involves changes over time in the concept instances. This is true whether instances are part of ontology or not

The issue of temporal data is of high importance in situations where data are changing continuously such as stock prices or weather temperature. Both *price* in the *stock* ontology and *temperature* in the *weather* ontology are properties of concepts whose instances change over time. A query answer evaluator that compares temperature values or stock prices represented in two different ontologies may produce different results at different points in time. Not accounting for time dependency can lead to faulty query answer assessments.

Assume that there is a network of peers that provide weather information for different cities, each with weather ontology similar to that shown in Figure 5. Also assume that we want to find the

coldest city in the network. One way to achieve this is by running a query similar to the following over all related cities and subsequently compare the results:

Q: Find the *Location* with the lowest *temperature*

If query propagation is delayed for some reason, or queries were posed at different times to each peer, the result will not reflect the correct weather temperature. This fault is not the result of differences in semantic representation (all peers use the same ontology), but rather due to the temporal nature of the temperature concept. This fault could be temporary or permanent, based on whether temporal concepts are accounted for or not in the ontology. Something similar could be said about a query to find the cheapest stock price. Other examples related to temporal changes of ontology concepts are presented in (Zhu, 2004).

The temporal issue is not limited to the concept instances. Similar issues also apply to temporal ontologies. However, while the issues relevant to the temporal schemas have extensively been studied in Database, the temporal issue is still an open area of research for ontologies (Gutierrez, 2005, Hurtado, 2006).

Figure 5. Partial weather ontology[j]

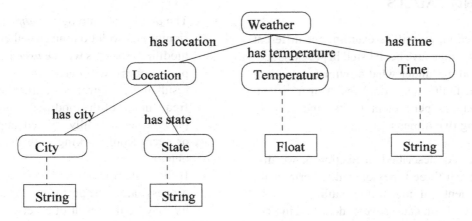

Unavailability of Data Sources

It has been pointed out by (Gal, 2001) that the design of the conceptual schema for information services possesses special properties. These include (1) a rapid change of data sources and meta-data, and (2) instability, since there is no control over the information sources. The *availability* of information sources is solely dependent upon information source providers. A possible scenario is the temporary unavailability of information when such information is needed. This possibility is particularly acute during query execution.

Misbehavior of Peers

Correctness of semantic mapping depends on the honest conduct of peers. A peer could be dishonest or biased in his interaction with other peers during the mapping process for reasons such as selfishness and greed. There are various ways through which a peer could influence the mapping process. These ways include (1) not forwarding a query to other peers during transitive mapping process, or, (2) not forwarding answers to the other peers during mapping, and, (3) altering or delaying queries (results) before forwarding

them to other peers. In all of these situations the mapping will be incorrect.

Working in a hostile or uncooperative environment gives rise to situations where peers are permanently hostile or uncooperative. This may lead to permanent faults. However, in the case of unintentional misinterpretation or incorrect implementation of mappings, faults are produced from "noise-like" actions, and it will be correct to assume that they are non-permanent.

There is some similarity between the information source unavailability described in the subsection 4.4 and peers misbehavior, but they are not quite the same. While the former is caused by information unavailability, the latter results in the information unavailability. Thus, we decided to present them separately.

In the above scenarios we need to differentiate between permanent and temporary mapping faults. The knowledge about different types of faults along the temporal dimension will help us determine when peers should be excluded from further interaction. This helps in better consensus formation, which in turn contributes to solving the semantic interoperability problem.

CLASSIFICATION OF TEMPORAL MAPPING FAULTS

In this section, we will re-examine the different fault causes that have been listed in previous section to find out under what circumstances each individual fault cause could result in transient, intermittent or permanent faults, and classify them along two dimensions:

- *Type*. As described in Section 3, we distinguish three types of faults: permanent, transient and intermittent faults.
- *Cause*. Fault causes were identified in Section 4. Below, we describe when they occur and identify their associated fault types.

Since we assume that local mappings between ontologies already exist, our classification will focus on what faults may occur during *mapping execution*, rather than on faults that may occur because of errors in the *mapping logic*, e.g. substituting a concept by its hypernyms or hyponyms. Hence, mapping faults caused by meaning and representations of concepts are not included in this classification. For this type of fault we refer reader to (Naiman, 1995; Ram, 2004; Glushko, 2005). Also, In order to simplify the analysis we sometimes refer to both intermittent and transient type errors as non-permanent faults.

Permanent Mapping Faults

The following situations could result in permanent mapping faults:

- Mapping *temporal* concepts without a representation of time constraints in the ontology leads to permanent faults. This is because temporal ontology concepts are continuously changing with time. Even if the mapping process produces (by accident) some correct mappings without consideration for time

constraints, eventually the system will fail completely.

- The *degree* of ontology *modification* (versioning and evolution), and whether or not the modified concepts will be *used* in the mapping process, will determine the mapping result. A high degree of modification and the frequent use of the modified concepts may prevent semantically related applications or peers from working with the modified ontology.
- If the system is *unavailable*, the mapping process cannot be performed. Unavailability may be the result of a network or peer failure.
- Working in a hostile or *uncooperative* environment can create conditions where peers are permanently hostile or uncooperative.[k]

We would like to point out that *query context and static mapping* will less likely lead to permanent faults. If this were not the case, it would indicate that the existing mapping is incomplete. Hence, a better concept mapping would be required.

Non-permanent Mapping Faults

Except from those situations identified in the first case, all other situations will result in non-permanent faults. These situations include:

- A change in *query context* which can give rise to intermittent faults. This is because every time an existing correspondence between two concepts, i.e. an existing static mapping, is used when mapping for contexts other than the contexts for which the relation was defined for, an error may occur.
- A *denial of service* request due to *temporary* server crashes or the disappearance and reappearance of peers which will result in a non-permanent fault.

- *time constraints* represented in temporal ontology concepts: e.g., if a *delay* is experienced during transitive query rewritten, i.e. $q_{\_start} + q_{\_delivary} > d_{\_time}$, where $q_{\_start}$ refers to the time when the query is submitted to other peers, $q_{\_delivary}$ refers to the length of time a query takes to propagate from a peer A to a peer B, and $d_{\_time}$ refers a point in time where the information on the remote site is correct, query result evaluator could falsely concludes that the query result is unavailable or nil. Depending on the frequency of query propagation delays this will lead to intermittent or transient faults.

- Circumstances where *ontology evolution* is not a complete substitution of the previous ontology, it is possible for related peers or applications to continue operating. In this scenario there can be intermittent faults. Faults will occur, because there are situations, where semantically related peers are unable to interpret the meanings of concepts in a modified ontology.

Moreover, the ontology modification procedure also has an impact on the fault type. Modification procedure could result in either (1) the unavailability of the information source for a short period of time, if the ontology is locked for updating or (2) a *race* condition between the information source provider and information user, if the ontology user is informed about the change after the modification. That is, the modification problem becomes an instance of the unavailability or temporal problems described above. From this observation we may conclude that every ontology modification can lead to a non-permanent fault.

- Unintentional *misinterpretation* or incorrect implementation of mappings gives rise to an incorrect mapping. Since the faults are produced from "noise-like "actions, it will be correct to assume that they are non-permanent.

The observations about ontology modification, unavailability and temporal ontology concepts can be generalized as follows:

- The effect of an ontology modification is not as severe as the effect of unavailability. This is because we assume that modifications to ontologies are less frequent than an information source becoming unavailable.
- The probability of transient faults may be higher than that for intermittent faults. Again, this is for the same reason.

It is important to note that, in this section, we have looked at causes of faults one cause at a time. For example, we studied the effect of query context, temporal aspects, and ontology modification separately. It will be interesting to explore whether a fault can be the result of multiple causes, and whether we need to distinguish between different fault causes, when a fault occurs. However, the approach that we will take in the next section to detect and remedy faults does not require knowledge of the underlying cause. Table 1 summarizes this classification.

CRITICAL REVIEW OF EMERGENT SEMANTICS

This section starts by describing the steps used by current methods to emergent semantic as documented in the literature (Aberer, 2003, 2004; Larry, 2006; Staab, 2002). These steps (shown in Figure 6) are:

1. Peers join a network after finding the first peer with a compatible knowledge representation. That is, peers establish mappings to the semantically related peers[1]. Subsequently, peers submit queries to their neighboring peers using concepts in their own personalized local ontologies.

Table 1. Classification of temporal faults

	Transient Fault	Intermittent Fault	Permanent Fault
Temporal Semantic Conflict	One-time message delay	Frequent message delays	Unsupported time constraint
Versioning and Evolution	During changes	During changes	Unsupported change management
Query Context and Static Mapping	Unsupported Query Context	Unsupported Query Context	Disqualify
Unavailability of Data Sources	Unavailability > Timeout	Frequent unavailability	Unavailability = infinity
Peers Misbehavior	Misbehavior for short period of time	Repeated misbehavior	Permanent misbehavior

2. Upon receiving a query, each peer starts processing the query locally, if the concepts used to formulate the query are compatible with concepts in its local ontology, and sends back query results to the querying peer. Otherwise, it forwards the query to other peers for which they have a direct mapping, after invoking the translation facilitator. Query forwarding will continue, until either (1) the query reaches the query initiator[m], (2) the query exceeds a specified number of query forwards ("hops"), or (3) the time to live for the query message expires.

3. The querying peer (query initiator) collects all answers returned, and *evaluates* them. If the answers were satisfactory, the query initiator will inform the neighbors involved about the result. Thus, the entire translation paths will be informed of the result of a successful query[n].

4. By comparing (mapping) list of query concepts to the list of concepts from the query result, the querying peer could conclude if the semantic relation along the translation path has been preserved. The semantic preservation is used to increase (decrease) peers confidence in their immediately connected peers. For mapping query concepts to the concepts of query answer, semantic affinity between concepts should be defined and used by mapping process. For example, the semantic affinity of $\{ \subset, \supset, \equiv, \perp \}$ between two concepts could be defined as $\{0.5, 0.5, 1, 0\}$ respectively. Similarly, peers could use satisfaction (dissatisfaction) of the query answers to reward (punish) their directly connected peers. The latter case is more appropriate for situation where emergent semantics is not the issue of the concern. Combing both described methods also possible. Query semantic would be considered preserved if (1) key concepts in the query did not drop during semantic mapping chain, and (2) the average value of the semantic preservation were greater than or equal to some threshold. The value of the threshold could be set by system administrator, where higher value means that higher semantic affinity between concepts of query and query answer is required. Query answers could be considered satisfactory if they meet query constraints.

The described steps could be conceived as a process of constructing a directed graph, where anytime a local peer P encounters another peer P` that provides a correct answer to its query, i.e. a peer with a comparable semantic representation,

Figure 6. Main steps of the current emergent semantic process

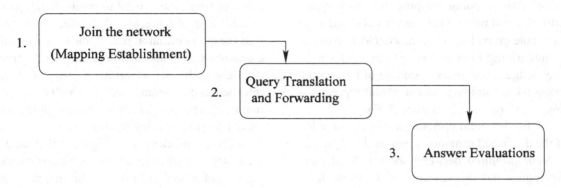

the existing semantic mapping between these peers will be further reinforced. That is, semantically related peers are discovered and linked to each other during the normal operation of the system—search and query forwarding. Figure 7 depicts such a graph. In the Figure, the highlighted peer is the query initiator, labels on the links represent a mapping from source to target

and semantically related peers are connected by a link. The graph will be used by peers for future collaboration, e.g. when initiating or forwarding a similar query.

The graph is a snapshot of a network where peers are connected by semantic mappings. The whole graph is not stored at any peer in the network, it is a distributed graph. Each peer in the

Figure 7. Semantically related peers without temporal fault handling

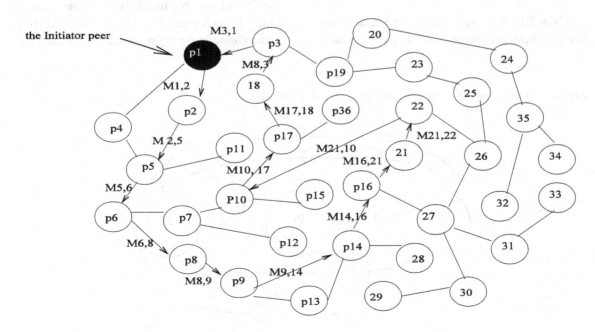

network has knowledge through the confidence value of its out-going mapping links to semantically relevant peers. However, peers could store the whole graph locally, if they decided to do so, by integrating foreign concepts into their local knowledge repositories. Example of integrating foreign concepts into local knowledge representation is described in (Castano, 2003).

A fundamental prerequisite for the creation of the described semantic graph is the existence of *local mappings* between peers with different ontologies and the *correctness* of those local mappings. Thus, when peers are unable to answer queries or provide correct answers to them, how this failure is handled can become a source of problems. We need to make a subtle distinction between permanent and non-permanent semantic mapping faults or risk the erroneous labeling of peers as having incompatible knowledge representations.

To give an idea of the consequences of erroneously labeling peers as incompatible we consider the effect on the number of outgoing mapping links each peer has to other peers in the network. We will consider two cases:

Case 1 In this case, one of the peers on the mapping path used to answer the query has only

one outgoing link. By mapping path we mean the chain of translations used to produce the query result. Figure 8 represents this case, where peer P_1 is the query initiator, peer P_k the peer with one outgoing link M_k, and all links from peer P_{k+1} from different paths participating in query answers returned to the initiator peer P_1. Small circles on the edges of the graph indicate that multiple peers participated in forming the results.

It should be clear from Figure 8 that unless the system can distinguish between transient and permanent mapping faults, if the mapping M_k between Peer P_k and peer P_{k+1} is not successful, even only for a short period of time, peer P_1 will conclude that the outgoing mapping link M_1 is not entirely reliable, that is, its confidence in the outgoing mapping link M_1 will be reduced.

This is because even a temporary failure of a mapping link, M_k, results in incorrectness of all paths MP_1, MP_2, MP_3 and MP_4, following that mapping link. That is, mapping faults are dependent. Hence, all the results originated from peer P_k will be considered incorrect for a particular query. Based on (1) the current state of the link M, i.e., its prior value, and (2) the rate of fault occurrence, peer P_k and all other peers on the mapping paths going through peer P_k could be excluded from participation in emerging shared semantics.

Figure 8. A peer on the mapping path with one outgoing link

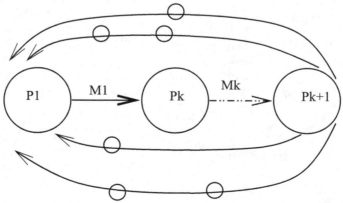

Figure 9. Peers on the mapping path have multiple outgoing links

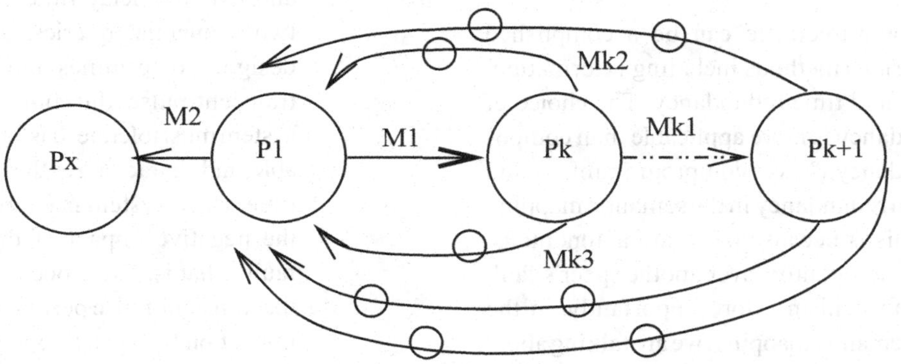

Case 2 In this case, we are considering a situation when peers have k outgoing mapping links and k > 1. Figure 9 represents this case. It shows that P_k has three outgoing mapping links {M_{k1}, M_{k2}, M_{k3}}. Hence, the decision on the reliability or trustworthiness of the outgoing link M_1 does not depend entirely on the outgoing link M_{k1}, as it was the situation in case 1. Nonetheless, not distinguishing between transient and permanent mapping faults, i.e., treating the mapping link M_k as permanently faulty, will have an impact on the perception about the correctness of the outgoing mapping link M_1.

The wrong perception about any outgoing mapping link, when peers have k outgoing links, could impact the way subsequent queries will be routed. Consider the situation shown in Figure 9. If the original trust in the outgoing links M_1 and M_2 were X and Y respectively and X-Y = d, then, if a transient fault on the mapping link M_{k1} downgrades the trust value of M_1 by a value Z, where Z > d, the peer P_k will favor M_2 over M_1 the next time it needs to forward a query. This, could, in turn, isolate other peers from participating in future collaborations, and lower the precision and recall of query results because of a lower number of peers participating in answering the query.

These cases lead us to believe that a complete semantic emergence between independent and heterogeneous ontologies is not possible without tolerating temporary semantic mapping faults. In the next section, we will propose a solution to non-permanent semantic mapping faults for emergent semantics.

Fault-Tolerant Emergent Semantics

Not all existing fault recovery techniques, e.g. checkpoints, rollback, and error log analysis are appropriate for P2P networks. Some of the existing solutions are difficult to implement and others are not appropriate for the context of semantic mapping.

We propose a solution to detect and correct non-permanent semantic mapping faults. Our solution is simple in concept and easy to apply. It is based on the *time redundancy* technique, which is well-known in the fault tolerance literature (Anghel, 2000; Avizienis 1995; Dupont 2002; Paradhan , 1996).

In this context, we refer to the replication of a query and checking for the query answer consistency as time redundancy.

Time Redundancy

Software fault-tolerance can be accomplished through various methods including information, component and time redundancy. The choice of time redundancy is more applicable than component redundancy (N-version programming) and information redundancy in the semantic mapping context. This is because peers are autonomous, and no peer has control over another peer's fault handling mechanism. More importantly, in the context of semantic mapping, we are talking about peers sending queries to other peers and not getting correct responses. Hence, the most appropriate way to determine whether a fault is permanent in such a setting is to resend the query.

The time-redundancy technique can be used to add fault-tolerance capabilities to semantic mapping-based systems in at least two ways: (1) querying the peer service provider more than once at different times and comparing the obtained results, and (2) preparing a test query for which the querying peer knows the answer. In both of these cases, the query initiator can directly verify whether the related peers executed correctly (Papalilo, 2005).

Proposed Algorithm

The procedure of our proposed algorithm for tolerating non-permanent semantic mapping faults comprises of two main parts: fault detection and fault recovery. The algorithms steps are:

1. To detect faults, peers will be tested with a repeated query as follows:
    a. Submit K sequential queries in place of one query every time query submission or query forwarding is performed. Queries are separated from each other by a time Δ. For instance, if K is set to 2 then the origin query and its clone will be separated by Δ time. That is, the second query will be posed at $t_0 +$

Δ, where t_0 is the time for initial query and Δ is the delay time between the two sequential queries. The system designer determines the maximum transient-pulse duration Δ that the system must tolerate. It is a system variable, and characterizes the length of the time which system is guarded against the negative impact of the transient fault. That is, faults occurring during the transient-pulse period will have no impact on the system operational.

b. Query answers from replicated queries are compared for consistency. The inconsistency among answers for the same query is a deciding criterion for the transient fault occurrences. The consistency checking leads to the following two cases:
    i. If query answers were consistent and incorrect then querying peer concludes that the queried peer is incapable of providing an answer to the query. Hence, it is permanently faulty relative to the posed query.
    ii. If query answers were inconsistent, then a transient fault must have occurred, and an action should take place to eliminate its negative impact.

The consistency relation is a system-defined relation. An example of consistency relations between two answers A_{s1} and A_{s2} is $\{\subset, \supset, \equiv\}$ where answers $A_{s1} \subset A_{s2}$ means that A_{s1} is less general than A_{s2}, $A_{s1} \supset A_{s2}$ means that A_{s1} is more general than A_{s2} and $A_{s1} \equiv A_{s2}$ means that A_{s1} and A_{s2} are identical.

2. A transient fault recovery action comprises two steps:
    a. **Query answer cancellation:** If a transient fault is detected, the infected

query impact on the semantic relation between peers should be ignored. This is achieved by sending a *cancel* signal to the peer that originally initiated the query. This signal indicates that answers resulting from the query should be ignored. The cancel signal has one parameter, a *query-id*. The query-id identifies the query for the semantic mapping under investigation. As each peer returns the cancel signal to the peer it received the query from, the signal reaches the query initiator and the result of a query with the query-id in the cancel signal will be ignored. The result of query will be ineffective on grounds of the trust peers have in their outgoing links.

b. **Query re-submission:** In order for queries to recover from the impact of the transient faults, query re-submission needs to take place. This happens after waiting for Δ_2 length of the time from the last time a transient fault is detected and query re-submission could take place. The query re-submission can be repeated up to K times. The Δ_2 value and the *number of query retry* are system parameters. These values will be set by system administration in such a way that a system will maximize the recall for the least additional queries. These values could be determined experimentally. Further, Yinglong et at. (2007), suggests that ontology update notification in distributed systems should be enforced and performed within a time window. In the latter case the Δ_2 value will be set equal to time constraint.

We can make the following observations about this algorithm:

- Query consistency checking could be accomplished in two different ways: Central Checking and Distributed Checking.
  i. **Distributed Checking:** when peers receive identical queries separated from each other by Δ time, they can use this knowledge for testing their immediate neighbors on the mapping path. This will be done by comparing query answer results. An inconsistency among query answers would be an indication of transient faults.
  ii. **Centralized Checking:** the querying peer will receive all answers for repeated identical queries. That is, the querying peer will receive a number of answer sets of different size and checks for consistency by comparing the answer sets. An inconsistency among answer sets would be used for transient fault detection.

There are tradeoffs for each approach. In the distributed fault detection approach, peers are required to perform some extra functionality, and send an extra message once a fault has been detected. In the centralized approach, a new policy for query re-submission and out-going mapping link reward (punishment) could be adapted. For example, queries could re-submit only when the all answers of the first query were wrong resulting in a reduced number of messages exchanged. However, the heavy computation that has to be done on querying peer and computation capabilities of existing peers will not be used.

- The impact of submitting multiple queries in place of one query on the level of the confidence peers have in their out-going mapping links has to eliminate. This could be done by assigning unique IDs to queries. Multiple queries with the same ID will be treated as one query. A querying peer will reward (punish) an out-going mapping link only once for receiving multiple answers from multiple queries with same query ID.

- Re-submitting queries in working environment with frequent transient faults could end-up repeating queries forever. To cope with this situation, our proposed solution will tolerate up to x transient faults, where x is a system variable whose value is determined as a ratio of queries to transient faults. Peers need to do some extra computation and book keeping works in order to determine the value of x.

- All peers run the same algorithm, and they update their confidence value in out-going mapping links based on the results they obtain from their own queries. The updating policy could be changed by requesting querying peers to propagate their acceptance (rejection) to query answers along the mapping path(s). This will help peers along the mapping path to update their confidence value in their out-going mapping links, based on the use by other peers.

Figure 10 shows a diagram of our proposed solution, where K = 2 and the delay between queries is Δ. The two arrows, **As1** and **As2** represent the query answers. In a case when there is no answer to a query, the arrow represents the time-out signal from the system clock. Having each peer check and capture transient mapping faults, we will build a robust system where the chances for expelling peers for non-permanent semantic mapping faults are minimized.

The algorithm is valuable, not only because it is simple in concept and easy to apply, but also because it is capable of detecting a range of faults without the need for knowing the causes of the faults. However, the algorithm will increase in the number of messages exchanged, could increase in computation time and will not detect all faults (e.g. faults caused by static mapping and context will not be detected).

Alternative Approaches

A key element for fault-tolerance is *redundancy*. That is, additional resources to provide capability

Figure 10. Query replication and answer consistency checking steps

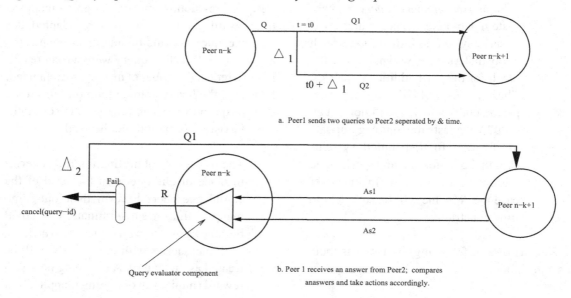

a. Peer1 sends two queries to Peer2 seperated by & time.

b. Peer 1 receives an answer from Peer2; compares anaswers and take actions accordingly.

for detecting/tolerating faults which will not be used if the fault-tolerant were not required (Laura, 2001). In the following we discuss briefly some alternatives to the described time redundancy technique.

Inspired by hardware redundancy, *Software Redundancy* techniques have emerged to tolerate software faults. It encompasses additional software programs, components, modules or codes in the system to support fault tolerance. Software redundancy could be used for tolerating software faults originating from requirement specification, design and/or coding errors. Different versions of the same software with the same functionality would be developed by different teams and possibly in different programming languages. Each software version would run on a separate machine, with same input. The program outputs are then compared for consistency.

Performing multiple computations in a dynamic environment such as P2P semantic knowledge sharing systems is difficult and subject to termination, thus depriving peers from opportunities to produce responses. A reasonable alternative would be the duplication of critical variables and/or blocks of code and comparing the output of these code blocks and variables at different stages of the execution of the same program.

Information or data redundancy, some times grouped with software redundancy, utilizes diverse data, i.e., variations in the input format or structure, to assist in fault tolerance. A data re-expression algorithm could be used to generate multiple formats of data with same content but different representations. The generated data, multiple identical queries in the context of P2P semantic knowledge sharing systems, is then used as input into different versions of the same programs or, software component, for detecting and tolerating faults.

One more way to enable P2P semantic knowledge sharing systems to be fault-tolerant is by using the *majority voting technique*, a well-known technique used for determining

consensus outcome from the results delivered by multiple computation sources. Consider the P2P semantic knowledge sharing system presented in Figure 11, where nodes represent peers, links represent mapping among peers and directed paths represented query answers to the query Q initiated by peer A.

The selection (de-selection) of a query result among multiple results returned from different translation paths by *query initiator* could by done using simple majority voting technique. The voting technique here would serve three purposes: (1) reduces number of answers to one answer, (2) increase the confidence in the query result since it is been asserted by the majority of mapping paths, and (3) increases the trust in the decision that will be made about correctness of the out-going mapping links.

In summary, there are various techniques for improving system fault-tolerance capability. Some of these techniques are well-known for handling faults in certain situations. As discussed above, the time redundancy, software block redundancy and voting techniques are more suitable than others for

Figure 11. Multiple answers use voting for consensus

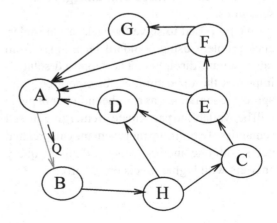

adding fault-tolerance to the P2P semantic knowledge sharing systems. Developing software, time and information redundancy based algorithms for tolerating faults in P2P semantic knowledge sharing systems, and carrying out empirical studies in order to determine the best possible usage of redundancy techniques for tolerating faults is a significant contribution to the science.

CONCLUSION

In this chapter, we identified one of the shortcomings of existing research on emergent semantics: current approaches fail to distinguish between permanent and transient semantic mapping faults. Instead, they treat all faults as permanent.

We identified a list of different situations that could cause non-permanent semantic mapping faults and classified them along temporal dimension.

We demonstrated that it is difficult to reach a complete state of emergent semantics among independent, heterogeneous and distributed local ontologies, unless the system can eliminate or reduce the impact of temporary semantic mapping faults. The reason is that treating all faults as permanent may result in the erroneous labeling of peers as having incompatible knowledge representations, which reduces the number of peers that can participate in emerging shared semantics.

We proposed to solve the lack of fault-tolerance problem using standard techniques from fault-tolerant discipline. The proposed solution improves the opportunities for emerging more agreeable semantics, as a higher number of peers will be available to participate in emerging shared semantics. Teaming up more semantically related peers with one another also could enable query answers with higher precision (recall).

FUTURE RESEACH DIRECTION

In addition to the demand for augmenting fault-tolerance capability, we believe that having more intelligent peers than those used in current emergent semantics system is another viable and open research area. Peers participating in the emergent semantic could be equipped with *learning* capability. They could make use of the discovered semantic affinity between their own concepts and concept from other peers' ontologies for better query routing answering.

Storing network *locations* of foreign concepts that are identified, during query processing and answering, as complementary concepts or properties to the peers' own concepts, constitute the learning capability peers lack today. Another important learning issue would be aligning or integrating semantically related foreign concepts into local ontologies. Peers should preserve their state. State maintenance refers to the endowment of peers with the ability to preserve the knowledge they acquire from the interaction with other peers in the network between sessions, i.e. between peers disconnection and reconnection to the network.

Investigating emergent semantics system performance would be another important issue to be considered in future research. This includes further study on query answer caching, overcoming point-to-point semantic mapping limitation without the need for query broadcasting.

Studying the effect of non-permanent semantic mapping faults in areas such as consensus formation, semantic Web services and semantic negotiation is an important matter worth investigating.

We consider the above-mentioned issues to be viable and open research subjects which need further study and attention from research communities.

ACKNOWLEDGMENT

I would like to thank Dr. Abdulghany Mohamed from Sprott School of Business, Carleton University for his valuable time, thoughts and discussions we had throughout writing this chapter.

REFERENCES

Aberer K., Cudre-Mauroux P., & Hauswirth, M. (2003). Start making sense: The chatty Web approach for global semantic agreements. *Journal of Web Semantics, 1*(1), 89-114.

Aberer K., Catarci T. et al. (2004). Emergent semantics systems. *In Lecture Notes in Computer Science, 3226*, 14-43.

Anghel L., Alexandrescu, D., & Nicolaidis, M. (2000). Evaluation of a soft error tolerance technique based on time and/or space redundancy. In Proceedings of *13th Symposium on Integrated Circuits and Systems Design*, IEEE Computer Society, 237 – 242.

Avizienis, A. (1995). The methodology of N-version programming. In M. R. Lyu (ed.), *Software fault tolerance*, Wiley, 23-46.

Axelrod R. (1997). The complexity of cooperation. Princeton University Press.

Bahceci E., Soysal O., & Sahin E. (2003). *A review: Pattern formation and adaptation in multi-robot systems. Report* CMU-RI-TR-03-43, Robotics Institute, Carnegie Mellon University.

Bondavalli A., Giandomenico F. D., & Grandoni, F. (2000). Threshold-based mechanisms to discriminate transient from intermittent faults. *IEEE Trans. on Computers, 49*(3), 230-45.

Bondavalli A., Chiaradonna, S., et al (1997). Discriminating fault rate and persistency to improve fault treatment. In *Digest of Papers. Twenty-Seventh Annual Intl. Symposium on Fault-Tolerant Computing*, 354-62.

Bonifacio M., Bouquet P., et al. (2002). KEx: A peer-to-peer solution for distributed knowledge management. In Karagiannis D., & Reimer U.(Eds.) *Practical aspects of knowledge management, 4th International Conference, LCNS*, Springer, 490-500.

Bouquet P., Giunchiglia F., et al (2003). C-OWL: Contextualizing ontologies. In *2nd Intl. Semantic Web Conf.*, 2870, 164-179. Springer: LNCS.

Castano S., Ferrara A., & Montanelli S. (2003). H-Match: An algorithm for dynamically matching ontologies in peer-based systems. In the *1st VLDB Int. Workshop on Semantic Web and Databases (SWDB)*, 231-250.

Dupont E., Nicolaidis M., & Rohr P. (2002). Embedded robustness IPs for transient-error-free ICs. *IEEE Design & Test, 19*(3), 56-70.

Fergus P., Mingkhwan A., et al.(2003). Distributed emergent semantics in P2P networks. In *Second IASTED Intl. Conf. on Information and Knowledge Sharing*,75-82.

McGuinees, D. L. (2003). *Ontologies come of age. Book chapter in spinning the Semantic Web: Bringing the World Wide Web to its full potential*, Fensel D. Hendler J. Lieberman H., et al. (eds). The MIT Press.

Gal, A. (2001). Semantic interoperability in information services: Experiencing with CoopWARE. *SIGMOD Record, 28*(1), 68-75.

Ghidini, C., & Giunchiglia, F. (2001). Local models semantics, or contextual reasoning = Locality + Compatibility. *Artificial Intelligence Archive, 127*(2), 221-259.

Glushko, R. J., & McGrath, T. (2005). Document engineering, Cambridge, Massachusetts: The MIT Press.

Gomez-Perez, A., Fernandez-Lopez, M., & Corcho, O. (2003). Ontological engineering. London: Springer Publishing.

Gruber, T. R. (1993). A translation approach to portable ontology specifications. *Knowledge Acquisition Archive, 5*(2), 199-220.

Guarino, N. (1998). Formal ontology and information systems. *Proceedings of Formal Ontology in Information Systems,* 3-15.

Gutierrez, C., Hurtado, C., & Vaisman, A. (2005). Temporal RDF. *The Semantic Web: Research and Applications, Second European Semantic Web Conference, ESWC 2005. Proceedings Lecture Notes in Computer Science, 3532,* 93-107

Haase P., Broekstra J., et al. (2004). Bibster -- A semantics-based bibliographic peer-to-peer system. In *Third Intl. Semantic Web Conf. (ISWC),* 122-136.

Halevy A., Ives Z., et al. (2003). Piazza: Mediation and integration infrastructure for Semantic Web data. *In the Intl. Worldwide Web Conf. WWW-03.*

Hurtado, C., & Vaisman, A. (2006). Reasoning with temporal constraints in RDF. *Principles and Practice of Semantic Web Reasoning. 4th International Workshop, PPSWR 2006. Revised Selected Papers Lecture Notes in Computer Science,. 4187,*164-78.

Larry, K., Hanjo, J., & Wooju, K. (2006). Emergent semantics in knowledge sifter: An evolutionary search agent based on Semantic Web services. *Journal on Data Semantics 6,* 187-209.

Laura, L. P. (2001). Software fault tolerance techniques and implementation. Norwood, Mass Publication.

Mawlood-Yunis, A-R., Weiss, M., & Santoro, N. (2007). Fault classification in P2P semantic mapping. *In Workshop on Semantic Web for Collaborative Knowledge Acquisition (SWeCKa)} at Intl. Conf. on Artificial Intelligence (IJCAI).*

Mena E., Illarramendi, A., et al. (2000). OBSERVER: An approach for query processing in global information systems based on interpretation across pre-existing ontologies. *Distributed and Parallel Databases, 8*(2), 223-71.

Mika, P. (2005). Ontologies are us: A unified model of social networks and semantics. In *4th Intl. Semantic Web Conference,* 522-36.

Naiman, C. F., & Ouskel, A.M. (1995). A classification of semantic conflicts in heterogeneous database systems. *Journal of Organizational Computing, 5*(2), 167-193.

Noy, N. F., & Musen, M. A. (2004a). Ontology versioning in an ontology management framework. *IEEE Intelligent Systems, 19*(4), 6-13.

Noy, N. F., & Klein, M. (2004b). Ontology evolution: Not the same as schema evolution. *Knowledge and Information Systems, 6*(4), 428-440.

Ouksel, A.M. (1999). Ontologies are not the panacea in data integration: A flexible coordinator to mediate context construction. *Distributed and Parallel Databases, 15*(1), 7-35.

Paradhan, D. K. (1996). *Fault-tolerant computing system design.* Prentice-Hall PTR publication.

Papalilo E., Friese, et al. (2005). Trust shaping: Adapting trust establishment and management to application requirements in a service-oriented grid environment. In *Proc. 4th Intl. Conf. on Grid and Cooperative Computing (GCC),* LNCS 3795, 47-58,

Pizza, M., Strigini L., et al. (1998). Optimal discrimination between transient and permanent faults. In *Third IEEE Intl. High-Assurance Systems Engineering Symposium,* 214-223.

Ram, S., & Park, J. (2004). Semantic conflict resolution ontology (SCROL): An ontology for detecting and resolving data and schema-level semantic conflicts. *IEEE Transactions on Knowledge and Data Engineering, 16*(2), 189-202.

Robert. Mc., et al. (2005). Mapping maintenance for data integration systems. In *Proceedings of the 31st international conference on VLDB*, 1018-1029.

Roddick, J. F. (1995). A survey of schema versioning issues for database systems. *Information and Software Technology, 37*(7), 383-393.

Rousset, M. C. (2004). Small can be beautiful in the Semantic Web. In *Third Intl. Semantic Web Conf.*, 6-16.

Rousset, P., Chatalic, et al. (2006). Somewhere: A scalable P2P infrastructure for querying distributed ontologies. *5th Intl. Conf. on Ontologies Databases and Applications of Semantics*, 698-703.

Staab, S. (2002). Emergent semantics. *IEEE Intelligent Systems, 17*(1), 78-86.

Staab, S.(2005) Social networks applied. *IEEE Intelligent Systems, 20*(1), 80-93.

Staab, S., & Stuckenschmidt, S. (2006). *Semantic Web and peer-to-peer*, Springer-Verlag, Berlin Heidelberg, Germany.

Stephens, L.M., & Huhns, M.N.(2001). Consensus ontologies. Reconciling the semantics of Web pages and agents. In *IEEE Internet Computing, 5*(5), 92-95.

Tempich, C., Staab, S., & Wranik, A. (2004). RE-MINDIN': Semantic query routing in peer-to-peer networks based on social metaphors. *In 13th Intl. Conf. on the World Wide Web*, 640-649.

Tempich, C., Pinto, H.S., et al. (2005). An argumentation ontology for distributed, loosely-controlled and evolving engineering processes of ontologies (DILIGENT). *In Second European Semantic Web Conf. (ESWC)*, LNCS *3532*, 241-56.

Wu, J., & Axelrod, R.(1995). How to cope with noise in the iterated prisoner's dilemma. *Journal of Conflict Resolution, 39*(1), 183-189.

Yinglong, M., et al. (2007). A timing analysis model for ontology evolutions based on distributed environments. In (Zhi-Hua Zhou, Hang Li, Qiang Yang (Eds.): *Advances in Knowledge Discovery and Data Mining, 11th Pacific-Asia Conference, PAKDD, LNCS 4426*, 183-192.

Zhu, H., Madnick, S. E., & Siegel, M.D. (2004). Effective data integration in the presence of temporal semantic conflicts. In *11th Intl. Symposium on Temporal Representation and Reasoning*, 109-114.

SUGGESTED ADDITIONAL READING

Antoniou G., & Harmelen F. V. (2004). *A Semantic Web primer*. Cambridge, Massachusetts, The MIT Press, USA.

Berners-Lee T. (2000). Weaving the Web: The original design and ultimate destiny of the World Wide Web. New York, USA: Collins Publishing.

Bonifacio M., Bouquet P., et al. (2004). Peer-mediated distributed knowledge management. Abecker A., Dignum, V., & Elst L. V. (Ed.), *Agent-Mediated Knowledge Management: International Symposium Amkm*, Springer, 31-47.

Cardoso J., & Sheth A. P. (Eds.) (2006). Semantic Web services, processes, and applications, Springer publication, USA.

Elmagarmid A., Rusinkiewicz, M., & Sheth A. (1999). Management of heterogeneous autonomous database systems, San Francisco, CA: Morgan Kaufmann Publication.

Klein M., Kiryakov A. et al. (2002). Finding and characterizing changes in ontologies. In *Conceptual Modeling – ER, 21st International Conference on Conceptual Modeling* Proceedings, 79-89.

Lacy, L. W. (2005). OWL: Representing information using the Web ontology language, Victoria, BC, Canada.

Mawlood-Yunis, A-R., Weiss W., & Santoro, N. (2006). Issues for robust consensus building in P2P networks. In *Intl. Workshop on Ontology Content and Evaluation in Enterprise (OnToContent)*, *LNCS 4278*, 1020-1028.

Mena E., Kashyap V., et al. (2000). Imprecise answers in distributed environments: Estimation of information loss for multi-ontology-based query processing. *Journal of Cooperative Information Systems*, *9*(4), 403-25.

Stuckenschmidt H., & Harmelen F. V. (2005). Information sharing on the Semantic Web. Germany: Springer publication.

Spaccapietra, Stefano (Ed.). *Journal on data semantics*, *1-6*. Springer Publishing.

ENDNOTES

[a] Emergent Semantic depends on the adaptive query routing algorithm. Checking for semantically related peers are embedded in the method. There is little chance for *unrelated peers to interact.*

[b] http://www.w3.org/XML/

[c] http://www.w3.org/RDF/

[d] http://iridia.ulb.ac.be/~mdorigo/ACO/ACO.html

[e] http://del.icio.us/

[f] http://www.flickr.com

[g] For information on instance data and schemas, we refer interested readers to (http://jena.sourceforge.net/ontology/common-problems.html#aBox-tBox; http://www.w3.org/TR/owl-guide/).

[h] (Noy, 2004b) argues that the issue of versioning and evolving are same in the context of ontology mapping. What we see as important is that both versioning and evolving introduce modifications to the existing ontology.

[i] see these following links as well: http://www.w3.org/TR/owl-guide/, http://jena.sourceforge.net/ontology/common-problems.html#aBox-tBox

[j] Note that this weather ontology is a partial ontology with instances

[k] If multiple peers cooperate and misbehave intentionally, this will create a different type of fault known as *Byzantine* fault, which is not considered in this chapter.

[l] Peers join the network by crafting their own mappings. Thus, it is reasonable to assume that they start with correct mappings. It is when ontologies change or evolve, mapping faults become a serious issue. Similar assumption is made by (Robert, 2005).

[m] The query must stop here, otherwise an infinite forwarding loop would be possible.

[n] A successful query result implies a successful series of mappings.

APPENDIX: QUESTION FOR DISCUSSION

Basic:

1. Define the semantic heterogeneity and semantic interoperability problems.
2. Define the concept of semantic reconciliation.
3. What are semantic mapping faults?
4. What is the difference between a semantic mapping fault and a *temporal* semantic mapping fault?
5. What are advantages/disadvantages of common upper ontologies?
6. What are advantages/disadvantages of local ontologies?
7. Why do some researchers prefer simple, less expressive ontologies over complex ontologies for open and dynamic environments?

Intermediate:

1. Name two consequences of failing to tolerate temporal semantic mapping faults.
2. How could peers extend their local ontologies using the proposed fault-tolerant emergent semantics?
3. Can you think of causes of temporal semantic mapping faults other than those described in the chapter?

Advanced:

1. Can you describe a technique, other than time redundancy, to solve temporal semantic mapping faults?
2. Using the provided algorithm, is it possible to identify precisely the cause of temporal faults any time a fault occurs? How important is that?
3. Should we design a set of criteria for selecting query answers, and what are they?
4. How would you measure the effect of non-permanent semantic mapping faults on emergent semantics?
5. Create a simulation model for transient semantic mapping faults?

Chapter VIII
Association Analytics for Network Connectivity in a Bibliographic and Expertise Dataset

Boanerges Aleman-Meza
University of Georgia, USA

Sheron L. Decker
University of Georgia, USA

Delroy Cameron
University of Georgia, USA

I. Budak Arpinar
University of Georgia, USA

ABSTRACT

This chapter highlights the benefits of semantics for analysis of the collaboration network in a bibliography dataset. Metadata of publications was used for extracting keywords and terms, which can be the starting point towards building a taxonomy of topics. The aggregated effect of the topics over all publications of an author can be used to determine his/her areas of expertise. We also highlight the value of using a taxonomy of topics in searching experts on a given topic.

INTRODUCTION

Large-scale bibliography datasets are becoming increasingly available for use by Semantic Web applications. For example, DBLP is a high-quality bibliography of Computer Science literature. Its data is available in XML but it has also been made available in RDF as DR2Q-generated RDF data (Bizer, 2003), also in the SwetoDblp ontology of DBLP data (http://lsdis.cs.uga.edu/projects/semdis/swetodblp/), and Andreas Harth's DBLP dataset in RDF (sw.deri.org/~aharth/2004/07/dblp/). DBLP data has been used to analyze co-authorship, collaborations, degrees of separation and other social network analysis measures. We claim that further and more detailed analysis is possible by using semantically marked-up data. In this paper, we describe a study of network connectivity in bibliography data. Our work expands upon earlier studies that have used subsets of DBLP data for analysis of collaborations in the field of databases (Elmacioglu & Lee, 2005; Nascimento et al., 2003). The dataset we use includes not only the data of publications in database field. It also includes data of publications in areas such as Artificial Intelligence, Web and Semantic Web.

Further analysis of bibliography data is possible when information of topics or research areas is available. Metadata of publications from DBLP can be used for the creation of a dataset of topics in Computer Science. In addition, keywords and terms that appear in abstracts of publications can be used for finding the most common topics or research areas. Based on this, we were able to identify potential terms to be used in building a taxonomy of Computer Science topics. The main benefit is that when these topics are suggested to human, the time required to build a taxonomy of topics could be shortened. Additionally, the suggested terms come from (and reflect) the domain in question (e.g., Computer Science). The identified terms can be analyzed to determine which ones appear only in the last few years. This can lead to the identification of possible new topics or emerging research trends. After the topics of a publication have been identified, it can be said that all authors of a paper have (at least some) knowledge on such topics. Thus, if we look at an author in particular, it is possible to determine the topics on which s/he has expertise/knowledge based on her/his publication track. This is the basis of our method to identify researchers that have high expertise on certain topics. We perform a study to validate this measure of expertise against well-known lists of recognized researchers (e.g., based on available lists of ACM fellows and IEEE fellows). We argue that this type of study can be done with existing Semantic Web technologies that are able to handle large datasets. We also describe the datasets used, which are freely available online.

In summary, the objectives of this chapter are to highlight the benefits of using semantics for analysis of the underlying collaboration network in a bibliography dataset. We describe how keywords and terms can be extracted and linked to metadata of publications. Then, we rely on the aggregated effect of terms/keywords of all publications of an author to determine his/her areas of expertise. We explain how analysis of terms and keywords of publications can help human to create a taxonomy of topics by identifying the most common terms as well as terms commonly occurring together. The use of topics to glean expertise of researchers is validated when top experts on certain topics compared quite well with researchers that have received awards such as ACM Fellows. In doing so, we highlight the value of using a taxonomy of topics to better match expertise of researchers.

BACKGROUND

Bibliography datasets have been used to measure how authors are connected, publication output, citations, etc. The motivation of such analysis typically is gaining insight of how a community evolves and the characteristics of the social or collaborative interactions among authors. Many techniques for analysis of bibliography data have their roots or are related to social networks analysis, which focuses on the analysis of patterns of relationships among people, organizations, states and such social entities.

A quite common analysis in networks is that of determining whether the small-world phenomenon exists. If it is the case, then most elements of a network can be reached, on average, by a small number of links. The intuition comes from the "six degrees of separation" experiment by Milgram (1967). Many networks where humans participate exhibit a small-world phenomenon. Bibliography data is no exception. It could be said that a network (where humans participate) that does not exhibit such phenomenon might require revising whether the data has been correctly extracted. Thus, we verify in our analysis that the collaboration network indeed exhibits a social network phenomenon.

Related efforts in the literature that have addressed analysis of publications include analysis of publication venues in the field of Databases (Elmacioglu & Lee, 2005; Nascimento et al., 2003). In the area of Semantic Web, Golbeck et al. (2006) addressed analysis of co-authorship, citation, and affiliation for authors of ISWC conferences. Similarly, analysis of communities in the Semantic Web has taken place by querying a search engine with names of researchers and research topics to determine associations between people and concepts (Staab et al., 2005). Their focus was more on visualization and data collection as compared as our approach highlighting the benefits of the use of explicit semantics (as defined by Sheth et al. (2005)).

We exploit the value of relating keywords and terms to authors in publications for the purpose of determining areas of expertise of researchers. Al-Sudani et al. (2006) described this idea intended for finding knowledgeable personnel in certain areas of interest. However, they used a much smaller dataset of publications. In fact, they point out that data collection/extraction is a time-consuming task. We believe that our approach circumvents such problem by using the metadata itself of publications for selecting URLs that contain keywords and terms metadata to be extracted (from other Web sources). Some manual work has to be done, in our case, for the creation of a web-scrapper for a specific web source such as ACM Digital Library. The advantage is that once such metadata is extracted, it can be safely assumed that it is not going to change. That is, the keywords of a published article will always remain the same. However, we note that other methods can bring additional useful metadata such as tagging.

Analysis of expertise of people has been addressed for finding experts in one of the tracks of the Text Retrieval Conferences (TREC, http://trec.nist.gov). Our work differs in the sense that in the TREC track, it is expected to analyze a corpus of documents (e.g., web pages) to determine human experts in various topics. For example, the "Spree" system finds experts by building profiles derived from documents (Metze et al., 2007). In our work, we use metadata of research publications instead. Sriharee and Punnarut (2007) use a combination of extracted data together with Web content to determine associations between people in academic environment that leads to find experts or groups of experts. Associations between people have been used to exploit referral information for finding experts (Kautz et al., 1997).

The benefits of using semantics for expressing expertise or areas of interest for persons have been highlighted in a variety of scenarios and applications (Aleman-Meza et al., 2007). In fact, the ExpertFinder Initiative intends to identify use cases, challenges, techniques, etc. for semantics-based representation, retrieval, and processing of expertise data (rdfweb.org/topic/ExpertFinder). There is a close relationship between determining topics of papers to the use of such topics in determining expertise of authors. In addition, the topics of papers can be used, together with their date, to find trends in research areas (Decker et al., 2007; Tho et al., 2003).

ANALYTICS IN THE BIOBLIOGRAPHY DATASET

We selected several of the techniques for network analysis that were part of earlier studies of the Databases community (Elmacioglu & Lee, 2005; Nascimento et al., 2003). However, instead of simply replicating their work with an updated dataset, we aim at demonstrating that further insight is possible by using RDF-encoded data. The data we use comes or is derived from DBLP. Where indicated, we used a subset of DBLP publications in the areas of Artificial Intelligence, Databases, Data Mining, Information Retrieval, Web and Semantic Web. We will refer to this subset as DBLP-subset.

Statistics about Authors

Centrality. There are known methods to identify participants in a network that are highly connected to the others. The *closeness centrality* measure identifies how close an author is, on average, to all other authors in the network. Authors with low

closeness values are connected to many authors within short path distances. Hence, it could be said that their 'influence' in the network is high. We computed centrality as the average of the shortest path that an author has to each author. Table 1 lists the top 10 *central* authors from the largest connected component in DBLP-subset. The value of centrality is computed as the average of each (shortest) path length from an author to other authors in the network. The first column lists authors with their centrality value computed by simply taking their name as they appear in DBLP.

It has been noted that DBLP does not have unique ID for authors (Elmacioglu & Lee, 2005). However, the name of an author plays the role of a primary key. For the cases when two different persons have the same name, DBLP appends a numerical value in the name to differentiate the two entries in DBLP. For the cases when the same person is referred to in two (or more) forms, then DBLP explicitly relates such names (i.e., aliases) as being the same person. We refer to these as 'same-as' in spirit of the 'sameAs' property of the OWL vocabulary. In fact, the explicit representation of the data uses such *sameAs* property. Common reasons for people having two names are the use of a shortened name (e.g., Tim and Timothy) and changes due to addition of hyphened name or middle initial. There are very few entries in

Table 1. Top 10 centrality authors in DBLP-subset, with and without same-as information

Centrality using name		Centrality using *same-as* information	
Value	**Author Name**	**Value**	**Author Name**
4.0578	Gio WiederHold	3.9859	Gio WiederHold
4.1527	Richard T. Snodgrass	4.0517	Umeshwar Dayal
4.1900	Umeshwar Dayal	4.0616	Richard T. Snodgrass
4.2020	Philip A. Bernstein	4.0825	Elisa Bertino
4.2025	Elisa Bertino	4.1028	Christos Faloutsos
4.2087	Christos Faloutsos	4.1335	Philip A. Bernstein
4.2232	Kenneth A. Ross	4.1431	Christian S. Jensen
4.2299	Hector Garcia-Molina	4.1487	Jiawei Han
4.2340	David Maier	4.1535	Kenneth A. Ross
4.2427	Christian S. Jensen	4.1605	Erich J. Neuhold

DBLP data for authors with more than one name – probably due to the difficulty of detecting such ambiguities automatically. For example, Aleman-Meza et al. (2006) addressed reconciling entities across and within DBLP and FOAF data. Another problem is distinguishing between people that have same name (i.e., name collision). Yin et al. (2007) have addressed that problem and shown examples of names of people in DBLP that are in fact different persons in real life. Hence, it is quite important to make use of information stating that two names refer to the same person. Otherwise, the publications of an author that has two names would be incorrectly counted. Similarly, co-authorship measures would miss out due to incorrectly counting the right number of co-authors. We compared results obtained when 'same-as' information is used in computing the centrality of authors. The second column of Table 1 shows the top 10 central authors when *same-as* information is used. It can be seen how various of the authors have changed positions yet their value of centrality of a smaller number indicates that their paths to other authors, are, on the average shorter than before. Table 2 lists examples of authors that appear in DBLP-subset with more than one name. Each name appears with its own computed value of centrality. In this table, it is noticeable how much of a change exists for the case of Alon Y. Halevy when both of his names spellings are considered. In the case of Timothy W. Finin, his centrality is also smaller but his position among all computed centrality values

moves from 94 to 101. This happens because the positions of authors computed using same-as information affect not only authors that have more than one name, but also affect other authors in the network. This is also evident in the second column in Table 1.

Collaborators Distribution. The distribution of number of collaborators per author, shown in Figure 1, clearly exhibits the power-law tail. This indicates that a large number of authors have a small number of collaborators (up to around 10). A much smaller number of authors have around 100 collaborators. A small number of authors have many publications (e.g., over 150). They would be the most likely authors to have many collaborators. Overall, the distribution of collaborators per authors indicates that the data exhibits a small-world phenomenon.

Collaboration Strength. Lastly, we measured the collaboration strength among authors. This method helps on identifying pairs of authors that collaborate frequently. For example, is expected that pairs of researchers with highest collaboration strength are those who work at the same organization for a long time and collaborate frequently. Instead of simply finding authors with highest frequent co-authors, we use a method that takes into account the number of authors in a paper as well as the number of papers that two people co-authored (Newman, 2001). The method adds a weight of $1/(n-1)$ to the collaboration strength of two authors for each paper they co-authored together (n is the number of authors in a paper).

Table 2. Examples of improved centrality score by considering the 'same-as' information available.

Using 'same-as' information		Without 'same-as' information	
Name of researcher	Centrality value	Names of researcher in the dataset	Centrality value
Alon Y. Halevy (37)	4.2707	Alon Y. Levy (51)	4.4026
		Alon Y. Halevy (111)	4.5498
Timothy W. Finin (101)	4.4051	Timothy W. Finin (94)	4.5123
		Tim Finin (1430)	5.0747

Figure 1. Distribution of collaborators per author

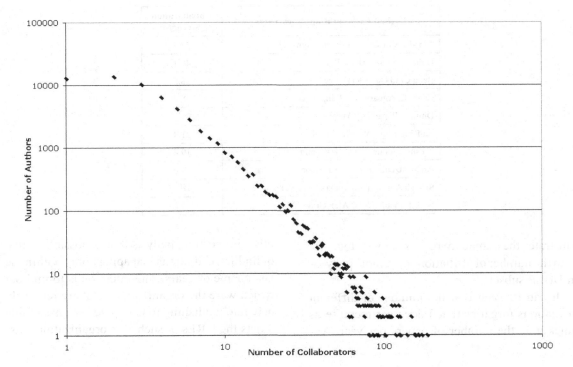

This measure captures quite well the collaboration among authors where a publication has very few authors. The assumption is that their collaboration strength is higher than in the case of publications with a large number of co-authors. Given that the computed collaboration strength for any two co-authors is symmetric, we show in Table 3 the highest ten pairs of collaborating researchers in the DBLP-subset. As expected, most of the collaborating researchers (in Table 3) work/worked at the same organization. Only a few of them do not work at the same place. Information of strength of collaboration is of importance for applications such as determining conflict of interest (Aleman-Meza et al., 2006) where it is need to determine the level of interaction between participants. It is also possible to use collaboration strength to find small groups of people that frequently work together.

Statistics about Papers

Common statistics about papers include computing the number of papers per authors and number of papers per year. However, our intention is to demonstrate that other statistics can be computed with a dataset represented using Semantic Web techniques. Hence, we chose to determine the number of different affiliations per year. This requires authors of papers to have affiliation information. Data from DBLP alone does not contain such information. We used the SwetoDblp ontology, which is created from DBLP data and includes affiliation data for some of the authors. SwetoDblp extracts affiliation of authors based on their homepage (whenever possible). DBLP contains homepage information for little over 10K authors. SwetoDblp extracts affiliation information for 7K of them (as of June 2007). Figure 2

Table 3. Highest ten pairs of collaborating researchers in DBLP-subset

Highest Collaborating Researchers	Collaboration Strength
Amr-El Abbadi – Divyakant Agrawal	57.3
Didier Dubois – Henri Prade	42.1
Beng Chin Ooi – Kian-Lee Tan	28.5
Charu C. Aggarwal – Philip S. Yu	28.4
Dimitris Papadias – Yufei Tao	21.4
Ee-Peng Lim – Wee-Keong Ng	21.4
Katsushi Inoue – Itsuo Takanami	19.4
Paolo Atzeni – Riccardo Torlone	19.0
Rakesh Agrawal – Ramakrishnan Srikant	18.0
Nick J. Fiddian – W. Alex Gray	17.8

illustrates the number of papers per year together with the number of affiliations of authors per year in DBLP-subset.

It can be seen that the number of different affiliations (organizations) does not increase as quickly as the number of papers per year. An-other interesting analysis that is possible is that of finding affiliations that appear only within the last couple of years. The intention is to find out which were the organizations that are relatively new into publishing in Computer Science. Table 4 lists the URLs of such *new* organizations (us-

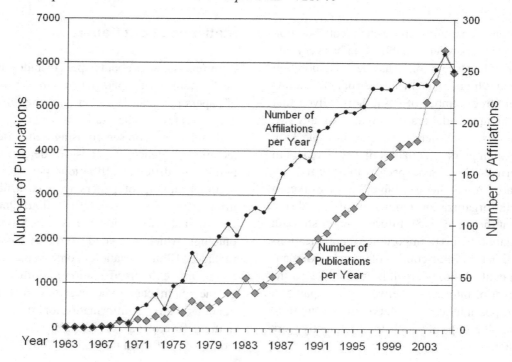

Table 4. Affiliations identified as only appearing within the last three years

Relatively Newly Appearing Affiliations
www.curtin.edu.au, www.fudan.edu.cn, www.hartford.edu, www.isu.edu, www.nuaa.edu.cn, www.qc.edu, www.research.ibm.com/beijing, www.seu.edu.cn, www.uoguelph.ca, www.ustc.edu.cn, www.zjnu.edu.cn, www.zju.edu.cn

ing data of DBLP-subset). These results could be more accurate if the homepage (and affiliation) of authors were completely available and up to date. In fact, only about 1.8% of authors in DBLP have *homepage* information. This is a good example where semantic techniques depend on availability of data to fully demonstrate newer capabilities. For example, if the information of organizations also is related to geographic data, it could be possible to provide further insight by displaying information on a map.

LINKING BIBLIOGRAPHY DATA TO EXPERTISE DATA

Identification of researchers that have expertise on a specific research topic could be of great value. The value of extracting expertise data has been noted in other efforts (Hezinger & Lawrence, 2004; Mika, 2005). For example, the National Science Foundation (NSF) is an agency that funds projects in a wide arrange of research areas. They may wish to inquire on the productivity of their funded research with respect to specific research areas. Identifying experts on topics could help validate that their funding within certain areas has had a positive/productive impact in the research community. Moreover, a researcher on a new area could determine which publications are of importance for background information based on which researchers were identified to be experts in the area. To help facilitate the discovery of such individuals, publications entities in a RDF dataset can be related to topics within a taxonomy. The authors of papers can then be implicitly related

to topics for the purpose of identifying who is knowledgeable or has expertise on specific topics. The assumption is that all authors of a paper have expertise on the topics of their papers.

In our previous work, we created a taxonomy of computer science topics, mostly in areas of Databases, Web and Semantic Web (Decker et al., 2007). The majority of topics within the taxonomy were based on brainstorming, discussion and feedback amongst several colleagues. However, we feel that the taxonomy was limited in regards to only the knowledge we pertain. Therefore, the decision was made to construct a taxonomy from scratch using data extraction methods from reliable computer science sources in order to obtain relevant terms from the data itself. Arguably, this would allow for the taxonomy to include past, present and emerging topics. At a later stage, the taxonomy was manually revised and adjusted based on the AKT ontology (Shadbolt et al., 2004) and CoMMa ontology (Gandon, 2001), both of which include descriptions of concepts of topic areas in Computer Science.

Bootstrapping the Creation of a Taxonomy of Topics in Computer Science

Building a thorough taxonomy of topics in Computer Science is an arduous task due to the human effort involved. There are classification systems readily available that could have been re-used in our approach. For instance, ACM's Computing Classification System (www.acm.org/class/1998/) provides a categorization of computer science related topics intended to reflect the current state of the field. It contains eleven primary research areas each including numerous subtopics. However, the system is comprised of a very "broad" four-level tree of topics that would not be very beneficial recognizing topics that are manifesting today. For example, a publication entitled "Semantic analytics on social networks: experiences in addressing the problem of conflict of interest detection" was classified with ACM's CCS with the primary topic 'Information Systems' because no other topics such as social networks, semantic analytics, or conflict of interest were available. Therefore, we developed our own taxonomy of computer science topics that would help identify "newer" terms. Identification of newer terms is advantageous for the purpose of recognizing possible emerging trends that might be included in a taxonomy of topics.

In order to ensure that our taxonomy was comprised of the most relevant topics, we decided to use extracted data from DBLP. A number of publication venues (over 50 conference series and journals) were selected that include areas of Web, Databases, Semantic Web, and Artificial Intelligence. We selected papers in such publication venues for extracting data that will be used in creating a taxonomy of topics. The main aspect of our approach is how we retrieved metadata of papers with the use of the *electronic edition* (ee) URL of individual papers (in DBLP). URLs having prefixes such as dx.doi.org/10.1016, doi.acm.org, or doi.ieeecomputerscociety.org were crawled to retrieve "keywords" and "abstracts" for the purpose of identifying a surplus of terms that are related to computer science. We experimented using metadata of keywords and abstracts separately. Using keywords alone brings data with

added value as compared to the research areas included in ACM's Computing Classification System. On the other hand, by incorporating terms extracted from the abstracts the method aided in identifying "newer" terms. The extraction of terms from abstracts identifies phrases and terms from a given input text. Instead of implementing a specific technique for term extraction, we used the Term Extraction capability provided by Yahoo! API (Term Extraction v1, developer.yahoo.com). We define newer terms as terms that have not appeared within abstracts of publications before a certain year, in this case we selected the year 2005. Table 5 lists examples of terms that best illustrate newer terms identified with our approach. This was accomplished by determining which papers within our dataset labeled each term as keywords or included the term within its abstract and then retrieved the dates of those publications. A benefit of this approach is that it can keep up with changes in the field. In fact, Hepp (2007) pointed out the need for ontology engineering methods to quickly reflect domain changes to keep ontologies up to update. Our approach is based on whatever terms are contained in the data (keywords and abstracts) instead of creating a taxonomy by only brainstorming or similar methods. Hence, our intent is to not limit the taxonomy with just personal knowledge of topics in the field. Additionally, our method uses the metadata of keywords and abstracts, without having to process the whole document content.

Our approach retrieved more than 280 potential topics to consider for building the taxonomy. However, methods were used to narrow the results list because several of the terms and phrases were not relevant to computer science. As a means

Table 5. Some of the identified terms appearing on year 2005 and afterwards

Friendship, grid middleware, grid technology, phishing, protein structures, service oriented architecture (SOA), social network analysis, spam, wikipedia

Table 6. Few of the top terms identified within last few years

Topic	1998	1999	2000	2001	2002	2003	2004	2005	2006
Algorithm(s)	87	99	111	89	219	222	381	418	608
Classifier(s)	0	7	1	2	33	30	47	80	94
Data Mining	12	10	20	13	46	62	88	104	184
Databases	13	17	19	19	28	32	43	53	63
Semantic Web	0	0	0	4	13	24	102	85	96
Semantics	19	16	26	22	28	24	90	75	86
Web Service(s)	0	0	0	0	4	2	67	82	69
XML	0	4	4	11	22	20	36	58	54

to retain the most common research topics accumulated, we kept a record of how many times each potential topic appeared. This allowed us to identify terms and phrases that were highly used as keywords and words within abstracts. Table 6 lists ten of the most frequently identified terms within the last few years.

In identifying some of the most frequently appearing, we were able to make three key observations pertaining to the results. First, we noticed that terms can be covered in a wide arrange of areas. Therefore, this may constitute for an extremely high volume count of a term compared to other terms. For example, the term *Algorithms* has become a very broad term that is not only used as a reference to a specific research area but also as a means of defining or describing a particular method or technique. This is probably the reason why it appears so many times. Secondly, for a term such as *Databases*, which one would expect to appear more times than shown, we discovered that the total number of appearances is relatively small due to the large amount of synonyms used to represent this particular term. For example, data base, data-bases, database management system, database management systems, and DBMS. Hence, if *Databases* is a topic in a taxonomy, then its synonyms should be added as alternate spellings of the term. Thirdly, we were able to identify broader terms, such as the term *Semantics*,

which has been used in literature for several years. Although this term has been long used, we were able to detect related terms that have emerged within recent years, case in point being the term *Semantic Web*. This shows that the total number of appearances for these broader terms could be due to newer terms that are related to terms that have been used for a longer time.

The structure of our taxonomy was put together by first determining which topics are related. Our approach began by first retrieving all the URLs of the publications of each term from which the terms were included within. We then added each URL into a *set* for each term. Relationships among terms were identified using measures calculated from the intersection of the sets of two terms divided by the union of the sets. This would produce a measure ranging from 0 (which implies the two topics are not related) to 1. Pairs of terms with a value above 0.05 were considered to be related terms. The identification of relationships aids in building a tree-level organization of topics that can later turn into a taxonomy. Figure 3 illustrates examples of topics and their identified relations. For example, human can use this information to explicitly define *subtopic-of* relationships such as "XQuery *subtopic-of* XML." Similarly, human might decide that certain links or nodes should be just removed. Other approaches have done similar work in identifying relationships of top-

Figure 3. Snippet of identified closely related terms

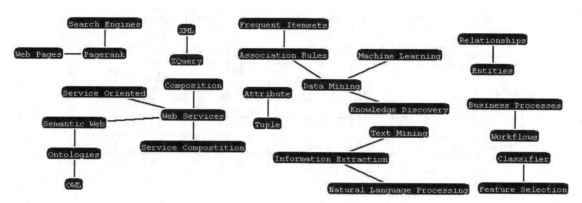

ics. In the work by Mika (2005), research topics were identified specifically from the interests of researchers within a Semantic Web community. The associations between the topics were based on the number of researchers who have an interest in the given pair of topics. Our approach instead identifies computer science topics by means of using the DBLP dataset and further data extraction, whereas in their work the topics were already known based on the supplied interests of researchers from FOAF. The work of Velardi et al. (2007) is an example of research on taxonomy learning. Similarly, TaxaMiner framework is intended to bootstrap building a taxonomy (Kashyap et al., 2005). In our work, we intend to demonstrate that the basic steps for suggesting terms in building a taxonomy can be achieved with off-the-shelf tools available on the Web such as Yahoo! Term Extraction. However, we are short of using the whole DBLP catalog as the effort to build a taxonomy of all Computer Science topics is significant.

Measuring Expertise

A dataset abundant with publication data is important for accurately characterizing the knowledge areas and/or expertise of a researcher. The greater the number of publications that can be linked to various topics, the more accurately "Expertise Profiles" can be captured and represented for a researcher. We exploit this principle in order to obtain rich and accurate expertise profiles for each researcher. It is noteworthy to emphasize that the publication venue of a publication is also helpful in determining the commensurate weight of a publication. For example, a workshop publication might have lesser impact than an article in a high impact journal. Existing data of publication-impact of various publication venues (conferences, journals, etc) thus play a role in determining the expertise of researchers. In fact, both the publication venues and the topics of expertise organized hierarchically have the characteristics of providing further information through richer queries than that of traditional database systems. The hierarchical organization of topics in the taxonomy is a dimension for complex querying (Fagin et al., 2005).

In our previous work, we detailed an approach for measuring expertise in order to find relevant reviewers for Program Committee (PC) membership in a Peer-Review process (Cameron, 2007). Such expertise measure considered the number of publications in developing the profile of a researcher. In addition, the impact of the publication venues was also taken into account. The use of a taxonomy of topics provided the additional benefits of organizing topics in a hierarchy for querying and/or aggregation. An evaluation of such approach yielded plausible results through comparison with PCs of past conferences. However, a thorough evaluation of methods that compute expertise of researchers is a challenging task due to the many factors in which expertise can be compared (many of which are of subjective nature). We expand the evaluation of measuring expertise by exploiting the availability of bibliography data. This can be achieved by comparing detected top *experts* by the system against experts or influential individuals that are determined (or selected) by humans.

Comparison with 'Social' Measures of Technical Achievements and Recognitions

Recognitions of outstanding research accomplishments are an important aspect of many research communities. Professional associations such as the Association of Computing Machinery (ACM) and IEEE recognize distinguished fellows annually across a wide variety of areas in Computer Science. IEEE has a history of distinction of deciding with some unanimity those worthy of recognition across many areas of Engineering and Technology at large. We perceive these organizations as credible sources for validating experts. However, newer forms of recognition include sites such as Wikipedia (www.wikipedia.org). The content of Wikipedia is compiled from a large number of participants. However, the mechanisms in Wikipedia make it extremely difficult to create (and keep) a new Wikipedia entry for a person. That is, a Wikipedia page about a person can be created only if such person is arguably famous, has an important position, has important achievements, etc. Hence, we assume that Wikipedia entries about Computer Science researchers can be viewed as evidence of their important contributions. In fact, there are many Wikipedia pages for pioneers in Computer Science research. Table 7 shows our findings from the comparison of our SEMEF (Cameron, 2007) application and the Class of 2007 ACM Fellow Inductees, Wikipedia and IEEE Fellows. SEMEF is an application that uses semantics to find experts using DBLP data and a taxonomy of Computer

Table 7. Comparing experts identified by the system against recognized experts by humans

Researcher	Rank without Taxonomy	Rank with Taxonomy	Award or Recognition	Topic	Contributions/Explanation of the Award or Recognition
Rakesh Agrawal	6	4	ACM Fellow	Data Mining	"... data mining"
Ming-Syan Chen	15	16	ACM Fellow	Data Mining	"... query processing and data mining"
Susan B. Davidson	11	12	ACM Fellow	XML	"... distributed databases, ... semi-structured data ..."
C. Lee Giles	78	19	ACM Fellow	Search	"... information processing and web analysis"
Jiawei Han	1	1	ACM Fellow	Data Mining	"... knowledge discovery and data mining"
Rudi Studer	20	33	Wikipedia Person	Ontologies	"... query processing and data mining"
Philip S. Yu	2	2	ACM Fellow	Data Mining	"... theory and practice of analytical performance modeling of database systems"
Amit P. Sheth	40	3	IEEE Fellow	Web	"... information integration and workflow management"

Science publications. Other measures of researchers with high impact are based on their citation impact. For example, the h-index (Hirsch, 2005) could be used to validate experts determined by our method. However, it would require extensive manual work to determine the h-index of researchers by topic, mostly due to the fact that citation information is needed. The data of DBLP contains only a small fraction of citation information. The use of other sources such as Citeseer of Google Scholar would bring along well-known challenges of entity-disambiguation.

We make a couple of observations based on these preliminary results. First, we recognize the importance of using a taxonomy of topics for finding experts. For example, consider the case of researcher C. Lee Giles, he appears to have a significantly larger number of publications in the subtopics of research topic "Search" rather than the topic itself. His rank on this research topic increased almost 60 spots when including publications under the subtopics of Search within the taxonomy. A similar situation is also evident for researcher Amit P. Sheth. Many of his recent publications span subtopics of the "Web" topic (e.g., Semantic Web and Web Services). On the other hand, researchers Rudi Studer and Ming-Syan Chen had their expertise-rank decreased when considering their publications in subtopics of the listed topic. This alerts us that there may be in many cases other experts whose expertise in those subtopics surpasses them, while not true for the topic itself. In other cases still, including Phillip S. Yu, Susan B. Davidson and Jiawei Han, the inclusion of the taxonomy of topics does not affect their ranking in the topics listed in the table – an indication that the larger percentage of their publications are in data mining itself. We present the following conclusion based on these findings. The taxonomy of topics is important in determining expertise at finer levels of granularity. In many cases it identifies experts whose areas of expertise are at very specific levels, while not particularly broad in scope given a specific top-

ics. In other cases, experts whose expertise is of greatest relevance are identified quite easily. Lastly, researchers whose expertise is distributed with some degree of consistency across the topic and subtopics of the given research area are also easily identifiable.

The second major observation we make based on the results in Table 7 is the "Extent of Overlap" of the topics of expertise of the researchers identified by computer system and the actual explanation listed in their recognition (e.g., award) according to their appropriate areas of expertise. For example, the area of Data Mining produced based on our application produced close to 1,400 researchers with some expertise in the field. Many of the Fellows we show in the Table 7 are in the top 1% of those experts identified by the system. We feel that this overlap shows promise of the validity of using a computer system for identifying experts. A key difference to just using Google Scholar is that our method can find experts when the input from user is the name of a topic. In addition, semantics are utilized to match the topic and its subtopics (through the use of the taxonomy).

EXPERIMENTS SETUP

Most of the data used in this study comes or is derived from DBLP (as of June 2007). The analysis that uses topics of expertise was done using data of publications in the areas of Artificial Intelligence, Databases, Data Mining, Information Retrieval, Web and Semantic Web. The selection of publications on these areas was achieved selecting 28 journals and 112 conferences, symposiums and workshops. The publication venues selected is a superset of those used by Elmacioglu & Lee (2003). Selecting a subset of DBLP publications might seem a tedious task but it was relatively easy due to the naming convention that DBLP uses for BibTex entries of publications. For example, all publications in the World Wide Web Conference have "http://dblp.uni-trier.de/rec/bibtex/conf/

www/" as prefix. The list of all prefixes used to create the subset we used, as well as other datasets mentioned here, are available online (http://lsdis. cs.uga.edu/~aleman/research/sa/).

The list of Computer Science authors that appear in Wikipedia was extracted in part from DBpedia (Auer, 2007) and by selecting authors in DBLP that have as homepage a Wikipedia entry. Most of the analysis was done with the SwetoDblp dataset in RDF containing DBLP data plus additions such as affiliations and organizations. We utilized BRAHMS system (Janik & Kochut, 2005) for fast processing of the 919MB rdf/xml file. The DBLP-subset (file size of 100MB) was created from such file. BRAHMS does not support the *sameAs* OWL property natively. We implemented the functionality by merging entities linked with *sameAs* relations dynamically. It did not seem to have a penalty on performance, probably due to the relatively small number of *sameAs* relations in the dataset.

CONCLUSION

We presented some of the benefits of using semantics for analysis in a bibliographic dataset. For example, it was possible to determine that the total number of universities affiliated with researchers is on the rise yet not at the same pace of publications from year to year. Centrality measures were also determined for researchers of publications included in our dataset. However, it was quite clear that there are benefits of using, if available, information of researchers that have more than one name or alias. Without the use of 'same-as' information of researchers, the computation of centrality values won't be accurate. We were able to create a taxonomy of topics using metadata of keywords and terms from abstracts, taking as starting point links of publications from DBLP. Our methods for extracting potential terms for the taxonomy were very effective in identifying topics that have been researched for many years and

topics that are currently emerging. For example, terms that appear most frequently in the last few years include *phishing*, *spam*, and *wikipedia*. Then, using the terms related to papers, it is possible to determine areas of expertise of the authors. We used lists of ACM and IEEE fellows to compare with the experts determined using computer method. The areas for which such recognized researchers received their awards did match quite well with topics for which they are ranked very high in the computer method. In addition, we compared their rank with and without the use of a taxonomy of topics and found that by using the taxonomy, the rank of the experts is a better match to what their expertise actually is. That is, they rank higher when the taxonomy is used to consider a topic and all its subtopics. The current study and its evaluation show evidence of the promise for measuring experts on topics using a taxonomy-based approach but for future work we plan to do an analysis in more detail by considering multiple topics of expertise of a person.

FUTURE RESEARCH DIRECTIONS

It is relatively straightforward to analyze bibliography data yet data about researchers also spans aspects such as social networks, events and blogs. Interlinking these aspects can provide options for analysis such as finding how certain communities interact. For example, which communities are more active in the blogsphere? Or, which community has a denser social network, independent of its collaboration network. In addition, data quality issues remain, such as affiliation data. In our experiments, we found that special attention should be paid for organizations that have divisions that are referred or named in a variety of different ways. For example, it is useful to keep affiliation information of a researcher at IBM India Research Labs yet at the same time, a query or inference should take into account that such affiliation implies that it is part of IBM Corporation.

The compilation of metadata from papers based on its keywords and abstracts can be improved. In our work, we found that the information on some publishers' websites was somewhat difficult to extract. Thus, it is possible that the detected *new* terms might not have been new in reality as the extracted data is not complete. There are efforts by some publishers to make their information easier to access, such as by means of content feeds in XML. However, they rarely provide all relevant metadata items of a publication. The benefits of making available such information in machine processable formats can lead to better dissemination of the latest publications. Moreover, using richer metadata for determining topics on the field can lead to improved measures of the areas of expertise of researchers. A key aspect in this respect is to assign identifiers (e.g., URIs) for authors of papers. This would be very helpful when dealing with ambiguity issues. The use of metadata notation for bibliography data has been proposed by using semantic vocabularies (Korfiatis et al., 2007). The expected benefits include enhancements of the accuracy of source data for bibliometric analysis.

The measures of expertise of researchers could be somewhat controversial. However, this issue could be turned around so that authors themselves could help on improving the expertise data. For example, a researcher whose publications do not contain all metadata details might want to provide such data herself so that her expertise profile could be more complete (and therefore accurate). Citation-count is an important indicator of the impact of research. For example, the h-index (Hirsch, 2005) requires citation data to compute the h-number of a researcher. It might be difficult to convince someone to provide machine processable details of the citations included in her papers. However, she might have a motivation to indicate which papers cite her papers because this type of data would directly impact her citation count. If a majority of researchers provide such information, existing measures of expertise or publications impact would have more practical value.

REFERENCES

Al-Sudani, S., Alhulou, R., Napoli, A., & Nauer, E. (2006). OntoBib: An ontology-based system for the management of a bibliography. Paper presented at the *17th European Conference on Artificial Intelligence*, Riva del Garcia, Italy.

Aleman-Meza, B., Nagarajan, M., Ramakrishnan, C., Ding, L., Kolari, P., Sheth, A.P., Arpinar, I.B., Joshi, A., & Finin, T. (2006). Semantic analytics on social networks: experiences in addressing the problem of conflict of interest detection. Paper presented at the *15th International World Wide Web Conference*. Edinburgh, Scotland.

Aleman-Meza, B., Bojars, U., Boley, H., Breslin, J. G., Mochol, M., Nixon, L. J. B., Polleres, A., & Zhdanova, A.V. (2007). Combining RDF vocabularies for expert finding. *Paper presented at the 4th European Semantic Web Conference*. Innsbruck, Austria.

Auer, S. & Lehmann, J. (2007). What have Innsbruck and Leipzig in common? Extracting semantics from Wiki content. *Paper presented at the Fourth European Semantic Web Conference*. Innsbruck, Austria.

Bizer, C. (2003). D2R MRP - A database to RDF mapping language. *Paper presented at the Twelfth International World Wide Web Conference*, Budapest, Hungary.

Cameron, D., Aleman-Meza, B., Decker, S., & Arpinar, I. B. (2007). SEMEF: *A taxonomy-based discovery of experts, expertise and collaboration networks*. (Tech. Rep. No. 1114806563). University of Georgia, Computer Science Department.

Cameron, D. (2007). *SEMEF: A taxonomy-based discovery of experts, expertise and collaboration networks*. MS Thesis, Computer Science Department, University of Georgia.

Decker, S. L., Aleman-Meza, B., Cameron, D., & Arpinar, I. B. (2007). *Detection of bursty and emerging trends towards identification of researchers at the early stage of trends.* (Tech. Rep. No. 11148065665). Computer Science Department, University of Georgia.

Elmacioglu, E., & Lee, D. (2005). On six degrees of separation in DBLP-DB and more. *SIGMOD Record, 34*(2), 33-40.

Fagin, R., Guha, R., Kumar, R., Novak, J., Sivakumar, D., & Tomkins, A. (2005). Multi-structural databases. *Paper presented at the Twenty-Fourth ACM Symposium on Principles of Database Systems*, Baltimore, Maryland, USA.

Gandon, F. (2001). Engineering an ontology for a multi-agent corporate memory system. *Paper presented at the Eighth International Symposium on the Management of Industrial and Corporate Knowledge.* Université de Technologie de Compiègne, France.

Golbeck, J., Katz, Y., Krech, D., Mannes, A., Wang, T. D., & Hendler, J. (2006). PaperPuppy: Sniffin the trail of Semantic Web publications. *Paper presented at the Fifth International Semantic Web Conference,* Athens, Georgia, USA.

Hepp, M. (2007). Possible ontologies: How reality constrains the development of relevant ontologies. *IEEE Internet Computing, 11*(1), 90-96.

Hezinger, M., & Lawrence, S. (2004). Extracting knowledge from the World Wide Web, *PNAS 101*(supplement 1), 5186-5191

Hirsch, J. E. (2005). An index to quantify an individual's scientific research output. *PNAS 102*(46), 16569-16572.

Janik, M., & Kochut, K. (2005). BRAHMS: A workBench RDF store and high performance memory system for semantic association discovery. *Paper presented at the Fourth International Semantic Web Conference.* Galway, Ireland.

Kashyap, V., Ramakrishnan, C., Thomas, C., & Sheth, A. (2005, September). TaxaMiner: An experimental framework for automated taxonomy bootstrapping. *International Journal of Web and Grid Services.*

Kautz, H., Selman, B., & Shah, M. (1997). The hidden web. *AI Magazine, 18*(2), 27-36.

Korfiatis, N., Poulos, M., & Bokos, G. (2007). Social metadata for the impact factor. *The Electronic Library, 25*(2), 166-175.

Metze, F., Bauckhage, C., & Alpcan, T. (2007). The "spree" expert finding system. *Paper presented at the First International Conference on Semantic Computing.* Irvine, California, USA.

Mika, P. (2005). Flink: Semantic Web technology for the extraction and analysis of social networks. *Journal of Web Semantics, 3*, 211-223.

Milgram, S. (1967). The small world problem. *Psychology Toda,y 2*, 60-70.

Nascimento, M. A., Sander, J., & Pound, J. (2003). Analysis of SIGMOD's co-quthorship Graph, *SIGMOD Record, 32*(3), 8-10.

Newman, M. E. J. (2001). Scientific collaboration networks: II. Shortest paths, weighted networks, and centrality, *Phys. Rev.,E, 64*, 016132

Shadbolt, N., Gibbins, N., Glaser, H., Harris, S., & Schraefel, M. M. C. (2004). CS AKTive space, or how we learned to stop worrying and love the Semantic Web. *IEEE Intelligent Systems 19*(3), 41-47.

Sheth, A.P., Ramakrishnan, C., & Thomas, C. (2005). Semantics for the Semantic Web: The implicit, the formal and the powerful. *International Journal Semantic Web Information Systems, 1*(1), 1-18.

Sriharee, N., & Punnarut, R. (2007). Constructing campus for academic collaboration. *Paper presented at the Second International ExpertFinder Workshop.* Busan, Korea.

Staab, S., Domingos, P., Mika, P., Golbeck, J., Ding, L., Finin, T. W., Joshi, A., Nowak, A., & Vallacher, R. R. (2005). Social networks applied. *IEEE Intelligent Systems, 20*(1), 80-93.

Tho, Q. T., Hui, S. C., & Fong, A. (2003). Web mining for identifying research trends. *Paper presented at the 6th International Conference on Asian Digital Libraries*. Kuala Lumpur, Malasya.

Velardi, P., Cucchiarelli, A., & Petit, M. (2007). A taxonomy learning method and its application to characterize a scientific Web community. *IEEE Transactions on Knowledge and Data Engineering, 19*(2), 180-191.

Yin, X., Han, J., & Yu, P.S. (2007). Object distinction: Distinguishing objects with identical names. *Paper presented at the IEEE 23rd International Conference on Data Engineering*. Istambul, Turkey.

ADDITIONAL READING

Barabási, A.-L. (2002). *Linked - The new science of networks. Cambridge*. MA: Perseus Publishing.

Berkowitz, S.D. (1982). *An introduction to structural znalysis: The network approach to social research*. Butterworth, Toronto.

Bojārs, U., & Breslin, J. G. (2007). ResumeRDF: Expressing skill information on the Semantic Web. *Paper presented at the 1st International ExpertFinder Workshop*. Berlin, Germany.

Cameron, D., Aleman-Meza, B., & Arpinar, I.B. (2007). Collecting expertise of researchers for finding relevant experts in a peer-review setting. *Paper presented at the 1st International Expert-Finder Workshop*. Berlin, Germany.

Griffiths, T. L., & Steyvers, M. (2004). Finding scientific topics, *PNAS 101*(supplement 1). 5228-5235.

Iofciu, T., Diederich, J., Dolog, P., & Balke W. T. (2007). ExpertFOAF recommends experts. *Paper presented at the 1st International ExpertFinder Workshop*. Berlin, Germany.

Kleinberg, J. (2000). The small-world phenomenon: An algorithm perspective. *Paper presented at the Thirty-second Annual ACM Symposium on Theory of Computing*. Portland, Oregon, USA.

Li, L., Alderson, D., Doyle, J. C., & Willinger, W. (2005). Towards a theory of scale-free graphs: Definition, properties, and implications. *Internet Mathematics, 2*(4), 431-523.

Liu, B., & Chin, C. W. (2002). Searching people on the Web according to their interests. *Poster presented at the Eleventh International World Wide Web Conference*. Honolulu, Hawaii, USA.

Liu, P., & Dew, P. (2004). Using Semantic Web technologies to improve expertise matching within academia, *Paper presented at the 2nd International Conference on Knowledge Management*. Graz, Austria.

Mane, K. K., & Börner, K. (2004). Mapping topics and topic bursts in PNAS. *PNAS 101*(supplement 1). 5287-5290.

Miki, T., Nomura, S., & Ishida, T. (2005). Semantic Web link analysis to discover social relationships in academic communities. *Paper presented at the 2005 Symposium on Applications and the Internet*.

Mochol, M., Jentzsch, A., & Wache, H. (2007). Suitable employees wanted? Find them with Semantic techniques. *Paper presented at the Workshop on Making Semantics Work for Business*. Vienna, Austria.

Mockus, A., & Herbsleb, J. A. (2002). Expertise browser: A quantative approach to indentifying expertise. *Paper presented at the International Conference on Software Engineering*. Orlando, Florida.

Ren, J., & Taylor, R. N. (2007). Automatic and versatile publications ranking for research institutions and scholars. *Communications of the ACM, 50*(6), 81-85.

Rodriguez, M. A., & Bollen, J. (2005). *An algorithm to determine peer-reviewers.* (Technical Report LA-UR-06-2261). Los Alamos National Laboratory.

Shadbolt, N., Hall, W., & Berners-Lee, T. (2006). The Semantic Web revisited. *IEEE Intelligent Systems, 21*(3), 96-101.

Smeaton, A. F., Keogh, G., Gurrin, C., McDonald, K., & Sødring, T. (2003). Analysis of papers from twenty-five years of SIGIR conferences: What have we been doing for the last quarter of a century? *ACM SIGIR Forum, 36*(2), 39-43.

Song, X., Tseng, B. L., Lin, C.-Y., & Sun, M.-T. (2005). ExpertiseNet: Relational and evolutionary expert modeling. *Paper presented at the Tenth International Conference on User Modeling.* Edinburgh, Scotland.

Takeda, H., Matsuzuka, T., & Taniguchi, Y. (2000). Discovery of shared topics networks among people - A simple approach to find community knowledge from WWW bookmarks. *Paper presented at the Sixth Pacific Rim International Conference on Artificial Intelligence.* Melbourne, Australia.

The Yahoo! Research Team. (2006). Content, metadata, and behavioral information: Directions for Yahoo! Research. *IEEE Data Engineering Bulletin, 31*(4). 10-18.

Thomas, C., & Sheth, A. P. (2006). On the expressiveness of the languages for the Semantic Web - Making a case for 'A Little More'. In E. Sanchez (Editor), *Fuzzy Logic and the Semantic Web.* Elsevier.

Wasserman, S., & Faust, K. (1994). *Social network analysis: Methods and applications.* Cambridge University Press.

Zhang, J., Ackerman, M. S., & Adamic, L. (2007). Expertise networks in online communities: Structure and algorithms. *Paper presented at the 16th International World Wide Web Conference.* Banff, Canada.

Zhou, D., Ji, X., Zha, H., & Giles, C. L. (2006). Topic evolution and social interactions: How authors effect research. *Paper presented at the 15th ACM International Conference on Information and Knowledge Management.* Arlington, Virginia, USA.

Zhou, D., Manavoglu, E., Li, J., Giles, C. L., & Zha, H. (2006). Probabilistic models for discovering E-Communities. *Paper presented at the 15th International World Wide Web Conference.* Edinburgh, Scotland.

APPENDIX: QUESTIONS FOR DISCUSSION

Beginner

Give examples of keywords that (i) are strong indication that a paper is related to a very specific topic; (ii) are indication of a broad topic; and (ii) are not sufficient to determine that a paper is related to a topic.

Answer:

(i) The keyword *PageRank* is strong indicator that a paper is related to the topic Search or Link Analysis. The keyword *XQuery* is a strong indicator that a paper is related to the topic XML.

(iii) The keywords *Data Mining*, *Semantic Web*, and *Databases* are examples that indicate that a paper is related to those (general) topics.

(iii) The keywords *algorithms*, and *evaluation* are not sufficient to determine that a paper is related to a topic.

Intermediate

Provide an example of ten topics in computer science organized with 'sub-topic' relationships and including a synonym for five of the topics. Collect the answer from few participants and collaboratively try to 'merge' the topics of all participants. Discuss your findings.

Answer: Web Services (synonym: Web Service) with subtopic Semantic Web Services (synonym: Semantic Web Service). Web Service Composition (synonym: Service Composition), which is subtopic of Web Services. Semantic Web with subtopic Semantic Web Services. Semantic Search, which is subtopic of Semantic Web. Search (synonym: Web Search) with subtopic Semantic Search. Intranet Search, which is subtopic of Search. Personalized Search, which is subtopic of Search. Discovery of Web Services (synonym: Web Services Discovery), which is subtopic of Web Services. Ontology Learning as a subtopic of Semantic Web.

Advanced

Explain the differences of using a taxonomy of topics for finding experts on a given topic versus not using a taxonomy of topics.

Answer. There is a case where there is not difference on using or not a taxonomy of topics for finding experts. This is the case where a topic is a leaf node in the taxonomy. However, depending on the depth of the hierarchy, finding experts on a given topic will very likely produce better results when the taxonomy is used. This is because it is expected that the subtopics of the input topic will be included when finding matches for experts. For example, if the topic of interest is *Web Search* and the taxonomy contains the topic *Link Analysis* as a subtopic of *Web Search*, then the papers that are related to *Link Analysis* would be considered as a match for the input topic. However, it could be possible that most papers in a topic might always include the general topic in addition to more specific subtopics. In such cases, retrieval of experts using the general topic might not change much with or without the use of a taxonomy. The other side of the coin is that retrieval of experts on a more specific topic would indeed bring good results regardless of whether the general topic is related to the papers. However, the more specific the topic is, the closer it would be up to reaching leaf nodes. As before mentioned, this case would be a match in exactly same way whether the taxonomy is used or not. In summary, there are benefits when a taxonomy of topics is used yet these benefits are not very evident when the topics are near or at the leaf level of the taxonomy.

Practical Exercises

Select one paper from the ACM Digital Library, one from the IEEE Digital Library and one from Springer. Make sure that all papers contain a list of keywords. Then, for every co-author in all papers, pick (if available) one paper for each of them and retrieve the keywords. Create a list of all keywords across all such papers, that is, three lists in total. Reorganize the lists by relating them to the authors whose papers are related to the keywords. If possible, determine the top experts on the keywords based on how many keywords are related to each author.

For every pair of collaborating researchers listed in Table 3, find out whether they collaborate often because they work at the same organization, or because they were in a advisor/advisee relationship and continue collaborating, or whether they are at different organizations yet collaborate frequently.

Chapter IX
Search Engine–Based Web Information Extraction

Gijs Geleijnse
Philips Research, The Netherlands

Jan Korst
Philips Research, The Netherlands

ABSTRACT

In this chapter we discuss approaches to find, extract, and structure information from natural language texts on the Web. Such structured information can be expressed and shared using the standard Semantic Web languages and hence be machine interpreted. In this chapter we focus on two tasks in Web information extraction. The first part focuses on mining facts from the Web, while in the second part, we present an approach to collect community-based meta-data. A search engine is used to retrieve potentially relevant texts. From these texts, instances and relations are extracted. The proposed approaches are illustrated using various case-studies, showing that we can reliably extract information from the Web using simple techniques.

INTRODUCTION

Suppose we are interested in *'the countries where Burger King can be found'*, *'the Dutch cities with a university of technology'* or perhaps *'the genre of the music of Miles Davis'*. For such diverse factual information needs, the World Wide Web in general and a search engine in particular can provide a solution. Experienced users of search engines are able to construct queries that are likely to access documents containing the desired information.

However, current search engines retrieve Web pages, not the information itself [1]. We have to search within the search results in order to acquire the information. Moreover, we make implicit use of our knowledge (e.g. of the language and the domain), to interpret the Web pages.

Apart from factual information, the Web is the de-facto source to gather community-based data as people with numerous backgrounds, interests and ideas contribute to the content of the Web. Hence the Web is a valuable source to extract opinions, characterizations and perceived relatedness between items.

In this chapter, the focus is on gathering and structuring information from the 'traditional' Web. This structured information can be represented (and shared) using the standard Semantic Web (SW) languages. Hence, this chapter focuses on the automatic creation of content for the SW. For simplicity, we abstract from the SW standards RDF(S)/OWL.

The Web-as-a-Corpus vs. Traditional Text Corpora

Information extraction (IE) is the task of identifying instances (or *named entities*) and relations between those instances in a collection of texts, called a text corpus.

In the nineties, the Message Understanding Conferences (MUC) focused on the recognition of named entities (such as names of persons and organizations) in a collection of texts (Chinchor, 1998). Initially, this work was mostly based on rules on the syntax and context of such named entities. For example, two capitalized words preceded by *mr.* will denote the name of a male person. As the creation of such rules is a laborious task, approaches became popular where named entities were recognized using machine learning (Mitchell, 1997), for example in (Zhou & Su, 2002; Brothwick, 1999; Finkel, Grenager, & Manning, 2005). However, such approaches typically make use of annotated training sets where instances (e.g. *'Microsoft'*) are labeled with their class (*'Organization'*).

Traditional information extraction tasks focus on the identification of named entities in large text corpora such as collections newspaper articles or biomedical texts. In this chapter however, we focus on the Web as a corpus. In Table 1 the most important differences between the two can be found.

Suppose that we are interested in a list of all countries in the world with their capitals. When we extract information from a collection of newspaper articles (e.g. 3 months of the New York Times), we cannot expect all information to be present. At best, we can try to discover every country-

Table 1. Comparison between the Web as a corpus and 'traditional' corpora

Web Corpus	Newspaper Corpus
Redundancy. Because of the size of the Web, we can expect information to be duplicated, or formulated in various ways. If we are interested in a fact, we have to be able to identify just one of the formulations to extract it.	**No or fewer redundancy**. Especially for smaller corpora, we cannot expect that information is redundantly present.
Temporal and unreliable. The content of the Web is created over several years by numerous contributors. The data is thus unreliable and may be out-dated.	**Constant and reliable**. In corpus-based IE, it is assumed that the information in the corpus is correct and up-to-date.
Multilingual and heterogeneous. The Web is not restricted to a single language and the texts are produced by numerous authors for diverse audiences.	**Often monolingual and homogeneous**. If the author or nature (e.g. articles from the Wall Street Journal) of the corpus is known beforehand, it is easier to develop heuristics or to train named entity recognizers.
No representative annotated corpora. As no representative annotated texts are available, the Web as a corpus is currently less suited for supervised machine learning approaches.	**Annotated test corpora available**. In order to train supervised learning based named entity recognizers (NERs), test corpora are available where instances of a limited number of classes are marked within the text.
Dynamic. The contents of the Web changes continuously, results of experiments may thus also change over time.	**Static**. Experimental results are independent of time and place as the corpora are static.
Facts and opinions. As a multitude of users contribute to the Web, its contents are also suited for opinion mining.	**Facts only**. Information Extraction tasks on Newspaper corpora mainly focus on the identification of facts.

capital combination that is expressed within the corpus. When we use the Web however, all the required information can be expected to be present. Moreover each of the combinations is likely to be expressed on various pages with multiple formulations. For example, *'Amsterdam is the capital of the Netherlands'* and *'The Netherlands and its capital Amsterdam (...)'* are different formulations of the same fact. In principle, we have to be able to interpret only one of the formulations to extract the country-capital combination. Hence, in comparison with a 'traditional' newspaper corpus, we can both set different objectives and apply different methods to extract information from the Web.

Heterogeneous vs. Homogeneous Sources

In this work we focus on unstructured natural language texts. Information extraction from structured sources is thoroughly described in for example (Chang, Kayed, Girgis, & Shaalan, 2006) and (Crescenzi & Mecca, 2004).These 'wrappers' make use of the homogeneous lay-out of large Web sites. Large Web sites such as *amazon.com* and *imdb.com* make use of a database and present automatically generated Web pages. The lay-out is uniform over the whole site, but the information changes from page to page. The performing artist, the title of the album and other catalogue data can be found on the exact same place on the page. The HTML-source of the two pages will also only differ at these places. For pages within a large Web site, a wrapper algorithm can be created the information of interest from an arbitrary page within the site. Wrappers are relatively simple and time efficient. However, they are Web site and thus domain dependent. Instead we focus on information from arbitrary Web sites in this chapter.

Fact Mining

The first part of this chapter discusses a method to extract factual information from the Web. To formalize the concept *information* we define an initial ontology on the domain of interest (e.g. movies, literature, hamburger restaurants). Given this initial ontology, we populate it with extracted knowledge. For example, if we consider an ontology with the classes *Movie* and *Actor*, we can populate the ontology by finding instances of these classes. Hence, if we identify the terms *'Top Gun'*, *'The Godfather'* as movie titles and the terms *'Tom Cruise'* and *'Marlon Brando'* as actors we can add these terms as instances to the ontology. Moreover if acts-in is a relation between Movie and Actor, then the challenge is to discover the instances of that relation from texts on the Web, e.g. (*Marlon Brando, The Godfather*).

In Section 2 of this chapter, we present an algorithm that—given a domain of interest—extracts, structures and combines information from the Web. With structured information available, we can easily find the information we are interested in. The extracted information can, e.g. be used by recommender systems to acquire additional metadata. This metadata can be used to make meaningful recommendations for music or TV programs. For example, suppose a user has expressed a preference for TV programs relating to Italy. The recommender system will be able to recognize regions as *Tuscany* and *Veneto* and cities as *Milano* and *Florence* using extracted information. Occurrences of such terms in a program guide description will mark a program as relevant. Likewise, if the user has expressed a preference for TV programs relating to photography the system will be able to recognize the names of famous photographers as *Cartier-Bresson* and *Moholy-Nagy.*

Community-Based Knowledge Mining

The Web is not only a well-suited text corpus to mine factual information. As a large community of users contributes to the contents of the Web, it can also be used to mine more subjective knowledge. For example, we call Paul Gauguin a post-impressionist and to be similar to Vincent van Gogh, *Christina Aguilera* a pop artist similar to *Britney Spears*. Such qualifications may not all be facts, but are thoughts shared by a large community.

In the second part of the chapter we focus on methods to automatically find such internet community-based meta-data. On the one hand we classify instances (e.g. pop artists) into categories and on the other hand identifying a distance matrix of related instances. The information found can be used to create an automated folksonomy: a knowledge base where items are tagged using implicit input from multiple users.

In restricted domains (e.g. Movies) in fact mining, the use of wrappers may be well usable. The Internet Movie Database[2] for example is a reliable, semi-structured source to extract data on movies. When we are interested in subjective data based on opinions of the Web community however, we cannot restrict ourselves to a single source. We combine data from multiple Web sites, and thus multiple contributors, to characterize instances. We can however use semi-structured data from social Websites such as *last.fm* as a benchmark on restricted domains like music (Geleijnse, Schedl, & Knees, 2007).

Related Work

Information extraction and ontology constructing are two closely related fields. For reliable information extraction, we need background information, e.g. an ontology. On the other hand, we need information extraction to generate broad and highly usable ontologies. An good overview on state-of-the-art ontology learning from text can be found in (Buitelaar, Cimiano, & Magnini, 2005).

Early work on relation identification from the Web can be found in (Brin, 1998). Brin describes a Web site-dependent system to identify hypertext patterns that express a given relation. For each Web site, such patterns are learned and explored to identify instances that are similarly related. SnowBall (Agichtein & Gravano, 2000) is a successor of Brin's system with an embedded named-entity recognizer. The idea of extracting relations using patterns is similar to one of the methods presented here. However, in Snowball the relations gathered are not evaluated.

KnowItAll is a hybrid named-entity extraction system (Etzioni et al., 2005) that finds lists of instances of a given class from the Web using a search engine. It combines hyponym patterns (Hearst, 1992) and learned patterns for instances of the class to identify and extract named-entities. Moreover, it uses adaptive wrapper algorithms (Crescenzi & Mecca, 2004) to extract information from html markup such as tables. Contrary to our method, it does not use instances to formulate queries. In (Downey, Etzioni, & Soderland, 2005) the information extracted by KnowItAll is evaluated using a combinatorial model based on the redundancy of information on the Web.

Cimiano and Staab (2004) describe a method to use a search engine to verify a hypothesis relation. For example, if we are interested in the 'is a' or hyponym relation and we have the instance Nile, we can use a search engine to query phrases expressing this relation (e.g. "rivers such as the Nile" and "cities such as the Nile"). The number of hits to such queries is used to determine the validity of the hypothesis. Per instance, the number of queries is linear in the number of classes (e.g. city and river) considered.

In (de Boer, van Someren, & Wielinga, 2007) a number of documents on art styles are collected. Names of painters are identified within these documents. The documents are evaluated by counting the number of painters in a training set (of e.g. expressionists) that appear in the document. Painters appearing on the best ranked documents are then mapped to the style. De Boer et al. use a training set and page evaluation, where we simply observe co-occurrences.

A document based technique in artist clustering is described in (Knees, Pampalk, & Widmer, 2004). For all music artists in a given set, a number of documents is collected using a search engine. For sets of related artists a number of discriminative terms is learned. These terms are used to cluster the artists using support vector machines. The documents are obtained in a similar way in our document-based method. However, we restrict ourselves to identifying names of artists and categories in the documents.

The number of search engine *hits* for pairs of instances can be used to compute a semantic distance between the instances (Cilibrasi & Vitanyi, 2007). The nature of the relation is not identified, but the technique can for example be used to cluster related instances. In (Zadel & Fujinaga, 2004) a similar method is used to cluster artists using search engine counts. In (Schedl, Knees, & Widmer, 2005), the number of search engine hits of combinations of artists is used in clustering artists. However, the total number of hits provided by the search engine is an estimate and not always reliable (Véronis, 2006). In (Geleijnse, Korst, & de Boer, 2006) an approach is presented where one instance is queried and the resulting texts are mined for occurrences of other instances. Such an approach is not only more efficient in the number of queries, but also gives better results.

In (Pang, Lee, & Vaithyanathan, 2002; Dave & Lawrence, 2003; Kim & Hovy, 2004; Pang & Lee, 2005) methods are discussed to identify opinions on reviewed products. For example, given is a set of reviews of some flat screen television mined from the Web. The task is to assign a grade to the product or its specific features (e.g. the quality of the speakers).

The extraction of social networks using Web data is a frequently addressed topic. For example, Mori et al. (2006) use tf·idf (see (Manning & Schütze, 1999)) to identify relations between politicians and locations and (Jin, Matsuo, & Ishizuka, 2006) use inner-sentence co-occurrences of company names to identify a network of related companies.

FACT MINING

In this first part of the chapter, we will describe a method to populate an ontology, given a domain of interest. Here we only consider factual information, i.e. opinions and the like are here not taken into account but will be considered in the second part of this chapter.

Problem Definition

The Semantic Web community (Berners-Lee, Hendler, & Lassila, 2001) is providing standards for machine readable and interpretable information on the Web. The languages RDF(S) and OWL are developed for this purpose by the World Wide Web Consortium[3]. Dedicated reasoners are created for the semantic Web languages for ontology-based question-answering services. As such, these reasoners are able to provide answers to information demands like the above, given a sufficiently populated ontology.

For our purposes we define an ontology as follows:

Definitions. A reference ontology O is a 4-tuple (C, I, P,T), with:

$C = (c_0, c_1, ..., c_{N-1})$, an ordered set of N classes,
$I = (I_0, I_1, ..., I_{N-1})$, with I_j, $0 \leq j < N$, the set of instances of class $c_j \in C$,
$P = (p_0, p_1, ..., p_{M-1})$, a set of M binary relations on the classes, with p_i: $c_{i,0} \times c_{i,1}$ $0 \leq i < M$, and $c_{i,0}, c_{i,1} \in C$, and

$\mathbf{T} = (T_0, T_1, \ldots, T_{M-1})$, is a set of instances of the relations in P with $T_i = \{(s,o) \mid p_i(s,o) \}$ for each i, $0 \leq i < M$

An *initial ontology* of O is defined as O' = (C, I', P,T'), where:

$I'_j \subseteq I_j$ for all j, $0 \leq j < N$,
$T'_i \subseteq T_i$ for all i, $0 \leq i < M$, and
$(s,o) \in T'_k \Rightarrow s \in I'_{k,0} \ o \in I'_{k,1}$ for some k

Popular search engines currently only give access to a limited list of possibly interesting Web pages. A user can get an idea of relevance of the pages presented by analyzing the title and the snippet presented. When a user has sent an accurate query to the search engine, the actual information required by the user can already be contained in the snippet.

We are interested whether the data in the snippets presented by a search engine is sufficient to extract information. With the definitions presented above, we formulate the information extraction problem as an ontology population problem:

Problem. Given an initial ontology O', extend O' to some O'' that maximizes the precision and/or recall.

We define precision and recall as measures of a class $c_j \in C$:

$$precision(c_j) = \frac{\left| I_j \cap I''_j \right|}{\left| I''_j \right|}$$

and

$$recall(c_j) = \frac{\left| I_j \cap I''_j \right|}{\left| I''_j \right|}$$

Similar measures can be formulated for relations p_i.

Global Outline

We choose to extract information from arbitrary Web sites. To find relevant Web sites—and thus relevant information—we use a state of the art search engine. Currently, both Google and Yahoo! allow a limited amount of automatic queries per day.

When using a search engine, we have to deal with the following restrictions.

1. The search engines return a limited number of search results per query (at most 5,000 per day using the *Yahoo! API*) .

2. We want to perform as few queries to a search engine as possible to limit the use of its services.

We therefore need accurate queries, for which we can expect the search engine to return relevant snippets. We therefore choose to use known instances in our queries to simultaneously find instances of classes and instances of relations. For example, given the instance *'Johan Cruijff'* in the initial ontology, we can use this instance in the query 'Johan Cruijff was born in' in order to retrieve a place in general and Cruijff's place of birth in particular. The place of birth, Amsterdam, can be extracted from the retrieved documents. Now, *'Amsterdam'* can be used in the query 'was born in Amsterdam' to discover other (Amsterdam-born) persons, like Willem Frederik Hermans and Paul Verhoeven.

For a given relation p_k, we thus use both an instance $I'_{k,0}$ and a natural language formulation of the relation in our queries. Subsequently, the snippets are scanned for instances of $I'_{k,1}$ and $(I'_{k,0}, I'_{k,1}) \in T'_k$. In Section 2.3 we focus on the identification of relation patterns. Section 2.4 handles the identification of instances of a class from the snippets. We combine these strategies into the ontology population algorithm as described in Section 2.5.

Identifying Effective Relation Patterns

Given is a relation p_k and a set T'_k of instances of p_k. For relation p_k, defined on $c_{k,0} \times c_{k,1}$, in the partial ontology O', we have to identify natural language formulations of this relation. We are thus interested in patterns P_k of the form "[$c_{k,0}$] expression [$c_{k,1}$]"[4] that express the relation p_k in natural language.

Say, for example, we consider the classes *'author'* and *'book title'* and the relation *'has written'*. We assume that we know some related instance-pairs, e.g. *('Leo Tolstoy', 'War and Peace')* and *('Günter Grass', 'Die Blechtrommel')*. We then want to find natural language phrases that relate authors to the titles of the books they wrote. If we find phrases that typically connect two related terms (i.e. patterns), we can expect them to also connect other related instance-pairs. Thus, if we query a pattern in combination with the name of an author (e.g. *'Umberto Eco wrote'*), we want the search results of this query to contain the books by this author.

Such patterns have to meet two criteria:

- **Precision:** Preferably, the phrase is unambiguous, i.e. the probability that the terms found do not belong to the intended class must be small. For example, consider the relation place of *birth(Person, City)*. The pattern *[Person] was born in [City]* is an ambiguous representation of this relation, since *[Person] was born in* can precede a date or the name of a country as well.
- **Recall:** The pattern must frequently occur on the Web. Rare patterns are not likely to give much search results when querying such a pattern in combination with an instance.

Identifying Relation Patterns

We focus on the relation p_k in our ontology O. For easy reference, we assume $p_k = c_q \times c_a$. The problem is to identify a set of patterns that lead to highly relevant search results when queried in combination with instances of c_q. We first generate a list of relation patterns with the use of the following algorithm. For evaluation purposes, we also compute the frequency of each pattern found.

- **Step 1:** Formulate queries using an instance-pair $(x,y) \in T'_k$. Since we are interested in phrases within sentences rather than in keywords or expressions in telegram style that often appear in titles of Web pages, we use the `allintext:` option. This gives us only search results with the queried expression in the bodies of the documents rather than in the titles. We query both `allintext:`" x * y " and `allintext:`" y * x ". The * is a regular expression operator accepted by both Google and Yahoo!. It is a placeholder for zero or more words.
- **Step 2:** Send the queries to the search engine and collect the snippets of the pages it returns for each query.
- **Step 3:** Extract all phrases matching the queried expressions and replace both x and y by the names of their classes.
- **Step 4:** Remove all phrases that are not within one sentence.
- **Step 5:** Normalize all phrases by removing all mark-up that is ignored by the search engine. Since the search engines are case-insensitive and ignore punctuation, double spaces and the like, we translate all phrases found to a normal form: the simplest expression that we can query that leads to the document retrieved.
- **Step 6:** Update the frequencies of all normalized phrases found.
- **Step 7:** Repeat the procedure for any unqueried pair $(x',y') \in T'_k$

We now have generated a list with relation patterns and their frequencies within the retrieved snippets.

Selecting Relation Patterns

From the list of relation patterns found, we are interested in the most effective ones. We are not only interested in the most precise ones. For example, the retrieved pattern "född 30 mars 1853 i" proved to be a 100% precise pattern expressing the relation between a person ('Vincent van Gogh') and his place of birth ('Zundert'). Clearly, this rare phrase is unsuited to mine instance-pairs of this relation in general. On the other hand, high frequency of some pattern is no guarantee for effectiveness either. The frequently occurring pattern "was born in London" (found when querying for Thomas Bayes * England) is well-suited to be used to find London-born persons, but in general the pattern is unsuited—since too narrow—to express the relation between a person and his or her country of origin. Taking these observations into account, we formulate three criteria for selecting effective relation patterns.

1. The patterns should *frequently* occur on the Web, to increase the probability of getting any results when querying the pattern in combination with an instance.

2. The pattern should be *precise*. When we query a pattern in combination with an instance in I_q, we want to have many search results containing instances from c_a.

3. If relation R is not functional, the pattern should be *broad*, i.e. among the search results when querying a combination of the pattern and an instance in I_q there must be as many distinct R-related instances from c_a as possible.

To measure these criteria, we use the following scoring functions for a relation pattern s.

1. **Frequency**. (shown in Box 1)
2. **Precision**.

$$f_{prec} = \sum_{x \in I'_q}^{n} \frac{P(s,x)}{|I'_q|}$$

For instances $x \in I'_q$, $I'_q \subseteq I_q$ we calculate $P(s,x)$ as follows.

$$P(s,x) = \frac{F_I(s,x)}{F_O(s,x)}$$

Where $F_I(s,x)$ and $F_O(s,x)$ are given as such in Box 2.

3. **Breadth**.

Box 1.

ffreq(s) = "number of occurrences of s in the snippets as found by the algorithm described in the previous subsection"

Box 2.

$F_I(s,x)$ = "the number of snippets after querying s in combination with x containing instances of c_a"

$F_O(s,x)$ = "the number of snippets found (at most 1,000)"

Box 3.

$B(s,x)$ = "the number of distinct instances of class c_a found after querying s in combination with x"

$$f_{spr} = \sum_{x \in I'_q} B(s, x)$$

Where B(s,x) is defined in Box 3.

The larger we choose the test set, the subset I'_q of I_q, the more reliable the measures for precision and breadth. However, the number of queries increases with the number of patterns found for each instance we add to I'_q. We finally calculate the score of the patterns by multiplying the individual scores:

$$score(s) = f_{freq} \cdot f_{prec} \cdot f_{spr}$$

For efficiency reasons, we only compute the scores of the patterns with the highest frequencies. The problem remains how to recognize a (possible multi-word) instance in the snippets. For an ontology alignment setting—where the sets I_q and I_a are not to be expanded—these problems are trivial: we determine whether $t \in I_a$ is accompanied by the queried expression. For a setting where the instances of c_a are not all known (e.g. it is not likely that we have a complete list of all books written in the world), we solve this problem in two stages. First we identify rules per class to extract candidate instances. Thereafter we use an additional query to verify if a candidate is indeed an instance of class c_a.

Instance Identification

A separate problem is the identification of terms in the text. An advantage is that we know the place in the text by construction (i.e. either preceding or following the queried expression). A disadvantage is that each class requires a different technique to identify its instances. Especially terms with a less determined format, such as movie titles, are hard to identify. We therefore design recognition functions f_i for each class.

For these functions f_i, we can adopt various techniques from the fields of (statistical) natural language processing in general and information extraction in particular. A regular expression that describes the instances of class c_i can be a part of the function f_i. The reader may also think of the use of part of speech tagging (Brill, 1992), N-gram models (Manning & Schütze, 1999; Downey, Broadhead, & Etzioni, 2007), off-the-shell named entity recognizers (Zhou & Su, 2002) or shallow parsers (Lin, 1998). We note that the HTML-markup can be of use as well, since terms tend to be emphasized, or made 'clickable'.

After extracting a term, we can perform an additional check to find out whether the extracted term is really an instance of the concerning class. We perform this check with the use of a search engine. We query phrases that express the term-class relation. Again, these phrases can be constructed semi-automatically. Hyponym patterns are candidates as well for this purpose (Hearst, 1992, 1998; Cimiano & Staab, 2004). A term is to be accepted as instance, when the number of hits of the queried phrase is at least a certain threshold. For example, we query the phrase 'Cities such as Eindhoven and' to check whether 'Eindhoven' is indeed an instance of the class City. When we use such a check function, we can allow ourselves to formulate less strict recognition functions f_i. That is, false instances that are accepted by f_i, are still rejected as an instance by the use of the check function.

Sketch of Algorithm

Per relation, we maintain a list of instances that already have been used in a query in combination with the patterns expressing this relation. Initially, these lists are thus empty. The following steps of the algorithm are performed until either some stop criterion is reached, or until no new instances or instance-pairs can be found.

- **Step 1:** Select a relation p_k on $c_{k,0} \times c_{k,1}$ and an instance v from either $I_{k,0}$ or $I_{k,1}$ we have not yet used in a query.

- **Step 2:** Combine the patterns expressing p_k (e.g. 'starring') with v (e.g. *'David Hasselhoff'*) and send these queries (*'starring David Hasselhoff'*) to the search engine.
- **Step 3:** Extract instances from the snippets using the instance identification rules for the class applicable.
- **Step 4:** Add the newly found instances to the corresponding instance set and add the instance-pairs found (thus with v) to $T'_{(k,0),(k,1)}$.
- **Step 5:** If there exists an instance that we can use to formulate new queries, then repeat the procedure.

Note that instances of class $c_{k,0} = c_{1,1}$ learned using the algorithm applied on relation p_k on $c_{k,0} \times c_{k,1}$ can be used as input for the algorithm applied to some relation p_l on $c_{1,0} \times c_{1,1}$ to populate the sets $I'_{1,0}$ and $T'_{(1,0),(1,1)}$.

Experimental Results

In this section, we discuss some experiments we conducted with this method. In Section 2.6, we investigate whether the learned patterns are indeed intuitive, by learning a list of relation patterns expressing the broader-narrower or hyponym relation. Section 2.6 handles the use of learned patterns to populate an ontology on restaurant chains and the countries where they can be found, while we populate a movie ontology in Section 2.6. Finally, we discuss the identification of a ranked list of historical persons and their biographical information in Section 2.6.

Learning Effective Hyponym Patterns

We are interested whether the effective surface text patterns are indeed intuitive formulations of some relation $p_k : c_q \times c_a$. As a test-case, we compute the most effective patterns for the hyponym relation using a test set with names of all countries.

Our experiment was set up as follows. We collected the complete list of countries in the world from the CIA World Factbook (footnote: http://www.cia.gov/cia/publications/factbook). Let I_a be this set of countries, and let I_q be the set { 'countries', 'country' }. The set T_k consists of all pairs (a,'countries') and (a , 'country'), for a $\in I_a$. We apply the surface text pattern learning algorithm on this set T_k.

The algorithm identified almost 40,000 patterns. We computed f_{spr} and f_{prec} for the 1,000 most frequently found patterns. In Table 2, we give the 25 most effective patterns found by the algorithm. Focusing on these patterns, we observe two groups: 'is a' and hyponym patterns as identified by Hearst (1992).

The hyponym patterns 'like' and 'such as' show to be the most effective. This observation is useful, when we want to minimize the amount of queries for hyponym patterns.

Expressions of properties that hold for each country and only for countries, for example the existence of a country code for dialing, are not trivially identified manually but are useful and reliable patterns.

The combination of 'is a', 'is an' or 'is the' with an adjective is a common pattern, occurring 2,400 times in the list. In future work, such adjectives can be identified in the snippets using a Part of Speech tagger (Brill, 1992) or a shallow parser (Lin, 1998 ; Marneffe, MacCartney, & Manning, 2006).

A Restaurant Ontology

The Text Retrieval Conference (TREC) question answering track in 2004 contains list question, for example 'Who are Nirvana's band members?' (Voorhees, 2004). We illustrate the use of our ontology population algorithm in the context of such list-question answering with a small case-study. Note that we do not consider the processing of the question itself in this research.

Table 2. Learned hyponym patterns and their scores given in descending order of effectiveness

pattern	freq	prec	spr
(countries) like	645	0.66	134
(countries) such as	537	0.54	126
is a small (country)	142	0.69	110
(country) code for	342	0.36	84
(country) map of	345	0.34	78
(countries) including	430	0.21	93
is the only (country)	138	0.55	102
is a (country)	339	0.22	99
(country) flag of	251	0.63	46
and other (countries)	279	0.34	72
and neighboring (countries)	164	0.43	92
(country) name republic of	83	0.93	76
(country) book of	59	0.77	118
is a poor (country)	63	0.73	106
is the first (country)	53	0.70	112
(countries) except	146	0.37	76
(country) code for calling	157	0.95	26
is an independent (country)	62	0.55	114
and surrounding (countries)	84	0.40	107
is one of the poorest (countries)	61	0.75	78
and several other (countries)	65	0.59	90
among other (countries)	84	0.38	97
is a sovereign (country)	48	0.69	89
or any other (countries)	87	0.58	58
(countries) namely	58	0.44	109

Inspired by one of the questions ('What countries is Burger King located in?'), we are interested in populating an ontology with restaurants and the countries in which they operate. We identify the classes 'country' and 'restaurant' and the relation 'located in' between the classes.

We hand the algorithm the instances of 'country', as well as two instances of 'restaurant': 'McDonald's' and 'KFC'. Moreover, we add three instance-pairs of the relation to the algorithm. We use these pairs and a subset $I'_{country}$ of size eight to compute a ranked list of the patterns. We extract terms consisting of one up to four capitalized words. In this test we set the threshold for the number of hits for the queries with the extracted terms to 50. After a small test with names of international restaurant branches, this seemed an appropriate threshold.

The algorithm learned, besides a ranked list of 170 surface text patterns (Table 3), a list of 54 instances of restaurant (Table 4). Among these instances are indeed the names of large international chains, Burger King being one of them. Less expected are the names of geographic locations and names of famous cuisines such as 'Chinese' and 'French'. The last category of false instances found that have not be filtered out, are a number of very common words (e.g. 'It' and 'There').

We populate the ontology with relations found between Burger King and instances from country using the 20 most effective patterns. The algorithm returned 69 instance-pairs with countries related to 'Burger King'. On the Burger King Web site[5] a list of the 65 countries can be found in which the hamburger chain operates. Of these 65 countries, we identified 55. This implies that our results have a precision of 55/69 = 80% and recall of 55/65 = 85%. Many of the falsely related countries—mostly in Eastern Europe—are locations where Burger King is said to have plans to expand its 'empire'.

Populating a Movie Ontology

For this case study, we have constructed a small partial ontology on the movie domain. It is defined as

$$O'_{movie} = \text{((Director, Actor, Movie),}$$
({'Steven Spielberg',
'Francis Ford Coppola'}, {}, {}),
('acts-in(Movie,Actor),
director-of(Movie,Director)),
({}, {})).

We thus only identify three classes, of which only the class Director has instances. Using our method, we want to find movies directed by these directors. The movies found are used to find starring actors, where those actors are the basis of the search for other movies in which they played, etc. The process continues until no new instances can be found.

Relation patterns. This small ontology contains two relations, acts in and director of. For these relations, we have manually selected the sets of patterns:

{"[Movie] starring [Actor]", "[Actor] and [Actor]"} and {"[Director]'s [Movie]", "[Movie], director: [Director]"}.

Instance identification. We identify a term as a Movie title, if it is placed in a text between quotation marks (Geleijnse & Korst, 2005; Sumida, Torisawa, & Shinzato, 2006). Although this may seem a severe restriction, in practice we can permit to loose information contained in other formulations since each query-result gives much redundant information. So, if a movie title is placed between quotation marks just once in the search results, we are able to recognize it.

A person's name (instances of the classes Director and Movie) is to be recognized as either two or three words each starting with a capital. Another feature of the recognition function is the use of lists with taboo words. If a taboo word is contained in an expression, we ignore it. We use a list of about 90 taboo words for the person names (containing words like 'DVD' and 'Biography'). For the movie titles we use a much shorter list, since movie titles can be much more diverse. We have constructed the taboo word lists based on the output of a first run of the algorithm.

We check each o the extracted candidate instances with the use of one of the following queries: "The movie [*Movie*]", "[*Actor*] plays", or "[*Director*] directed". A candidate is accepted, if the number of search results to the query exceeds a threshold. After some tests we choose 5 as a threshold value, since this threshold filtered out not only false instances but most of the common spelling errors in true instances as well.

Formulation of queries. The relation patterns lead to the following set of queries: {"[Director]'s", "[Movie] starring", "[Movie] director", "starring [Actor]"}. We have analyzed the first 100 snippets returned by the search engine after querying a pattern in combination with an instance.

Results

We first ran the algorithm with the names of two (well-known) directors as input: Francis Ford Coppola and Steven Spielberg. Afterwards, we

Table 3. Top learned patterns for the restaurant-country relation

pattern	prec	spr	freq
c_a restaurants of c_q	0.24	15	21
c_a restaurants in c_q	0.07	19	9
c_a hamburger chain that occupies villages throughout modern day c_q	1.0	1	7
c_a restaurant in c_q	0.06	16	6
c_a restaurants in the c_q	0.13	16	2
c_a hamburger restaurant in southern c_q	1.0	1	4

Table 4. Learned instances for restaurant

Chinese	Bank	Outback Steakhouse
Denny's	Pizza Hut	Kentucky Fried Chicken
Subway	Taco Bell	Continental
Holywood	Wendy's	Long John Silver's
HOTEL OR	This	**Burger King**
Japanese	West	Keg Steakhouse
You	BP	Outback
World	Brazil	San Francisco
Leo	Victoria	New York
These	Lyons	Starbucks
FELIX	Roy	California Pizza Kitchen
Marks	Cities	Emperor
Friendly	Harvest	Friday
New York	Vienna	Montana
Louis XV	Greens	Red Lobster
Good	It	There
That	Mark	Dunkin Donuts
Italia	French	Tim Hortons

experimented with larger sets of directors and small sets of beginning directors as input.

An interesting observation is that for this case study the output can be independent of the input sets. That is, when we take a subset of the output of an experiment as the input of another experiment, the outputs are the same, modulo some small differences due to the changes in the search results over time.

We have found 7,000 instances of the class Actor, 3,300 of Director and 12,000 of Movie. The number of retrieved instances increases, about 7%, when 500 query results are used instead of 100.

Precision. When we analyze the precision of the results, we use the data from the Internet Movie Database (IMDb) as a reference. An entry in our ontology is accepted as a correct one, if it can be found in IMDb. We have manually

Table 5. Recall of academy award winners

Category	Recall
Best Actor	96%
Best Actress	94%
Best Director	98%
Best Picture	87%

checked three sequences of 100 instances (at the beginning, middle and end of the generated file) of each class. We estimate a precision of 78%. Most misclassified instances were misspellings or different formulations of the same entity (e.g. ''Leo DiCaprio'' and ''Leonardo DiCaprio''). In the future, we plan to add post processing to recognize these flaws. We can analyze the context (e.g. when 2 actors act in the same set of movies) and use approximate string matching techniques to match these cases.

Likewise, we have also analyzed the precision of the relations. We estimate the precision of the relation between movie and director around 85%, and between movie and actor around 90%.

Recall. The number of entries in IMDb exceeds our ontology by far. Although our algorithm performs especially well on recent productions, we are interested how well it performs on classic movies, actors and directors. First, we made lists of all Academy Award winners (1927-2005) in a number of relevant categories, and checked the recall (Table 5).

IMDb has a top 250 of best movies ever. The algorithm found 85% of them. We observe that results are strongly oriented towards Hollywood productions. We also made a list of all winners of the Cannes Film Festival, the 'Palme d'Or'. Alas, our algorithm only found 26 of the 58 winning movies in this category.

Extracting Information on Historical Figures

The second case study aims at extracting a long list of historical persons and in addition extract-

ing for each of them biographical information such as nationality, period of life, and profession. Using this additional information, we can create sublists of e.g. 17th-century Dutch painters. The information extraction is carried out in two phases. First a long list of historical persons is extracted, and secondly, additional information on these persons is gathered.

Relation Patterns and Query Formulation

It has been observed by e.g. (Ravichandran & Hovy, 2002) that a surface pattern as ''Wolfgang Amadeus Mozart ('' is very successful to determine the year of birth of in this case Mozart, as the open bracket will be often followed by the period of life of the person (in this case: 1756-1791). We decided to use this observation but in a different fashion (Korst, Geleijnse, De Jong, & Verschoor, 2006). Instead of looking for the year of birth of a given person, we use year intervals that possibly relate to the lifetime of a person to find historical persons. More precisely, we issued all year intervals ''$(y_1 - y_2)$'' as queries, with $y_1 \leq [1000 \ldots 1990]$, $y_2 - y_1 \leq [15 \ldots 110]$, and $y_2 \leq 2005$. In other words, we search for persons who were born during the last millennium and who died at an age between 15 and 110. Note that, in this way, we will only find persons that already passed away.

Instance Identification

For each of these issued queries, we scan the at most 1000 snippets that the search engine returned. In each of these snippets, we determine the first occurrence of the queried pair of numbers. Since search engines ignore non-alphanumeric characters, the queried pair of numbers may also occur as y_1 , y_2 or as y_1 / y_2. If the queried pair of numbers is in the intended context $(y_1 - y_2)$, i.e. if they are surrounded by brackets and separated by a hyphen, then the words directly preceding this first occurrence are stored for later analysis, to a maximum of six words. In this way, we obtain for each queried pair of numbers up to 1000 short text fragments that potentially contain person names. In addition, for each of the stored text fragments, we remove potential pre- and suffixes that normally cannot be part of a name. For example, we delete all words that precede a full stop (except when preceded by a single capital letter), a colon, or a semicolon. In addition, of words consisting of upper-case letters only we transform the upper-case into lower-case letters, except for the first one (with some specific exceptions concerning ordinal numbers of kings, queens, etc., composite names including hyphens or apostrophes, and Scottish and Irish names). This results in a set of candidate names.

The *check* phase consists of two filtering steps: one to filter out non-person names and one to filter out multiple variants of a single person name. These steps are next discussed in more detail. Not all text fragments we have found in the extraction phase will be person names. Typically, historic periods, art styles, geographic names, etc. can also directly precede a time interval. Table 6 illustrates the difficulties in discriminating between person names and other text fragments. We note that West Mae probably refers to the person name *Mae West* and that *Napoleon Hill* refers to a person as well as to a geographic location in the state Idaho (USA).

Table 6. Some examples to illustrate the difficulties in discriminating between persons names and other text fragments

Person Name	Non-Person Names
Art Blakey	Art Deco
West, Mae	West Virginia
Amy Beach	Miami Beach
HP Lovecraft	HP Inkjet
Napoleon Hill	Napoleon Hill

To filter out non-person names, we first constructed from dedicated Web sites a long list of the most common first names (boy's and girl's names). If a text fragment starts with such a name, then this is a strong indication that the text fragment is a person name. In addition, we constructed a long list of suspect words that typically do not occur in person names, as follows. From the many snippets that we gathered with the year interval queries we extracted all words, counting how often they occur with a capital and without a capital. If a word occurs most often without a capital, and it is not a special word as 'van', 'de', or 'la', then it is added to the long list of suspect words. We next apply a rule-based approach using these lists of first names and suspect words to filter out text fragments that probably do not relate to person names. In addition to filtering out non-person names, we also want to filter out multiple occurrences of the same person name. These occurrences are caused by variations in spelling of names and errors in the lifetimes. To this end, we carried out the following filtering steps.

1. **Keeping only the last name/lifetime variants that occur most often.** For each last name/lifetime combination, we often find different variants of first names preceding it. For example, Bach (1685–1750) is preceded by, e.g., Johann Sebastian, JS, and Johann S. Of all these variants we only store the one that is found most often, i.e., the variant that occurs most often in the text fragments we found in the 1000 snippets returned on query "(1685–1750)".

2. **Filtering out small variations in name.** If two names have exactly the same lifetime and the edit distance (Gusfield, 1997) between these full names is less than a given threshold, then only the variant that is found most often is kept. As threshold we use an edit distance of two.

3. **Filtering out single errors in lifetimes.** If two names are completely identical but their

lifetimes differ in only the year of birth *or* the year of death, then only the variant that is found most often is kept.

Experiments indicate that in this step we reduce the candidate set of names by approximately 25%.

Ordering Persons by Fame

To order the persons by fame, we use the number of hits (the 'Google Page Count' GPC) as our measure of fame. Now, the question is which query we should issue to the search engine to determine the GPC of a person. The query should be neither too general nor too specific. A single person is often identified in different ways, e.g. Johann Sebastian Bach, JS Bach, JOHANN SEBASTIAN BACH and Bach, Johann Sebastian all refer to the same person. The last variant is called an *inversion*. The latter two variants can be transformed into the first variant by substituting upper-case characters by lower-case ones and by adjusting the order of first and last names. Complicating factors in the identification of inversions are *(i)* that a comma between last name and first names is sometimes omitted and *(ii)* that many first names also occur as last names. An additional complication is that the first names sometimes vary per language (e.g. Charles vs. Karel). To achieve that we are less sensitive to these variants, we use the following query to determine the GPC:

''[last name] ([year of birth]–[year of death])''

For kings, queens, popes, etc., we use the Latin ordinal number as last name. In this way Charles V (1500–1558), Carlos V (1500–1558), and Karel V (1500–1558) are all covered by query ''V (1500–1558)''. Note that we assume the combination of last name and lifetime to be specific enough to uniquely identify historical persons.

Extracting Additional Information

The first phase, described above, resulted in a large list of historical persons that was ordered using GPC as measure of fame. For further details on this list we refer to (Korst, Geleijnse, De Jong, & Verschoor, 2006). In the next phase, we extracted additional information, such as gender, nationality, and professions. Also, we tried to retrieve related images and a few one-liners that already give a brief impression of how the person gathered fame. We extracted additional information for the top 10,000 of the list of historical persons that we obtained in the first phase. We next briefly describe how we gathered this additional material.

To acquire additional information, we again issued queries of the type ''Albert Einstein was'', i.e., we used the full name of a person followed by the word was, where we restrict ourselves to English language pages. From the snippets returned, we extracted complete sentences that contain the query. Hence, if only a fraction of a sentence was given in a snippet, then this fraction was simply ignored. These sentences were next used to identify specific words that indicate gender, nationality and professions.

Determining gender. We simply counted words that refer to the male gender, namely the words he, his, son of, brother of, father of, man and men. Likewise, we counted words that refer to the female gender, namely the words she, her, daughter of, sister of, mother of, woman, and women. We simply assigned the gender with the highest count.

Determining nationality. We extracted for each country from the CIA World Factbook Web site the country name (in conventional short form) and the corresponding adjective that indicates nationality, e.g. 'Belgium' and 'Belgian'. In addition, for some countries we added a number of additional terms relating to parts of the country, such as 'Flemish' for Belgium and 'English', 'Scottish', and 'Welsh' for the United Kingdom. To determine the nationality, we count for each country the number of word occurrences in the set of sentences, and simply assign the nationality with the highest count. So far, we did not consider country names of countries that do no longer exist, such as Prussia.

Determining professions. As for gender and nationality, we now simply count how often each of these profession names occur in the sentences. However, instead of only selecting the one with the highest count, we here want to be able to retain multiple professions. For that reason, we select the ones that have at least a count of $0.5 \cdot c_{max}$, where c_{max} is the score of the highest scoring profession, ordered by decreasing count.

Results

To give an impression of the results that we obtained in this case study, we present three tables. Table 7 gives the top of the persons born in the period 1880—1889, Table 8 gives the top of the persons that has as their highest scoring profession either artist or painter. For more details and examples we refer to (Korst, Geleijnse, De Jong, & Verschoor, 2006) and (Geleijnse and Korst, 2007).

Considering Table 9, we observe that Thomas Young is given the American nationality, while he is from the United Kingdom. This is due to the fact that Thomas Young is a common name,

Table 7. The 20 persons born between 1880 and 1889 with the highest GPC

Born In [1880–1889]		
James Joyce (1882-1941)	Ireland	author
Bela Bartok (1881-1945)	Hungary	composer
Pablo Picasso (1881-1973)	Spain	artist
Anton Webern (1883-1945)	Austria	musician, composer
HL Mencken (1880-1956)	United States	author, journalist
Niels Bohr (1885-1962)	Denmark	scientist, physicist
Adolf Hitler (1889-1945)	Germany	leader
Amedeo Modigliani (1884-1920)	Italy	artist, painter
Agustin Barrios (1885-1944)	Paraguay	musician, composer
Le Corbusier (1887-1965)	Switzerland	architect
John Maynard Keynes (1883-1946)	United Kingdom	economist
Ludwig Wittgenstein (1889-1951)	Austria	philosopher
Igor Stravinsky (1882-1971)	Russia	composer
TS Eliot (1888-1965)	United Kingdom	poet
Franz Kafka (1883-1924)	Czech Republic	author
Franklin D. Roosevelt (1882-1945)	United States	president
Marc Chagall (1887-1985)	Russia	painter, artist
Martin Heidegger (1889-1976)	Germany	philosopher
Kahlil Gibran (1883-1931)	Lebanon	poet, philosopher,...
Heitor Villa-Lobos (1887-1959)	Brazil	composer

Table 8. The 25 artists/painters with the highest GPC

Artists/Painters		
Leonardo da Vinci (1452–1519)	Italy	artist, scientist,...
Pablo Picasso (1881–1973)	Spain	artist
Vincent van Gogh (1853–1890)	Netherlands	artist, painter
Claude Monet (1840–1926)	France	artist, painter,...
Pierre-Auguste Renoir (1841–1919)	France	painter
Paul Gauguin (1848–1903)	France	painter
Edgar Degas (1834–1917)	France	artist, painter,...
Paul Cezanne (1839–1906)	France	painter, artist
Salvador Dali (1904–1989)	Spain	artist
Henri Michaux (1899–1984)	Belgium	artist, poet
Gustav Klimt (1862–1918)	Austria	painter, artist
Peter Paul Rubens (1577–1640)	Belgium	artist, painter
Katsushika Hokusai (1760–1849)	Japan	painter
Amedeo Modigliani (1884–1920)	Italy	artist, painter
JMW Turner (1775–1851)	United Kingdom	artist, painter
James McNeill Whistler (1834–1903)	United States	artist
Rene Magritte (1898–1967)	Belgium	artist, painter
Henri Matisse (1869–1954)	France	artist
Rembrandt van Rijn (1606–1669)	Netherlands	artist, painter
Edouard Manet (1832–1883)	France	artist, painter
Herm Albright (1876–1944)	—	artist, engraver,...
Marc Chagall (1887–1985)	Russia	painter, artist
Edvard Munch (1863–1944)	Norway	painter, artist
Wassily Kandinsky (1866–1944)	Russia	artist, painter
Francisco Goya (1746–1828)	Spain	artist, painter

thus many of the sentences starting with 'Thomas Young was' actually refer to different persons. Unfortunately, Marie Curie is not in this sublist. The only reason is that her only profession that is retained was 'scientist'. Otherwise, she would have ranked between Rutherford and Feynman. For the same reason, Robert Hooke would have ranked between Heisenberg and Volta, and Robert Wilhelm Bunsen would have ranked between Hahn and Curie. The first profession of Sir David Brewster is judge, resulting from the phrase "Sir David Brewster was afraid that the members could scarcely judge ...".

Recall. To get an impression of the performance of our algorithm, we estimate the recall by choosing a diverse set of six books containing short biographies of persons whom we would expect to find in our list. For each of these books, we determined for the persons that could potentially be found by our algorithm (i.e., the persons who are born in the intended time period and have died). Of these 1049 persons, 1033 were present in our

Table 9. The 40 physicists with the highest GPC

Albert Einstein (1879–1955)	scientist, physicist
Isaac Newton (1642–1727)	scientist, mathematician, physicist
Galileo Galilei (1564–1642)	astronomer, physicist, scientist
Niels Bohr (1885–1962)	scientist, physicist
Lord Kelvin (1824–1907)	physicist, scientist, mathematician
Christiaan Huygens (1629–1695)	astronomer, scientist, mathematician, physicist
Michael Faraday (1791–1867)	chemist, scientist, physicist
Georg Christoph Lichtenberg (1742–1799)	physicist, author, mathematician, astronomer
James Clerk Maxwell (1831–1879)	physicist
Max Planck (1858–1947)	physicist
Ernest Rutherford (1871–1937)	scientist, physicist
Richard Feynman (1918–1988)	physicist
Hermann von Helmholtz (1821–1894)	scientist, physicist
Werner Heisenberg (1901–1976)	physicist
Alessandro Volta (1745–1827)	physicist
Wolfgang Pauli (1900–1958)	physicist
Sir Arthur Eddington (1882–1944)	scientist, physicist, director, author
Heinrich Hertz (1857–1894)	scientist, physicist, explorer, author, researcher
Wilhelm Conrad Roentgen (1845–1923)	scientist, physicist, director
Paul Dirac (1902–1984)	physicist
Andre Marie Ampere (1775–1836)	physicist, mathematician
Joseph John Thomson (1856–1940)	scientist, physicist, explorer
James Prescott Joule (1818–1889)	scientist, physicist
Ludwig Boltzmann (1844–1906)	physicist
Thomas Young (1773–1829)	physicist, physician, scientist
Ernst Mach (1838–1916)	philosopher, physicist
Evangelista Torricelli (1608–1647)	physcist, mathematician
Charles Augustin Coulomb (1736–1806)	engineer, physicist, scientist
Otto Hahn (1879–1968)	chemist, physicist
Pierre Curie (1859–1906)	physicist
Otto von Guericke (1602–1686)	scientist, inventor, physicist
Sir David Brewster (1781–1868)	judge, physicist
William Henry Bragg (1862–1942)	physicist
Thomas Kuhn (1922–1996)	philosopher, physicist, historian
George Gamow (1904–1968)	physicist
Sadi Carnot (1796–1832)	physicist, engineer
Gustav Theodor Fechner (1801–1887)	physicist, psychologist, philosopher
Joseph Swan (1828–1914)	chemist, inventor, physicist
Louis de Broglie (1892–1987)	physicist
Augustin Fresnel (1788–1827)	inventor, physicist, engineer

list, which is a fraction of 0.98. For further details on the chosen books we refer to Korst, Geleijnse, De Jong, & Verschoor, 2006). We observe that the recall is close to one, for each of the six books, even for a more specialized topic as 17th century Dutch painters. Of the total 108 of these painters mentioned in one of the books, 106 were found. We note that of the 16 persons that did not appear in our list, there were 4 persons for which the books could not provide the lifetime. For the recall of the additional information, we observe that for the 10,000 persons that we considered all were given a gender, 77% were given a nationality, and 95% were given one or more professions.

Precision. All kinds of imperfections can still be observed in our list of historical persons, such as remaining inversions, missing parts of a name, and errors in lifetimes, although each of these occurs relatively infrequently. We concentrate on estimating the fraction of names that do not relate to persons. The corresponding precision that is obtained by the algorithm has been estimated as follows. We selected three decennia, namely 1220-1229, 1550-1559 and 1880-1889, and analyzed for each the candidate persons that were 'born' in this decennium. For the first two decennia we analyzed the complete list, for decennium 1880-1889 we analyzed only the first 1000 as well as the last 1000 names. This resulted in a precision of 0.94, 0.95, and 0.98, respectively. As the decennium of 1880-1889 resulted in considerably more names, we take a weighted average of these results. This yields an estimated precision for the complete list of 0.98 (Korst, Geleijnse, De Jong, & Verschoor, 2006). Regarding the precision of the property *lived-in*, we make the following observations. Considering the list of 450,000 potential instances that our algorithm found for this property, we observe that 235 were found with a GPC of at least 10,000 and 2450 were found with a GPC of at least 1000. Clearly, the probability that instances with a high GPC contain spelling errors in person name or lifetime is quite low, since accidental spelling errors in the last name or in the lifetime

will result in a low GPC. Indeed, we found that the accuracy of our results was better than that of the information in some of the books.

Biographical entries. To get a better impression of the quality of the biographical entries, we manually checked 50 persons, evenly distributed in the top-2500. Of these 50 persons, we observed that gender, nationality and professions were all correct for 38 persons. No errors in gender were detected in any of the 50 persons. For three persons the nationality was not found. All nationalities found proved to be correct. For two persons, all given professions were wrong. For eight others, one or more given professions were incorrect, but usually the professions with the highest count were correct.

COMMUNITY-BASED KNOWLEDGE MINING

In this second part of the chapter, we focus on more subjective knowledge. For example, we are interested the most appropriate genre for a musical artist, using the collective knowledge of the Web community. As such knowledge is not only expressed (directly) within sentences, we discuss two alternative methods to find relations, apart from the pattern-based method described in the previous part. Since we focus on subjective knowledge, multiple relations are possible, e.g. Madonna may both be a Rock and a Pop artist. We therefore assign a score for each of the relations found. For example, the aim is to find a higher score for the relation between ABBA and Disco than between ABBA and Dead Metal. As the focus is on scoring relations, we assume the classes to be complete. This second part of the chapter is organized as follows. In Section 3.1 we formally define the problem, while Section 3.2 discusses the three alternative methods to categorize instances. In Section 3.3 we discuss a similar method to find relatedness between the instances. The found relatedness scores can be used to improve the categorization (Section 3.4).

Experiments in two domains are discussed in Section 3.5. Finally we conclude this part of the chapter in Section 4.

Problem Description

We want to map a complete set of instances of class c_a - artists or items such as movies or paintings—to a set of categories: instances of class c_s. Given are two sets of instances I_a of size N and I_s of size M. Hence, I_a is a set with instances such as paintings, or artists. The set I_s contains categories like movements in art or genres. We are interested in a mapping $m : I_a \rightarrow I_s$.

Definition. We call a category m(b) *most appropriate* for b if a domain expert would select m(b) from the set I_s as the category best applicable to b.

Problem 1. Find for each $b \in I_a$ the most appropriate $m(b) \in I_s$.

Problem 2. Find for each pair of instances of c_a, *(b,c)* a score $\Gamma(b,c)$ expressing the extent of relatedness between b and c.

We use co-occurrences of instances in I_a and categories in I_s (e.g. Johnny Cash and country) on the Web to extract such information to compute a preliminary mapping. Additionally, we assume that related instances in I_a often share a category in I_s. We compute distances between instances using Web co-occurrences in order to identify the nearest neighbors for each instance. The preliminary mapping of each artist and its nearest neighbors are combined into a final mapping m.

Three Classification Methods

In this section, we present three methods to classify instances in I_a using Web data. The first method is based on analyzing the total numbers of co-occurrences of instances in I_a and categories

in I_s on the Web. To retrieve this data we again use a state of the art search engine. An important drawback of this page count method is that it has a high *Google Complexity*, i.e. it requires many queries to a search engine, namely $O(N \cdot M)$. For large sets this can be problematic, since search engines currently allow only a limited amount of automated queries per day (Cafarella, Downey, Soderland, & Etzioni, 2005). Moreover, the number of hits can fluctuate over time (Véronis, 2006), which hampers the reuse of old hit counts. We present two alternative methods that do not suffer from these drawbacks.

We are interested in a mapping m', based on co-occurrences of elements in I_a and I_s. In Section 3.4 we combine this mapping m' with a distance matrix between related instances in I_a to find a definite mapping *m*.

Page-Count-Based Mapping (PCM)

To obtain the mapping m' we perform a query "b","g" for each pair $(b,g) \in I_a \times I_s$. Per query, we extract the estimated number of *hits* co(*b,g*).

co(*b,g*) = 'the number of hits for query "b", "g"'

We assume that the order of the terms *b* and *g* in the query does not effect the number of hits, thus we assume co(*b,g*) = co(*g,b*).

This Page-Count-based Mapping (PCM) is simple and intuitive. If we are for example interested in categorizing music artists into genres, we analyze the number of hits to queries for combinations of the names of the artist and each genre. Assuming Johnny Cash to be a country artist, we expect that more documents contain both the terms *Country* and *Johnny Cash* than *Reggae* and *Johnny Cash*.

Per $b \in I_a$ we could map the $g \in I_s$ with the most hits. However, we observe that frequently occurring categories in I_s have a larger probability to be mapped to any instance in I_a. For example, the query '*Pop*' results in 8 times more hits than the query *'Disco'*. Although we consider *Boney M* as a *disco-act*, the query *'Boney M, pop'* gives twice the amount of hits as *'Boney M, disco'*. This observation leads to a normalized approach, inspired by the theory of pointwise mutual information (Manning & Schütze, 1999; Downey et al., 2005). For $b \in I_a$ and $g \in I_s$, we define a scoring function S(b,g) as follows.

$$S(b,g) = \frac{co(b,g)}{1 + \sum_{c \in Ia} co(c,g)} \qquad (1)$$

In the denominator we add 1 to the sum of all co-occurrences with g to avoid dividing by 0.

Having computed the scores for all pairs, we select a preliminary mapping *m'* for each $b \in I_a$. Per instance we select the category $g \in I_s$ with the highest score S.

$$m'(b) = \text{argmax}_{h \in Is} S(b,h) \qquad (2)$$

Using PCM we thus need to perform N · M queries.

Pattern-Based Mapping (PM)

The Pattern-based Mapping (PM) is based on occurrences of terms in phrases on the Web. We observe combinations of terms in phrases that express the relation we are interested in. For example, if we are interested in the relation between music artists (in I_a) and their genres (in I_s), an appropriate phrase that links terms of the two could be *'[artist] is one of the biggest [genre] artists'*. We can identify these patterns automatically by using a training set of related instances and categories; see (Ravichandran & Hovy, 2002; Geleijnse & Korst, 2006) and Section 2.3 of this chapter. Learning patterns can be done with $O(N)$ queries.

We use combinations of a pattern and an instance or a category as a query to the search engine. For example, if we have the pattern *''[genre] artist such as [artist]''*, we use *''artist such as''*

in queries in combinations with all names of genres and artists. We use this pattern e.g. both for the query *''Country artists such as''* and for the query *''artists such as Prince''*. In the snippets found with the first query, we identify instances in I_a, while in the results for the second query we search for categories in I_s related to Prince. These queries provide access to relevant data. From the snippets returned by the search engine, we thus identify the elements of either I_a or I_s to measure the number of co-occurrences of the pairs. Hence, using PM co(b,g) is defined as follows.

co(b,g) = 'number of occurrences of *b* by querying patterns with *g*' + 'number of occurrences of *g* by querying patterns with *b*'

Using PM we only need $O(M+N)$ queries. We use the same scoring function S(b,g) as given in (1) to obtain a preliminary mapping as given in (2).

Document-Based Mapping (DM)

In the Document-based Mapping (DM) approach we collect the first *k* URLs of the documents returned by the search engine for a given query. These *k* URLs are the most relevant for the query submitted based on the ranking used by the search engine (Brin & Page, 1998).

In the first phase of the algorithm, we query all instances in both I_a and I_s and collect the top *k* documents for each of the queries. For instances in I_a, we retrieve each document using the URLs found by the search engine. We count the occurrences of the categories in I_s (thus the names of the categories) in the retrieved documents for the intermediate mapping *m'*. From the documents retrieved with a category $g \in I_s$, we similarly extract the occurrences of instances in I_a.

The documents obtained using DM are the most relevant for each element $b \in I_a$. For the artists queried we expect biographies, fan pages, pages of museums, entries in database sites and so on. The categories in I_s (e.g. the genres or styles) mentioned in these pages will most probably reflect the genre of the artist queried.

Thus the co-occurrences function is here defined as follows.

co(b,g) = 'number of occurrences of b in documents found with g' + 'number of occurrences of g in documents found with b'

The co-occurrences of elements in I_a and I_s again are used for an intermediate mapping using the same scoring function. This method also requires only $O(M+N)$ queries. However, additional data communication is required since for each query up to k documents have to be downloaded instead of using only the data provided by the search engine.

Finding Related Instances

We use the same three co-occurrence-based methods to compute the relatedness between elements in I_a. We consider instances in I_a to be related, when they frequently co-occur in the same context. In Section 3.4, we use this information in a final mapping m between elements in I_a and I_s. Per pair (b,c) $\in I_a \times I_a$ we compute the score $\Gamma(b,c)$, similar to the score S in (1).

$$\Gamma(b,c) = \frac{co(b,c)}{\sum_{x, x \neq c} co(x,c)} \quad (3)$$

Again, we do not use a majority voting to prevent frequently occurring instances to be strongly related to many other instances.

In PCM we combine the names of two artists into a query and extract the number of *hits*. Using this method this phase requires N^2 queries.

If we use PM to obtain the numbers of co-occurrences of instances in I_a, we can specify the nature of the relatedness. For example, for instances of the class pop artist, we can solely be interested in artists who have played together. A

pattern such as *"[pop artist] recorded a duet with [pop artist]"* could be suitable for this purpose. This phase of the method consists of $k \cdot N$ queries (with k the number of patterns). In the documents obtained with the DM method we only expect occurrences of other terms in I_a that are strongly connected with the b $\in I_a$ queried. For DM no additional queries have to be performed in this phase, since we can reuse the documents obtained in the first phase.

Combining Results in Final Mapping

We use the assumption that related instances in I_a often share the same category. We investigate whether the use of relatedness between instances in I_a helps to improve to the precision of the mapping m'. We combine the scores Γ with the preliminary mapping m' as follows. Per b $\in I_a$, we inspect m' to determine the category that is assigned most often to b and its n closest related instances. We thus expect that the most appropriate category g for b is most often mapped by m' among b and its nearest neighbors.

Per instance b $\in I_a$, we construct an ordered list B(n) with b and its n nearest neighbors

B(n) = $(b_0, b_1, \ldots, b_n)$
with b = b_0 as its first element and
$\Gamma(b, b_i) \geq \Gamma(b, b_{i+1})$, for i < 0

For a final mapping m of instances b $\in I_a$ to a category in I_s, we inspect the most occurring category mapped by m' to b and its n nearest neighbors.

$$m(b,n) = \mathrm{argmax}_{h \in I_s} \sum_{c \in B(n)} \tau(c,h)$$

with

$$\begin{aligned} \tau(c,h) &= 1 & \text{if } m'(b_i) = h \\ &= 0 & \text{otherwise} \end{aligned}$$

If two categories have an equal score, we select the first occurring one. That is, the category that is mapped by *m'* to b or to the artist most related to b.

Experimental Results

We evaluate the methods discussed in this part of the chapter as follows. First, we evaluate the instance-similarity scoring using the three methods PM, DM and PCM. These similarities are used in the subsequent part to classify musical artists into genres. Finally, we repeat this experiment on a different domain to classify painters into art movements.

Musical Artist Similarity

We use the common test set I_{224} of 224 artists, equally divided over 14 genres as defined by Knees et al. (2004)[6] to evaluate the computed

Table 10. patterns for artist—artist relation

"like I_{224} and I_{224}"
"such as I_{224} and I_{224} "
"including I_{224} and I_{224} "
"for example I_{224} and I_{224} "
"namely I_{224} and I_{224}"
" I_{224} and I_{224} "
" I_{224} I_{224} and other"

artist similarities $\Gamma(b,c)$. We consider two artists to be similar, if they share a genre in the test set. In these experiments, we only evaluate precision. If for an $b \in I_a$ no mapping or related instance could be found, we consider the result to be incorrect.

For PCM we added the extra term music for finding co-occurrences of the artists. For example the terms Bush and Inner Circle co-occurred a lot on the Web, due to American politics. By adding the term music we restrict ourselves to documents handling music.

Figure 1. Precision for classification of the 224 musical artists

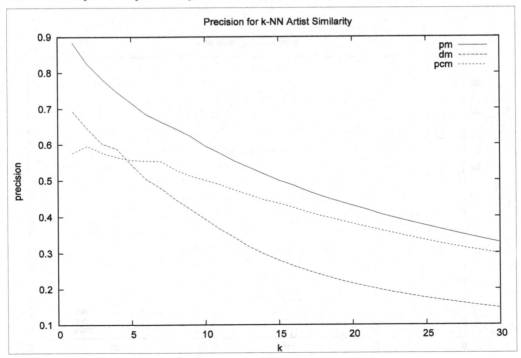

Since we are not interested in the nature of the relatedness between artists, for PM we selected general enumeration patterns (Table 10) to obtain co-occurrences.

Figure 1 shows the average precision of the similarity of the artists and their *k*-NN for the sets of 224 artists. We can conclude that the pattern based method PM gives good results and outperforms both DM and PCM. For smaller values of *k* the method most inefficient in the number of queries is outperformed by both DM and PM. The performance of DM drops quickly due to the fact that only few related artists are mentioned among the best ranked pages for the queried instances.

Musical Artist Genre Tagging

In this experiment, I_{224} is again the set of all artist names in the list composed by Knees, Pampalk

Table 11. The patterns for the artist-genre relation

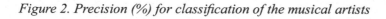

"I_g (artists OR bands OR acts OR musicians) like I_{224}"
"I_g (artists OR bands OR acts OR musicians) such as I_{224}"
"I_g (artists OR bands OR acts OR musicians) for example I_{224}"
"I_{224} and other I_g (artists OR bands OR acts OR musicians)"

& Widmer (2004). This list consists of 14 genres, each with 16 artists.

To find a mapping between I_{224} and the set of genres I_g, the genres mentioned in the list are not all suitable for finding co-occurrences. For example, the term *classical* is ambiguous and *Alternative Rock/Indie* is an infrequent term. We therefore manually rewrote the names of the genres into unambiguous ones (such as *classical music*) and added some synonyms. After collecting the numbers of co-occurrences of artists and genres, we summed up the scores of the co-occurrences for synonyms. Thus, for each artist *b* the number of co-occurrences with the terms *Indie*

Figure 2. Precision (%) for classification of the musical artists

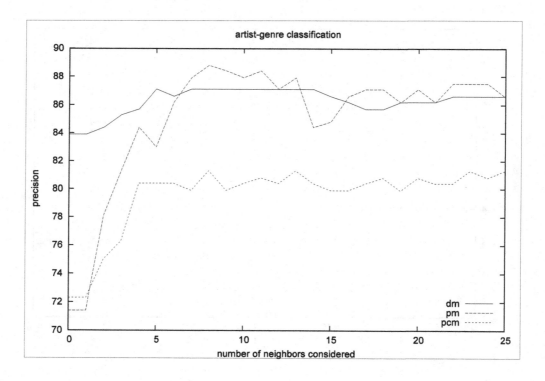

Table 12. Precision (%) without related artists and best precision per method

method	n=0	best	(corresponding n)
PCM	71.4	81.3	(13)
PM	72.2	88.8	(8)
DM	83.9	87.1	(5)

Table 13. Best scoring learned patterns for painter—movement relation

> "$I_a I_s$"
> "$I_s I_a$"
> "I_a and other I_s"
> "I_a and I_s"
> "I_a tog initiativ til I_s"
> "I_a and the I_s"
> "I_a surrealism I_s"
> "I_a synthetic I_s"
> "I_s artist I_a"
> "I_a express I_s"
> "I_a of the I_s"
> "I_a uit de I_s"
> "I_a experimenting with I_s"
> "I_a arte I_s"
> "I_s painter I_a"

and *Alternative Rock* are added to the co-occurrences of *b* with the genre *Alternative Rock/Indie*. Motivated by the results in (Schedl et. al, 2005), for PCM we used the `allintitle` option in the artist classification experiment.

For PM we selected for the genre-artist relations the patterns in Table 11 from a list of patterns found expressing this relation.

For all three methods, we reuse the computed artist similarities.

In Table 12 the performance of the preliminary mapping can be found for the three methods (n = 0). We were able to map all artists to a genre. Co-occurrences between genres and artists thus could be found using PCM, PM as well as DM. The latter performs best. With respect to the preliminary mapping, the method with the smallest amount of Google queries performs best. The data found on the best ranked documents is thus reliable.

Using DM only few related artists can be found on the documents visited. This leads to a stable performance for the final mapping when expanding the list of related artists (Figure 2). That is, we only consider artists that co-occur at least once. Contrary to especially PCM, large numbers of n do not deteriorate the precision.

The performance of the pattern-based method strongly improves by considering related artists, the best performance is obtained for n = 8. All methods perform best for values of n between 5 and 13. The *Rock n' Roll* artists proved to be the most problematic to categorize. The artists in the genres *classical*, *blues* and *jazz* were all correctly categorized with the best scoring settings. With the supervised music artist clustering method discussed in (Knees et al., 2004) a precision of 87% was obtained using complex machine learning techniques and a relatively large training set. In (Schedl et al., 2005) a precision of up to 85% was obtained using $O(N^2)$ queries. We can conclude that our simple and unsupervised method produces similar results. Moreover, we compute a classification of artists into genres instead of clusters of artists.

Painter Movement Classification

For this experiment, we constructed a list of painters I_a and a list of movements I_s in art using Wikipedia and map the two. From Wikipedia we extracted a set I_a of 1,280 well-known painters from the article *List of painters* and a set I_s of 77 movements in art from *List of art movements*[7]. We tested the performance of the algorithm on the subset of 160 painters who could be extracted from the Wikipedia pages describing movements (e.g. from the page on Abstract Expressionism). The other 1,120 painters are either not mentioned on the pages describing styles or are mentioned on more than one page. However, when computing similarities between the painters, we take all 1,280 painters into account. For the elements of I_s in this test no synonyms were added. For fairness,

Figure 3. Precision (%) for classification of the painters

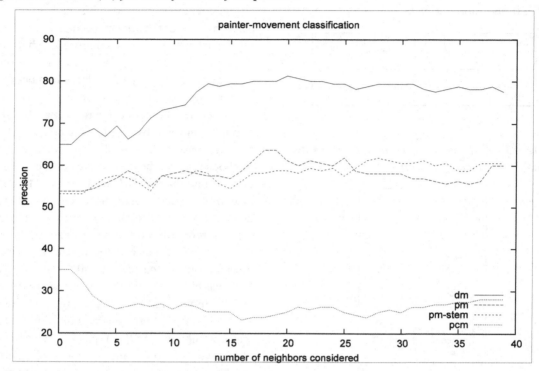

Table 14. Precision (%) without related instances and best precision per method

method		Painter-Movement	
	N = 0	best	(corresp. n)
PCM	35.0	35.0	(0)
PM	53.8	63.8	(18)
DM	65.0	81.2	(20)
PM-STEMMING	53.2	61.9	(28)

we excluded pages from the domain wikipedia.org in the search queries.

For PM, we selected learned patterns for the mapping between the elements in I_a and I_s. For learning, we used instance-pairs outside the test set. The best scoring patterns can be found in Table 13. For the relation between the instances in I_a, these patterns found were mostly enumeration patterns, e.g. *"including b and"*. The complete details of both experiments and the patterns used

in PM can be found on the Web (**footnote** http:// gijsg.dse.nl/Webconmine/). Due to the rareness of some of the painters and names of movements, we did not use any additional terms in the queries for DM or PCM.

In Table 14 the performance of the preliminary mapping *m'* can be found for the three methods (n = 0). The experiments show that in general the use of related instances improves the classification (see Table 14 and Figure 3). It shows again that the methods with the lowest Google Complexity thus PM and DM perform better than PCM.

Although in the painter-movement experiment the number of categories identified (77) is much larger than in the previous experiment (16), the performance of PM and especially DM is still good. The results of PCM indicate that when the precision of the intermediate mapping is low (35%), the use of related instances does not improve the results. In this experiment we even observe a deterioration of the performance. Here DM clearly outperforms PM. This can be explained by the fact that using PM considerably less painter-movement pairs could be extracted. We expected the recall of PM to increase when applying stemming on the names of movements and the texts extracted (Porter, 1997). Although the number of pairs extracted slightly increases, the precision does not improve (Table 14).

CONCLUSION

In Section 2 we have presented a framework algorithm for ontology population using queried expressions to mine factual information. We combine patterns expressing relations and an instance of a class into queries to generate highly usable search engine snippets. From these snippets we simultaneously extract instances of the classes and instance pairs of the relations. The results of the experiments are convincing. When submitting effective queries, the snippets provide enough data to populate an ontology with good recall and precision. The method is simple and easily adaptable to different domains. In the second part, we have discussed three alternative methods PCM, PM and DM to obtain co-occurrences of terms using a search engine. These methods are applied to gain a preliminary mapping between instances such as artists or painters and categories such as genres or art-movements. The distance between related instances is used to obtain a more reliable mapping. The three alternatives used have a different complexity with respect to the number of queries to a search engine. The method using patterns and the one using complete documents are linear in the number of items in the sets of instances and categories, where the page-count-based mapping is quadratic. This distinction is important for classifying large sets of instances, since search engines allow only a limited amount of automated queries per day. We can precisely classify artists to genres, where the most efficient

methods with respect to the Google complexity perform best. A second experiment consisted of the mapping of painters to their movements. This experiment underlines that the document-based and pattern-based method outperform the query-expensive method based on the number of search engine hits. We showed that simple and unsupervised methods can be used for a reliable classification. Using related instances indeed helps to improve the classification of instances. The experiments show an increase of the performance in both experiments. However, the Google count based method in painter classification shows that this additional step deteriorates the precision, if the classification is very unreliable.

FUTURE RESEARCH DIRECTIONS

We have shown that the pattern based approach in general gives access to highly relevant snippets. For future work, it is the process of identifying the instances within the snippets that needs further research.

The creation of precise rules is a laborious task, especially since each class requires its specific set of rules. The experiments in Part I showed that the challenge lies in the improvement of the precision of the recognition rules and the check functions.

The use of check functions based on enumeration of candidate instance has potential. Part II showed us that enumeration patterns are reliable to identify related instances. Now, if our ontology contains the instances *KFC* and *McDonald's*, we can formulate enumeration queries containing these instances and candidate instances. Fore example, the enumeration *'KFC, Chinese and McDonald's'* is not found by Google, where *'KFC, Burger King and McDonald's'* gives 31 hits.

With the known instances and the instances learned using the rules, we can automatically create an annotated corpus. This annotated corpus can be used to train a named entity recognizer. Such a named entity recognizer should be robust and consider only the local context of the named entities, as the snippets contain incomplete sentences. Approaches using only fully parsed sentences are therefore less usable. Memory-based learning (Daelemans & van den Bosch, 2005) is a technique that does not abstract from the learned instances. Moreover, only a small window of words is taken into account. If the information is redundantly available within the snippets, this technique may lead to satisfactory results.

The use of named entity recognizers based on machine learning also gives the possibility to compare the various approaches. When we collect the downloaded snippets, this comparison can be made on the same data.

With respect to the community-based data, in this chapter we assumed that the mapping was functional, i.e. only one category could be assigned to an instance. However, in some tasks multiple categories can apply to an instance. We therefore want to adapt the system such that multiple categories accompanied with a confidence mark can be assigned to an instance, analogue to the Web 2.0 concept of social tagging (O'Reilly, 2005). Moreover, methods can be exploited to learn other words related to some category, e.g. with the $tf \cdot idf$-approach (Knees et al., 2004; Manning & Schütze, 1999).

REFERENCES

Agichtein, E., & Gravano, L. (2000). Snowball: Extracting relations from large plain-text collections. In *Proceedings of the fifth ACM international conference on digital libraries*.

Balog, K., Mishne, G., & De Rijke, M. (2006). Why are they excited? Identifying and explaining spikes in blog mood levels. In *Conference companion of the 11th meeting of the European chapter of the association for computational linguistics (eacl 2006)* (pp. 207-210). Trento, Italy.

Berners-Lee, T., Hendler, J., & Lassila, O. (2001, May). The Semantic Web. In *Scientific American*.

Blackburn, P., & Bos, J. (2005). *Representation and inference for natural language. A first course in computational semantics*. CSLI.

Boer, V. de, Someren, M. van, & Wielinga, B. J. (2007). A redundancy-based method for the extraction of relation instances from the Web. *International Journal of Human-Computer Studies, 65*(9), 816-831.

Brill, E. (1992). A simple rule-based part-of-speech tagger. In *Proceedings of the third conference on applied natural language processing (ANLP'92)* (pp. 152-155). Trento, Italy.

Brin, S. (1998). Extracting patterns and relations from the World Wide Web. *In Webdb workshop at sixth international conference on extending database technology (EDBT'98)*.

Brin, S., & Page, L. (1998). The anatomy of a large-scale hypertextual Web search engine. *Computer Networks and ISDN Systems, 30*(1-7), 107-117.

Brooks, C. H., & Montanez, N. (2006). Improved annotation of the blogosphere via autotagging and hierarchical clustering. *In Proceedings of the 15th international conference on world wide Web (www2006)* (pp. 625-632). Edinburgh, UK.

Brothwick, A. (1999). *A maximum entropy approach to named entity recognition*. Unpublished doctoral dissertation, New York University.

Buitelaar, P., Cimiano, P., & Magnini, B. (Eds.). (2005). Ontology learning from text: Methods, evaluation and applications, *123*. IOS Press.

Bunt, H., & Muskens, R. (Eds.). (2000). Computing meaning, *1*(73) Kluwer. Cafarella, M. J., Downey, D., Soderland, S., & Etzioni, O. (2005). Knowitnow: Fast, scalable information extraction from the Web. In *Proceedings of human language technology conference and conference on empirical methods in nlp* (pp. 563-570). Vancouver, Canada.

Chang, C.-H., Kayed, M., Girgis, M. R., & Shaalan, K. F. (2006). A survey of Web information systems. *IEEE Transactions on Knowledge and Data Engineering, 18*(10), 1411-1428.

Chinchor, N. A. (Ed.). (1998). *Proceedings of the seventh message understanding conference (muc-7)*. Fairfax, Virginia: Morgan Kaufmann.

Cilibrasi, R., & Vitanyi, P. (2007). The Google similarity distance. *IEEE Transactions on Knowledge and Data Management, 19*(3), 370-383.

Cimiano, P., & Staab, S. (2004). Learning by Googling. SIGKDD Explorations Newsletter, *6*(2), 24-33.

Crescenzi, V., & Mecca, G. (2004). Automatic information extraction from large Web sites. *Journal of the ACM, 51*(5), 731-779.

Cunningham, H., Maynard, D., Bontcheva, K., & Tablan, V. (2002). Gate: A framework and graphical development environment for robust nlp tools and applications. In *Proceedings of the 40th annual meeting of the association for computational linguistics (acl 2002)*. Philadelphia, PA.

Daelemans, W., & Bosch, A. van den. (2005). *Memory-based language processing.* Cambridge University Press.

Dave, D., & Lawrence, S. (2003). Mining the peanut gallery: Opinion extraction and semantic classification of product reviews. In *Proceedings of the twelfth international World Wide Web conference (www2003)* (pp. 519-528). Budapest, Hungary: ACM Press.

Downey, D., Broadhead, M., & Etzioni, O. (2007). Locating complex named entities in Web text. In *Proceedings of the twentieth international joint conference on artificial intelligence (ijcai'07)*. Hyderabad, India.

Downey, D., Etzioni, O., & Soderland, S. (2005). A probabilistic model of redundancy in information extraction. In *19th international joint conference on arti_cial intelligence (ijcai'05)* (pp. 1034-1041). Edinburgh, UK.

Duda, R. O., Hart, P. E., & Stork, D. G. (2000). *Pattern classification.* Wiley-Interscience Publication.

Dumais, S., Banko, M., Brill, E., Lin, J., & Ng, A. (2002). Web question answering: Is more always better? *In Sigir '02: Proceedings of the 25th annual international acm sigir conference on research and development in information retrieval* (pp. 291-298). New York, NY, USA: ACM Press.

Etzioni, O., Cafarella, M. J., Downey, D., Popescu, A., Shaked, T., Soderland, S., et al. (2005). Unsupervised named-entity extraction from the Web: An experimental study. *Artificial Intelligence, 165*(1), 91-134.

Finkel, J. R., Grenager, T., & Manning, C. D. (2005). Incorporating non-local information into information extraction systems by Gibbs sampling. In *Proceedings of the 43rd annual meeting of the association for computational linguistics (acl 2005)*. Ann Arbor ,MI.

Geleijnse, G., & Korst, J. (2005). *Automatic ontology population by googling.* In K. Verbeeck,

Geleijnse, G., & Korst, J. (2006). Learning effective surface text patterns for information extraction. In *Proceedings of the eacl 2006 workshop on adaptive text extraction and mining (atem 2006)* (pp. 1-8). Trento, Italy: Association for Computational Linguistics.

Geleijnse, G., & Korst, J. (2007). Creating a dead poets society: Extracting a social network of historical persons from the Web. In K. Aberer et al. (Eds.), *Proceedings of the Sixth International Semantic Web Conference and the Second Asian Semantic Web Conference (iswc + aswc 2007), Busan, Korea, 4825 of Lecture Notes in Com-*

puter Science (LNCS), pp 156-168). Heidelberg, Germany: Springer.

Geleijnse, G., Korst, J., & De Boer, V. (2006). Instance classification using co-occurrences on the Web. In *Proceedings of the iISWC 2006 Workshop on Web Content Mining with Human Language Technologies (Webconmine).* Athens, GA. (http://orestes.ii.uam.es/workshop/3.pdf)

Geleijnse, G., Schedl, M., & Knees, P. (2007). The quest for ground truth in musical artist tagging in the social Web era. In S. Dixon, D. Bainbridge, & R. Typke (Eds.), *Proceedings of the Eighth International Conference on Music Information Retrieval (ismir'07)* (pp. 525-530).Vienna, Austria: Austrian Computer Society.

Gusfield, D. (1997). Algorithms on strings, trees, and sequences: Computer science and computational biology. Cambridge, UK: Cambridge University Press.

Hearst, M. (1992). Automatic acquisition of hyponyms from large text corpora. In *Proceedings of the 14th Conference on Computational Linguistics* (pp. 539-545). Nantes, France.

Hearst, M. (1998). Automated discovery of wordnet relations. In C. Fellbaum (Ed.), *Wordnet: An Electronic Lexical Database.* Cambridge, MA: MIT Press.

Jin, Y., Matsuo, Y., & Ishizuka, M. (2006). Extracting a social network among entities by Web mining. In *Proceedings of the ISWC 2006 Workshop on Web Content Mining with Human Language Technologies (Webconmine).* Athens, GA.

Jurafsky, D., & Martin, J. H. (2000). *Speech and language processing.* Prentice Hall.

Kim, S.-M., & Hovy, E. (2004). Determining the sentiment of opinions. In *Coling '04: Proceedings of the 20th International Conference on Computational Linguistics* (p. 1367). Morristown, NJ, USA: Association for Computational Linguistics.

Knees, P., Pampalk, E., & Widmer, G. (2004, October). Artist classification with Web-based data. In *Proceedings of 5th International Conference on Music Information Retrieval (ismir'04)* (pp. 517-524). Barcelona, Spain.

Korst, J., Geleijnse, G., De Jong, N., & Verschoor, M. (2006). Ontology-based extraction of information from the World Wide Web. In W. Verhaegh, E. Aarts, & J. Korst (Eds.), Intelligent Algorithms in Ambient and Biomedical Computing (pp. 149-167). Heidelberg, Germany: Springer.

Lin, D. (1998). Dependency based evaluation of minipar. In *Proceedings of the Workshop on the Evaluation of Parsing Systems at the First International Conference on Language Resources and Evaluation.* Granada, Spain.

Manning, C. D., & Schütze, H. (1999). Foundations of statistical natural language processing. Cambridge, Massachusetts: The MIT Press.

Marneffe, M.-C. de, MacCartney, B., & Manning, C. D. (2006). Generating Typed Dependency Parses from Phrase Structure Parses. In *Proceedings of the IEEE/ACL 2006 Workshop on Spoken Language Technology.*

McCallum, A. (2005). Information extraction: Distilling structured data from unstructured text. *ACM Queue, 3*(9), 48-57.

Mika, P. (2007). Ontologies are us: A unified model of social networks and semantics. *Journal of Web Semantics, 5*(1), 5-15.

Mishne, G. (2007). *Applied text analysis for blogs.* Unpublished doctoral dissertation, University of Amsterdam

Mitchell, T. (1997). *Machine learning.* McGraw Hill.

Mori, J., Tsujishita, T., Matsuo, Y., & Ishizuka, M. (2006). Extracting relations in social networks from the Web using similarity between collective contexts. In *Proceedings of the 5th International*

Semantic Web Conference (iswc 2006), 4273, 487-500. Athens, GA: Springer.

O'Reilly, T. (2005). What is Web 2.0. (http://www.oreillynet.com/pub/a/oreilly/tim/news/2005/09/30/what-is-Web-20.html)

Pang, B., & Lee, L. (2005). Seeing stars: Exploiting class relationships for sentiment categorization with respect to rating scales. In *Proceedings of the 43th Annual Meeting of the Association for Computational Linguistics (acl 2005)* (pp. 115-124). Ann Arbor, MI.

Pang, B., Lee, L., & Vaithyanathan, S. (2002). Thumbs up? Sentiment classification using machine learning techniques. In *Proceedings of the 2002 Conference on Empirical Methods in Natural Language Processing (emnlp)* (pp. 79-86).

Porter, M. F. (1997). An *algorithm for suffix stripping. In Readings in information retrieval* (pp. 313-316). San Francisco, CA: Morgan Kaufmann Publishers Inc.

Ravichandran, D. (2005). *Terascale knowledge acquisition.* Unpublished doctoral dissertation, University of Southern California.

Ravichandran, D., & Hovy, E. (2002). Learning surface text patterns for a question answering system. In *Proceedings of the 40th Annual Meeting of the Association for Computational Linguistics (acl 2002)* (pp. 41-47). Philadelphia, PA.

Schedl, M., Knees, P., & Widmer, G. (2005, June). A Web-Based approach to assessing artist similarity using co-occurrences. In *Proceedings of the Fourth International Workshop on Content-Based Multimedia Indexing (CBMI'05).* Riga, Latvia.

Sumida, A., Torisawa, K., & Shinzato, K. (2006). Concept-instance relation extraction from simple noun sequences using a full-text search engine. In *Proceedings of the ISWC 2006 Workshop on Web Content Mining With Human Language Technologies (Webconmine).* Athens, GA.

Tuyls, K., Nowe, A., Kuijpers, B., & Manderick, B. (Eds.), *Proceedings of the seventeenth belgium-netherlands conference on artificial intelligence (bnaic 2005)* (pp. 120-126). Brussels, Belgium: Koninklijke Vlaamse Academie van Belge voor Wetenschappen en Kunsten.

Véronis, J. (2006). Weblog. (http://aixtal.blogspot.com)

Voorhees, E. (2004). Overview of the trec 2004 question answering track. In *Proceedings of the 13th Text Retrieval Conference (trec 2004).* Gaithersburg, Maryland.

Zadel, M., & Fujinaga, I. (2004, October). Web services for music information retrieval. In *Proceedings of 5th International Conference on Music Information Retrieval (ismir'04).* Barcelona, Spain.

Zhou, G., & Su, J. (2002). Named entity recognition using an hmm-based chunk tagger. In *Proceedings of the 40th Annual Meeting of the Association for Computational Linguistics (acl 2002)* (pp. 473-480). Philadelphia, PA.

ADDITIONAL READING

A solid introduction into the field of statistical natural language processing is the book by Manning and Schütze (1999). It is well readable as it contains both chapters discussing elementary mathematical notions and the linguistic essentials. Sentence parsing, word sense disambiguation and term identification are some of the introduced topics that are relevant for Web Information Extraction. An alterative is (Jurafsky & Martin, 2000).

In (2005) McCallum introduces the problem of information extraction to a broad audience. A list of relevant papers is provided for further reading as well as a number of URLs of tools for information extraction, for instance the GATE framework (Cunningham, Maynard, Bontcheva, & Tablan,

2002). Not named by McCallum, but nevertheless interesting is the KnowItAll project by the group of Oren Etzioni (2005). In one of the KnowItAll papers, (Downey et al., 2005), the redundancy of information on the Web is exploited to identify instances on the Web without supervision. The same paradigm is the basis of (De Boer et al., 2007) where relations between painters and art movements are learned.

In this work, we used a set of rules to identify the instances within the texts. However, when an annotated training set is available (or can be created), instances can also be recognized using machine learning. In (Manning and Schütze,1999) a thorough introduction to Hidden Markov Models is given and their applications in natural language processing. Daelemans and Van den Bosch use Memory-based learning to identify named-entities (2005). A broad overview of machine learning and pattern classification techniques can be found in (Duda, Hart, & Stork, 2000).

The above mentioned approaches are based on statistical techniques. In (Blackburn & Bos, 2005) and (Bunt & Muskens, 2000) models are discussed where the meaning of a texts can be represented in a formal language.

A field closely related to Information Extraction is Question Answering. Given a corpus, answers to questions like 'Who is the Mayor of San Francisco?' need to be answered. In (Ravichandran, 2005; Dumais, Banko, Brill, Lin, & Ng, 2002) question answering systems are presented that use the Web as a corpus.

In the second part of this chapter, the tagging of items is discussed. Previous work addresses the 'auto tagging' of Weblogs (Brooks & Montanez, 2006; Balog, Mishne, & De Rijke, 2006; Mishne, 2007). Given a post on a Weblog, the question is which tags are appropriate labels for this post.

ENDNOTES

[1] The question-answering services of http://www.google.com or http://www.ask.com do not provide answers to these (simple) questions.

[2] http://imdb.com

[3] http://w3c.org

[4] We use the $[c_k]$ notation to denote a variable instance of class c_k

[5] http://www.whopper.com

[6] http://www.cp.jku.at/people/knees/publications/artistlist224.html

[7] www.wikipedia.org Both pages visited April 2006

APPENDIX: QUESTIONS FOR DISCUSSION

1. Why is it hard to compare two different approaches in ontology population from the Web? (The obtained query results differ.)

2. Alike the SW languages (introduced in chapter X by Cardoso), we consider *binary* relations between instances. Show that these can also be used to express associations with more than two instances.

3. Suppose that you have created an ontology with the class City. How would you identify instances of this class? How about instances of the class Texan Cities, cities within the state Texas?

4. What is the *Google Complexity* of the ontology population method applied on the movie ontology in Section 2.6?

5. In the second part of the Chapter, relations are given a score. How would you model this scoring using the SW languages, cf. (Mika, 2007)?

6. Suppose you are interested in a ordered list of all American presidents from George Washington to George W. Bush. Formulate classes and relations that describe this information demand. What would be appropriate patterns to populate this ontology?

7. KnowItAll is a system that extracts information from the Web from both structured sources (e.g. tables and lists) and unstructured Web texts. Can you think of information demands where the extraction of data from tables is less usable?

Chapter X
From Databases to Ontologies

Guntis Barzdins
University of Latvia, Latvia

Janis Barzdins
University of Latvia, Latvia

Karlis Cerans
University of Latvia, Latvia

ABSTRACT

This chapter introduces the UML profile for OWL as an essential instrument for bridging the gap between the legacy relational databases and OWL ontologies. We address one of the long-standing relational database design problems where initial conceptual model (a semantically clear domain conceptualization ontology) gets "lost" during conversion into the normalized database schema. The problem is that such "loss" makes database inaccessible for direct query by domain experts familiar with the conceptual model only. This problem can be avoided by exporting the database into RDF according to the original conceptual model (OWL ontology) and formulating semantically clear queries in SPARQL over the RDF database. Through a detailed example we show how UML/OWL profile is facilitating this new and promising approach.

INTRODUCTION

In this chapter we describe the role of Semantic Web languages, such as RDF and OWL, in transforming the field of traditional relational databases towards more open "world" based on shared ontologies. The purpose of this chapter is not to describe a novel theoretical result, but rather to gather and illustrate a broad range of techniques involved in what is nowadays called "Semantic Web". Special focus is devoted to the use of the UML profile for OWL (ODM, 2007) as an essential instrument for the described transformations. Although tools for some of these technologies are still rather infantile, they are sufficient to demonstrate the full spectrum of possibilities enabled by these new technologies compared to the traditional relational databases. The novelty of this chapter is that through a detailed "almost real life" example we illustrate how these theoretically known benefits can be implemented today with the currently available (though still largely experimental) tools and frameworks.

Semantic Web initially (in the seminal paper by Berners-Lee (2001)) was positioned as a meta-layer for adding meta-information to the unstructured documents stored on the traditional World Wide Web. However, OWL (2004), an ontology language developed for the Semantic Web, is lately emerging as the "lingua franca" for a wide variety of information exchange tasks, including the ones, which traditionally have been handled by the relational databases and their design frameworks, such as ER-models and UML. In this chapter we will consider only the later aspect of the Semantic Web – the applicability of OWL and its UML profile to the field of the traditional Information Systems.

The key idea of the Semantic Web is to unite the semantics of the data (metadata) and the actual data itself. For decades in the Information Systems based on the relational databases these two parts have been artificially separated – the conceptual model (metadata) often used in the design phase of the database was "lost" during the coding phase, were it got substituted by the normalized database schemas and low-level executable code of the user interfaces. Also data itself got buried in the database tables together with abundance of implementation-specific information that made this data hardly understandable to anyone but the programmers of the system. The key purpose of this chapter is to illustrate how semantic web technology is resolving this long standing database design problem and making data again easy accessible through the queries formulated in the terms of the high-level conceptual model (ontology).

Here we need to make an important note about terminology used in this chapter: OWL ontologies formally may contain both the concept definitions (referred to as "Tbox" in the underlying description logics theory) and the actual data ("Abox"). Meanwhile in the semantic web literature it is more common to use term "ontology" only for the concept definitions (Tbox) and to use term "RDF data" for the actual data (Abox). We will conform to this later terminology throughout this chapter.

The reminder of the chapter is structured as follows. In Section 2 we discuss the historic background of the techniques presented in the rest of the chapter and the overall motivation for the proposed approach. Section 3 introduces a legacy university enrollment Information System, which will serve as an example for the rest of the discussion. Section 4 starts the main part of the chapter illustrating in detail the use of the latest Semantic Web tools for re-engineering the university enrollment system to meet the basic Semantic Web requirements. Section 5 illustrates the database consistency constraint mapping to OWL reasoning. Finally, we conclude with the brief summary of the described methods and their potential future developments.

BACKGROUND

Systems for exporting relational database data to RDF have existed since the beginning of the Semantic Web (Berners-Lee, 1998). The need for such export initially was motivated purely by the web-related issues – that vast majority of the structured data on the web is currently buried in the traditional relational databases (so called "deep web") and is presented to the human viewer only through the dynamically generated web pages, where data and its semantics is mostly incomprehensible to the remote "software agents". In this approach relational databases are viewed as data-rich web nodes that need to be turned inside out (through the export to RDF), so that remote "software agents" could directly crawl and integrate structured data from across the web. Although technologies for partial recovering of the structured data from the deep web have been devised, such as "web scraping", "web services" and lately SPARQL, this semantic web vision has been slow to materialize on the large scale due to the underestimated complexity of disparate data source ontology mapping and due to the information safeguarding desire of the deep web data owners.

The renewed interest into exporting relational database data to RDF is lately coming from a completely different community – information system software engineering, which traditionally has been involved with issues like ER or UML diagram design and database schema normalization. Despite significant performance penalty of today's RDF databases compared to the relational databases, presenting enterprise data into RDF format solves one of the long-standing relational database design problems (Yuan, 2007). Namely, the established three-level database design methodology starts from the conceptual design (usually an ER or UML diagram, a semantically clear domain conceptualization ontology), then followed by the logical design, and finally the physical design. The problem is that during implementation the conceptual model gets substituted by the normalized database schema to guarantee the integrity of data in the database, and thus the conceptual model is being "lost" during the implementation. This loss of the conceptual model leads to the incapability for the domain experts understanding the conceptual model (domain ontology) to directly query the database – their queries need to be translated into the terms of the implementation-specific database schema by a programmer familiar with this schema. This problem can be largely solved by exporting the database into RDF according to the original conceptual model (OWL ontology) and formulating semantically clear queries in SPARQL over

exported RDF data (see Section 4). Optionally, the SPARQL query engine can be integrated with a powerful description logic reasoner, if the conceptual model designers are willing to invest an extra effort to make the domain ontology OWL DL or OWL 1.1 compliant (see Section 5).

This renewed interest into RDF access to the relational database data has lately fueled development of the number of advanced export tools such as D2RQ, Virtuoso, SquirrelRDF and others. For example, the popular D2RQ tool (Bizer, 2006) uses a special D2RQ mapping language (see Section 4 for an example) to define mapping between the relational database schema and the conceptual model described as an OWL ontology. With D2RQ mapping provided, the D2RQ tool can be used to either export to RDF the entire relational database, or more conveniently – to query by SPARQL the data still stored in the original relational database (this is achieved by translating SPARQL queries into a set of SQL queries according to the D2RQ mapping provided).

Historically, the link between the real-life relational databases and their conceptual modeling along with logic reasoning has been around for decades in the community of Knowledge Representation and Reasoning (Borgida, 2007 and Laborda, 2006), which has been the driving force for the development of the Description Logics field. Nowadays these early results have largely been re-branded as OWL DL / OWL 1.1 ontology language and associated reasoners (e.g. FaCT++ and Pellet) for the Semantic Web. This has lead to the re-discovery of these techniques by the wider community mainly thanks to the "Semantic Web" name and vision coined by Berners Lee (2001). This re-discovery has created lot of initial hype, which was largely pinned on the false assumption that conversion of data into the semantically enriched ontological representation would automatically lead to the seamless global integration of all this data. It took some time to realize, that integration of disparate ontologies is very hard due to slight meaning shifts in disparate ontologies (and even in simple taxonomies or vocabularies) for seemingly similar classes, objects and their relationships (Hepp, 2007).

Formalisms for uniting data and its semantics (metadata) did not hit the "mainstream" relational database development practice until definition and wider adoption of UML modeling language, where the semantics of the data (metadata) is primarily encoded in the form of UML class diagrams. This has greatly improved the human readability of the metadata, governing the internal structure of the actual data stored and manipulated in the relational databases. But UML alone was not able to fully bring these two worlds back together, because UML typically is used only at the design phase of the Information System and is largely abandoned, once the designed Information System is finally implemented in the low-level executable code and schemas of the relational database.

This is where the Semantic Web languages are coming into the picture and are offering a profound change to the existing Information Systems landscape. This is because Semantic Web languages cover both the semantics of the stored data (metadata) expressed in the form of ontologies (in this chapter we will use UML profile for OWL (ODM, 2007) as the metadata description language) and the storage of the actual data in the form of massive amounts of RDF triples. And what is most important – this integration of the semantics (metadata) and the actual data itself within the common RDF/OWL framework applies not only to the system design phase (as it was with UML), but it persists throughout the whole lifecycle of the Information System.

It has to be noted, however, that RDF/OWL technology still has a long way to go to become a de facto standard in the database and Information System engineering. There are among others the issues of technology maturity and support, data and system security, system building and data access management tools that need to be solved on a satisfactory scale before the technology can be universally accepted. Also the languages for

querying RDF/OWL based resources, such as SPARQL (2007), are much less mature than its counterpart SQL in the relational database world. On the other hand, even in the case of potential full superiority of RDF/OWL technology over the traditional relational databases, the latter will continue to live for decades because of existing databases, their applications, and people trained to work in this framework.

Therefore it appears reasonable to look at mutually beneficial co-existence of the two approaches, where the outstanding benefits of RDF/OWL are complemented with the interfacing techniques such as D2RQ allowing the vast amounts of the raw data to be still stored in the traditional relational databases.

EXAMPLE OF A LEGACY INFORMATION SYSTEM

Throughout the chapter we will use a simple yet expressive example of the simplified university enrollment Information System.

We assume that the legacy implementation of this Information System uses a regular relational database, just the way a typical SQL database programmer would most likely implement it. Figure 1 shows an Entity Relationship (ER) diagram of the database structure for this system, extracted from the real SQL database automatically by the MS VisualStudio or similar tool.

The main data originally are in tables 'Student', 'Program', 'Course' and 'Teacher', as shown in Figure 2. The table 'Level' includes key information for levels that can be associated with records of table 'Teacher'. The table 'Registration' contains records for student registration to courses. The foreign key mechanisms are employed to record student-to-program, registration-to-student, registration-to-course, course-to-program, course-to-teacher and teacher-to-level relations. All tables except 'Level' are equipped with an automatically generated primary key column 'AutoID'.

Figure 1. Physical schema of the university enrollment system legacy database

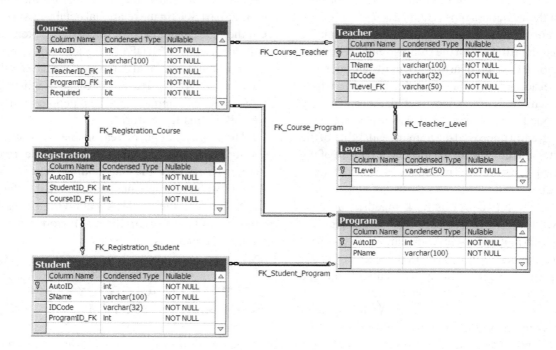

In Figure 2 we also show the actual data tables of the legacy database – this specific data set will be used as an example throughout the rest of the chapter.

At this point the "meaning" of some database fields might be already rather clear from the table and column names used and from the actual table contents shown. Meanwhile the meaning of other fields, such as "Required" column of the "Course" table, could be less obvious. The purpose and meaning for such less obvious fields is typically coming from the constraints enforced by the "business logic" of the Information System. To understand their meaning, let us list the main constraints, which should be enforced by "our university" enrollment Information System:

1. There is a fixed list of Academic Programs (table Programs) in our university. Each Course is assigned to exactly one Academic Program. Also each student is enrolled into exactly one Academic Program. Students are allowed to take only those Courses, which are assigned to the same Academic Program as to which the Student himself is enrolled.

2. Some of the courses are Optional, while others are Mandatory (indicated by value "1" in the "Required" column of the "Course" table). The students are obliged to take all Mandatory courses of the Program to which they have enrolled. Moreover, there is a restriction that Mandatory courses may be taught only by the Teachers who are Professors (table Level).

3. It is permitted that a Student may also be a Teacher for some course. The only restriction is that the same Person (as a Student) may not take the Course which he himself is teaching (as a Teacher). The PersonID ("IDcode" column in the "Student" and

Figure 2. The actual data-tables of the legacy database

Table Program

A uto ID	N an e
1	Computer Science
2	Computer Engineering

Table Level

T le vle
Assistant
Associate Professor
Professor

Table Course

A uto ID	CN an e	P ro ga mID FK	Te ahceD FK	Re cure d
1	Programming Basics	2	3	0
2	Semantic Web	1	1	1
3	Computer Networks	2	2	1
4	Quantum Computations	1	2	0

Table Teacher

A uto ID	TN an e	D Co de	Te vle FK
1	Alice	999999999	Professor
2	Bob	777777777	Professor
3	Charlie	555555555	Assistant

Table Student

A uto ID	SN an e	D Co de	Pro ga mID FK
1	Dave	123456789	1
2	Eve	987654321	2
3	Charlie	555555555	1
4	Ivan	345453432	2

Table Registration

A uto ID	Stu dertID FK	Cous eD FK
1	1	2
2	1	4
3	2	1
4	2	3
5	3	2

"Teacher" tables) is used to uniquely identify Persons.

In the legacy Information System such "business logic" constraints can be enforced either in the client applications working with the database, or directly in the database through the integrity triggers to preclude any client application from inserting inconsistent data into the database.

As an example, let us consider the constraint that only professors are allowed to teach mandatory courses. It can be modeled on the database integrity level by triggers for insert and update events attached to both tables Course and Teacher.

These triggers raise an error whenever a teacher that is not recorded to be a professor is attempted to be attached to a course that is labeled as required (mandatory).

```
Create Trigger Course_IUT_Professor On dbo.Course
For Insert, Update As
If Update(TeacherID_FK) or Update(Required) begin
    if exists (select * from inserted I inner join Teacher T on I.TeacherID_FK = T.AutoID
        where I.Required = 1 and isnull(T.TLevel_FK,'') <> 'Professor') begin
```

```
        raiserror 50000 'Only professors are
allowed to teach mandatory courses'
        rollback tran
    end end


    Create Trigger Teacher_IUT_Required-
Course On dbo.Teacher
    For Insert, Update As
    If Update(TLevel_FK) begin
    if exists (select * from inserted I inner join
Course C on C.TeacherID_FK = I.AutoID
        where C.Required = 1 and isnull(I.
TLevel_FK,") <> 'Professor') begin
        raiserror 50000 'Only professors are
allowed to teach mandatory courses'
        rollback tran
    end end
```

The condition that a person may not simultaneously be a student and a teacher for the same course would normally be checked either on the level of a client application working with the database, or on the level of procedures for data entry and update in database tables. The integrity check on the database integrity level for this constraint would be rather complicated and would involve a combination of triggers attached to all involved tables 'Student', 'Teacher', 'Course' and 'Registration'.

Besides the mentioned ones, there are even more integrity constraints which would need to be enforced by the actual Information System, such as to ensure that the same student does not register for the same course twice, and similar. We will not detail all constraints here, as they will be addressed more formally in the following Sections.

SEMANTIC RE-ENGINEERING OF THE LEGACY INFORMATION SYSTEM

In this section by means of the university enrollment database example we will illustrate the process for making a legacy relational database semantics and data available in the OWL/RDF format of the Semantic Web.

Although the techniques discussed here are readily available, yet they are presently seldom practically used due to their perceived "complexity". In this Section we would like to illustrate that these techniques are within the reach for pragmatic use, once their intended role, possibilities, and limitations are sufficiently understood.

The key enabling technique for the described approach is the UML profile for OWL (ODM, 2007) which formally is a syntactic dialect of the W3C standard Semantic Web ontology language OWL. The outstanding characteristic of this dialect is that from one side it is fully compatible with the OWL language for describing Semantic Web ontologies, but from the other side it is compatible with the UML language widely accepted for the design of traditional Information Systems.

The first step towards semantic re-engineering is to recover the conceptual model "lost" in the normalized physical schema (Figure 1) of our legacy database – this is a pure application of the classic UML based methodology, which has formally nothing to do with the Semantic Web. This methodology is most often used for the design of new Information Systems, but it can also be applied for reverse-engineer an existing system, in our case, the university enrollment legacy Information System described in the previous Section. Figure 3 shows the result of such reverse-engineering – a UML class-diagram along with the OCL statements capturing the defined consistency constraints[a].

Such reverse-engineered is equivalent to the creation of an ontology (UML class diagram defines an OWL ontology) and therefore is the most important and creative step of the whole process, where it is possible to re-use the successful elements of the legacy database design, to harmonize the structure and object naming with other similar ontologies, and finally, to fix the design inefficiencies typically accumulating

Figure 3. Traditional UML class diagram (with OCL constraints) of the university enrollment system

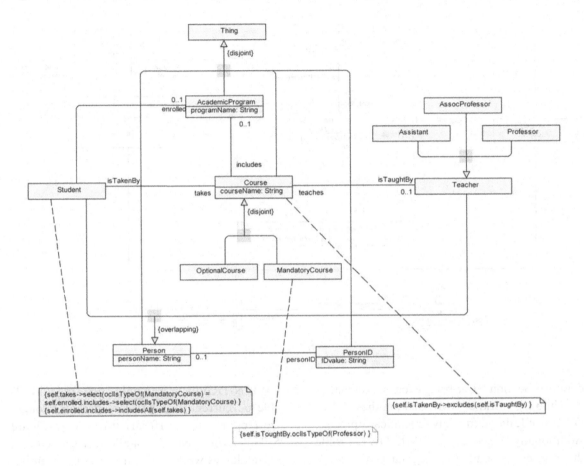

over the life-cycle of the Information System. Although semi-automatic methodologies have been proposed for extracting an ontology from the legacy database schema (Kupfer, 2006; Borgida, 2005), we suggest to use them only as a guidance for creating a clean and well-designed ontology manually. The designed ontology must reflect the consensus of the domain experts, because the true value of the ontology is in making it public and shared – then it can later be used to formulate semantically precise queries in SPARQL or be reused in related databases to ensure semantic compatibility of information systems even on the national scale (Barzdins, 2006; Hyvonen, 2007;

Niemann, 2007). Note that this goal of public and shared ontologies was not easy to achieve within the pure UML-based realm (before UML profile for OWL) due to semi-formal UML semantics and wide variety of vendor-specific UML implementations and interchange formats.

The above problem is finally solved by the outstanding properties of the UML profile for OWL (ODM, 2007): from one side it corresponds to a traditional UML class diagram, but from the other side it can be interpreted as a regular OWL ontology. Since large subsets of OWL Full (OWL 1.1 and its subsets OWL DL, OWL Lite) have completely formal semantics (to be discussed in

Figure 4. UML/OWL profile ontology (without constraints) of the university enrollment system

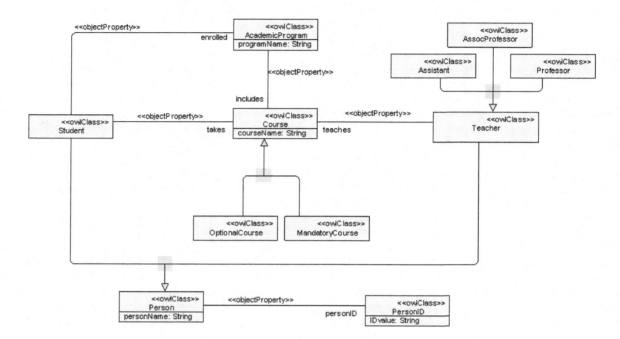

detail in Section 5), it brings formal semantics also into the world of UML making these UML OWL profile diagrams truly semantically precise. Additionally, since every UML OWL profile diagram corresponds to a regular OWL ontology, they can be universally exchanged through the W3C standard OWL serialization formats. Figure 4 shows the traditional UML diagram of Figure 3 converted into the syntax of UML OWL profile, except for consistency constraints, which are intentionally omitted – we will revert to constraints in UML OWL profile later in the Section 5. It should be obvious from these two drawings, that apart from the constraints, the UML OWL profile diagram is just a syntactic variation of the classic UML class diagram.

At this point we are facing the need for a tool to enter this kind of UML OWL profile diagrams and to convert them to/from W3C standard OWL serialization formats, such as OWL/XML or OWL/N-TRIPLES. The only such freely available tool currently is IODT[b] (Integrated Ontology Development Toolkit) from IBM, shown in Figure 5. This Eclipse-based tool allows visual editing of ontologies while simultaneously maintaining the OWL/XML representation of the ontology and possibly several visual views of it. Although presently this tool only partially allows to visualize UML OWL profile diagrams (e.g. it lacks visualization support for inverse properties and other advanced features), this tool is sufficient for entering a simple UML OWL profile diagram shown in Figure 4 and converting it into the standard OWL/N-TRIPLES serialization shown in Figure 6[c]. The tools for this crucial step will most likely improve, once the UML OWL profile will become a standard. Until that, more complex UML OWL profile ontologies can be re-entered into OWL manually with Protégé or similar ontology editor.

Figure 5. A screenshot of IODT (Integrated Ontology Development Toolkit)

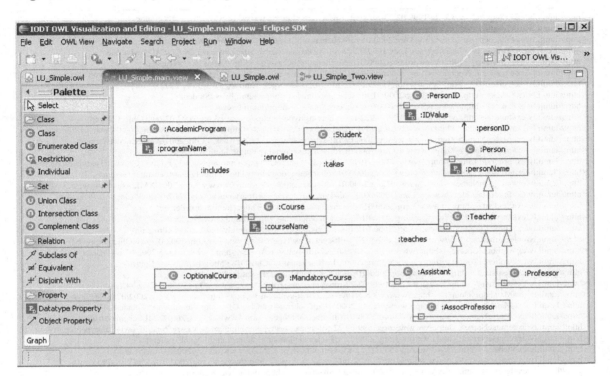

OWL ontology even without constraints included is a quite useful resource for the Information System being re-engineered. Although this ontology use case is slightly naïve (the other use case with constraints included will be considered in Section 5), due to performance considerations and universal applicability it is the most pragmatic one. The lack of constraints in this use case is not crucial, as long as all data is coming solely from the legacy database, where the constraints are enforced by the legacy means (as was illustrated at the end of Section 3).

As long as we are not interested in OWL constraints, the ultimate goal of the whole exercise is to make the data originally stored in the legacy database (Figure 2) available also in the RDF triples format structured according to the given OWL ontology (Figure 6). RDF triples format ("RDF triples" is just another name for the same OWL/N-TRIPLES format) is well suited for data exchange between the isolated Information Systems and can be stored also permanently in the RDF databases (sometimes called "triple-stores") such as Sesame or Oracle 10g from where they can be accessed by means of standard SPARQL query language.

As an example of how the re-engineered OWL ontology and RDF data triples generated from the legacy database could be used, consider the university accounting system, which would need to access the data from our enrollment database in order to calculate tuitions for the students depending on the number of courses taken by each student. In the legacy approach, the two databases (enrollment database and accounting system) would need to be linked by some custom-programmed data transfer procedure to feed the subset of information stored in the enrollment database (number of courses taken by each student) into the accounting system. In the new Semantic

Figure 6. OWL/N-TRIPLES corresponding to the UML OWL profile ontology

```
<http://lumii.lv/ex> <http://www.w3.org/1999/02/22-rdf-syntax-ns#type> <http://www.w3.org/2002/07/owl#Ontology> .
<http://lumii.lv/ex#Teacher> <http://www.w3.org/1999/02/22-rdf-syntax-ns#type> <http://www.w3.org/2002/07/owl#Class> .
<http://lumii.lv/ex#Teacher> <http://www.w3.org/2000/01/rdf-schema#subClassOf> <http://lumii.lv/ex#Person> .
<http://lumii.lv/ex#Professor> <http://www.w3.org/1999/02/22-rdf-syntax-ns#type> <http://www.w3.org/2002/07/owl#Class> .
<http://lumii.lv/ex#Professor> <http://www.w3.org/2000/01/rdf-schema#subClassOf> <http://lumii.lv/ex#Teacher> .
<http://lumii.lv/ex#AcademicProgram> <http://www.w3.org/1999/02/22-rdf-syntax-ns#type> <http://www.w3.org/2002/07/owl#Class> .
<http://lumii.lv/ex#PersonID> <http://www.w3.org/1999/02/22-rdf-syntax-ns#type> <http://www.w3.org/2002/07/owl#Class> .
<http://lumii.lv/ex#takes> <http://www.w3.org/2000/01/rdf-schema#domain> <http://lumii.lv/ex#Student> .
<http://lumii.lv/ex#takes> <http://www.w3.org/2000/01/rdf-schema#range> <http://lumii.lv/ex#Course> .
<http://lumii.lv/ex#takes> <http://www.w3.org/1999/02/22-rdf-syntax-ns#type> <http://www.w3.org/2002/07/owl#ObjectProperty> .
<http://lumii.lv/ex#personName> <http://www.w3.org/1999/02/22-rdf-syntax-ns#type> <http://www.w3.org/2002/07/owl#DatatypeProperty> .
<http://lumii.lv/ex#personName> <http://www.w3.org/2000/01/rdf-schema#range> <http://www.w3.org/2001/XMLSchema#string> .
<http://lumii.lv/ex#personName> <http://www.w3.org/2000/01/rdf-schema#domain> <http://lumii.lv/ex#Person> .
<http://lumii.lv/ex#programName> <http://www.w3.org/1999/02/22-rdf-syntax-ns#type> <http://www.w3.org/2002/07/owl#DatatypeProperty> .
<http://lumii.lv/ex#programName> <http://www.w3.org/2000/01/rdf-schema#domain> <http://lumii.lv/ex#AcademicProgram> .
<http://lumii.lv/ex#programName> <http://www.w3.org/2000/01/rdf-schema#range> <http://www.w3.org/2001/XMLSchema#string> .
<http://lumii.lv/ex#Student> <http://www.w3.org/1999/02/22-rdf-syntax-ns#type> <http://www.w3.org/2002/07/owl#Class> .
<http://lumii.lv/ex#Student> <http://www.w3.org/2000/01/rdf-schema#subClassOf> <http://lumii.lv/ex#Person> .
<http://lumii.lv/ex#enrolled> <http://www.w3.org/2000/01/rdf-schema#domain> <http://lumii.lv/ex#Student> .
<http://lumii.lv/ex#enrolled> <http://www.w3.org/2000/01/rdf-schema#range> <http://lumii.lv/ex#AcademicProgram> .
<http://lumii.lv/ex#enrolled> <http://www.w3.org/1999/02/22-rdf-syntax-ns#type> <http://www.w3.org/2002/07/owl#ObjectProperty> .
<http://lumii.lv/ex#OptionalCourse> <http://www.w3.org/1999/02/22-rdf-syntax-ns#type> <http://www.w3.org/2002/07/owl#Class> .
<http://lumii.lv/ex#OptionalCourse> <http://www.w3.org/2000/01/rdf-schema#subClassOf> <http://lumii.lv/ex#Course> .
<http://lumii.lv/ex#Assistant> <http://www.w3.org/2000/01/rdf-schema#subClassOf> <http://lumii.lv/ex#Teacher> .
<http://lumii.lv/ex#Assistant> <http://www.w3.org/1999/02/22-rdf-syntax-ns#type> <http://www.w3.org/2002/07/owl#Class> .
<http://lumii.lv/ex#MandatoryCourse> <http://www.w3.org/1999/02/22-rdf-syntax-ns#type> <http://www.w3.org/2002/07/owl#Class> .
<http://lumii.lv/ex#MandatoryCourse> <http://www.w3.org/2000/01/rdf-schema#subClassOf> <http://lumii.lv/ex#Course> .
<http://lumii.lv/ex#courseName> <http://www.w3.org/2000/01/rdf-schema#range> <http://www.w3.org/2001/XMLSchema#string> .
<http://lumii.lv/ex#courseName> <http://www.w3.org/1999/02/22-rdf-syntax-ns#type> <http://www.w3.org/2002/07/owl#DatatypeProperty> .
<http://lumii.lv/ex#courseName> <http://www.w3.org/2000/01/rdf-schema#domain> <http://lumii.lv/ex#Course> .
<http://lumii.lv/ex#Person> <http://www.w3.org/1999/02/22-rdf-syntax-ns#type> <http://www.w3.org/2002/07/owl#Class> .
<http://lumii.lv/ex#teaches> <http://www.w3.org/1999/02/22-rdf-syntax-ns#type> <http://www.w3.org/2002/07/owl#ObjectProperty> .
<http://lumii.lv/ex#teaches> <http://www.w3.org/2000/01/rdf-schema#range> <http://lumii.lv/ex#Course> .
<http://lumii.lv/ex#teaches> <http://www.w3.org/2000/01/rdf-schema#domain> <http://lumii.lv/ex#Teacher> .
<http://lumii.lv/ex#AssocProfessor> <http://www.w3.org/2000/01/rdf-schema#subClassOf> <http://lumii.lv/ex#Teacher> .
<http://lumii.lv/ex#AssocProfessor> <http://www.w3.org/1999/02/22-rdf-syntax-ns#type> <http://www.w3.org/2002/07/owl#Class> .
<http://lumii.lv/ex#IDValue> <http://www.w3.org/2000/01/rdf-schema#range> <http://www.w3.org/2001/XMLSchema#string> .
<http://lumii.lv/ex#IDValue> <http://www.w3.org/2000/01/rdf-schema#domain> <http://lumii.lv/ex#PersonID> .
<http://lumii.lv/ex#IDValue> <http://www.w3.org/1999/02/22-rdf-syntax-ns#type> <http://www.w3.org/2002/07/owl#DatatypeProperty> .
<http://lumii.lv/ex#includes> <http://www.w3.org/2000/01/rdf-schema#domain> <http://lumii.lv/ex#AcademicProgram> .
<http://lumii.lv/ex#includes> <http://www.w3.org/1999/02/22-rdf-syntax-ns#type> <http://www.w3.org/2002/07/owl#ObjectProperty> .
<http://lumii.lv/ex#includes> <http://www.w3.org/2000/01/rdf-schema#range> <http://lumii.lv/ex#Course> .
<http://lumii.lv/ex#Course> <http://www.w3.org/1999/02/22-rdf-syntax-ns#type> <http://www.w3.org/2002/07/owl#Class> .
<http://lumii.lv/ex#personID> <http://www.w3.org/2000/01/rdf-schema#domain> <http://lumii.lv/ex#Person> .
<http://lumii.lv/ex#personID> <http://www.w3.org/1999/02/22-rdf-syntax-ns#type> <http://www.w3.org/2002/07/owl#ObjectProperty> .
<http://lumii.lv/ex#personID> <http://www.w3.org/2000/01/rdf-schema#range> <http://lumii.lv/ex#PersonID> .
```

Web inspired implementation, the data transfer from the enrollment database to the accounting system would be straightforward – the accounting system manager looks up the public OWL ontology of the enrollment database (preferably via graphic UML OWL profile in Figure 5) and requests by SPARQL query language the RDF triples with the relevant enrollment data.

So, let us proceed with making the data originally stored in the legacy database available also in the RDF triples format structured according to given OWL ontology. Figure 7 shows the overall workflow of the transformation.

Although semi-automatic methods for constructing such data transformation have been investigated since early days of Semantic Web

Figure 7. The relational database to RDF/OWL mapping scheme

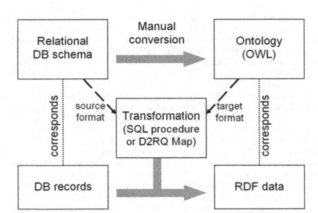

[10,20], no purely automatic procedure there is possible due to necessity to manually map the legacy database schema elements to the OWL ontology concepts. It is not difficult to write from scratch an SQL batch-procedure (Figure 10) for data export from the legacy database (Figure 2) into the RDF triples format (Figure 8) corresponding to the OWL ontology (Figure 6).

Meanwhile a more advanced approach is made possible by the D2RQ tool and the corresponding D2RQ (Bizer, 2006) mapping language illustrated in Figure 9 – this D2RQ mapping produces the same RDF export results as the SQL batch procedure shown in Figure 10. D2RQ mapping is somewhat more user friendly than plain SQL for triple generation and additionally can be used also in D2RQ tool for SPARQL queries over the data still stored in the original relational database, thus avoiding the need for the actual RDF data export and associated problems of data synchronization (this is achieved by translating SPARQL query into a set of SQL queries according to the D2RQ mapping provided).

Although the use of the advanced D2RQ tool for RDF access to the legacy database might be useful in some applications, we would also like to stress that the simple SQL batch-procedure shown in Figure 10 is of comparable complexity and allows for manual optimization, especially in

the case of subclass hierarchies, for which D2RQ language is rather inefficient. Therefore we would like to briefly explain this approach.

Such batch-procedure most conveniently can be implemented in the same legacy database by adding a new table Triples with columns Subject, Predicate and Object and filling it with the required RDF triples through a custom programmed SQL procedure. The table Triples later can be exported into the W3C standard N-TRIPLES format. The triple insertion is performed via view v_Triples that is defined to contain following columns.

CREATE VIEW v_Triples AS SELECT Subject, Predicate, Object FROM Triples

The triple generation with every record in the principal database tables (all tables except 'Registration' and 'Level') associates a resource of the form '<http://lumii.lv/ex#' ^ <table_name> ^ <ID value> ^ '>', where <table_name> is the name of the table and <ID value> is the value of 'AutoID' column in this record.

The triple generation procedure starts with assigning type information to these resources. The correspondence between table names and ontology classes is used to define this type information. In some cases ('Student', 'Teacher') the ontology class name is exactly the same, as

Figure 8. RDF data triples corresponding to the data in Figure 2

```
<http://lumii.lv/ex#Student1> <http://www.w3.org/1999/02/22-rdf-syntax-ns#type> <http://lumii.lv/ex#Student> .
<http://lumii.lv/ex#Student2> <http://www.w3.org/1999/02/22-rdf-syntax-ns#type> <http://lumii.lv/ex#Student> .
<http://lumii.lv/ex#Student3> <http://www.w3.org/1999/02/22-rdf-syntax-ns#type> <http://lumii.lv/ex#Student> .
<http://lumii.lv/ex#Student4> <http://www.w3.org/1999/02/22-rdf-syntax-ns#type> <http://lumii.lv/ex#Student> .
<http://lumii.lv/ex#Teacher1> <http://www.w3.org/1999/02/22-rdf-syntax-ns#type> <http://lumii.lv/ex#Professor> .
<http://lumii.lv/ex#Teacher2> <http://www.w3.org/1999/02/22-rdf-syntax-ns#type> <http://lumii.lv/ex#Professor> .
<http://lumii.lv/ex#Teacher3> <http://www.w3.org/1999/02/22-rdf-syntax-ns#type> <http://lumii.lv/ex#Assistant> .
<http://lumii.lv/ex#Program1> <http://www.w3.org/1999/02/22-rdf-syntax-ns#type> <http://lumii.lv/ex#AcademicProgram> .
<http://lumii.lv/ex#Program2> <http://www.w3.org/1999/02/22-rdf-syntax-ns#type> <http://lumii.lv/ex#AcademicProgram> .
<http://lumii.lv/ex#Course1> <http://www.w3.org/1999/02/22-rdf-syntax-ns#type> <http://lumii.lv/ex#OptionalCourse> .
<http://lumii.lv/ex#Course2> <http://www.w3.org/1999/02/22-rdf-syntax-ns#type> <http://lumii.lv/ex#MandatoryCourse> .
<http://lumii.lv/ex#Course3> <http://www.w3.org/1999/02/22-rdf-syntax-ns#type> <http://lumii.lv/ex#MandatoryCourse> .
<http://lumii.lv/ex#Course4> <http://www.w3.org/1999/02/22-rdf-syntax-ns#type> <http://lumii.lv/ex#OptionalCourse> .
<http://lumii.lv/ex#Student1> <http://lumii.lv/ex#personName> "Dave"^^<http://www.w3.org/2001/XMLSchema#string> .
<http://lumii.lv/ex#Student2> <http://lumii.lv/ex#personName> "Eve"^^<http://www.w3.org/2001/XMLSchema#string> .
<http://lumii.lv/ex#Student3> <http://lumii.lv/ex#personName> "Charlie"^^<http://www.w3.org/2001/XMLSchema#string> .
<http://lumii.lv/ex#Student4> <http://lumii.lv/ex#personName> "Ivan"^^<http://www.w3.org/2001/XMLSchema#string> .
<http://lumii.lv/ex#Teacher1> <http://lumii.lv/ex#personName> "Alice"^^<http://www.w3.org/2001/XMLSchema#string> .
<http://lumii.lv/ex#Teacher2> <http://lumii.lv/ex#personName> "Bob"^^<http://www.w3.org/2001/XMLSchema#string> .
<http://lumii.lv/ex#Teacher3> <http://lumii.lv/ex#personName> "Charlie"^^<http://www.w3.org/2001/XMLSchema#string> .
<http://lumii.lv/ex#Program1> <http://lumii.lv/ex#programName> "Computer Science"^^<http://www.w3.org/2001/XMLSchema#string> .
<http://lumii.lv/ex#Program2> <http://lumii.lv/ex#programName> "Computer Engineering"^^<http://www.w3.org/2001/XMLSchema#string> .
<http://lumii.lv/ex#Course1> <http://lumii.lv/ex#courseName> "Programming Basics"^^<http://www.w3.org/2001/XMLSchema#string> .
<http://lumii.lv/ex#Course2> <http://lumii.lv/ex#courseName> "Semantic Web"^^<http://www.w3.org/2001/XMLSchema#string> .
<http://lumii.lv/ex#Course3> <http://lumii.lv/ex#courseName> "Computer Networks"^^<http://www.w3.org/2001/XMLSchema#string> .
<http://lumii.lv/ex#Course4> <http://lumii.lv/ex#courseName> "Quantum Computations"^^<http://www.w3.org/2001/XMLSchema#string> .
<http://lumii.lv/ex#PersonID123456789> <http://www.w3.org/1999/02/22-rdf-syntax-ns#type> <http://lumii.lv/ex#PersonID> .
<http://lumii.lv/ex#PersonID345453432> <http://www.w3.org/1999/02/22-rdf-syntax-ns#type> <http://lumii.lv/ex#PersonID> .
<http://lumii.lv/ex#PersonID555555555> <http://www.w3.org/1999/02/22-rdf-syntax-ns#type> <http://lumii.lv/ex#PersonID> .
<http://lumii.lv/ex#PersonID777777777> <http://www.w3.org/1999/02/22-rdf-syntax-ns#type> <http://lumii.lv/ex#PersonID> .
<http://lumii.lv/ex#PersonID987654321> <http://www.w3.org/1999/02/22-rdf-syntax-ns#type> <http://lumii.lv/ex#PersonID> .
<http://lumii.lv/ex#PersonID999999999> <http://www.w3.org/1999/02/22-rdf-syntax-ns#type> <http://lumii.lv/ex#PersonID> .
<http://lumii.lv/ex#PersonID123456789> <http://lumii.lv/ex#IDValue> "123456789"^^<http://www.w3.org/2001/XMLSchema#string> .
<http://lumii.lv/ex#PersonID345453432> <http://lumii.lv/ex#IDValue> "345453432"^^<http://www.w3.org/2001/XMLSchema#string> .
<http://lumii.lv/ex#PersonID555555555> <http://lumii.lv/ex#IDValue> "555555555"^^<http://www.w3.org/2001/XMLSchema#string> .
<http://lumii.lv/ex#PersonID777777777> <http://lumii.lv/ex#IDValue> "777777777"^^<http://www.w3.org/2001/XMLSchema#string> .
<http://lumii.lv/ex#PersonID987654321> <http://lumii.lv/ex#IDValue> "987654321"^^<http://www.w3.org/2001/XMLSchema#string> .
<http://lumii.lv/ex#PersonID999999999> <http://lumii.lv/ex#IDValue> "999999999"^^<http://www.w3.org/2001/XMLSchema#string> .
<http://lumii.lv/ex#Student1> <http://lumii.lv/ex#personID> <http://lumii.lv/ex#PersonID123456789> .
<http://lumii.lv/ex#Student2> <http://lumii.lv/ex#personID> <http://lumii.lv/ex#PersonID987654321> .
<http://lumii.lv/ex#Student3> <http://lumii.lv/ex#personID> <http://lumii.lv/ex#PersonID555555555> .
<http://lumii.lv/ex#Student4> <http://lumii.lv/ex#personID> <http://lumii.lv/ex#PersonID345453432> .
<http://lumii.lv/ex#Teacher1> <http://lumii.lv/ex#personID> <http://lumii.lv/ex#PersonID999999999> .
<http://lumii.lv/ex#Teacher2> <http://lumii.lv/ex#personID> <http://lumii.lv/ex#PersonID777777777> .
<http://lumii.lv/ex#Teacher3> <http://lumii.lv/ex#personID> <http://lumii.lv/ex#PersonID555555555> .
<http://lumii.lv/ex#Student1> <http://lumii.lv/ex#enrolled> <http://lumii.lv/ex#Program1> .
<http://lumii.lv/ex#Student2> <http://lumii.lv/ex#enrolled> <http://lumii.lv/ex#Program2> .
<http://lumii.lv/ex#Student3> <http://lumii.lv/ex#enrolled> <http://lumii.lv/ex#Program1> .
<http://lumii.lv/ex#Student4> <http://lumii.lv/ex#enrolled> <http://lumii.lv/ex#Program2> .
<http://lumii.lv/ex#Program2> <http://lumii.lv/ex#includes> <http://lumii.lv/ex#Course1> .
<http://lumii.lv/ex#Program1> <http://lumii.lv/ex#includes> <http://lumii.lv/ex#Course2> .
<http://lumii.lv/ex#Program2> <http://lumii.lv/ex#includes> <http://lumii.lv/ex#Course3> .
<http://lumii.lv/ex#Program1> <http://lumii.lv/ex#includes> <http://lumii.lv/ex#Course4> .
<http://lumii.lv/ex#Teacher3> <http://lumii.lv/ex#teaches> <http://lumii.lv/ex#Course1> .
<http://lumii.lv/ex#Teacher1> <http://lumii.lv/ex#teaches> <http://lumii.lv/ex#Course2> .
<http://lumii.lv/ex#Teacher2> <http://lumii.lv/ex#teaches> <http://lumii.lv/ex#Course3> .
<http://lumii.lv/ex#Teacher2> <http://lumii.lv/ex#teaches> <http://lumii.lv/ex#Course4> .
<http://lumii.lv/ex#Student1> <http://lumii.lv/ex#takes> <http://lumii.lv/ex#Course2> .
<http://lumii.lv/ex#Student1> <http://lumii.lv/ex#takes> <http://lumii.lv/ex#Course4> .
<http://lumii.lv/ex#Student2> <http://lumii.lv/ex#takes> <http://lumii.lv/ex#Course1> .
<http://lumii.lv/ex#Student2> <http://lumii.lv/ex#takes> <http://lumii.lv/ex#Course3> .
<http://lumii.lv/ex#Student3> <http://lumii.lv/ex#takes> <http://lumii.lv/ex#Course2> .
```

Figure 9. The D2RQ Map program for generating RDF triples from the legacy database data

```xml
<?xml version="1.0"?>
<d2r:Map xmlns:d2r="http://www.wiwiss.fu-berlin.de/suhl/bizer/D2RMap/0.1#" d2r:versionInfo="$Id: iswcMap.d2r,xml, v 0.1 2003/01/15 19:44:09
Chris Exp $">
    <d2r:ProcessorMessage d2r:outputFormat="N-TRIPLES"/>
    <d2r:DBConnection d2r:odbcDSN="RDF_Uni"/>
    <d2r:Namespace d2r:prefix="lumii" d2r:namespace="http://lumii.lv/ex#"/>
    <d2r:Namespace d2r:prefix="rdf" d2r:namespace="http://www.w3.org/1999/02/22-rdf-syntax-ns#"/>
    <!--Students-->
    <d2r:ClassMap d2r:type="lumii:Student" d2r:sql="SELECT Student.*, CourseID_FK FROM Student LEFT OUTER JOIN Registration ON
StudentID_FK = Student.AutoID" d2r:groupBy="Student.AutoID" d2r:uriPattern="http://lumii.lv/ex#Student{column('AutoID')}">
        <d2r:ObjectPropertyBridge d2r:property="lumii:personID" d2r:referredClass="lumii:PersonID" d2r:referredGroupBy="IDCode"/>
        <d2r:ObjectPropertyBridge d2r:property="lumii:enrolled" d2r:referredClass="lumii:AcademicProgram" d2r:referredGroupBy="ProgramID_FK"/>
        <d2r:ObjectPropertyBridge d2r:property="lumii:takes" d2r:referredClass="lumii:OptionalCourse" d2r:referredGroupBy="CourseID_FK"/>
        <d2r:ObjectPropertyBridge d2r:property="lumii:takes" d2r:referredClass="lumii:MandatoryCourse" d2r:referredGroupBy="CourseID_FK"/>
        <d2r:DatatypePropertyBridge d2r:property="lumii:personName" d2r:column="SName" d2r:datatype="string"/>
    </d2r:ClassMap>
    <!-- Teachers, Professors -->
    <d2r:ClassMap d2r:type="lumii:Professor" d2r:sql="SELECT Teacher.*,Course.AutoID as CAutoID FROM Teacher LEFT OUTER JOIN Course On
TeacherID_FK = Teacher.AutoID WHERE TLevel_FK='Professor'" d2r:groupBy="Teacher.AutoID" d2r:uriPattern="
http://lumii.lv/ex#Teacher{column('AutoID')}">
        <d2r:ObjectPropertyBridge d2r:property="lumii:personID" d2r:referredClass="lumii:PersonID" d2r:referredGroupBy="IDCode"/>
        <d2r:ObjectPropertyBridge d2r:property="lumii:teaches" d2r:referredClass="lumii:OptionalCourse" d2r:referredGroupBy="CAutoID"/>
        <d2r:ObjectPropertyBridge d2r:property="lumii:teaches" d2r:referredClass="lumii:MandatoryCourse" d2r:referredGroupBy="CAutoID"/>
        <d2r:DatatypePropertyBridge d2r:property="lumii:personName" d2r:column="TName"/>
    </d2r:ClassMap>
    <!-- Teachers, AssocProfessors -->
    <d2r:ClassMap d2r:type="lumii:AssocProfessor" d2r:sql="SELECT Teacher.*,Course.AutoID as CAutoID FROM Teacher LEFT OUTER JOIN
Course On TeacherID_FK = Teacher.AutoID WHERE TLevel_FK='Associate Professor'" d2r:groupBy="Teacher.AutoID" d2r:uriPattern="
http://lumii.lv/ex#Teacher{column('AutoID')}">
        <d2r:ObjectPropertyBridge d2r:property="lumii:personID" d2r:referredClass="lumii:PersonID" d2r:referredGroupBy="IDCode"/>
        <d2r:ObjectPropertyBridge d2r:property="lumii:teaches" d2r:referredClass="lumii:OptionalCourse" d2r:referredGroupBy="CAutoID"/>
        <d2r:ObjectPropertyBridge d2r:property="lumii:teaches" d2r:referredClass="lumii:MandatoryCourse" d2r:referredGroupBy="CAutoID"/>
        <d2r:DatatypePropertyBridge d2r:property="lumii:personName" d2r:column="TName"/>
    </d2r:ClassMap>
    <!-- Teachers, Assistants -->
    <d2r:ClassMap d2r:type="lumii:Assistant" d2r:sql="SELECT Teacher.*,Course.AutoID as CAutoID FROM Teacher LEFT OUTER JOIN Course On
TeacherID_FK = Teacher.AutoID WHERE TLevel_FK='Assistant'" d2r:groupBy="Teacher.AutoID" d2r:uriPattern="
http://lumii.lv/ex#Teacher{column('AutoID')}">
        <d2r:ObjectPropertyBridge d2r:property="lumii:personID" d2r:referredClass="lumii:PersonID" d2r:referredGroupBy="IDCode"/>
        <d2r:ObjectPropertyBridge d2r:property="lumii:teaches" d2r:referredClass="lumii:OptionalCourse" d2r:referredGroupBy="CAutoID"/>
        <d2r:ObjectPropertyBridge d2r:property="lumii:teaches" d2r:referredClass="lumii:MandatoryCourse" d2r:referredGroupBy="CAutoID"/>
        <d2r:DatatypePropertyBridge d2r:property="lumii:personName" d2r:column="TName"/>
    </d2r:ClassMap>
    <!-- Programs -->
    <d2r:ClassMap d2r:type="lumii:AcademicProgram" d2r:sql="SELECT Program.*, Course.AutoID as CAutoID FROM Program LEFT OUTER JOIN
Course on ProgramID_FK = Program.AutoID" d2r:groupBy="Program.AutoID" d2r:uriPattern="http://lumii.lv/ex#Program{column('AutoID')}">
        <d2r:ObjectPropertyBridge d2r:property="lumii:includes" d2r:referredClass="lumii:OptionalCourse" d2r:referredGroupBy="CAutoID"/>
        <d2r:ObjectPropertyBridge d2r:property="lumii:includes" d2r:referredClass="lumii:MandatoryCourse" d2r:referredGroupBy="CAutoID"/>
        <d2r:DatatypePropertyBridge d2r:property="lumii:programName" d2r:column="PName"/>
    </d2r:ClassMap>
    <!-- Courses, Optional -->
    <d2r:ClassMap d2r:type="lumii:OptionalCourse" d2r:sql="SELECT * FROM Course WHERE Required = 0" d2r:groupBy="Course.AutoID"
d2r:uriPattern="http://lumii.lv/ex#Course{column('AutoID')}">
        <d2r:DatatypePropertyBridge d2r:property="lumii:courseName" d2r:column="Course.CName"/>
    </d2r:ClassMap>
    <!-- Courses, Mandatory -->
    <d2r:ClassMap d2r:type="lumii:MandatoryCourse" d2r:sql="SELECT * FROM Course WHERE Required = 1" d2r:groupBy="Course.AutoID"
d2r:uriPattern="http://lumii.lv/ex#Course{column('AutoID')}">
        <d2r:DatatypePropertyBridge d2r:property="lumii:courseName" d2r:column="Course.CName"/>
    </d2r:ClassMap>
    <!-- Person IDs -->
    <d2r:ClassMap d2r:type="lumii:PersonID" d2r:sql="SELECT IDCode FROM STUDENT UNION SELECT IDCode FROM Teacher" d2r:groupBy="IDCode"
d2r:uriPattern="http://lumii.lv/ex#PersonID{column('IDCode')}">
        <d2r:DatatypePropertyBridge d2r:property="lumii:IDValue" d2r:column="IDCode"/>
    </d2r:ClassMap>
</d2r:Map>
```

Figure 10. The SQL procedure for generating RDF triples from the legacy database data

```
CREATE Procedure sp_GenerateTriples As

declare @strExample varchar(100), @strRDFType varchar(100),
                @strString varchar(100), @strOWL varchar(100)

set @strExample = '<http://lumii.lv/ex#'
set @strRDFType = '<http://www.w3.org/1999/02/22-rdf-syntax-ns#type>'
set @strString = '^^<http://www.w3.org/2001/XMLSchema#string>'
set @strOWL = '<http://www.w3.org/2002/07/owl#'

delete from Triples

-- rdf#Type
insert into v_Triples select @strExample + 'Student' + convert(varchar,AutoID) + '>',
                @strRDFType, @strExample + 'Student'+ '>' from Student
insert into v_Triples select @strExample + 'Teacher' + convert(varchar,AutoID) + '>',
                @strRDFType, @strExample +
                case TLevel_FK when 'Assistant' then 'Assistant'
                        when 'Associate Professor' then 'AssocProfessor'
                        when 'Professor' then 'Professor' end + '>' from Teacher
insert into v_Triples select @strExample + 'Program' + convert(varchar,AutoID) + '>',
                @strRDFType, @strExample + 'AcademicProgram' + '>' from Program
insert into v_Triples select @strExample + 'Course' + convert(varchar,AutoID) + '>',
                @strRDFType, @strExample + case when Required = 1 then 'MandatoryCourse'
                else 'OptionalCourse' end + '>' from Course
-- Attributes
insert into v_Triples select @strExample + 'Student' + convert(varchar,AutoID) + '>',
@strExample + 'personName>', char(34) + SName + char(34) + @strString
from Student where SName is not null

insert into v_Triples select @strExample + 'Teacher' + convert(varchar,AutoID) + '>',
@strExample + 'personName>', char(34) + TName + char(34) + @strString
from Teacher where TName is not null

insert into v_Triples select @strExample + 'Program' + convert(varchar,AutoID) + '>',
@strExample + 'programName>', char(34) + PName + char(34) + @strString
from Program where PName is not null

insert into v_Triples select @strExample + 'Course' + convert(varchar,AutoID) + '>',
@strExample + 'courseName>', char(34) + CName + char(34) + @strString
from Course where CName is not null

-- Attributes as classes
insert into v_Triples select distinct
@strExample + 'PersonID' + IDCode + '>', @strRDFType, @strExample + 'PersonID' + '>'
from (select IDCode from Student where IDCode is not null
union select IDCode from Teacher where IDCode is not null) A

insert into v_Triples select distinct @strExample + 'PersonID' + IDCode + '>',
@strExample + 'IDValue>', char(34) + IDCode + char(34) + @strString
from (select IDCode from Student union select IDCode from Teacher) A
where IDCode is not null

insert into v_Triples select @strExample + 'Student' + convert(varchar,AutoID) + '>',
@strExample + 'hasID>', @strExample + 'PersonID' + IDCode + '>'
from Student where IDCode is not null

insert into v_Triples select @strExample + 'Teacher' + convert(varchar,AutoID) + '>',
@strExample + 'personID>', @strExample + 'PersonID' + IDCode + '>'
from Teacher where IDCode is not null
```

continued on following page

Figure 10. continued

```
-- Links
insert into v_Triples select @strExample + 'Student' + convert(varchar,AutoID) + '>',
@strExample + 'enrolled>', @strExample + 'Program' + convert(varchar, ProgramID_FK) + '>'
from Student where ProgramID_FK is not null

insert into v_Triples select @strExample + 'Program' + convert(varchar,ProgramID_FK) + '>',
@strExample + 'includes>', @strExample + 'Course' + convert(varchar, AutoID) + '>'
from Course where ProgramID_FK is not null

insert into v_Triples select @strExample + 'Teacher' + convert(varchar,TeacherID_FK) + '>',
@strExample + 'teaches>', @strExample + 'Course' + convert(varchar, AutoID) + '>'
from Course where TeacherID_FK is not null

insert into v_Triples select @strExample + 'Student' + convert(varchar,StudentID_FK) + '>',
@strExample + 'takes>', @strExample + 'Course' + convert(varchar, CourseID_FK) + '>'
from Registration where StudentID_FK is not null and CourseID_FK is not null

return
```

the table name in the database. In some cases ('Program') the type to be assigned to all instances corresponding to records in a table has another name ('AcademicProgram'). Further on, a case distinction may be required on the basis of table record's attribute, to determine the type of instance that corresponds to the record in the table (for instance, the table 'Course' corresponds to two classes in the ontology: 'MandatoryCourse' and 'OptionalCourse').

The values of 'IDCode' fields in tables 'Student' and 'Teacher' are to be rendered as instances of class 'PersonID' with the additional requirement that equal codes that correspond to different records in either 'Student' or 'Teacher' tables, do get merged into a single instance of this class. The corresponding SQL mechanism that ensures the uniqueness of codes corresponding to 'PersonID' resources is 'select distinct'. This mechanism is first applied to generate the identity and type information for resources in 'PersonID' and then for assigning a literal attribute value to every resource in this class. Furthermore, the links of concrete student and teacher instances to the instances of corresponding 'PersonID's are created on the basis of information in 'IDCode' fields in 'Student' and 'Teacher' tables.

The links between instances corresponding to records in the database are generated from foreign key information that is contained in the database. In this way, a relation between 'Student' and 'Program' record instances is created on the basis of correspondence of 'AutoID' and 'ProgramID_FK' fields in 'Student' table. In a similar manner the relations between 'Course' and 'Program', and 'Course' and 'Teacher' tables are created.

The relation 'takes' between instances that correspond to 'Student' and 'Course' table records is generated directly on the basis of 'Registration' table, as correspondence between 'StudentID_FK' and 'CourseID_FK' values. In this way it is possible not to include the instances of 'Registration' table as separate resources in the output in the triple form.

The generated RDF data triples in Figure 8 along with the OWL ontology in Figure 6 can be stored in RDF database, such as Sesame or Oracle 10g, from where they can be accessed by the SPARQL query language. For example, the following SPARQL query could be used to lookup names of the persons taking a course that is taught by a teacher named 'Alice'.

```
select ?name
where {
    ?person <http://lumii.lv/ex#personName>
?name .
    ?person <http://www.w3.org/1999/02/22-
rdf-syntax-ns#type> <http://lumii.lv/
ex#Person> .
        ?person <http://lumii.lv/ex#takes>
?course .
        ?teacher <http://lumii.lv/ex#teaches>
?course .
    ?teacher<http://lumii.lv/ex#personName>
"Alice"^^<http://www.w3.org/2001/
XMLSchema#string> .
    }
```

This query would return the names of two students {Dave, Charlie}. At this point it is essential to observe an important difference from SQL: the SPARQL query was able to use the rdfs: subClassOf relation from the OWL ontology to infer that students are persons. In this way SPARQL queries in RDF databases go slightly beyond the traditional SQL, where queries could be stated over data only. Meanwhile SPARQL inference capabilities in regular RDF databases (unlike real reasoners discussed in Section 5) are typically limited to the RDFS entailment inference – apart from that RDF database implements only a straightforward Basic Graph Patterns (BGP) matching over explicitly asserted RDF triples in the database.

By this we have achieved the main goal hinted previously: the university enrollment legacy database data now can be accessed by the university accounting system through looking up the OWL ontology and querying the necessary RDF triples via standard SPARQL interface.

UML PROFILE FOR OWL CONSTRAINTS AND REASONING

The techniques discussed in the previous Section 4 were universally applicable to a wide range of legacy Information Systems for making their content adherent to the Semantic Web formats. Compared to that, in this section we are stepping into the realm of resoning, which historically often has been attributed to the area of "artificial intelligence" where many of the reasoning problems are algorithmically unsolvable.

The field of formal reasoning in a sense was initiated by D.Hilbert around 1900, when he tried to develop a theory in which all valid theorems of mathematics could be inferred. Contrary to Hilbert's intuition, K.Goedel in 1931 proved that such universal theory is impossible; moreover, he showed that no fixed theory could infer all true theorems of integer arithmetic.

Despite this pessimistic result of Goedel, the First Order Logic (FOL) theory is commonly considered to cover most of the practically necessary inferences. The only problem with FOL is that its formula satisfiability checking (reasoning) is not guaranteed to terminate (A.Church, A.Turing, 1936), which makes FOL reasoning problematic. Therefore a subset of FOL called Description Logic[d] (Baader, 2003) has been introduced for which formula satisfiability checking is algorithmically solvable and efficient reasoners (based on the tableaux algorithm) can be implemented.

At this point we shall assume that the reader is familiar with the different subsets of OWL language: OWL Lite, OWL DL, OWL Full and, finally, the upcoming OWL 1.1[e] version. OWL 1.1 (2006) corresponds to the Description Logic (DL) part of FOL and therefore is supported by the efficient reasoners of Description Logic such as Pellet (Sirin, 2007a) or FaCT++ (Tsarkov, 2006). Although some OWL reasoning tasks might go

Figure 11. UML/OWL profile ontology with constraints

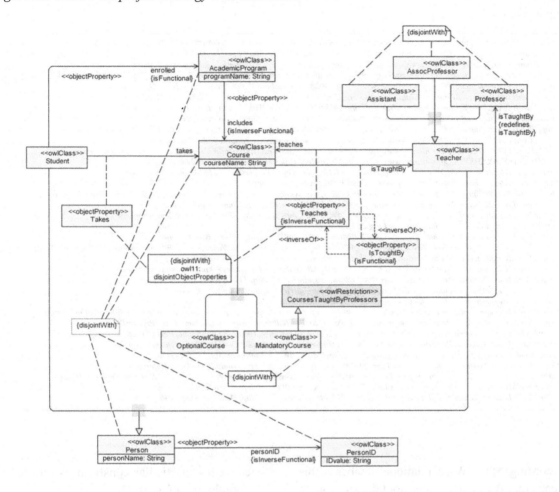

beyond the resources of today's computers, for most practical problems the existing reasoner performance tends to be acceptable.

Figure 11 shows UML profile for OWLontology with constraints corresponding to the traditional UML diagram with OCL constraints shown in Figure 3. Unlike traditional UML diagrams, the UML profile for OWLontologies can be interpreted through fully formal semantics of Description Logics. This gives the possibility to formally express many (although not all) UML OCL constraints into OWL 1.1 and to automatically verify them with OWL reasoners. The only UML OCL constraint of our example which cannot

be expressed in OWL 1.1 is the one shown with gray background in Figure 3: it states that Students are allowed to take only Courses included in the AcademicProgram into which they have enrolled and that they must take all mandatory courses of that program.

In this chapter we will not go into the details of what constraints can and what cannot be expressed in OWL 1.1, but will only mention, that in part they are related also to the closed world assumption (CWA) used in relational databases and open world assumption (OWA) used on OWL. For example, in our legacy database (Figure 2) student Ivan is not asserted to take any course.

Figure 12. Additional OWL/N-TRIPLES defining the constraints added to the OWL/N-TRIPLES ontology in Figure 6

```
<http://lumii.lv/ex#Course> <http://www.w3.org/2002/07/owl#disjointWith> <http://lumii.lv/ex#PersonID> .
<http://lumii.lv/ex#Course> <http://www.w3.org/2002/07/owl#disjointWith> <http://lumii.lv/ex#Person> .
<http://lumii.lv/ex#Course> <http://www.w3.org/2002/07/owl#disjointWith> <http://lumii.lv/ex#AcademicProgram> .
<http://lumii.lv/ex#includes> <http://www.w3.org/1999/02/22-rdf-syntax-ns#type> <http://www.w3.org/2002/07/owl#InverseFunctionalProperty> .
<http://lumii.lv/ex#MandatoryCourse> <http://www.w3.org/2002/07/owl#disjointWith> <http://lumii.lv/ex#OptionalCourse> .
<http://lumii.lv/ex#OptionalCourse> <http://www.w3.org/2002/07/owl#disjointWith> <http://lumii.lv/ex#MandatoryCourse> .
<http://lumii.lv/ex#AssocProfessor> <http://www.w3.org/2002/07/owl#disjointWith> <http://lumii.lv/ex#Professor> .
<http://lumii.lv/ex#AssocProfessor> <http://www.w3.org/2002/07/owl#disjointWith> <http://lumii.lv/ex#Assistant> .
<http://lumii.lv/ex#MandatoryCourse> <http://www.w3.org/2000/01/rdf-schema#subClassOf> _:AX5fXX3aXX40XX5fXX3aXA0 .
_:AX5fXX3aXX40XX5fXX3aXA0 <http://www.w3.org/2002/07/owl#onProperty> <http://lumii.lv/ex#isToughtBy> .
_:AX5fXX3aXX40XX5fXX3aXA0 <http://www.w3.org/1999/02/22-rdf-syntax-ns#type> <http://www.w3.org/2002/07/owl#Restriction> .
_:AX5fXX3aXX40XX5fXX3aXA0 <http://www.w3.org/2002/07/owl#allValuesFrom> <http://lumii.lv/ex#Professor> .
<http://lumii.lv/ex#takes> <http://www.w3.org/2006/12/owl11#disjointObjectProperties> <http://lumii.lv/ex#teaches> .
<http://lumii.lv/ex#isToughtBy> <http://www.w3.org/1999/02/22-rdf-syntax-ns#type> <http://www.w3.org/2002/07/owl#FunctionalProperty> .
<http://lumii.lv/ex#isToughtBy> <http://www.w3.org/1999/02/22-rdf-syntax-ns#type> <http://www.w3.org/2002/07/owl#ObjectProperty> .
<http://lumii.lv/ex#isToughtBy> <http://www.w3.org/2002/07/owl#inverseOf> <http://lumii.lv/ex#teaches> .
<http://lumii.lv/ex#PersonID> <http://www.w3.org/2002/07/owl#disjointWith> <http://lumii.lv/ex#AcademicProgram> .
<http://lumii.lv/ex#PersonID> <http://www.w3.org/2002/07/owl#disjointWith> <http://lumii.lv/ex#Course> .
<http://lumii.lv/ex#PersonID> <http://www.w3.org/2002/07/owl#disjointWith> <http://lumii.lv/ex#Person> .
<http://lumii.lv/ex#teaches> <http://www.w3.org/1999/02/22-rdf-syntax-ns#type> <http://www.w3.org/2002/07/owl#InverseFunctionalProperty> .
<http://lumii.lv/ex#teaches> <http://www.w3.org/2002/07/owl#inverseOf> <http://lumii.lv/ex#isToughtBy> .
<http://lumii.lv/ex#teaches> <http://www.w3.org/2006/12/owl11#disjointObjectProperties> <http://lumii.lv/ex#takes> .
<http://lumii.lv/ex#Person> <http://www.w3.org/2002/07/owl#disjointWith> <http://lumii.lv/ex#AcademicProgram> .
<http://lumii.lv/ex#Person> <http://www.w3.org/2002/07/owl#disjointWith> <http://lumii.lv/ex#PersonID> .
<http://lumii.lv/ex#Person> <http://www.w3.org/2002/07/owl#disjointWith> <http://lumii.lv/ex#Course> .
<http://lumii.lv/ex#personID> <http://www.w3.org/1999/02/22-rdf-syntax-ns#type> <http://www.w3.org/2002/07/owl#InverseFunctionalProperty> .
<http://lumii.lv/ex#AcademicProgram> <http://www.w3.org/2002/07/owl#disjointWith> <http://lumii.lv/ex#PersonID> .
<http://lumii.lv/ex#AcademicProgram> <http://www.w3.org/2002/07/owl#disjointWith> <http://lumii.lv/ex#Course> .
<http://lumii.lv/ex#AcademicProgram> <http://www.w3.org/2002/07/owl#disjointWith> <http://lumii.lv/ex#Person> .
<http://lumii.lv/ex#Assistant> <http://www.w3.org/2002/07/owl#disjointWith> <http://lumii.lv/ex#Professor> .
<http://lumii.lv/ex#Assistant> <http://www.w3.org/2002/07/owl#disjointWith> <http://lumii.lv/ex#AssocProfessor> .
<http://lumii.lv/ex#enrolled> <http://www.w3.org/1999/02/22-rdf-syntax-ns#type> <http://www.w3.org/2002/07/owl#FunctionalProperty> .
<http://lumii.lv/ex#Professor> <http://www.w3.org/2002/07/owl#disjointWith> <http://lumii.lv/ex#Assistant> .
<http://lumii.lv/ex#Professor> <http://www.w3.org/2002/07/owl#disjointWith> <http://lumii.lv/ex#AssocProfessor> .
```

According to the CWA of relational databases, this means that Ivan indeed does not take any course (even the mandatory courses) and this would raise a database integrity error. Meanwhile according to the OWA of OWL, instead of raising an error, a reasoner would infer that Ivan is taking the mandatory course ComputerNetworks which he is obliged to take according to the constraint that students must take all mandatory courses of the AcademicProgram into which they are enrolled. In some sense this CWA and OWA inconsistency problem is tackled in OWL 1.1 (2006), where NegativeObjectPropertyAssertion and DisjointObjectProperties (e.g. "takes" and "doesNotTake") are introduced. The described problem does not show up in the reminder of this Section only because this particular constraint is omitted in the ontology on Figure 11.

The UML OWL profile ontology in Figure 11 is a superset of the UML OWL profile ontology in Figure 4 with only constraints are added. Therefore OWL/N-TRIPLES representation of the Figure 11 ontology includes all triples of Figure 6 along with new triples shown in Figure 12 defining the added constraints. To generate these OWL/N-TRIPLES theoretically we could have used the IODT tool illustrated in Figure 5, but due to its limited functionality, presently we have created them manually with the help of Protégé 4.0 ontology editor. The RDF data triples for the new ontology remain unchanged from Figure 8.

Figure 13. SPARQL query submitted through the command line interface of Pellet reasoner

```
C:\pellet>java -jar lib/pellet.jar -s off -ifmt N-TRIPLE -if ex.owl -r -qf query.sparql
Input file: file:/C:/pellet/ex.owl
Consistent: Yes
Time: 1094 ms (Loading: 1031 Consistency: 16 Classification: 16 Realization: 0 )

Classification:
owl:Thing
    ex:PersonID - (ex:PersonID123456789, ex:PersonID555555555, ex:PersonID999999999,
            ex:PersonID345453432, ex:PersonID987654321, ex:PersonID777777777)
    ex:Course
        ex:OptionalCourse - (ex:Course1, ex:Course4)
        ex:MandatoryCourse - (ex:Course2, ex:Course3)
    ex:AcademicProgram - (ex:Program1, ex:Program2)
    ex:Person
        ex:Student - (ex:Student2, ex:Student1, ex:Student3, ex:Student4, ex:Teacher3)
        ex:Teacher
            ex:Professor - (ex:Teacher1, ex:Teacher2)
            ex:AssocProfessor
            ex:Assistant - (ex:Student3, ex:Teacher3)

Query:
select ?person ?name ?courseTakes ?courseTeaches ?personID
where {
 ?person <http://lumii.lv/ex#personName> ?name .
 ?person <http://www.w3.org/1999/02/22-rdf-syntax-ns#type> <http://lumii.lv/ex#Teacher> .
 ?person <http://lumii.lv/ex#takes> ?courseTakes .
 ?person <http://lumii.lv/ex#teaches> ?courseTeaches .
 ?person <http://lumii.lv/ex#personID> ?personID .
}
-----------------------------------------------------
Query Results (2 answers):
person    | name          | courseTakes | courseTeaches | personID
=============================================================
ex:Student3 | "Charlie"^^xsd:string | ex:Course2 | ex:Course1    | ex:PersonID555555555
ex:Teacher3 | "Charlie"^^xsd:string | ex:Course2 | ex:Course1    | ex:PersonID555555555
```

The added constraints in Figure 12 syntactically belong to OWL 1.1 ontology language, which means that we are within the completely formal and safe part of OWL Full language where reasoners such as Pellet and FaCT++ are guaranteed to terminate and produce answers for most kinds of queries.

Once we are within OWL 1.1, the safe area of OWL language, the actual reasoning is not much different from queering RDF database via SPARQL[f] (Sirin, 2007b) shown at the end of Section 4 – in fact the same SPARQL query could be given to the OWL 1.1 reasoner instead of RDF database, and the result would be exactly the same. The only difference is that with the help of OWL 1.1 reasoner we can query not only for RDF triples explicitly asserted in the database, but also for the previously non-existent RDF triples inferred by the reasoner according to the formal OWL 1.1 semantics. In Figure 13 we illustrate a more advanced SPARQL query executed within Pellet, an OWL 1.1 reasoner, where file "ex.owl" contains our full ontology with constraints and individuals from Figures 6, 8, 12[g].

We will conclude this Section by discussing the output produced by Pellet reasoner in Figure 13.

The actual SPARQL query and results appear at the end of the output. The SPARQL query is formulated to search for Teachers who are not only teaching but also taking some Course in our university – apparently this query can be satisfied only by persons who are registered both as students and as teachers. The query succeeds and outputs the data about one such person found. Needless to stress, that such SPARQL query would produce no result in the regular RDF database, because no Teacher is explicitly asserted to take any Course – this can only be inferred from the InverseFunctionalProperty (bold line in Figure 12) asserted about the "personID" ObjectProperty leading to the conclusion that Student3 and Teacher3 actually is the same individual and therefore can both teach and take some courses. Note that OWL does not use a Unique Name Assumption (UNA), making it possible to denote the same object by two different names (Student3 and Teacher 3). The beauty of OWL 1.1 reasoning is that it always terminates and produces a correct result – this is guaranteed by the relatively tough syntactic limitations on OWL 1.1 expressivity – remember, that due to these limitations we could not express in OWL 1.1 one of the original (not so complex) constraints, that students may take only courses included in the same AcademicProgram to which the student has enrolled.

The next block of reasoner output is Classification. This output is not directly relevant for specific SPARQL queries, but is considered useful for other ontology applications – it shows the inferred subsumption graph between all classes and the most specific class for each individual. Even for our university enrollment dataset this classification result clearly shows that Student3 and Teacher3 have dual roles.

Finally, the line "Consistent: Yes" is one of the most important output lines. It assures that the whole ontology, its constraints, and data are consistent (do not lead to any logical contradictions). Consistency there is checked in a rather strong manner: the reasoner checks that all ontology classes are satisfiable (can possibly have any instances). This is a very useful ontology debugging tool, because, obviously, it makes no

sense to have unsatisfiable classes in the ontology and therefore clearly indicates an error. In case ontology turns out to be inconsistent (unsatisfiable), the Pellet reasoner outputs a detailed explanation of which ontology triples have caused the contradiction.

We will conclude this very brief introduction to OWL 1.1 reasoning with restating that reasoning can be viewed as a very powerful extension to the SPARQL querying engine of the more traditional RDF databases. But this extension comes at a cost – slower query execution and OWL 1.1 limitations compared to the OWL Full expressivity. Nevertheless, it is always advisable to try to stay within OWL 1.1 limits – even if not everyone will use such ontologies with a reasoner, the reasoning possibility enables much deeper level of debugging and more flexible uses for such ontologies.

CONCLUSION

In this chapter we have discussed the new outstanding possibilities enabled by the use of RDF/OWL technology besides with the traditional relational database systems. The benefits range from reuniting the conceptual model of the database (OWL ontology) with the actual data (RDF data) for enabling direct semantically meaningful SPARQL queries, to the possibility of using a powerful description logic reasoner for advanced queries and conceptual model debugging.

Not any database is complete in itself – almost all databases contain information that can be combined with the information in other databases. Connecting these diverse data sources is a challenging task which can be supported by ontologies describing them. Although there are traditional meta-search engines and data mining tools for a number of databases relying on hand-fitted interfaces, these have to be refitted after every change in the database schema. The new approach would allow for more generic query systems and ontology and data browsing applications, including graphic ones in the style of (Athanasis, 2004; Berners-Lee, 2006). This would substantially ease the task for a user to find data across different databases which use these ontologies.

ONGOING AND FUTURE RESEARCH DIRECTIONS

Here we would like to bring attention to the few more radical development directions, which have been largely omitted in the main body of the chapter due to their present immaturity. Nevertheless, following research directions are likely to shape the future of this research area.

- Integration of multiple databases through their ontology mapping to the common upper ontology. This approach has generally failed on the global semantic web scale, but it is completely realistic on even a large enterprise scale. Development of standard and widely accepted ontologies (or just vocabularies) for narrow domains, such as DublinCore, FOAF, and lately SIOC are facilitating this process, along with national ontology standardization initiatives (Hyvonen, 2007; Niemann, 2007).
- Need for bidirectional SPARQL extension with support for CREATE, DELETE, UPDATE statements. Semantic web initially was envisioned as a distributed read-only medium similar to the classic web, but the current embracing of these technologies as a potential substitute for the relational databases requires also a bidirectional query language. One of the developments in this direction is SPARQL/Update language (nicknamed "SPARUL").
- RDF quad stores is a new trend in RDF database design, where each RDF triple is complemented with a fourth URI pointing to the "Named Graph" (source file or database)

from which this particular RDF triple has been generated. Quad stores is a simple and yet effective solution to RDF data versioning, access-rights management, and finally also to the management of trust into various RDF data sources.

REFERENCES

An, Y., Borgida, A., & Mylopoulos, J. (2005). Inferring complex semantic mappings between relational tables and ontologies from simple correspondences. In *ODBASE'05,* (pp.1152-1169).

Athanasis, N., Christophides, V., & Kotzinos, D. (2004). Generating on the fly queries for the Semantic Web: The ICS-FORTH Graphical RQL interface (GRQL). In *LNCS, 3298,* 486-501.

Baader, F., Calvanese, D., McGuinness, D.L., Nardi, D., & Patel-Schneider, P.F. (2003). *The description logic handbook: Theory, implementation, applications.* Cambridge University Press.

Barzdins, J., Barzdins, G., Balodis, R., Cerans, K., et.al. (2006). Towards semantic latvia. In *Communications of 7th International Baltic Conference on Databases and Information Systems* (pp.203-218).

Berners-Lee, T. (1998). *Relational databases on the Semantic Web.* Retrieved December 15, 2007, from http://www.w3c.org/DesignIssues/RDB-RDF.html

Berners-Lee, T., et.al. (2006). Tabulator: Exploring and analyzing linked data on the Semantic Web. *LNCS, 4273,* 158-171.

Berners-Lee, T., Hendler, J., & Lassila, O. (2001, May 29-37). The Semantic Web. *Scientific American.*

Bizer, C., & Cyganiak, R. (2006). D2R server - Publishing releational databases on the Semantic Web. In *Poster at the 5th International Semantic*

Web Conference. Retrieved December 15, 2007, from http://sites.wiwiss.fu-berlin.de/suhl/bizer/pub/Bizer-Cyganiak-D2R-Server-ISWC2006.pdf

Borgida, A. (2007). Knowledge representation meets databases – A view of the symbiosis. In *Proceedings of the 20th international workshop on Description Logics*. CEUR Workshop Proceedings, *250*, 1-11. Retrieved December 15, 2007, from http://ceur-ws.org/Vol-250/invited_3.pdf

Hepp, M., & Bruijn, J. (2007). GenTax: A generic methodology for deriving OWL and RDF-S ontologies from hierarchical classification, thesauri, and inconsistent taxonomies. *LNCS, 4519*, 129-144.

Hyvonen, E., Viljanen, K., Makela, E., et al. (2007). Elements of a National Semantic Web infrastructure - Case study Finland on the Semantic Web. In *Proceedings of the First International Semantic Computing Conference (IEEE ICSC 2007)*, IEEE Press.

Kupfer, A., Eckstein, S., Neumann, K., & Mathiak, B. (2006). Keeping track of changes in database schemas and related ontologies. In *Communications of 7th International Baltic Conference on Databases and Information Systems* (pp.63-68).

Laborda, C.P., & Conrad, S. (2006). Bringing relational data into the Semantic Web using sparql and relational.owl. In *Proc. of the 22nd Int. Conf. on Data Engineering Workshops (ICDEW'06)*, (pp. 55-62).

Niemann, B.L. (2007). New enterprise data management strategy for the U.S. Government: Support for the Semantic Web. In *W3C Workshop on RDF Access to Relational Databases*. Retrieved December 15, 2007, from http://www.w3.org/2007/03/RdfRDB/papers/niemann.doc

ODM (2007). Ontology definition metamodel. *OMG Adopted Specification,* Document Number: ptc/2007-09-09. Retrieved December 15, 2007, from http://www.omg.org/docs/ptc/07-09-09.pdf

OWL (2004). Web ontology language (OWL). *W3C Specification*. Retrieved December 15, 2007, from http://www.w3.org/2004/OWL/

OWL 1.1 (2006). OWL 1.1 Web ontology language. *Submission Request to W3C*. Retrieved December 15, 2007, from http://www.w3.org/Submission/2006/10/

Sirin, E., & Parsia, B. (2007b). SPARQL-DL: SPARQL Query for OWL-DL. In *Proceedings of the 3rd OWL Experiences and Directions Workshop (OWLED-2007)*. CEUR Workshop Proceedings, Vol 258. Retrieved December 15, 2007, from http://ceur-ws.org/Vol-258/paper14.pdf

Sirin, E., Parsia, B., Cuenca Grau, B., Kalyanpur, A., & Katz, Y. (2007a). Pellet: A practical OWL-DL reasoner. *Web Semantics: Science, Services and Agents on the World Wide Web, 5*(2), 51-53.

SPARQL (2007). SPARQL query language for RDF. *W3C proposed recommendation*. Retrieved December 15, 2007, from http://www.w3.org/TR/rdf-sparql-query

Tsarkov, D., & Horrocks, I. (2006). FaCT++ description logic reasoner: System description. *Lecture Notes in Artificial Intelligence, 4130*, 292-297.

Yuan, J., & Jones, G.H. (2007). Enabling Semantic access to enterprise RDB data. In *W3C Workshop on RDF Access to Relational Databases*. Retrieved December 15, 2007, from http://www.w3.org/2007/03/RdfRDB/papers/yuan.html

ADDITIONAL READING

As it was mentioned in the introduction, most of the tools and approaches described in this chapter are still under active research or development. Therefore it is impossible to recommend any solid introductory textbook, which would not be outdated. To follow up to date developments, our recommended additional reading starting-point is materials of the latest W3C Workshop on RDF Access to Relational Databases, available online.

ENDNOTES

a   The class „Thing" is introduced in the UML diagram only to state that classes „Person", „Course", „PersonID", and „AcademicProgram" are disjoint. Due to semi-formal semantics of classic UML, such high-level disjointness statements are seldom used in traditional UML diagrams – it is typically assumed that these diagrams will be used only by humans capable to guess disjointness of the classes from their meaningfull names. As a counter-example, classes „Student" and „Female", if used within the same UML diagram, would not be assumed to be disjoint by the human reader.

b   A similar commercial tool VOM (Visual Ontology Modeler) is developed by Sandpiper company and is available as an add-in to IBMs Rational Rose product.

c   Throughout this chapter we will use OWL/N-TRIPLES ontology serialization format, because it is equivalent to the „RDF triples" format used later for data export and SPARQL queries over RDF databases. Unfortunately, many tools, such as Protégé and IODT store ontologies in OWL/XML format and do not support OWL/N-TRIPLE format directly. As a workaround, Sesame RDF database (discussed at the end of this Section) can be used to convert ontologies between OWL/XML and OWL/N-TRIPLES formats.

d   Description Logic is a generic term for a wide variety of specific (syntactically recognizable) subsets of FOL. For example, OWL 1.1 corresponds to the SROIQ subset of FOL.

e   OWL 1.1 is the largest algorithmically decidable subset of OWL Full, for which complete reasoners like Pellet and FaCT++ are available. OWL Lite and OWL DL are subsets of OWL 1.1 introduced at earlier stages of OWL language development. In this chapter we use OWL 1.1.

f   OWL reasoners are often used via DIG or OWL API interface from ontology editors like Protege, but for the purposes of this chapter more adequate is the native SPARQL interface of Pellet reasoner.

g   Pellet reasoner can read OWL/N-TRIPLES format directly. Therefore N-TRIPLES from mentioned Figures 6,8,12 can be literally given to Pellet to reproduce the results shown in Figure 13.

APPENDIX: QUESTIONS FOR DISCUSSION

1. Why it is hard to merge ontologies of disparate data sources even if they include complementary information about the same objects? (Conceptualizations used in different application domains are often incompatible.)

2. Why relational databases and SQL queries are generally faster than corresponding RDF stores and SPARQL queries? (RDF can encode an arbitrary graph, not just linked tables.)

3. Why OWL reasoners (such as Pellet or FaCT++) are not universally applicable? (Because not all real-life integrity constraints can be encoded in OWL 1.1)

Chapter XI
RapidOWL:
A Methodology for Enabling Social Semantic Collaboration

Sören Auer

University of Pennsylvania, USA & Institut für Informatik, Universität Leipzig, Germany

ABSTRACT

In this chapter we give a brief overview on the recently emerging concepts of Social Software and Web 2.0. Both concepts stress the adaptive, agile methodological character of communication and collaboration. In order to lift the adaptive collaboration and communication patterns of Social Software and the Web 2.0 towards a truly semantic collaboration, we outline an adaptive knowledge engineering methodology–RapidOWL. It is inspired by adaptive software development methodologies from software engineering and emphasises support for small end-user contributions to knowledge bases.

INTRODUCTION

Examples from software development, communication and knowledge management show that the support for agile collaboration scenarios has an enormous potential for the reduction of resources, reducing development times and increase of quality. In software engineering, for example, the shift towards more adaptability in processes started long ago with methodologies like eXtreme Programming, Scrum and Adaptive Software Development. These individual approaches were later unified by the "Manifesto for Agile Software Development" (Beck et al. 2001). Subsequently, agile methods in software engineering led to the creation of complex software applications like the GNU/Linux operating system, the Web browser Mozilla Firefox, and the office software OpenOffice. But the success of adaptive methodologies is by far not limited to software engineering: just recently, adaptive communication methods of social software (such as blogs, the Jabber or

Skype networks and platforms like LinkedIn) have enabled entirely new communication patterns. The domain of collaborative publishing and content management was revolutionized by blog and wiki technologies, which resulted in far reaching news networks without central control and made the creation of the most comprehensive encyclopedia possible, which is edited solely by volunteers - Wikipedia.

The aim of RapidOWL now is to take advantage of the potential of adaptive processes for collaborative Knowledge Engineering. The major aim of RapidOWL is to make the elicitation, structuring and processing of knowledge and thus the cooperation among domain experts and knowledge engineers more efficient. The RapidOWL methodology is based on the idea of iterative refinement, annotation and structuring of a knowledge base. Central to the paradigm for the RapidOWL methodology is the attention given to the smallest possible information chunks (i.e. RDF statements). The collaborative aspect comes into its own by allowing those information chunks to be selectively added, removed, or annotated with comments and/or ratings. Design rationales for the RapidOWL methodology are to be light-weight, easy-to-implement, and supportive spatially distributed and highly collaborative scenarios.

RapidOWL is, on the one hand, inspired by the XP.K methodology (eXtreme Programming of Knowledge-based systems, (Knublauch 2002)), which extends Extreme Programming to an agile methodology for the development of knowledge-based systems. On the other hand, RapidOWL is influenced by the Wiki idea (Leuf & Cunningham 2001}, which established agile practices for collaborative text editing. However, contrary to XP.K the RapidOWL methodology stresses the generic nature of a knowledge base and thus focuses on development of knowledge bases, whose final usage scenario is either not a priori known or a single usage scenario is not easily definable. This is usually the case for conceptualizations targeting at information integration as well as for shared classification systems and vocabularies. Different from the Wiki idea on the other side RapidOWL's artifacts are structured information and knowledge represented in statements rather than the Wiki's unstructured text documents. Wiki's are commonly seen as part of a development described by the terms Social Software or Web 2.0.

The concepts *Social Software* and *Web 2.0* were coined to characterize a variety of (sometimes minimalist) services on the Web, which rely on social interactions to determine additions, annotations, or corrections from a multitude of potentially minor user contributions. Non-profit, *collaboration-centered* projects such as the free encyclopedia Wikipedia belong to this class of services, as well as commercial applications that enable users to publish, classify, rate and review objects of a certain content type. Examples for this class of *content-centered* Web 2.0 projects are del.iciou.us (for Web links), Digg.com (for news), Flickr (for images), YouTube (for movies). *Communication-centered* services such as MySpace or XING enable individual communication and search for and within spatially distributed communities. So-called Web 2.0 *mashups* integrate and visualize the collected data and information in novel ways, unforeseen by the original content providers. The most prominent examples of mashups are based on Google Maps and overlay external content on a map. All these developments have a common approach of collecting metadata by making participation and contribution as easy and rewarding as possible.

Even before Social Software and Web 2.0 applications emerged, prior attempts had been made to enable rapid assembly of data on the Web into more informative content: the most well-known such project is the *Semantic Web*, although researchers had been working on "information integration for the Web" for many years prior (Ambite et al. 1998, Garcia-Molina 1997), with very different methodologies but a similar end goal. The Semantic Web is conceived as an extension of the existing Web to enable machine reasoning and inference:

Table 1. Similarities and differences between Social Software and the Semantic Web

Social Software & Web 2.0	Semantic Web
Collaboration and integration focused Based on the Web Provide enhanced means for search and navigation	
End-user and business centred	Technology centred
Community intelligence	Artificial intelligence
Post-encoding of semantics	Pre-encoding of semantics
Opaque, homogeneous content	Complex, heterogeneous content
Light-weight standards & technologies	Heavy-weight standards & technologies

a prerequisite to this is that "information is given well-defined meaning" (Berners-Lee, 2001). This approach is based on a standardized description model (Resource Description Framework, RDF (Lassila et. al, 1999)) and semantic layers on top for semantic nets and taxonomies (RDF-Schema) as well as ontologies, logic axioms and rules (OWL and SWRL). However, the Semantic Web is not ubiquitous to this point, in part because of the high level of effort involved in annotating data and developing knowledge bases to support the Semantic Web.

The Web 2.0 and Semantic Web efforts, which have largely gone on simultaneously, pose an interesting study in contrasting methods to achieve a similar goal. Both approaches aim at integrating dispersed data and information to provide enhanced search, ranking, browsing, and navigation facilities for the Web. However, Web 2.0 mainly relies on aggregate *human* interpretation (the collaborative "ant" intelligence of community members) as the basis of its metadata creation, conflict resolution, ranking, and refinement; the Semantic Web relies on complex but sophisticated knowledge representation languages and machine inference (cf. Table 1). A natural question to ask is whether the different approaches can be combined in a way that leads to synergies. We discuss in this chapter how the question is being answered in the affirmative by providing an adaptive methodology – RapidOWL – for the creation of comprehensive knowledge bases. The main goal of this meth-

odology is to support collaborative knowledge engineering in social networks, with high reward and little effort. After some preliminary concepts in Section 2, we exhibit the paradigms RapidOWL bases on in Section 3. In Sections 4 we describe the RapidOWL process in the light of its values, principles and practices. We give an overview on how these can be successfully combined in Section 5 and conclude with remarks concerning future challenges in Section 6.

PRELIMINARIES

Social Software and Web 2.0

The concepts social software (Webb, 2004) and Web 2.0 (O'Reilly 2005) were recently conceived to explain the phenomenon that computers and technology are becoming more and more important for human communication and collaboration. In particular the following aspects are important with respect to software enabling social collaboration: (1) usability, (2) community and participation, (3) economic aspects, (4) standardization, (5) reusability and convergence. In addition to that, a precise delimitation of the concept social software is due to heterogeneity of applications, applicants and application domains complex. It was proposed (Shirky 2003), to define the concept of social software not just with respect to characteristics of a certain software, but also

Table 2. Typical communication patterns for social software

Pattern	Name	Partner	Direction	Example
	Point-to-point	1:1		Email, SMS/MMS
	Bi-directional	1:1		IM, VoIP
	Star-like	1:n		Webpages, Blogs, Podcasts
	Net-like	n:m		Wikis, content communities

with regard to communication patterns leading to the formation of a virtual community. Typical communication patterns of Social Software are depicted in Table 2.

On the technological side the popularity of social software is related to the development and use of the software development- and communication paradigms AJAX (Asyncrounous JAvascript and XML), REST (Representational State Transfer), and JSON (JavaScript Object Notation). These, in comparison to their counterparts Web-services, RPC or remote desktop light-weight, technologies enable completely new adaptive and interactive application architectures and services.

Based on these technologies a number of methods for user-interaction established, which encourage and simplify spontaneous contributions, help to organize a multiplicity of contributions, as well as to syndicate and mutually integrate the gained data. These include:

- **Folksonomies:** Content annotation by means of tags (i.e. self-describing attributes attached to content objects) enables the fuzzy but intuitive organization of comprehensive content bases (Golder et. al. 2006). Tag clouds visualize tags to support navigation and filtering. Tags are co-located in a tag cloud when jointly used and emphasized differently to stress their usage frequency.
- **Architecture of participation:** Already the usage of an application creates an added

value. For example, the added value can be generated by interactively evaluating usage statistics to determine popular content objects or by collecting ratings from users to classify content with respect to quality.

- **Instant-Gratification:** Active users are rewarded with enhanced functionality and their reputation in the user community is visibly increased. This promotes contributions and helps to establish a collaboration culture.
- **Mashups and feeds:** The content collected in the system is syndicated for other services (e.g. as RSS feeds, JSON exports or public APIs). This allows seamless integration of different data end transforms the Web into a Service Oriented Architecture.

From a methodological point of view these Web 2.0 and Social Software methods contribute to make communication and participation on the Web more adaptive.

Knowledge Engineering Methodology

Concerning the way humans think, the notion of knowledge is difficult to define. There has been a debate on the topic for millenniums and the field of epistemology dealing with it continues to be vibrant and dynamic. With regard to computer systems, knowledge is commonly differentiated from data and information. Since all three ultimately have to be stored as bits in the computer's memory, it is obvious that the borders between them are not clearly marked. However, within the CommonKADS methodology (de Hoog et al. 1996) a characterization system has been proposed. This is demonstrated in the following example.

Data are supposed to be "raw signals", such as the name of a person (e.g. "Vincent van Gogh").

Information attaches meaning to data, such as the statement that a person is male (e.g. "Vincent van Gogh is male").

Knowledge in turn attaches purpose and competence to information, potential to generate action, e.g. "A human male must be a man."

Knowledge Engineering now subsumes the process of eliciting information and condensing the elicited information into knowledge by structuring, formalizing, and operationalizing. According to a widely accepted viewpoint this process is mainly carried out in order to construct a knowledge-based system that can perform a difficult task adequately (cf. (de Hoog et al. 1996)). From our point of view another aspect is important too: the structured sharing and exchange of knowledge between humans (and computer systems). The initial aim of such an approach is no longer the imitation of human intelligence by problem-solving methods of a single knowledge-based system, but the generation of human "swarm intelligence". In other words, relevant knowledge fragments from different sources can be dynamically combined, aggregated and visualized. We are convinced that such an interlinking of knowledge can have a similar impact as the interlinking of hypertext documents on the World Wide Web had.

In this document we will adopt the view of Alistair Cockburn (2000), who defines a methodology as "an agreement of how multiple people

will work together. It spells out what roles they play, what decisions they must reach, how and what they will communicate".

A *knowledge engineering methodology* is an agreement of how multiple people will work together. It defines a process in which domain experts and knowledge engineers will build a knowledge base. This knowledge base is represented in a knowledge representation language with suitable tools. Processes, languages and tools are based on knowledge representation paradigms.

The RapidOWL methodology is presented in this document following other agile methodologies. Figure 3 summarizes the important ingredients, i.e. people, paradigms, processes, models and tools. RapidOWL is grounded on paradigms (see Section Paradigms). Paradigms influence the process (see Section Process), they lay the foundation for the models, and have to be internalized by people. Last but not least, tools implement the collaboration processes between people on the basis of the methodologies models. This document primarily aims at characterizing the agile Knowledge Engineering process of RapidOWL. However, prospective strategies supporting the methodology are mentioned whenever possible.

Figure 1. The way of portraying agile methodologies according to Alistair Cockburn

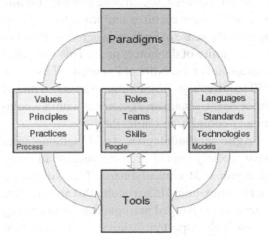

Existing Approaches

Related approaches can be roughly classified into two groups. Accompanied by the formation of knowledge engineering as an independent field of research several Knowledge Engineering methodologies were developed. Most of them are much inspired by Software Engineering methodologies. In the Software Engineering domain, in the 90's several Agile Software Engineering methodologies emerged. Triggered by the fact that flexibility, in particular fast and efficient reactions on changed prerequisites, becomes increasingly important, agile methodologies recently also appeared in other areas than Software Engineering. The most prominent representatives from each of these directions are briefly presented in the following.

Knowledge engineering. Traditional knowledge engineering methodologies, such as the ones by (Uschold 1996), (Grüninger and Fox 1995), (Methontology 1997), CommonKADS (de Hoog et al. 1996) take a task as the starting point, i.e. they suggest performing knowledge base construction with the knowledge base's usage scenarios in mind. This requires significant initial effort and makes changes to and reuse of the resulting ontologies inherently difficult. More recent approaches such as DOGMA (Spyns 2002), Diligent (Pinto et al. 2004), HCOME (Kotis et al. 2004) appeared, which conceive the building of knowledge structures and knowledge bases more in the sense of finding an agreement within a community of domain experts. This is a major step towards reusability of knowledge bases, but still requires significant initial efforts and makes processes to obtain an agreement within a community complex and inflexible.

Agile methodologies. Agile methodologies have recently gained growing success in many economic and technical spheres. This is due to the fact that flexibility, in particular fast and efficient reactions to changed prerequisites, is becoming increasingly important in the information society.

This development started in Software Engineering after the realization in the mid 1990's that the traditional "heavy" methodologies do not work well in settings where requirements are uncertain and change frequently. Several adaptive or agile Software Engineering methodologies subsequently evolved (e.g. eXtreme Programming (Beck & Andres 2004), Crystal Clear (Cockburn 2004), Scrum (Schwaber & Beedle 2001) Adaptive Software Development (Orr & Highsmith 2000), Feature Driven Development). Agile methodologies are especially suited for small co-located teams and for the development of non life-threatening applications. Since the problem of uncertain, changing requirements is not limited to the Software Engineering domain, the idea of establishing adaptive methodologies, which can react to changing prerequisites, was also adopted by other domains than Software Engineering. These include "The Wiki Way" (Leuf & Cunningham 2001) for Content Management, Rapid Prototyping (Gebhardt 2003) for Industrial Engineering. Also, the Lean Management method was used to some extent in the business management domain.

SPECIFIC CHARACTERISTICS OF KNOWLEDGE ENGINEERING

The analysis of the application of the existing knowledge engineering methodologies and tools shows that they are up to now virtually not used in practice (Knublauch 2002, p 16). This stands in contrast to the often proclaimed necessity for knowledge engineering. What can be the reason for this discrepancy? Most of the existing knowledge engineering methodologies adopt techniques and apply process models from software engineering. However, in many scenarios required knowledge engineering tasks reveal specific characteristics, which a knowledge engineering methodology should be aware of. In the following, we describe some specific characteristics of Knowledge Engineering important for RapidOWL.

Knowledge engineering is not a business in itself. There is no market for Knowledge Engineering as there is for Software Development. This is not because Knowledge Engineering is less important in the economic sphere, but due to the fact that the flow of knowledge in most cases accompanies the development of products and services, rather than being an economic asset itself. Hence, Knowledge Engineering services are often required when spatially distributed users have to collaborate on a semantic level. For example, this is the case when a common terminology has to be established, dispersed information must be integrated, or when shared classification systems and taxonomies have to be developed. This type of semantic cooperation is for example often required for Virtual Organizations (Appel & Behr 1996), scientific communities or standardization boards, or intra-organizational use. Thus, the actors within Knowledge Engineering processes are often not bound together by a legal contract, or the Knowledge Engineering processes are not part of such a contract. Since this is usually the case for Software Development processes, some practices from agile software development methodologies seem to be out of place in the context of Knowledge Engineering.

Lack of a unique knowledge serialization. Agile methodologies rely heavily on sophisticated versioning and evolution strategies due to their focus on small incremental changes. However, agile methodologies, as well as their respective versioning and evolutions strategies within software development, do not seem to be reasonably applicable to knowledge engineering. For example, contrary to software development paradigms, most knowledge representation paradigms do not provide unique serializations. In other words, the ordering of statements or axioms in a knowledge base is irrelevant, while the ordering of source-code lines in software is fixed. Consequently, the use of existing software versioning strategies (e.g.

delta method) and their respective implementations (e.g. CVS, Subversion) is not suitable.

Spatial separation of parties. Most agile Software Development methodologies assume a small team of programmers working closely (especially spatially) with domain experts. This is a reasonable assumption for commercial software development, where a client requests software developers to implement certain functionality. But when the involved parties are spatially separated, the use of a formal, tool-supported Knowledge Engineering becomes particularly important. Furthermore, the knowledge engineering tasks of establishing common classification systems, shared vocabularies and conceptualizations are is especially important in distributed settings. When teams are co-located implicit knowledge representation in the form of text documents in conjunction with verbal communication turns out to be more efficient and for a long time established.

Involvement of a large number of parties. The growing together of the world by Internet and Web technologies enabled completely new mechanisms of collaboration. Open source software projects as for example the Linux kernel or collaborative content authoring projects as Wikipedia demonstrate this power of scalable collaboration impressively. However, Knowledge Engineering is especially challenging when a large number of domain experts have to be integrated into the knowledge-engineering process. Agile software development methodologies claim to be best suited for small to medium sized development scenarios. This is mainly due to the accent on and need for instant communication. On the other hand, the interlinking of people and tools using internet technologies facilitates scaling of agile cooperation scenarios. Knowledge Engineering scenarios in most cases differ from software development scenarios: it is usually not optional, but crucial to integrate a large number of domain experts, knowledge engineers and finally users of the knowledge bases.

PARADIGMS

In this section we outline the paradigms Rapid-OWL is based on. The basic paradigms of conventional knowledge engineering methodologies are the generic architecture of knowledge-based systems, ontologies and problem-solving methods. We argue that the paradigms of an agile knowledge engineering methodology, with a focus on Semantic-Web knowledge representation standards, must both reflect the distributed interlinked nature of the Web and recognize statements as being the smallest building blocks of Semantic-Web knowledge bases.

Generic Architecture of Knowledge-Based Systems

As widely accepted, ontologies and problem-solving methods are the central components in a generic architecture for knowledge-based systems (cf. (Fensel et al. 2003; Grosso et al. 1999)). One question, however, is whether real problems can be solved on a major scale by problem-solving methods alone, or are tighter interactions with humans needed in order to perform (real) intellectual tasks? In the latter case, knowledge-based systems should initially focus more on the efficient provision of knowledge for use by humans. Thus, the RapidOWL methodology is based on a generic architecture, the core components of which are semantic enabled user interfaces in conjunction with efficient querying and aggregation strategies. The main benefit of a knowledge-based system seen from this point of view will not be achieved by the application of elaborated problem-solving methods, but by providing a scalable platform for a semantic collaboration between humans and a semantic inter-operation between machines.

Semantic-Web Data Model

The notion of ontology, from our point of view, is too vague for the RapidOWL methodology to be based on. However, in the context of the Semantic-Web activity, the use of RDF triples provides a precise frame for knowledge representation. Statements consisting of subject, predicate and object can be viewed as the smallest manageable pieces of knowledge (cf. (Kiryakov et al. 2002)). More complex facts can be expressed by using several statements with the same subject or by connecting two statements by using the object of the first statement as subject of the second one. This mechanism has proved to be reasonable to build vocabularies, classification systems and ontologies including instance data adhering to these (cf. RDF (Klyne & Carroll 2004), OWL (Bechhofer 2004)). An ontology of a distinct species is now an allowed combination of statements as, for example, has been defined in the OWL lite, OWL DL or OWL Full standards. All higher level constructs such as classes, properties or axioms can be broken down to a number of statements. For novices, moreover, this way of representing knowledge on the basis of simple subject-predicate-object statements is very easy to understand, yet expressive enough to formalize complex relationships.

Web Technologies

RapidOWL inherently requires the use of Web technologies when interlinking parties and tools in the Knowledge Engineering process. Universal Resource Identifier (URI) enable the unique global referencing of resources and concepts. Consequently, URI references can on the one hand build the basis for the referencing of arbitrary entities within RDF statements. On the other hand, they can be used within tools supporting RapidOWL to locate information about the referenced entity on the Web. The HTTP family of protocols here facilitates the exchange of digital resources, while the UTF encoding and XML technologies aim at easing the exchange and transformation of information in a serialized form. Such a procedure is simple, intuitive and eases the implementation. Beside this rather technical aspect of basing on

Web technologies, RapidOWL projects should be socially Web-centered, too. Domain experts, knowledge engineers and software developers commit themselves to using the Web as a primary medium for publication and communication.

PROCESS

Conventional methodologies distinguish different phases within the life-cycle of either software or knowledge. Agile methodologies give the importance of applying a change a much higher value than being located in a certain stage of the life cycle. Consequently agile methodologies do not provide a phase model. Instead, they propose values from which (on the basis of paradigms) principles are derived for the engineering process in general, as well as practices for establishing those principles in daily life. We will describe RapidOWL along these dimensions in the following subsections, and then give an overview of how they can be combined and applied in practice.

Values

RapidOWL adopts the values of eXtreme Programming, namely Communication (to enable collaborative ontology development), Feedback (to enable evolution), Simplicity (to increase knowledge base maintainability) and Courage (to be able to escape modeling dead-ends). However, RapidOWL combines the values of Communication and Feedback in its Community value. This includes the social constructs that underlie the communication and subsumes feedback as a special form of communication. In addition to XP's values, RapidOWL includes the value of Transparency. These values are explained in the sequel.

Community. The Semantic-Web knowledge representation paradigm that RapidOWL bases on is especially suited to represent terminological knowledge, i.e. shared classification systems, vo-

cabularies and conceptualizations. To be applied and used in a broad scope, such terminological knowledge has to be agreed on by a community. The value of community thereby induces the involvement of the community in the process of knowledge elicitation, modeling and knowledge base evolution. Since fluent communication is not easily achieved RapidOWL supports and even strengthens communication with the use of several practices such *as interactive cooperation*, *joint ontology design*, and *community modeling.*

Simplicity. In many areas it was recognized long ago that simplicity is a key factor for achieving efficiency, usability and maintainability. See for example David Ungar's and Randall B. Smith's influencing paper about simplicity in Software Development (Ungar & Smith 1991), Kristiina Karvonen's article about "The Beauty of Simplicity" for user interface design (Karvonen 2000) or Jack Trout's book on employing simplicity in the economic sphere (Trout 1998). For knowledge representation, however, the biggest opponent of simplicity is expressivity. A variety of incompatible knowledge representation languages emerged, each of them finding a different compromise between simplicity and expressivity. However, there is hope that on the basis of the RDF statement paradigm these different representation languages can be smoothly integrated into a layered architecture with increasing expressiveness. Hence, RapidOWL demands and promotes simplicity in both, the knowledge representation paradigm which it is based on and the modeling achieved by making use of this representation paradigm.

Courage. Courage enables domain experts and knowledge engineers to make relatively big changes in order to solve problems that cannot be solved with only minor changes. Courage is especially important because modeling in RapidOWL is deliberately performed with little pre-planning. Courage can be also seen as an analogue to the Wiki philosophy of "making it easy to correct mistakes, rather than making it hard to make them". In that, the value of courage also advocates to trust the expert's intuition and creativity instead of putting him on a leash of rigid processes and relying on hierarchical decision-making.

Transparency. All activities can be watched and reviewed by any other party. All changes to the knowledge model and to the instance data agreeing on it can be easily and timely observed by interested parties. This attracts attention and invites people to collaborate. Transparency results in an instant gratification of the contributing domain expert or knowledge engineer, since his contributions can be seen instantly by others. In addition to establish transparency to humans other software systems should be enabled to instantly obtain changed parts of the knowledge base, too. This enables different Semantic-Web applications (or knowledge-based systems) to interact smoothly. Transparency is (amongst others) promoted by the RapidOWL practices of *view generation*, *simple knowledge model* and *observable development*.

Principles

Based on the four values which represent long-term goals, the RapidOWL development process is guided in the mid-term by various principles. They are partly inspired by Ward Cunningham's design goals for the first Wiki system (Cunningham 2003). The principles describe the single RapidOWL process axiomatically in the sense that they define characteristics the RapidOWL process should possess. In the next section concrete practices are derived from the principles aiming at achieving these desired characteristics in daily routine without prescribing a rigid process.

Open-world. Should a concept be found to be incomplete or poorly described, any domain expert can add and change the description of the concept as they see fit. Contributions by domain experts should require little or no initial investment. Knowledge engineers are enabled to provide

more detailed ontological descriptions, classifications and axiomatizations at any time.

Incremental change. Concepts can refer other concepts, including ones that have not been described yet. This promotes (small) changes by people, even if they are aware of required additional work to be done. In that it supports collaboration between people with different knowledge.

Organic evolution. The knowledge base is open to editing and evolution. Contributors need not worry about destroying something because all changes are tracked and easy roll-back mechanisms are in place. To implement reliable applications it is possible to access the state of the knowledge base at a certain point of time.

Uniform authoring. The mechanisms of modeling and organizing are the same as those of data acquisition, so that any data contributor is automatically a modeler and an organizer. Furthermore, this is very useful as the borderline between model and instance data is often not clear.

WYSIWYM. What You See Is What You Modeled - the visual representation of the knowledge bases content will suggest the input required to reproduce it. A knowledge base is usually structured on different levels: statements, classes and instances. This structuring should be made visually explicit, so that it is easy to understand which information represents a statement, which information stands for an instance etc.

Observable development. Making the authoring of the knowledge base observable is important for two reasons. Firstly, it should be possible for any interested party to watch and review activity within the knowledge base. In conjunction with effortlessness of contributing this stimulates people to actively participate. Secondly, changes and contributions should be published instantly to ensure direct editor gratification for his (hopefully) minor effort.

Rapid feedback. Observers can provide direct feedback on every single addition or change to the knowledge base. This feedback would either encourage the original contributor to intensify his efforts or to rethink his modeling decisions. Ideally, this alternation of changes and feedback leads to conceptualizations which are really shared by the parties of a community, since they are result of a clash of different (or similar) viewpoints in a social ecosystem.

Convergent. Duplication can be discouraged or removed by finding, proposing and referring to similar or related concepts. This results on the one hand in simpler and smaller knowledge bases and on the other hand allows inaugurating new insights due to the increased interlinking of the knowledge base.

Traveling light. RapidOWL suggests focusing on a single modeling artifact. This artifact is the domain model expressed in the form of statements. This model can be enriched with documentation, feedback and comments. Instead of maintaining multiple models for the different levels of abstraction, RapidOWL promotes the use of different views.

Practices

The practices of RapidOWL are inspired by the practices of eXtreme Programming (XP) and from Holger Knoblauch's modifications for software / knowledge base co-design XP.K (Knublauch 2002). Due to the specific characteristics of knowledge engineering (cf. Section 3) not all practices from XP have an equivalent in RapidOWL and inversely. However, as in XP the practices support each other, so that the weakness of one practice is overcome by the strengths of other practices. This implies that most benefit from using RapidOWL lies in applying all of the practices together. In contrast to software development, where the team of full-time programmers can be easily instructed to put the values and principles of XP into daily routine, RapidOWL aims to turn domain experts into part-time knowledge engineers by keeping practices as simple as possible and by proposing strategies to support them with tools.

Interactive cooperation. Instead of requiring an on-site customer (or as in XP.K an On-Site domain expert) we propose to establish methods of interactive on-line cooperation between domain experts and knowledge engineers. A first step, is to transparently and timely publish ontologies and traces of changes for easy access by other modeling or reviewing parties. This can be technologically supported by interactively publishing the ontology and changes on the Web. Current developments of equipping Wiki systems with support for representing semantic relationships (cf. (Aumüller 2005), (Krötzsch et al. 2005)) are good candidates to accomplish this task. By applying recent content syndication standards (such as RSS (Winer 2002) or ATOM (Nottingham & Sayre 2005)) for the announcement of changes, experts can be timely and conveniently kept up to date.

Joint ontology design. Based on the simple subject-predicate-object statement paradigm, domain experts initially only define and describe concepts in a quite spontaneous manner. For this, they make use of worldwide unique concept identifiers (URI references) as subjects, predicates and objects within statements (i.e. RDF triples). After the information is thus represented, it can be enriched by more experienced domain experts or knowledge engineers with more detailed categorizations, classifications and logical descriptions (e.g. OWL axioms or SWRL rules).

Community modeling. To enable collaborative semantic cooperation, domain experts can attach comments to the statements and vote on how usefulness of the statements. In order to technically achieve this, RDF reifications may come into effect. To observe changes on higher conceptual levels than that of additions and deletions of statements, multiple added or deleted statements can be put into change sets. This is comparable to the way that patches subsume multiple atomic changes in software source-code versioning. Hierarchically organizing changes even allow change reviews on different levels of detail.

Information integration. The awareness of the need for developing a knowledge base often arises when a multiplicity of information sources exists and their interrelations are hard to maintain. Hence, it is crucial for the success of a knowledge engineering project to integrate existing information sources. Two approaches are possible to achieve this goal: *Importing information* into the common knowledge base - all further maintenance of the information has to be done within the knowledge base. This method can be easily applied for simple structured information sources as for example Excel sheets containing tabular information (Powl as described in (Auer 2005) contains such functionality). The other possibility is to *interlink existing data sources* with the knowledge base. This method will be the preferred way if information sources are highly structured (such as e.g. relational databases or LDAP directories), existing applications rely on access to the information sources in conventional ways and the maintenance of the information should be performed in established processes. For relational databases the problem is tackled by D2RQ (Bizer & Seaborn 2004). LDAP2OWL (Dietzold 2005) is an approach to make information from LDAP directories accessible to knowledge bases.

View generation. An aim of classical knowledge engineering is to realize problem-solving capabilities comparable to a domain expert (Studer et al. 1998)). In addition knowledge engineering can be seen as a support strategy helping users and experts to transfer knowledge between individuals or to gain new insights by presenting knowledge in unforeseen ways. Generating different views on a knowledge base will support greatly the latter mentioned aspects of knowledge engineering. Views select and combine certain parts of the knowledge base for human users. On type of views are user generated views, where the user or viewer is identical to the generator to the view. Such 'self service' views can be realized in a user friendly manner by provision of full-text searches in combination with filtering and sorting functionality. However, for certain investigations more sophisticated selection strategies than filtering and sorting might be needed or the presentation for humans should be tuned. In this case view generation will require either a more experienced user, able to cope with query languages and aware of the knowledge structures or knowledge engineers assisting in generating the view. Fresnel (Bizer et al. 2004) for example is a declarative way to encode presentation knowledge in RDF with the primary goal of reusability across different representation paradigms.

Modeling standards. Modeling Standards are the counterpart to the XP practice of Coding Standards. Modeling Standards are agreed-upon naming conventions (e.g., "properties should start with a verb") and syntax rules (e.g., "classes start with an uppercase letter"). Since the ontology language RapidOWL bases on (i.e., OWL) is much simpler than programming languages, it only requires the use of a few standards. In (Knublauch 2002, p 74) standards are described as being "essential to enable model exchange, collaborative modeling, and to minimize the dependency of the team on specific members. Furthermore, they contribute to the original vision of ontology research to enable global knowledge sharing". Whilst it is relatively easy to enforce syntax rules within tools, the compliance check for naming convention could prove more challenging. The prefixing of properties with verbs though, can be checked with the aid of electronic thesauri (e.g. WordNet (Fellbaum 1998)).

Ontology evolution. Ontology evolution is the counterpart for the XP practice Refactoring. The more spontaneous new modelings and information is integrated into the knowledge base the higher is the demand later to adopt modelings and migrate instance data accordingly. Many approaches to ontology evolution emerged recently ((Stojanovic 2004) gives an overview), most of them, however, presuppose a well-defined and fixed set of possible knowledge base changes. To be able to review changes on different levels

Figure 2. The building blocks of RapidOWL: Values, Principles, Practices

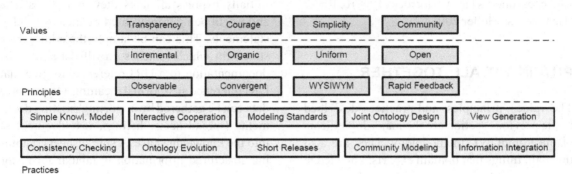

of detail (e.g. statement, ontology, domain level) we developed a hierarchical versioning strategy (cf. (Auer & Herre 2006)) which also facilitates automatic migration of instance data by providing a framework for the detection of ontology evolution patterns.

Short releases. A long-lasting develop-release cycle as in traditional software engineering would not adequately reflect the continuous information integration and knowledge structure evolution, which is characteristic for shared classification systems, vocabularies and conceptualizations. Instead we propose to make the development process as transparent as possible, by publishing changes immediately and releasing stable versions frequently. The sooner an ontology is released to the public, the easier it is to discuss changes and the earlier it is that potential problems become visible. Short releases will be facilitated if the consequences of changes to the ontology are known, i.e. if data adhering to the ontology has to be migrated or if queries about and views on the data have to be adopted.

Simple knowledge model. According to XP.K, simplicity is a "key to making models easy to understand, communicate, and maintain" (Knublauch 2002, p 75). Hence, the best knowledge model for RapidOWL is the model that has the fewest possible classes, properties and instances, provides semantic transparency for users as well

as software systems, provides the needed querying facilities and passes consistency checks without violations. RapidOWL envisions a middle-out strategy for concept identification to implicitly achieve simple modelings: Domain experts are required to initially integrate all that information into the knowledge base they assume being relevant and worth represented. Such instance and sample data is in the following only thus far condensed into classifications and enriched with logical axiomatizations as needed for querying and/or reasoning services provided to the users. Hence, a RapidOWL knowledge base is not required to anticipate (all) future requirements a priori. Increasing complexity is therefore mainly driven by domain experts (i.e. users) of the knowledge base, thus ensuring comprehensibility.

Consistency checking. RapidOWL envisions the successive enrichment of a knowledge base with additional structure and logical representations according to the Semantic-Web language stack. However, this process should be mainly driven by users insofar as the increased semantics gives them real benefits with regard to querying and reasoning capabilities. Due to the size of real-life knowledge bases a strategy to enable reasoning services is to extract distinct parts or "slices" of the knowledge base adhering to a distinct OWL species or a rule language (e.g. SWRL (Horrocks et al. 2003)) to perform constraint and/or consistency checks (e.g. by means of Description Logic reasoner as FaCT (Horrocks 1998) or Racer (Haarslev & Möller 2001).

PUTTING IT ALL TOGETHER

The values, principles, and practices described in the previous section are the major ingredients of the RapidOWL methodology. They are also the main things that domain experts, knowledge engineers and especially tool developers for RapidOWL enabled knowledge engineering and management systems, should be aware of. In contrast to systematic engineering methodologies, RapidOWL does not prescribe a sequence of modeling activities that should be precisely followed. Furthermore, RapidOWL does not waste resources on comprehensive analysis and design activities. Instead, it follows the philosophy of agile methodologies, in which agility in the face of changing requirements and knowledge models is a major goal.

The individual tasks and contributions of prospectively involved parties in building a knowledge base on the basis of the RapidOWL principles are presented in the next paragraphs.

RapidOWL encourages *domain experts* to initially express all facts they assume as true and worth being, represented by means of RDF statements. This can be simply the adding of a statement which attaches an rdfs:label or rdfs: documentation to a URI reference, to give that URI reference an informal meaning. Or, instance data can be gathered by importing existing documents (spreadsheets, listings, text documents) into the knowledge base. A spreadsheet containing structured information in tabular form, for example, can be interpreted as a class, where columns indicate properties and rows usually represent instances. This activity promotes a shallow learning curve, since domain experts can instantly participate. As soon as an expert starts working on such a knowledge representation, other experts can observe every single step. They can add comments, vote about the usefulness of certain representations, add their own knowledge fragments and/or delete other ones.

More *experienced domain experts* assist in restructuring, interlinking and consolidating the gathered data. Importing information from legacy documents often results in duplicates, because, for example, columns in different spreadsheet documents representing the same information are not labeled in a uniform manner. Such duplications

Figure 3. Collaboration between different parties on the basis of RapidOWL

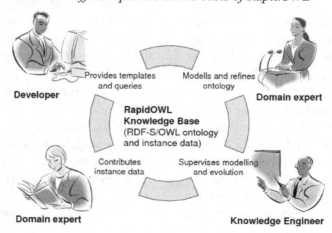

have to be detected and eliminated (e.g. by merging the respective properties into one). To reduce the costs of such changes, RapidOWL will rely on implemented wizards assisting in the detection of frequent modeling errors and by providing (semi-)automatic resolution to support evolution and migration. It might also be necessary to convert literal data, as, for example, two properties to be merged can represent the same information differently (e.g. names like "Auer, Sören" or "Sören Auer"). This kind of consolidation activity also includes the establishing of relationships which are not yet represented.

Knowledge engineers can support such a community of domain experts with advice for reasonable representation methods and by providing ontology evolution and data migration strategies. Knowledge engineers can further enrich the knowledge base with logical ontology axioms. This includes property characteristics (e.g. transitivity) and restrictions (e.g. cardinality restrictions). Class descriptions are refined with set operators (owl:intersectionOf, owl:unionOf, owl:complementOf). The knowledge engineer can also extract distinct parts or "slices" of the knowledge base adhering to the OWL species, DL and lite to perform consistency checks using a Description Logic reasoner. Since RapidOWL does not restrict domain experts in their usage of RDF it is likely that the knowledge base does not fall into the OWL DL or OWL lite categories. The species validation of an OWL reasoner, however, can give hints about how the knowledge base has to be modified. Another task is the testing of existing queries and views on the knowledge base after changes have been incorporated.

RapidOWL focuses primarily on establishing conceptualizations for information integration as well as the establishing of shared classification systems and vocabularies. Hence, tools supporting RapidOWL will have a rather generic than domain specific nature. However, *software developers* participate in the collaboration by developing domain specific applications providing specific views onto the knowledge base,

or by assisting domain experts and knowledge engineers in formulation more complex queries to the knowledge base.

RapidOWL does not enforce a distinct succession; neither does it require all the just mentioned tasks and activities to be accomplished by the respective parties. The quality of the knowledge base, however, is determined by carefully performing activities related to consolidation, restructuring and modeling as well as consistency checking. Tools on the other hand, can highly automatize and integrate these activities into the Gathering activity.

In order to provide tool support for RapidOWL we developed OntoWiki (cf. Figure 5). OntoWiki facilitates the visual presentation of a knowledge base as an information map, with different views on instance data. It enables intuitive authoring of semantic content, with an inline editing mode for editing RDF content, similar to WYSIWYG for text documents. It fosters social collaboration aspects by keeping track of changes, allowing comments and discussions on every single part of a knowledge base, enabling to rate and measure the popularity of content and honoring the activity of users. OntoWiki enhances the browsing and retrieval by offering semantic enhanced search strategies. All these techniques are applied with the ultimate goal of decreasing the entrance barrier for projects and domain experts to collaborate using semantic technologies. In the spirit of the Web 2.0 OntoWiki implements an "architecture of participation" that allows users to add value to the application as they use it. It is available as open-source software and a demonstration platform can be accessed at http://demo.ontowiki. net. OntoWiki is described in detail in (Auer et at. 2006).

CONCLUSION

The purpose of RapidOWL is to bring about a stable state of the knowledge base through

Figure 4. Screenshot of the RapidOWL tool OntoWiki

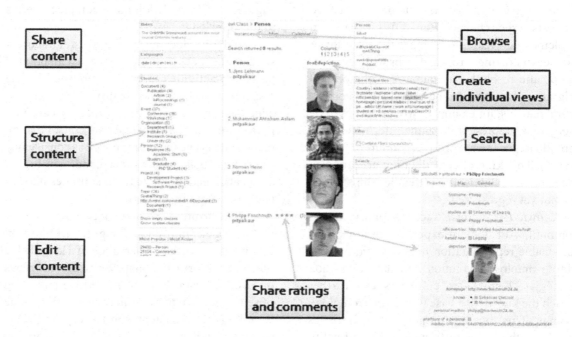

small incremental changes from a multiplicity of contributors. To achieve that, RapidOWL applies various techniques and practices with the explicit goal of reducing the cost of change. Much of the assumption that the cost of change can be reduced is based on the value of *Transparency*. The practice *Short Releases* for example promotes that ontologies are published quickly and frequently, so that expensive misunderstandings can be uncovered and eliminated early, when the costs of changing them are still low. *View Generation* furthermore enables domain experts to timely review the representations from different perspectives. *Joint Ontology Design* and *Community Modeling* promote communication between domain experts (and knowledge engineers) and thus help by detecting errors earlier and spreading the knowledge. *Ontology Evolution* enables to undo problematic changes and to estimate prospective effects on instance data. Early *Information Integration* helps that the ontology really

captures needed conceptualizations adequately. The *Simple Knowledge Model* of the statement based approach of Semantic-Web knowledge representation standards is very easy to understand. In conjunction with *Modeling Standards* domain experts are thus enabled to efficiently contribute to a knowledge base, even in absence of knowledge engineers. Finally, *Consistency Checking* helps to build robust and terminologically correct knowledge bases.

Although each of these practices has weaknesses when applied individually, their benefits greatly outweigh their weaknesses when they are used as a combined approach. In other words, the practices of RapidOWL support one and other. This analogous to other agile methodologies (cf. (Beck & Andres 2004), (Knublauch 2002)) and due to the "axiomatic" description of their single process. An example for individual weaknesses and mutual compensation of such is the interplay of the practices of *Short Releases* and *Ontology*

Figure 5. RapidOWL's placement in terms of predictive vs. adaptive methodologies

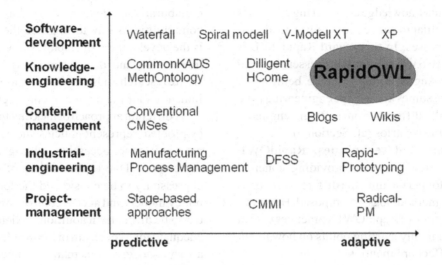

Software-development	Waterfall	Spiral modell	V-Modell XT	XP
Knowledge-engineering	CommonKADS MethOntology	Dilligent HCome	**RapidOWL**	
Content-management	Conventional CMSes		Blogs	Wikis
Industrial-engineering	Manufacturing Process Management	DFSS	Rapid-Prototyping	
Project-management	Stage-based approaches	CMMI	Radical-PM	

predictive ⟶ adaptive

Evolution. Short Releases of the ontologies may result in instabilities of the resulting knowledge-based systems. However, *Ontology Evolution* supports the early detection of prospective problems and enables the revoke of individual problematic changes in a simple way.

In (Fernández-López 1999) a number of criteria for analyzing methodologies were proposed. In the following we discuss RapidOWL in the light of these criteria.

Detail of the methodology. RapidOWL is a rather lightweight methodology. This is primarily due to the recognition that knowledge engineering is usually not a business in itself and thus significant resources for evaluating the methodology and later controlling the compliance of the processes with the methodology are not available. RapidOWL rather banks on tools supporting it than on exhaustive documentation.

Recommendations for knowledge formalization. RapidOWL bases on representation of all knowledge in the form of triples, i.e. RDF statements. A concrete degree of formalization is not prescribed. However, RapidOWL proposes to justify the degree of formalization according to

the required reasoning capabilities of the resulting knowledge base.

Strategy for building ontologies. Regarding this criterion it is questioned whether the strategy to develop ontologies is (a) application-dependent, (b) application-semi-dependent, or (c) application-independent. RapidOWL focuses on the development of rather application-independent ontologies. However, RapidOWL is primarily suited for information integration tasks and tasks related to the establishing of shared classification systems, vocabularies and conceptualizations.

Strategy for identifying concepts. RapidOWL here follows a middle-out strategy, i.e. from the most relevant to the most abstract and most concrete. By stressing the collecting of example or instance data RapidOWL tries to abolish knowledge elicitation by means of face-to-face communication between domain experts and knowledge engineers.

Recommended life cycle. Due to its adaptive nature RapidOWL does not explicitly propose a rigid life cycle. However, many aspects of stages in the life cycle of conventional methodologies can be discovered in RapidOWL's single process.

Differences between the methodology and IEEE 1074-1995. This criterion is related to the conviction that knowledge engineering processes should be similar to conventional software development processes. In this regard RapidOWL is different in two ways: Firstly it stresses the need to react on changed prerequisites, i.e. being agile. Secondly it assumes knowledge engineering to be fundamentally different from software engineering in certain scenarios (cf. Section 3).

Recommended techniques. RapidOWL stresses the importance of providing concrete techniques for performing the different practices of which the methodology is composed. However, in the description of RapidOWL's practices within this document only starting points on how to put them into effect are mentioned.

Usage and application. Due to the fact that RapidOWL is rather new and significant resources had not been at our disposal for a broad evaluation the number of successfully realized RapidOWL projects is still small. However, ontologies and applications have been building on the basis of RapidOWL containing approximately 20,000 concepts and serving 3,000 parties (cf. the case study in (Auer & Pieterse, 2005)). Also, the large DBpedia multi-domain ontology extracted from Wikipedia (Auer et al. 2007), can be seen as a confirmation and working example for large-scale social semantic collaboration in the spirit of RapidOWL.

FUTURE RESEARCH DIRECTIONS

As we already mentioned earlier, a pivotal Social Software concept is the collaborative tagging of content leading to folksonomies (i.e. taxonomies created by folks). Applied to the sphere of the Semantic Web the challenge is to employ human "swarm intelligence" in the spirit of tagging to create not just *comprehensive* but also consistent knowledge bases. Consistent here is meant less from a logical point of view than from the perspective of achieving an agreement in the user community. When knowledge bases are collaboratively developed by loosely-coupled communities a way to improve the consistency is the development of RapidOWL extensions for moderation and decision processes. A field of future research is also the investigation of possible indicators for the degree of consistency.

A different approach of tackling the consistency problem represent policies and access control mechanisms for accessing, editing and annotating content. Due to the variety of the possible expressivity to be considered the formulation of policy models and access control strategies turns out to be difficult. In addition, policies should be adequate for a spectrum of knowledge bases with a varying degree of semantic richness.

Another challenge, lying less in the scientific than the software engineering field, is to increase the flexibility and robustness of storage backends, libraries and frameworks for the development of social Semantic Web applications. In addition to that standards for semantic widgets and user interface elements can support user acceptance and interoperability.

Last but not least *economic aspects* play a crucial role to make the Semantic Web a success. Due to the fact that semantic collaboration is in many cases not a direct business in itself, specific business models are needed, which are focused on services and products supporting the generation and curation of semantic content by communities.

REFERENCES

Ambite, J. L., Ashish, N., Barish, G., Knoblock, C. A., Minton, S., Modi, P. J., Muslea, I., Philpot, A. & Tejada, S. (1998). *ARIADNE: A System for Constructing Mediators for Internet Sources, Proceedings of ACM SIGMOD.*

Appel, W. P., & Behr, R. (1996). *Towards the theory of virtual organizations: A description of their formation and figure (Arbeitspapiere Wirtschaftsinformatik)*. Justus-Liebig-Universität Gießen Fachbereich Wirtschaftswissenschaften.

Auer, S. (2005, May 30). Powl: A Web-based platform for collaborative Semantic Web development. In *Proceedings of the 1ˢᵗ Workshop on Scripting for the Semantic Web (SFSW05)*. Hersonissos, Crete, Greece.

Auer, S., Bizer, C., Lehmann, J., Kobilarov, G., Cyganiak, R., & Ives, Z. (2007, November 11-15) DBpedia: A nucleus for a Web of open data. In Aberer et al. (Eds.): *The Semantic Web, 6th International Semantic Web Conference, 2nd Asian Semantic Web Conference, ISWC 2007 + ASWC 2007*, Busan, Korea. Lecture Notes in Computer Science 4825 Springer 2007, ISBN 978–3–540–76297–3.

Auer, S., Bizer, C., & Miller, L. (Eds.). (2005, May 30). *Proceedings of the 1st Workshop on Scripting for the Semantic Web (SFSW05)*. Hersonissos, Crete, Greece (No. 135).

Auer, S., & Herre, H. (2006, September 27-30). A versioning and evolution framework for RDF knowledge bases, in *Proc. of Sixth International Conference Perspectives of System Informatics*, Novosibirsk, Russia.

Auer, S., & Pieterse, B. (2005). "Vernetzte Kirche": Building a Semantic Web. In *Proceedings of ISWC Workshop Semantic Web case studies and best practices for E-Business (SWCASE05)*.

Aumüller, D. (2005a, May). Semantic authoring and retrieval within a Wiki (Wik-SAR). In *Demo Session at the Second European Semantic Web Conference (ESWC2005)*. Available at http://wik-sar.sf.net.

Aumüller, D. (2005b). SHAWN: Structure helps a Wiki navigate. In *Proceedings of the BTW-Workshop "WebDB meets IR"*.

Bechhofer, S., Harmelen, F. van, Hendler, J., Horrocks, I., McGuinness, D. L., Patel-Schneider, P. F., et al. (2004). *OWL Web ontology language reference*. W3C Recommendation (http://www.w3.org/TR/owl-ref/).

Bizer, C., Lee, R., & Pietriga, E. (2004). *Fresnel - Display vocabulary for RDF*.

Bizer, C., & Seaborne, A. (2004). D2RQ -treating non-RDF databases as virtual RDF graphs. *Poster at Third International Semantic Web Conference (ISWC2004)*. Hiroshima, Japan.

Cockburn, A. (2000). Selecting a project's methodology. *IEEE Software, 17*(4).

Cockburn, A. (2004). *Crystal clear*. Addison-Wesley Professional.

Dietzold, S. (2005). *Generating RDF models from LDAP directories*.

Fellbaum, C. (Ed.) (1998). *Wordnet - An electronic lexical database*. MIT Press.

Fensel, D., Motta, E., Harmelen, F. van, Benjamins, V. R., Crubezy, M., Decker, S., et al. (2003). The unified problem-solving method development language UPML. *Knowl. Inf. Syst, 5*(1), 83-131.

Fernandez, M., Perez, G. A., & Juristo, N. (1997). METHONTOLOGY: From ontological art towards ontological engineering. *Proceedings of the AAAI97 Spring Symposium Series on Ontological Engineering, Stanford*. USA, 1997.

Fernandez-Lopez, M. (1999). Overview of methodologies for building ontologies. In IJCAI99 Workshop on Ontologies and Problem-Solving Methods: Lessons Learned and Future Trends.

Garcia-Molina, H., Papakonstantinou, Y., Quass, D., Rajaraman, A., Sagiv, Y., Ullman, J., & Widom, J. (1997). The TSIMMIS project: Integration of heterogeneous information sources. *Journal of Intelligent Information Systems*.

Gebhardt, A. (2003). *Rapid prototyping*. Hanser Gardner Pubns.

Golder, S., Huberman, B. A. (2006). Usage patterns of collaborative tagging systems. *Journal of Information Science, 32*(2), 198-208.

Grosso, W., Eriksson, H., Fergerson, R., Gennari, J., Tu, S., & Musen, M. (1999). Knowledge modeling at the millennium (the design and evolution of Protégé-2000. In *Proceedings of the Twelfth Workshop on Knowledge Acquisition, Modeling and Management.*

Gruber, T. R. (1993). A translation approach to portable ontologies. *Knowledge Acquisition, 5*(2), 199-220.

Gruninger, M., & Fox, M. S. (1995). Methodology for the design and evaluation of ontologies. *Proceedings of the Workshop on Basic Ontological Issues in Knowledge Sharing, International Joint Conference on Artificial Intelligence*, Montreal, Canada, 1995.

Haarslev, V., & Möller, R. (2001, June 18-23). RACER system description. In R. Goré, A. Leitsch, & T. Nipkow (Eds.), *International Joint Conference on Automated Reasoning, IJCAR'2001*, Siena, Italy (pp. 701-705). Springer-Verlag.

de Hoog, R., Benus, B., Vogler, M., & Metselaar, C. (1996). The commonKADS organization model: Content, usage and computer support. *Expert Systems with Applications, 11*(1), 1996.

Horrocks, I. (1998). The fact system. In H. de Swart (Ed.), *Automated Reasoning With Analytic Tableaux and Related Methods: International Conference Tableaux '98* (pp. 307-312). Springer-Verlag.

Horrocks, I., Patel-Schneider, P. F., Boley, H., Tabet, S., Grosof, B., & Dean, M. (2003). SWRL: A Semantic Web rule language combining OWL and RuleML. http://www.daml.org/2003/11/swrl/.

Karvonen, K. (2000). The beauty of simplicity. In J. Scholtz & J. Thomas (Eds.), *Proceedings of the 2000 Conference on Universal Usability (CUU-00,)* (pp. 85-90). NY: ACM Press.

Kiryakov, A., Ognyanov, D., Fensel, D., Klein, M., & Lab, O. (2002, June 28). Ontology versioning and change detection on the Web. In *Proceedings of the 13th International Conference on Knowledge Engineering and Knowledge Management (EKAW02)*, SigUenza, Spain October 1-4, 2002.

Klyne, G., & Carroll, J. J. (2004). *Resource Description Framework (RDF): Concepts and abstract syntax*. W3C Recommendation (http://www.w3.org/TR/rdf-concepts).

Knublauch, H. (2002). *An agile development methodology for knowledge-based systems*. Unpublished doctoral dissertation, University of Ulm.

Kotis, K., Vouros, G. A., & Alonso, J. P. (2004). HCOME: Tool-Supported methodology for collaboratively devising living ontologies, *Proceedings of the 2nd International Workshop of Semantic Web and Databases*, Toronto, Canada, 2004.

Krötzsch, M., Vrandecic, D., & Völkel, M. (2005). Wikipedia and the Semantic Web - The missing links. In J. Voss & A. Lih (Eds.), *Proceedings of Wikimania 2005*, Frankfurt, Germany.

McGuinness, D., Ding, L., Glass, A., Chang, C., Zeng, H., & Furtado, V. (2006, November 6). Explanation interfaces for the Semantic Web: Issues and Models, SWUI 2006 - *The 3rd International Semantic Web User Interaction Workshop*, Athens, Georgia, USA

Mika, P. (2005). Social networks and the Semantic Web: The next challenge. *IEEE Intelligent Systems 20*(1), 80-93

Nottingham, M., & Sayre, R. (2005). *The atom syndication format* (Tech. Rep.). Internet Engineering Task Force (IETF).

Orr, K., & Highsmith, J. A. (2000). *Adaptive software development: A collaborative approach to managing complex systems.* Dorset House Publishing Co.

Palmer, S. R., & Felsing, J. M. (2002). *A practical guide to the feature-driven development.* Prentice Hall PTR.

Pinto, H. S., Tempich, C., & Staab, S. (2004). Diligent: Towards a fine-grained methodology for distributed, loosely-controlled and evolving engineering of ontologies, *Proceedings of the 16th European Conference on Artificial Intelligence*, Valencia, Spain, 2004.

Schreiber, G., Akkermans, H., Anjewierden, A., Hoog, R. de, Shadbolt, N., Velde, W. V. de, et al. (2000). *Knowledge engineering and management: The commonKADS methodology.* MITpress.

Schwaber, K., & Beedle, M. (2001). *Agile software development with scrum* (1st ed.). Prentice Hall.

Shirky, C. (2003, April). A group is its own worst enemy. *Rede zur ETech Conference*, online http://www.shirky.com/writings/group_enemy.html.

Spyns, P., Meersman, R., & Jarrar, M. (2002). Data modelling versus ontology engineering. *SIGMOD Record (ACM Special Interest Group on Management of Data), 31*(4).

Stojanovic, L. (2004). *Methods and tools for ontology evolution.* Unpublished doctoral dissertation, Institut für Angewandte Informatik und Formale Beschreibungsverfahren, Universität Karlsruhe (TH).

Trout, J., & Rivkin, S. (1998). *The power of simplicity.* Mcgraw-Hill.

Uschold, M. (1996). Building ontologies: Towards a unified methodology. *Proceedings of the 16th Annual Conference of the British Computer Society Specialist Group on Expert Systems*, Cambridge, UK, 1996.

Vanderwal, T. (2005, November, 5). *Off the top*: Folksonomy Entries.

Winer, D. (2002). *RSS 2.0 specification* (Available at http://blogs.law.harvard.edu/tech/rss). Berkman Center for Internet & Society at Harvard Law School.

ADDITIONAL READING

Beck, K., Beedle, M., van Bennekum, A., Cockburn, A., Cunningham, W., Fowler, M. Grenning, J., Highsmith, J., Hunt, A., Jeffries, R., Kern, J., Marick, B., Martin, R., Mellor, S., Schwaber, K., Sutherland, J., & Thomas, D. (2001). *Manifesto for agile software development.* http://agilemanifesto.org

Auer, S., Dietzold, S., & Riechert, T. (2006, November 5-9): OntoWiki - A tool for social, semantic collaboration, in I. Cruz et al., (ed.) *Proc. of 5th International Semantic Web Conference*, Athens, GA, USA, Springer-Verlag Berlin Heidelberg, , pp. 736-749.

Bächle, M. (2006), Social Software., *Informatik Spektrum 29*(2), 121-124.

O'Reilly, T. (2005). *What Is Web 2.0 - Design patterns and business models for the next generation of software*, online http://www.oreillynet.com/pub/a/oreilly/tim/news/2005/09/30/what-is-Web-20.html

Webb, M. (2004). *On social software*, Online http://interconnected.org/home/2004/04/28/on_social_software

Beck, K., & Andres, C. (2004). *Extreme programming explained: Embrace change, second edition.* Addison Wesley Professional.

Cunningham, W. (2003). *Wiki design principles.* http://c2.com/cgi/wiki?WikiDesignPrinciples.

Leuf, B., & Cunningham, W. (2001). The wiki way: Collaboration and sharing on the internet. Addison-Wesley Professional.

Studer, R., Benjamins, V. R., & Fensel, D. (1998). Knowledge engineering: Principles and methods. *Data & Knowledge Engineering, 25*(1-2), 161-197.

Ungar, D., & Smith, R. B. (1991). *SELF: The power of simplicity. Lisp and Symbolic Computation, 4*(3), 187-205.

APPENDIX: QUESTIONS FOR DISCUSSION

Name three adaptive methodologies in different domains.

Extreme Programming in software engineering, "the Wiki Way" for content management, Rapid Prototyping for industrial engineering are adaptive methodologies in different domains.

What are smallest possible information chunks in RapidOWL knowledge bases?

RapidOWL is based on statements in the shape of RDF triples consisting of subject, predicate and object.

How can the unique identification of entities be assured on the Web?

Universal Resource Identifier (URI) enable the unique global referencing of resources and concepts, both within RDF statements and for retrieving further information about the referenced entity from the Web.

What are the typical ingredients of adaptive methodologies?

Adaptive methodologies can be described on the basis of their roles, paradigms, processes, models and tools. Paradigms influence the process; they lay the foundation for models, and have to be internalized by people. Tools support the collaboration processes on the basis of the methodologies models.

How can we distinguish data, information and knowledge?

Data are supposed to be "raw signals", such as the name of a person. Information attaches meaning to data, such as the statement that a person is male. Knowledge in turn attaches purpose and competence to information, potential to generate action.

Which roles of participating actors are envisioned by RapidOWL in the creation of knowledge bases?

RapidOWL envisions domain experts, knowledge engineers and software developers to participate in semantic collaboration scenarios. However, RapidOWL is primarily focused on domain experts and should be applicable even in the absence of knowledge engineers and developers.

How is the creation of knowledge bases different from the creation of software?

Knowledge Engineering is usually not a business model in itself. It also lacks unique knowledge serializations as there are with source code for software. Knowledge engineering scenarios mostly have to deal with a large number of spatially separated parties.

Describe differences and similarities of Social Software and the Semantic Web

Both paradigms are collaboration and integration focused, based on the Web and provide enhanced means for search and navigation. They differ, however, with regard to the involvement of communities, the incorporation of business aspects as well as the complexity of content and technologies.

What are the typical communication patterns for social software?

Typical communication patterns for social software are point-to-point, bi-directional, star-like, net-like communication.

Chapter XII
The Social Semantic Desktop:
A New Paradigm Towards Deploying the Semantic Web on the Desktop

Ansgar Bernardi
German Research Center for Artificial Intelligence (DFKI) GmbH, Kaiserslautern, Germany

Stefan Decker
National University of Ireland, Ireland

Ludger van Elst
German Research Center for Artificial Intelligence (DFKI) GmbH, Kaiserslautern, Germany

Gunnar Aastrand Grimnes
German Research Center for Artificial Intelligence (DFKI) GmbH, Kaiserslautern, Germany

Tudor Groza
National University of Ireland, Ireland

Siegfried Handschuh
National University of Ireland, Ireland

Mehdi Jazayeri
University of Lugano, Switzerland

Cédric Mesnage
University of Lugano, Switzerland

Knud Möller
National University of Ireland, Ireland

Gerald Reif
University of Lugano, Switzerland

Michael Sintek
German Research Center for Artificial Intelligence (DFKI) GmbH, Kaiserslautern, Germany

Leo Sauermann
German Research Center for Artificial Intelligence (DFKI) GmbH, Germany

ABSTRACT

This chapter introduces the general vision of the Social Semantic Desktop (SSD) and details it in the context of the NEPOMUK project. It outlines the typical SSD requirements and functionalities that were identified from real world scenarios. In addition, it provides the design of the standard SSD architecture together with the ontology pyramid developed to support it. Finally, the chapter gives an overview of some of the technical challenges that arise from the actual development process of the SSD.

Copyright © 2009, IGI Global, distributing in print or electronic forms without written permission of IGI Global is prohibited.

INTRODUCTION

A large share of everybody's daily activities centres around the handling of information in one way or the other. Looking for information, digesting it, writing down new ideas, and sharing the results with other people are key activities both in work as well as in manifold leisure activities. The abundance of PCs and the Web in today's world result in new numbers and qualities of information exchange and interaction which are seen both as chance and as threat by the users. Supporting personal and shared information handling is thus a highly requested but yet unsolved challenge.

In traditional desktop architectures, applications are isolated islands of data – each application has its own data, unaware of related and relevant data in other applications. Individual vendors may decide to allow their applications to interoperate, so that, e.g., the email client knows about the address book. However, today there is no consistent approach for allowing interoperation and a system-wide exchange of data between applications. In a similar way, the desktops of different users are also isolated islands – there is no standardized architecture for interoperation and data exchange between desktops. Users may exchange data by sending emails or uploading it to a server, but so far there is no way of seamless communication from an application used by one person on their desktop to an application used by another person on another desktop.

The problem on the desktop is similar to that on the Web – also there, we are faced with isolated islands of data and no generic way to integrate and communicate between various Web applications (i.e., Web Services). The vision of the SW offers solutions for both problems. RDF[a] is the common data format which builds bridges between the islands, and Semantic Web Service technology offers the means to integrate applications on the Web.

The Social Semantic Desktop (SSD) paradigm adopts the ideas of the SW paradigm for the desktop. Formal ontologies capture both a shared conceptualization of desktop data and personal mental models. RDF serves as a common data representation format. Web Services – applications on the Web – can describe their capabilities and interfaces in a standardized way and thus become Semantic Web Services. On the desktop, applications (or rather: their interfaces) will therefore be modelled in a similar fashion. Together, these technologies provide a means to build the semantic bridges necessary for data exchange and application integration. The Social Semantic Desktop will transform the conventional desktop into a seamless, networked working environment, by loosening the borders between individual applications and the physical workspace of different users.

By realizing the Social Semantic Desktop, we contribute to several facets of an effective personal information handling:

- We offer the individual user a systematic way to structure information elements within the personal desktop. Using standard technology to describe and store structures and relations, users may easily reflect and express whatever is important in their personal realm.
- Standardized interfaces enable the integration of all kinds of available desktop applications into the personal information network. Investments in programs, data collections, and hard-learned working styles are not lost but augmented and connected into a comprehensive information space.
- Based on the SW technology basis, all kinds of automated and semi-automatic support are possible, like, e.g., text classification services, image categorization, document relevance assessments, etc.
- The exchange of standard data formats between individual work spaces is supported not only on the technical level (e.g., standard

communication protocols), but also on the semantic level (via sharing and alignment of ontologies and the corresponding annotated information elements). The integration with formal ontologies eases the sharing and understanding between different persons.

- Ultimately, we thus contribute to a solution for the initialization problem of the SW: As the individual user will receive immediate benefit from the semantic annotation within the personal workspace, the motivation is high to invest the necessary structuring and formalization work. As the standards used allow for an effortless sharing of such work, the amount of semantically annotated information which can be made available in the Web grows dramatically – which in turn makes it worthwhile to develop new SW-based services.

In this chapter we describe in detail the core components which are necessary for building a Social Semantic Desktop. We illustrate the necessary standard framework and describe the role and structure of the ontologies which support the spectrum from personal to social information handling. We outline the implementation decisions which need to be observed in order to realize a consequently ontology-oriented system, which is able to deal with the numerous flexibilities required within the Semantic Web. Finally, we show examples of the benefits obtained from the realization and use of an SSD.

The ideas and implementation principles presented in this chapter are distilled from our experiences in the NEPOMUK Project[b]. For each section we will describe the general motivation and principles and then give details on how the particular challenges have been solved in the NEPOMUK project.

BACKGROUND

The Social Semantic Desktop vision has been around for a long time: visionaries like Vannevar Bush (1945) and Doug Engelbart (1962) have formulated and partially realized these ideas. However, for the largest part their ideas remained a vision for far too long, since the necessary foundational technologies were not yet invented – figuratively speaking, these ideas were proposing jet planes when the rest of the world had just invented the parts to build a bicycle. Only in the recent years several technologies and research streams began to provide a foundation which will be combined and extended to realize the envisioned collaborative infrastructure of the SSD.

Figure 1 shows the highest-level architecture and connections between components of the SSD, i.e., the social networks, the P2P infrastructure, and the individual desktops. Traditional semantics, knowledge representation, and reasoning research are now interacting. While none of them can solve the problem alone, together they may have the explosive impact of the original Web:

The Semantic Web effort provides standards and technologies for the definition and exchange of metadata and ontologies. Available standard proposals provide ways to define the syntax (RDF) and semantics of metadata based on ontologies (Web Ontology Language – OWL (McGuiness et. al, 2004), RDF Schema – RDFS). Research covering data transfer, privacy, and security issues is now also under development.

Social Software maps the social connections between different people into the technical infrastructure. As an example, Online Social Networking makes the relationships between individuals explicit and allows the discovery of previously unknown relationships. The most recent Social Networking Sites also help form new virtual communities around topics of interest and provide means to change and evolve these communities.

Figure 1. Component architecture of the Social Semantic desktop

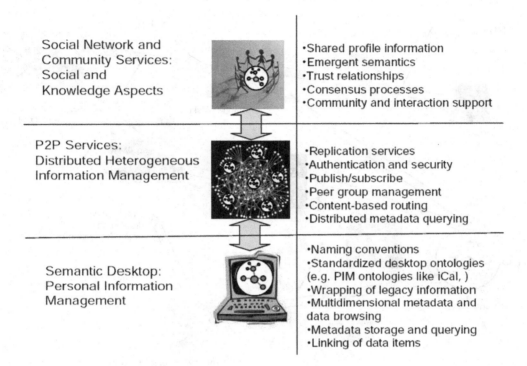

Social Network and
Community Services:
Social and
Knowledge Aspects

•Shared profile information
•Emergent semantics
•Trust relationships
•Consensus processes
•Community and interaction support

P2P Services:
Distributed Heterogeneous
Information Management

•Replication services
•Authentication and security
•Publish/subscribe
•Peer group management
•Content-based routing
•Distributed metadata querying

Semantic Desktop:
Personal Information
Management

•Naming conventions
•Standardized desktop ontologies
(e.g. PIM ontologies like iCal,)
•Wrapping of legacy information
•Multidimensional metadata and
data browsing
•Metadata storage and querying
•Linking of data items

P2P and Grid computing develops technology to network large communities without centralized infrastructures for data and computation sharing. P2P networks have technical benefits in terms of scalability and fault tolerance, but a main advantage compared to central sites is a political one: they allow to build communities without centralized nodes of control, much as the Internet grew as fast as it did because it was based on reciprocity – it avoided political debate as to who gets to own big, expensive central facilities. Recent research has provided initial ways of querying, exchanging and replicating data in P2P networks in a scalable way.

By projecting the trajectory of current trends, we can simplify this picture by stating that next generation desktop applications will support collaboration and information exchange in a P2P network, connecting online decentralized social networks, and enabling shared metadata creation and evolution by a consensus process. The result of this process will be the Social Semantic Desktop. Figure 2 depicts the phases in which the relevant co-evolving technologies are combined to achieve the final goal, i.e., the realization of the Social Semantic Desktop.

SCENARIOS

Before we move on to the specific functionalities that a Social Semantic Desktop supports and discuss how they are implemented, we will first present some scenarios that will illustrate what an SSD is, how it will be used, and how it will change the way we do knowledge work. We chose the scenarios such that they illustrate the different dimensions of an SSD: Sect. *The Semantic*

Figure 2. Phases towards the Social Semantic desktop

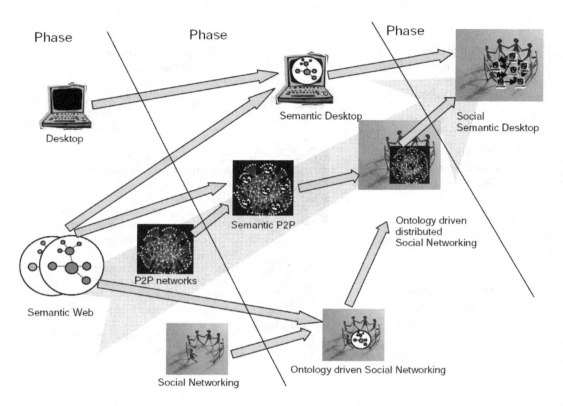

Dimension describes example usage that shows the use of semantics on the desktop, and Sect. *The Social Dimension* will show the social dimension of an SSD, i.e., the interaction between desktops of different users. The scenarios give an overview of what is possible and how the SSD presents itself to the user.

The Semantic Dimension

A typical use of a single Semantic Desktop is to organize ones data: files, emails, pictures, etc. Users are able to tag those information resources with concepts from a network of ontologies. The ontologies also contain relations (or properties, to use RDF terminology), which can be used to link information resources on the desktop. Organizing information resources in this way helps users

to find what they are looking for quicker, and makes it possible for the Semantic Desktop itself to aid the user in their daily work. When a user first begins using the Semantic Desktop, many often-used concepts and properties are already present. E.g., there are basic concepts such as **Person**, **Meeting** or **Place**, and properties such as **knows** or **located-in**. Also, we can assume that useful things like an ontology of all countries are already in place. Then, as the need arises, users can extend the existing ontologies – e.g., they can add concepts for a particular meeting they attend or people they know, such as **Executive-Committee-Meeting-07/06/07**, **Jane-Doe** or **Hans-Schmidt**. The following two scenarios give examples of this kind of Semantic Desktop usage. We will use two imaginary users (*personas*[c]) flesh them out:

Dirk, who works in a research group for some company in Germany, and Claudia, who is the group leader and his boss. Both Dirk and Claudia work on a project called Torque.

Organizing pictures (*Annotation*). Dirk just got back from his holidays in Norway, where he took a lot of pictures. Using his Semantic Desktop, he now wants to organize them, so that he can later find the pictures he wants to easier, generate photo albums for particular topics, etc. A lot of the important concepts probably already exist on his desktop, such as Norway, or the cities he has visited: **Oslo**, **Bergen** and **Trondheim**. Other concepts will be added by Dirk himself, such as **Holidays-in-Norway-2007** and tourist sights like **Preikestolen** or **Holmenkollen**. Since these concepts are more than just tags, Dirk can also say things *about* them, e.g., that **Holidays-in-Norway-2007** was a **Trip** and took place in **2007**, and that **Preikestolen** is a **Location** in **Norway**. Dirk even managed to take a picture of Prince Håkon and Princess Mette-Marit, so he creates two more concepts **Håkon** and **Mette-Marit**. There are many ways in which Dirk can link (or tag) his pictures to the relevant concepts – however, part of the Semantic Desktop are intuitive user interfaces, which hide most of the intricacies that go on under the hood from the user. E.g., Dirk might have an application that shows all the concepts that he is interested in the form of a tag cloud. Linking the pictures would then simply require him to drag them onto the desired concept in the cloud.

Planning a trip (*Context*). Later, Dirk finds out that he has to go on a work trip: a conference in Oslo. The Semantic Desktop assists him in planning and organizing this trip, through the notion of *context*. Dirk can create a new **Trip** object **Trip-to-OOC2007-Oslo** and tell his desktop that he is now in the context of this trip. This means that everything he does from this moment on will be interpreted as happening in that context, until he quits the context again. When he books a flight in his Web browser, the

destination field will automatically be filled in with "Oslo", similarly the departure field. Afterwards, when he books a hotel room, he will be assisted similarly. Dirk will receive a number of email confirmations, such as the flight itinerary and booking confirmation for his hotel. These emails and their attachments will automatically be filed as belonging to the **Trip-to-OOC2007-Oslo** context, so that Dirk can easily find them again later. Once he knows his exact flight dates and where his hotel will be, he enters this information into his calendar, which is also context-aware and will therefore remember that these entries belong to Dirk's trip.

The Social Dimension

Users will have a lot of benefit from just using the Semantic Desktop on their own. However, by connecting to others, a number of additional possibilities arise.

Assigning tasks in a group (*Social Interaction*). In the previous scenario, Dirk found out he had to go on a business trip. In fact, he found out about this because he was notified by his boss Claudia, who also uses a Semantic Desktop. Claudia plans to travel to the OOC2007 conference in Oslo to present a research prototype her group has developed as part of the *Torque* project. She does not want to travel alone, so she first needs to find out who of her group members are available while the conference runs. Through the network of Social Semantic Desktops, her calendar application has access to the calendars (or parts of them) of all her contacts. She can ask the calendar to give her a list of all people in her group (**My-Research-Group**) who are working on the *Torque* project (**Torque-Project**) and are free when OOC2007 is on. She finds out that Dirk is free at the desired time. Just like Dirk in the previous scenario, she creates a **Trip-to-OOC2007-Oslo** object and makes it her current context. She also links the trip to the **Torque-Project**. Now, she creates a new **Task** object

Dirk-Prepare-Trip-To-OOC2007, with a subtask **Dirk-Prepare-Presentation-Slides** and afterwards sends an email to Dirk, asking him to accompany her to the conference, book flights and hotel rooms, and prepare slides for the conference presentation. Her email and the task will of course be automatically linked to the proper context. Also, in this version of the scenario, Dirk no longer has to create the **Trip-to-OOC2007-Oslo** object himself – instead, it will be added to his Semantic Desktop automatically when he gets Claudia's mail.

FUNCTIONALITIES

In this section we describe a list of functionalities that are needed to support the scenarios mentioned above, as well as other scenarios developed during the NEPOMUK project. The SSD is a platform used to develop different kinds of social and semantic applications. These applications share common functionalities which must be supported by the SSD. We have divided them into five groups, which can be considered different aspects of the SSD. Tab. 1 shows the five different aspects and the individual functionalities within each group. Below we briefly describe the use of each functionality.

Desktop. At the *desktop* level, the semantic functionality common to most applications is the ability to add information about any resource. **Annotation** comprises the facilities to store and retrieve semantic relations about anything on the desktop. When Dirk annotates his photos from his trip, he does it from his most favorite photo application (such as Picasa or iPhoto), the annotations are then stored by the SSD. We name this functionality **Application Integration**; applications interact with the SSD by means of different services. When Dirk got notified about the trip to Oslo, this was an example of **Notification Management**. The SSD handles different kinds of mechanisms such as emails, RSS, or text messaging. When Dirk creates a new concept or even a new file on the SSD, the application he uses interacts with the **Resource Management** facilities of the SSD, creating the needed semantics according to the current context and setup. Some of the information Dirk needs when booking his trip are stored on Claudia's desktop. If she is not connected to the network, the **Offline Access** facility exports the relevant information to another desktop. **Desktop Sharing** is the ability for different users of the SSD to work on the same resources. Claudia might write a report of the trip together with Dirk: the resource management is done on Dirk's desktop, but Claudia can access and edit it remotely.

Search. The semantic network created on the desktop unleashes a whole new way of searching on the SSD. **Search** uses the semantic relations as well as social relations to retrieve relevant items. Once an item is found a user can also **Find Related Items**. For instance, when Dirk searches for a flight to Oslo, he can also search for related

Table 1. Functionalities of the Social Semantic desktop

Desktop	Annotation, Offline Access, Desktop Sharing, Resource Management, Application Integration, Notification Management
Search	Search, Find Related Items
Social	Social Interaction, Resource Sharing, Access Rights Management, Publish/Subscribe, User Group Management
Profiling	Training, Tailor, Trust, Logging
Data Analysis	Reasoning, Keyword Extraction, Sorting and Grouping

items and may find out that another company is actually cheaper, based on the experience of his social contacts.

Social. The SSD provides different means of **Social Interaction**, e.g., the embedding of semantic information in emails or text messaging, or the ability to annotate another user's resources. Some desktop level functionalities such as desktop sharing and offline access require the SSD to enable **Resource Sharing**. When Dirk and Claudia collaborate on the trip's report, Dirk might make it accessible to the whole group by adding it to a shared information space. When sharing resources or information on the network, the **Access Rights Management** of the SSD provides ways to define specific rights relations between users, groups and resources. The SSD's **User Group Management** system makes it easy for the rapid creation of new groups from a list of users. These groups can then be used to modify access rights or for resource sharing in a shared information space. E.g., some of Dirk's friends may have subscribed to get notifications of new pictures that Dirk annotates and makes available. The **Publish/Subscribe** mechanism of the SSD facilitates the creation of feeds of relevant information.

Profiling. If enabled, the **Logging** functionality of SSD logs user activity, which may help to detect the current user's context. The *profiling* of the SSD can be done automatically by **Training**: the SSD learns to predict the user's behavior. The user can still **Tailor** the SSD's intelligent behaviors: some learned contexts can become irrelevant and may need to be re-adapted or removed. The notion of **Trust** on the SSD between people or information sources is also a result of the profiling of the desktop. Dirk might define that he trusts Claudia's information, or Claudia's SSD might learn that Dirk is a trustworthy source of information regarding the *Torque* project.

Data analysis. To support the training behaviors of the SSD or querying related items, the SSD provides different *data analysis* mechanisms such as **Reasoning**. For instance, when Dirk tags

a picture with **Preikestolen** and **Norway**, the SSD may infer that Preikestolen is in Norway. This information can later be reused for search. **Sorting and Grouping** supports applications that perform search. The SSD returns items from many sources and people and sorts and groups these items regarding different criteria, using the semantics defined on these resources. The **Keyword Extraction** from resources such as text resources is useful for automatically tagging or summarizing.

ONTOLOGIES

Ontologies form a central pillar in Semantic Desktop systems, as they are used to model the environment and domain of the applications. The common definition of an ontology is "a formal, explicit specification of a shared conceptualization" (Gruber, 1995)

We distinguish four levels of ontologies for the SSD: *Representational*, *Upper-Level*, *Mid-Level and Domain*. The main motivation for having these layers is that ontologies at the foundational levels can be more stable, reducing the maintenance effort for systems committed to using them. A core principle of the Semantic Desktop is that ontologies are used for personal knowledge management. Each user is free to create new concepts or modify existing ones for his *Personal Information Model*. This modeling takes place on the domain-ontology level, but the user is of course free to copy concepts from the other layers and modify them to fit his or hers own needs. In order of decreasing generality and stability the four layers are:

Representation(al) Ontology. Representational ontologies (i.e., ontology definition languages) define the vocabulary with which the other ontologies are represented; examples are RDFS and OWL. The relationship of a representational ontology to the other ontologies is quite special: while upper-level ontologies generalize mid-level ontologies, which in turn generalize domain ontologies, all these ontologies can be understood as instances of the representational ontology. Concepts that might occur in the Representational Ontology level include: classes, properties, constraints, etc.

Upper-Level Ontology. "An upper ontology [...] is a high-level, domain-independent ontology, providing a framework by which disparate systems may utilize a common knowledge base and from which more domain-specific ontologies may be derived. The concepts expressed in such an ontology are intended to be basic and universal concepts to ensure generality and expressivity for a wide area of domains. An upper ontology is often characterized as representing common sense concepts, i.e., those that are basic for human understanding of the world. Thus, an upper ontology is limited to concepts that are meta, generic, abstract and philosophical. Standard upper ontologies are also sometimes referred to as foundational ontologies or universal ontologies." (Semy et. al, 2004) In the upper-level ontology you will find concepts like: `Person`, `Organization`, `Process`, `Event`, `Time`, `Location`, `Collection`, etc.

Mid-Level Ontology. "A mid-level ontology serves as a bridge between abstract concepts defined in the upper ontology and low-level domain specific concepts specified in a domain ontology. While ontologies may be mapped to one another at any level, the mid-level and upper ontologies are intended to provide a mechanism to make this mapping of concepts across domains easier. Mid-level ontologies may provide more concrete representations of abstract concepts found in the upper ontology. These commonly used ontologies are sometimes referred to as utility ontologies." (Semy et. al, 2004). The mid-level ontologies may include concepts such as: `Company`, `Employer`, `Employee`, `Meeting`, etc.

Domain Ontology. "A domain ontology specifies concepts particular to a domain of interest and represents those concepts and their relationships

from a domain specific perspective. While the same concept may exist in multiple domains, the representations may widely vary due to the differing domain contexts and assumptions. Domain ontologies may be composed by importing mid-level ontologies. They may also extend concepts defined in mid-level or upper ontologies. Reusing well established ontologies in the development of a domain ontology allows one to take advantage of the semantic richness of the relevant concepts and logic already built into the reused ontology. The intended use of upper ontologies is for key concepts expressed in a domain ontology to be derived from, or mapped to, concepts in an upper-level ontology. Mid-level ontologies may be used in the mapping as well. In this way ontologies may provide a web of meaning with semantic decomposition of concepts. Using common mid-level and upper ontologies is intended to ease the process of integrating or mapping domain ontologies." (Semy et. al, 2004). Domain ontologies consist of concepts like: **Group Leader, Software Engineer, Executive Committee Meeting, Business Trip, Conference**, etc.

Figure 3 shows how these four layers relate to the four ontologies created and used in the NEPOMUK Project. As detailed in Sect. *"Technology"*, we were hesitant to make use of OWL for the representational ontology level in NEPOMUK, and in its place we developed the NEPOMUK Representational Language (Sintek et. al, 2007) (NRL). NRL defines an extension to the semantics offered by RDF and RDFS; the main contribution of NRL is the formalization of the semantics of named graphs. NRL allows multiple semantics (such as open and closed world) to coexist in the same application, by allowing each named graph to have separate semantics. The NEPOMUK Annotation Ontology (NAO) is a basic schema for describing annotations of resources, this is essentially a formalization of the tagging paradigm of Web2.0 applications. A specialized part of NAO is the NEPOMUK Graph Metadata schema (NGM) which allows the

Figure 3. NEPOMUK ontology pyramid

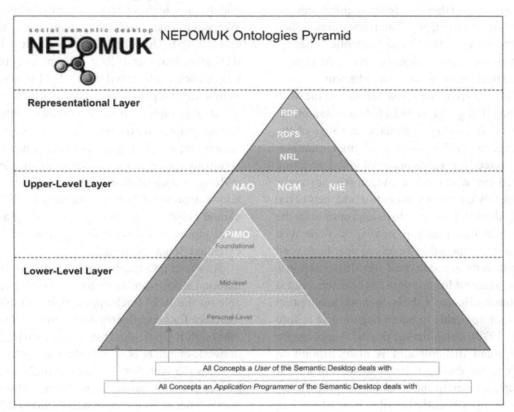

description of named graphs, defining meta-data properties such as the author, modification dates and version data.

Finally, the NEPOMUK Information Elements ontology (NIE) contains classes and properties for describing objects found on the traditional desktop, such as files (Word documents, images, PDFs), address book entries, emails, etc. NIE is based on existing formats for file meta-data such as EXIF for image meta-data, MPEG7 for multimedia annotations, ID3 for music files, iCal, and others.

TECHNOLOGY

The Social Semantic Desktop deploys the Semantic Web on the desktop computer. Therefore, the technology stack proposed for the Semantic Web (the famous "Layercake"[d] adapted in Figure 4) is adopted for the SSD as well.

However, there are some specific considerations for the desktop scenario: everything on the desktop should identifiable by URIs. This is partially solved for files, where RFC1738[e] specifies the form of file:// URIs, but requires considerable care for other applications which may not represent their data entities as individual files, such as address books or email clients.

Secondly, one can note that for the single desktop scenario there are fewer requirements on aspects such as trust, proof, and signatures. When one progresses to the Social Semantic Desktop, which involves interactions between many users, these aspects must be considered again.

In NEPOMUK we chose not to use the Web Ontology Language (OWL) (McGuiness et. al, 2004) as an ontology language, because of the challenge of dealing with (and implementing) OWL correctly; because our ontological modeling requirements were modest, and, most importantly, because OWL enforces an open-world view of the world, which did not seem to be appropriate for the (local) Semantic Desktop. In a World Wide Web context it is impossible for an application to read all available data, and an open-world assumption is natural, since additional data can be discovered at any moment. However, the open-world assumption makes it impossible to adopt negation as failure (Clark, 1978) which makes practical application development difficult and is also difficult to explain to the end-user. In the context of a local desktop application the situation is quite different, here it is perfectly possible to read all data available, and the closed world assumption makes much more sense. In place of OWL we developed our own ontology specification language called NRL, which uses the closed-world assumption.

An additional RDF-based technology that we use widely, but which does not feature in the Semantic Web stack is the concept of named graphs (Caroll et. al, 2005). This allows one to divide a larger RDF store into sets of RDF statements (graphs), where each is identified with a URI (the name). In this way it is possible to make meta-statements about each graph, such as provenance information. Named graphs thus become an alternative to RDF reification, which also allows making statements about other statements, but is harder to implement and creates a significant overhead. NRL does also allows applying different semantics for different named graphs, thus allowing us to integrate the local closed-world with the open-world of the extended Semantic Web.

As noted previously, applications on the Semantic Desktop are analogous to services available on the Web. Each application will offer an interface for exposing the functionality it offers. Although a single desktop is not distributed, a network of SSDs is. It therefore suggests itself to adopt the Web Service stack of tools for inter-service communication for the Semantic Desktop: the Web Service Description Language (WSDL)[f] which is used for describing the interfaces of services offered, XML Schema (XSD)[g] which is used for primitive type definitions, and finally the Simple Object Access Protocol (SOAP)[h] which

Figure 4. The Semantic Web technology stack

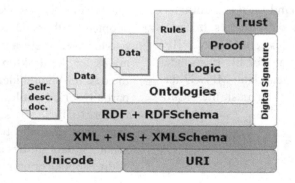

is used for the invocation of services. In Sect. *"Implementation and Engineering Principles"* we give further details on how these technologies work in relation to the Semantic Web technologies presented above.

ARCHITECTURE

In our vision, the standard architecture comprises a small set of standard interfaces which allow application developers to easily extend it and ultimately lead to an evolving ecosystem. Figure 5 depicts this set of interfaces transposed into services, together with their placement in the NEPOMUK architecture. The architecture has to reflect the two aspects of the scenarios introduced in Sect. *"Scenarios"*, i.e., the semantic (which can operate on a single desktop) and the social aspect (which is relevant in a network of desktops). To cover these requirements and the functionalities discussed in Sect. *"Functionalities"*, the SSD is organized as a Service Oriented Architecture (SOA). Each service has a well defined WSDL interface and is registered at the *Service Registry*. The social aspect of sharing resources over the network is enabled by the peer-to-peer (P2P) infrastructure of the architecture. In the following we present the services of the SSD.

The architecture, as show in Figure 5, is organized in three layers. Like current desktop systems, the desktop environment builds on top of the *Operating System* core, such as the file system, kernel, and network environment. On the SSD the desktop environment is pooled in the *Social Semantic Desktop Middleware* Layer (SSD Middleware). The SSD Middleware groups the services of the SSD to be used in the Presentation Layer, which provides the user with SSD enabled applications that take advantages of the functionalities of the SSD.

The SSD is made up by individual desktops, which are organized in a P2P fashion. To support the communication between the peers, the SSD

Middleware provides *P2P Network communication Services*. To enable information sharing between individual desktops, the RDF metadata of shared resources is stored in the *distributed index* of the P2P system. In NEPOMUK, the P2P system is based on GridVine (Aberer et. al, 2004), which in turn is built on top of P-Grid (Aberer et. al, 2003) and provides a distributed index with RDQL query supports.

Network Communication Services provide an *Event-based System*, which is responsible for the distribution of the events between the SSD peers. On the SSD, the event-based system is used to support the publish/subscribe system. Users as well as other services can use RDF to describe the kind of information they are interested in (e.g., new pictures of Norway become available, the status of a document changes to final, etc.). These subscriptions are stored in the distributed index of the P2P system. An event that was fired carries an RDF query as payload, which is matched against all subscriptions and triggers the notification of the subscriber. In addition, the *Messaging Routing* system uses RDF information to route messages to receiver.

The *Data Services* are responsible to control the insertion, modification, deletion, and retrieval of resources on the SSD. A resource can be a user, a document, a calendar entry, an email, and so on. It provides a service to store the RDF metadata in the *Local Storage*. Resources and their RDF descriptions can either be added to the SSD manually, or the *Data Wrapper* or *Text Analysis* service extracts the information from desktop applications such as email clients or calendars. Data Wrappers are used to extract metadata form structured data sources (e.g., email headers, calendar entries, etc.). In NEPOMUK, data wrappers are implemented based on Aperture (Aperture, 2007). The Text Analysis service is used to extract metadata from unformatted text (e.g., email bodies, word processing documents, etc.). For local queries and for offline working the RDF metadata is stored in the *Local Storage*. If a

Figure 5. Layered architecture of the Social Semantic desktop

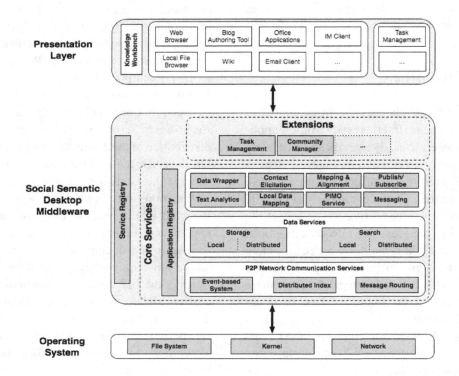

resource is shared with other users in an information space, the meta-data is also uploaded to the distributed index of the peer-to-peer file sharing system. The *Search* service can either issue a *local* search in the local storage or a *distributed* search in the underlying P2P system.

Before new metadata can be added to the repository, we have to check whether this metadata describes resources that are already instantiated (i.e., an URI has been assigned) in the RDF repository. In this case, the URI of the resource should be reused, rather then creating a new one. This process is known as information integration (Bergamaschi et. al, 2001). The *Local Data Mapper* service takes over this responsibility in the SSD Middleware. E.g., the Data Wrapping service extracts contact information from the address

book and stores the metadata in the repository. Since this is the first time information about the contacts is added to the RDF repository, a new URI is generated for each person. If later the Data Wrapping service extracts information from an email header, the Local Data Mapping service is responsible to lookup whether information about the sender of the email is already in the repository and reuse the corresponding URI instead of creating a new one (Sauermann et. al, 2006).

Ideally only one ontology exists for a domain of interest such as contact data, calendar events. In reality, however, we are faced with many ontologies of (partly) overlapping domains (e.g., FOAF and vCard for contact data, or different personal information models). Since individual users share information over the SSD, it is likely to happen that they use different ontologies for their annotations even when talking about similar domains. Therefore, the SSD Middleware provides a *Mapping & Alignment* service that can be used by other middleware services and services in higher layers to translate RDF graphs from a source ontology to a target ontology.

The SSD Middleware logs the actions a user performs on the resources on his desktop. The logged data is stored in the Local Storage and analyzed by the *Context Elicitation* service to capture the current working context of the user. The context can for example be used to adapt the user interface or to suggest meaningful annotations to the users, depending on the task they are currently working on.

As discussed in Sect. *"Technology"*, the services on the SSD use RDF to exchange data. Therefore, services need the capability to generate and process RDF graphs. To simplify the handling of the RDF graphs, the *Ontology Service* provides an easy way to create and manipulate concepts in RDF graphs.

The *Publish/Subscribe System* allows users or other SSD services to subscribe to events on the SSD. The subscriptions are stored as RDF graphs in the distributed index. If an event occurs, the RDF query of the event is matched against the subscriptions. When the subscription, i.e., the RDF query, matches the event, the *Messaging* service looks up the preferred notification media (e.g., email, instant messaging, SMS) and delivers the messages. The Messaging System is further used for synchronous and asynchronous communication between SSD users.

The *Core Services* of the SSD Middleware comprise the services which provide the basic functionalities of the SSD. These services can be accessed via the SSD Application Programming Interface (API). If a developer wants to exploit the SSD Core Services to build his domain-specific application, he can do this as an *extension* of the SSD Middleware. An example for such an extension is the *Task Management* which provides

functionalities such as creating, delegating, and manipulating of tasks. Finally, the *Application registry* allows applications from the Presentation Layer to register call back methods at the SSD Middleware if they need to be notified by SSD services, e.g., when a message arrives and has to be displayed to the user in an Instant Messaging Client.

The top layer of the architecture is the presentation layer. It provides a user interface to the services provided by the SSD, and is built using the SSD API. Many desktop applications are possible sources for resources that should be managed by the SSD. Therefore, each desktop application should integrate support for the SSD Middleware. Since this assumption does not hold for most of the current off-the-shelf applications, we developed plug-ins and add-ons to enable a seamless integration with existing applications. These plugins for example extract email or calendar data and add them as resources to the SSD. However, within NEPOMUK we also develop dedicated applications that make use of the SSD API directly, such as a semantic *Wiki* or *Blogging Tools*. (Möller et. al, 2006)

In addition, the *Knowledge Workbench* is the central place to browse, query, view, and edit resources and their metadata. In this way the Knowledge Workbench aims to replace current file management tools such as the MS File Explorer. If the SSD is extended by usage extensions, the application programmer also has to provide the corresponding user interface in the Presentation Layer (e.g., for Task Management, Community Management, etc.).

IMPLEMENTATION AND ENGINEERING PRINCIPLES

As detailed in Sect. *"Architecture"*. we deem a Service Oriented Architecture (SOA) to be most suitable for the SSD framework. Furthermore, we decided to use the industry standard SOAP (Simple

Object Access Protocol) for exchanging messages between our components. For traditional applications the names and structure of SOAP messages is specified using the Web Service Description Language (WSDL), which in turn uses XML schema data-types to specify the form of the objects being exchanged. However, since the formal modeling of the target domain using ontologies is the core idea of a Semantic Desktop application, the best-practices for SOAs are slightly different. In this section we will discuss some important differences from a traditional SOA system.[i] Basing a system architecture on underlying domain ontologies is similar in nature to Model Driven Architectures (MDA)[j]. However, on the SSD, ontologies take the place of UML models.

Working with RDF

Sect. "*Ontologies*" described the substantial effort that went into the modeling of our domains as ontologies in a formal language. These ontologies give us a very powerful and flexible modeling language, although the structure of instances of such ontologies at first sight seem much more constrained than complex XML schema data-types, the flexibility of RDF introduces some additional requirements for developers of components that should handle RDF instances:

- The structure of the RDF instances received may not be fully known at design time. This means one must take great care that the code does not break when encountering unknown properties in the data, and these unknown properties must also be preserved. In general, programming services for the Semantic Desktop is more like programming services for the web, rather than for traditional desktop applications, and one should follow the general rule of web-programming: "Be strict in what you send and tolerant in what you receive."

- Conversely, other services might not be aware of all the properties the local service uses. Therefore each service must be programmed to be tolerant of missing data and do their best with the data that was provided.

Passing Instances in Messages

Normally, when using SOAP in connection with WSDL and XML schema for data modeling, some mapping is used that will convert the XML schema definition to class definitions in the programming language of choice. Furthermore, stubs and skeletons will be generated for the service themselves, so that the details of communication are hidden. Programming against remote services is then indistinguishable from programming against a local object. However, when using services that pass instances for which the structure is defined by ontologies, the mapping is not so straight forward. Although interaction with RDF data can always be done on a completely general level using basic RDF APIs we are interested in facilitating the job of programmers consuming our services, and allowing them to work on a higher level than RDF triples. We identify three alternatives for programming web services where parameters are instances from an ontology:

- Starting with the ontologies, a number of tools[k] can be used to create a set of Java classes from the ontologies. The service interface is written using parameters of these types, and another tool is used to generate the WSDL and associated XML schema types from these. By sharing the URIs of the concepts in the ontologies with the URIs of the XML schema types, the semantics of messages is retained. The benefit of this approach is that much of the SOAP technology is retained, existing tools may be reused. Also, developers who are not familiar with Semantic Web technology will find that developing and using these services is unchanged from a normal Java environment. The main problem with this approach comes from the fact that ontologies are in general more dynamic than Java class definitions. In particular, as noted in Sect. *"Ontologies"*, we expect the personal information models to change frequently. This approach requires a complete re-run of the whole tool chain and a recompile of the system when an ontology changes, as well as introducing some constraints on the ontologies.

- On the other end of the spectrum it is possible to bypass the parameter passing of SOAP all together, and rely more on the Semantic Web technology. Each method offered by a service will take a single RDF document (possibly including several named-graphs), and all the details about the message are given in these RDF graphs. An additional ontology for messages and parameters must be constructed, and some named-graph aware serialization (e.g., TriG or TriX[l]) of RDF is used to construct the XML SOAP messages. This approach was, for instance, used in the SmartWeb project[m]. The benefit of this approach is that the effort that has gone into modeling the ontologies is not duplicated for modeling objects. Also, the full expressivity of RDF may be used when modeling, as it not required that the instances fit into another representation. The backside to this flexibility is that it is significantly harder to program with RDF graphs than with simple Java objects, and both service developers and consumers need good knowledge about RDF. One can of course envisage new tools that facilitate programming with such RDF messages, but since all the interesting details are hidden inside the RDF parameter, existing SOAP tools for development or debugging are no longer very useful.

- Finally, a hybrid approach of the two methods is possible. Here each method will retain multiple arguments, but each argument is represented by an RDF resource. We envisage two possibilities for doing this: either each parameter is given as a (*named-graph-uri, uri*) tuple pointing into an RDF document given as a special parameter; or, alternatively, each parameter is in itself an RDF graph plus the URI of the actual parameter (each RDF graph may contain several resources). The benefit of this method is that the changes in the ontology do no longer require a recompile of the system, while at the same time allowing slightly more compatibility with existing SOAP tools. The problem with this method remains that both client and server programmers need in-depth knowledge of RDF and the ontologies used.

Regardless of which of the three alternatives one chooses, it remains an important issue to make sure that the formal description of the services (i.e., the WSDL+XML Schema definitions) remain semantically correct and retain the pointers to the ontology concepts which the parameters represent. As mentioned, for the first approach this can be handled by well chosen URIs for the XMLSchema types. For the second and third approach the parameters have the form of simple string objects in both the WSDL definition and the SOAP messages, since the RDF serialization is represented as a string. However, both versions of WSDL available at the time of writing allow extensions to the WSDL format itself[n], and additional constraints on the type or form of the RDF instances contained inside the string parameters may be specified here. This is the approach taken by the *Semantic Annotation for WSDL and XML Schema* (SAWSDL) working group[o] and the NEPOMUK project makes use of their standard.

In this section we have considered a very lightweight approach to semantically enriching SOAP Web Services by passing RDF-based parameters. If a more powerful approach is required, the reader is advised to look into OWL-S[p] and the Web Service Modeling Language (WSML)[q], both defining much more sophisticated frameworks for Semantic Web Services.

RELATED WORK

In the following we review relevant research and development approaches for the Social Semantic Desktop. After providing a brief description, we discuss the lessons learned and state our conclusions.

Gnowsis (Sauermann, 2003) was among the first research projects targeting a Semantic Desktop system. Its goal is to complement established desktop applications and the desktop operating system with Semantic Web features, rather than replacing them. The primary focus of Gnowsis is on *Personal Information Management* (PIM). It also addresses the issues of identification and representation of desktop resources in a unified RDF graph. Gnowsis uses a Service Oriented Architecture (SOA), where each component defines a certain interface and it is available as an XML/RPC service.

The **Haystack** (Quan et. al, 2003) project presents a good example for an integrated approach to the SSD field. Inter-application barriers are avoided by simply replacing these applications with Haystack's own word processor, email client, image manipulation, instant messaging, etc. Haystack allows users to define their own arrangements and connections between views of information, thus making it easier to find information located in the personal space. The Haystack architecture can be split into two distinct parts: the Haystack Data Model (HDM) and the Haystack Service Model (HSM). The Data Model is the means by which the user's infor-

mation space is represented, similar to what has been discussed in Sect. *"Ontologies"*. The set of functionalities within Haystack is implemented by objects in the Haystack Service Model (HSM). Haystack has a standard three-tiered architecture, consisting of a user interface layer (the client), a server/service layer, and a database. Haystack was ground-breaking in terms of the dynamic creation of user interfaces, but the project ended before establishing any standards.

Another relevant personal information management tool is the **Semex System** (SEMantic EXplorer) (Dong et. al, 2005). Like other tools, it organizes data according to a domain ontology that offers a set of classes, objects and relationships. Semex leverages the Personal Information Management (PIM) environment to support on-the-fly integration of personal and public data. Information sources are related to the ontology through a set of mappings. Domain models can be shared with other users in order to increase the coverage of their information space. When users are faced with an information integration task, Semex aids them by trying to leverage data collected from previous tasks performed by the user or by others. Hence, the effort expended by one user later benefits others. Semex begins by extracting data from multiple sources and for these extractions it creates instances of classes in the domain model. It employs multiple modules for extracting associations, as well as allowing associations to be given by external sources or to be defined as views over other sets of associations. To combine all these associations seamlessly, Semex automatically reconciles multiple references to the same real-world object. The user browses and queries all this information through the domain model.

A similar idea is exploited by the **IRIS** Semantic Desktop (Cheyer et. al, 2005) ("Integrate. Relate. Infer. Share"), an application framework that enables users to create a "personal map" across their office-related information objects. IRIS offers integration services at three levels:

- Information resources (e.g., email messages, calendar appointments) and applications that create and manipulate them must be accessible to IRIS for instrumentation, automation, and query. IRIS offers a plug-in framework, in the style of the Eclipse architecture, where "applications" and "services" can be defined and integrated within IRIS. Apart from a very small, lightweight kernel, all functionality within IRIS is defined using a plug-in framework, including user interface, applications, back end persistence store, learning modules, harvesters, etc. Like Haystack, inter-application barriers do not exists, because all applications are made from scratch for IRIS.

- A Knowledge Base provides the unified data model, persistence store, and query mechanisms across the information resources and semantic relations among them. The IRIS user interface framework allows plug-in applications to embed their own interfaces within IRIS and to interoperate with global UI services, such as notification pane, menu toolbar management, query interfaces, the link manager, and suggestion pane.

DeepaMehta (Richter et. al, 2005) is an open source Semantic Desktop application based on the Topic Maps standard[r]. The DeepaMehta UI, which runs through a Web browser, renders Topic Maps as a graph, similar to concept maps. Information of any kind as well as relations between information items can be displayed and edited in the same space. The user is no longer confronted with files and programs. DeepaMehta has a layered, service oriented architecture. The main layer is the application layer, which offers various ways for the presentation layer to communicate with it via the communication layer (API, XML Topic Maps (XTM) export, EJB, SOAP). Finally, the storage layer holds all topics and their data either in a relational database or simply in the file system.

Other relevant projects include **Beagle++** (Brunkhorst et. al, 2005), a semantic search engine which provides the means for creating and retrieving relational metadata between information elements present on the destkop, **DBIN** (Tummarello et. al, 2006), which is similar to a file sharing client and connects directly to other peers, **PHLAT** (Cutrell et. al, 2006), a new interface for Windows, enabling users to easily specify queries and filters, attempting to integrate search and browse in one intuitive interface, or **MindRaider**[s], a Semantic Web outliner, trying to connect the tradition of outline editors with emerging SW technologies. The **MyLifeBits** project by Microsoft Research is a lifetime store of multimedia data. Though the system does not intent to be a SSD, one can learn from it how to integrate data, i.e., how to manage the huge amount of media and how to classify/retrieve the data (Gemmell et. al, 2002). It combines different approaches from HCI (Computer-Human Interaction) and information integration, while it lacks a conceptual layer beyond files. The **Apogée**[t] project deals with data integration in applications related to Enterprise Development Process (ECM). It aims at building a framework to create Enterprise Development Process-oriented desktop applications, independent from vendor or technologies. Finally, starting from the idea that everything has to do with everything, has a relationship with everything, **Fenfire**[u] is a Free Software project developing a computing environment in which you can express such relationships and benefit from them.

Although the systems we have looked at focus on isolated and complementary aspects, they clearly influenced the vision of the SSD presented here. Some of the architectural decisions made in the NEPOMUK project and presented in this chapter are similar to those of platforms like Haystack, IRIS, and DeepaMetha, e.g., in that we present a User Interface Layer, a Service and a Data Storage Layer. The modular architecture, also identified within the Haystack, SEMEX, and

DeepaMetha systems, as well as the standardized APIs offer an easy way of introducing new components. Our approach guarantees that each component may be changed without affecting other components it interacts with. The interaction has to suffer only in the case in which the API of the component is modified. The NEPOMUK Architecture also provides service discovery functionalities: the NEPOMUK Registry providing a proper support for publishing and discovering the existing NEPOMUK Services by using a standard interface.

CONCLUSION

We presented the Social Semantic Desktop as a comprehensive approach to information handling. Oriented at the needs of knowledge workers, this approach centers around supporting the main information-oriented activities: The articulation of knowledge and the generation of new information items; the structuring, relating, and organization of information, and the sharing of formal and informal information within networks of co-operating people. From this, we derived key functionalities of the desktop, but also for search, social interaction, profile building, and data analysis.

Building the SSD relies on basic principles: Whatever appears within the personal workspace is treated as an information item. Content, relations, special services all refer to formal annotations of such information items, which in turn link between information items and personal information models. Unifying the flexibility and personal liberty of expressing whatever concepts seem relevant with the commitment to socially shared conceptualizations results in a layered hierarchy of ontologies which allow the necessary differences in stability, sharing scope, and formality. Integrating the tools of everyday information processing asks for an easy and flexible integra-

tion of existing desktop applications. Finally, the adoption of Semantic Web standard technology for representation and communication enables the easy transgression from personal annotated information to shared Semantic Web content.

Consequently, the architecture of the SSD combines standards-based data repositories with a rich middleware, which in particular allows for manifold service integrations and communications. On top of that, various presentation clients and specific applications support whatever activities are performed on the desktop. Such applications may be highly domain-specific, although core functionalities of knowledge work trigger standard applications, e.g., for document processing, task management, communication, etc.

The design decisions presented result in particular implementation and engineering principles; we outlined the adaptation to RDF, the service integration, and the message passing mechanisms in particular.

In summary, the SSD offers the basic technology and tools for everyday information processing by knowledge workers. In order to reach the intended wide acceptance and broad uptake, care was taken to make the central software components available under open source licenses, and to encourage the development and contribution of application-specific enhancements and adaptations. The concept of the SSD is promising and relies on a number of techniques which reach their maturity right now – consequently, a number of research and development projects are under way and contribute to the overall evolution of the concept.

Following the realizations described in this chapter, we see the SSD as a basis for the self-motivated generation of semantically annotated information, which will not only help the individual by allowing multitudes of specific services and support, but will also initiate a wide movement to populate the Semantic Web.

FUTURE RESEARCH DIRECTIONS

Although the ideas of the Social Semantic Desktop are based on solid foundations as presented here, the research areas surrounding this topic are still in their infancies. We will briefly discuss some of the pre-dominant challenges in the coming years:

Trust and Privacy. As pointed out in the Semantic Web technology stack presented earlier, a crucial component for any high-level Semantic Web service is the issue of trust and privacy. Trust touches on a wide range of issues, from the technical issues of cryptographic signatures and encryption, to the social issues of trust in groups and among individuals. These issues are all as valid for the Social Semantic Desktop as for the Semantic Web in general, or perhaps even more so, as people are less critical of putting personal data on their personal desktop.

User, group, and rights management. When a single personal Semantic Desktop allows easy sharing of information with the network of Social Semantic Desktops, determining access rights for this information becomes very important. The Social Semantic Desktop sets new requirements for distributed authentication, flexible group management, and fine-grained access rights, all the while remaining intuitive and unobtrusive for the end user.

Integration with the wider Semantic Web and Web 2.0. Currently we are talking about the Social Semantic Desktop as a network of Semantic Desktops built on the same standards. It is important to remember that the key benefit of Semantic technology is the easy access to integration with anyone using the same representational languages and ontologies. The growth of feature-rich Web applications is growing rapidly, and ensuring a strong bond between the Semantic Desktop and these services is a continuous challenge.

Ontologies and Intelligent Services. To date ontologies have been used to introduce a common vocabulary for knowledge exchange. On the Social Semantic Desktop ontologies are used to formalize and categorize personal information. This introduces many interesting issues around ontology versioning, ontology mapping, and ontology evolution. Furthermore, using ontologies with well-defined semantics will allow intelligent services to be built (e.g., using reasoning) that allow for much more than just browsing and (simple) searching.

User Evaluation. The underlying thesis of the whole (Social) Semantic Desktop effort is that the added semantics will improve productivity and enable new forms of cooperation and interaction which were not previously possible. In-depth empirical evaluation with real users of a Social Semantic Desktop systems are required to determine if this thesis really holds.

REFERENCES

Aberer, K., & Cudré-Mauroux, P., Datta, A., Despotovic, Z., Hauswirth, M., Punceva, M., & Schmidt. R. (2003). P-Grid: A self-organizing structured P2P system. *SIGMOD Record, 32*(3), 29-33.

Aberer, K., Cudré-Mauroux, P., Hauswirth, M., & Pelt, T.V. (2004). Gridvine: Building Internet-scale semantic overlay networks. In S. A. McIlraith, D. Plexousakis, F. van Harmelen (Eds.), *The Semantic Web – ISWC 2004: Third International Semantic Web Conference*, 107-121. Springer Verlag.

Aperture: A Java framework for getting data and metadata, Last visited March 2007. http://aperture.sourceforge.net/.

Bergamaschi, S., Castano, S., Vincini, M., & Beneventano, D. (2001). Semantic integration and query of heterogeneous information sources. *Data & Knowledge Engineering, 36*(3), 215-249.

Berners-Lee, T., & Fischetti, M. (1999). *Weaving the Web – The original design and ultimate destiny of the World Wide Web by its inventor.* Harper San Francisco.

Berners-Lee, T., Hendler, J., & Lassila, O. (2001). The Semantic Web. *Scientific American.*

Brunkhorst, I., Chirita, P. A., Costache, S., Gaugaz, J., Ioannou, E., Iofciu, T., Minack, E., Nejdl, W., & Paiu. R. (2006). *The Beagle++ Toolbox: Towards an extendable desktop search architecture (Technical report)*, L3S Research Centre, Hannover, Germany.

Bush, V. (1945, July). *As we may think.* The Atlantic Monthly.

Carroll, J. J., Bizer, C., Hayes, P., & Sticker, P. (2005). Named graphs, provenance and trust, In A Ellis, T. Hagino (Eds.), *WWW 2005: The World Wide Web Conference*, 613-622.

Cheyer, A., Park, J., & Giuli, R. (2005, November 6). IRIS: Integrate. Relate. Infer. Share. In S. Decker, J. Park, D. Quan, L. Sauermann (Eds.), *Semantic Desktop Workshop at the International Semantic Web Conference*, Galway, Ireland, *175.*

Clark, K. L. (1978). Negation as failure. In J. Minker (Ed.), *Logic and Data Bases*, Plenum Press, New York, 293-322.

Cutrell, E., Robbins, D.C., Dumais, S.T., & Sarin, R. (2006, April 22-27). Fast, flexible filtering with PHLAT – Personal search and organization made easy. R. E. Grinter, T. Rodden, P. M. Aoki, E Cutrell, R. Jeffries, G. M. Olson (Eds.), *Proceedings of the 2006 Conference on Human Factors in Computing Systems*, CHI 2006, Montréal, Québec, Canada. ACM 2006, ISBN 1-59593-372-7.

Decker, S., & Frank, M. (2004, May 18). The networked semantic desktop. In C. Bussler, S. Decker, D., Schwabe, O. Pastor (Eds.), *Proceedings of the WWW2004 Workshop on Application Design, Development and Implementation Issues in the Semantic Web*, New York, USA.

Dong, X., & Halevy, A.Y. (2005). A platform for personal information management and integra-tion. In M. Stonebraker, G. Weikum, D. DeWitt (Eds.), *Proceedings of 2005 Conference on Innovative Data Systems Research Conference*, 119-130

Engelbart, D.C. (1962). *Augmenting human intellect: A conceptual framework (Summary report)*, Stanford Research Institute (SRI).

Gemmell, J., Bell, G., Lueder, R., Drucker, S., & Wong, C. (2002, December 1-6). MyLifeBits: Fulfilling the memex vision. In *ACM Multimedia*, Juan-les-Pins, France, 235–238.

Gifford, D.K., Jouvelot, P., Sheldon, M.A., & O'Toole, J.W. Jr. (1991, October). Semantic file systems. In 13th *ACM Symposium on Operating Systems Principles.*

Gruber, T.R. (1995). Toward principles for the design of ontologies used for knowledge sharing. In *International Journal of Human-Computer Studies, 43*, 907-928.

Hendler, J. (2001, March/April). Agents and the SemanticWeb. *IEEE Intelligent Systems, 16*(2), 30–-37.

McGuinness, D.L., & van Harmelen, F. (2004, February). *OWL Web Ontology Language Overview (Technical report)*. http://www.w3.org/TR/2004/REC-owl-features-20040210/.

Möller, K., Bojārs, U., & Breslin, J.G. (2006, June 11-14). Using semantics to enhance the blogging experience. In Y. Sure, J. Domingue (Eds.), *The Semantic Web: Research and Applications, 3rd European Semantic Web Conference*, ESWC 2006 Proceedings, Budva, Montenegro, 679-696.

Nelson, T.H. (1965). A file structure for the complex, the changing, and the indeterminate. In *ACM 20th National Conference Proceedings*, 84-100, Cleveland, Ohio.

Oren, E. (2006). An overview of information management and knowledge work studies: Lessons for the semantic sesktop. In S. Decker, J.

Park, L. Sauermann, S. Auer, S. Handschuh (Eds.), *Proceedings of the Semantic Desktop and Social Semantic Collaboration Workshop (SemDesk 2006) at ISWC 2006*. Athens, GA, USA.

Quan, D., Huynh, D., & Karger, D.R. (2003). Haystack: A platform for authoring end user Semantic Web applications. In D. Fensel, K.P. Sycara, J. Mylopoulos (Eds.), *The Semantic Web – ISWC 2003: International Semantic Web Conference*, Proceedings, 738-753.

Richter, J., Völkel, M., & Haller, H. (2005). DeepaMehta – A Semantic desktop. In *Proceedings of the 1st Workshop on the Semantic Desktop - Next Generation Personal Information Management and Collaboration Infrastructure* at ISWC 2005, Galway, Ireland.

Sauermann, L., Grimnes, G. AA., Kiesel, M., Fluit, C., Maus, H., Heim, D., Nadeem, D., Horak, B., & Dengel, A. (2006). Semantic desktop 2.0: The gnowsis experience. In I. Cruz, S. Decker, D. Allemang, C. Preist, D. Schwabe, P. Mika, M. Uschold, L. Aroyo (Eds.), *The Semantic Web – ISWC 2006: 5th International Semantic Web Conference*, Athens, GA, Proceedings.

Sauermann, L. (2003). The Gnowsis – *Using Semantic Web Technologies to Build a Semantic Desktop*. Diploma Thesis, Technical University of Vienna, 2003.

Semy, S.K., Pulvermacher, M.K., & Obrst, L.J. (2004). *Toward the use of an upper ontology for U.S. Government and U.S. Military domains: An evaluation. (Technical report)*. MITRE, September 2004.

Sintek, M., van Elst, L., Scerri, S., & Handschuh, S. (2007). Distributed knowledge representation on the social semantic desktop: Named graphs, views and roles in NRL. In E. Franconi, M. Kifer, W. May (Eds.), *The Semantic Web – ESWC 2007: The 4th European Semantic Web Conference (ESWC 2007) Proceedings*.

Tummarello, T., Morbidoni, C., & Nucci, M. (2006). Enabling Semantic Web communities with DBin: An overview. In I. Cruz, S. Decker, D. Allemang, C. Preist, D. Schwabe, P. Mika, M. Uschold, L. Aroyo (Eds.), *The Semantic Web – ISWC 2006: 5th International Semantic Web Conference*, Athens, GA, Proceedings, 943-950.

ADDITIONAL READINGS

From a historical perspective, the most important references in the Social Semantic Desktop domain are those by Vannevar Bush (1945) and Doug Engelbart (1962) which we mentioned in Sect. "*Background*". Another important early influence is certainly Ted Nelson's work on hypertext (Nelson, 1965). A modern vision of those ideas is a paper by Decker and Frank (2004), which also coined the term "Semantic Desktop". Of course, any work that is based on the ideas of the Semantic Web is not complete without references to seminal papers such as (Berners-Lee et. al, 2001) or (Hendler, 2001). In fact, the original vision of the World Wide Web itself already contained the idea of an information space that would reach from "mind to mind" (Berners-Lee, 1999); a thought that is central to the SSD.

Current and recent research and development in the SSD domain has already been presented in Sect. "*Related Work*". However, one influence that has not been covered in this chapter so far, but is closely related to the idea of a Semantic Desktop is the concept of *Semantic File Systems* – file systems in which files are not organized hierarchically, but rather according to their metadata. The concept and an early implementation are described in detail in (Gifford et. al, 2001).

Most of the references given in this chapter are of a technical nature. However, one has to keep in mind that the SSD is a tool for *information management* and *knowledge work*, and thus psychological and sociological research into the nature of knowledge work in any form are relevant as well. Oren (2006) provides a detailed overview of literature in this field, with the intention of applying the lessons learned to the development of the Semantic Desktop.

Finally, as another entry point for additional reading, we would like to point the reader to the series of *Semantic Desktop Workshops* which were co-located with the International Semantic Web Conferences in 2005[v] and 2006[w].

ENDNOTES

[a] RDF: http://www.w3.org/RDF/

[b] The NEPOMUK Project is supported by the European Union IST fund, grant FP6-027705

[c] Within the NEPOMUK Project, these personas were created by distilling typical users from a series of interviews and evaluations with our use-case partners.

[d] Tim Berners-Lee talk, XML and the Web: http://www.w3.org/2000/Talks/0906-xml-web-tbl/

[e] RFC1738: http://tools.ietf.org/html/rfc1738

[f] WSDL: http://www.w3.org/TR/wsdl

[g] XML Schema: http://www.w3.org/XML/Schema

[h] SOAP: http://www.w3.org/TR/soap

[i] In this chapter we make the assumption that a modern object-oriented programming language like Java will be used for implementation, but observations and solutions are equally valid for most other languages.

[j] MDA: http://www.omg.org/mda/

[k] RDFReactor: http://wiki.ontoworld.org/wiki/RDFReactor; RDF2Java: http://rdf-2java.opendfki.de; Elmo: http://openrdf.org, etc.

[l] TriG/TriX: http://www.w3.org/2004/03/trix/

[m] SmartWeb: http://www.smartweb-project.de/

[n] Language Extensibility in WSDL1: http://www.w3.org/TR/wsdl#_language and in WSDL2: http://www.w3.org/TR/wsdl20#language-extensibility

[o] SAWSDL: http://www.w3.org/TR/sawsdl/

[p] OWL-S: http://www.daml.org/services/owl-s/

[q] WSML: http://www.wsmo.org/wsml/

[r] ISO/EIC 13250:2003: http://www.y12.doe.gov/sgml/sc34/document/0129.pdf

[s] MindRaider: http://mindraider.sourceforge.org/

[t] Apogée: http://apogee.nuxeo.org/

[u] Fenfire: http://www.fenfire.org/

[v] SemDesk2005: http://tinyurl.com/yuxpld

[w] SemDesk2006: http://tinyurl.com/2hqfak

APPENDIX: QUESTIONS FOR DISCUSSION

Q: I prefer to handle my photo collection in a web 2.0 photo sharing environment. Is this compatible with the Social Semantic Desktop? May I keep the work I have invested here?

A: Yes. Every photo in your collection can be reached via a specific URI, thus it can be handled as a particular information item in the SSD. You might implement a suitable wrapper to transfer local annotations from your SSD onto the photo sharing platform, if you intend to disclose this information.

Q: The Social Semantic Desktop presupposes that everything is an information item. What about entities which are not information but real-world objects? Can I manage them in the SSD and add comments about them, e.g., about my friend's cat?

A: The solution is easy: Just create an appropriate description of the real world object within your SSD, thus creating an URI for the object in question. Let's say you create an instance of the class pet in your SSD (assuming you have this category within your SSD) and describe it as 'well-known house cat'. Then you can link this instance to, e.g., a photo of the animal, or you add an 'owns' link which connects it to the URI of your friend, and so on. Making an arbitrary object re-appear as a formal instance within the SSD models is often called 're-birthing', btw.

Q: Think about scenarios you encounter every day, and where the SSD can make your work easier.

A: The answer is of course a personal one, but for a typical knowledge worker (researchers, students, journalists, etc.) here are some example ideas:

- Show me related appointments when composing emails to a person, i.e., You also have lunch with Claudia next week.
- Show me previously viewed PDF documents on the same topic when researching on Wikipedia.
- Remember my meal and window preferences when booking flights.
- Remind me of my previous idea of combining topic A with topic B when reviewing my topic A notes.
- Let me connect an incoming email from a student to the colleague who introduced me to that student.

Q: What are the benefits of the Social Semantic Desktop compared to solution such as Microsoft Exchange server or the tight integration of applications on MacOSX? They also fulfil many of the functionalities required by the scenarios outline in this chapter.

A: The Social Semantic Desktop is different because of the standards used to build it. Firstly, by basing the representational layers of the Semantic Desktop on the existing (Semantic) Web standards we enable interoperability by a wide range of existing projects, and secondly, by creating new standards for desktop integration and data-formats we encourage future software developers to build on top of the Semantic Desktop. On the Semantic Desktop both the applications and the data encourages open access, and this exactly the opposite of the vendor lock-in that for instance Exchange Server aims for.

Q: Inspect the current state of the Semantic Web and the data available. What data-sources and/or ontologies do you think could be useful for integration with the Semantic Desktop?

A: The answer will of course change as the Semantic Web evolves, but at the time of writing relevant ontologies include:

- The Friend-of-a-Friend project – http://xmlns.com/foaf/spec
- The Description-of-a-Project schema – http://usefulinc.com/doap
- The Semantically Interlinked Online Communities project – http://siocproject.org/
- Dublin Core for basic meta-data – http://dublincore.org/

Useful data-sources and/or web-services include:

- GeoNames for (reverse) geocoding – http://www.geonames.org/
- DBpedia for a Semantic Web view of Wikipedia – http://DBpedia.org/

Chapter XIII
Uncertainty Representation and Reasoning in the Semantic Web

Paulo Cesar G. Costa
George Mason University, USA

Kathryn Blackmond Laskey
George Mason University, USA

Thomas Lukasiewicz
Oxford University Computing Laboratory, UK

ABSTRACT

This chapter is about uncertainty representation and reasoning for the Semantic Web (SW). We address the importance, key issues, state-of-the-art approaches, and current efforts of both the academic and business communities in their search for a practical, standard way of representing and reasoning with incomplete information in the Semantic Web. The focus is on why uncertainty representation and reasoning are necessary, its importance to the SW vision, and the major issues and obstacles to addressing uncertainty in a principled and standardized way. Although some would argue that uncertainty belongs in the "rule layer" of the SW, we concentrate especially on uncertain extensions of ontology languages for the Semantic Web.

WHY CARE ABOUT UNCERTAINTY?

After some years of SW research, the subject remains rife with controversy, and there is still some disagreement on how uncertainty should be handled in SW applications. Thus, it is no surprise that little was said on the subject in previous chapters of this book. A major reason for the present state of affairs is that the most popular technologies employed in SW applications are rooted in traditional knowledge representation formalisms that have historically ignored uncertainty. The most compelling examples are Frame Systems (Minsky, 1975), and Description Logics, which evolved from the so-called "Structured

Inheritance Networks" (Brachman, 1977), and form the logical basis for the ontology language OWL.

The spotlight is not on the *status quo*, but on what the future holds. To answer this question, we begin with a comprehensive analysis of the major challenges to be faced by the SW community, including what kinds of interactions, scenarios, demands, and obstacles must be addressed to make the SW promises a reality. Next, we assess whether protocols that rely only on complete, deterministic information will suffice to address these challenges. Although much progress has been made by tackling problems in which uncertainty is inessential or can be circumvented, addressing the full range of challenges inherent in the Semantic Web vision will require optimal use of *all* available information. In this Chapter, we argue that a principled framework for representing and reasoning with incomplete information is necessary to realizing the SW vision. Because uncertainty is a ubiquitous aspect of most real-world problems, any representation scheme intended to model real-world entities, properties and processes must be able to cope with uncertain phenomena. Current SW technologies' inability to represent and reason about uncertainty in a sound and principled manner raises an unnecessary barrier to the development of new, powerful features for general knowledge application, a limitation that threatens to derail the original vision for the Semantic Web as a whole. In other words, we argue that realizing the SW as envisioned by Tim Berners-Lee (Berners-Lee & Fischetti, 2000) requires a principled framework for representing and reasoning with uncertainty.

The Semantic Web envisions effortless cooperation between humans and computers, seamless interoperability and information exchange among web applications, and rapid and accurate identification and invocation of appropriate Web services. While considerable progress has been achieved toward realization of the Semantic Web vision, it is increasingly apparent that a sound and

principled technology for handling uncertainty is an important requirement for continued progress. Uncertainty is an unavoidable factor in knowledge interchange and application interoperability. Different applications have different ontologies, different semantics, and different knowledge and data stores. Legacy applications are usually only partially documented and may rely on tacit usage conventions that even proficient users do not fully understand or appreciate. Furthermore, data that is exchanged in the context of the semantic web is often incomplete, inconsistent, and inaccurate. This suggests that recent work in the application of probability, fuzzy logic, and decision theory to complex, open-world problems could be of vital importance to the success of the Semantic Web. Incorporating these new technologies into languages, protocols, and specifications for the Semantic Web is fundamental to realizing the Semantic Web vision.

Typical Problems Needing Uncertainty Representation and Reasoning. The following web-relevant reasoning challenges illustrate the kinds of problems for which reasoning under uncertainty is important.

- Information extracted from large information networks such as the World Wide Web is typically incomplete. The ability to exploit partial information is useful for identifying sources of service or information. For example, the fact that an online service deals with greeting cards may be evidence that it also sells stationery. It is clear that search tools capable of utilizing probabilistic knowledge could increase search effectiveness.
- Much information on the World Wide Web is likely to be uncertain. Common examples include weather forecasts and gambling odds. A canonical method for representing and integrating such information and the uncertainty associated with it is necessary for communicating such information in a seamless fashion.

- Web information is also often incorrect or only partially correct, raising issues related to trust or credibility. Uncertainty representation and reasoning helps to resolve tensions amongst information sources for purposes of approximating appropriately.
- The Semantic Web will require numerous distinct but conceptually overlapping ontologies to co-exist and interoperate. Ontology mapping will benefit from the ability to represent and reason with information about partial overlap, such as likelihoods of membership in Class A of Ontology 1 given membership in Class B of Ontology 2.

Section 5 below discusses some use cases, based on the work of the W3C Uncertainty Reasoning for the World Wide Web Incubator Group (URW3-XG). These use cases exhibit the above characteristics, and are representative of the kinds of challenges that the SW must address. Despite the potential that a principled framework for representing uncertainty would have in contributing to the development of robust SW solutions, for historical reasons, research on the Semantic Web started with little support for representing and reasoning in the presence of uncertain, incomplete knowledge. As interest in and application of SW technology grows, there is increasing recognition of the need for uncertain reasoning technology, and increasing discussion of the most appropriate ways to address this need.

Should Ontologies Represent Uncertainty?
A major impediment to widespread adoption of technologies for representing and reasoning with incomplete information is the dominance of the classical logic paradigm in the field of ontological engineering. There is a plethora of definitions of the term ontology in the field of information systems. Among these, a common underlying assumption is that classical logic would provide the formal foundation for knowledge representation and reasoning. Until recently, theory and methods for representing and reasoning with uncertain and

incomplete knowledge have been neglected almost entirely. However, as research on knowledge engineering and applications of ontologies matures, the ubiquity and importance of uncertainty across a wide array of application areas has generated consumer demand for ontology formalisms that can capture uncertainty. Although recognition of the need for uncertainty reasoning is growing, there is disagreement about its appropriate place in the Semantic Web architecture. We have argued elsewhere (e.g., Costa, 2005; Costa and Laskey, 2006), that there is a need to represent declarative knowledge about likelihood in domain ontologies. In environments in which noisy and incomplete information is the rule, likelihood information is a key aspect of domain knowledge. Furthermore, much of the key semantic content needed to enable interoperability involves information about plausibility. For this reason, we have argued, knowledge about likelihoods should be included in formal domain ontologies.

This viewpoint is not universal. A counter-argument to our position is that probability is inherently epistemic, whereas formal ontology should represent phenomena as they exist in the world. Carried to its extreme, however, this philosophical stance would preclude the use of virtually every ontology that has yet been developed. To explore this idea further, we note that if computational ontologies had existed in the 17th century, Becher and his followers might well have developed an ontology of phlogiston. We may chuckle now at their naïveté, but who among our 17th century predecessors had the foresight to judge which of the many scientific theories then in circulation would stand the test of time? Researchers in medicine, biology, defense, astronomy, and other communities have developed a plethora of domain ontologies. It is virtually certain that at least some aspects of some of these ontologies will, as human knowledge progresses, turn out in retrospect to be as well founded as the theory of phlogiston. Shall we outlaw use of all these ontologies until the day we can prove they contain only that which is ontological, and nothing that is mere epistemology? Moreover, many aspects of our common, shared knowledge of these domains are inherently probabilistic. Well-established statistical regularities are a key element of expert reasoning. A principled means of representing these probabilistic aspects of domain knowledge is needed to facilitate interoperability and knowledge sharing.

Similar questions arise with the representation of vagueness. Fuzzy logic has been applied extensively to problems of reasoning with imprecisely defined terms. For example, fuzzy reasoning might be applied to retrieve and sort responses to a query for "inexpensive" patio furniture. A fuzzy reasoner would assign each furniture set a degree of membership in the fuzzy set "inexpensive," and would sort the retrieved sets by their membership in the fuzzy set. There is an analogous question of whether it is legitimate to extend ontology formalisms to allow representation of fuzzy membership values, or whether fuzziness is inherently epistemological and does not belong in an ontology.

There is a valid, important, and as yet unresolved philosophical clash between those who believe that we live in a deterministic world in which uncertainty is entirely epistemic, and those who believe the world includes phenomena that are ontologically stochastic and/or imprecise and should be represented as such. From an engineering standpoint, we cannot wait for the debate to be resolved before we move forward with building and using ontologies.

Although our ultimate scientific objective is to seek the truth about reality as it is, this ultimate objective is unattainable in the lifetime of any human. Therefore, no "perfect ontology of all things" is reachable, regardless of one's philosophical view on uncertainty. Nevertheless, from a pragmatic perspective, it is necessary and desirable to do the best we can with the knowledge we have, even if this causes the ontology to be under-specified due to incomplete information.

Formal ontology provides a useful means of communicating domain knowledge in a precise and shareable manner, and of extending and revising our descriptions as human knowledge accrues. Accepting only complete knowledge would leave us with too little information to solve most of the interesting problems that ontologies are capable of addressing.

Not surprisingly, as ontology engineering research has achieved a greater level of maturity, the need for uncertainty representation and reasoning for the Semantic Web has become more and more clear. Correspondingly, interest is increasing in extending traditional ontology formalisms to include standard mechanisms for representing and reasoning with uncertainty. Whether the ultimate consensus is that ontology formalisms should be capable of representing information about uncertainty, or that ontologies should represent the space of possibilities and that information about uncertainty should be conveyed in a different semantic layer, principled means of representing and reasoning with uncertainty are increasingly seen as necessary.

Uncertainty in Rule Languages. A related stream of research has focused on augmenting SW rule languages to handle uncertainty (Damásio *et al.*, 2006; Lukasiewicz, 2005, 2006; Lukasiewicz & Straccia, 2007). Although there is as yet no standard rule language for the Semantic Web, the W3C's Rule Interchange Format (RIF) Working Group has recently released working draft documents specifying use cases, requirements, and a core design for a format that allows rules to be translated between rules languages[a]. The use cases and requirements document does not mention uncertainty, but the core design mentions the need to translate between rule languages that handle uncertainty, and makes brief mention of syntactic and semantic implications of the need to treat uncertainty. This brief treatment is far from sufficient to address the full range of issues that need to be addressed to achieve semantic interoperability between systems that express and reason with uncertainty. For space reasons, we do not address rule language research in detail in this chapter. We note, however, that augmenting ontologies to express uncertainty generates a requirement to augment rule languages to take advantage of the information expressed in uncertainty-enhanced ontologies.

Towards a Pragmatic View. Apart from the historical and philosophical issues, as research on SW leaves the conceptual level and reaches a level of maturity in which the actual challenges are better understood, realization has grown that many SW applications require a principled means for representing uncertainty and performing plausible reasoning with incomplete data. As the interest in uncertainty representation techniques grows, the focus of SW shifts from philosophical issues toward "down to earth" engineering issues. Important challenges are to identify the kinds of information management problems that would benefit most from mechanisms for reasoning with uncertainty, to assess the scalability of uncertainty representation approaches, to evaluate the suitability of different forms of representation and reasoning to solve specific use cases, and others.

This pragmatic, focused view has pushed researchers from many different domains of knowledge into an appreciation of the need for a forum to discuss the ways in which uncertainty reasoning can contribute to addressing their respective challenges, and to evaluate the strengths and weaknesses of different approaches to representing and reasoning under uncertainty. Although uncertainty-related papers were sometimes presented in other venues, the first forum explicitly geared towards answering the above issues was the workshop on Uncertainty Representation for the Semantic Web (URSW workshop), held in conjunction with the Fourth International Semantic Web Conference (ISWC 2005). The intention of the URSW workshop was to provide an open forum to all forms of uncertainty representation and reasoning, without being prejudicial in favor of any particular approach. At the second workshop (URSW 2006), a consensus was reached that the most important tasks were (1) to develop a set of use cases for uncertainty in the SW; and (2) to assess how each approach (or combination of approaches) would address appropriate challenges set out in the use cases. In the end, a much improved understanding of those issues would led to identification of best practices involving uncertainty reasoning in the SW.

The strong interest in the URSW and similar venues prompted the W3C to create, in March 2007, the Uncertainty Reasoning for the World Wide Web Incubator Group (URW3 XG), with the objective of better defining the challenge of working with incomplete knowledge. The URW3 adopted the same "approach-independent" stance as the URSW, with an initial focus on the problem itself rather than a particular approach to solving it. At the time of this writing, the URW3 is actively pursuing its development of use cases, and planning for a third URSW is underway. The next two sections present a brief view of the major approaches for uncertainty in the SW being discussed in fora such as the URW3 and URSW.

PROBABILISTIC APPROACHES TO UNCERTAINTY IN THE SEMANTIC WEB

Bayesian probability provides a mathematically sound representation language and formal calculus for rational degrees of belief, which gives different agents the freedom to have different beliefs about a given hypothesis. This provides a compelling framework for representing uncertain, incomplete knowledge that can come from diverse agents. Not surprisingly, there are many distinct approaches using Bayesian probability for the Semantic Web.

Bayesian knowledge representation and reasoning systems have their formal basis in the axioms of probability theory (e.g., Ramsey, 1931;

Kolmogorov, 1960/1933). Probability theory allows propositions to be assigned truth-values in the range from zero, meaning certain falsehood, to one, meaning certain truth. Values intermediate between zero and one reflect degrees of likelihood of a proposition that may be either true or false. *Bayes Rule*, a theorem that can be derived from the axioms of probability theory, provides a method of updating the probability of a proposition when information is acquired about a related proposition. The standard format of Bayes rule is:

$$P(B|A) = \frac{P(A|B)P(B)}{P(B)}$$

On the right side of the formula, *P(A)* is called the prior probability of *A*, and represents our belief in event *A* before obtaining information on event *B*. Likewise, *P(B)* is called the prior probability of *B*. There is also *P(A|B)*, which is the likelihood of event *A* given that event *B* has happened. On the left side of the formula there is *P(B|A)*, which is the posterior probability of *B*, and represents our new belief in event *B* after applying Bayes rule with the information collected from event *A*. Bayes rule provides the formal basis for the active and rapidly evolving field of Bayesian probability and statistics. In the Bayesian view, inference is a problem of belief dynamics. Bayes rule provides a principled methodology for belief change in the light of new information.

Bayesian Networks (BNs). BNs provide a means of parsimoniously expressing joint probability distributions over many interrelated hypotheses. A Bayesian network consists of a directed acyclic graph (DAG) and a set of local distributions. Each node in the graph represents a random variable. A random variable denotes an attribute, feature, or set of hypotheses about which we may be uncertain. Each random variable has a set of mutually exclusive and collectively

Figure 1. A BN for pizzas and wines

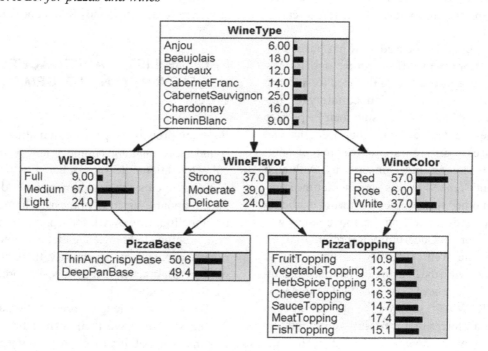

exhaustive possible values. That is, exactly one of the possible values is or will be the actual value, and we are uncertain about which one it is. The graph represents direct qualitative dependence relationships; the local distributions represent quantitative information about the strength of those dependencies. The graph and the local distributions together represent a joint probability distribution over the random variables denoted by the nodes of the graph.

Bayesian networks have been successfully applied to create consistent probabilistic representations of uncertain knowledge in diverse fields. Heckerman *et al.* (1995) provide a detailed list of recent applications of Bayesian Networks. The prospective reader will also find comprehensive coverage of Bayesian Networks in a large and growing literature on this subject, such as Pearl (1988), Neapolitan (1990, 2003), and others. Figure 1 shows an example of a BN representing part of a highly simplified ontology for wines and pizzas.

In this toy example[b], we assume that domain knowledge about gastronomy was gathered from sources such as statistical data collected among restaurants and expertise from sommeliers and pizzaiolos. Moreover, the resulting ontology also considered incomplete knowledge to establish a probability distribution among features of the pizzas ordered by customers (i.e. type of base and topping) and characteristics of the wines ordered to accompany the pizzas.

Consider a customer who enters a restaurant and requests a pizza with cheese topping and a thin and crispy base. Using the probability distribution stored in the BN of Figure 1, the waiter can apply Bayes rule to infer the best type of wine to offer the customer given his pizza preferences the body of statistical and expert information previously linking features of pizza to wines. Such computation would be difficult when there are very many features. Bayesian networks provide a parsimonious way to express the joint

Figure 2. BN after entering evidence

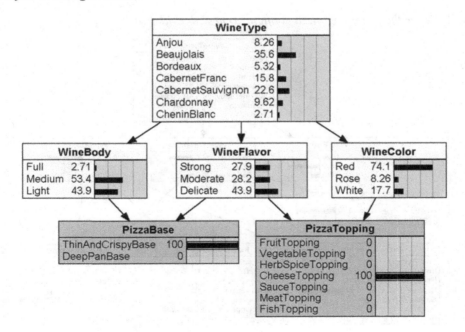

distribution and a computationally efficient way to implement Bayes rule. This inferential process is shown in Figure 2, where evidence (i.e., the customer's order) was entered in the BN and its result points to Beaujolais as the most likely wine the customer would order, followed by Cabernet Sauvignon, and so on.

Although this is just a toy example, it is useful to show how incomplete information about a domain can be used to improve decisions. In an ontology without uncertainty, there would not be enough information for a logical reasoner to infer a good choice of wine to offer the customer, and the decision would have to be made without optimal use of all the information available.

As Bayesian networks have grown in popularity, their shortcomings in expressiveness for many real-world applications have become increasingly apparent. More specifically, Bayesian Networks assume a simple attribute-value representation – that is, each problem instance involves reasoning about the same fixed number of attributes, with only the evidence values changing from problem instance to problem instance. In the pizza and wine example, the PizzaTopping random variable conveys general information about the class of pizza toppings (i.e., types of toppings for a given pizza and how it is related to preferences over wine flavor and color), but the BN in Figures 1 and 2 is valid for pizzas with only one topping. To deal with more elaborate pizzas, it is necessary to build specific BNs for each configuration, each one with a distinct probability distribution. Figure 3 depicts a BN for a 3- topping pizza with a specific customer preference displayed. Also, the information conveyed by the BNs (i.e., for 1-topping, 2-toppings, etc.) relates to the class of pizza toppings, and not to specific instances of those classes. Therefore, the BN in Figure 3 cannot be used for a situation in which the costumer asks for two 3-topping pizzas. This type of representation is inadequate for many problems of practical importance. Similarly, these BNs cannot be used to reason about a situation in which a customer orders several bottles of wine that may be of different varieties. Many domains require reason-

Figure 3. A BN for the 3-topping pizza configuration with evidence

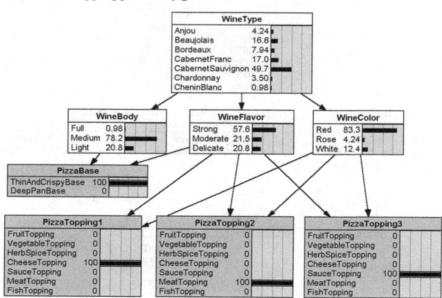

ing about varying numbers of related entities of different types, where the numbers, types, and relationships among entities usually cannot be specified in advance and may have uncertainty in their own definitions.

In spite of their limitations, BNs have been used in specific applications for the SW where the limitations on expressivity can be overcome by clever knowledge engineering workarounds. One example is BayesOWL (Ding and Peng, 2004; Ding, 2005), which augments OWL semantics to allow probabilistic information to be represented via additional markups. The result is a probabilistic annotated ontology that could then be translated to a Bayesian network. Such a translation is based on a set of translation rules that rely on the probabilistic information attached to individual concepts and properties within the annotated ontology. After successfully achieving the translation, the resulting Bayesian network will be associated with a joint probability distribution over the application domain. Although a full translation of an ontology to a standard BN is impossible given the limitations of the latter in terms of expressivity, the scheme can be successfully used to tackle specific problems involving uncertainty.

Also focusing on Bayesian extensions geared towards the Semantic Web is the work of Gu *et al.* (2004), which takes an approach similar to that of BayesOWL. A related effort is the set of RDF extensions being developed by Yoshio Fukushige (2004). Generally speaking, SW approaches that rely on BNs will have to compensate for their lack of expressiveness by specializing in a specific type of problem, such as the BN-focused approaches for solving the ontology mapping problem (e.g., Mitra *et al.*, 2004; and Pan *et al.*, 2005; Peng *et al.*, 2007).

Probabilistic Extensions to Description Logics. Most of the probabilistic extensions aimed at the ontology engineering domain are based on description logics (DLs), which Baader and Nutt (2003, page 47) define as a family of knowledge representation formalisms that represent the knowledge of an application domain (the "world") by first defining the relevant concepts and roles of the domain (its terminology), which represent classes of objects/individuals and binary relations between such classes, respectively, and then using these concepts and roles to specify properties of objects/individuals occurring in the domain (the world description).

Description logics divide a knowledge base into two components: a terminological box, or T-Box, and the assertional box, or A-Box. The first introduces the terminology (i.e., the vocabulary) of an application domain, while the latter contains assertions about instances of the concepts defined in the T-Box. Description logics are a subset of first-order logic (FOL) that provide a very good combination of decidability and expressiveness. In fact, an important desired property of description logics is the decidability of their reasoning tasks. Description logics are also the basis of the web ontology language OWL, whose sublanguages OWL Lite and OWL DL correspond to the expressive description logics $SHIF(\mathbf{D})$ and $SHOIN(\mathbf{D})$, respectively.

There are several probabilistic extensions of description logics in the literature, which can be classified according to the generalized description logics, the supported forms of probabilistic knowledge, and the underlying probabilistic reasoning formalism.

Heinsohn (1994) presents a probabilistic extension of the description logic ALC (a member of the AL-languages (Schmidt-Schauß & Smolka, 1991) obtained by including the full existential quantification and the union constructors to the basic AL (attributive language)), which allows representation of terminological probabilistic knowledge about concepts and roles, and which is essentially based on probabilistic reasoning in probabilistic logics. Heinsohn, however, does not allow for assertional knowledge about concept and role instances. Jaeger (1994) proposes another probabilistic extension of the description logic

ALC, which allows for terminological and assertional probabilistic knowledge about concepts and roles and about concept instances, respectively, but does not support assertional probabilistic knowledge about role instances (but he mentions a possible extension in this direction). The uncertain reasoning formalism in (Jaeger, 1994) is essentially based on probabilistic reasoning in probabilistic logics, as the one in (Heinsohn, 1994), but coupled with cross-entropy minimization to combine terminological probabilistic knowledge with assertional probabilistic knowledge. Jaeger's recent work (2006) focuses on interpreting probabilistic concept subsumption and probabilistic role quantification through statistical sampling distributions, and develops a probabilistic version of the guarded fragment of first-order logic.

The work by Koller *et al.* (1997) gives a probabilistic generalization of the CLASSIC description logic, called P-CLASSIC. In short, each probabilistic component is associated with a set P of p-classes, and each p-class C in set P is represented using a Bayesian network. Like Heinsohn's work (1994), the work by Koller *et al.* (1997) allows for terminological probabilistic knowledge about concepts and roles, but does not support assertional probabilistic knowledge about instances of concepts and roles. However, differently from (Heinsohn, 1994), it is based on inference in Bayesian networks as underlying probabilistic reasoning formalism. Closely related work by Yelland (2000) combines a restricted description logic close to *FL* with Bayesian networks. It also allows for terminological probabilistic knowledge about concepts and roles, but does not support assertional knowledge about instances of concepts and roles.

Another DL with a probabilistic extension is *SHOQ*(**D**) (Horrocks & Sattler, 2001). *SHOQ*(**D**) is the basis of DAML+OIL (Horrocks, 2002), the language that came from merging two ontology languages being developed in the US (DAML) and Europe (OIL) and has been superseded by OWL. Its probabilistic extension is called P-

SHOQ(**D**) (Giugno & Lukasiewicz, 2002) (see also (Lukasiewicz, 2008)) and allows for expressing both terminological probabilistic knowledge about concepts and roles, as well as assertional probabilistic knowledge about instances of concepts and roles. P-*SHOQ*(**D**) is based on probabilistic lexicographic entailment from probabilistic default reasoning (Lukasiewicz, 2002) as underlying probabilistic reasoning formalism, which treats terminological and assertional probabilistic knowledge in a semantically very appealing way as probabilistic knowledge about random and concrete instances, respectively.

Description logics are highly effective and efficient for the classification and subsump-tion problems that they were designed to address. However, their ability to represent and reason about other commonly occurring kinds of knowledge is limited. One restrictive aspect of DL languages is their limited ability to represent constraints on the instances that can participate in a relationship. As an example, a probabilistic Description Logics version of the toy example in Figures 1 to 3 would allow us to instantiate (say) three pizzas. However, suppose we want to express that for a given pizza to be compatible with another pizza in a specific type of situation (e.g., a given mixture of toppings for distinct pizzas), it is mandatory that the two individuals of class pizza involved in the situation are not the same. In DLs, making sure that the two instances of class pizza are different in a specific situation is only possible if we actually instantiate/specify the tangible individuals involved in that situation. Indeed, stating that two "fillers" (i.e., the actual individuals of class Pizza that will "fill the spaces" of concept pizza in our statement) are not equal without specifying their respective values would require constructs such as *negation* and *equality role-value-maps*, which cannot be expressed in description logics. While equality and role-value-maps provide additional useful means to specify structural properties of concepts, their inclusion makes the logic undecidable (Calvanese & De Giacomo, page 223).

First-Order Probabilistic Approaches. In recent years, a number of languages have appeared that extend the expressiveness of probabilistic graphical models in various ways. This trend reflects the need for probabilistic tools with more representational power to meet the demands of real world problems, and goes to the encounter of the needs for Semantic Web representational schemes compatible with incomplete, uncertain knowledge. A clear candidate logic to fulfill this requirement for extended expressivity is first-order logic (FOL), which according to Sowa (2000, page 41) "has enough expressive power to define all of mathematics, every digital computer that has ever been built, and the semantics of every version of logic, including itself."

FOL was invented independently by Frege and Pierce in the late nineteenth century (Frege, 1879/1967; Pierce, 1898) and is by far the most commonly used, studied, and implemented logical system. A theory in first-order logic assigns definite truth-values only to sentences that have the same truth-value (either true or false) in all interpretations of the theory. The most that can be said about any other sentence is that its truth-value is indeterminate. A logical system is *complete* if all valid sentences can be proven and *negation complete* if for every sentence, either the sentence or its negation can be proven. Kurt Gödel proved both that first-order logic is complete, and that no consistent logical system strong enough to axiomatize arithmetic can be negation complete (cf. Stoll, 1963; Enderton, 2001). However, systems based on classical first-order logic lack a theoretically principled, widely accepted, logically coherent methodology for reasoning under uncertainty. Below are some of the approaches addressing this issue.

Object-Oriented Bayesian Networks (Koller & Pfeffer, 1997; Bangsø & Wuillemin, 2000; Langseth & Nielsen, 2003) represent entities as instances of object classes with class-specific attributes and probability distributions. Probabilistic Relational Models (PRM) (Pfeffer *et al.*, 1999; Getoor *et al.*, 2000; Getoor *et al.*, 2001; Pfeffer, 2001) integrate the relational data model (Codd, 1970) and Bayesian networks. PRMs extend standard Bayesian Networks to handle multiple entity types and relationships among them, providing a consistent representation for probabilities over a relational database. PRMs cannot express arbitrary quantified first-order sentences and do not support recursion. Although PRMs augmented with DBNs can support limited forms of recursion, they still do not support general recursive definitions. Jaeger (1997) extends relational probabilistic models to allow recursion, but it is limited to finitely many random variables. Plates (Buntine, 1994; Gilks *et al.*, 1994; Spiegelhalter *et al.*, 1996) represent parameterized statistical models as complex Bayesian networks with repeated components.

DAPER (Heckerman *et al.*, 2004) combines the entity-relational model with DAG models to express probabilistic knowledge about structured entities and their relationships. Any model constructed in Plates or PRM can be represented by DAPER. Thus, DAPER is a unifying language for expressing relational probabilistic knowledge. DAPER expresses probabilistic models over finite databases, and cannot represent arbitrary first-order sentences involving quantifiers. Therefore, like other languages discussed above, DAPER does not achieve full first-order representational power.

MEBN (Laskey and Mahoney, 1997; Laskey and Costa, 2005; Laskey, 2007) represents the world as consisting of entities that have attributes and are related to other entities. Knowledge about the attributes of entities and their relationships to each other is represented as a collection of MEBN fragments (MFrags) organized into MEBN Theories (MTheories). An MFrag represents a conditional probability distribution for instances of its resident random variables given their parents in the fragment graph and the context nodes. An MTheory is a set of MFrags that collectively satisfies consistency constraints ensuring the existence of a unique joint probability distribution over instances of the random variables represented in each of the MFrags within the set. MEBN semantics integrates the standard model-theoretic semantics of classical first-order logic with random variables as formalized in mathematical statistics.

Although the above approaches are promising where applicable, a workable solution for the Semantic Web requires a general-purpose formalism that gives ontology designers a range of options to balance tractability against expressiveness. Current research on SW formalisms using first-order probabilistic logics is still in its infancy, and generally lack a complete set of publicly available tools. Examples include PR-OWL (Costa, 2005), which is an upper ontology for building probabilistic ontologies based on MEBN logic[c], and KEEPER (Pool and Aiken, 2005), an OWL-based interface for the relational probabilistic toolset Quiddity*Suite, developed by IET, Inc. Their constructs are similar in spirit and provide an expressive method for representing uncertainty

in OWL ontologies. Costa (2005) gives a definition for Probabilistic Ontologies, develops rules for constructing PR-OWL ontologies in a manner that can be translated into Quiddity*Suite, and describes how to perform the translation.

As an illustration of the expressiveness of a first-order probabilistic logic, Figure 4 presents a graphical depiction of the MFrags for the wine and pizza toy example.[d] It conveys both the structural relationships (implied by the arcs) among the nodes and the numerical probabilities (embedded in the probability distributions and not depicted in the figure). The MFrags depicted in Figure 4 form a consistent set that allows to reason probabilistically about a domain and can be stored in an OWL file using the classes and properties defined in the PR-OWL upper ontology. The MFrags can be used to instantiate situation specific Bayesian networks to answer queries about the domain of application being modeled. In other words, a PR-OWL probabilistic ontology consists of both deterministic and probabilistic information about

Figure 4. MFrags representing the wine and pizza example

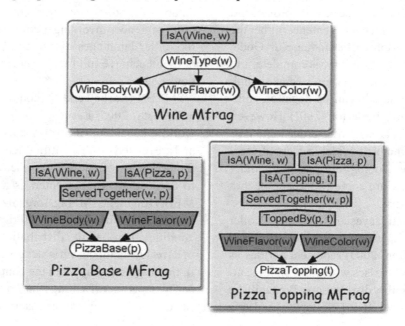

the domain of discussion (e.g., wines and pizzas), stored in an OWL file that can be used for answering specific queries for any configuration of the instances given the evidence at hand.

In particular, the toy ontology of Figure 4 can be applied to reason about situations involving any number of pizzas with any number of toppings on each, accompanied by any number of bottles of wine, and including any possible interactions among specific instances of those. Figure 5 illustrates this concept, depicting a situation in which evidence a customer has ordered one thin and crispy pizza with three toppings (cheese, meat, and sauce) and is planning to order one bottle of wine. The BN represents the response to a request to suggest a good wine to go with the pizzas.

In MEBN syntax[e], the knowledge base is augmented by an instance of pizza (!P0), three instances of topping types (!T0, !T1, !T2), and an instance of wine (!W0). To answer the query on the wine suggestion, a probabilistic reasoner will use the evidence available to build a Situation Specific Bayesian Network (SSBN). This example was constructed to yield the same BN as Figure 3. This illustrates the point that the MFrags in Figure 4 have captured all information that is needed to build SSBNs for any specific configuration of pizzas and wines for this toy example.

Clearly, this example is oversimplified, but it suffices to illustrate how PR-OWL can be used to build a probabilistic ontology combining legacy ontologies of pizzas and wines. This example illustrates the use of an expressive probabilistic language to capture knowledge that cannot be expressed with standard Bayesian networks. Probabilistic ontologies are an increasingly important topic in forums devoted to best practices in systems development. Given the nature of the domain knowledge embedded in their systems, system developers in general would profit most from the advantages of being able to convey such knowledge with a principled treatment for uncertainty.

Figure 5. SSBN constructed from the MFrags of Figure 4

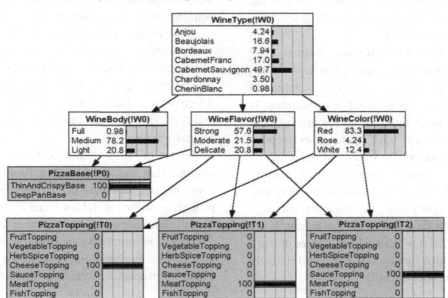

FUZZY FORMALISMS APPLIED TO THE SEMANTIC WEB

In contrast to probabilistic formalisms, which allow for representing and processing degrees of uncertainty about ambiguous pieces of information, fuzzy formalisms allow for representing and processing degrees of truth about vague (or imprecise) pieces of information. The following examples illustrate the difference between degrees of uncertainty and degrees of truth.

Consider the statement "it will rain tomorrow". This statement is *uncertain*, that is, it is either true or false, depending on the weather conditions of tomorrow, but we generally do not have a complete knowledge about whether it will rain tomorrow or not. In probabilistic formalisms, we thus assume a set of possible worlds, each of which is associated with a probability. Intuitively, we are uncertain about which possible world is the right one. In each world, we only allow for binary truth-values, and thus in each world the statement "it will rain tomorrow" is either true or false. This way, we can quantify our ignorance about whether it will rain tomorrow or not. For example, we may say that the probability that it will rain tomorrow is 0.7, which means that the probabilities of all worlds in which it will rain tomorrow sum up to 0.7.

Consider next the statement "John is tall." This statement is *vague*, that is, it is more or less true, depending on the body height of John, but we are unable to say whether this statement is completely true or false due to the involvement of the vague concept "tall," which does not have a precise definition. In fuzzy formalisms, we assume fuzzy interpretations, which directly generalize binary interpretations by mapping elementary vague propositions into a truth value space between false and true. For example, we may say that John is tall with the degree of truth 0.7, which intuitively means that John is relatively tall but not completely tall.

It is also important to point out that vague statements are truth-functional, that is, the degree of truth of a vague complex statement (which is constructed from elementary vague statements via logical operators) can be calculated from the degrees of truth of its constituents, while uncertain complex statements are generally not a function of the degrees of uncertainty of their constituents (Dubois and Prade, 1994).

Vagueness abounds especially in multimedia information processing and retrieval. Another typical application domain for vagueness and thus fuzzy formalisms are natural language interfaces to the Web. Furthermore, fuzzy formalisms have also been successfully applied in ontology mapping, information retrieval, and e-commerce negotiation tasks.

Fuzzy Propositional Logics. Rather than being restricted to a binary truth value among false and true, *vague propositions* may also have a truth value strictly between false and true. One often assumes the unit interval $[0, 1]$ as the set of all possible truth values, where 0 and 1 represent the ordinary binary truth values false and true, respectively. For example, the vague proposition "John is tall" may be more or less true, and it is thus associated with a truth value in $[0, 1]$, depending on the body height of John.

To combine and modify the truth values in $[0, 1]$, one assumes *combination functions*, namely, *conjunction, disjunction, implication*, and *negation functions*, denoted $\otimes, \oplus, \triangleright$, and $\ominus$, respectively, which are functions $\otimes, \oplus, \triangleright: [0, 1] \times [0, 1] \to [0, 1]$ and $\ominus: [0, 1] \to [0, 1]$ that generalize the ordinary logical operators $\wedge, \vee, \to$, and $\neg$, respectively, to the set of truth values $[0, 1]$. As usual, we assume that the combination functions have some natural algebraic properties, namely, the properties shown in Tables 1 and 2. Note that in Table 1, Tautology and Contradiction follow from Identity, Commutativity, and Monotonicity. Note also that conjunction and disjunction functions (with the properties shown in Table 1) are also

Table 1. Axioms for conjunction and disjunction functions

Axiom Name	Conjunction Function	Disjunction Function
Tautology / Contradiction	$a \otimes 0 = 0$	$a \oplus 1 = 1$
Identity	$a \otimes 1 = a$	$a \oplus 0 = a$
Commutativity	$a \otimes b = b \otimes a$	$a \oplus b = b \oplus a$
Associativity	$(a \otimes b) \otimes c = a \otimes (b \otimes c)$	$(a \oplus b) \oplus c = a \oplus (b \oplus c)$
Monotonicity	if $b \leq c$, then $a \otimes b \leq a \otimes c$	if $b \leq c$, then $a \oplus b \leq a \oplus c$

Table 2. Axioms for implication and negation functions

Axiom Name	Implication Function	Negation Function
Tautology / Contradiction	$0 \rhd b = 1$, $a \rhd 1 = 1$, $1 \rhd 0 = 0$	$\ominus 0 = 1$, $\ominus 1 = 0$
Antitonicity	if $a \leq b$, then $a \rhd c \geq b \rhd c$	if $a \leq b$, then $\ominus a \geq \ominus b$
Monotonicity	if $b \leq c$, then $a \rhd b \leq a \rhd c$	

Table 3. Combination functions of various fuzzy logics

	Łukasiewicz Logic	Gödel Logic	Product Logic	Zadeh Logic
$a \otimes b$	$\max(a + b - 1, 0)$	$\min(a, b)$	$a \cdot b$	$\min(a, b)$
$a \oplus b$	$\min(a + b, 1)$	$\max(a, b)$	$a + b - a \cdot b$	$\max(a, b)$
$a \rhd b$	$\min(1 - a + b, 1)$	$\begin{cases} 1 & \text{if } a \leq b \\ b & \text{otherwise} \end{cases}$	$\min(1, b/a)$	$\max(1 - a, b)$
$\ominus a$	$1 - a$	$\begin{cases} 1 & \text{if } a = 0 \\ 0 & \text{otherwise} \end{cases}$	$\begin{cases} 1 & \text{if } a = 0 \\ 0 & \text{otherwise} \end{cases}$	$1 - a$

called *triangular norms* and *triangular co-norms* (Hájek, 1998), respectively. The combination functions of some well-known fuzzy logics are shown in Table 3.

More formally, a *fuzzy (propositional) interpretation I* maps each elementary vague proposition p into the set of truth values [0,1], and is then extended inductively to all (complex) vague propositions (which are constructed from the elementary vague propositions by using the binary and unary logical operators $\land$, $\lor$, $\rightarrow$, and $\neg$) as follows (where $\otimes$, $\oplus$, $\rhd$, and $\ominus$ are conjunction, disjunction, implication, and negation functions, respectively, as described above):

$$I(\phi \land \psi) = I(\phi) \otimes I(\psi)$$
$$I(\phi \lor \psi) = I(\phi) \oplus I(\psi)$$
$$I(\phi \rightarrow \psi) = I(\phi) \rhd I(\psi)$$
$$I(\neg \phi) = \ominus I(\phi)$$

A fuzzy (propositional) knowledge base consists of a finite set of *fuzzy formulas*, which have one of the forms $\varphi \geq 1$, $\varphi \leq 1$, $\varphi > l$, or $\varphi < l$, where φ is a vague proposition, and l is a truth value from [0,1]. Such statements express that φ has a degree of truth of at least, at most, greater than, and lower than l, respectively. For example, *tall_John* ≥ 0.6 says that *tall_John* has a degree of truth of at least 0.6. Any such fuzzy knowledge base represents a set of fuzzy interpretations, which can be used to define the notions of *satisfiability, logical consequence,* and *tight logical consequence,* as usual. Here, it is important to point out the difference from Bayesian networks: rather than encoding one single probability distribution (over a set of binary interpretations), fuzzy knowledge bases encode a set of fuzzy interpretations.

Fuzzy Description Logics and Ontology Languages. In fuzzy description logics and ontology languages, concept assertions, role assertions, concept inclusions, and role inclusions have a degree of truth rather than a binary truth value. Semantically, this extension is essentially obtained by (i) generalizing binary first-order interpretations to fuzzy first-order interpretations and (ii) interpreting all the logical operators by a corresponding combination function. Syntactically, as in the fuzzy propositional case, one then also allows for formulas that restrict the truth values of concept assertions, role assertions, concept inclusions, and role inclusions. Some important new ingredients of fuzzy description logics are often also fuzzy concrete domains, which include fuzzy predicates on concrete domains, and fuzzy modifiers (such as "very" or "slightly"), which are unary operators that change the membership functions of fuzzy concepts.

As a fictional example, an online shop may use a fuzzy description logic knowledge base to classify and characterize its products. For example, suppose (1) textbooks are books, (2) PCs and laptops are mutually exclusive electronic products, (3) books and electronic products are mutually exclusive products, (4) PCs have a price, a memory size, and a processor speed, (5) *pc1* is a PC with the price 1300€, the memory size 3 GB, and the processor speed 4 GHz, (6) *pc2* is a PC with the price 500€, the memory size 1 GB, and the processor speed 2 GHz, (7) *pc3* is a PC with the price 900€, the memory size 2 GB, and the processor speed 3 GHz, (8) *ibm, acer,* and *hp* are the producers of *pc1, pc2,* and *pc3,* respectively. These relationships are expressed by the following description logic knowledge base:

(1)   *Textbook* $\sqsubseteq$ *Book*;

(2)   *PC* $\sqcup$ *Laptop* $\sqsubseteq$ *Electronics*; *PC* $\sqsubseteq$ ¬*Laptop*;

(3)   *Book* $\sqcup$ *Electronics* $\sqsubseteq$ *Product*; *Book* $\sqsubseteq$ ¬*Electronics*;

(4)   *PC* $\sqsubseteq$ $\exists$*hasPrice.Integer* $\sqcap$ $\exists$*hasMemorySize. Integer* $\sqcap$ $\exists$*hasProcessorSpeed.Integer*;

(5)   (*PC* $\sqcap$ $\exists$*hasPrice.*1300 $\sqcap$ $\exists$*hasMemorySize.*3 $\sqcap$ $\exists$*hasProcessorSpeed.*4)(*pc1*);

(6)   (*PC* $\sqcap$ $\exists$*hasPrice.*500 $\sqcap$ $\exists$*hasMemorySize.*1 $\sqcap$ $\exists$*hasProcessorSpeed.*2)(*pc2*);

(7)   (*PC* $\sqcap$ $\exists$*hasPrice.*900 $\sqcap$ $\exists$*hasMemorySize.*2 $\sqcap$ $\exists$*hasProcessorSpeed.*3)(*pc3*);

(8)   *produces*(*ibm, pc1*); *produces*(*acer, pc2*); *produces*(*hp, pc3*).

The notions "expensive PCs", "PCs having a large memory", and "PCs having a fast processor" can then be defined as fuzzy concepts by adding the following three fuzzy concept definitions:

ExpensivePC $\equiv$ *PC* $\sqcap$ $\exists$*hasPrice.PCExpensive,*

LargeMemoryPC $\equiv$ *PC* $\sqcap$ $\exists$*hasMemorySize. MemoryLarge,*

FastProcessorPC $\equiv$ *PC* $\sqcap$ $\exists$*hasProcessorSpeed.ProcessorFast.*

Here, *PCExpensive, MemoryLarge,* and *ProcessorFast* are fuzzy unary datatype predicates, which are defined by *PCExpensive*(x) = $rs(x; 600, 1200)$, *MemoryLarge*(x) = $rs(x; 1, 3)$, and *ProcessorFast*(x) = $rs(x; 2, 4)$, respectively, where $rs(x; a, b)$ is the so-called right-shoulder function (see Figure 6). Informally, as for the fuzzy concept "expensive PCs", every PC costing at least 1200€ (resp., at most 600€) is definitely expensive (resp., not expensive), while every PC costing between 600€ and 1200€ is expensive to some degree between 0 and 1.

Similarly, the notions "costs at most about 1000€" and "has a memory size of around 2 GB" in a buyer's request can be expressed through the following fuzzy concepts *C* and *D*, respectively:

$C \equiv \exists hasPrice.LeqAbout1000$ and $D \equiv \exists has\text{-}MemorySize.Around2,$

where $LeqAbout1000 = ls(500, 1500)$ and $Around2 = tri(1.5, 2, 2.5)$ (see Figure 6).

The literature contains many different approaches to fuzzy extensions of description logics and ontology languages. They can be roughly classified according to (a) the description logics or the ontology languages that they generalize, (b) the fuzzy constructs that they allow, (c) the fuzzy logics that they are based on, and (d) their reasoning algorithms.

One of the earliest works is due to Yen (1991), who proposes a fuzzy extension of a quite restricted sublanguage of *ALC*. Yen considers fuzzy terminological knowledge, along with fuzzy modifiers, but no fuzzy assertional knowledge, and he uses Zadeh Logic as underlying fuzzy logic. Yen's work also includes a reasoning algorithm, which allows for testing crisp subsumptions. Tresp and Molitor's work (1998) presents a more general fuzzy extension of *ALC*. Like Yen's work, it also includes fuzzy terminological knowledge, along with a special form of fuzzy modifiers, but no fuzzy assertional knowledge, and it is based on Zadeh Logic. The reasoning algorithm of Tresp and Molitor's work is a tableaux calculus for computing subsumption degrees.

Another important fuzzy extension of *ALC* is due to Straccia (1998, 2001), who allows for both fuzzy terminological and fuzzy assertional knowledge, but not for fuzzy modifiers, and again assumes Zadeh Logic as underlying fuzzy logic. Straccia's work also includes a tableaux calculus for deciding logical consequences and computing tight logical consequences. Hölldobler *et al.* (2002, 2005) extend Straccia's fuzzy *ALC* with fuzzy modifiers of the form $f_m(x) = x^\beta$, where $\beta > 0$, and present a sound and complete reasoning algorithm for the graded subsumption problem.

Straccia (2004) shows how reasoning in fuzzy *ALC* under Zadeh Logic can be reduced to reasoning in classical *ALC*. This idea has also been explored by Li *et al.* (2005a, 2005b).

Approaches towards more expressive fuzzy description logics include the works by Sanchez and Tettamanzi (2004, 2006), who consider the description logic *ALCQ*. They introduce the new notion of *fuzzy quantifiers*. As underlying fuzzy logic, they also assume Zadeh Logic. Their reasoning algorithm calculates the satisfiability interval for a fuzzy concept. Straccia (2005c) defines the semantics of a fuzzy extension of *SHOIN(D)*, which is the description logic that stands behind OWL DL. Stoilos *et al.* (2005a) use this semantics to define a fuzzy extension of the OWL language, and also propose a translation of fuzzy OWL to fuzzy *SHOIN*.

6. (a) triangular function tri(x; a, b, c), (b) left-shoulder function ls(x; a, b), and (c) right-shoulder function rs(x; a, b)

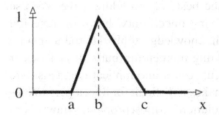 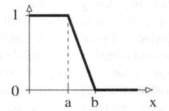 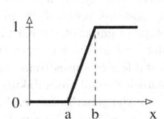

Other works include the one by Hájek (2005, 2006), who considers *ALC* under arbitrary t-norms and proposes especially a reasoning algorithm for testing crisp subsumptions. Bonatti and Tettamanzi (2006) provide some complexity results for reasoning in fuzzy description logics.

Recent works by Straccia (2005b, 2005a) present a calculus for *ALC(D)*, which works whenever the connectives, the fuzzy modifiers, and the concrete fuzzy predicates are representable as bounded mixed integer linear programs. For example, Łukasiewicz logic satisfies these conditions. The method has been extended to fuzzy *SHIF(D)*, which is the description logic standing behind OWL Lite, and a reasoner (called *fuzzyDL*) supporting Zadeh, Łukasiewicz, and classical semantics has been implemented and is available from Straccia's web page.

Towards reasoning in fuzzy *SHOIN(D)*, Stoilos *et al.* (2005, 2005b) show results providing a tableaux calculus for fuzzy *SHIN* without fuzzy general concept inclusions and under the Zadeh semantics. Stoilos et al. (2006) provide a generalization thereof that additionally allows for fuzzy general concept inclusions. In closely related work, Li *et al.* (2006) provide a tableaux calculus for fuzzy *SHI* with fuzzy general concept inclusions.

FUTURE RESEARCH DIRECTIONS

As the Semantic Web makes its transition from a vision to implementation, many of its stakeholders begin to feel the need to represent and reason under uncertainty. SW applications being developed for domains of knowledge in which uncertainty plays a significant role must include a means to store and retrieve incomplete knowledge. To cite just a few examples from the medical domain[f], statistical regularities linking a given protein to (say) Alzheimer's disease, the predisposition of patients with gene X towards developing cancer Y, or gene ontology evidence codes in support of a particular GO annotation of a gene can be all considered specific instances of more general cases in which a principled means for representing incomplete knowledge is needed. Similar situations can be observed in other domains of knowledge currently being studied in the context of the Semantic Web, which makes uncertainty representation and reasoning a rapidly growing field of SW research.

In early 2007, the W3C approved an incubator group to focus on uncertain knowledge. The URW3-XG[g] has the overall mission of better defining the challenge of reasoning with and representing uncertain information available through the WWW and related technologies. Accomplishing this mission involves identifying problems for which uncertainty is an essential aspect, to produce use cases, and to identify requirements for knowledge representation and reasoning when crisp truth-values are unknown or inappropriate. It is important to emphasize the fact that the group's scope does not include recommending a single methodology, but to investigate whether standard representations of uncertainty can be identified that will support requirements across a wide spectrum of reasoning approaches.

This stance is compatible with what we see as the future in this area. For most domains of knowledge, the task of representing the various distinct forms of uncertainty that might have a strong influence in the way knowledge is represented and applied is complex enough that the search for a "silver bullet" is inadvisable. That is, selecting a specific approach to be the definitive one for representing uncertainty would be a recipe for failure. In fact, a combination of approaches might be the best way to address the SW use cases involving uncertainty. For now, research on uncertain knowledge applied to the Semantic Web is gaining momentum but still lacks clear definitions, use cases, and applications. This state of affairs makes it difficult for developers to create useful solutions to most problems drawn from uncertainty-plagued domains, but the current rate of progress makes it clear to us that major change is near at hand.

REFERENCES

Baader, F., & Nutt, W. (2003). Basic description logics. In Baader, F., Calvanese, D., McGuiness, D., Nardi, D., & Patel-Schneider, P. (Eds.), *The Description Logics Handbook: Theory, Implementation and Applications.* 1st edition, *2*, 47-100. Cambridge, UK: Cambridge University Press.

Bangsø, O., & Wuillemin, P.-H. (2000). *Object oriented Bayesian networks: A framework for topdown specification of large Bayesian networks and repetitive structures.* Technical Report No. CIT-87.2-00-obphw1. Department of Computer Science, Aalborg University, Aalborg, Denmark.

Berners-Lee, T., & Fischetti, M. (2000). *Weaving the Web: The original design and ultimate destiny of the World Wide Web by its inventor.* 1st edition. New York: HarperCollins Publishers.

Bonatti, P., & Tettamanzi, A. (2006). Some complexity results on fuzzy description logics. In Di Gesu, V., Masulli, F., & Petrosino, A. (Eds.), *Fuzzy logic and applications, 2955 of LNCS*, 19-24. Springer.

Brachman, R. J. (1977). What's in a concept: Structural foundations for Semantic networks. *International Journal of Man-Machine Studies*, *9*(2), 127-152.

Buntine, W. L. (1994). *Learning with graphical models.* Technical Report No. FIA-94-03. NASA Ames Research Center, Artificial Intelligence Research Branch.

Calvanese, D., & De Giacomo, G. (2003). Expressive description logics. In Baader, F., Calvanese, D., McGuiness, D., Nardi, D., & Patel-Schneider, P. (Eds.), *The Description Logics Handbook:*

Theory, Implementation and Applications. 1st edition, *5*, 184-225. Cambridge, UK: Cambridge University Press.

Charniak, E. (1991). Bayesian networks without tears. *AI Magazine*, 12, 50-63.

Codd, E. F. (1970). A relational model for large shared data banks. *Communications of the ACM*, *13*(6), 377-387.

Costa, P. C. G., & Laskey, K. B. (2006, November 9-11). PR-OWL: A framework for probabilistic ontologies. In *Proceedings of the International Conference on Formal Ontology in Information Systems (FOIS 2006)*. Baltimore, MD, USA.

Costa, P. C. G. (2005). *Bayesian Semantics for the Semantic Web*. Doctoral dissertation. Department of Systems Engineering and Operations Research, George Mason University: Fairfax, VA, USA. p. 312.

Damasio, C., Pan, J., Stoilos, G., & Straccia, U. (2006). An approach to representing uncertainty rules in RuleML. In *Proceedings of the 2nd International Conference on Rules and Rule Markup Languages for the Semantic Web (RuleML-06)*. IEEE Computer Society. Available at http://2006.ruleml.org/online-proceedings/submission_24.pdf

Ding, Z. (2005). *BayesOWL: A probabilistic framework for Semantic Web*. Doctoral dissertation. Computer Science and Electrical Engineering. University of Maryland, Baltimore County: Baltimore, MD, USA. p. 168.

Ding, Z., & Peng, Y. (2004, January 5-8). A probabilistic extension to ontology language OWL. In *Proceedings of the 37th Annual Hawaii International Conference on System Sciences (HICSS'04)*. Big Island, Hawaii, USA.

Dubois, D., & Prade, H. (1994). Can we enforce full compositionality in uncertainty calculi? *Proceedings AAAI-1994*, 149-154. AAAI Press.

Frege, G. (1879). *Begriffsschrift*, 1879, translated in Jean van Heijenoort, ed., *From Frege to Gödel*, Cambridge, MA: Harvard University Press.

Fukushige, Y. (2004). Representing probabilistic knowledge in the Semantic Web, *W3C Workshop on Semantic Web for Life Sciences*. Cambridge, MA, USA.

Getoor, L., Friedman, N., Koller, D., & Pfeffer, A. (2001). *Learning probabilistic relational models*. New York, NY, USA: Springer-Verlag.

Getoor, L., Koller, D., Taskar, B., & Friedman, N. (2000). Learning probabilistic relational models with structural uncertainty. *Paper presented at the ICML-2000 Workshop on Attribute-Value and Relational Learning:Crossing the Boundaries*. Stanford, CA, USA.

Gilks, W., Thomas, A., & Spiegelhalter, D. J. (1994). A language and program for complex Bayesian modeling. *The Statistician, 43*, 169-178.

Giugno, R., & Lukasiewicz, T. (2002, September 23-26). P-SHOQ(D): A probabilistic extension of SHOQ(D) for probabilistic ontologies in the Semantic Web. In Flesca, S.; Greco, S.; Leone, N.; and Ianni, G. (Eds.), *Proceedings of the Eight European Conference on Logics in Artificial Intelligence (JELIA 2002)* Cosenza, Italy (LNCS 2424, pp. 86-97). Berlin, Germany: Springer-Verlag.

Hájek, P. (1998). *Metamathematics of fuzzy logic*. Kluwer.

Hájek, P. (2005). Making fuzzy description logics more expressive. *Fuzzy Sets and Systems, 154*(1), 1-15.

Hájek, P. (2006). What does mathematical fuzzy logic offer to description logic? In Sanchez, E. (Ed.), *Capturing Intelligence: Fuzzy Logic and the Semantic Web*. Elsevier.

Heckerman, D., Mamdani, A., & Wellman, M. P. (1995). Real-world applications of Bayesian networks. *Communications of the ACM, 38*(3), 24-68.

Heckerman, D., Meek, C., & Koller, D. (2004). *Probabilistic models for relational data*. Technical Report MSR-TR-2004-30, Microsoft Corporation, March 2004. Redmond, WA, USA.

Heinsohn, J. (1994, July 29-31). Probabilistic description logics. *Paper presented at the Tenth Conference on Uncertainty in Artificial Intelligence (UAI-94)*.Seattle, WA, USA.

Hölldobler, S., Khang, T. D., & Störr, H.-P. (2002). A fuzzy description logic with hedges as concept modifiers. In *Proceedings InTech/VJFuzzy-2002*, 25-34.

Hölldobler, S., Nga, N. H., & Khang, T. D. (2005). The fuzzy description logic ALC_{FLH}. In *Proceeedings DL-2005*.

Horridge, M., Knublauch, H., Rector, A., Stevens, R., & Wroedn, S. (2004). *A practical guide to building OWL ontologies using the Protégé-OWL plugin and CO-ODE tools*. The University of Manchester. Retrieved June 9, 2007, from http://www.co-ode.org.

Horrocks, I. (2002). DAML+OIL: A reasonable Web ontology language. Keynote talk at the WES/CAiSE Conference. Toronto, Canada.

Horrocks, I., & Sattler, U. (2001, August 4-10). Ontology reasoning in the SHOQ(D) description logic. In *Proceedings of the Seventeenth International Joint Conference on Artificial Intelligence (IJCAI 2001)*. Seattle, WA, USA.

Jaeger, M. (1994, May 24-27). Probabilistic reasoning in terminological logics. *Paper presented at the Fourth International Conference on Principles of Knowledge Representation and Reasoning* (KR94). Bonn, Germany.

Jaeger, M. (1997, August 1-3). Relational Bayesian networks. *Paper presented at the 13th Annual Conference on Uncertainty in Artificial Intel-*

ligence (UAI-97).Providence, RI, USA.

Jaeger, M. (2006). Probabilistic role models and the guarded fragment. In *Proceedings IPMU-2004*, pp. 235–242. Extended version in *Int. J. Uncertain. Fuzz.*, *14*(1), 43-60.

Koller, D., Levy, A. Y., & Pfeffer, A. (1997, July 27-31). P-CLASSIC: A tractable probabilistic description logic. *Paper presented at the Fourteenth National Conference on Artificial Intelligence (AAAI-97)*. Providence, RI, USA.

Koller, D., & Pfeffer, A. (1997). Object-oriented Bayesian networks. *Paper presented at the Thirteenth Conference on Uncertainty in Artificial Intelligence (UAI-97)*. San Francisco, CA, USA.

Kolmogorov, A. N. (1960). *Foundations of the Theory of Probability*. 2nd edition. New York, NY, USA: Chelsea Publishing Co. Originally published in 1933.

Langseth, H., & Nielsen, T. (2003, July). Fusion of domain knowledge with data for structured learning in object-oriented domains. *Journal of Machine Learning Research*, Special Issue on the Fusion of Domain Knowledge with Data for Decision Support, *4*, 339-368.

Laskey, K. B. (2007). MEBN: A language for first-order Bayesian knowledge bases. *Artificial Intelligence*, 172(2-3).

Laskey, K. B., & Costa P. C. G. (2005). Of Klingons and starships: Bayesian logic for the 23rd Century, in *Uncertainty in Artificial Intelligence: Proceedings of the Twenty-first Conference*. Edinburgh, Scotland: AUAI Press.

Laskey, K. B., & Mahoney, S. M. (1997, August). Network fragments: Representing knowledge for constructing probabilistic models. In *Proceedings of the Thirteenth Conference on Uncertainty in Artificial Intelligence (UAI-97)*. Providence, RI, USA.

Li, Y., Xu, B., Lu, J., & Kang, D. (2006). Discrete tableau algorithms for *SHI*. In *Proceeedings DL-2006*.

Li, Y., Xu, B., Lu, J., Kang, D., & Wang, P. (2005a). Extended fuzzy description logic *ALCN*. In *Proceedings KES-2005, 3684 of LNCS,* 896-902. Springer.

Li, Y., Xu, B., Lu, J., Kang, D., & Wang, P. (2005b). A family of extended fuzzy description logics. In *Proceedings COMPSAC-2005,* 221-226. IEEE Computer Society.

Lukasiewicz, T. (2002). Probabilistic default reasoning with conditional constraints. *Ann. Math. Artif. Intell.*, *34*(1-3), 35-88.

Lukasiewicz, T. (2008). Expressive probabilistic description logics. *Artificial Intelligence*, *172*(6-7), 852-883.

Minsky, M. L. (1975). Framework for representing knowledge. In *The Psychology of Computer Vision*. P. H. Winston (Eds.), 211-277. New York, NY: McGraw-Hill.

Mitra, P., Noy, N. F., & Jaiswal, A. R. (2004, November). OMEN: A probabilistic ontology mapping tool. *Workshop on Meaning Coordination and Negotiation at the Third International Conference on the Semantic Web (ISWC-2004)*. Hisroshima, Japan.

Neapolitan, R. E. (1990). *Probabilistic reasoning in expert systems: Theory and algorithms*. New York, NY, USA: John Wiley and Sons, Inc.

Neapolitan, R. E. (2003). *Learning Bayesian networks*. New York: Prentice Hall.

Pan, R., Ding, Z., Yu, Y., & Peng, Y. (2005, November). A Bayesian approach to ontology mapping. In *Proceedings of the Fourth International Semantic Web Conference (ISWC-2005)*. Galway, Ireland.

Pearl, J. (1988). *Probabilistic reasoning in intelligent systems: Networks of plausible inference*. San Mateo, CA, USA: Morgan Kaufmann Publishers.

Peng, Y., Ding, Z., Pan, R., Yu, Y., Kulvatunyou, B., Izevic, N., Jones, A., & Cho, H. (2007, May). A probabilistic framework for semantic similarity and ontology mapping. In *Proceedings of the 2007 Industrial Engineering Research Conference (IERC)*. Nashville, TN, USA.

Peirce, C. S. (1885). On the algebra of logic. *American Journal of Mathematics, 7*, 180-202.

Pfeffer, A. (2001, August 4-10). IBAL: A probabilistic rational programming language international. In *Proceedings of the Seventeenth International Joint Conference on Artificial Intelligence (IJCAI-2001), 1*, 733-740. Seattle, WA, USA.

Pfeffer, A., Koller, D., Milch, B., & Takusagawa, K. T. (1999, July-August 1). SPOOK: A system for probabilistic object-oriented knowledge representation. In *Proceedings of the Fifteenth Conference on Uncertainty in Artificial Intelligence*, 541-550. Stockholm, Sweden

Pool, M., & Aikin, J. (2004, July 6-9). KEEPER and protégé: An elicitation environment for Bayesian inference tools. *Paper presented at the Workshop on Protégé and Reasoning held at the Seventh International Protégé Conference.* Bethesda, MD, USA.

Ramsey, F. P. (1931). *The Foundations of Mathematics and other Logical Essays*. London, UK: Kegan Paul, Trench, Trubner & Co.

Sanchez, D., & Tettamanzi, A. (2004). Generalizing quantification in fuzzy description logics. In *Proceedings 8th Fuzzy Days in Dortmund*.

Sanchez, D., & Tettamanzi, A. (2006). Fuzzy quantification in fuzzy description logics. In Sanchez, E. (Ed.), *Capturing Intelligence: Fuzzy Logic and the Semantic Web*. Elsevier.

Schmidt-Schauß, M., & Smolka, G. (1991). Attributive concept descriptions with complements. *Artificial Intelligence, 48*(1), 1-26.

Spiegelhalter, D. J., Thomas, A., & Best, N. (1996). Computation on graphical models. *Bayesian Statistics, 5*, 407-425.

Stoilos, G., Stamou, G. B., Tzouvaras, V., Pan, J. Z., & Horrocks, I. (2005b). The fuzzy description logic *f-SHIN*. In *Proceedings URSW-2005*, 67-76.

Stoilos, G., Straccia, U., Stamou, G., & Pan, J. Z. (2006). General concept inclusions in fuzzy description logics. In *Proceedings ECAI-2006*, 457-61. IOS Press.

Stoilos, G., Stamou, G., Tzouvaras, V., Pan, J. Z., & Horrock, I. (2005). A fuzzy description logic for multimedia knowledge representation. In *Proceedings of the International Workshop on Multimedia and the Semantic Web*.

Straccia, U. (1998). A fuzzy description logic. In *Proceedings AAAI-1998*, 594-599. AAAI Press/MIT Press.

Straccia, U. (2001). Reasoning within fuzzy description logics. *J. Artif. Intell. Res., 14*, 137-166.

Straccia, U. (2004). Transforming fuzzy description logics into classical description logics. In *Proceedings JELIA-2004, 3229 of LNCS*, 385-399. Springer.

Straccia, U. (2005a). Description logics with fuzzy concrete domains. In *Proceedings UAI-2005*, 559-567. AUAI Press.

Straccia, U. (2005b). Fuzzy *ALC* with fuzzy concrete domains. In *Proceeedings DL-2005*, 96-103.

Tresp, C., & Molitor, R. (1998). A description logic for vague knowledge. In *Proceedings ECAI-1998*, 361-365. J. Wiley & Sons.

Yen, J. (1991). Generalizing term subsumption languages to fuzzy logic. In *Proceedings IJCAI-1991,* 472-177. Morgan Kaufmann.

Yelland, P. M. (2000). An alternative combination of Bayesian networks and description logics. In *Proceedings KR-2000*, 225–234. Morgan Kaufmann.

ADDITIONAL READING

Due to the initial stage of research on the subject, there are no specifications yet for representing and reasoning with uncertainty and thus no SW applications based on commonly accepted standards. The first step towards standardization is already being taken by the W3C via the already cited URW3 XG incubator group. At the time of this writing, the group was finishing its report and listing use cases for possible uncertainty-aware SW applications.

The interested reader is strongly encouraged to browse the use cases being studied by the XG, which convey formalized details of some of the most promising use cases analyzed by the group. The use cases are described in the XG Report, available from http://www.w3.org/2005/Incubator/urw3/. The use cases there were taken from a large list initially considered, and included various domains of knowledge such as discovery, appointment making, Healthcare and Life Sciences, ontology mapping, belief fusion and opinion pooling, shopping software agents, large-scale database retrieval and reasoning, and many others.

In addition, the literature listed below includes recent material on distinct approaches to representing and reasoning with uncertainty:

Costa, P. C. G., Laskey, K. B., Laskey, K. J., & Pool, M. (2005. November 7). *Proceedings of the ISWC Workshop on Uncertainty Reasoning for the Semantic Web (URSW 2005).* Galway, Ireland. Available at http://ftp.informatik.rwth-aachen.de/Publications/CEUR-WS/Vol-173/.

Costa, P. C. G., Fung, F., Laskey, K. B., Laskey, K. J., & Pool, M. (2006, November 5). *Proceedings of the ISWC Workshop on Uncertainty Reasoning for the Semantic Web (URSW 2006).* Athens, GA, USA. Available at http://ftp.informatik.rwth-aachen.de/Publications/CEUR-WS/Vol-218/.

Jousselme, A. L., Maupin, P., & Bosse, E. (2003, July 8-12). Uncertainty in a situation analysis Perspective. In *Proceedings of the Sixth International Conference of Information Fusion, 2,* 1207-1214. 2003, Cairns, Queensland, Australia.

Lukasiewicz, T. (2006). Fuzzy Description Logic Programs under the Answer Set Semantics for the Semantic Web. In *Proceedings of the 2nd International Conference on Rules and Rule Markup Languages for the Semantic Web (RuleML-06),* 89-96. IEEE Computer Society. Extended version: *Fundamenta Informaticae 82,* 1-22, 2008.

Lukasiewicz, T. (2005). Probabilistic Description Logic Programs. In *Proceedings ECSQARU 2005,* Barcelona, Spain, July 2005, *3571* of *LNCS,* pp. 737-749. Springer. Extended version: *International Journal of Approximate Reasoning 45*(2), 288-307, 2007.

Lukasiewicz, T., & Straccia, U. (2007). Description logic programs under probabilistic uncertainty and fuzzy vagueness. In *Proceedings ECSQARU 2007,* Hammamet, Tunisia, October/November 2007, *4724* of *LNCS,* 187-198. Springer.

Mitra, P., Noy, N., & Jaiswal, A. R. (2005, November 7). Ontology mapping discovery with uncertainty. presented at the *Fourth International Semantic Web Conference (ISWC 2004).* Galway, Ireland.

Pan, J. Z., Stoilos, G., Stamou, G., Tzouvaras, V., & Horrocks, I. (2006). f-SWRL: A Fuzzy Extension of SWRL. In *Data Semantics*, special issue on Emergent Semantics, *4090*/2006: 28-46.

Parsons, S. (1996, June). Current approaches to handling imperfect information in data acknowledgement bases. In *IEEE Transactions on Knowledge and Data Engineering*, 8(3), 353-372. Los Alamitos, CA, USA: IEEE Computer Society.

Sanchez, E. (2006). *Fuzzy logic and the Semantic Web*. 1ˢᵗ edition, April 3, 2006. Oxford, UK: Elsevier Science.

Straccia, U. (2005c). Towards a fuzzy description logic for the Semantic Web. In *Proceedings of the Second European Semantic Web Conference, ESWC 2005*.

Stoilos, G., Stamou, G., Tzouvaras, V., Pan, J. Z., & Horrocks, I. (2005a). Fuzzy OWL: Uncertainty and the Semantic Web. In *Proceedings of the International Workshop on OWL: Experience and Directions (OWL-ED2005)*.

Yang, Y., & Calmet, J. (2005). OntoBayes: An ontology-driven uncertainty model. *Presented at the International Conference on Intelligent Agents, Web Technologies and Internet Commerce (IAWTIC2005)*. Vienna, Austria. Available at http://iaks-www.ira.uka.de/iaks-calmet/papers/IAWTIC05_yang.pdf.

ENDNOTES

[a] See http://www.w3.org/TR/2006/WD-rif-ucr-20060710/ and http://www.w3.org/TR/rif-core/.

[b] Inspired by the wine ontology available at http://protege.cim3.net/cgi-bin/wiki.pl?ProtegeOntologiesLibrary and the pizza ontology presented in Horridge *et al.* (2004).

[c] PR-OWL is available from http://www.pr-owl.org.

[d] The pentagon nodes are context nodes, representing constraints that must be satisfied for the distributions in the MFrag to apply. The trapezoid nodes are input nodes, whose probability distribution is defined outside the MFrag. The oval nodes are resident nodes, whose distributions are defined in the MFrag.

[e] In MEBN, RVs take arguments that refer to entities in the domain of application. An interpretation of the theory uses entity identifiers as labels to refer to entities in the domain. Entity identifiers are written either as numerals or as alphanumeric strings beginning with an exclamation point, e.g., !M3, 48723.

[f] See http://esw.w3.org/topic/HCLS/UncertaintyUseCases for a more comprehensive analysis.

[g] Charter available at http://www.w3.org/2005/Incubator/urw3/charter.

APPENDIX: QUESTIONS FOR DISCUSSION

1. Cite a typical problem needing uncertainty representation and reasoning within the context of the Semantic Web.
2. Figure 2 displays the Bayesian Network from Figure 1 after evidence on pizza topping and base was included. Based on the results, which wine should a waiter suggest to the customer? Why?
3. What is "under the hood" of that reasoning process? How did the BN arrive at its conclusion?
4. What is the major limitation of BNs when applied to the SW?
5. What is the major advantage of using probabilistic extensions to DLs?
6. If Probabilistic FOL approaches cannot guarantee decidability in many cases, why should anyone care about using them?
7. What is the difference between uncertainty and vagueness?
8. Which are typical application areas for fuzzy formalisms?
9. What is the difference between probabilistic and fuzzy propositional interpretations? What is the difference between the semantics of Bayesian Networks and fuzzy propositional knowledge bases?

Answers:

1. See Introduction of this chapter.
2. According to the knowledge stored in that BN and the evidence entered, the waiter should suggest a red wine with medium to light body, delicate flavor. His first choice should be Beaujolais. Expert information from sommeliers and statistical regularities on previous orders were used to build this model, which allows it to make the best choice possible with the available information. For purposes of this example, "best" means the most likely wine a customer would order given the evidence.
3. The BN model uses Bayes rule to update the beliefs displayed in each of its nodes. After evidence was entered, an algorithm performed the belief updating in real time. See Charniak (1991) for a good introduction on BNs.
4. Apart from their flexibility and inferential power, BNs have only assertional expressivity and cannot represent situations where each problem instance involves reasoning about the same fixed number of attributes, with only the evidence values changing from problem instance to problem instance. This is insufficient for most SW problems. However, BNs can be applied in very specific cases, for which the representational power of BNs is sufficient.
5. Description logics are highly effective and efficient for the classification and subsumption problems they were designed to address. They provide decidability and their probabilistic extensions allow for representation of both numerical and structural aspects of a probabilistic model.
6. First Order Probabilistic Approaches have sufficient representational power for most real world problems. Additionally, they can provide ontology designers with a range of options to balance tractability against expressiveness.

7. Uncertainty expresses the lack of knowledge about binary statements, while vague-ness expresses the inherent imprecision of many-valued statements.

8. Some typical application areas for fuzzy formalisms are multimedia information processing and retrieval, natural language interfaces to the Web, ontology mapping, information retrieval, and e-commerce negotiation tasks.

9. A probabilistic propositional interpretation maps binary interpretations to a degree of likelihood in [0, 1], while a fuzzy propositional interpretation maps elementary vague propositions to a degree of truth in [0, 1]. A Bayesian Network encodes a probability distribution over a set of binary interpretations, while a fuzzy propositional knowledge bases encodes a set of fuzzy propositional interpretations.

Chapter XIV
Benchmarking in the Semantic Web

Raúl García-Castro
Universidad Politécnica de Madrid, Spain

Asunción Gómez-Pérez
Universidad Politécnica de Madrid, Spain

ABSTRACT

The Semantic Web technology needs to be thoroughly evaluated for providing objective results and obtaining massive improvement in its quality; thus, the transfer of this technology from research to industry will speed up. This chapter presents software benchmarking, a process that aims to improve the Semantic Web technology and to find the best practices. The chapter also describes a specific software benchmarking methodology and shows how this methodology has been used to benchmark the interoperability of ontology development tools, employing RDF(S) as the interchange language.

INTRODUCTION

The Semantic Web technology has considerably improved since the 1990's, when the first tools were developed; although it has mainly been applied in research laboratories, in recent years companies have started to be interested in this technology and its application.

To transfer the Semantic Web technology from the academia, its current niche, to the industrial world it is necessary that this technology reaches a maturity level that enables it to comply with the quality requirements of the industry. Therefore, the Semantic Web technology needs to be thoroughly evaluated both for providing objective results and for attaining a massive improvement in its quality.

Until recently, the Semantic Web technology was seldom evaluated; now, however, this technology is widely used and numerous studies concerning its evaluation have appeared in the last few years. So now it seems quite necessary that researchers increase the quality of their evaluations and improve the technology collectively by benchmarking it, employing for this a methodological process.

Evaluating and benchmarking this technology within the Semantic Web can be quite costly because most of the people involved do not know how to carry out these processes and also because no standard nor agreed methods to follow now exist. On the other hand, since it is quite difficult to reuse the results and put into practice the lessons learnt in previous activities, it is necessary to develop new methods and tools every time this technology has to be evaluated or benchmarked.

Software benchmarking is presented in this chapter as a continuous process whose aim is to improve software products, services, and processes by evaluating and comparing them with those considered the best. Although software evaluations are performed inside the benchmarking activities, benchmarking provides some benefits that cannot be obtained from evaluations, as for example, the continuous improvement of software, or the extraction of the best practices used to develop the software.

Within the Knowledge Web[a] European Network of Excellence a new methodology for benchmarking Semantic Web technology has been developed; this methodology is now being adopted in different benchmarking studies and applied to the different types of Semantic Web technologies (ontology development tools, ontology alignment tools, ontology-based annotation tools, and reasoners). The methodology focuses on the special interests of the industry and research fields and on their different needs. At the end of the chapter, we describe how we have followed this methodology during one of the activities performed to benchmark the interoperability of ontology development tools, employing RDF(S) as the interchange language.

EVALUATION AND BENCHMARKING IN THE LITERATURE

Software Evaluation

Software evaluation plays an important role in different areas of Software Engineering, such as Software Measurement, Software Experimentation or Software Testing. In this section, we present a general view of these areas.

According to the ISO 14598 standard (ISO/IEC, 1999), software evaluation is *the systematic examination of to which extent an entity is capable of fulfilling specified requirements*; this standard considers software not just as a set of computer programs but also as a set of procedures, documentation and data.

Software evaluation can take place all along the software life cycle. It can be performed during the software development process by evaluating intermediate software products or when the development has finished.

Although evaluations are usually carried out inside the organisation that develops the software, other independent groups such as users or auditors can also make them. When independent third parties evaluate software, they are usually very effective, though their evaluations can become very expensive (Rakitin, 1997).

The goals of evaluating software vary since they depend on each specific case, but in general, they can be summarised (Basili et al., 1986; Park et al., 1996; Gediga et al., 2002) as follows:

- To **describe** the software in order to understand it and establish baselines for comparisons.
- To **assess** the software with respect to some quality requirements or criteria and determine the degree of quality required from the software product and its weaknesses.

- To **improve** the software by identifying opportunities and, thus, improving its quality. This improvement is measured by comparing the software with the baselines.
- To **compare** alternative software products or different versions of a same product.
- To **control** software quality by ensuring that it meets the required level of quality.
- To **predict** new trends in order to take decisions and establish new goals and plans for accomplishing them.

It is understood that the methods to follow to evaluate software vary from one author to another and from one Software Engineering area to another. However, from the methods proposed in the areas of a) Software Evaluation (ISO/IEC, 1999; Basili, 1985), b) Software Experimentation (Basili & Selby, 1991; Perry et al., 2000; Freimut et al., 2002), c) Software Measurement (Park et al., 1996; IEEE, 1998), and d) Software Testing (Abran et al., 2004) we can extract a common set of tasks that must be carried out in software evaluations. These tasks are the following:

1. To establish the evaluation requirements by setting its goals, the entities to evaluate, and their relevant attributes.
2. To define the evaluation by explaining the data to collect, the evaluation criteria to follow, and the mechanisms to collect data and implement these mechanisms.
3. To produce the evaluation plan.
4. To execute the evaluation and to collect data.
5. To analyse the collected data.

Benchmarking in the Literature

In the last decades, the word benchmarking has become relevant within the business management community. The most well-known definitions of the term are those by Camp (1989) and Spendolini (1992). Camp defines benchmarking as *the search for industry best practices that lead to superior performance*; on the other hand, Spendolini has expanded Camp's definition by adding that benchmarking is *a continuous, systematic process for evaluating the products, services, and work processes of organisations that are recognised as representing best practices for the purpose of organisational improvement*. In this context, best practices are good practices that have worked well elsewhere, are proven and have produced successful results (Wireman, 2003).

These definitions highlight the two main benchmarking characteristics:

- Continuous improvement.
- Search for best practices.

The Software Engineering community does not share a common benchmarking definition but several. Here we present some of the most representative:

- Both Kitchenham (1996) and Weiss (2002) define benchmarking as a software evaluation method suitable for system comparisons. Whereas for Kitchenham benchmarking is *the process of running a number of standard tests using a number of alternative tools/methods and assessing the relative performance of the tools in those tests*, for Weiss benchmarking is *a method of measuring performance against a standard, or a given set of standards*.
- Wohlin et al. (2002) have adopted the benchmarking definition from the business world, that is, they consider benchmarking as a continuous improvement process that strives to be the best of the best through the comparison of similar processes in different contexts.

Software Benchmarking

In this section, we have followed the notions that support continuous improvement and search for best practices within business management benchmarking; these notions have led us to consider software benchmarking as a continuous improvement process instead of as a punctual activity. Equally important for us are the concept of comparing software through evaluations and that of carrying out the benchmarking activity through a systematic procedure.

All these concepts permit us to define **software benchmarking** as a continuous process whose aim is to improve software products, services, and processes by systematically evaluating and comparing them with those considered to be the best.

This definition, however, does not specify the type of the entities considered in benchmarking (software products, services or processes), nor does it determine the software life-cycle phase when benchmarking is performed, and nor does it explain who is responsible for benchmarking. However, software benchmarking is usually performed on software products already developed and is executed by their developers.

The reason for benchmarking software products instead of just evaluating them is to gain those benefits that cannot be obtained from software evaluations. When we evaluate software we can observe its weaknesses and its compliance to quality requirements. If, on the other hand, several software products are involved in the evaluation, then we can have a comparative analysis of these products and provide some recommendations. But when we benchmark several software products, in addition to all the benefits commented, we obtain products that are continuously improved, recommendations for developers on the practices used and, from these practices, those that can be considered the best.

Software Evaluation in Benchmarking Activities

To evaluate software is not a straightforward task; however, as this is an issue that has been thoroughly examined both in theory and practice, several authors have proposed different recommendations to consider (Basili et al., 1986; Perry et al., 2000; Freimut et al., 2002; Juristo & Moreno, 2001; Kitchenham et al., 2002).

These recommendations are also applicable to the software evaluations made during the benchmarking activities. However, when we have to define this kind of software evaluations, we must take into account some additional recommendations.

And the most important recommendation is that the evaluation of the benchmarking procedure must be an **improvement-oriented activity**. Its intended results will not only be used for comparing the different software products, but for learning how to improve such products. This requires that the evaluation yield not only some comparative results but also that it show the practices that produced these results.

Another recommendation is that benchmarking evaluations should be as **general** as possible since they will be performed by different groups of people in different locations and on different software.

Benchmarking is a process driven by a community; therefore, to gain credibility, effectiveness and impact, its evaluations should also be **community-driven**.

Additionally, benchmarking evaluations should be **reproducible** since they are intended to be used not only by the people participating in the benchmarking, but by the whole community. This requires that the evaluation be thoroughly detailed, providing public data and procedures.

To perform the evaluations consumes significant resources; these evaluations, on the other hand, must be made by several groups of people. Therefore, evaluations should be as **economical** as possible, employing for this activity common evaluation frameworks and, when this is not possible, limiting the scope of the evaluation.

Furthermore, as benchmarking is a continuous process, benchmarking evaluations should have a **limited scope**, leaving other objectives for the next benchmarking iterations and incrementing progressively the complexity of the evaluations. We must add here that a broader evaluation scope does not entail better results but more resources.

As the next section shows, most of these recommendations should also be adopted in the benchmark suites. Therefore, it is advisable to **use benchmark suites** in the evaluations.

Benchmark Suites

A benchmark suite is a collection of benchmarks, being a benchmark *a test or set of tests used to compare the performance of alternative tools or techniques* (Sim et al., 2003).

A benchmark definition must include the following:

- The **context** of the benchmark, namely, which tools and which of their characteristics are measured with it (efficiency, interoperability, portability, usability, etc.).
- The **requirements** for running the benchmark, namely, the tools (hardware or software), data, or people needed.
- The **input variables** that affect the execution of the benchmark and the values that the variables will take.
- The **procedure** to execute the benchmark and obtain its results.
- The **evaluation criteria** followed to interpret these results.

A benchmark suite definition must include the definitions of all its benchmarks. Generally, all these benchmarks share some of their charac-

teristics, such as context or requirements. These characteristics, therefore, must be specified at the benchmark suite level, and not individually for each benchmark.

Desirable Properties of a Benchmark Suite

The properties below, which are extracted from the works of different authors (Bull et al., 1999; Shirazi et al., 1999; Sim et al., 2003; Stefani et al., 2003), can help both to develop new benchmark suites and to assess the quality of the existing ones before being used.

Although a good benchmark suite should have most of these properties, each evaluation will require considering some of them previously. However, we must not forget that achieving these properties completely is not possible since the increment of some properties has a negative effect on the others.

- **Accessibility.** A benchmark suite must be accessible to anyone interested. This involves providing (a) the necessary software to execute the benchmark suite, (b) the software documentation, and (c) the software source code to increase transparency. Then the results obtained from executing the benchmark suite should be made public so that anybody can execute it and then compare his/her results with those available.
- **Affordability.** Using a benchmark suite normally entails a number of costs regarding human, software, and hardware resources. Thus, the costs of using a benchmark suite must be lower than those of defining, implementing, and carrying out any other experiments that fulfil the same goal. On the other hand, the resources consumed in the execution of a benchmark suite can be reduced by (a) automating the execution of the benchmark suite, (b) providing components for data collection and analysis, and (c) facilitating its use in different heterogeneous systems.

- **Simplicity.** The benchmark suite must be simple and interpretable and should be well documented; therefore, whoever wants to use it must be able to understand how it works and the results that it yields. If the benchmark suite is not transparent enough, its results will be questioned and may be interpreted incorrectly. To avoid this, the elements of the benchmark suite should have a common structure and use, and common inputs and outputs. Measurements, on the other hand, should have the same meanings across the benchmark suite.

- **Representativity.** The actions that perform the benchmarks composing the benchmark suite must be representative of the actions normally performed on the system.

- **Portability.** The benchmark suite should be executed on a wide range of environments and should be applicable to as many systems as possible. Besides, it should be specified at a high enough level of abstraction to ensure that it can be transferred to different tools and techniques and that is not biased against other technologies.

- **Scalability.** The benchmark suite should be parameterised to allow scaling the benchmarks with varying input rates. In addition, it should work with tools or techniques of different levels of maturity and should be applicable to research prototypes and commercial products.

- **Robustness.** The benchmark suite must allow for unpredictable environment behaviours and should not be sensitive to factors irrelevant to the study. When running the same benchmark suite on a given system and under the same conditions several times, the results obtained should not vary considerably.

- **Consensus.** The benchmark suite must be developed by experts capable of applying their knowledge of the domain and of identifying the key problems. Additionally,

it should be assessed and agreed on by the whole community.

EVALUATION AND BENCHMARKING WITHIN THE SEMANTIC WEB

This section provides an overview of the evaluation and benchmarking trends now occurring in the Semantic Web area; it also describes to what extent the evaluation and benchmarking activities performed on the Semantic Web technology can be partially or totally reused in different tools, and the facilities provided for doing so.

To this end, we have performed a survey of the main conferences on the Semantic Web field and of the workshops whose main topic is Semantic Web technology evaluation. We have examined the proceedings of five conferences: International Semantic Web Conference (ISWC), European Semantic Web Conference (ESWC), Asian Semantic Web Conference (ASWC), International Conference on Knowledge Capture (K-CAP), and International Conference on Knowledge Engineering and Knowledge Management (EKAW); and we have studied five workshops: Workshop on Evaluation of Ontology-based Tools (EON), Workshop on Scalable Semantic Web Knowledge Base Systems (SSWS), Workshop on Practical and Scalable Semantic Systems (PSSS), International Workshop on Ontology Matching (OM), and Workshop on Integrating Ontologies (IntOnt). The survey includes all the papers accepted in these conferences and workshops from 2000 to 2006.

It is clear that the papers examined, which were presented in the conferences and workshops above commented, do not provide exhaustive information, but they can provide an overview of the current trends.

We consider that fulfilling the desirable properties of a benchmark suite and the recommendations for defining evaluations in benchmarking activities, both defined in the previous section, is an indication of evaluation reusability. And thus, with these desirable properties and recommendations in mind we have produced a questionnaire that should be filled in for each of the selected papers. As an example, the questions asked for assessing the portability of an evaluation approach are the following:

- *In which type of tools can the evaluation be performed?*
- *Can the evaluation approach be transferred to other tools?*
- *On which of the operating systems/platforms can the evaluation be performed?*

Figure 1. Evaluation-related papers in conferences

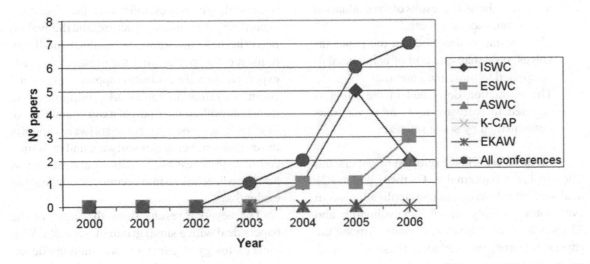

Figure 2. Evaluation-related papers in workshops

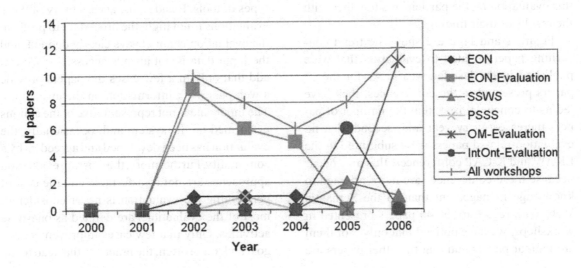

Although software evaluations are frequent in research papers, we focused on those papers where the evaluation approaches followed are reusable to a certain extent. However, we did not distinguish between evaluations that are performed within the benchmarking activities and evaluations that are not, nor did we distinguish between these benchmarking activities that use benchmark suites and those that do not. Thus, the criteria we followed to select the papers are:

- The paper describes how to evaluate several tools, or it shows the results of the evaluation over several tools, or both.
- The evaluation described in the paper involves more than one tool or is intended to be applied to more than one tool.
- The evaluation described in the paper is targeted to software tools or to methods implemented by some software.

With these criteria we selected 61 papers and filled in the questionnaire. Of these papers, 21 deal with the description and application of an evaluation, 7 simply describe an evaluation, and 33 show how an evaluation is made. Among the papers selected, we included those workshop papers that present proposals for performing a common evaluation and the papers written on this evaluation by the participants together with the results of their findings.

Figure 1 and Figure 2 show the trend concerning papers related to evaluation that were published in the last few years. As for the 17 papers presented in the conferences, they have led us to conclude, first, that the number of papers increases every year and, second, that no evaluation-related papers were submitted to the EKAW and K-CAP conferences; this may occur because these conferences are more oriented to knowledge management than to the Semantic Web. With regard to the 44 papers presented in workshops, we have noticed that only 7 of them are regular papers and that the other papers are either evaluation proposals or evaluation results. There is a call for participation in evaluations every year; we have observed that in these evaluations the number of evaluation contributions varies, whereas the number of regular papers is more or less constant.

Our survey shows the results of the reusability of the evaluation approaches in which it can be observed that some of them are positive and some, negative.

The positive results confirm that, in general, the evaluation approaches are easy to understand because they clearly establish both the input data, according to a common structure, and the evaluation criteria for analysing the results. In addition, in most cases, performing the evaluations is not expensive since the evaluation approaches provide common evaluation frameworks and, quite often, the whole evaluation or part of it can be automated. In other cases, however, some software supports the evaluation, being this software and its source code usually accessible. Scalability and robustness have also been taken into account throughout the evaluations.

The negative results show that most of the papers deal with a small group of Semantic Web tools (ontology alignment tools, ontology development tools and ontology repositories) and that, in general, evaluations are not applicable to other types of tools. Besides, the accessibility of these evaluations is not high, the procedure to perform the evaluation is not always clearly defined, and the input data is not always accessible. We can add that only in a few cases the papers provide a web page with information on the evaluation. The input data is not representative of the actions performed on the system and, occasionally, the evaluation has been developed and agreed on by a community. Furthermore, the existing evaluation approaches are not transferrable and the cost of performing the evaluation is never considered; most of the evaluations are defined as one-time activities. Only in a few cases improvement is a goal and, quite often, the practices that lead to the

Figure 3. Histogram of the reusability metric

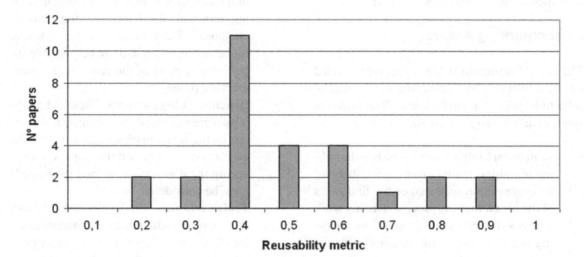

results or improvement recommendations cannot be obtained directly from these results.

As we mentioned before, each of the questions of the questionnaire is related to one of the desirable properties of a benchmark suite. Therefore, we have described the reusability of the evaluation presented in each paper taking into account the number of questions answered positively for each of these properties. For each paper, we have calculated the percentage of positive answers for each dimension and the mean of all these percentages. The resulting value ranges from 0 (not reusable at all) to 1 (totally reusable). Even though this is not a robust metric, it gives us a hint of the reusability of the evaluations.

Figure 3 presents the histogram of the reusability metric used with the 28 papers that describe how to perform an evaluation over several tools. The horizontal axis represents the different ranges of the reusability metric, whereas the vertical axis represents the number of papers in each range. We can clearly observe that most of the papers have low values and are far from the ideal situation.

As a summary of this section we can conclude that although the number of evaluation and benchmarking activities is continuously increasing in

the Semantic Web area, such number is still not good enough to ensure a high quality technology, and that the activities carried out involved just a few types of Semantic Web technologies. Consequently, the reusability of the evaluation approaches is not high enough, which is a hindrance for their use.

THE BENCHMARKING METHODOLOGY FOR SEMANTIC WEB TECHNOLOGY

This section summarises the benchmarking methodology for Semantic Web technology developed by the authors in the Knowledge Web European Network of Excellence. A detailed description of this methodology can be found in (García-Castro et al., 2004).

The methodology has been inspired by works of quality improvement from different fields. The main inputs for this methodology were the benchmarking methodologies of the business management community and their notions of continuous improvement and best practices. We have also taken into account the evaluation and improvement processes proposed in the Software Engineering area such as those cited in Section 2.1.

Benchmarking Actors

The tasks of the benchmarking process are carried out by different actors according to the kind of roles to be performed in each task. The different types of actors involved are the following:

- **Benchmarking initiator.** The benchmarking initiator is the member (or members) of an organisation who makes the first tasks of the benchmarking process. His/her work consists in preparing a proposal for carrying out the benchmarking activity in the organisation and in obtaining the management approval to perform it.
- **Organisation management.** The organisation management plays a key role in the benchmarking process: this actor must approve the benchmarking activity and the changes that result from it. The organization management must also assign resources to the benchmarking and integrate the benchmarking planning into the organisation planning.

- **Benchmarking team.** Once the organisation management approves the benchmarking proposal, the benchmarking team is composed. Their members have to belong to the organisation and are responsible for performing most of the remaining benchmarking processes.
- **Benchmarking partners.** The benchmarking partners are the organisations participating in the benchmarking activity. All the partners must agree on the steps to follow during the benchmarking, and their needs must be considered.
- **Tool developers.** The developers of the tool must implement the necessary changes in the tool to improve it. Some of the developers may also be part of the benchmarking team and, if so, care must be taken to minimise bias.

Benchmarking Process

The benchmarking methodology for Semantic Web technology describes a benchmarking process together with the main phases to follow when benchmarking this technology and it

Figure 4. The software benchmarking methodology

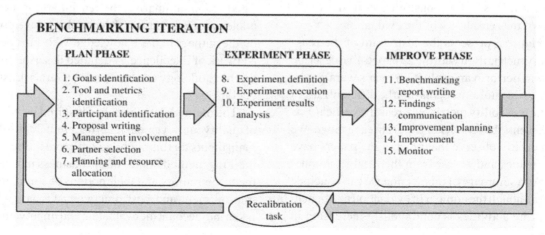

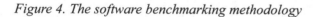

also provides a set of guidelines. Therefore, this methodology has a twofold use: to help carry out software benchmarking activities, and to know, at a specific time, which is the actual progress of a benchmarking activity.

The benchmarking process defined in this methodology is composed of a benchmarking iteration that is repeated forever. Each iteration, as shown in Figure 4, is composed of three phases (*Plan*, *Experiment* and *Improve*) and ends with a *Recalibration* task.

Plan Phase

The *Plan* phase is composed of the different tasks that must be performed (1) to prepare the benchmarking proposal, (2) to obtain support from the organisation management, (3) to find other organisations willing to participate in benchmarking, and 4) to plan benchmarking. These tasks are the following:

P1. Goals identification. In this task, the *benchmarking initiator* (the member or members of the organisation who are aware of the need for benchmarking) must identify the benchmarking goals according to the goals and strategies of the organization as well as the benefits and costs involved in carrying out benchmarking. However, every organization may have its own goals and these can be quite different. For example, some may be interested in assessing the performance and improving the quality of the software over its lifetime, others, in comparing their software with the software that is considered the best, whereas some others are interested in establishing or creating standards by analysing the different existing software.

P2. Software and metrics identification. In this task, the *benchmarking initiator* should make an analysis of the software products developed in the organisation in order to understand and document them, identifying the weaknesses and functionalities that require improvement. Then,

he/she must select the products to be benchmarked, the functionalities relevant to the study and the evaluation criteria to follow to assess these functionalities; these criteria must take into account the organisation's software, the benchmarking goals, the benefits and costs identified in the previous task as well as other factors considered critical by the organisation, such as quality requirements, end-user needs, etc.

P3. Participant identification. In this task, the *benchmarking initiator* must identify and contact the members concerned with the software and the functionalities selected (managers, developers, end users, etc.) and other relevant participants that do not belong to the organisation (customers or consultants). The benchmarking initiator is responsible for organizing the benchmarking team and, quite often, he is a member of the team. The team should be small and include those organisation members whose work and interest are related to the software, who have a thorough understanding of the software and have gained valuable experience with it. They must be aware of the time they will spend in the benchmarking activity and of their responsibilities, and they should be trained in the tasks they will have to perform.

P4. Proposal writing. In this task, the *benchmarking team* (and the *benchmarking initiator*, if he does not belong to the team) must write a document with the benchmarking proposal. The proposal will be used as a reference along the benchmarking process and must include all the relevant information on the process: the information identified in the previous benchmarking tasks (goals, benefits, costs, software, metrics, members involved, and benchmarking team), a description of the benchmarking process, and a full detailed description of the benchmarking costs along with the resources needed. To do this, the benchmarking team should take into consideration the different intended readers of the benchmarking proposal, namely, the organisation managers, the organisation developers, the members of partner organisations, and the members of the benchmarking team.

P5. Management involvement. In this task, the *benchmarking initiator* must bring the benchmarking proposal to the *organisation management*. This task is of great significance because the management approval is required if we want to continue with the benchmarking process. Management support will also be requested in the future, when the changes required for benchmarking will have to be implemented, either in the software or in the organisation processes that affect the software.

P6. Partner selection. In this task, the *benchmarking team* must collect and analyse information on the software products that are to be compared with the software selected, and on the organisations that develop the products. The benchmarking team must also select the software employed in the benchmarking study taking into account its relevance and use in the community or in the industry, its public availability, how the software has adopted the latest technological tendencies, etc. In order to obtain better results with benchmarking, the software selected should be the software considered the best. Then, the benchmarking team must contact the people from the organisations that develop these software products to find out whether they are interested in becoming *benchmarking partners*. These partners will also have to establish a team and to take the proposal to their own organisation management for approval. During this task, the benchmarking proposal will be modified by incorporating the partners' opinions and requirements. This will result in an updated proposal that, depending on the magnitude of the modifications, should be presented again to each organisation management for approval.

P7. Planning and resource allocation. In this task, the *organisation managements* and the *benchmarking teams* must specify the planning of the remainder of the process, considering the

different resources that will be devoted to it, and finally they must reach a consensus. This planning must be given careful consideration and should be integrated into each organisation planning.

Experiment Phase

The *Experiment* phase is composed of the tasks in which the experimentation on the software products is performed. These tasks are the following:

E1. Experiment definition. In this task, the *benchmarking teams* of each organization must establish the experiment that will be performed on each of the software products, and then the members must agree on it. The experiment must be defined according to the benchmarking goals, the software functionalities selected, and their corresponding criteria, as stated in the benchmarking proposal. The experiment must also provide objective and reliable software data not just of its performance, but also of the reasons of its performance; in addition, its future reusability must be also be considered. The benchmarking teams must determine and agree on the planning to follow during the experimentation; this new planning must be decided according to the benchmarking planning established previously.

E2. Experiment execution. As indicated in the experimentation planning, explained in the previous task, the *benchmarking teams* must perform the established experiments on their software products. Then the data obtained from all the experiments must be compiled, documented, and written in a common format to facilitate its future analysis.

E3. Experiment results analysis. In this task, the *benchmarking teams* must analyse the results, detect and document any significant differences found in them, and determine the practices leading to these different results in order to identify whether, among the practices found, some of them can be considered the best practices. Then, the benchmarking teams should write a report with all the findings of the experimentation, that is, the experimentation results, the differences in the results, the practices and the best practices found, etc.

Improve Phase

The *Improve* phase comprises the tasks where the results of the benchmarking process are produced and then communicated to the benchmarking partners; it also comprises the tasks where, in several cycles, the improvement of the different software products takes place. The tasks are the following:

I1. Benchmarking report writing. In this task, the *benchmarking teams* must write the benchmarking report. This report is intended to provide an understandable summary of the benchmarking carried out, and it should be written bearing in mind its different audiences: managers, benchmarking teams, developers, etc. The benchmarking report must include a) an explanation of the process followed, together with all the relevant information of the updated version of the benchmarking proposal; and b) the results and conclusions of the experiments presented in the experiment report, including the practices found and highlighting the best practices. The report should also contain the recommendations provided by the benchmarking teams for improving the software products according to the experiment results, the practices found, and the best practices implemented by the community.

I2. Findings communication. Here, the *benchmarking teams* must communicate, in successive meetings, the results of the benchmarking to their organisations and, particularly, to all the members concerned and identified when planning benchmarking. The goals of these meetings are:

- To obtain feedback from the members concerned on the benchmarking process, the results, and the improvement recommendations.

- To obtain support and commitment from the organisation members for implementing the improvement recommendations on the software.

Any feedback received during these communications must be collected, documented and analysed. This analysis may finally involve having to review the work done and to update the benchmarking report.

I3. Improvement planning. The last three tasks of the *Improve* phase (*Improvement planning*, *Improvement* and *Monitor*) form a cycle that must be carried out separately in each organisation. The *benchmarking teams* and the *organisation managements* must identify, from the benchmarking report and the monitoring reports, which are the changes needed to improve their software products. Besides, they must forecast the improvements to be achieved after performing these changes. Both the organisation management and the benchmarking team must provide mechanisms for ensuring improvements in their organisation and for measuring the software functionalities. These last mechanisms can be obtained from the *Experiment* phase. Then, the organisation management and the benchmarking team must establish a planning for improving the software benchmarked, taking into account the different resources devoted to the improvement. This planning must be then integrated into the organisation planning.

I4. Improvement. It is in this task where the *developers* of each of the software product must implement the necessary changes to achieve the desired results. For this, they must measure the state of the software before and after implementing any changes, using for that purpose the measurement mechanisms provided by the benchmarking team in the previous task. Then, the developers must compare the resulting measurements with those that were obtained before implementing the changes and with the improvement forecasted.

I5. Monitor. In each organisation, the *benchmarking team* must provide *software developers* with means for monitoring the organisation's software. Software developers must periodically monitor the software and write a report with the results of this process. These results may show the need for new improvements in software and may also mean the beginning of a new improvement cycle which involves having to perform again the two tasks previously mentioned: *Improvement Planning* and *Improvement*.

Recalibration Task

The recalibration task is performed at the end of each iteration. Here the *benchmarking teams* must recalibrate the process by applying the lessons learnt while performing it. Thus, the organisation (and the whole community) achieves improvement not just in the software, but also in the benchmarking process. This recalibration is needed because both the software and the organisations evolve and innovate over time.

BENCHMARKING THE INTEROPERABILITY OF ONTOLOGY DEVELOPMENT TOOLS USING RDF(S) AS THE INTERCHANGE LANGUAGE

This section presents how we have applied the software benchmarking methodology, presented in the previous section, to one important problem of the Semantic Web: technology interoperability.

Ontologies permit interoperability among heterogeneous Semantic Web technologies, and ideally, one could use all the existing technologies seamlessly. The technologies appear in different forms (ontology development tools, ontology repositories, ontology alignment tools, reasoners, etc.), but although all these tools use different kinds of ontologies, not all of them share a common knowledge representation model.

This diversity in the representation formalisms of the tools causes problems when the tools try to interoperate. This is so because the tools require translating their ontologies from their own knowledge models to a common model and vice versa, and these problems occur even when we employ standard APIs for managing ontologies in the common knowledge model.

As we have observed in previous workshops on Evaluation of Ontology-based Tools (EON) (Sure & Corcho, 2003), interoperability among different ontology tools is not straightforward. Finding out why interoperability fails is cumbersome and not at all trivial because any assumption made for translating ontologies within one tool may easily prevent the successful interoperability with other tools.

To solve this problem, the Knowledge Web European Network of Excellence organized a benchmarking of interoperability of ontology development tools using RDF(S) as the interchange language. Its goal was to assess and improve the interoperability of the tools.

The section that follows describes such benchmarking activity. The methodology presented in the previous section provides the general guidelines that can be adapted to this case. So we present here how this new benchmarking was organized, the experiments conducted on the participating tools, and its results.

Organising the Benchmarking

The goals of benchmarking the interoperability of ontology development tools are related to the benefits pursued through it, and these are:

- To *evaluate and improve* their interoperability.
- To acquire a *deep understanding* of the practices used to develop the importers and exporters of these tools, and to extract from these practices those that can be considered the *best practices*.

Table 1. Ontology tools participating in the benchmarking

Tool	Knowledge model	Version	Developer	Experimenter
Corese	RDF(S)	2.1.2	INRIA	INRIA
Jena	RDF(S)	2.3	HP	U. P. Madrid
KAON	RDF(S) extension	1.2.9	U. Karlsruhe	U. Karlsruhe
Sesame	RDF(S)	2.0 alpha 3	Aduna	U. P. Madrid
Protégé	Frames	3.2 beta build 230	Stanford U.	U. P. Madrid
WebODE	Frames	2.0 build 109	U. P. Madrid	U. P. Madrid

- To produce *recommendations* on their interoperability for users.
- To create *consensual processes* for evaluating their interoperability.

These goals concern different communities that somehow are related to the ontology development tools, namely, the research community, the industrial community, and the tool developers.

Participation in the benchmarking was open to any organisation irrespective of being a Knowledge Web partner or not. To involve other organisations in the process with the aim of having the best-in-class tools participating, several actions were taken:

- The benchmarking proposal, the document being used as a reference along the benchmarking, was published as a public web page[b] and included all the relevant information about the benchmarking: motivation, goals, benefits and costs, tools and people involved, planning, related events, and a complete description of the experimentation and the benchmark suites.
- Research was carried out on the existing ontology development tools, both the freely available and the commercial versions, which could export and import to and from RDF(S); In addition, their developers were contacted. Any tool capable of importing and exporting RDF could participate in

the benchmarking or will benefit from the created benchmarks in a near future.
- The interoperability benchmarking was announced with a call for participation through the main mailing lists of the Semantic Web area and through lists specific to ontology development tools.

Six tools took part in the benchmarking, three of which are ontology development tools: KAON[c], Protégé[d] (using its RDF backend), and WebODE[e]; the other three are RDF repositories: Corese[f], Jena[g] and Sesame[h]. As Table 1 shows, the tools do not share a common knowledge model and benchmarking was not always performed by the tool developers.

The experimentation conducted on the tools aimed to obtain results for interoperability improvement. Therefore, other quality attributes such as performance, scalability, interoperability, robustness, etc. were not considered. However, an approach for benchmarking the performance and scalability of ontology development tools can be found in (García-Castro & Gómez-Pérez, 2005).

The experimentation was carried out taking into account the most common ways of interchanging ontologies that ontology tools provide, such as the following:

- Interchanging ontologies by exporting them from a tool into an interchange language and then importing them into the other tool.

- Using RDF(S) as the interchange language, and serializing the ontologies into the RDF/XML syntax. A future benchmarking activity inside Knowledge Web will cover the case of using OWL as the interchange language.

The interoperability of ontology tools using an interchange language depends on the capabilities of the tools to import and export ontologies from/ to this language. Therefore, the experimentation included not only the evaluation of the interoperability but also of the RDF(S) import and export functionalities.

The evaluation criteria must describe in depth the import, export and interoperability capabilities of the tools, whereas the experiments to be performed in the benchmarking must provide data explaining how the tools comply with these criteria. Therefore, to obtain detailed information about these capabilities, we need to know:

- The elements of the *internal knowledge model* of an ontology development tool that can be imported from RDF(S), exported to RDF(S) and interchanged with other tool, using RDF(S) as the interchange language.
- The *secondary effects* of importing, exporting, and interchanging these components, such as insertion or loss of information.
- The *subset of elements* of the internal knowledge models that these tools may use to interoperate correctly.

To obtain these experimentation data, we defined three benchmark suites that evaluate the capabilities of the tools (García-Castro et al., 2006), which were common for all the tools. Since the quality of the benchmark suites to be used is essential for the results, the first step was to agree on the definition of the suites. Then, we decided to make the import and export experiments before the interoperability one because the

results of the first experiments affected those of the second.

A benchmark execution comprises (a) the definition of the expected ontology that results from importing, exporting or interchanging the ontology described in the benchmark, (b) the import, export, or interchange of the ontology defined in the benchmark, and (c) the comparison of the expected ontology with the imported, exported or interchanged ontology, checking whether there is some addition or loss of information. The steps to follow to execute the three benchmark suites are similar.

The benchmark suites were intended to be executed manually but, as they contained many benchmarks, it was highly recommended to execute them (or part of them) automatically. In the cases of Corese, Jena, Sesame, and WebODE, most of the experiment was automated. In the other cases, it was performed manually.

The benchmarking web page[i] contains the results of the experiments and a complete and detailed description of (a) the benchmark suites, (b) all the files to be used in the experiments, and (c) the templates for collecting the results.

Benchmark Suites

The benchmark suites check the correct import, export and interchange of ontologies that model a simple combination of ontology components (classes, properties, instances, etc.). Because one of the goals of benchmarking is to improve the tools, the benchmark ontologies are kept simple on purpose in order to isolate the causes of the problems and to identify possible problems.

As the ontology tools that participated in benchmarking had different internal knowledge models, both the experimentation and the analysis of the results were based on a common group of ontology modelling primitives, available both in RDF(S) and in these tools. On the other hand, covering this common group exhaustively would yield a huge number of benchmarks; so we only considered the components most widely used for modelling ontologies in ontology development tools: classes, instances, properties with domain and range, literals, and class and property hierarchies. The remainder of the components has not been dealt with so far.

The **RDF(S) Import Benchmark Suite** contains 82 benchmarks[j], which define a simple RDF(S) ontology serialized in a RDF/XML file, which must be loaded into the ontology development tool.

In order to isolate the factors that affect the correct import of an ontology, we defined two types of import benchmarks: one that evaluates the import of the different combinations of components of the RDF(S) knowledge model, and the other type that evaluates the import of the different variants of the RDF/XML syntax, as stated in the RDF/XML specification.

Table 2 shows the categories of the RDF(S) Import Benchmark Suite, the number of benchmarks, and the components used. All the RDF(S) files to be imported can be downloaded from a single file; besides, templates are provided for collecting the execution results.

The **RDF(S) Export Benchmark Suite** comprises 66 benchmarks[k], which describe an ontology that must be modelled in the tool and saved to a RDF(S) file.

We have defined two types of benchmarks for isolating the two factors that affect the correct export of an ontology: one type evaluates the correct export of the combinations of components of the ontology development tool knowledge model, and the other evaluates the export of ontologies using concepts and properties whose names have characters restricted by RDF(S), such as those characters that are forbidden when representing RDF(S) or XML URIs.

Table 3 shows the categories of the benchmark suite. The table contains the number of benchmarks and the components used in each category. Templates are also provided for collecting the execution results.

Since the factors that affect both the correct interchange of an ontology (besides the correct functioning of the importers and exporters) and the knowledge model (used for defining the ontologies) are the same as those that affect the RDF(S) Export Benchmark Suite, the ontologies described in the RDF(S) Interoperability Bench-

Table 2. Categories of the import benchmarks

Category	No.	Components used
Class	2	*rdfs:Class*
Metaclass	5	*rdfs:Class, rdf:type*
Subclass	5	*rdfs:Class, rdfs:subClassOf*
Class and property	6	*rdfs:Class, rdf:Property, rdfs:Literal*
Property	2	*rdf:Property*
Subproperty	5	*rdf:Property, rdfs:subPropertyOf*
Property with domain and range	24	*rdfs:Class, rdf:Property, rdfs:Literal, rdfs:domain, rdfs:range*
Instance	4	*rdfs:Class, rdf:type*
Instance and property	14	*rdfs:Class, rdf:type, rdf:Property, rdfs:Literal*
Syntax and abbreviation	15	*rdfs:Class, rdf:type, rdf:Property, rdfs:Literal*

Table 3. Categories of the export benchmarks

Category	No.	Components used
Class	2	*class*
Metaclass	5	*class, instanceOf*
Subclass	5	*class, subClassOf*
Class and object property	4	*class, object property*
Class and datatype property	2	*class, datatype property, literal*
Object property	14	*object property*
Datatype property	12	*datatype property*
Instance	4	*class, instanceOf*
Instance and object property	9	*class, instanceOf, object property*
Instance and datatype property	5	*class, instanceOf, datatype property, literal*
URI character restrictions	4	*class, instanceOf, object property, datatype property, literal*

mark Suite are identical to those of the RDF(S) Export Benchmark Suite.

The evaluation criteria are common for the three benchmark suites, and are defined as follows:

- **Modelling** (*YES/NO*). The ontology tool can model the ontology components described in the benchmark.
- **Execution** (*OK/FAIL*). The execution of the benchmark is normally carried out seamlessly, and the tool always produces the expected result. However, when an execution fails, the following information is required:
  - The causes of the failure.
  - The changes performed if the tool had been previously corrected to pass a benchmark correctly.
- **Information added or lost.** The information added to or lost in the ontology interchange when executing the benchmark.

In the export and interoperability benchmark suites, if a benchmark describes an ontology that cannot be modelled in a certain tool, such benchmark cannot be executed in the tool, be-

ing the *Execution* result *N.E.* (Non Executed). However, in the import benchmark suites, even if a tool cannot model some components of the ontology, it should be able to import the rest of the components correctly.

Import and Export Results

The results obtained when importing from and exporting to RDF(S) depend mainly on the knowledge model of the tool that executes the benchmark suite. The tools that natively support the RDF(S) knowledge model (Corese, Jena and Sesame, essentially the RDF repositories) do not need to perform any translation in the ontologies when importing/exporting them from/to RDF(S). The RDF repositories import and export correctly all the combinations of components from/to RDF(S) because these operations do not require any translation.

In the case of tools with non-RDF knowledge models (KAON, Protégé and WebODE, the ontology development tools), some of their knowledge model components can also be represented in RDF(S), but some others cannot, and these tools do need to translate ontologies between their

Table 4. Combinations of components modelled by the tools

Combination of components	RDF repos.	KAON	Protégé	WebODE
Classes	Y	Y	Y	Y
...instance of metaclasses	Y	Y	Y	N
Class hierarchies without cycles	Y	Y	Y	Y
...with cycles	Y	N	N	N
Datatype properties without domain or range	Y	Y	Y	N
...with multiple domains	Y	Y	N	N
...whose range is String	Y	Y	Y	Y
...whose range is a XML Schema datatype	Y	Y	N	Y
Object properties without domain or range	Y	Y	Y	N
...with multiple domains or ranges	Y	Y	N	N
...with a domain and range	Y	Y	Y	Y
Instances of a single class	Y	Y	Y	Y
...of multiple classes	Y	Y	Y	N
...related via object or datatype properties	Y	Y	Y	Y
...related via datatype properties whose range is a XML Schema datatype	Y	N	N	Y

knowledge models and RDF(S). Finally, we must add that not all the combinations of components of the RDF(S) knowledge model that have been considered can be modelled into all the tools, as Table 4 shows.

Next, we present an analysis of the results of importing and exporting in the ontology development tools that participated in the benchmarking.

Import Results

In general, the ontology development tools import correctly from RDF(S) all or most of the combinations of components that they model; they seldom add or lose information. The only exceptions are:

- Protégé, which presents problems, but only when it imports classes or instances that are instances of multiple classes.

- WebODE, which presents problems, but only when it imports properties with a XML Schema datatype as range.

When the tools import ontologies with combinations of components that they cannot model, they lose the information about these components. Nevertheless, these tools usually try to represent such components partially using for this other components from their knowledge models. In most cases, the importing is performed correctly. The only exceptions are:

- KAON, which causes problems when it imports class hierarchies with cycles.
- Protégé, which causes problems when it imports class and property hierarchies with cycles and properties with multiple domains.
- WebODE, which causes problems when it imports properties with multiple domains or ranges.

When dealing with the different variants of the RDF/XML syntax, we can observe that the ontology development tools

- Import correctly resources with the different URI reference syntaxes.
- Import correctly resources with different syntaxes (shortened and unshortened) of empty nodes, of multiple properties, of typed nodes, of string literals, and of blank nodes. The only exceptions are: KAON when it imports resources with multiple properties in the unshortened syntax; and Protégé when it imports resources with empty and blank nodes in the unshortened syntax. Do not import language identification attributes (*xml:lang*) in tags.

Export Results

In general, the ontology development tools export correctly to RDF(S) all or most of the combinations of components that they model with no loss of information. In particular:

- KAON causes problems only when it exports to RDF(S) datatype properties without range and datatype properties with multiple domains plus a XML Schema datatype as range.
- Protégé causes problems only when it exports to RDF(S) classes or instances that are instances of multiple classes and template slots with multiple domains.

When ontology development tools export components present in their knowledge model that cannot be represented in RDF(S), such as their own datatypes, they usually insert new information in the ontology, but they also lose some.

When dealing with concepts and properties whose names do not fulfil URI character restrictions, each ontology development tool behaves differently:

- When names do not start with a letter or "_", some tools leave the name unchanged, whereas others replace the first character with "_".
- Spaces in names are replaced by "-" or "_", depending on the tool.
- URI reserved characters and XML delimiter characters are left unchanged, replaced by "_", or encoded, depending on the tool.

Interoperability Results

The RDF repositories (Corese, Jena and Sesame) interoperate correctly between themselves, because they always import and export from/to RDF(S) correctly. This produces that the interoperability between the ontology development tools and the RDF repositories depends only on the capabilities of the former to import and export from/to RDF(S); therefore, the results of this interoperability are identical to those presented in the previous section.

The import and export results presented in previous sections indicate that some problems arise in the process of importing and exporting ontologies, whereas the interoperability results, on the other hand, show more problems.

As a general comment we can say that interoperability between the tools depends on

a. the correct functioning of their RDF(S) importers and exporters and
b. the way chosen for serializing the exported ontologies in the RDF/XML syntax.

Furthermore, we have observed that the problems affecting any of these factors also affect the results of not just one but several benchmarks. This means that, in some cases, to correct a single import or export problem, or to change the way of serializing ontologies can produce significant interoperability improvements.

Below we list the components that can be interchanged between the tools. These components are

Table 5. Components interchanged between the tools

Combination of components	K-K	P-P	W-W	K-P	K-W	P-W	K-P-W
Classes	Y	Y	Y	Y	Y	Y	Y
...instance of a single metaclass	Y	Y	-	N	-	-	-
...instance of a multiple metaclasses	Y	N	-	N	-	-	-
Class hierarchies without cycles	Y	Y	Y	Y	Y	Y	Y
Datatype properties without domain or range	Y	Y	-	N	-	-	-
...with multiple domains	Y	-	-	-	-	-	-
...whose range is String	Y	Y	Y	N	N	Y	N
...whose range is a XML Schema datatype	Y	-	Y	-	Y	-	-
Object properties without domain or range	Y	Y	-	Y	-	-	-
...with multiple domains or ranges	Y	-	-	-	-	-	-
...with a domain and range	Y	Y	Y	Y	Y	Y	Y
Instances of a single class	Y	Y	Y	Y	Y	Y	Y
...of multiple classes	Y	N	-	N	-	-	-
...related via object properties	Y	Y	Y	Y	Y	Y	Y
...related via datatype properties	Y	Y	Y	N	Y	Y	N
...related via datatype properties whose range is a XML Schema datatype	-	-	Y	-	-	-	-

summarized in Table 5; each column of the table shows whether the combination of components can be interchanged between a group of tools[1]. The "-" character means that the component cannot be modelled in some of the tools and, therefore, cannot be interchanged between them.

Interoperability Using the Same Tool

Ontology development tools seem to pose no problems when the source and the destination of an ontology interchange are the same tool. The only exception is Protégé when it interchanges classes that are instances of multiple metaclasses and instances of multiple classes; this is so because Protégé does not import resources that are instances of multiple metaclasses.

Interoperability between Each Pair of Tools

The interoperability between different tools varies depending on the tools. As the detailed interoperability results show, in some cases, the tools are able to interchange certain components from one tool to another, but not the other way round.

When **KAON** interoperates with **Protégé**, they can interchange correctly some of the common components that these tools are able to model. However, with components such as classes that are instances of a single metaclass or of multiple metaclasses, datatype properties without domain or range, datatype properties whose range is *String*, instances of multiple classes, and instances related through datatype properties, we have encountered some problems.

When **KAON** interoperates with **WebODE**, they can interchange correctly most of the common components that these tools can model, but when they interchange datatype properties with domain and whose range is *String,* the results are not the same.

When **Protégé** interoperates with **WebODE**, they can interchange correctly all the common components that these tools can model.

Interoperability between All the Tools

Interoperability between **KAON**, **Protégé** and **WebODE** can be achieved by most of the common components that these tools can model. The only components that these tools cannot use are datatype properties with domain and whose range is *String,* and instances related through datatype properties.

Therefore, interoperability was achieved among the tools that participated in the benchmarking by using classes, class hierarchies without cycles, object properties with domain and with range, instances of a single class, and instances related through object properties.

Interoperability Regarding URI Character Restrictions

Interoperability is low when tools interchange ontologies containing URI character restrictions in class and property names. This is so because tools usually encode some or all the characters that do not comply with these restrictions, which provokes changes in class and property names.

Recommendations

Recommendations for Ontology Engineers

This section offers recommendations for ontology engineers which use more than one ontology tool to build ontologies. Depending on the tools

used, the level of interoperability may be higher or lower, as can be seen in Section 5.4.

If the ontology is being developed bearing in mind interoperability, ontology engineers should be aware of the components that can be represented in the ontology development tools and in RDF(S). And they should try to use the common knowledge components that these tools have so as to avoid the knowledge losses commented above.

Ontology engineers should also be aware of the semantic equivalences and differences between the knowledge models of the tools and the interchange language. For example, in Protégé, multiple domains in template slots are considered the union of all the domains, whereas in RDF(S) multiple domains in properties are considered the intersection of all the domains; in WebODE, on the other hand, instance attributes are local to a single concept, whereas in RDF(S) properties are global and can be used in any class.

It is not recommended to name resources using spaces or any character that is restricted in the RDF(S), URI, or XML specifications.

When the RDF repositories interoperate, even though these repositories export and import correctly to RDF(S), ontology engineers should consider the limitations that other tools have when they export their ontologies to RDF(S).

Recommendations for Tool Developers

This section includes general recommendations for improving the interoperability of the tools while developing them. In (García-Castro et al., 2006), we offer full detailed recommendations regarding the results and practices gathered to improve each of the participant tools. Although it is not compulsory to follow these recommendations, they help correct interoperability problems as we could observe when we analysed the results.

The interoperability between ontology tools (using RDF(S) as the interchange language) depends on how the importers and exporters of these tools work; on the other hand, how these importers and exporters work depends on the development decisions made by the tool developers, and these are different people with different needs. Therefore, to provide general recommendations for developers is not straightforward, though some comments can be extracted from the analysis of the benchmarking results.

In some occasions, a development decision will produce interoperability improvement with some tools and interoperability loss with others. For example, when exporting classes that are instances of a metaclass, some tools require that the class be defined as instance of *rdfs:Class*, whereas other tools require the opposite.

Tool developers, therefore, should analyze the collateral consequences of the development decisions. Thus, if a datatype is imported as a class in the ontology, then the literal values of this datatype should be imported as instances in the ontology, which would complicate the management of these values.

They also should be aware of the semantic equivalences and differences between the knowledge models of their tool and the interchange language; on the other hand, the tools should notify the user when the semantics is changed.

The first requirement for achieving interoperability is that the importers and exporters of the tools be robust and work correctly when dealing with unexpected inputs. Although this is an obvious comment, the results show that this requirement is not achieved by the tools and that some tools even crash when importing some combinations of components.

Above all, tools should deal correctly with the combinations of components that are present in the interchange language but cannot be modelled in them. For example, although cycles in class and property hierarchies cannot be modelled in some ontology development tools, these tools should be able to import these hierarchies by eliminating the cycles.

If developers want to export components that are commonly used by ontology development tools, the components should be completely defined in the file. This means that metaclasses and classes in class hierarchies should be defined as instances of *rdfs:Class*, properties should be defined as instances of *rdf:Property*, etc.

Exporting complete definitions of other components can cause problems if these are imported by other tools. And not every tool deals with datatypes defined as instances of *rdfs:Datatype* in the file, or with *rdf:datatype* attributes in properties.

If the document does not define a default namespace, every exported resource should have a namespace.

CONCLUSION

This chapter states the need to evaluate and benchmark the Semantic Web technology and provides some references that can be helpful in these activities. It also presents the authors' approach to software benchmarking and compares it with other existing evaluation and benchmarking approaches.

We have tried to explain how the benchmarking methodology can help assess and improve software, whereas the use of benchmark suites is advisable when performing evaluations in benchmarking.

One of the strong points we make on benchmarking is its community-driven approach. Benchmarking should be performed by the experts of the community since the benefits obtained after performing it affect the whole community.

Benchmarking does not imply comparing the results of the tools but comparing the practices that lead to these results. Therefore, experimentation should be designed to obtain these practices as well as the results.

However, as we have seen, benchmarking is not the solution to every case. In a preliminary step, developers would have to asses whether benchmarking is the correct approach; as benchmarking is useful when the goals are to improve the software and to extract the practices performed by others.

Benchmarking is an activity that takes long time to perform because it requires tasks that are not immediate: announcements, agreements, etc. Therefore, benchmarking activities should start early in time, and the benchmarking planning should consider a realistic duration of the benchmarking and the resources needed for carrying them out.

We have also shown how we have applied the benchmarking methodology to a concrete case in the Semantic Web area: interoperability of ontology development tools using RDF(S) as interchange language.

Providing benchmark suites in the benchmarking allows evaluating other tools with RDF(S) import and export capabilities without their having to participate in the benchmarking; this can be useful both while the tools are being developed and afterwards, when their development has finished. In addition, the benchmarking results can be used by ontology development tool users that may find problems when interchanging ontologies or may want to foresee the results of a future interchange.

Although it is not required that the tool developers participate in the benchmarking and perform the experiments over their tool, their involvement facilitates the execution and analysis of the experimentation results to a large extent. In all the cases where tool developers carried out the experimentation over their own tools, a great improvement occurred before the *Improve* phase of the methodology because developers were able to detect problems and correct their tools while executing the benchmark suites.

We have observed that the manual execution of the experiments and the analysis of the results cause the benchmark suite to be costly. Consequently, tool developers often automate the execution of the benchmark suites, but not always. Another drawback of the manual execution of

experiments is that the results obtained depend on the people performing these experiments, on their expertise with the tools, and on their ability to extract the practices performed.

FUTURE RESEARCH DIRECTIONS

As shown in Section 3, current evaluation and benchmarking activities over the Semantic Web technology are scarce and a hindrance to the full development and maturity of this technology. The Semantic Web needs to produce methods and tools for evaluating the technology at great scale and in an easy and economical way. This requires defining technology evaluations focusing on their reusability.

In the last few years, evaluation and benchmarking efforts have mainly focused on some types of technologies and on some of their metrics, namely, the interoperability of ontology development tools, the precision and recall of ontology alignment tools, and the efficiency and scalability of ontology repositories. But now we think that new efforts are required, first, to involve other Semantic Web technologies (ontology learning tools, ontology annotation tools, ontology population tools, etc.) and, second, to broaden the scope of these evaluations by considering a wider range of evaluation metrics for the technology (latency, robustness, security, usability, etc.).

The role of the research community when defining and performing benchmarking activities is crucial. Community-driven benchmarking connects experts and allows obtaining high quality results and increasing the credibility of the benchmarking and its results.

However, future research must focus on performing evaluations centred on the user of the Semantic Web technology. And it would be advisable to consider audiences from beyond the research community itself as recipients of the evaluation results.

REFERENCES

Abran, A., Moore, J. W., Bourque, P., & Dupuis, R. (Ed.). (2004). *SWEBOK: Guide to the software engineering body of knowledge.* IEEE Press.

Basili, V. R., & Selby, R. W. (1991). Paradigms for experimentation and empirical studies in software engineering. *Reliability Engineering and System Safety, 32,* 171-191.

Basili, V. R., Selby, R. W., & Hutchens, D. H. (1986). Experimentation in software engineering. *IEEE Transactions on Software Engineering, 12*(7), 733-743.

Basili, V. R. (1985, September). Quantitative evaluation of software methodology. In *1st Pan-Pacific Computer Conference,* Melbourne, Australia.

Bull, J. M., Smith, L. A., Westhead, M. D., Henty, D. S., & Davey, R. A. (1999). A methodology for benchmarking Java grande applications. In the *ACM 1999 conference on Java Grande* (pp. 81-88).

Camp, R. (1989). *Benchmarking: The search for industry best practices that lead to superior performance.* Milwaukee, ASQC Quality Press.

Freimut, B., Punter, T., Biffl, S., & Ciolkowski, M. (2002). *State-of-the art in empirical studies.* Technical Report ViSEK/007/E, Visek.

García-Castro, R., & Gómez-Pérez, A. (2005, November). Guidelines for benchmarking the performance of ontology management APIs. In Y. Gil, E. Motta, R. Benjamins, & M. Musen (Ed.), *4th International Semantic Web Conference (ISWC2005), 3729* in LNCS, 277-292. Galway, Ireland: Springer-Verlag.

García-Castro, R., Maynard, D., Wache, H., Foxvog, D., & González-Cabero, R. (2004). *D2.1.4 Specification of a methodology, general criteria and benchmark suites for benchmarking ontology tools.* Technical report, Knowledge Web.

García-Castro, R., Sure, Y., Zondler, M., Corby, O., Prieto-González, J., Paslaru Bontas, E., Nixon, L., & Mochol, M. (2006). *D1.2.2.1.1 Benchmarking the interoperability of ontology development tools using RDF(S) as interchange language.* Technical report, Knowledge Web.

Gediga, G., Hamborg, K., & Duntsch, I. (2002). Evaluation of software systems. In *Encyclopedia of Computer Science and Technology, 44,* 166-192.

IEEE. (1998) *IEEE Std 1061-1998 IEEE Standard for a software quality metrics methodology.*

ISO/IEC (1999) *ISO/IEC 14598-1: Software product evaluation - Part 1: General overview.*

Juristo, N., & Moreno, A. (2001). *Basics of software engineering experimentation.* Kluwer Academic Publishers.

Kitchenham, B. A., Pfleeger, S. L., Pickard, L. M., Jones P. W., Hoaglin, D. C., El-Emam, K., & Rosenberg, J. (2002). Preliminary guidelines for empirical research in Software Engineering. *IEEE Transactions on Software Engineering 28*(8), 721-734.

Kitchenham, B. (1996). *DESMET: A method for evaluating Software Engineering methods and tools.* Technical Report TR96-09, Department of Computer Science, University of Keele, Staffordshire, UK.

Park, R. E., Goethert, W. B., & Florac, W. A. (1996). *Goal-driven software measurement - a guidebook.* Technical Report CMU/SEI-96-HB-002, Software Engineering Institute.

Perry, D. E., Porter, A. A., & Votta L. G. (2000). Empirical studies of Software Engineering: a roadmap. In A. Finkelstein (Ed.), *The Future of Software Engineering,* 345-355. ACM Press.

Rakitin, S. R. (1997). *Software Verification and Validation, a practitioner's guide.* Artech House.

Shirazi, B., Welch, L. R., Ravindran, B., Cavanaugh, C., Yanamula, B., Brucks, R., & Huh, E. (1999). Dynbench: A dynamic benchmark suite for distributed real-time systems. In the *11ᵗʰ IPPS/SPDP'99 Workshops*,1335-1349. Springer-Verlag.

Sim, S., Easterbrook, S., & Holt, R. (2003). Using benchmarking to advance research: A challenge to software engineering. In the *25th International Conference on Software Engineering (ICSE'03)*,74-83. Portland, OR.

Spendolini, M. J. (1992). *The benchmarking book.* New York, NY: AMACOM.

Stefani, F., Macii, D., Moschitta, A., & Petri, D. (2003, June). FFT benchmarking for digital signal processing technologies. In the *17th IMEKO World Congress.* Dubrovnik, Croatia.

Sure, Y., & Corcho, O. (Ed.) (2003). Proceedings of the *2nd International Workshop on Evaluation of Ontology-based Tools (EON2003)*, 87 of CEUR-WS. Florida, USA.

Weiss, A. R. (2002). *Dhrystone benchmark: History, analysis, scores and recommendations.* White paper, EEMBC Certification Laboratories, LLC.

Wireman, T. (2003). *Benchmarking best practices in maintenance management.* Industrial Press.

Wohlin, C., Aurum, A., Petersson, H., Shull, F., & Ciolkowski, M. (2002, June). Software inspection benchmarking - a qualitative and quantitative comparative opportunity. In the *8th International Software Metrics Symposium,* 118-130.

ADDITIONAL READING

Ahmed, P., & Rafiq, M. (1998). Integrated benchmarking: a holistic examination of select techniques for benchmarking analysis. *Benchmarking for Quality Management and Technology* 5, 225-242.

Basili, V. R., Caldiera, G., & Rombach, D. H. (1994). The Goal Question Metric approach. *Encyclopedia of Software Engineering*, 528-532. Wiley.

Basili, V. R. (1993). The experimental paradigm in Software Engineering: Critical assessment and future directions. In the *International Workshop on Experimental Software Engineering Issues*, 3-12. Springer-Verlag.

Beitz, A., & Wieczorek, I. (2000). Applying benchmarking to learn from best practices. *Product Focused Software Process Improvement, Second International Conference (PROFES 2000)*, 59-72.

Brickley, D., Guha, R. V. (Ed.) (2004). *RDF Vocabulary Description Language 1.0: RDF Schema.* W3C Recommendation 10 February 2004.

Brown, A., & Wallnau, K. (1996). A framework for evaluating software technology. *IEEE Software, 13*, 39-49.

Corcho, O. (2005). *A layered declarative approach to ontology translation with knowledge preservation.* Volume 116 of Frontiers in Artificial Intelligence and its Applications. IOS Press.

Dongarra, J., Martin, J. L., & Worlton, J. (1987). Computer benchmarking: paths and pitfalls. *IEEE Spectrum, 24*(7), 38-43.

Duineveld, A. J., Stoter, R., Weiden, M. R., Kenepa, B., & Benjamins V. R. (1999). Wondertools? A comparative study of ontological engineering tools. In the *12ᵗʰ International Workshop on Knowledge Acquisition, Modeling and Management (KAW'99)*, Banff, Canada: Kluwer Academic Publishers.

Dujmovic, J. J., (1998). Evaluation and design of benchmark suites. Chapter 12 in *State-of-the-art in performance modeling and simulation: theory, techniques and tutorials*,287-323. Gordon and Breach Publishers.

Feitelson, D. G. (2005). *Experimental computer science:The Need for a Cultural Change*.

Fenton, N. (1991). *Software metrics - a rigorous approach*. Chapman & Hall.

Fenton, N., & Neil, M. (2000). Software metrics: Roadmap. In the *Conference on the future of Software Engineering*, 357-370. ACM Press.

Fernandez, P., McCarthy, I., & Rakotobe-Joel, T. (2001). An evolutionary approach to benchmarking. *Benchmarking: An International Journal, 8*, 281-305.

García-Castro, R. (2006). Benchmarking como herramienta de transferencia tecnológica Invited talk in the *3er Encuentro Internacional de Investigadores en Informática*. Popayán, Colombia.

García-Castro, R. (2006). Keynote: Towards the improvement of the Semantic Web technology. In the *Second International Workshop on Scalable Semantic Web Knowledge Based Systems (SSWS2006)*.

García-Castro, R., & Gómez-Pérez, A. (2006). Benchmark suites for improving the RDF(S) importers and exporters of ontology development tools. In the *3rd European Semantic Web Conference (ESWC2006)*, 155-169. LNCS-4011.

García-Castro, R., Gómez-Pérez, A. (2006). Interoperability of Protégé using RDF(S) as interchange language. In the *9th International Protégé Conference*.

García-Castro, R. (2006) Keynote: Tecnologías de la Web Semántica: cómo funcionan y cómo interoperan. In the *4th Seminario Internacional Tecnologías Internet*. Popayán, Colombia.

García-Castro, R., & Gómez-Pérez, A. (2005). A method for performing an exhaustive evaluation of RDF(S) importers. In the *Workshop on Scalable Semantic Web Knowledge Based Systems (SSWS2005)*.

García-Castro, R. (2005). *D2.1.5 prototypes of tools and benchmark suites for benchmarking ontology building tools*. Technical report, Knowledge Web.

Gee, D., Jones, K., Kreitz, D., Nevell, S., O'Connor, B., & Ness, B. V. (2001). Using performance information to drive improvement. *Performance-Based Management Special Interest Group, 6*.

Goodman, P. (1993). *Practical implementation of software metrics*. McGraw Hill.

Grady, R., & Caswell, D. (1987). *Software metrics: Establishing a company-wide program*. Prentice-Hall.

Jones, C. (1995, October). Software benchmarking. *IEEE Computer*, 102-103.

Kitchenham, B., Linkman, S., & Law, D. (1994). Critical review of quantitative assessment. *Software Engineering Journal, 9*, 43-53.

Kitchenham, B., Pfleeger, S., & Fenton, N. (1995). Towards a framework for software measurement validation. *IEEE Transactions on Software Engineering, 21*, 929-944.

Kraft, J. (1997). *The Department of the Navy benchmarking handbook: a systems view*. Department of the Navy.

Lankford, W. (2000). Benchmarking: understanding the basics. *Coastal Business Journal*.

Lukowicz, P., Tichy, W. F., Prechelt, L., & Heinz E.A. (1995). Experimental evaluation in computer science: A quantitative study. *The Journal of Systems and Software*, 28(1),1-18.

Manola, F., & Miller, E. (2004, February 10). *RDF Primer*. W3C Recommendation.

OntoWeb (2002). *D1.3: A survey on ontology tools*. Technical report, IST OntoWeb Thematic Network.

Pfleeger, S. L. (1999). Understanding and improving technology transfer in software engineering. *Journal of Systems and Software* 47,111-124.

Sim, S. (2003). *A theory of benchmarking with applications to software reverse engineering.* PhD thesis. University of Toronto.

Sole, T., & Bist, G. (1995). Benchmarking in technical information. *IEEE Transactions on Professional Communication* 38, 77-82.

Tichy, W. (1998). Should computer scientists experiment more? *Computer* 31, 32-40.

Wache, H., Serafini, L., & García-Castro, R. (2004). *D2.1.1 survey of scalability techniques for reasoning with ontologies.* Technical report, KnowledgeWeb.

Wireman, T. (2003). *Benchmarking best practices in maintenance management.* Industrial Press.

ENDNOTES

[a] http://knowledgeweb.semanticweb.org/

[b] http://knowledgeweb.semanticweb.org/benchmarking_interoperability/rdfs/

[c] http://kaon.semanticweb.org/

[d] http://protege.stanford.edu/

[e] http://webode.dia.fi.upm.es/

[f] http://www-sop.inria.fr/acacia/soft/corese/

[g] http://jena.sourceforge.net/

[h] http://www.openrdf.org/

[i] http://knowledgeweb.semanticweb.org/benchmarking_interoperability/rdfs/

[j] http://knowledgeweb.semanticweb.org/benchmarking_interoperability/rdfs/rdfs_import_benchmark_suite.html

[k] http://knowledgeweb.semanticweb.org/benchmarking_interoperability/rdfs/rdfs_export_benchmark_suite.html

[l] The names of the tools have been shortened in the heading of the table: KAON=K, Protégé=P and WebODE=W.

APPENDIX: QUESTIONS FOR DISCUSSION

Beginner:

1. Which are the main characteristics of benchmarking?
2. Which is the goal of the *Recalibration* task in the benchmarking methodology?
3. Which are the factors that influence the correct interchange of an ontology between two Semantic Web tools?
4. When exporting one ontology from an ontology development tool to RDF(S) having interoperability in mind, is it advisable to export the complete definition of all its components?

Intermediate:

1. Which are the differences between evaluation and benchmarking?
2. Are the users of the software involved in the benchmarking?
3. Is management support needed in the *Improve* phase of the methodology?
4. Which RDF(S) components can be represented in KAON, Protégé and WebODE?

Advanced:

1. Which resources are needed for performing a benchmarking activity?
2. Why are there three different evaluation criteria to define the results of the RDF(S) Import, Export and Interoperability benchmark suites?
3. Why is it not enough to have a single ontology representation language to achieve interoperability between the Semantic Web technologies?

Practical Exercises:

1. Select one conference paper that presents some evaluation or benchmarking approach and then evaluate its reusability according to the desirable properties of a benchmark suite and the recommendations given for software evaluation in benchmarking activities.
2. Create a mid-size ontology using one ontology development tool. Can you anticipate the consequences of exporting that ontology to RDF(S)? And of importing it into another ontology development tool?
3. Then, export the ontology to RDF(S). Was your prediction correct? Has it had information addition or loss?
4. Finally, import the exported ontology into the other ontology development tool. Was your prediction correct? Has it had information addition or loss?

ANSWERS TO THE QUESTIONS FOR DISCUSSION

Beginner:

1. The main characteristics of benchmarking are continuous improvement and the search for best practices.
2. The goal of the *Recalibration* task is to improve the benchmarking process by recalibrating it and applying the lessons learnt while performing it.
3. The factors that influence the correct interchange of an ontology between two tools are the combinations of components of the knowledge model of the ontology development tool and the naming of the components present in the ontology.
4. It is advisable to export the complete definition of all its components only for components commonly used by ontology development tools.

Intermediate:

1. Benchmarking is a continuous process, whereas an evaluation is a punctual activity. In addition, benchmarking involves evaluating software but its goals are to obtain a continuous improvement on the software and the practices used when developing the tools.
2. Yes, the users of the software are identified in the *Participant identification* task and in the *Findings communication* task.
3. Yes, it is needed to implement the necessary changes in the software and in the organisation processes affecting the software.
4. Classes, class hierarchies without cycles, datatype properties with a class as a domain and a string range, object properties with a domain and a range, instances of a single class, instances related by object properties, and instances related by datatype properties with a string range.

Advanced:

1. The resources needed are human resources though some equipment and travel resources are also required, and these are mainly used in three tasks: benchmarking organisation, experimentation definition and execution, and result analysis.
2. Because these three evaluation criteria are necessary to represent the different situations and behaviours that can occur when two tools interchange one ontology.
3. Because different types of users need different tools; existing tools have different knowledge representation models; and tools need to translate their ontologies from their knowledge models to the common ontology representation language.

Compilation of References

Aberer K., Catarci T. et al. (2004). Emergent semantics systems. *In Lecture Notes in Computer Science, 3226*, 14-43.

Aberer K., Cudre-Mauroux P., & Hauswirth, M. (2003). Start making sense: The chatty Web approach for global semantic agreements. *Journal of Web Semantics, 1*(1), 89-114.

Aberer, K., & Cudré-Mauroux, P., Datta, A., Despotovic, Z., Hauswirth, M., Punceva, M., & Schmidt. R. (2003). P-Grid: A self-organizing structured P2P system. *SIGMOD Record, 32*(3), 29-33.

Aberer, K., Cudré-Mauroux, P., Hauswirth, M., & Pelt, T.V. (2004). Gridvine: Building Internet-scale semantic overlay networks. In S. A. McIlraith, D. Plexousakis, F. van Harmelen (Eds.), *The Semantic Web – ISWC 2004: Third International Semantic Web Conference*, 107-121. Springer Verlag.

Abran, A., Moore, J. W., Bourque, P., & Dupuis, R. (Ed.). (2004). *SWEBOK: Guide to the software engineering body of knowledge*. IEEE Press.

Adida, B., & Birbeck, M. (2007). *Rdfa primer 1.0: Embedding RDF in XHTML*, W3C Working Draft 12 March 2007. Retrieved June 16, 2007, from http://www.w3.org/TR/xhtml-rdfa-primer/

Aduna (2007). *Sesame*. Retrieved June 26, 2007, http://www.openrdf.org/.

Agichtein, E., & Gravano, L. (2000). Snowball: Extracting relations from large plain-text collections. In *Proceedings of the fifth ACM international conference on digital libraries*.

Aleman-Meza, B., Bojars, U., Boley, H., Breslin, J. G., Mochol, M., Nixon, L. J. B., Polleres, A., & Zhdanova, A.V. (2007). Combining RDF vocabularies for expert finding. *Paper presented at the 4th European Semantic Web Conference*. Innsbruck, Austria.

Aleman-Meza, B., Nagarajan, M., Ramakrishnan, C., Ding, L., Kolari, P., Sheth, A.P., Arpinar, I.B., Joshi, A., & Finin, T. (2006). Semantic analytics on social networks: experiences in addressing the problem of conflict of interest detection. Paper presented at the *15th International World Wide Web Conference*. Edinburgh, Scotland.

Al-Sudani, S., Alhulou, R., Napoli, A., & Nauer, E. (2006). OntoBib: An ontology-based system for the management of a bibliography. Paper presented at the *17th European Conference on Artificial Intelligence*, Riva del Garcia, Italy.

Alves, A., Arkin, A., Askary, S., Bloch, B., Curbera, F., & Goland, Y. (2006). *Web services business process execution language (WS-BPEL) Version 2.0* (Committee Draft): Organization for the Advancement of Structured Information Standards (OASIS).

Amardeilh, F. (2006a). OntoPop or how to annotate documents and populate ontologies from texts. *Proceedings of the Workshop on Mastering the Gap: From Information Extraction to Semantic Representation (ESWC'06), CEUR Workshop Proceedings, 187*, Budva, Montenegro. Retrieved February 21, 2008, from http://ftp.informatik.rwth-aachen.de/Publications/CEUR-WS/Vol-187/11.pdf

Amardeilh, F., & Francart, T. (2004). A Semantic Web portal with HLT capabilities. *Actes du Colloque Veille Stratégique Scientifique et Technologique (VSST'04), 2*, 481-492, Toulouse, France.

Amardeilh, F., Carloni, O., & Noel, L. (2006b). PressIndex: A Semantic Web press clipping application. *Proceedings of the ISWC 2006 Semantic Web Challenge*, Athens, Georgia, USA.

Amardeilh, F., Laublet, P., & Minel, J.-L. (2005a). Annotation documentaire et peuplement d'ontologie à partir d'extractions linguistiques. Actes de la Conférence Ingénierie des Connaissances (IC'05), Nice, France, pp. 160-172.

Amardeilh, F., Laublet, P., & Minel, J.-L. (2005b). Document annotation and ontology population from linguistic extractions. *Proceedings of the International Conference on Knowledge Capture (KCAP'05)*, Banff, Canada, pp. 161-168.

Ambite, J. L., Ashish, N., Barish, G., Knoblock, C. A., Minton, S., Modi, P. J., Muslea, I., Philpot, A. & Tejada, S. (1998). *ARIADNE: A System for Constructing Mediators for Internet Sources, Proceedings of ACM SIGMOD.*

An, Y., Borgida, A., & Mylopoulos, J. (2005). Inferring complex semantic mappings between relational tables and ontologies from simple correspondences. In *ODBASE'05,* (pp.1152-1169).

Anagnostopoulos, C. B., Tsounis, A., & Hadjiefthymiades, S. (2007). Context awareness in mobile computing environments. *Wireless Personal Communications 42*(3), 445-464.

Anghel L., Alexandrescu, D., & Nicolaidis, M. (2000). Evaluation of a soft error tolerance technique based on time and/or space redundancy. In Proceedings of *13th Symposium on Integrated Circuits and Systems Design*, IEEE Computer Society, 237 – 242.

Antoniou G., & Bikakis A. (2005). DR-Prolog: A system for reasoning with rules and ontologies on the Semantic Web. *Proceedings From 25th American National Conference on Artificial Intelligence (AAAI)* (pp. 1594-1595), Pittsburgh, Pennsylvania: AAAI Press.

Antoniou, G., & Harmelen, F.V. (2004a). *A Semantic Web primer.* Massachusetts: The MIT Press.

Antoniou, G., Baldoni, M., Baroglio, C., Baumgartner, R., Bry, F., Eiter, T., Henze, N., Herzog, M., May, W., Patti, V., Schaffert, S., Schindlauer, R., & Tompits., H. (2004b). Reasoning methods for personalization on the Semantic Web. *Annals of mathematics, computing and teleinformatics, 2*(1), *1-24.*

Aperture: A Java framework for getting data and metadata, Last visited March 2007. http://aperture.sourceforge.net/.

Appel, W. P., & Behr, R. (1996). *Towards the theory of virtual organizations: A description of their forma-* tion and figure (Arbeitspapiere Wirtschaftsinformatik). Justus-Liebig-Universität Gießen Fachbereich Wirtschaftswissenschaften.

Athanasis, N., Christophides, V., & Kotzinos, D. (2004). Generating on the fly queries for the Semantic Web: The ICS-FORTH Graphical RQL interface (GRQL). In *LNCS, 3298*, 486-501.

Auer, S. & Lehmann, J. (2007). What have Innsbruck and Leipzig in common? Extracting semantics from Wiki content. *Paper presented at the Fourth European Semantic Web Conference.* Innsbruck, Austria.

Auer, S. (2005, May 30). Powl: A Web-based platform for collaborative Semantic Web development. In *Proceedings of the 1st Workshop on Scripting for the Semantic Web (SFSW05)*. Hersonissos, Crete, Greece.

Auer, S., & Herre, H. (2006, September 27-30). A versioning and evolution framework for RDF knowledge bases, in *Proc. of Sixth International Conference Perspectives of System Informatics*, Novosibirsk, Russia.

Auer, S., & Pieterse, B. (2005). "Vernetzte Kirche": Building a Semantic Web. In *Proceedings of ISWC Workshop Semantic Web case studies and best practices for E-Business (SWCASE05).*

Auer, S., Bizer, C., & Miller, L. (Eds.). (2005, May 30). *Proceedings of the 1st Workshop on Scripting for the Semantic Web (SFSW05).* Hersonissos, Crete, Greece (No. 135).

Auer, S., Bizer, C., Lehmann, J., Kobilarov, G., Cyganiak, R., & Ives, Z. (2007, November 11-15) DBpedia: A nucleus for a Web of open data. In Aberer et al. (Eds.): *The Semantic Web, 6th International Semantic Web Conference, 2nd Asian Semantic Web Conference, ISWC 2007 + ASWC 2007*, Busan, Korea. Lecture Notes in Computer Science 4825 Springer 2007, ISBN 978–3–540–76297–3.

Aumüller, D. (2005a, May). Semantic authoring and retrieval within a Wiki (Wik-SAR). In *Demo Session at the Second European Semantic Web Conference (ESWC2005).* Available at http://wiksar.sf.net.

Aumüller, D. (2005b). SHAWN: Structure helps a Wiki navigate. In *Proceedings of the BTW-Workshop "WebDB meets IR".*

Aussenac, N., & Seguela, P. (2000). Les relations sémantiques : Du linguistique au formel. *Cahiers de grammaire*, Numéro spécial « Sémantique et Corpus », *25*, 175-198 Presses de l'UTM, Toulouse.

Avizienis, A. (1995). The methodology of N-version programming. In M. R. Lyu (ed.), *Software fault tolerance*, Wiley, 23-46.

Axelrod R. (1997). The complexity of cooperation. Princeton University Press.

Baader, F., & Nutt, W. (2003). Basic description logics. In Baader, F., Calvanese, D., McGuiness, D., Nardi, D., & Patel-Schneider, P. (Eds.), *The Description Logics Handbook: Theory, Implementation and Applications*. 1st edition, *2*, 47-100. Cambridge, UK: Cambridge University Press.

Baader, F., Calvanese, D., MacGuinness, D.L., Nardi, D., & Patel-Schneider, P. (Eds.) (2003). *The description logic handbook: Theory, implementation, and applications*. United Kingdom: Cambridge University Press.

Baader, F., Calvanese, D., McGiuness, D., Nardi, D., & Patel-Schneider, P. (2003). *The description logic handbook: Theory, implementation, and applications*. Cambridge: Cambridge University Press.

Baader, F., Calvanese, D., McGuinness, D.L., Nardi, D., & Patel-Schneider, P.F. (2003). *The description logic handbook: Theory, implementation, applications*. Cambridge University Press.

Bahceci E., Soysal O., & Sahin E. (2003). *A review: Pattern formation and adaptation in multi-robot systems*. Report CMU-RI-TR-03-43, Robotics Institute, Carnegie Mellon University.

Bailey, J., Bry, F., Furche, T., & Schaffert, S. (2005). Web and Semantic Web query anguages: A survey. In J. Maluszinsky and N. Eisinger (Eds.), *Reasoning Web Summer School 2005*, (pp. 35–133). Springer-Verlag.

Baldoni, M., Baroglio, C., & Henze, N. (2005). Personalization for the Semantic Web, *Reasoning Web, first international summer school 2005, LNCS Tutorial, 3564*, 173-212, Msida, Malta: Springer.

Baldoni, M., Baroglio, C., & Patti, V. (2004). Web-based adaptive tutoring: An approach based on logic agents and reasoning about actions. *Artificial Intelligence Review, 1*(22), 3-39.

Balog, K., Mishne, G., & De Rijke, M. (2006). Why are they excited? Identifying and explaining spikes in blog mood levels. In *Conference companion of the 11th meeting of the European chapter of the association for computational linguistics (eacl 2006)* (pp. 207-210). Trento, Italy.

Bangsø, O., & Wuillemin, P.-H. (2000). *Object oriented Bayesian networks: A framework for topdown specification of large Bayesian networks and repetitive structures*. Technical Report No. CIT-87.2-00-obphwl. Department of Computer Science, Aalborg University, Aalborg, Denmark.

Baral. C. (2003). *Knowledge representation, reasoning and declarative problem solving*. Cambridge, UK: Cambridge University Press.

Barber, K., & Martin, C. (1999, May 1). Agent autonomy: Specification, measurement, and ydnamic adjustment. In *Proceedings of the Autonomy Control Software Workshop at Autonomous Agents 1999* (Agents '99), 8-15. Seattle,WA.

Barzdins, J., Barzdins, G., Balodis, R., Cerans, K., et.al. (2006). Towards semantic latvia. In *Communications of 7th International Baltic Conference on Databases and Information Systems* (pp.203-218).

Basili, V. R. (1985, September). Quantitative evaluation of software methodology. In *1st Pan-Pacific Computer Conference*, Melbourne, Australia.

Basili, V. R., & Selby, R. W. (1991). Paradigms for experimentation and empirical studies in software engineering. *Reliability Engineering and System Safety, 32*, 171-191.

Basili, V. R., Selby, R. W., & Hutchens, D. H. (1986). Experimentation in software engineering. *IEEE Transactions on Software Engineering, 12*(7), 733-743.

Bassiliades, N., Antoniou, G., & Vlahavas, I. (2004). *A defeasible logic system for the Semantic Web*. In Principles and Practice of Semantic Web Reasoning (2004), LNCS 3208 (pp. 134-148). St Malo, France: Springer.

Baumgartner, R., Henze, N., & Herzog, M. (2005). The personal publication reader: Illustrating Web data extraction, personalization and reasoning for the Semantic Web. *Lecture Notes in Computer Science, 3532. In 2005 European Semantic Web Conference (ESWC 2005)* (pp. 515-530). Heraklion, Greece: Springer.

Bechhofer, S., Goble, C., Carr, L., Kampa, S., & Hall, W. (2003). COHSE: Conceptual open hypermedia service. *Annotation for the Semantic Web*, Handschuh S., & Staab, S. (Eds.), Frontiers in artificial intelligence and applications, Volume 96, 193-211. IOS Press, Springer-Verlag.

Bechhofer, S., Harmelen, F. van, Hendler, J., Horrocks, I., McGuinness, D. L., Patel-Schneider, P. F., et al. (2004).

OWL Web ontology language reference. W3C Recommendation (http://www.w3.org/TR/owl-ref/).

Beckett, D. (2004). *Turtle - Terse RDF triple language.* Retrieved June 16, 2007, from http://www.dajobe.org/2004/01/turtle/.

Beckett, D., & Broekstra, J. (2006). *SPARQL query results XML format.* W3C. http://www.w3.org/TR/rdf-sparql-XMLres/

Benjamins, V.R., Contreras, J., Blázquez, M., Niño, M., García, A., Navas, E., Rodríguez, J., Wert, C., Millán, R., & Dodero, J.M. (2005). ONTO-H: A collaborative semiautomatic annotation tool. *Proceedings of the 8th International Protégé Conference.* Madrid, Spain.

Bergamaschi, S., Castano, S., Vincini, M., & Beneventano, D. (2001). Semantic integration and query of heterogeneous information sources. *Data & Knowledge Engineering, 36*(3), 215-249.

Berners-Lee, T. (1998). *Relational databases on the Semantic Web.* Retrieved December 15, 2007, from http://www.w3c.org/DesignIssues/RDB-RDF.html

Berners-Lee, T. (2007). Web Services - Semantic Web. Retrieved May, 2007 from http://www.w3.org/2003/Talks/05-gartner-tbl.

Berners-Lee, T., & Fischetti, M. (1999). *Weaving the Web – The original design and ultimate destiny of the World Wide Web by its inventor.* Harper San Francisco.

Berners-Lee, T., & Fischetti, M. (2000). *Weaving the Web: The original design and ultimate destiny of the World Wide Web by its inventor.* 1st edition. New York: HarperCollins Publishers.

Berners-Lee, T., et.al. (2006). Tabulator: Exploring and analyzing linked data on the Semantic Web. *LNCS, 4273,* 158-171.

Berners-Lee, T., Hendler, J., & Lassila, O. (2001). The Semantic Web. *Scientific American.*

Berners-Lee, T., Hendler, J., & Lassila, O. (2001, May 29-37). The Semantic Web. *Scientific American.*

Berners-Lee, T., Hendler, J., & Lassila, O. (2001, May). The Semantic Web. In *Scientific American.*

Bizer, C. (2003). D2R MRP - A database to RDF mapping language. *Paper presented at the Twelfth International World Wide Web Conference,* Budapest, Hungary.

Bizer, C., & Cyganiak, R. (2006). D2R server - Publishing releational databases on the Semantic Web. In *Poster at the 5th International Semantic Web Conference.* Retrieved December 15, 2007, from http://sites.wiwiss.fu-berlin.de/suhl/bizer/pub/Bizer-Cyganiak-D2R-Server-ISWC2006.pdf

Bizer, C., & Seaborne, A. (2004). D2RQ -treating non-RDF databases as virtual RDF graphs. *Poster at Third International Semantic Web Conference (ISWC2004).* Hiroshima, Japan.

Bizer, C., Cyganiak, R. (2008). *Publishing Databases on the Semantic Web.* Retrieved February, 2008 from http://www4.wiwiss.fu-berlin.de/bizer/d2r-server/publishing.

Bizer, C., Lee, R., & Pietriga, E. (2004). *Fresnel - Display vocabulary for RDF.*

Blackburn, P., & Bos, J. (2005). *Representation and inference for natural language. A first course in computational semantics.* CSLI.

Blomqvist, E., & Sandkuhl, K. (2005). Patterns in ontology engineering: Classification of ontology patterns. In *International Conference on Enterprise Information Systems (ICEIS2005), 3,* 413-416. Setubal: INSTICC.

Boer, V. de, Someren, M. van, & Wielinga, B. J. (2007). A redundancy-based method for the extraction of relation instances from the Web. *International Journal of Human-Computer Studies, 65*(9), 816-831.

Bonatti, P., & Tettamanzi, A. (2006). Some complexity results on fuzzy description logics. In Di Gesu, V., Masulli, F., & Petrosino, A. (Eds.), *Fuzzy logic and applications, 2955 of LNCS,* 19-24. Springer.

Bondavalli A., Chiaradonna, S., et al (1997). Discriminating fault rate and persistency to improve fault treatment. In *Digest of Papers. Twenty-Seventh Annual Intl. Symposium on Fault-Tolerant Computing,* 354-62.

Bondavalli A., Giandomenico F. D., & Grandoni, F. (2000). Threshold-based mechanisms to discriminate transient from intermittent faults. *IEEE Trans. on Computers, 49*(3), 230-45.

Bonifacio M., Bouquet P., et al. (2002). KEx: A peer-to-peer solution for distributed knowledge management. In Karagiannis D., & Reimer U.(Eds.) *Practical aspects of knowledge management, 4th International Conference, LCNS,* Springer, 490-500.

Borgida, A. (2007). Knowledge representation meets databases – A view of the symbiosis. In *Proceedings of the 20th international workshop on Description Logics.* CEUR Workshop Proceedings, *250*, 1-11. Retrieved December 15, 2007, from http://ceur-ws.org/Vol-250/invited_3.pdf

Borgida, A., & Brachman, R.J. (2003). *Conceptual modelling with description logics.* In (Baader, 2003), chapter *10*, 349-372.

Borgida, A., & Serafini, L. (2003). Distributed description logics: Assimilating information from peer sources. *Journal of Data Semantics, 2800/2003*, 153-184.

Borgida, A., Lenzerini, M., & Rosati, R. (2003). Description logics for data bases. In Baader, F., Calvanese, D., MacGuinness, D.L., Nardi, D., Patel-Schneider, P. (Eds.) (2003). *The Description Logic Handbook: Theory, Implementation, and aApplications* (pp. 472-494). United Kingdom: Cambridge University Press.

Bouquet P., Giunchiglia F., et al (2003). C-OWL: Contextualizing ontologies. In *2nd Intl. Semantic Web Conf.*, 2870, 164-179. Springer: LNCS.

Brachman, R. J. (1977). What's in a concept: Structural foundations for Semantic networks. *International Journal of Man-Machine Studies, 9*(2), 127-152.

Brambilla, M., Celino, I., Ceri, S., Cerizza, D., Della Valle, E., & Facca, F.M. (2006, November 5-9). A software engineering approach to design and development of Semantic Web service applications. In *The Semantic Web - ISWC 2006, 5th International Semantic Web Conference, ISWC 2006, Athens, GA, USA, Proceedings* (pp. 172-186). Springer.

Bray, T., Paoli, J., Sperberg-McQueen, C. M., Maler, E., & Yergeau, F. (2006). *Extensible Markup Language (XML) 1.0 (Fourth Edition)* (W3C Recommendation). Retrieved May, 2007 from http://www.w3.org/TR/xml/.

Brill, E. (1992). A simple rule-based part-of-speech tagger. In *Proceedings of the third conference on applied natural language processing (ANLP'92)* (pp. 152-155). Trento, Italy.

Brin, S. (1998). Extracting patterns and relations from the World Wide Web. *In Webdb workshop at sixth international conference on extending database technology (EDBT'98).*

Brin, S., & Page, L. (1998). The anatomy of a large-scale hypertextual Web search engine. *Computer Networks and ISDN Systems, 30*(1-7), 107-117.

Broekstra, J., Kampman, A., & van Harmelen, F. (2002). Sesame: A generic architecture for storing and querying RDF and RDF schema. *First International Semantic Web Conference*, No. *2342*, 54-68: Springer Verlag.

Brooks, C. H., & Montanez, N. (2006). Improved annotation of the blogosphere via autotagging and hierarchical clustering. *In Proceedings of the 15th international conference on world wide Web (www2006)* (pp. 625-632). Edinburgh, UK.

Brothwick, A. (1999). *A maximum entropy approach to named entity recognition.* Unpublished doctoral dissertation, New York University.

Brunkhorst, I., Chirita, P. A., Costache, S., Gaugaz, J., Ioannou, E., Iofciu, T., Minack, E., Nejdl, W., & Paiu. R. (2006). *The Beagle++ Toolbox: Towards an extendable desktop search architecture (Technical report)*, L3S Research Centre, Hannover, Germany.

Buckman, T. (2005). *NATO network enabled capability feasibility study: Executive summary.* (Executive Summary). Brussels, Belgium: NATO Consultation, Command and Control Agency (NC3A).

Buitelaar, P., Cimiano, P., & Magnini, B. (Eds.). (2005). Ontology learning from text: Methods, evaluation and applications, *123*. IOS Press.

Bull, J. M., Smith, L. A., Westhead, M. D., Henty, D. S., & Davey, R. A. (1999). A methodology for benchmarking Java grande applications. In the *ACM 1999 conference on Java Grande* (pp. 81-88).

Bunt, H., & Muskens, R. (Eds.). (2000). Computing meaning, *1*(73) Kluwer. Cafarella, M. J., Downey, D., Soderland, S., & Etzioni, O. (2005). Knowitnow: Fast, scalable information extraction from the Web. In *Proceedings of human language technology conference and conference on empirical methods in nlp* (pp. 563-570). Vancouver, Canada.

Buntine, W. L. (1994). *Learning with graphical models.* Technical Report No. FIA-94-03. NASA Ames Research Center, Artificial Intelligence Research Branch.

Bush, V. (1945, July). *As we may think.* The Atlantic Monthly.

Cali, A., Calvanese, D., Colucci, S., Di Noia, T., & Donini, F.M. (2004). *A description logic-based approach for matching user profiles*, In Volker Haarslev, Ralf Möller (Eds.), *Proceedings of the 2004 International Workshop on Description Logics (DL2004). 104*, 110-119. Whistler, British Columbia, Canada: CEUR.

CALO (2008). http://www.ai.sri.com/project/CALO

Calvanese, D., & De Giacomo, G. (2003). Expressive description logics. In Baader, F., Calvanese, D., McGuiness, D., Nardi, D., & Patel-Schneider, P. (Eds.), *The Description Logics Handbook: Theory, Implementation and Applications.* 1ˢᵗ edition, 5, 184-225. Cambridge, UK: Cambridge University Press.

Calvanese, D., De Giacomo, G., Lenzerini, M. (2001, August). Ontology of integration and integration of ontologies. In *Proceedings of the 9th International Conference on Conceptual Structures* (ICCS'01), Stanford, CA, USA, August 2001.

Cameron, D. (2007). *SEMEF: A taxonomy-based discovery of experts, expertise and collaboration networks.* MS Thesis, Computer Science Department, University of Georgia.

Cameron, D., Aleman-Meza, B., Decker, S., & Arpinar, I. B. (2007). SEMEF: *A taxonomy-based discovery of experts, expertise and collaboration networks.* (Tech. Rep. No. 1114806563). University of Georgia, Computer Science Department.

Camp, R. (1989). *Benchmarking: The search for industry best practices that lead to superior performance.* Milwaukee, ASQC Quality Press.

Carroll, J. J., Bizer, C., Hayes, P., & Sticker, P. (2005). Named graphs, provenance and trust, In A Ellis, T. Hagino (Eds.), *WWW 2005: The World Wide Web Conference,* 613-622.

Carroll, J.J., Klyne, G. (2004). *Resource description framework (RDF): Concepts and abstract Syntax* (W3C Recommendation). Retrieved May, 2007 from http://www.w3.org/TR/rdf-concepts/.

Castano S., Ferrara A., & Montanelli S. (2003). H-Match: An algorithm for dynamically matching ontologies in peer-based systems. In the *1st VLDB Int. Workshop on Semantic Web and Databases (SWDB),* 231-250.

Casteleyn, S., Plessers, & P., Troyer, O.D. (2006, *July 11-14).* Generating semantic annotations during the Web design process. In *Proceedings of the 6th international Conference on Web Engineering (Palo Alto, California, USA). ICWE '06* (pp. 91-92). ACM Press.

Catarci, T., & Lenzerini, M. (1993). Representing and using interschema knowledge in cooperative information systems. *Journal of Intelligent and Cooperative Information Systems, 2*(4), 375-398.

Ceri, S., Fraternali, P., Bongio, A., Brambilla, M., Comai, S., & Matera, M. (2002). *Designing data-intensive Web applications.* Morgan Kauffmann

Chang, C.-H., Kayed, M., Girgis, M. R., & Shaalan, K. F. (2006). A survey of Web information systems. *IEEE Transactions on Knowledge and Data Engineering, 18*(10), 1411-1428.

Charniak, E. (1991). Bayesian networks without tears. *AI Magazine,* 12, 50-63.

Chen, P. (1976). The entity-relationship model - Toward a unified view of data. *ACM Transactions on Database Systems, 1*(1), 9-36 .

Cheyer, A., Park, J., & Giuli, R. (2005, November 6). IRIS: Integrate. Relate. Infer. Share. In S. Decker, J. Park, D. Quan, L. Sauermann (Eds.), *Semantic Desktop Workshop at the International Semantic Web Conference,* Galway, Ireland, *175.*

Chinchor, N. A. (Ed.). (1998). *Proceedings of the seventh message understanding conference (muc-7).* Fairfax, Virginia: Morgan Kaufmann.

Chinnici, R., Haas, H., Lewis, A., A., Moreau, J., Orchard, D., & Weerawarana, S. (2007). *Web services description language (WSDL).* Version 2.0 Part 2: Adjuncts. W3C, http://www.w3.org/TR/wsdl20-adjuncts/

Chinnici, R., Moreau, J-J., Ryman, A., & Weerawarana, S. (2007). *Web services description language (WSDL) Version 2.0 Part 1: Core language* (W3C Proposed Recommendation). Retrieved May, 2007 from http://www.w3.org/TR/wsdl20/.

Cilibrasi, R., & Vitanyi, P. (2007). The Google similarity distance. *IEEE Transactions on Knowledge and Data Management, 19*(3), 370-383.

Cimiano, P. (2006). *Ontology learning and population from text: Algorithms, evaluation, and applications.* New York, NY, USA: Springer-Verlag.

Cimiano, P., & Staab, S. (2004). Learning by Googling. SIGKDD Explorations Newsletter, *6*(2), 24-33.

Cimiano, P., Handschuh, S., & Staab, S. (2004). Towards the self-annotating Web. *Proceedings of the 13th International World Wide Web Conference (WWW'04),* pp. 462-471. New York, USA: ACM Press

Ciravegna, F., & Wilks, Y. (2003). Designing adaptive information extraction for the semantic web in Amilcare. *Annotation for the Semantic Web,* Handschuh, S., &

Staab, S. (Eds.), Frontiers in Artificial Intelligence and Applications, Volume 96, IOS Press, Springer-Verlag, pp. 112-127.

Ciravegna, F., Chapman, S., Dingli, A., & Wilks, Y. (2004). Learning to harvest information for the Semantic Web. *Proceedings of the 1st European Semantic Web Symposium (ESWS'04)*, Springer-Verlag, Heraklion, Crete, Greece, pp. 312-326.

Ciravegna, F., Dingli, A., Petrelli, D., & Wilks, Y. (2002). User-system cooperation in document annotation based on information extraction. *Proceedings of the 13th International Conference on Knowledge Engineering and Management (EKAW'02)*, LNCS 2473, Springer-Verlag, Madrid, Spain, pp. 122-138.

Clark, K. (2006). *SPARQL Protocol for RDF* (W3C Candidate Recommendation). Retrieved May, 2007 from http://www.w3.org/TR/rdf-sparql-protocol/.

Clark, K. L. (1978). Negation as failure. In J. Minker (Ed.), *Logic and Data Bases*, Plenum Press, New York, 293-322.

Cockburn, A. (2000). Selecting a project's methodology. *IEEE Software, 17*(4).

Cockburn, A. (2004). *Crystal clear*. Addison-Wesley Professional.

Codd, E. F. (1970). A relational model for large shared data banks. *Communications of the ACM, 13*(6), 377-387.

Corcho, O., Fernández-López, M., & Gómez-Pérez, A. (2003). Methodologies, tools and languages for building ontologies: Where is their meeting point? *Data Knowledge Engineering, 46*(81), 41-64.

Costa, P. C. G. (2005). *Bayesian Semantics for the Semantic Web*. Doctoral dissertation. Department of Systems Engineering and Operations Research, George Mason University: Fairfax, VA, USA. p. 312.

Costa, P. C. G., & Laskey, K. B. (2006, November 9-11). PR-OWL: A framework for probabilistic ontologies. In *Proceedings of the International Conference on Formal Ontology in Information Systems (FOIS 2006)*. Baltimore, MD, USA.

Cowell, A.J., McGuinness, D.L., Varley, C.F., & Thurman, D.A. (2006). Knowledge-worker requirements for next generation query answering and explanation systems. In the *Proceedings of the Workshop on Intelligent User Interfaces for Intelligence Analysis, International Conference on Intelligent User Interfaces* (IUI 2006), Sydney, Australia.

Cox, S.J.D. (2006). *Observations and measurements*. OpenGIS Discussion Paper, OGC document 05-087r4.

Crescenzi, V., & Mecca, G. (2004). Automatic information extraction from large Web sites. *Journal of the ACM, 51*(5), 731-779.

Cristani, M., & Cuel, R. (2005). A survey on ontology creation methodologies. *International Journal on Semantic Web & Information Systems, 1*(2), 49-69.

Cunningham, H., Maynard, D., Bontcheva, K., & Tablan, V. (2002). Gate: A framework and graphical development environment for robust nlp tools and applications. In *Proceedings of the 40th annual meeting of the association for computational linguistics (acl 2002)*. Philadelphia, PA.

Cutrell, E., Robbins, D.C., Dumais, S.T., & Sarin, R. (2006, April 22-27). Fast, flexible filtering with PHLAT – Personal search and organization made easy. R. E. Grinter, T. Rodden, P. M. Aoki, E Cutrell, R. Jeffries, G. M. Olson (Eds.), *Proceedings of the 2006 Conference on Human Factors in Computing Systems,* CHI 2006, Montréal, Québec, Canada. ACM 2006, ISBN 1-59593-372-7.

d'Aquin, M., Sabou, M., & Motta, E., (2006). Modularization: A key for the dynamic selection of relevant knowledge components. *Paper presented at First International Workshop on Modular Ontologies, 232*, 15-28. Athens, Georgia, USA: CEUR.

Daelemans, W., & Bosch, A. van den. (2005). *Memory-based language processing*. Cambridge University Press.

Damasio, C. V., Analyti, A., Antoniou, G., & Wagner, G. (2006). Supporting open and closed world reasoning on the Web. In José Júlio Alferes, J. Bailey and U. Schwertel (Eds.), *Lecture Notes in Computer Science Vol. 4187*, 149–163. Budva, Montenegro: Springer.

Damasio, C., Pan, J., Stoilos, G., & Straccia, U. (2006). An approach to representing uncertainty rules in RuleML. In *Proceedings of the 2nd International Conference on Rules and Rule Markup Languages for the Semantic Web (RuleML-06)*. IEEE Computer Society. Available at http://2006.ruleml.org/online-proceedings/submission_24.pdf

Dave, D., & Lawrence, S. (2003). Mining the peanut gallery: Opinion extraction and semantic classification of product reviews. In *Proceedings of the twelfth international World Wide Web conference (www2003)* (pp. 519-528). Budapest, Hungary: ACM Press.

de Hoog, R., Benus, B., Vogler, M., & Metselaar, C. (1996). The commonKADS organization model: Content, usage and computer support. *Expert Systems with Applications, 11*(1), 1996.

De Moor, A., De Leenheer, P., & Meersman, R. (2006). DOGMA-MESS: A meaning evolution support system for interorganizational ontology engineering. In *14th International Conference on Conceptual Structures (ICCS 2006)*, pp. 189-202. Aalborg, Denmark: Springer.

De Virgilio, R., Torlone, R., & Houben, G.J. (In Press). Rule-based adaptation of Web information systems, *World Wide Web Journal*, Springer.

Decker, S. L., Aleman-Meza, B., Cameron, D., & Arpinar, I. B. (2007). *Detection of bursty and emerging trends towards identification of researchers at the early stage of trends.* (Tech. Rep. No. 11148065665). Computer Science Department, University of Georgia.

Decker, S., & Frank, M. (2004, May 18). The networked semantic desktop. In C. Bussler, S. Decker, D., Schwabe, O. Pastor (Eds.), *Proceedings of the WWW2004 Workshop on Application Design, Development and Implementation Issues in the Semantic Web*, New York, USA.

Del Rio, N., & Pinheiro da Silva, P. (2007, June). Identifying and explaining map imperfections through knowledge provenance visualization. *Technical report UTEP-CS-07-43a*, University of Texas at El Paso, El Paso, TX.

Del Rio, N., & Pinheiro da Silva, P. (2007a, November 26-28). Probe-It! Visualization support for provenance. In *Proceedings of the Third International Symposium on Visual Computing (ISVC 2007)*, Lake Tahoe, NV/CA.

Dent, L., Boticario, J., McDermott, J. et al. (1992). A personal learning apprentice. In *Proceedings of the 10 National Conference on Artificial Intelligence*, San Jose, California: AAAI Press, pp. 96-103.

Dietzold, S. (2005). *Generating RDF models from LDAP directories.*

Dill, S., Eiron, N., Gibson, D., Gruhl, D., Guha, R., Jhingran, A., Kanungo, T., Rajagopalan, S., Tomkins, A., Tomlin, J.A., & Zien, J.Y. (2003a). SemTag and Seeker: Bootstrapping the Semantic Web via automated semantic annotation. *Proceedings of the 12th International World Wide Web Conference (WWW'03)*, ACM Press, Budapest, Hungry, pp. 178-186.

Dill, S., Eiron, N., Gibson, D., Gruhl, D., Guha, R., Jhingran, A., Kanungo, T., Mccurley, K.S., Rajagopalan, S., & Tomkins, A. (2003b). A case for automated large-scale semantic annotation. *Journal of Web Semantics, Science, Services and Agents on the World Wide Web, 1*(1), 115-132. Elsevier.

Ding, Z. (2005). *BayesOWL: A probabilistic framework for Semantic Web*. Doctoral dissertation. Computer Science and Electrical Engineering. University of Maryland, Baltimore County: Baltimore, MD, USA. p. 168.

Ding, Z., & Peng, Y. (2004, January 5-8). A probabilistic extension to ontology language OWL. In *Proceedings of the 37th Annual Hawaii International Conference on System Sciences (HICSS'04)*. Big Island, Hawaii, USA.

Dingli, A. (2003a). Next generation annotation interfaces for adaptive information extraction. *Proceedings of the 6th Annual Computer Linguists UK Colloquium (CLUK'03)*, Edinburgh, UK.

Dingli, A., Ciravegna, F., & Wilks, Y. (2003b). Automatic semantic annotation using unsupervised information extraction and integration. *Proceedings of the Workshop on Knowledge Markup and Semantic Annotation (KCAP'03)*, Sanibel, Florida.

Dolby, J., Fokoue, A., Kalyanpur, A., Kershenbaum, A., Schonberg, E., & Srinivas, K. (2007). Scalable semantic retrieval through summarization and refinement. In *22nd AAAI Conference on Artificial Intelligence (AAAI-07)*, pp. 209-304. Vancouver, British Columbia: AAAI Press.

Dolog, P., Henze, N., Nejdl, W., & Sintek, M. (2004). The personal reader: Personalizing and enriching learning resources using Semantic Web technologies. In *Proceedings of the 3nd International Conference on Adaptive Hypermedia and Adaptive Web-Based Systems (AH 2004)*, LNCS 3137 (pp. 85–94). Eindhoven, The Netherlands: Springer.

Dong, X., & Halevy, A.Y. (2005). A platform for personal information management and integration. In M. Stonebraker, G. Weikum, D. DeWitt (Eds.), *Proceedings of 2005 Conference on Innovative Data Systems Research Conference*, 119-130

Downey, D., Broadhead, M., & Etzioni, O. (2007). Locating complex named entities in Web text. In *Proceedings of the twentieth international joint conference on artificial intelligence (ijcai'07)*. Hyderabad, India.

Downey, D., Etzioni, O., & Soderland, S. (2005). A probabilistic model of redundancy in information extraction. In *19th international joint conference on arti_cial intelligence (ijcai'05)* (pp. 1034-1041). Edinburgh, UK.

Dubois, D., & Prade, H. (1994). Can we enforce full compositionality in uncertainty calculi? *Proceedings AAAI-1994*, 149-154. AAAI Press.

Duda, R. O., Hart, P. E., & Stork, D. G. (2000). *Pattern classification*. Wiley-Interscience Publication.

Dumais, S., Banko, M., Brill, E., Lin, J., & Ng, A. (2002). Web question answering: Is more always better? *In Sigir '02: Proceedings of the 25th annual international acm sigir conference on research and development in information retrieval* (pp. 291-298). New York, NY, USA: ACM Press.

Dupont E., Nicolaidis M., & Rohr P. (2002). Embedded robustness IPs for transient-error-free ICs. *IEEE Design & Test, 19*(3), 56-70.

Dzbor, M., Motta, E., & Domingue, J.B. (2004). Opening up magpie via semantic services. In McIlraith et al. (eds), The Semantic Web - ISWC 2004, *Third International Semantic WebConference*. Hiroshima, Japan. *Lecture Notes in Computer Science*, 3298,Springer-Verlag.

Eiter, T., Ianni, G., Polleres, A., Schindlauer, R., & Tompits, H. (2006). Reasoning with rules and ontologies. In *Proceedings of Summer School Reasoning Web 2006* (pp. 93-127). Lisbon, Portugal: Springer.

Eiter, T., Lukasiewicz, T., Schindlauer, R., & Tompits, H. (2004). Combining answer set programming with description logics for the semantic Web. In *Proceedings KR-2004*, (pp. 141–151), TU Wien: Publisher.

Elmacioglu, E., & Lee, D. (2005). On six degrees of separation in DBLP-DB and more. *SIGMOD Record, 34*(2), 33-40.

Engelbart, D.C. (1962). *Augmenting human intellect: A conceptual framework (Summary report)*, Stanford Research Institute (SRI).

Etzioni, O., Cafarella, M. J., Downey, D., Popescu, A., Shaked, T., Soderland, S., et al. (2005). Unsupervised named-entity extraction from the Web: An experimental study. *Artificial Intelligence, 165*(1), 91-134.

Euzenat, J. (2005). L'annotation formelle de documents en 8 questions. *Ingénierie des connaissances*, Teulier R., Charlet J & Tchounikine P. (Eds.), L'Harmattan, Paris, pp. 251-271.

Fagin, R., Guha, R., Kumar, R., Novak, J., Sivakumar, D., & Tomkins, A. (2005). Multi-structural databases. *Paper presented at the Twenty-Fourth ACM Symposium on Principles of Database Systems*, Baltimore, Maryland, USA.

Fellbaum, C. (Ed.) (1998). *Wordnet - An electronic lexical database*. MIT Press.

Feng, J. Q., Smith, J. S., Wu, Q. H., & Fitch, J. (2005). Condition assessment of power system apparatuses using ontology systems. In *Transmission and Distribution Conference*, pp. 1-6. Dalian, China: IEEE/PES.

Feng, J. Q., Wu, Q. H., & Fitch, J. (2004). An ontology for knowledge representation in power systems. In *Control 2004 Conference, 35*, 1-5. University of Bath, UK.

Fensel, D., Lausen, H., Polleres, A., de Bruijn, J., Stollberg, M., Roman, D., & Domingue, J. (2006). *Enabling Semantic Web services: The Web service modeling ontology*. New York: Springer-Verlag.

Fensel, D., Motta, E., Harmelen, F. van, Benjamins, V. R., Crubezy, M., Decker, S., et al. (2003). The unified problem-solving method development language UPML. *Knowl. Inf. Syst, 5*(1), 83-131.

Fergus P., Mingkhwan A., et al. (2003). Distributed emergent semantics in P2P networks. In *Second IASTED Intl. Conf. on Information and Knowledge Sharing*,75-82.

Fernandez, M., Perez, G. A., & Juristo, N. (1997). METHONTOLOGY: From ontological art towards ontological engineering. *Proceedings of the AAAI97 Spring Symposium Series on Ontological Engineering, Stanford. USA*, 1997.

Fernandez, Y. B., Arias, J. J. P., Nores, M. L., Solla, A. G., & Cabrer, M. R. (2006). AVATAR: An improved solution for personalized TV based on semantic inference, *IEEE Transactions on Consumer Electronics* (pp. 223-231). IEEE Consumer Electronics Society.

Fernandez-Lopez, M. (1999). Overview of methodologies for building ontologies. In IJCAI99 Workshop on Ontologies and Problem-Solving Methods: Lessons Learned and Future Trends.

Fernández-López, M. (1999). Overview of methodologies for building ontologies. In *IJCAI Workshop on Ontologies and Problem-Solving Methods*, pp. 1-12. Stockholm, Sweden: CEUR Publications.

Fernández-López, M., Gómez-Pérez, A., & Juristo, N. (1997). Methontology: From ontological art towards ontological engineering. In *AAAI Spring Symposium on Ontological Engineering*, pp 33-40. Stanford: AAAI Press.

Ferraiolo, J., Jun, F., & Jackson, D. (2003). Scalable vector graphics (SVG) 1.1 Specification (W3C Recommendation). Retrieved May, 2007 from http://www.w3.org/TR/SVG11/.

Fielding, R.T. (2000). *Architectural styles and the design of network-based software architectures*. Doctoral dissertation, University of California, Irvine, CA, USA.

Finkel, J. R., Grenager, T., & Manning, C. D. (2005). Incorporating non-local information into information extraction systems by Gibbs sampling. In *Proceedings of the 43rd annual meeting of the association for computational linguistics (acl 2005)*. Ann Arbor ,MI.

Foster, I., Kesselman, C., Nick, J., & Tuecke, S. (Eds.) (1999). *The grid: Blueprint for a new computing infrastructure*. San Francisco, CA, USA: Morgan-Kaufmann Publishers Inc.

Frege, G. (1879). *Begriffsschrift*, 1879, translated in Jean van Heijenoort, ed., *From Frege to Gödel*, Cambridge, MA: Harvard University Press.

Freimut, B., Punter, T., Biffl, S., & Ciolkowski, M. (2002). *State-of-the art in empirical studies*. Technical Report ViSEK/007/E, Visek.

Fuchs, F., & Berger, M. (2006). Towards scalable retrieval of distributed and dynamic ontology instances. In *5th International Semantic Web Conference (ISWC), Workshop Scalable Semantic Web Knowledge Base Systems*, pp. 89-100. Athens, GA, USA: Springer LNCS 4273.

Fuchs, F., Henrici, S., Pirker, M., Berger, M., Langer, G., & Seitz C. (2006). Towards semantics-based monitoring of large-scale industrial systems. In *Conference on Computational Intelligence for Modelling, Control and Automation*, pp. 261-266. Sydney: IEEE Computer Society.

Fuchs, F., Lewis, R., Pirker, M., Roberts, C., Berger, M., & Langer, G. (2006). Applying semantic technologies to railway decision support. In *Semantics 2006 International Conference*, pp. 217-227.Vienna: Oesterreichische Computer Gesellschaft.

Fukushige, Y. (2004). Representing probabilistic knowledge in the Semantic Web, *W3C Workshop on Semantic Web for Life Sciences*. Cambridge, MA, USA.

Furche, T., Linse, B., Bry, F., Plexousakis, D., & Gottlob, G. (2006). RDF querying: Language constructs and evaluation methods compared. In *Proceedings of Summer School Reasoning Web 2006*, Lisbon (pp. 1–52). Springer.

Gal, A. (2001). Semantic interoperability in information services: Experiencing with CoopWARE. *SIGMOD Record, 28*(1), 68-75.

Gandon, F. (2001). Engineering an ontology for a multi-agent corporate memory system. *Paper presented at the Eighth International Symposium on the Management of Industrial and Corporate Knowledge*. Université de Technologie de Compiègne, France.

García-Castro, R., & Gómez-Pérez, A. (2005, November). Guidelines for benchmarking the performance of ontology management APIs. In Y. Gil, E. Motta, R. Benjamins, & M. Musen (Ed.), *4th International Semantic Web Conference (ISWC2005)*, 3729 in LNCS, 277-292. Galway, Ireland: Springer-Verlag.

García-Castro, R., Maynard, D., Wache, H., Foxvog, D., & González-Cabero, R. (2004). *D2.1.4 Specification of a methodology, general criteria and benchmark suites for benchmarking ontology tools*. Technical report, Knowledge Web.

García-Castro, R., Sure, Y., Zondler, M., Corby, O., Prieto-González, J., Paslaru Bontas, E., Nixon, L., & Mochol, M. (2006). *D1.2.2.1.1 Benchmarking the interoperability of ontology development tools using RDF(S) as interchange language*. Technical report, Knowledge Web.

Garcia-Molina, H., Papakonstantinou, Y., Quass, D., Rajaraman, A., Sagiv, Y., Ullman, J., & Widom, J. (1997). The TSIMMIS project: Integration of heterogeneous information sources. *Journal of Intelligent Information Systems*.

Gardiner, T., Tsarkov, D., & Horrocks, I. (2006). Framework for an automated comparison of description logic reasoners. In *5th International Semantic Web Conference (ISWC)*, pp. 654-667. Athens, GA, USA: Springer LNCS 4273.

Gartner, G., Frank, A., & Retscher, G. (2004). Pedestrian navigation system for mixed indoor/outdoor environments - The NAVIO project. In: Schrenk, M. (Ed.): *Proceedings of the CORP 2004 and Geomultimedia04 Symposium* (pp. 165-171). Vienna, Austria.

Gebhardt, A. (2003). *Rapid prototyping*. Hanser Gardner Pubns.

Gediga, G., Hamborg, K., & Duntsch, I. (2002). Evaluation of software systems. In *Encyclopedia of Computer Science and Technology, 44*, 166-192.

Geleijnse, G., & Korst, J. (2005). *Automatic ontology population by googling*. In K. Verbeeck,

Geleijnse, G., & Korst, J. (2006). Learning effective surface text patterns for information extraction. In *Proceedings of the eacl 2006 workshop on adaptive text extraction and mining (atem 2006)* (pp. 1-8). Trento, Italy: Association for Computational Linguistics.

Geleijnse, G., & Korst, J. (2007). Creating a dead poets society: Extracting a social network of historical persons from the Web. In K. Aberer et al. (Eds.), *Proceedings of the Sixth International Semantic Web Conference and the Second Asian Semantic Web Conference (iswc + aswc 2007), Busan, Korea, 4825 of Lecture Notes in Computer Science (LNCS)*, pp 156-168). Heidelberg, Germany: Springer.

Geleijnse, G., Korst, J., & De Boer, V. (2006). Instance classification using co-occurrences on the Web. In *Proceedings of the iISWC 2006 Workshop on Web Content Mining with Human Language Technologies (Webconmine)*. Athens, GA. (http://orestes.ii.uam.es/workshop/3.pdf)

Geleijnse, G., Schedl, M., & Knees, P. (2007). The quest for ground truth in musical artist tagging in the social Web era. In S. Dixon, D. Bainbridge, & R. Typke (Eds.), *Proceedings of the Eighth International Conference on Music Information Retrieval (ismir'07)* (pp. 525-530). Vienna, Austria: Austrian Computer Society.

Gemmell, J., Bell, G., Lueder, R., Drucker, S., & Wong, C. (2002, December 1-6). MyLifeBits: Fulfilling the memex vision. In *ACM Multimedia*, Juan-les-Pins, France, 235–238.

Getoor, L., Friedman, N., Koller, D., & Pfeffer, A. (2001). *Learning probabilistic relational models*. New York, NY, USA: Springer-Verlag.

Getoor, L., Koller, D., Taskar, B., & Friedman, N. (2000). Learning probabilistic relational models with structural

uncertainty. *Paper presented at the ICML-2000 Workshop on Attribute-Value and Relational Learning:Crossing the Boundaries*. Stanford, CA, USA.

Ghidini, C., & Giunchiglia, F. (2001). Local models semantics, or contextual reasoning = Locality + Compatibility. *Artificial Intelligence Archive, 127*(2), 221-259.

Gifford, D.K., Jouvelot, P., Sheldon, M.A., & O'Toole, J.W. Jr. (1991, October). Semantic file systems. In 13th *ACM Symposium on Operating Systems Principles*.

Gilks, W., Thomas, A., & Spiegelhalter, D. J. (1994). A language and program for complex Bayesian modeling. *The Statistician, 43*, 169-178.

Giugno, R., & Lukasiewicz, T. (2002, September 23-26). P-SHOQ(D): A probabilistic extension of SHOQ(D) for probabilistic ontologies in the Semantic Web. In Flesca, S.; Greco, S.; Leone, N.; and Ianni, G. (Eds.), *Proceedings of the Eight European Conference on Logics in Artificial Intelligence (JELIA 2002)* Cosenza, Italy (LNCS 2424, pp. 86-97). Berlin, Germany: Springer-Verlag.

Glass, A., McGuinness, D., & Wolverton, M. (2008). Toward establishing trrust in adaptive agents. In *Proceedings of the International Conference on Intelligent User Interfaces (IUI'08)*, Gran Canaria, Spain. Also, KSL Technical Report KSL-07-04.

Glushko, R. J., & McGrath, T. (2005). Document engineering, Cambridge, Massachusetts: The MIT Press.

Golbeck, J., Katz, Y., Krech, D., Mannes, A., Wang, T. D., & Hendler, J. (2006). PaperPuppy: Sniffin the trail of Semantic Web publications. *Paper presented at the Fifth International Semantic Web Conference,* Athens, Georgia, USA.

Golder, S., Huberman, B. A. (2006). Usage patterns of collaborative tagging systems. *Journal of Information Science, 32*(2), 198-208.

Goldfarb, C.F. (1991). *The SGML handbook*. New York, USA: Oxford University Press.

Gomez-Perez, A., Fernandez-Lopez, M., & Corcho, O. (2003). Ontological engineering. London: Springer Publishing.

Graham, S., Hull, D., & Murray, B. (2006). *Web services base notification 1.3 (WS-BaseNotification)* (Public Review Draft): Organization for the Advancement of Structured Information Standards (OASIS).

Grosof, B. N., Horrocks, I., Volz, R., & Decker, S. (2003). *Description logic programs: Combining logic programs with description logic.* In *Twelfth International World Wide Web Conference (WWW 2003)* (pp. 48-57). Budapest, Hungary: ACM.

Grosso, W., Eriksson, H., Fergerson, R., Gennari, J., Tu, S., & Musen, M. (1999). Knowledge modeling at the millennium (the design and evolution of Protégé-2000. In *Proceedings of the Twelfth Workshop on Knowledge Acquisition, Modeling and Management.*

Gruber, T. R. (1993). A translation approach to portable ontologies. *Knowledge Acquisition, 5*(2), 199-220.

Gruber, T. R. (1993). A translation approach to portable ontology specifications. *Knowledge Acquisition Archive, 5*(2), 199-220.

Gruber, T.R. (1995). Toward principles for the design of ontologies used for knowledge sharing. In *International Journal of Human-Computer Studies, 43*, 907-928.

Gruninger, M., & Fox, M. S. (1995). Methodology for the design and evaluation of ontologies. *Proceedings of the Workshop on Basic Ontological Issues in Knowledge Sharing, International Joint Conference on Artificial Intelligence*, Montreal, Canada, 1995.

Guarino, N. (1998). Formal ontology and information systems. *Proceedings of Formal Ontology in Information Systems, 3*-15.

Gudgin, M., Hadley, M., Mendelsohn, N., Moreau, J-J., & Nielsen, H. F. (2007). *SOAP Version 1.2 Part 1: Messaging framework (Second Edition)* (W3C Recommendation). Retrieved May, 2007 from http://www.w3.org/TR/soap12-part1/.

Guha, R., & McCool, R. (2003). Tap: A Semantic Web platform. *Computer Networks, 42*(5), 557-577.

Gusfield, D. (1997). Algorithms on strings, trees, and sequences: Computer science and computational biology. Cambridge, UK: Cambridge University Press.

Gutierrez, C., Hurtado, C., & Vaisman, A. (2005). Temporal RDF. *The Semantic Web: Research and Applications, Second European Semantic Web Conference, ESWC 2005. Proceedings Lecture Notes in Computer Science, 3532,* 93-107

Haarslev, V., & & Möller, R. (2001). *RACER system description. Hamburg*, Germany: University of Hamburg, Computer Science Department.

Haarslev, V., & Möller, R. (2001, June 18-23). RACER system description. In R. Goré, A. Leitsch, & T. Nipkow (Eds.), *International Joint Conference on Automated Reasoning, IJCAR'2001*, Siena, Italy (pp. 701-705). Springer-Verlag.

Haase P., Broekstra J., et al. (2004). Bibster -- A semantics-based bibliographic peer-to-peer system. In *Third Intl. Semantic Web Conf. (ISWC)*, 122-136.

Haase, P., Broekstra, J., Eberhart, A., & Volz, R. (2004, November 7-11). A comparison of RDF query languages. In *Proceedings of the third International Semantic Web Conference, Hiroshima, Japan,* (pp. 502–517). Springer.

Habert, B. (2005). *Instruments et ressources électroniques pour le français*, Collection «L'essentiel Français», Ophrys, Paris, p. 169

Hájek, P. (1998). *Metamathematics of fuzzy logic.* Kluwer.

Hájek, P. (2005). Making fuzzy description logics more expressive. *Fuzzy Sets and Systems, 154*(1), 1-15.

Hájek, P. (2006). What does mathematical fuzzy logic offer to description logic? In Sanchez, E. (Ed.), *Capturing Intelligence: Fuzzy Logic and the Semantic Web.* Elsevier.

Halevy A., Ives Z., et al. (2003). Piazza: Mediation and integration infrastructure for Semantic Web data. *In the Intl. Worldwide Web Conf. WWW-03.*

Handschuh, S. (2005). *Creating ontology-based metadata by annotation for the Semantic Web.* PhD Thesis, Karlsruhe University, p. 225.

Handschuh, S., Staab, S., & Ciravegna, F. (2002). S-CREAM - Semi-automatic creation of metadata. *Proceedings of the 13th International Conference on Knowledge Engineering and Management (EKAW'02)*, LNCS 2473, Springer-Verlag, Madrid, Spain.

Handschuh, S., Staab, S., & Maedche, A. (2001). CREAM - Creating relational metadata with a component-based, ontology-driven annotation. *Proceedings of the Knowledge Capture Conference (KCAP'01)*, Banff, Canada, pp. 76-83.

Happel, H.-J., & Seedorf, S. (2006). *Applications of ontologies in software engineering. Paper presented at Workshop on Semantic Web Enabled Software Engineering (SWESE) on the 5th International Semantic Web Conference (ISWC 2006)*, Athens, Georgia, USA.

Hearst, M. (1992). Automatic acquisition of hyponyms from large text corpora. In *Proceedings of the 14th Conference on Computational Linguistics* (pp. 539-545). Nantes, France.

Hearst, M. (1998). Automated discovery of wordnet relations. In C. Fellbaum (Ed.), *Wordnet: An Electronic Lexical Database*. Cambridge, MA: MIT Press.

Heckerman, D., Mamdani, A., & Wellman, M. P. (1995). Real-world applications of Bayesian networks. *Communications of the ACM, 38*(3), 24-68.

Heckerman, D., Meek, C., & Koller, D. (2004). *Probabilistic models for relational data*. Technical Report MSR-TR-2004-30, Microsoft Corporation, March 2004. Redmond, WA, USA.

Heflin, J., & Hendler, J. A. (2001). A portrait of the Semantic Web in action. *IEEE Intelligent Systems, 16*(2), 54-59. IEEE.

Heinsohn, J. (1994, July 29-31). Probabilistic description logics. *Paper presented at the Tenth Conference on Uncertainty in Artificial Intelligence (UAI-94)*. Seattle, WA, USA.

Hendler, J. (2001, March/April). Agents and the Semantic Web. *IEEE Intelligent Systems, 16*(2), 30--37.

Henze, N., & Herrlich, M. (2004a). The personal reader: A framework for enabling personalization services on the Semantic Web. In *Proceedings of the Twelfth GI-Workshop on Adaptation and User Modeling in Interactive Systems (ABIS 04)*, Berlin, Germany.

Henze, N., & Kriesell, M. (2004b). Personalization functionality for the Semantic Web: Architectural outline and first sample implementations. In *Proccedings of the 1st International Workshop on Engineering the Adaptive Web (EAW 2004)*, co-located with AH 2004, Eindhoven, The Netherlands.

Hepp, M. (2007). Possible ontologies: How reality constrains the development of relevant ontologies. *IEEE Internet Computing, 11*(1), 90-96.

Hepp, M., & Bruijn, J. (2007). GenTax: A generic methodology for deriving OWL and RDF-S ontologies from hierarchical classification, thesauri, and inconsistent taxonomies. *LNCS, 4519*, 129-144.

Hezinger, M., & Lawrence, S. (2004). Extracting knowledge from the World Wide Web, *PNAS 101*(supplement 1), 5186-5191

Hirsch, J. E. (2005). An index to quantify an individual's scientific research output. *PNAS 102*(46), 16569-16572.

Hölldobler, S., Khang, T. D., & Störr, H.-P. (2002). A fuzzy description logic with hedges as concept modifiers. In *Proceedings InTech/VJFuzzy-2002, 25-34*.

Hölldobler, S., Nga, N. H., & Khang, T. D. (2005). The fuzzy description logic ALC_{FLH}. In *Proceeedings DL-2005*.

Horridge, M., Knublauch, H., Rector, A., Stevens, R., & Wroedn, S. (2004). *A practical guide to building OWL ontologies using the Protégé-OWL plugin and CO-ODE tools*. The University of Manchester. Retrieved June 9, 2007, from http://www.co-ode.org.

Horrocks, I. (1998). The fact system. In H. de Swart (Ed.), *Automated Reasoning With Analytic Tableaux and Related Methods: International Conference Tableaux '98* (pp. 307-312). Springer-Verlag.

Horrocks, I. (2002). DAML+OIL: A reasonable Web ontology language. Keynote talk at the WES/CAiSE Conference. Toronto, Canada.

Horrocks, I., & Sattler, U. (2001, August 4-10). Ontology reasoning in the SHOQ(D) description logic. In *Proceedings of the Seventeenth International Joint Conference on Artificial Intelligence (IJCAI 2001)*. Seattle, WA, USA.

Horrocks, I., Li, L., Turi, D., & Bechhofer, S. (2004a). *The instance store: DL reasoning with large numbers of individuals*. In *Proc. Of the 2004 Description Logic Workshop (DL-2004)*, (pp. 31-40). Whistler, British Columbia, Canada

Horrocks, I., Patel-Schneider, P. F., Boley, H., Tabet, S., Grosof, B., & Dean, M. (2003). SWRL: A Semantic Web rule language combining OWL and RuleML. http://www.daml.org/2003/11/swrl/.

Horrocks, I., Patel-Schneider, P.F., Boley, H., Tabet, S., Grosof, B., & Dean, M. (2004b). *SWRL: A Semantic Web rule language combining OWL and RuleML*, W3C Member Submission, 21 May 2004. Retrieved June 13, 2007, from http://www.w3.org/Submission/SWRL/.

HP (2007). *Jena a Semantic Web framework for Java*. Retrieved June 26, 2007, http://jena.sourceforge.net.

Hurtado, C., & Vaisman, A. (2006). Reasoning with temporal constraints in RDF. *Principles and Practice of Semantic Web Reasoning. 4th International Workshop, PPSWR 2006. Revised Selected Papers Lecture Notes in Computer Science,. 4187,*164-78.

Hustadt, U., Motik, B., & Sattler, U. (2004). Reducing SHIQ⁻ description logic to disjunctive datalog programs. In *9th International Conference on Knowledge Representation and Reasoning (KR2004)*, pp. 152-162. Whistler, BC, Canada: AAAI Press.

Huynh, D., Mazzocchi, S., Karger, D. (2005, November 6-10). Piggy bank: Experience the Semantic Web inside your Web browser. In Gil et al. (eds), *The Semantic Web - ISWC 2005, 4th International Next Generation Semantic Web Applications ISWC 2005*. Galway, Ireland. *Lecture Notes in Computer Science*, 3729 Springer-Verlag.

Hyvönen, E., Mäkelä, E., Salminen, M., Valo, A., Viljanen, K., Saarela, S., Junnila, M., & Kettula, S. (2005). MuseumFinland - Finnish museums on the Semantic Web. *Journal of Web Semantics, 3*(2), 25.

Hyvonen, E., Viljanen, K., Makela, E., et al. (2007). Elements of a National Semantic Web infrastructure - Case study Finland on the Semantic Web. In *Proceedings of the First International Semantic Computing Conference (IEEE ICSC 2007)*, IEEE Press.

IEEE. (1998) *IEEE Std 1061-1998 IEEE Standard for a software quality metrics methodology.*

ISO/IEC (1999) *ISO/IEC 14598-1: Software product evaluation - Part 1: General overview.*

Jaeger, M. (1994, May 24-27). Probabilistic reasoning in terminological logics. *Paper presented at the Fourth International Conference on Principles of Knowledge Representation and Reasoning* (KR94). Bonn, Germany.

Jaeger, M. (1997, August 1-3). Relational Bayesian networks. *Paper presented at the 13th Annual Conference on Uncertainty in Artificial Intelligence (UAI-97)*. Providence, RI, USA.

Jaeger, M. (2006). Probabilistic role models and the guarded fragment. In *Proceedings IPMU-2004*, pp. 235–242. Extended version in *Int. J. Uncertain. Fuzz., 14*(1), 43-60.

Jang, M., & Sohn, J-C. (2004). Bossam: An extended rule engine for OWL inferencing. Hiroshima, Japan: In *Workshop on Rules and Rule Markup Languages for the Semantic Web at the 3rd International Semantic Web Conference* (LNCS 3323), (pp. 128-138). Hirosima, Japan: Springer-Verlag.

Janik, M., & Kochut, K. (2005). BRAHMS: A work-Bench RDF store and high performance memory system for semantic association discovery. *Paper presented at the Fourth International Semantic Web Conference*. Galway, Ireland.

Jena, A. *Semantic Web framework for java*, Retrieved June 13, 2007, from http://jena.sourceforge.net/

Jess, The rule engine for the Java Platform, Retrieved June 13, 2007, from http://www.jessrules.com/jess/index.shtml

Jin, Y., Decker, S., & Wiederhold, G. (2001, July 30-August 1). OntoWebber: Model-Driven ontology-based Web site management. In I.F. Cruz, S. Decker, J. Euzenat, & D.L. McGuinness (Eds.), *Proceedings of SWWS'01, The First Semantic Web Working Symposium,* Stanford University, California, USA. (pp. 529–547)

Jin, Y., Matsuo, Y., & Ishizuka, M. (2006). Extracting a social network among entities by Web mining. In *Proceedings of the ISWC 2006 Workshop on Web Content Mining with Human Language Technologies (Webconmine)*. Athens, GA.

Jones, D.M., Bench-Capon, T.J.M., & Visser, P.R.S. (1998). Methodologies for ontology development. In *15th World Computer Congress, Conference on Information Technology and Knowledge Systems*. Budapest: IFIP.

Jurafsky, D., & Martin, J. H. (2000). *Speech and language processing*. Prentice Hall.

Juristo, N., & Moreno, A. (2001). *Basics of software engineering experimentation*. Kluwer Academic Publishers.

Kahan, J., Koivunen, M.R., Prud'Hommeaux, E., & Swick, R. (2001). Annotea: An open RDF infrastructure for shared Web annotations. *Proceedings of the 10ᵗʰ International World Wide Web Conference (WWW'01)*, ACM Press, Hong-Kong, pp. 623-632.

Kalyanpur, A., Parsia, B., Sirin, E., Cuenca-Grau, B., & Hendler, J. (2005). Swoop: A 'web' ontology editing browser. *Journal of Web Semantics, 4*(2).

Karvonen, K. (2000). The beauty of simplicity. In J. Scholtz & J. Thomas (Eds.), *Proceedings of the 2000 Conference on Universal Usability (CUU-00,)* (pp. 85-90). NY: ACM Press.

Karvounarakis, G., Magkanaraki, A., Alexaki, S., Christophides, V., Plexousakis, D., Scholl, M., & K. Tolle (2004). RQL: A functional query language for RDF. In Gray, P., King, P., & Poulovassilis, A. (Eds.),

The Functional Approach to Data Management (pp. 435–465). Springer-Verlag.

Kashyap, V., Ramakrishnan, C., Thomas, C., & Sheth, A. (2005, September). TaxaMiner: An experimental framework for automated taxonomy bootstrapping. *International Journal of Web and Grid Services.*

Kautz, H., Selman, B., & Shah, M. (1997). The hidden web. *AI Magazine, 18*(2), 27-36.

Kay, J., & Lum, A., (2003). Ontology-based User Modelling for the Semantic Web. *10th International Conference on User Modeling, Workshop: Personalisation for the Semantic Web* (pp. 11-19). Edinburgh, Scotland.

Keller et al. (2005). *State of the art of supporting ICT systems for collaborative planning and execution within supply networks.* Deliverable D4.2/5.2. of the ILIPT project. Available through http://www.ilipt.org.

Kendall, G. C. (2006). *SPARQL Protocol for RDF.* W3C. http://www.w3.org/TR/rdf-sparql-protocol/

Kikiras P., Tsetsos V., & Hadjiefthymiades S. (2006). Ontology-based user modeling for pedestrian navigation systems, *Paper presented at ECAI 2006 Workshop on Ubiquitous User Modeling (UbiqUM)*, Riva del Garda, Italy.

Kim, S., Alani, H., Hall, W., Lewis, P., Millard, D., Shadbolt, N., & Weal, M. (2002). Artequakt: Generating tailored biographies with automatically annotated fragments from the Web. *Proceedings of the Workshop on Semantic Authoring, Annotation & Knowledge Markup (SAAKM'02)*, Lyon, France, pp. 1-6.

Kim, S.-M., & Hovy, E. (2004). Determining the sentiment of opinions. In *Coling '04: Proceedings of the 20th International Conference on Computational Linguistics* (p. 1367). Morristown, NJ, USA: Association for Computational Linguistics.

Kiryakov, A., Ognyanov, D., Fensel, D., Klein, M., & Lab, O. (2002, June 28). Ontology versioning and change detection on the Web. In *Proceedings of the 13th International Conference on Knowledge Engineering and Knowledge Management (EKAW02)*, SigUenza, Spain October 1-4, 2002.

Kiryakov, A., Popov, B., Terziev, I., Manov, D., Kirilov, A., & Goranov, M. (2005). Semantic annotation, indexing, and retrieval. *Journal on Web Semantics, Science,*

Services and Agents on the World Wide Web, 2(1), 49-79. Elsevier.

Kitchenham, B. (1996). *DESMET: A method for evaluating Software Engineering methods and tools.* Technical Report TR96-09, Department of Computer Science, University of Keele, Staffordshire, UK.

Kitchenham, B. A., Pfleeger, S. L., Pickard, L. M., Jones P. W., Hoaglin, D. C., El-Emam, K., & Rosenberg, J. (2002). Preliminary guidelines for empirical research in Software Engineering. *IEEE Transactions on Software Engineering 28*(8), 721-734.

Klapsing, R., Neumann, G., & Conen, W. (2001, November). Semantics in Web engineering: Applying the resource description framework. *IEEE MultiMedia, 8(2)*, 62-68. IEEE Computer Society.

Klyne, G., & Carroll, J. J. (2004). *Resource Description Framework (RDF): Concepts and abstract syntax.* W3C Recommendation (http://www.w3.org/TR/rdf-concepts).

Knees, P., Pampalk, E., & Widmer, G. (2004, October). Artist classification with Web-based data. In *Proceedings of 5th International Conference on Music Information Retrieval (ismir'04)* (pp. 517-524). Barcelona, Spain.

Knublauch, H. (2002). *An agile development methodology for knowledge-based systems.* Unpublished doctoral dissertation, University of Ulm.

Kogut, P., & Holmes, W. (2001). AeroDAML: Applying information extraction to generate DAML annotations from Web pages. *Proceedings of the Workshop on Knowledge Markup and Semantic Annotation (KCAP'01)*, Victoria, Canada. Retrieved February 21, 2008, from http://semannot2001.aifb.uni-karlsruhe.de/positionpapers/AeroDAML3.pdf

Koller, D., & Pfeffer, A. (1997). Object-oriented Bayesian networks. *Paper presented at the Thirteenth Conference on Uncertainty in Artificial Intelligence (UAI-97).* San Francisco, CA, USA.

Koller, D., Levy, A. Y., & Pfeffer, A. (1997, July 27-31). P-CLASSIC: A tractable probabilistic description logic. *Paper presented at the Fourteenth National Conference on Artificial Intelligence (AAAI-97).* Providence, RI, USA.

Kolmogorov, A. N. (1960). *Foundations of the Theory of Probability.* 2nd edition. New York, NY, USA: Chelsea Publishing Co. Originally published in 1933.

Korfiatis, N., Poulos, M., & Bokos, G. (2007). Social metadata for the impact factor. *The Electronic Library, 25*(2), 166-175.

Korst, J., Geleijnse, G., De Jong, N., & Verschoor, M. (2006). Ontology-based extraction of information from the World Wide Web. In W. Verhaegh, E. Aarts, & J. Korst (Eds.), Intelligent Algorithms in Ambient and Biomedical Computing (pp. 149-167). Heidelberg, Germany: Springer.

Kotis, K., Vouros, G. A., & Alonso, J. P. (2004). HCOME: Tool-Supported methodology for collaboratively devising living ontologies, *Proceedings of the 2nd International Workshop of Semantic Web and Databases*, Toronto, Canada, 2004.

Krötzsch, M., Vrandecic, D., & Völkel, M. (2005). Wikipedia and the Semantic Web - The missing links. In J. Voss & A. Lih (Eds.), *Proceedings of Wikimania 2005*, Frankfurt, Germany.

Kumar, S., Kunjithapatham, A., Sheshagiri, M., Finin, T., Joshi, A., Peng, Y., & Cost, R.S. (2002). A personal agent application for the Semantic Web. In *AAAI Fall Symposium on Personalized Agents* (pp. 43-58), North Falmouth, MA: AAAI Press.

Kupfer, A., Eckstein, S., Neumann, K., & Mathiak, B. (2006). Keeping track of changes in database schemas and related ontologies. In *Communications of 7th International Baltic Conference on Databases and Information Systems* (pp.63-68).

Kutz, O., Lutz, C., Wolter, F., & Zakharyaschev, M. (2003). E-Connections of description logics. In *International Workshop on Description Logics*. Rome, Italy: CEUR-WS.

Laborda, C.P., & Conrad, S. (2006). Bringing relational data into the Semantic Web using sparql and relational. owl. In *Proc. of the 22nd Int. Conf. on Data Engineering Workshops (ICDEW'06)*, (pp. 55-62).

Lanfranchi, V., Ciravegna, F., & Petrelli, D. (2005). Semantic Web-based document: Editing and browsing in AktiveDoc. *Proceedings of the 2nd European Semantic Web Conference (ESWC'05)*, LNCS 3532, Springer-Verlag, Heraklion, Crete, Greece, pp. 623-632.

Langseth, H., & Nielsen, T. (2003, July). Fusion of domain knowledge with data for structured learning in object-oriented domains. *Journal of Machine Learning Research*, Special Issue on the Fusion of Domain Knowledge with Data for Decision Support, *4*, 339-368.

Larry, K., Hanjo, J., & Wooju, K. (2006). Emergent semantics in knowledge sifter: An evolutionary search agent based on Semantic Web services. *Journal on Data Semantics 6*, 187-209.

Lashkari, Y., Metral, M., & Maes, P. (1994). Collaborative interface agents. In *Proceedings of the 12 National Conference on Artificial Intelligence*. Seattle, WA: AAAI Press, pp. 444-450.

Laskey, K. B. (2007). MEBN: A language for first-order Bayesian knowledge bases. *Artificial Intelligence, 172*(2-3).

Laskey, K. B., & Costa P. C. G. (2005). Of Klingons and starships: Bayesian logic for the 23rd Century, in *Uncertainty in Artificial Intelligence: Proceedings of the Twenty-first Conference*. Edinburgh, Scotland: AUAI Press.

Laskey, K. B., & Mahoney, S. M. (1997, August). Network fragments: Representing knowledge for constructing probabilistic models. In *Proceedings of the Thirteenth Conference on Uncertainty in Artificial Intelligence (UAI-97)*. Providence, RI, USA.

Laublet, P. (2007). Web Sémantique et ontologies. *Nouvelles Technologies Cognitives et Concepts des Sciences Humaines et s Sociales, 1*. Humanités Numériques, Hermès, Paris.

Laura, L. P. (2001). Software fault tolerance techniques and implementation. Norwood, Mass Publication.

Lee, R. (2004). *Scalability report on triple store applications* (SIMILE project report). Cambridge: Massachusetts Institute of Technology.

Leone, N., Pfeifer, G., Faber, W., Eiter, T., Gottlob, G., Perri, S., & Scarcello F. (2005). The DLV System for Knowledge Representation and Reasoning. ACM Transactions on Computational Logic, ACM

Levy, A. Y. (2000). Logic-based techniques in data integration. In Jack Minker, editor, *Logic Based Artificial Intelligence*. Kluwer Academic Publishers, 2000.

Lewis, R., Fuchs, F., Pirker, M., Roberts, C., & Langer, G. (2006). Using ontology to integrate railway condition monitoring data. In *Conference on Railway Condition Monitoring (RCM)*, pp. 149-155. Birmingham, UK: IET.

Li, L., & Horrocks, I. (2003, May). A software framework for matchmaking based on Semantic Web technology. *Paper presented at WWW2003*, Budapest, Hungary.

Li, Y., Xu, B., Lu, J., & Kang, D. (2006). Discrete tableau algorithms for *SHI*. In *Proceeedings DL-2006*.

Li, Y., Xu, B., Lu, J., Kang, D., & Wang, P. (2005a). Extended fuzzy description logic *ALCN*. In *Proceedings KES-2005, 3684 of LNCS*, 896-902. Springer.

Li, Y., Xu, B., Lu, J., Kang, D., & Wang, P. (2005b). A family of extended fuzzy description logics. In *Proceedings COMPSAC-2005*, 221-226. IEEE Computer Society.

Lieberman, H., & Kumar, A. (2005, September). Providing expert advice by analogy for on-line help, *IEEE/ACM Conference on Web Intelligence & Intelligent Agent Technology*, Compiègne, France.

Liebig, T. (2006). *Reasoning with OWL – System support and insights* (Technical Report 2006-04). Ulm: Ulm University.

Lima, F., & Schwabe, D. (2003). Application modeling for the Semantic Web. In *1st Latin American Web Congress (LA-WEB 2003), Empowering Our Web,, Sanitago, Chile, Proceedings* (pp. 93–102). IEEE Computer Society.

Lin, D. (1998). Dependency based evaluation of minipar. In *Proceedings of the Workshop on the Evaluation of Parsing Systems at the First International Conference on Language Resources and Evaluation*. Granada, Spain.

Lopez, V., Motta, E., & Uren, V. (2006, June 11-14). PowerAqua: Fishing the Semantic Web. In York Sure and John Domingue (eds.), *The Semantic Web: Research and Applications, 3rd European Semantic Web Conference, ESWC 2006*, Budva, Montenegro. *Lecture Notes in Computer Science 4011*, Springer, ISBN 3-540-34544-2.

Lukasiewicz, T. (2002). Probabilistic default reasoning with conditional constraints. *Ann. Math. Artif. Intell., 34*(1-3), 35-88.

Lukasiewicz, T. (2008). Expressive probabilistic description logics. *Artificial Intelligence, 172*(6-7), 852-883.

Lutz, C. (2003). Description logics with concrete domains—A survey. *Advances in Modal Logics*, (4), 265-296.

Maedche, A., Motik, B., Silva, N., & Volz, R. (2002). MA-FRA – A mapping framework for distributed ontologies in *Knowledge Engineering and Knowledge Management: Ontologies and the Semantic Web*, Volume *2473*(/2002), :pp. 69-75. Springer Berlin / Heidelberg.

Maes, P. (1994). *Agents that reduce work and information overload communications of the ACM, 37*(7), 31-40.

Manning, C. D., & Schütze, H. (1999). Foundations of statistical natural language processing. Cambridge, Massachusetts: The MIT Press.

Manola, F., & Miller, E. (2004). *RDF primer*. W3C. http://www.w3.org/TR/rdf-primer/

Marneffe, M.-C. de, MacCartney, B., & Manning, C. D. (2006). Generating Typed Dependency Parses from Phrase Structure Parses. In *Proceedings of the IEEE/ACL 2006 Workshop on Spoken Language Technology*.

Mawlood-Yunis, A-R., Weiss, M., & Santoro, N. (2007). Fault classification in P2P semantic mapping. *In Workshop on Semantic Web for Collaborative Knowledge Acquisition (SWeCKa)} at Intl. Conf. on Artificial Intelligence (IJCAI)*.

Maybury, M. (2003). New directions on question and answering, *AAAI Spring Sysmposium*, TR-SS-03-07, Stanford, CA.

McCallum, A. (2005). Information extraction: Distilling structured data from unstructured text. *ACM Queue, 3*(9), 48-57.

McGuinees, D. L. (2003). *Ontologies come of age. Book chapter in spinning the Semantic Web: Bringing the World Wide Web to its full potential*, Fensel D. Hendler J. Lieberman H., et al. (eds). The MIT Press.

McGuinness, D. L. (1996). Explaining reasoning in description logics. Ph.D. Thesis, Rutgers University. Technical Report LCSR-TR-277. Rutgers Department of Computer Science Technical Report Series.

McGuinness, D. L., & Wright, J. R. (1998). An industrial strength description logic-based configurator platform. *IEEE Intelligent Systems, 13*(4), 69-77.

McGuinness, D., Ding, L., Glass, A., Chang, C., Zeng, H., & Furtado, V. (2006, November 6). Explanation interfaces for the Semantic Web: Issues and Models, SWUI 2006 *- The 3rd International Semantic Web User Interaction Workshop*, Athens, Georgia, USA

McGuinness, D., Fox, P., Cinquini, L., West, P., Garcia, J., Benedict, J.L., & Middleton, D. (2007a, July 22-26). The virtual solar-terrestrial observatory: A deployed Semantic Web application case study for scientific research. In *proceedings of the Nineteenth Conference on Innovative Applications of Artificial Intelligence (IAAI-07)*. Vancouver, BC, Canada.

McGuinness, D.L., & Pinheiro da Silva, P. (2004, October). Explaining answers from the Semantic Web: The inference Web approach. *Journal of Web Semantics, 1*(4), 397-413.

McGuinness, D.L., & van Harmelen, F. (2004). *OWL Web ontology language* (W3C Recommendation). Retrieved May 2007 from http://www.w3.org/TR/owl-features/.

McGuinness, D.L., & van Harmelen, F. (2004, February). *OWL Web Ontology Language Overview (Technical report).* http://www.w3.org/TR/2004/REC-owl-features-20040210/.

McGuinness, D.L., Ding, L., Glass, G., Chang, C., Zeng, H., & Furtado, V. (2006a) Explanation interfaces for the Semantic Web: Issues and models. Presented in the *3rd International Semantic Web User Interaction Workshop (SWUI'06),* Co-located with the *International Semantic Web Conference,* Athens, Georgia, USA.

McGuinness, D.L., Ding, L., Glass, G., Chang, C., Zeng, H., & Furtado, V. (2006a) Explanation interfaces for the Semantic Web: Issues and models. Presented in the *3rd International Semantic Web User Interaction Workshop (SWUI'06),* Co-located with the *International Semantic Web Conference,* Athens, Georgia, USA.

McGuinness, D.L., Ding, L., Pinheiro da Silva, P., & Chang, C. (2007). A modular explanation interlingua. In the *Proceedings of the Explanation-aware Computing Workshop (ExaCt-2007)* co-located with the *Association for the Advancement of Artificial Intelligence,* Vancouver, BC.

McGuinness, D.L., Zeng, H., Pinheiro da Silva, P., Ding, L., Narayanan, D., & Bhaowal. M. (2006b, May 22). Investigations into trust for collaborative information repositories: A Wikipedia case study. *WWW2006 Workshop on the Models of Trust for the Web (MTW'06),* Edinburgh, Scotland.

Mena E., Illarramendi, A., et al. (2000). OBSERVER: An approach for query processing in global information systems based on interpretation across pre-existing ontologies. *Distributed and Parallel Databases, 8*(2), 223-71.

Metze, F., Bauckhage, C., & Alpcan, T. (2007). The "spree" expert finding system. *Paper presented at the First International Conference on Semantic Computing.* Irvine, California, USA.

Mika, P. (2005). Flink: Semantic Web technology for the extraction and analysis of social networks. *Journal of Web Semantics, 3,* 211-223.

Mika, P. (2005). Ontologies are us: A unified model of social networks and semantics. In *4th Intl. Semantic Web Conference,* 522-36.

Mika, P. (2005). Social networks and the Semantic Web: The next challenge. *IEEE Intelligent Systems 20*(1), 80-93

Mika, P. (2007). Ontologies are us: A unified model of social networks and semantics. *Journal of Web Semantics, 5*(1), 5-15.

Milgram, S. (1967). The small world problem. *Psychology Toda,y 2,* 60-70.

Miller, L., & Brickley, D. (2000). *Foaf project.* Retrieved June 16, 2007, from http://www.Foaf-project.org.

Minsky, M. L. (1975). Framework for representing knowledge. In *The Psychology of Computer Vision.* P. H. Winston (Eds.), 211-277. New York, NY: McGraw-Hill.

Mishne, G. (2007). *Applied text analysis for blogs.* Unpublished doctoral dissertation, University of Amsterdam

Mitchell, T. (1997). *Machine learning.* McGraw Hill.

Mitra, P., Noy, N. F., & Jaiswal, A. R. (2004, November). OMEN: A probabilistic ontology mapping tool. *Workshop on Meaning Coordination and Negotiation at the Third International Conference on the Semantic Web (ISWC-2004).* Hisroshima, Japan.

Möller, K., Bojārs, U., & Breslin, J.G. (2006, June 11-14). Using semantics to enhance the blogging experience. In Y. Sure, J. Domingue (Eds.), *The Semantic Web: Research and Applications, 3rd European Semantic Web Conference,* ESWC 2006 Proceedings, Budva, Montenegro, 679-696.

Mori, J., Tsujishita, T., Matsuo, Y., & Ishizuka, M. (2006). Extracting relations in social networks from the Web using similarity between collective contexts. In *Proceedings of the 5th International Semantic Web Conference (iswc 2006),* 4273, 487-500. Athens, GA: Springer.

Morley, D., & Myers, K. (2004). The SPARK agent framework. In *Proceedings of the Third International Joint Conference on Autonomous Agents and Multi Agent Systems (AAMAS-04),* New York, NY.

Mota, E., & Sabou, M. (2006). *Next generation Semantic Web applications,* ASWC.

Motik, B., & Sattler, U. (2006). A comparison of reasoning techniques for querying large description logic ABoxes. In *13th International Conference on Logic for Programming Artificial Intelligence and Reasoning*, pp. 227-241. Phnom Penh, Cambodia: Springer LNCS 4246.

Motik, B., Shearer, R., & Horrocks, I. (2007). A hypertableau calculus for *SHIQ*. In *International Workshop on Description Logics, pp. 419-426. Brixen, Italy:* CEUR.

Muller, K. (2000, June). *NATO and XML.* Paper presented at XML Europe 2000, Paris, France.

Multilateral Interoperability Programme – MIP (2005). *Command and control information exchange data model (C2IEDM) sSpecifications.* Retrieved May, 2007 from http://www.mip-site.org/publicsite/03-Baseline_ 2.0/C2IEDM-C2_Information_Exchange_Data_ Model/C2IEDM-Main-UK-DMWG-Edition6.15e-2005-12-02.pdf.

Murdock, J.W., McGuinness, D.L., Pinheiro da Silva, P., Welty, C., & Ferrucci, D. (2006, November 5-9). Explaining conclusions from diverse knowledge sources. In the *Proceedings of the Fifth International Semantic Web Conference,* Athens, Ga.

Nadalin, A., Kaler, C., Monzillo, R., & Hallan-Baker, P. (2004). *Web services security: SOAP message security 1.0 (WS-Security 2004)* (OASIS Standard): Organization for the Advancement of Structured Information Standards (OASIS).

Naiman, C. F., & Ouskel, A.M. (1995). A classification of semantic conflicts in heterogeneous database systems. *Journal of Organizational Computing, 5*(2), 167-193.

Nascimento, M. A., Sander, J., & Pound, J. (2003). Analysis of SIGMOD's co-quthorship Graph, *SIGMOD Record, 32*(3), 8-10.

NATO (2007). *NATO Standardization Agreements.* Retrieved May, 2007 from http://www.nato.int/docu/ standard.htm#STANAG.

NATO (2007b). *NATO Response Force (NRF).* Retrieved May, 2007 from http://www.nato.int/issues/nrf.

NATO (2008). *NATO Ground Moving Target Indicator Format (GMTIF).* Retrieved January, 2008 from http:// www.nato.int/docu/stanag/4607/4607_home.htm.

Neapolitan, R. E. (1990). *Probabilistic reasoning in expert systems: Theory and algorithms.* New York, NY, USA: John Wiley and Sons, Inc.

Neapolitan, R. E. (2003). *Learning Bayesian networks.* New York: Prentice Hall.

Nelson, T.H. (1965). A file structure for the complex, the changing, and the indeterminate. In *ACM 20th National Conference Proceedings*, 84-100, Cleveland, Ohio.

Newman, M. E. J. (2001). Scientific collaboration networks: II. Shortest paths, weighted networks, and centrality, *Phys. Rev.,E, 64,* 016132

Niedere, C., Stewart, A., Mehta, B., & Hemmje, M. (2004). *A multi-dimensional, unified user model for cross-system personalization. Paper presented at Advanced Visual Interfaces (AVI2004) Workshop on Environments for Personalized Information Access,* Gallipoli, Italy.

Niemann, B.L. (2007). New enterprise data management strategy for the U.S. Government: Support for the Semantic Web. In *W3C Workshop on RDF Access to Relational Databases.* Retrieved December 15, 2007, from http://www.w3.org/2007/03/RdfRDB/papers/niemann.doc

Nierle, J. E. (1996). *Internetworking: Technical sStrategy for iImplementing the nNext gGeneration Internet pProtocol (IPV6) in the Marine Corps tTactical dData nNetwork.* Msc. Thesis, Naval Postgraduate School, Monterey, CA, USA.

Nottingham, M., & Sayre, R. (2005). *The atom syndication format* (Tech. Rep.). Internet Engineering Task Force (IETF).

Noy, N. F., & Klein, M. (2004b). Ontology evolution: Not the same as schema evolution. *Knowledge and Information Systems, 6*(4), 428-440.

Noy, N. F., & Musen, M. A. (2004a). Ontology versioning in an ontology management framework. *IEEE Intelligent Systems, 19*(4), 6-13.

Noy, N.F., Sintek, M., Decker, S., Crubezy, M., Fergerson, R.W., & Musen, M.A. (2001). Creating Semantic Web contents with Protègè 2000. *IEEE Intelligent Systems 16(2),* 60-71. IEEE Computer Society.

O'Connor, M. J., Knublauch, H., Tu, S. W., Grossof, B., Dean, M., Grosso, W.E., & Musen, M.A. (2005). Supporting rule system interoperability on the Semantic Web with SWRL. *Fourth International Semantic Web Conference* (pp. 974-986). Galway, Ireland: Springer.

O'Reilly, T. (2005). What is Web 2.0. (http://www. oreillynet.com/pub/a/oreilly/tim/news/2005/09/30/what-is-Web-20.html)

Oaks, S., Gong, L., & Traversat, B. (2002), *JXTA in a nNutshell*. Sebastopol, CA, USA: O'Reilly & Associates, Inc.

Oberle, D., Ankolekar, A., Hitzler, P., & al. (2006). *DOLCE ergo SUMO: On foundational and domain models in SWIntO (SmartWeb Integrated Ontology)* (Technical Report). Karlsruhe: University of Karlsruhe, AIFB.

ODM (2007). Ontology definition metamodel. *OMG Adopted Specification,* Document Number: ptc/2007-09-09. Retrieved December 15, 2007, from http://www.omg.org/docs/ptc/07-09-09.pdf

OGC (Open Geospatial Consortium), Inc. (2007). *Sensor Web enablement WG*. Retrieved June 4, 2007, from http://www.opengeospatial.org/projects/groups/sensorweb

Oren, E. (2006). An overview of information management and knowledge work studies: Lessons for the semantic sesktop. In S. Decker, J. Park, L. Sauermann, S. Auer, S. Handschuh (Eds.), *Proceedings of the Semantic Desktop and Social Semantic Collaboration Workshop (SemDesk 2006) at ISWC 2006*. Athens, GA, USA.

Orr, K., & Highsmith, J. A. (2000). *Adaptive software development: A collaborative approach to managing complex systems*. Dorset House Publishing Co.

Ouksel, A.M. (1999). Ontologies are not the panacea in data integration: A flexible coordinator to mediate context construction. *Distributed and Parallel Databases, 15*(1), 7-35.

OWL (2004). Web ontology language (OWL). *W3C Specification*. Retrieved December 15, 2007, from http://www.w3.org/2004/OWL/

OWL 1.1 (2006). OWL 1.1 Web ontology language. *Submission Request to W3C*. Retrieved December 15, 2007, from http://www.w3.org/Submission/2006/10/

Palmer, S. R., & Felsing, J. M. (2002). *A practical guide to the feature-driven development*. Prentice Hall PTR.

Pan, R., Ding, Z., Yu, Y., & Peng, Y. (2005, November). A Bayesian approach to ontology mapping. In *Proceedings of the Fourth International Semantic Web Conference (ISWC-2005)*. Galway, Ireland.

Pang, B., & Lee, L. (2005). Seeing stars: Exploiting class relationships for sentiment categorization with respect to rating scales. In *Proceedings of the 43th Annual Meeting of the Association for Computational Linguistics (acl 2005)* (pp. 115-124). Ann Arbor, MI.

Pang, B., Lee, L., & Vaithyanathan, S. (2002). Thumbs up? Sentiment classification using machine learning techniques. In *Proceedings of the 2002 Conference on Empirical Methods in Natural Language Processing (emnlp)* (pp. 79-86).

Papalilo E., Friese, et al. (2005). Trust shaping: Adapting trust establishment and management to application requirements in a service-oriented grid environment. In *Proc. 4th Intl. Conf. on Grid and Cooperative Computing (GCC)*, LNCS 3795, 47-58,

Paradhan, D. K. (1996). *Fault-tolerant computing system design*. Prentice-Hall PTR publication.

Park, R. E., Goethert, W. B., & Florac, W. A. (1996). *Goal-driven software measurement - a guidebook*. Technical Report CMU/SEI-96-HB-002, Software Engineering Institute.

Parsia, B., & Sirin, E. (2004). Pellet: An OWL DL reasoner. In *International Semantic Web Conference (ISWC)*. Hiroshima, Japan: Springer LNCS.

Parsia, B., Sirin, E., & Kalyanpur, A. (2005) Debugging owl ontologies. In the *Proceedings of the World Wide Web Conference*, pp. 633-640.

Patel-Schneider, P.F., & Horrocks, I. (2007*). OWL 1.1 Web oOntology lLanguage – Overview*. Retrieved May, 2007 from http://webont.org/owl/1.1/overview.html

Pearl, J. (1988). *Probabilistic reasoning in intelligent systems: Networks of plausible inference*. San Mateo, CA, USA: Morgan Kaufmann Publishers.

Peirce, C. S. (1885). On the algebra of logic. *American Journal of Mathematics, 7*, 180-202.

Peng, Y., Ding, Z., Pan, R., Yu, Y., Kulvatunyou, B., Izevic, N., Jones, A., & Cho, H. (2007, May). A probabilistic framework for semantic similarity and ontology mapping. In *Proceedings of the 2007 Industrial Engineering Research Conference (IERC)*. Nashville, TN, USA.

Perry, D. E., Porter, A. A., & Votta L. G. (2000). Empirical studies of Software Engineering: a roadmap. In A. Finkelstein (Ed.), *The Future of Software Engineering*, 345-355. ACM Press.

Pfeffer, A. (2001, August 4-10). IBAL: A probabilistic rational programming language international. In *Proceedings of the Seventeenth International Joint Conference on Artificial Intelligence (IJCAI-2001), 1*, 733-740. Seattle, WA, USA.

Pfeffer, A., Koller, D., Milch, B., & Takusagawa, K. T. (1999, July-August 1). SPOOK: A system for probabilistic object-oriented knowledge representation. In *Proceedings of the Fifteenth Conference on Uncertainty in Artificial Intelligence*, 541-550. Stockholm, Sweden

Pinto, H. S., Tempich, C., & Staab, S. (2004). Diligent: Towards a fine-grained methodology for distributed, loosely-controlled and evolving engineering of ontologies, *Proceedings of the 16th European Conference on Artificial Intelligence*, Valencia, Spain, 2004.

Pizza, M., Strigini L., et al. (1998). Optimal discrimination between transient and permanent faults. In *Third IEEE Intl. High-Assurance Systems Engineering Symposium*, 214-223.

Plessers, P, & Troyer, O. D. Resolving inconsistencies in evolving ontologies. In the *Proceedings of the European Semantic Web Conference*, pp. 200-214.

Pool, M., & Aikin, J. (2004, July 6-9). KEEPER and protégé: An elicitation environment for Bayesian inference tools. *Paper presented at the Workshop on Protégé and Reasoning held at the Seventh International Protégé Conference*. Bethesda, MD, USA.

Popov, B., Kiryakov, A., Kirilov, A., Manov, D., Ognyanoff, D., & Goranov, M. (2003). KIM – A Semantic Annotation Platform. In D. Fensel, K. Sycara, and J. Mylopoulos (eds.), *The Semantic Web - ISWC 2003, Second International Semantic Web Conference. Lecture Notes in Computer Science*, 2870, Springer-Verlag.

Popov, B., Kiryakov, A., Manov, D., Kirilov, A., Ognyanoff, D., & Goranov, M. (2003). Towards Semantic Web information extraction. *Proceedings of the Human Language Technologies Workshop (ISWC'03)*, Sanibel, Florida, pp. 1-22.

Porter, M. F. (1997). An *algorithm for suffix stripping. In Readings in information retrieval* (pp. 313-316). San Francisco, CA: Morgan Kaufmann Publishers Inc.

Prié, Y., & Garlatti, S. (2004). Méta-données et annotations dans le Web Sémantique. *Le Web sémantique*, Charlet, J., Laublet, P., & Reynaud, C. (Ed.), Hors série de la *Revue Information - Interaction - Intelligence* (I3), 4(1), 45-68. Cépaduès, Toulouse.

Prud'hommeaux, E. (2004). *Algae RDF query language*. Retrieved June 16, 2007, from http://www.w3.org/2004/05/06-Algae/.

Prud'hommeaux, E., & Seaborne, A. (2006). *SPARQL Query Language for RDF*. W3C. http://www.w3.org/TR/rdf-sparql-query/

Prud'Hommeaux, E., & Seaborne, A. (2007). *SPARQL Query Language for RDF* (W3C Working Draft). Retrieved May, 2007 from http://www.w3.org/TR/rdf-sparql-query/.

Puhretmair, F., Rumetshofer, H., & Schaumlechner, E. (2002). Extended decision making in tourism information dystems. *Lecture Notes in Computer Science, 2455* ,57-66. Aix-en-Provence, France: Springer-Verlag.

Pulvermacher, M.K., Stoutenburg, S., & Semy, S. (2004). *Net-centric sSemantic lLinking: An approach for eEnterprise sSemantic iInteroperability.* (Tech. Paper). Bedford, Massachusetts, USA: The MITRE Corporation.

Pynadath, D.V., & Tambe, M. (2002). Electric elves: Adjustable autonomy in real-world multiagent environments. In socially intelligent agents – *Creating relationships with computers and robots*. Kluwer Academic Publishers.

Quan, D., Huynh, D., & Karger, D.R. (2003). Haystack: A platform for authoring end user Semantic Web applications. In D. Fensel, K.P. Sycara, J. Mylopoulos (Eds.), *The Semantic Web – ISWC 2003: International Semantic Web Conference*, Proceedings, 738-753.

Racer Systems (2007). *RacerPro*. Retrieved June 16, 2007, from http://www.racer-systems.com/.

RacerPro, Retrieved June 13, 2007, from http://www.racer-systems.com/products/racerpro/index.phtml http://www.racer-systems.com/products/racerpro/index.phtml

Rakitin, S. R. (1997). *Software Verification and Validation, a practitioner's guide*. Artech House.

Ram, S., & Park, J. (2004). Semantic conflict resolution ontology (SCROL): An ontology for detecting and resolving data and schema-level semantic conflicts. *IEEE Transactions on Knowledge and Data Engineering, 16*(2), 189-202.

Ramsey, F. P. (1931). *The Foundations of Mathematics and other Logical Essays*. London, UK: Kegan Paul, Trench, Trubner & Co.

Raskin, R. (2003). Semantic Web for earth and environmental terminology (SWEET). In *3rd Annual Earth Science Technology Conference*. Earth Science Technology Office, NASA.

Ravichandran, D. (2005). *Terascale knowledge acquisition*. Unpublished doctoral dissertation, University of Southern California.

Ravichandran, D., & Hovy, E. (2002). Learning surface text patterns for a question answering system. In *Proceedings of the 40th Annual Meeting of the Association for Computational Linguistics (acl 2002)* (pp. 41-47). Philadelphia, PA.

Rector, A. (2005). Representing specified values in OWL: "value partitions" and "value sets". *W3C Best Practice Working Group Note*, http://www.w3.org/TR/swbp-specified-values.

Rhodes, B.J., & Starner, T. (1996). Remembrance agent: A continuously automated information retrieval system. *Proceedings, First international Conference on the Practical Application of Intelligent Agents and Multi-Agent Technology*. London, UK.

Ricci, F., Arslan, B., Mirzadeh, N., & Venturini, A (2002). ITR: A case-based travel advisory system, *Lecture Notes in Artificial Intelligence, 6th European Conference on Case Based Reasoning 2416*, 613-627. Aberdeen, Scotland: Springer-Verlag.

Richter, J., Völkel, M., & Haller, H. (2005). DeepaMehta – A Semantic desktop. In *Proceedings of the 1st Workshop on the Semantic Desktop - Next Generation Personal Information Management and Collaboration Infrastructure* at ISWC 2005, Galway, Ireland.

Rinaldi, F., Dowdall, J., Hess, M., Ellman, J., Zarri, G.-P., Persidis, A., Bernard, L., & Karanikas, H. (2003). Multilayer annotations in Parmenides. *Proceedings of the Knowledge Markup and Semantic Annotation Workshop*, Sanibel, Florida, USA, pp.33-40.

Robert. Mc., et al. (2005). Mapping maintenance for data integration systems. In *Proceedings of the 31st international conference on VLDB*, 1018-1029.

Roddick, J. F. (1995). A survey of schema versioning issues for database systems. *Information and Software Technology, 37*(7), 383-393.

Rousset, M. C. (2004). Small can be beautiful in the Semantic Web. In *Third Intl. Semantic Web Conf.*, 6-16.

Rousset, P., Chatalic, et al. (2006). Somewhere: A scalable P2P infrastructure for querying distributed ontologies. *5th Intl. Conf. on Ontologies Databases and Applications of Semantics*, 698-703.

RSS-DEV Working Group (2000). RDF Site Summary (RSS) 1.0. Retrieved June 16, 2007, from http://web.resource.org/rss/1.0/spec.

RuleML, Rule Markup Initiative, Retrieved June 13, 2007, from http://www.ruleml.org/

Russell, S.J., & Norvig, P. (2003). *Artificial iIntelligence: Aa modern approach*. Upper Saddle River, N.J.: Prentice Hall.

Saint-Andre, P. (Ed.) (2004). *Extensible mMessaging and pPresence pProtocol (XMPP): Core* (RFC 3920): Jabber Software Foundation.

Sanchez, D., & Tettamanzi, A. (2004). Generalizing quantification in fuzzy description logics. In *Proceedings 8th Fuzzy Days in Dortmund*.

Sanchez, D., & Tettamanzi, A. (2006). Fuzzy quantification in fuzzy description logics. In Sanchez, E. (Ed.), *Capturing Intelligence: Fuzzy Logic and the Semantic Web*. Elsevier.

Sanchez, E. (2006). *Fuzzy logic and the Semantic Web*. Elsevier Science & Technology.

Sauermann, L. (2003). The Gnowsis – *Using Semantic Web Technologies to Build a Semantic Desktop*. Diploma Thesis, Technical University of Vienna, 2003.

Sauermann, L., Grimnes, G. AA., Kiesel, M., Fluit, C., Maus, H., Heim, D., Nadeem, D., Horak, B., & Dengel, A. (2006). Semantic desktop 2.0: The gnowsis experience. In I. Cruz, S. Decker, D. Allemang, C. Preist, D. Schwabe, P. Mika, M. Uschold, L. Aroyo (Eds.), *The Semantic Web – ISWC 2006: 5th International Semantic Web Conference*, Athens, GA, Proceedings.

Schedl, M., Knees, P., & Widmer, G. (2005, June). A Web-Based approach to assessing artist similarity using co-occurrences. In *Proceedings of the Fourth International Workshop on Content-Based Multimedia Indexing (CBMI'05)*. Riga, Latvia.

Schmidt-Schauß, M., & Smolka, G. (1991). Attributive concept descriptions with complements. *Artificial Intelligence, 48*(1), 1-26.

Schraefel, M.C., Shadbolt, N.R., Gibbins, N., Glaser, H., & Harris, S. (2004). CS AKTive space: Representing computer science in the Semantic Web. In *Proceedings of the 13th International World Wide Web Conference*.

Schreiber, G., Akkermans, H., Anjewierden, A., Hoog, R. de, Shadbolt, N., Velde, W. V. de, et al. (2000). *Knowl-*

edge engineering and management: The commonKADS methodology. MITpress.

Schröder, A., Laresgoiti, I., Werlen, K., Schowe-von der Brelie, B., & Schnettler, A. (2007). Intelligent self-describing power grids. In *International Conference on Electricity Distribution*. Vienna, Austria: CIRED.

Schwabe, D., & Rossi, G. (1998, October). An object-oriented approach to Web-based application design. In *Theory and Practice of Object Systems (TAPOS)*, 207–225. John Wiley & Sons

Schwaber, K., & Beedle, M. (2001). *Agile software development with scrum* (1st ed.). Prentice Hall.

Semy, S.K., Pulvermacher, M.K., & Obrst, L.J. (2004). *Toward the use of an upper ontology for U.S. Government and U.S. Military domains: An evaluation. (Technical report)*. MITRE, September 2004.

Shadbolt, N., Gibbins, N., Glaser, H., Harris, S., & Schraefel, M. M. C. (2004). CS AKTive space, or how we learned to stop worrying and love the Semantic Web. *IEEE Intelligent Systems 19*(3), 41-47.

Sheth, A.P., Ramakrishnan, C., & Thomas, C. (2005). Semantics for the Semantic Web: The implicit, the formal and the powerful. *International Journal Semantic Web Information Systems, 1*(1), 1-18.

Shirazi, B., Welch, L. R., Ravindran, B., Cavanaugh, C., Yanamula, B., Brucks, R., & Huh, E. (1999). Dynbench: A dynamic benchmark suite for distributed real-time systems. In the *11th IPPS/SPDP'99 Workshops*,1335-1349. Springer-Verlag.

Shirky, C. (2003, April). A group is its own worst enemy. *Rede zur ETech Conference*, online http://www.shirky.com/writings/group_enemy.html.

Sim, S., Easterbrook, S., & Holt, R. (2003). Using benchmarking to advance research: A challenge to software engineering. In the *25th International Conference on Software Engineering (ICSE'03)*,74-83. Portland, OR.

Sintek, M., & Decker S. (2002). TRIPLE - A Query, inference, and transformation language for the Semantic Web. In *1st International Semantic Web Conference, ISWC 2002, Chia, Sardinai, Italy, Proceedings* (pp. 364 - 378). Springer.

Sintek, M., van Elst, L., Scerri, S., & Handschuh, S. (2007). Distributed knowledge representation on the social semantic desktop: Named graphs, views and roles in NRL. In E. Franconi, M. Kifer, W. May (Eds.), *The Semantic Web – ESWC 2007: The 4th European Semantic Web Conference (ESWC 2007) Proceedings*.

Sirin, E., & Parsia, B. (2004, May). Pellet: An OWL DL rReasoner. *Paper presented at Workshop on Application Design, Development and Implementation Issues in the Semantic Web*, New York, NY, USA.

Sirin, E., & Parsia, B. (2007b). SPARQL-DL: SPARQL Query for OWL-DL. In *Proceedings of the 3rd OWL Experiences and Directions Workshop (OWLED-2007)*. CEUR Workshop Proceedings, Vol 258. Retrieved December 15, 2007, from http://ceur-ws.org/Vol-258/paper14.pdf

Sirin, E., Parsia, B., Cuenca Grau, B., Kalyanpur, A., & Katz, Y. (2007a). Pellet: A practical OWL-DL reasoner. *Web Semantics: Science, Services and Agents on the World Wide Web, 5*(2), 51-53.

Sirin, E., Parsia, B., Grau, .B. C., Kalyanpur, A., & Katz, Y. (2007). Pellet: A Practical OWL-DL Reasoner. *Journal of Web Semantic,s 5(2)*, 51-53. Elsevier.

Sirin, E., Parsia, B., Grau, B. C., Kalyanpur, A., & Katz, Y. (2007). Pellet: A practical OWL-DL reasonerr, *Journal of Web Semantics, 5*(2), 51-53

Sølvberg, A., Hakkarainen, S., Brasethvik, T., T., Su, X., & Matskin, M. (2002, October). *Concepts on eEnriching uUnderstanding and rRetrieving the sSemantics on the Web*. ERCIM News No. 51, October 2002.

Sowa, J. (2000). *Knowledge representation: Logical, philosophical and computational foundations*, Brooks Cole Publishing Co., Pacific Grove, p. 594.

SPARQL (2007). SPARQL query language for RDF. *W3C proposed recommendation*. Retrieved December 15, 2007, from http://www.w3.org/TR/rdf-sparql-query

Spendolini, M. J. (1992). *The benchmarking book*. New York, NY: AMACOM.

Spiegelhalter, D. J., Thomas, A., & Best, N. (1996). Computation on graphical models. *Bayesian Statistics, 5*, 407-425.

Spyns, P., Meersman, R., & Jarrar, M. (2002). Data modelling versus ontology engineering. *SIGMOD Record (ACM Special Interest Group on Management of Data), 31*(4).

Sriharee, N., & Punnarut, R. (2007). Constructing campus for academic collaboration. *Paper presented at the Second International ExpertFinder Workshop*. Busan, Korea.

Srivihok, A., & Sukonmanee, P. (2005). *Intelligent agent for e-Tourism: Personalization travel support agent using reinforcement learning. Proceeding of The 14th International World Wide Web Conference (WWW2005) Workshop*. Chiba, Japan: Keio University.

Staab, S. (2002). Emergent semantics. *IEEE Intelligent Systems, 17*(1), 78-86.

Staab, S.(2005) Social networks applied. *IEEE Intelligent Systems, 20*(1), 80-93.

Staab, S., & Stuckenschmidt, S. (2006). *Semantic Web and peer-to-peer*, Springer-Verlag, Berlin Heidelberg, Germany.

Staab, S., Domingos, P., Mika, P., Golbeck, J., Ding, L., Finin, T. W., Joshi, A., Nowak, A., & Vallacher, R. R. (2005). Social networks applied. *IEEE Intelligent Systems, 20*(1), 80-93.

Staab, S., Maedche, A., & Handschuh, S. (2001a). An annotation framework for the Semantic Web. *Proceedings of the 1ˢᵗ International Workshop on MultiMedia Annotation*, Tokyo, Japan.

Staab, S., Maedche, A., & Handschuh, S. (2001b). *Creating metadata for the Semantic Web: An annotation framework and the human factor.* Technical Report, AIFB Institut, Karlsruhe University, Germany, p. 25.

Stefani, F., Macii, D., Moschitta, A., & Petri, D. (2003, June). FFT benchmarking for digital signal processing technologies. In the *17th IMEKO World Congress*. Dubrovnik, Croatia.

Stephanidis, C., & Savidis, A. (2001). Universal access in the information society: Methods, tools, and interaction technologies, *Universal Access in the Information Society, 1*(1), 40-55.

Stephens, L.M., & Huhns, M.N.(2001). Consensus ontologies. Reconciling the semantics of Web pages and agents. In *IEEE Internet Computing, 5*(5), 92-95.

Stoilos, G., Stamou, G. B., Tzouvaras, V., Pan, J. Z., & Horrocks, I. (2005b). The fuzzy description logic *f-SHIN*. In *Proceedings URSW-2005, 67*-76.

Stoilos, G., Stamou, G., Tzouvaras, V., Pan, J. Z., & Horrock, I. (2005). A fuzzy description logic for multimedia knowledge representation. In *Proceedings of the International Workshop on Multimedia and the Semantic Web*.

Stoilos, G., Straccia, U., Stamou, G., & Pan, J. Z. (2006). General concept inclusions in fuzzy description logics. In *Proceedings ECAI-2006, 457*-61. IOS Press.

Stojanovic, L. (2004). *Methods and tools for ontology evolution*. Unpublished doctoral dissertation, Institut für Angewandte Informatik und Formale Beschreibungsverfahren, Universität Karlsruhe (TH).

Straccia, U. (1998). A fuzzy description logic. In *Proceedings AAAI-1998, 594*-599. AAAI Press/MIT Press.

Straccia, U. (2001). Reasoning within fuzzy description logics. *J. Artif. Intell. Res., 14,* 137-166.

Straccia, U. (2004). Transforming fuzzy description logics into classical description logics. In *Proceedings JELIA-2004, 3229* of *LNCS*, 385-399. Springer.

Straccia, U. (2005a). Description logics with fuzzy concrete domains. In *Proceedings UAI-2005, 559*-567. AUAI Press.

Straccia, U. (2005b). Fuzzy *ALC* with fuzzy concrete domains. In *Proceeedings DL-2005, 96*-103.

Sullivan, D., Grosz, B., & Kraus, S. (2000). Intention reconciliation by collaborative agents. In *Proceedings of the Fourth International Conference on Multi-Agent Systems, IEEE Computer Society Press*, Boston, MA.

Sumida, A., Torisawa, K., & Shinzato, K. (2006). Concept-instance relation extraction from simple noun sequences using a full-text search engine. In *Proceedings of the ISWC 2006 Workshop on Web Content Mining With Human Language Technologies (Webconmine)*. Athens, GA.

Sure, Y., & Corcho, O. (Ed.) (2003). Proceedings of the *2nd International Workshop on Evaluation of Ontology-based Tools (EON2003), 87* of CEUR-WS. Florida, USA.

Sure, Y., Erdmann, M., Angele, J., Staab, S., Studer, R., & Wenke D. (2002). OntoEdit: collaborative ontology development for the Semantic Web. In *1st International Semantic Web Conference, ISWC 2002, Chia, Sardinai, Italy, Proceedings* (pp. 221 - 235). Springer.

SweetRules, *Tools for Semantic Web rules and ontologies, including translation, inferencing, analysis, and uathoring*, Retrieved June 13, 2007, from http://sweetrules.projects.semWebcentral.org/

Tallis, M. (2003). Semantic word processing for content authors. *Proceedings of the Knowledge Markup and Semantic Annotation Workshop (SEMANNOT'03)*, CEUR

Workshop Proceedings, 101, Sanibel, Florida. Retrieved February 21, 2008, from ftp.informatik.rwth-aachen.de/Publications/CEUR-WS/Vol-101/Marcelo_Tallis.pdf

Tempich, C., Pinto, H.S., et al. (2005). An argumentation ontology for distributed, loosely-controlled and evolving engineering processes of ontologies (DILIGENT). *In Second European Semantic Web Conf. (ESWC)*, LNCS 3532, 241-56.

Tempich, C., Staab, S., & Wranik, A. (2004). REMIN-DIN': Semantic query routing in peer-to-peer networks based on social metaphors. *In 13th Intl. Conf. on the World Wide Web*, 640-649.

Terziyan, V., & Katasonov A. (2007). *Global understanding environment: Applying Semantic Web to industrial automation.* Retrieved December 12th, 2007, from University of Jyvaskyla, Department for Artificial Intelligence: http://www.cs.jyu.fi/ai/papers/Chapter_Emergent_Technologies_IS-2007.pdf

Tho, Q. T., Hui, S. C., & Fong, A. (2003). Web mining for identifying research trends. *Paper presented at the 6th International Conference on Asian Digital Libraries.* Kuala Lumpur, Malasya.

Thompson, H., Beech, D., Maloney, M., & Mendelsohn, N. (2004). *XML sSchema Part 1: Structures sSecond eEdition* (W3C Recommendation). Retrieved May, 2007 from http://www.w3.org/TR/xmlschema-1/.

Tran, T., Cimiano, P., & Ankolekar, A. (2006). Rules for an ontology-based approach to adaptation. In *Proceedings of the 1st International Workshop on Semantic Media Adaptation and Personalization* (pp. 49-54). Athens, Greece: IEEE Computer Society.

Tresp, C., & Molitor, R. (1998). A description logic for vague knowledge. In *Proceedings ECAI-1998,* 361-365. J. Wiley & Sons.

Trout, J., & Rivkin, S. (1998). *The power of simplicity.* Mcgraw-Hill.

Tsarkov, D., & Horrocks, I. (2006). Fact++ Description logic reasoner: System description. In *International Joint Conference on Automated Reasoning (IJCAR 2006),* pp.292-297. Springer LNCS 4130.

Tsarkov, D., & Horrocks, I. (2006). FaCT++ description logic reasoner: System description. *Lecture Notes in Artificial Intelligence, 4130,* 292-297.

Tsetsos, V., Anagnostopoulos, C., Kikiras, P., & Hadjiefthymiades, S. (2006). Semantically-enriched navigation for indoor environments. *International Journal of Web and Grid Services, 2*(4)*, 473-47.,* Inderscience Publishers.

Tummarello, T., Morbidoni, C., & Nucci, M. (2006). Enabling Semantic Web communities with DBin: An overview. In I. Cruz, S. Decker, D. Allemang, C. Preist, D. Schwabe, P. Mika, M. Uschold, L. Aroyo (Eds.), *The Semantic Web – ISWC 2006: 5th International Semantic Web Conference,* Athens, GA, Proceedings, 943-950.

Tuyls, K., Nowe, A., Kuijpers, B., & Manderick, B. (Eds.), *Proceedings of the seventeenthbelgium-netherlands conference on artificial intelligence (bnaic 2005)* (pp. 120-126). Brussels, Belgium: Koninklijke Vlaamse Academie van Belge voor Wetenschappen en Kunsten.

Undercoffer, J. (2004). *Intrusion etection: Modeling system state to detect and classify aberrant behaviors.* Doctoral dissertation, University of Maryland, Baltimore.

Undercoffer, J., Joshi, A., Finin, T., & Pinkston, J. (2004). A target centric ontology for intrusion detection: Using DAML+OIL to classify intrusive behaviors. *Knowledge Engineering Review,* 18, 221-241.

Uschold, M. (1996). Building ontologies: Towards a unified methodology. *Proceedings of the 16th Annual Conference of the British Computer Society Specialist Group on Expert Systems,* Cambridge, UK, 1996.

Vallet, D., Mylonas, P., Corella, M. A., Fuentes, J. M., Castells, P., & Avrithis, Y. (2005). A semantically-enhanced personalization framework for knowledge-driven media services. *IADIS WWW/Internet Conference (ICWI 2005).* Lisbon, Portugal: IADIS Press.

Vanderwal, T. (2005, November, 5). *Off the top*: Folksonomy Entries.

Vargas-Vera, M., Motta, E., Domingue, J., Lanzoni, M., Stutt, A., & Ciravegna, F. (2002a). MnM: Ontology driven tool for semantic markup. *Proceedings of the Workshop on Semantic Authoring, Annotation & Knowledge Markup (SAAKM'02),* Lyon, France, pp. 43-47.

Vargas-Vera, M., Motta, E., Domingue, J., Lanzoni, M., Stutt, A., & Ciravegna, F. (2002b). MnM: ontology driven semi-automatic and automatic support for semantic markup. *Proceedings of the 13th International Conference on Knowledge Engineering and Management (EKAW'02),* LNCS 2473, Springer-Verlag, Madrid, Spain, pp. 379-391.

Vargas-Vera, M., Domingue, J., Motta, E., Buckingham Shum, S., & Lanzoni, M. (2001). Knowledge extraction by using an ontology-based annotation tool. *Proceedings of the Workshop Knowledge Markup & Semantic Annotation (KCAP'01)*, Victoria, Canada, pp. 5-12.

Vdovjak, R., Frasincar, F., Houben, G.J., & Barna, P. (2003). Engineering Semantic Web information systems in Hera. *Journal of Web Engineering, 2(1-2)*, 3-26. Rinton Press

Velardi, P., Cucchiarelli, A., & Petit, M. (2007). A taxonomy learning method and its application to characterize a scientific Web community. *IEEE Transactions on Knowledge and Data Engineering, 19*(2), 180-191.

Véronis, J. (2006). Weblog. (http://aixtal.blogspot.com)

Voorhees, E. (2004). Overview of the trec 2004 question answering track. In *Proceedings of the 13th Text Retrieval Conference (trec 2004)*. Gaithersburg, Maryland.

W3C (2004a, February). *OWL Web ontology language overview: W3C recommendation*. Retrieved June 16, 2007, from http://www.w3.org/TR/owl-features/.

W3C (2004b, February). *RDF Primer: W3C recommendation*. Retrieved June 16, 2007, from http://www.w3.org/TR/owl-features/

W3C (2004c, February). *RDF Vocabulary Description Language 1.0: RDF Schema W3C Recommendation*. Retrieved June 16, 2007, from http://www.w3.org/TR/rdf-primer/

W3C (2007). *Semantic Web*. Retrieved May, 2007 from http://www.w3.org/2001/sw.

W3C (2007, June). SPARQL Query Language for RDF: W3C Candidate Recommendation. Retrieved June 26, 2007, from http://www.w3.org/TR/rdf-sparql-query.

Wagner, E., & Lieberman, H. (2003, January). End-user debugging for electronic commerce. *ACM Conference on Intelligent User Interfaces*, Miami Beach.

WebModels s.r.l. (2007). *Webratio tool*. Retrieved June 16, 2007, from http://www.webratio.com

Weiss, A. R. (2002). *Dhrystone benchmark: History, analysis, scores and recommendations*. White paper, EEMBC Certification Laboratories, LLC.

Weissenberg, N., Gartmann, R., & Voisard, A. (2006). An ontology-based approach to personalized situation-aware mobile service supply. *Geoinformatica 10*(1), 55-90.

Weitzner, D.J., Abelson, H., Berners-Lee, T., Hanson, C.P., Hendler, J., Kagal, L., McGuinness, D.L., Sussman, G.J., Krasnow-Waterman, K. (2006). Transparent accountable inferencing for privacy risk management. *Proceedings of AAAI Spring Symposium on The Semantic Web meets eGovernment*. Stanford University, USA: AAAI Press Also available as MIT CSAIL Technical Report-2006-007 and Stanford KSL Technical Report KSL-06-03.

Welty, C., Murdock, J.W., Pinheiro da Silva, P., McGuinness, D.L., Ferrucci, D., & Fikes, R. (2005). Tracking information extraction from intelligence documents. In *Proceedings of the 2005 International Conference on Intelligence Analysis (IA 2005)*, McLean, VA, USA.

Wessel, M., & Möller, R. (2005). *A high performance Semantic Web query answering engine*. In *International Workshop on Description Logics (DL2005)*. Edinburgh, UK: CEUR.

Winer, D. (2002). *RSS 2.0 specification* (Available at http://blogs.law.harvard.edu/tech/rss). Berkman Center for Internet & Society at Harvard Law School.

Wireman, T. (2003). *Benchmarking best practices in maintenance management*. Industrial Press.

Wohlin, C., Aurum, A., Petersson, H., Shull, F., & Ciolkowski, M. (2002, June). Software inspection benchmarking - a qualitative and quantitative comparative opportunity. In the *8th International Software Metrics Symposium*, 118-130.

Wu, J., & Axelrod, R.(1995). How to cope with noise in the iterated prisoner's dilemma. *Journal of Conflict Resolution, 39*(1), 183-189.

Yelland, P. M. (2000). An alternative combination of Bayesian networks and description logics. In *Proceedings KR-2000*, 225–234. Morgan Kaufmann.

Yen, J. (1991). Generalizing term subsumption languages to fuzzy logic. In *Proceedings IJCAI-1991*, 472-177. Morgan Kaufmann.

Yin, X., Han, J., & Yu, P.S. (2007). Object distinction: Distinguishing objects with identical names. *Paper presented at the IEEE 23rd International Conference on Data Engineering*. Istambul, Turkey.

Yinglong, M., et al. (2007). A timing analysis model for ontology evolutions based on distributed environments. In (Zhi-Hua Zhou, Hang Li, Qiang Yang (Eds.): *Advances in Knowledge Discovery and Data Mining, 11th Pacific-Asia Conference, PAKDD, LNCS 4426*, 183-192.

Yuan, J., & Jones, G.H. (2007). Enabling Semantic access to enterprise RDB data. In *W3C Workshop on RDF Access to Relational Databases*. Retrieved December 15, 2007, from http://www.w3.org/2007/03/RdfRDB/papers/yuan.html

Zadel, M., & Fujinaga, I. (2004, October). Web services for music information retrieval. In *Proceedings of 5th International Conference on Music Information Retrieval (ismir'04)*. Barcelona, Spain.

Zhou, B., Siu, C., & Fong, A. (2005). Web usage mining for Semantic Web personalization. *Presented at Personalizati*

Zhou, G., & Su, J. (2002). Named entity recognition using an hmm-based chunk tagger. In *Proceedings of the 40th Annual Meeting of the Association for Computational Linguistics (acl 2002)* (pp. 473-480). Philadelphia, PA.

Zhu, H., Madnick, S. E., & Siegel, M.D. (2004). Effective data integration in the presence of temporal semantic conflicts. In *11th Intl. Symposium on Temporal Representation and Reasoning*, 109-114.

Zimmermann, H. (1980, April). OSI rReference mModel - The ISO mModel of aArchitecture for oOpen sSystems iInterconnection. *IEEE Transactions on Communications, vol. 28(, no. 4)*, April 1980, pp. 425 - 432.

398

About the Contributors

Jorge Cardoso joined SAP Research (Germany) in 2007. He is also Professor at the University of Madeira (Portugal) and the director of the of the SEED Laboratory. He previously gave lectures at the University of Georgia (USA) and at the Instituto Politécnico de Leiria (Portugal). Dr. Cardoso received his PhD in Computer Science from the University of Georgia in 2002. While at the University of Georgia, he was part of the LSDIS Lab. where he did extensive research on workflow management systems. In 1999, he worked at the Boeing Company on enterprise application integration. Dr. Cardoso was the organizer of several international conferences on Semantic Web and Information Systems. He has published over 80 refereed papers in the areas of workflow management systems, semantic Web, and related fields. He has also edited 3 books on semantic Web and Web services. He is on the Editorial Board of the *Enterprise Information Systems Journal, the International Journal on Semantic Web and Information Systems, and the International Journal of Information Technology*. He is also member of the Editorial Advisory Review Board of IGI Global. Prior to joining the University of Georgia, he worked for two years at CCG, Zentrum fur Graphische Datenverarbeitung, where is did research on Computer Supported Cooperative Work.

Miltiadis D. Lytras is an Assistant Professor in the Computer Engineering and Informatics Department-CEID (University of Patras). His research focuses on semantic web, knowledge management and e-learning, with more than 100 publications in these areas. He has co-edited / co-edits, 25 special issues in International Journals (e.g. IEEE Transaction on Knowledge and Data Engineering, IEEE Internet Computing, IEEE Transactions on Education, Computers in Human Behaviour etc) and has authored/[co-]edited 12 books [e.g. Open Source for Knowledge and Learning management, Ubiquitous and Pervasive Knowledge Management, Intelligent Learning Infrastructures for Knowledge Intensive Organizations, Semantic Based Information systems] . He is the founder and officer of the Semantic Web and Information Systems Special Interest Group in the Association for Information Systems (http://www.sigsemis.org). He serves as the (Co) Editor in Chief of 12 international journals [e.g. *International Journal of Knowledge and Learning, International Journal of Technology Enhanced Learning, International Journal on Social and Humanistic Computing, International Journal on Semantic Web and Information Systems, International Journal on Digital Culture and Electronic Tourism, International Journal of Electronic Democracy, International Journal of Electronic Banking, International Journal of Electronic Trade*] while he is associate editor or editorial board member in seven more.

* * *

Boanerges Aleman-Meza received a PhD in Computer Science and a Masters degree in Applied Mathematics from the University of Georgia in 2007 and 2001, respectively. His BE in Computer Engineering is from the Chihuahua II Technological Institute in Mexico. He was recipient of a Fulbright/Conacyt Fellowship. His research interests are in databases and semantic technologies for search and analytics. He is also interested in national security applications that combine semantic annotation of documents with geospatial data. Since October 2007, he holds a Research Fellowship position at the Institute for Infocomm Research (I2R), in Singapore. He is member of the ACM and IEEE Computer Society.

Florence Amardeilh leads the R&D Department of Mondeca since 2007, working on knowledge acquisition and semantic annotation since 2002. In 2001, she graduated as a Research Engineer in the fields of Information Systems and Knowledge Management, specialised on Text Mining solutions. From 2003 to 2007, she did a PhD in Language Processing at the University of Paris 10, sponsored by Mondeca. The thesis dealt with combining Natural Language Processing and Semantic Web methods and tools to create domain-oriented applications for ontology population and semantic annotation. She gave lectures in semantics, knowledge representation and semantic web at the universities of Paris 4 (Sorbonne) and Paris 10. Her current research interests include ontologies modelling, semantic knowledge bases, linguistic tools and especially the ontology-based information extraction engines, automatic knowledge acquisition and semantic annotation.

I. Budak Arpinar is an associate professor in Computer Science at the University of Georgia. His research interests include workflow management, Semantic Web, semantic search and knowledge discovery, and Web service composition. His funded research includes grants from the National Science Foundation. Arpinar received PhD and MS degrees in Computer Science from the Middle East Technical University in Turkey in 1998 and 1993, respectively. He is member of the ACM and IEEE Computer Society.

Søren Auer leads the research group Agile Knowledge Engineering and Semantic Web (AKSW) at the department Business Information Systems (University of Leipzig) and collaborates with the database research group at the University of Pennsylvania, USA. Søren is founder of several high-impact research and community projects such as the Wikipedia semantification project DBpedia, the open-source innovation platform Cofundos.org or the social Semantic Web toolkit OntoWiki. Søren is author of over 50 peer-reviewed scientific publications, co-organiser of several workshops, chair of the first Social Semantic Web conference and member of the advisory board of the Open Knowledge Foundation.

Guntis Barzdins is a professor in Computer Science at the University of Latvia and a senior researcher at the Institute of Mathematics and Computer Science, University of Latvia. He received his Ph.D in Computer Science from Academy of Sciences (Novosibirsk), Russia in 1990. His research interests include knowledge representation and reasoning, computational linguistics, and computer networking.

Janis Barzdins is a professor in Computer Science at the University of Latvia. From 1997 to 2006, he was also Director of the Institute of Mathematics and Computer Science, University of Latvia. He received his Doctor of Science degree (Mathematics) from the Institute of Mathematics (Novosibirsk), Academy of Science, Russia in 1976. He has also worked with industry in developing system modeling tools. His current research interests include system modeling languages and tools, as well as system engineering methods based on metamodeling and model transformations.

Michael Berger holds a diploma in Electrical Engineering and a PhD in computer science from Dresden University of Technology. He has been involved in Computer Science research for the last 14 years, specializing in Distributed Systems, Mobile and Ubiquitous Systems, and Intelligent-Agent and Multi-Agent Systems research. Since 1997 Dr. Berger is a member of Siemens Corporate Technology, Intelligent Autonomous Systems, in Munich and currently competence field leader for "Agent Technologies". Dr. Berger has many scientific publications, is actively involved in workshops and conferences, is reviewer for the EU commission and lecturer in the area of Agent Technologies as well as Mobile and Ubiquitous Computing at Dresden University of Technology and Ludwig-Maximilians-University in Munich.

Ansgar Bernardi is deputy head of the Knowledge Management research department of the German Research Center on Artificial Intelligence – DFKI GmbH, which develops technologies for the effective support of corporate knowledge work. He conducted numerous projects on learning organizations, knowledge management, distributed organizational memories, and their application in industrial settings. In his PhD thesis he applied knowledge management to the maintenance of complex machines. In 2006--2008, Dr. Ansgar Bernardi is the co-ordinator of the EU Integrated Project NEPOMUK. Under his guidance, 16 partners from 6 European countries develop the concepts, technologies, and open-source implementations of a Social Semantic Desktop.

Marco Brambilla is assistant professor at Politecnico di Milano. He graduated cum laude in 2001 and got his PhD in Information Engineering in 2004. His research interests include Web modeling methodologies, Web design patterns, conceptual design of data-intensive Web applications, workflow-based Web applications, service oriented applications, and Semantic Web application modeling. He has collaborated as application analyst in several industrial projects; among others, he worked with Acer Europe, Cisco System (San José, CA), and WebRatio. He has a wide teaching experience in Databases, Computer Science, and Web Engineering. In 2004 he spent six months as visiting researcher at University of California, San Diego. He is author of several conference and journal papers, of teaching books, and of the book "Designing Data-Intensive Web Applications", Morgan-Kauffman, USA.

Delroy Cameron is a PhD student in Computer Science at the Kno.e.sis Center at Wright State University. He received a MS in Computer Science from the University of Georgia, where he was a Research Assistant at the Complex Carbohydrate Research Center. He graduated with a BS in Computer Science Technology from Savannah State University 2005. His research interests are in Semantic Web, Semantic Web Services and Social Networks.

Karlis Cerans is a senior researcher at the Institute of Mathematics and Computer Science, University of Latvia and an associate professor in Computer Science at the University of Latvia. He received his Dr.Sc.comp degree from University of Latvia in 1992. His research interests include system engineering, modeling tool development, and mathematical models of software and biological systems.

Cynthia Chang is a research scientist in the computer science department at Rensselaer Polytechnic Institute. Before moving to RPI, she held various positions for many years at Stanford University, TIAA-CREF, State University of New York, and Vanderbilt University. Her recent research interests are in semantic web and related areas. She holds a masters degree in computer science.

Paulo C. G. Costa, PhD, is affiliate professor at George Mason University's Center of Excellence in C4I, an invited expert at the W3C, and an invited professor at both the Brazilian Air Force Institute of Technology (ITA) and the University of Brasilia. Dr. Costa is a pioneer researcher in the field of probabilistic ontologies and developed a probabilistic extension to the OWL Web Ontology Language, called Pr-OWL, which extends the former to first-order Bayesian expressiveness using Multi-Entity Bayesian Networks. He is also a key contributor to the development of UnBBayes-MEBN, an open source, freely available, java-based probabilistic reasoner and PR-OWL GUI that enables reasoning with probabilistic ontologies. His interests and contributions encompass areas such as systems engineering, probabilistic reasoning, knowledge representation, multi-source data fusion, decision theory, and service-oriented architectures. Dr. Costa received his BS degree in engineering with honors from the Brazilian Air Force Academy, and both his MS degree in system engineering and his PhD degree in Information Technology from George Mason University, where he became a recipient of the Excellence in Systems Engineering award in 1999.

Sheron L. Decker received a MS in Computer Science from the University of Georgia. He received a BS in Computer Science in 2003 from South Carolina State University. His research interests are in Software Engineering and Semantic Web.

Stefan Decker is a professor at the National University of Ireland, Galway, and Director of the Digital Enterprise Research Institute. Previously he worked at ISI, University of Southern California (2 years, Research Assistant Professor and Computer Scientist), Stanford University, Computer Science Department (Database Group) (3 Years, PostDoc and Research Associate), and Institute AIFB, University of Karlsruhe (4 years, PhD Student and Junior Researcher). He is one of the most widely cited Semantic Web scientists, and he current research interests include semantics in collaborative systems, Web 2.0, and distributed systems.

Li Ding is a research scientist of the Tetherless World Constellation in the computer science department at the Rensselaer Polytechnic Institute. He has over 10 years' experiences in the application of Artificial Intelligence; and he is currently working on explainable systems, information integration, the Semantic Web, and social computing. Mr. Ding received his Bachelor's and Master's degree in computer science from Peking University, China, and his PhD in computer science from University of Maryland, Baltimore County. He is a former Postdoctoral Fellow of the Knowledge Systems, Artificial Intelligence Laboratory at Stanford University.

Ludger van Elst is a research scientist at the German Research Center for Artificial Intelligence (DFKI GmbH) Kaiserslautern. Within the DFKI Knowledge Management Lab, he investigates tools for building, maintaining, and using personal and organizational memory information systems. He is especially interested in the role of formal conceptualizations in such systems. Currently, he is leading the Mymory project which investigates support for multiple work contexts and the use of attention elicitation for semantic personal memory systems.

Federico Michele Facca is a final year PhD candidate in Computer and Automation Engineering at Politecnico of Milano. His research is mainly focused on Web Mining, Adaptive Hypermedia Modeling and Semantic Web application Modeling. He has collaborated as application analyst in WebModels s.r.l. and he has been visiting researcher at DERI Innsbruck in 2007 for 6 months. He has published papers at international conferences and journals; recently he won the "Highly Commended Paper Award" at ICWE 2005. One of his paper on Web Usage Mining is currently in the TOP25 articles within the journal "Data and Knowledge Engineering" (Elsevier).

Florian Fuchs is a PhD candidate in Computer Science at Siemens Corporate Technology, Intelligent Autonomous Systems and the Mobile and Distributed Systems Group at Ludwig-Maximilians-University Munich. He received his Master's degree (Diplom) in Computer Science from Technical University of Munich. His research interests include semantic modelling and reasoning for context-aware applications. In the context of infrastructure monitoring, he investigates appropriate system architectures and ontology patterns for modeling system faults and states. A major focus of his work are reasoning over distributed knowledge bases and reasoning by exploiting infrastructure topologies.

Vasco Furtado is professor of computer science at University of Fortaleza (UNIFOR), Brazil, where he also leads a team of researchers in the Knowledge Engineering group that studies agent-based simulation and agent's explanation on the web. He is consultant of the State of Ceara IT Company (ETICE) where he has coordinated and developed research and development projects on the law enforcement domain. Furtado holds a PhD in Informatique from the University of Aix-Marseille III, France. He has spent one year (2006-07) during his sabbatical in the Knowledge Systems Laboratory at Stanford University. Further information about publications and projects is available at http://www.mentores.com.br/vasco.

Raúl García-Castro is a PhD student at the Computer Science School at the Universidad Politécnica de Madrid (UPM). After 3 years as a software engineer, he has been working at UPM since he graduated in Computer Science (2003) in several EU-funded initiatives: Esperonto, KnowledgeWeb NoE, OntoGrid, and NeOn and in the Spanish CICYT project Infraestructura tecnológica de servicios semánticos para la web semántica. He is one of the developers of the WebODE ontology engineering workbench and his research focuses on the evaluation and benchmarking of Semantic Web technology. Nowadays he is leading an activity for benchmarking the interoperability of Semantic Web technology.

Gijs Geleijnse was born on June 12, 1979 in Breda, the Netherlands. From 1997 to 2004 he studied Computing Science at the Eindhoven University of Technology. His graduation project was supervised by Rob Nederpelt and focused on formal languages for mathematics. After graduating with honors, he started working as a PhD candidate at Philips Research in Eindhoven. Supervised by Jan Korst and Emile Aarts, Gijs works on the extraction of information from unstructured texts on the Web. He has filed a handful of patent applications and his work has been published and presented at several international conferences.

Alyssa Glass is completing her PhD in Computer Science in the Artificial Intelligence Laboratory at Stanford University. Her research involves explaining task execution and machine learning in adaptive agents, to make learning-based systems more trustworthy for users. Prior to starting doctoral work at Stanford, Alyssa was a computer scientist in the Artificial Intelligence Center at SRI International, where she still works part-time, doing research on planning and execution systems. Before joining SRI, she worked at PARC Incorporated (previously Xerox PARC). She received her Bachelor's degree in computer science and economics from Harvard University.

Asunción Gómez-Pérez is full professor at the Computer Science School at Universidad Politécnica de Madrid, Spain. She is the director of the Ontology Engineering Group since 1995. The most representative projects she is participating are: SEEMP, NeOn, OntoGrid as project coordinator, Knowledge Web NoE acting as Scientific Vice-director, Esperonto, the OntoWeb thematic network, and also the MKBEEM project. She has published more than 100 papers on the above issues. She is author of one book on Ontological Engineering and co-author of a book on Knowledge Engineering. She has been co-director of the summer school on Ontological Engineering and the Semantic Web in 2003, 2004, 2005, 2006 and 2007. She was program chair of ESWC'05 and EKAW'02. She has been co-organizer of conferences, workshops and tutorials. She acts as reviewer in many conferences and Journals.

Gunnar Aastrand Grimnes is originally from Norway, but completed his undergraduate studies in Aberdeen in Scotland. Currently, he is in the process of completing his PhD at Aberdeen University, on the topic of applying machine-learning techniques to learn from Semantic Web data, and using planning techniques for Semantic Web agents to autonomously chose what to learn. Since 2005 he is also working at DFKI GmbH in Kaiserslautern, Germany. There he mainly spends his time on the NEPOMUK project, for which he has been the Technical Director since 2007.

Tudor Groza received is MSc. degree in Computer Science from the Technical University of Cluj Napoca in partnership with DaimlerChrysler AG Berlin. In 2005, he joined Digital Enterprise Research Institute (DERI) Galway as a PhD student under the supervision of Siegfried Handschuh and Stefan Decker. His PhD topic is semantic authoring and publishing. Since the beginning of 2006 he is actively involved in the NEPOMUK Project, where he deals with building the Architecture for the NEPOMUK platform. He has written a number of papers on topics such as semantic authoring and publishing or the Semantic Desktop, which were published at major international conferences.

Stathes Hadjiefthymiades received his B.Sc., M.Sc., PhD degrees (in Computer Science) from the University of Athens (UoA), Athens, Greece and a Joint Engineering-Economics M.Sc. from the National Technical University of Athens. Since 1992, he was with the consulting firm Advanced Services Group. He has been a member of the Communication Networks Laboratory of the UoA. He has participated in numerous EU-funded and national projects. He served as visiting Assistant Professor at the University of Aegean, Dept. of Information and Communication Systems Engineering. He joined the faculty of Hellenic Open University (Patras, Greece) as an Assistant Professor. Since December 2003 he belongs to the faculty of the Department of Informatics and Telecommunications, UoA, where he is an Assistant Professor. His research interests are in the areas of mobile/pervasive computing and networked multimedia applications. He is the author of over 100 publications in the above areas.

Siegfried Handschuh is an adjunct lecturer at the National University of Ireland, Galway (NUIG), where he lectures a master course in ``Digital Information and Multimedia Semantics`` at the Huston School of Film and Digital Media. He is a project leader at the Digital Enterprise Research Institute

(DERI), Galway and leader of the research group for, *Semantic Information Systems and Language Engineering (SmILE)*, Siegfried holds Honours Degrees in both Computer Science and Information Science. He received his PhD from the University of Karlsruhe (Germany). His current research interests include: Annotation for the Semantic Web, Semantic Desktop, Knowledge Acquisition and Social Semantic Collaboration.

Víctor Rodríguez Herola is Ingeniero Principal de Sistemas, ISDEFE, S.A., Dirección de Sistemas de Defensa y Seguridad, Espana. Prior to this he was with **NATO C3 Agency working as a** Principal Scientist, in the Department of Technology in NATO offices at La Haya Holland.

Mehdi Jazayeri is the founding Dean of the Faculty of Informatics and Professor of Computer Science at the University of Lugano, Switzerland. From 1994 to 2007, he held the chair of distributed systems at the Technical University of Vienna and was the head of the distributed systems group. He spent many years in software research and development at several Silicon Valley companies, including ten years at Hewlett-Packard Laboratories in Palo Alto, California. His recent work has been concerned with component-based software engineering of distributed systems, particularly Web-based systems. He is a co-author of Programming Language Concepts, (John Wiley, 3 rd edition, 1998), Fundamentals of Software Engineering, (Prentice-Hall, 2nd edition, 2002), and Software Architecture for Product Families (Addison-Wesley, 2000). He was elected a Fellow of the IEEE in 2007. He is a member of ACM, Swiss, German, and Austrian Computer Societies.

Jan Korst received his M.Sc. degree in mathematics from Delft University of Technology, and his PhD degree from Eindhoven University of Technology, both in the Netherlands. Since 1985, he has been with the Philips Research Laboratories in Eindhoven. Over the years he has been working mainly on the design and analysis of algorithms in the field of combinatorial optimization. Application fields include scheduling, resource management, IC design, multimedia systems and information extraction. Jan coauthored three books and twelve u.s. patents. His email address is jan.korst@philips.com.

Kathryn B. Laskey, PhD is Associate Professor of Systems Engineering and Operations Research at George Mason University, where she teaches and performs research on computational decision theory and evidential reasoning. Professor Laskey's research involves methods for representing knowledge in forms that can be processed by computers, extending traditional knowledge representation methods to represent uncertainty, eliciting knowledge from human experts, applying probability theory to draw conclusions from evidence arising from multiple sources. She has applied her research to problems such as modeling the emplacement of improvised explosive devices, predicting aircraft delays, managing terrorist risk at public facilities, judicial reasoning, and planning military engagements. Dr. Laskey developed multi-entity Bayesian networks (MEBN), a language and logic that extends classical first-order logic to support Bayesian probability. She was a key contributor to the development of PR-OWL, an upper ontology that allows MEBN theories to be represented in OWL ontologies. Dr. Laskey is an invited expert to the W3C, and is co- chair of the W3C Uncertainty Reasoning for the World Wide Web Incubator Group, http://www.w3.org/2005/Incubator/urw3/. She has served on several National Academy of Sciences committees, and is currently a member of the Committee on Applied and Theoretical Statistics of the National Academy of Sciences. Dr. Laskey received the BS degree in mathematics from the University of Pittsburgh, the MS degree in mathematics from the University of Michigan, and the PhD degree in statistics and public policy from Carnegie Mellon University.

Thomas Lukasiewicz is currently holding a Heisenberg Fellowship by the German Research Foundation (DFG), affiliated both at the Oxford University Computing Laboratory and at the Institute of Information Systems of the Vienna University of Technology. He holds a PhD in Computer Science from the University of Augsburg, Germany, and the Dozent degree (venia legendi) in Practical and Theoretical Computer Science from the Vienna University of Technology, Austria. Thomas Lukasiewicz's main research interests are in AI, the Semantic Web, and databases.

Abdul-Rahman Mawlood-Yunis, PhD candidate, School of Computer Science at Carleton University. Masters in Science and Information System Science, School of Computer Science at Carleton University (2003), and Bachelor in Chemical Engineering, Technology University Baghdad (1991). His research interest include: Distributed Computing, P2P Networking, Information Systems, E-Commerce, Fault-tolerance, Mobile Agent, Software Agent and Software Engineering.

Deborah L. McGuinness is the Tetherless World Senior Constellation Chair and Professor of Computer Science and Cognitive Science at Rensselaer Polytechnic Institute. Deborah's research focuses on the semantic web, ontologies and ontology evolution environments, explanation, trust, and semantic eScience. Until recently, Deborah led the Knowledge Systems, Artificial Intelligence Lab at Stanford University. Deborah is also the CEO of McGuinness Associates consulting and acting Chief Scientist for Sandpiper Software. Deborah received her BS degree from Duke University, MS from the University of California at Berkeley, and her PhD from Rutgers University.

Cédric Mesnage is a PhD student of the university of Lugano under the direction of Mehdi Jazayeri. He received his Master's degree in Computer Science from the University of Caen, France, with specialization in Algorithmics and Information Modeling. His diploma thesis was on visualization of software evolution artifacts. He works in the NEPOMUK European Project where he focuses on the architecture, the functionalities and services overview of the social semantic desktop. His research question regards the nature of Software Engineering and the usage of Social Sciences methods.

Knud Möller received an MA in Computational Linguistics, English and Scandinavian Languages from the Universität zu Köln in Germany in 2003. Since 2004, he is working at DERI at the National University of Ireland in Galway, where he is pursuing a PhD in Computer Science, on the topic of generating metadata for the Semantic Web. He has written a number of papers on topics such as semantic blogging, annotation or the Semantic Desktop, which were published at major international conferences, has co-organized the Semantic Annotation and Authoring Workshop in 2006, and been on the organizing committee for the International Semantic Web Conferences 2006 and 2007 as metadata co-chair. Knud is a member of the NEPOMUK team at DERI since 2005.

Vassilis Papataxiarhis received his BSc in Informatics from the Department of Informatics & Telecommunications at the University of Athens, Greece, in 2006. He is currently a postgraduate student in the division of "Advanced Information Systems" at the same department and member of the Pervasive Computing Research Group. He has been involved as software designer and developer in several national projects. His research interests are in the areas of Semantic Web technologies, Pervasive Computing and Artificial Intelligence.

Paulo Pinheiro da Silva is an Assistant Professor of Computer Science and the leader of the Trust Laboratory at the University of Texas at El Paso (UTEP), Texas. At UTEP, Paulo is a member of the NSF-funded Cyber-ShARE Center of Excellence for Cyber-Infrastructure Applications. Paulo received his Bachelor's degree in Mathematics and his MSc degree in computer science both from the Federal University of Minas Gerais, Brazil, and his PhD in computer science from Manchester University, United Kingdom. He is a former Postdoctoral Fellow of the Knowledge Systems, Artificial Intelligence Laboratory at Stanford University.

Michael Pirker works for the Intelligent Autonomous Systems group at Siemens Corporate Technology. He received his Master's degree in Information and Communication Technologies from Technical University Graz, Austria. He has been working on the application of diverse software agent and ambient intelligence technologies in industrial contexts like automation, business communication, and transportation. Examples for applied technologies are agent interaction protocols, higher level ad-hoc network communication mechanisms, rule engines, OWL ontologies, and DL reasoners. His recent work particularly addresses practical problems of systems emerging in industry that realize semantic information integration together with automated information processing.

Gerald Reif got his MSc from the Graz University of Technology in 2000 and his PhD from the Vienna University of Technology in June 2005. The topic of the PhD thesis was „WEESA - Web Engineering for Semantic Web Applications" in which he has designed and implemented WEESA, a mapping from XML documents to ontologies that enables the automatic generation from RDF meta-data out of XML documents. After finishing his PhD Gerald Reif started as postdoc in the Software Engineering group at the University Zurich in September 2005 to further pursue his research in the area of Semantic Web Applications.

Nicola Santoro, PhD, is professor of Computer Science at Carleton University. Dr. Santoro has been involved in distributed computing from the beginning of the field. He has contributed extensively on the algorithmic aspects, authoring many seminal papers. He is a founder of the main theoretical conferences in the field (PODC, DISC, SIROCCO). His current research is on distributed algorithms for mobile agents, autonomous mobile robots, and mobile sensor networks.

Michael Sintek studied Computer Science and Economics at the University of Kaiserslautern and received the Diplom (master's degree) in 1996. Since then, he is as a research scientist at the German Research Center for Artificial Intelligence (DFKI GmbH) Kaiserslautern, where he worked on several knowledge management, e-learning, and Semantic Web projects. He was a visiting researcher at the Stanford Medical Informatics department (1999 and 2000/2001) where he developed several extensions for Protégé-2000. As a visiting researcher at the Stanford Database Group and at ISI 2002, he developed (together with Stefan Decker) the Semantic Web rule language TRIPLE. Currently, he is co-head of the Competence Center Semantic Web (CCSW) at DFKI.

Vassileios Tsetsos received his BSc in Informatics from the Department of Informatics & Telecommunications at the University of Athens, Greece, in 2003, and his MSc in the division of Communication Systems and Data Networks from the same department in 2005. He is currently a PhD student in the same department and member of the Pervasive Computing Research Group. He has been involved as software designer and developer in several national and European R&D projects. His research interests are in the areas of mobile and pervasive computing, semantic web, ontological engineering, and web applications.

Michael Weiss an associate professor in the Department of Systems and Computer Engineering at Carleton University in Ottawa and a member of the Technology Innovation Management (TIM) program. His research interests include open source ecosystems, service-oriented architectures, mashups/Web 2.0, business process modeling, product architecture and design, and pattern languages. Between 2000 and 2007, he was a professor of Computer Science at Carleton University. From 1994 to 1999, he was a member of the Strategic Technology group at Mitel. Michael obtained his PhD (Dr.rer.nat.) from the University of Mannheim in 1993. He is author of over 70 peer-reviewed publications in leading journals and conferences.

Index